First & Second
Maryland Cavalry
C. S. A.

Robert J. Driver Jr.

Rockbridge Publishing
an imprint of
HOWELL PRESS, INC.
Charlottesville, Virginia

Published by
Rockbridge Publishing
an imprint of
HOWELL PRESS, INC.
1713-2D Allied Lane • Charlottesville, VA 22903
(804) 977-4006
http://www.howellpress.com

A Katherine Tennery Book

Library of Congress Cataloging-in-Publication Data

Driver, Robert J.
    First & second Maryland Cavalry, C.S.A. / Robert J. Driver, Jr.
    p.   cm.
    Includes bibliographical references (p.   ) and index.
    ISBN 1-883522-24-2
    1. Confederate States of America. Army. Maryland Cavalry Battalion, 1st. 2.
Confederate States of America. Army. Maryland Cavalry Battalion, 2nd. 3.
Confederate States of America. Army. Maryland Cavalry. Davis's Battalion. 4.
Maryland–History–Civil War, 1861-1865–Regimental histories. 5. United States–
History–Civil War, 1861-1865–Regimental histories. 6. Maryland–History–Civil War,
1861-1865–Cavalry operations. 7. United States–History–Civil War, 1861-1865–
Cavalry operations. 8. Soldiers–Maryland–Registers. 9. United States–History–Civil
War, 1861-1865–Registers. [ ] I. Title. II. Title: First and second Maryland Cavalry,
Confederate States of America
    E566.6 1st .D75 1999
    973.7'452–dc21   98-49753
                                                                              CIP

Printed in Canada.

Contents

To those gallant Maryland cavalrymen who came to the aid of Virginia in its hour of need—lest we forget.

Introduction

First Maryland Cavalry

The First Maryland Cavalry, Confederate States Army, was formed in May 1862 of veterans of the Howard County (Maryland) Dragoons and the First Virginia Cavalry. The Marylanders had served with the Second Virginia Cavalry during Stonewall Jackson's Valley Campaign, at the second battle of Manassas, and in the Maryland Campaign of 1862. They returned to the Shenandoah Valley, where six additional companies were organized, armed, and equipped. The First Maryland served as part of the Maryland Line in and around Winchester in the fall and winter of 1862.

The Maryland Line was the designation of Maryland troops during the Revolutionary War and the War of 1812, an effort by the Marylanders to have all of their units—infantry, artillery, and cavalry—serve in one command. The attempt to organize them in that way met with limited success during the Civil War, as infantry and cavalry were organized into brigades comprising regiments of at least ten companies each and artillery into battalions. The Marylanders, usually lacking the minimum number of companies, were designated battalions. The Line was broken up numerous times, the last time in May 1864.

During the spring of 1863 the Maryland troopers participated in the Jones-Imboden raid into western Virginia that reached the Ohio River. Under the gallant Ridgely Brown, the First fought with distinction at Brandy Station, Gettysburg, Williamsport, Leesburg, and other actions in 1863. In October 1863 the battalion rejoined the Maryland Line at Hanover Junction, Virginia, northeast of Richmond.

In the spring of 1864 the First was called to repel Federal incursions into the area, including Dahlgren's raid on Richmond. With the opening of Grant's campaign to capture the capital of the South, the Marylanders fought Sheridan's cavalry at Beaver Dam, Pollard's Farm, and along the South Anna near Ashland, losing Lieutenant Colonel Brown in the last action.

They then joined Gen. Jubal Early in the Valley and participated in his raid on Washington, D.C., in July. They were sent to free the Confederate prisoners held at Point Lookout, Maryland, but were recalled from this endeavor. The battalion did penetrate the outskirts of Baltimore, where its men destroyed trains, bridges, and telegraph communications.

They returned to the Valley and rode with Gen. John McCausland; they aided in the burning of Chambersburg, Pennsylvania. Near Moorefield, now West Virginia, the battalion was surprised by Gen. William W. Averell's Federal cavalry and suffered heavy losses.

The First rejoined Early in the Valley and fought at Smithfield, Winchester, and Cedar Creek. The Marylanders helped defend the Luray Valley and stopped Custer and Torbert from capturing Gordonsville.

They were then ordered to Petersburg to act as part of the rear guard for Lee's Army of Northern Virginia as it retreated to Appomattox Court House. On the morning of April 9, 1865, the First Maryland led the charge that broke through the Federal lines and rode on to Lynchburg. The unit disbanded at Cloverdale, Virginia, on April 28, 1865.

Davis's Battalion of Maryland Cavalry

Thomas Sturgis Davis organized his command during September 1863. Davis had seen service in the Seventh Virginia Cavalry and as Gen. Turner Ashby's assistant adjutant general. The unit was raised with the expectation that it would become a part of the First Maryland Cavalry, but this plan never came to pass. Davis's original company was eventually assigned to the First, but many of the other officers and men of the battalion were Virginians, so in keeping with the general practice, the Confederate War Department assigned these companies to Virginia units.

Davis's Battalion spent the winter of 1863–64 scouting and on outpost duty in the Shenandoah Valley. Major Davis served as Gen. John D. Imboden's chief of scouts. The battalion fought at New Market, Piedmont, Buford's Gap, and Winchester. Davis was wounded and captured during the last battle, and the remnants of his unit served with the First and Second Maryland until the end of the war.

Second Maryland Cavalry

The Second Maryland Cavalry, Confederate States Army, was organized by Maj. Harry W. Gilmor of Baltimore in May 1863. Gilmor had served with the Twelfth Virginia Cavalry, and most of his first company were Marylanders who had served with him. "Gallant Harry" commanded the First and Second Maryland during the first part of the Gettysburg campaign. He returned to the Shenandoah Valley, where he raised six companies by September 1863. During the remainder of 1863 and in early 1864 the Second served around Winchester while making raids on Union outposts, wagon trains, and the Baltimore and Ohio Railroad.

The battalion served with Early in his advance on Washington. Gilmor led the First and Second into the suburbs of Baltimore, where they burned trains and bridges. The Second returned to the Valley and participated in the Chambersburg raid with McCausland. As was the case with the First Maryland, the Second was surprised and lost heavily at Moorefield. Gilmor and his men rejoined Early; the major fought in numerous cavalry skirmishes and battles until seriously wounded. The men of the Second, much reduced in numbers, went on to serve as scouts.

In 1865 Gilmor's men rode with Virginia partisan ranger units in western Virginia, but following Gilmor's capture in February 1865, little is known of the activities of the Second Maryland.

First Maryland
Cavalry

Guidon of the First Maryland Cavalry, Confederate States Army.
(Museum of the Confederacy)

Chapter I

1861

"Maryland, My Maryland!"

T he seizure of the United States Arsenal at Harpers Ferry, Virginia, on October 16, 1859, by the abolitionist John Brown and his followers brought an immediate reaction from the citizens of Maryland, which lies just across the Potomac River. Brown's action caused the white population, which knew of the violence that had plagued Missouri and Kansas for years, to fear a Negro uprising. That fear in turn prompted the state legislature to consider a bill that would stop the manumission of slaves and regulate the employment of free blacks. The bill failed, but the Marylanders did pass declarations in support of Southern rights of secession.

In the national presidential election of 1860, the people of Maryland split their vote between John C. Breckinridge of Kentucky, supported by Southern Democrats, and John Bell of Tennessee, backed by the Constitutional Union party. Breckinridge carried Maryland by less than one percent, with his support coming from Baltimore City and Charles, Prince George's, St. Mary's, Talbot, and Worcester counties. Abraham Lincoln of Illinois won the election because of similar splits in all of the Southern and border states; in all of Maryland he received only 1,211 votes. Stephen A. Douglas received even fewer. Lincoln's election heightened tensions between the North and South.

South Carolina seceded from the Union on December 20, 1860. When other states rapidly followed her, Maryland came under pressure from both the North and South. The governor of Maryland, Thomas H. Hicks, although himself a slave owner, refused to call a special session of the general assembly, in part because it was dominated by representatives from slave-holding southern Maryland and the Eastern Shore. Some lawmakers wanted to assemble immediately in Baltimore, but most politicians preferred to wait until the results of the Virginia secession convention were known.

The situation in Baltimore reflected the dilemma of all Marylanders. The city was a major commercial seaport with the financial characteristics of New York, Philadelphia, and Boston in the North. Its social and cultural ties, however, were with the slave-holding South; the Chesapeake Bay society, for example, was closely tied to Virginia. The Baltimore and Ohio Railroad linked the city to large western markets, and industry thrived. Western Maryland, on the other hand, was predominantly rural, agricultural, and non-slave-holding.

Lincoln's furtive passage through the state on his way to his inauguration in Washington did little to gain the respect of Marylanders, and his inaugural address did nothing to ease the tensions between the North and South.

South Carolina's attack on Fort Sumter, on April 12, 1861, began the war that few Marylanders wanted. Lincoln's call on April 15 for volunteers to put down the rebellion prompted Virginia and the upper Southern states to secede. Troops from the Northern states prepared to assemble in Washington.

It was immediately clear that, because of its important railroad connections, many Northern troops would pass through Maryland en route to Washington. On April 19 some two thousand soldiers from Massachusetts and Pennsylvania entered Baltimore on the Philadelphia, Wilmington, and Baltimore Railroad. They were to proceed to Washington on the Baltimore and Ohio line, but since the railway companies used different depots, the troops were forced to march from one to the other through the streets of Baltimore. The Sixth Massachusetts Regiment came under attack by a mob of citizens who hurled verbal abuse, stones, and bricks.

The unseasoned troops opened fire in response. Francis X. Ward, a Baltimore attorney, attempted to seize a flag from the Massachusetts militiamen and was shot in the hip for his efforts. The ball passed through him and killed a citizen nearby. Edward W. Beatty, a customs officer, picked up a musket dropped by a Federal and returned fire. George W. Booth, who was returning from overnight duty with the Maryland militia, provided Beatty with ammunition from his pockets. All three men would later serve in the Confederate army.

At the end of the fray, twelve Baltimoreans were dead and scores injured. Forty-two soldiers had been killed or wounded. News of the Baltimore 'riots' spread around the country like wildfire.

A portrait of James Ryder Randall, author of the poem set to music that became the anthem of Southern partisans in Maryland, "Maryland, My Maryland," is seen here behind the battle flag of the Second Maryland Cavalry, C.S.A., at the state house in Annapolis. (Goldsborough 1900)

In Louisiana James Ryder Randall, a schoolteacher from Baltimore, read of the tragic debacle in the local newspaper. Francis Ward, Randall's former roommate at Georgetown College, was listed as mortally wounded. Grieving and sickened by the supposed loss of his friend, Randall wrote a poem that expressed his anger over the subjugation of his home state. It was published three days later and was soon put to music as "Maryland, My Maryland!" Ward's blood became the rallying cry for Southern sympathizers in Maryland.

In an effort to prevent further bloodshed, the Maryland legislature sent a committee to Washington to request that Lincoln send no more troops through Baltimore. When the request was refused, Governor Hicks ordered two companies of militia to burn the railroad bridges north of Baltimore to prevent the arrival of more troops. He and George W. Brown, the mayor of Baltimore, appealed to the citizens to remain calm. George P. Kane, the Baltimore chief of police and a Southern sympathizer, requested militia reinforcements. Bradley T. Johnson's company from Frederick answered the call and arrived in Baltimore on April 20. Other companies arrived and occupied the Federal arsenal at Pikesville.

The next day the Baltimoreans prepared for the arrival of Federal troops then camped at Cockeysville. Among the militiamen arriving in the city were Capt. George Ridgely Gaither Jr.'s Howard County Dragoons. Frank A. Bond's company

Capt. Frank A. Bond, Co. A., First
Maryland Cavalry. (Ridgely B. Bond Jr.)

from Anne Arundel County seized Annapolis Junction and cut the railroad and telegraph lines between Washington and Baltimore. Lincoln then relented and had the troops withdrawn from Cockeysville, but at the same time Gen. Benjamin F. Butler and his Federal troops seized Annapolis and moved into southern Maryland.

Gen. Winfield Scott, commander of the Union army, understood the importance of the Baltimore and Ohio Railroad and the Chesapeake and Ohio Canal, which paralleled the railroad through parts of western Maryland, to the defense of Washington. The Confederates, who had seized Harpers Ferry on April 18, were already receiving supplies from Baltimore over the rail line.

Governor Hicks finally called the legislature into session at Frederick on April 26, choosing that city over Annapolis because of the presence of Federal troops in the state capital. The hopes of Southern sympathizers in Maryland were dashed when the state senate and house of delegates refused to vote on an ordinance of secession. The arrest of pro-Confederate members of both houses predetermined this result.

After the war Bradley Johnson condemned the legislature and Governor Hicks for their inactivity during the crisis. Johnson believed that a "small body of influential, honorable and sincere members were opposed to *hasty action*. They dallied and delayed and lost a *week*. A *week* in war, never to be recovered. A *week* in Revolution—a century in the tranquil current of civil affairs."[1]

Maryland's failure to join the Confederacy prompted immediate Federal action. General Butler seized the Relay House south of Baltimore, the key railroad junction that controlled the flow of traffic in and out of the city. On the night of May 13–14, Butler occupied Baltimore and seized Federal Hill, which overlooks downtown Baltimore and the harbor. The attempt by the citizens to support the rebellion was over.

1.   *Southern Historical Society Papers*, Vol. XI, 348

By the end of June, Kane, the Baltimore police chief, had been arrested and imprisoned in Fort McHenry for his Southern leanings. In protest over his arrest the police commissioners disbanded the entire Baltimore police force. Col. John R. Kenley of the First Maryland Infantry, U.S.A., was appointed to replace Kane. One of Kenley's first acts as chief was to arrest the police commissioners and others believed to be supporting the rebellion.

Many of the Southern-sympathizing militia units called out by the governor chose to leave Maryland to serve in Virginia state units. Captain Gaither led twenty-three of his Howard County Dragoons from Baltimore to Point of Rocks, where they crossed the Potomac into Virginia. Although few in number, they were armed with U.S. sabres and Colt revolvers and equipped for service. Other members of the Howard Dragoons followed in small parties until at least sixty of the original troop were sworn into Virginia service at Leesburg on May 14. Gaither gathered up other Marylanders who crossed the river in small groups, thus swelling his ranks to a total of seventy-five men who took the oath to Virginia. Gaither, a prominent Baltimore merchant, was elected captain, George W. Howard first lieutenant, and Samuel W. Dorsey second lieutenant.

The company was assigned to Turner Ashby, who placed it on picket duty on the Virginia side of Edwards's Ferry. The Howard troop maintained its position on outpost duty until ordered to Winchester on June 15. There Gaither's troopers were placed under the command of Col. Angus McDonald, an elderly West Point graduate who commanded the companies organized by Ashby. McDonald led the units toward Romney, where they scouted and picketed northward to the Potomac River.

On July 15 McDonald was ordered to bring his troopers to Winchester and unite with Gen. Joseph E. Johnston's command. Johnston had received orders to join Gen. P. T. G. Beauregard at Manassas on July 18. Gaither's troop was assigned the mission of screening the infantry's march from Union forces near Berryville, which it did. When the last rifleman crossed the Shenandoah River, Gaither led his company eastward, following Johnston's men. The Howard Dragoons had been acting in concert with the First Virginia Cavalry under Col. James Ewell Brown "Jeb" Stuart, and Stuart was apparently impressed by the Marylanders. While they were en route to Manassas, he had them assigned to his regiment.

During the battle of Bull Run on July 21 the Marylanders came under Federal artillery fire but suffered no casualties. When the Union army began to retreat, Gaither's troop joined in the pursuit, taking prisoners and capturing large amounts of arms and equipment. Stuart led his troopers on to Fairfax Court

Lt. Col. RIDGELY BROWN.

*Lt. Col. Ridgely Brown. (Goldsborough
1900)*

House, taking more wagons and supplies. The cavalrymen were able to arm, equip, and clothe themselves from the booty.

Stuart was then ordered to picket the area toward the defenses of Washington City. On July 24 Gaither led a patrol to Mason's Hill, which was unoccupied by the Federals although within sight of the capitol. Upon hearing of Gaither's success Stuart moved to the hill with the rest of the regiment, supported by the First Maryland Infantry, C.S.A. Outposts were established at Fairfax Station, Falls Church, and Mason's, Munson's, and Upton's hills.

Despite the heavy demands for his troopers, Stuart adhered to a strict training program of drills and evening dress parades. The First Virginia cavalrymen learned the discipline that was lacking in the Southern troops in the battle of Bull Run.

During this period Lieutenants Howard and Dorsey resigned, and Ridgely Brown was elected first lieutenant, Frank A. Bond second lieutenant, and Thomas Griffith third lieutenant. The Howard County Dragoons were mustered into Confederate service at Fairfax Court House on August 1.

While on patrol on the Falls Church–Lewinsville road on September 10, a detachment of the Dragoons was ambushed by a large force of the Seventy-ninth New York Infantry, which had been led to the wooded site by a Union man who lived nearby. Fortunately the New Yorkers fired high; only one man was wounded and captured, and one horse was killed and another captured.

Gaither's troopers were still on the picket the next day, when the Federals advanced toward Lewinsville. The Marylanders, on outpost duty, were spread out from that small village northward to Great Falls on the Potomac, so Gaither had few men present to face the enemy. Stuart soon arrived with infantry and artillery reinforcements and drove the Yankees back. Pvt. Otho Scott Lee of the Dragoons wrote:

> The tents occupied by the regiment and all camp equipment, including wagons, ambulances, cooking utensils, etc. had been recently captured from the enemy, and were branded in large letters U.S. You would have

thought to see the camp we were U.S. troops. . . . While picketing and scouting we had daily drills on horseback and on foot, two or three times a day. Roll call came at day light, stable call, then mess call, and late in the afternoon dress parade.[2]

Stuart was promoted to brigadier general on September 24, and Capt. William E. "Grumble" Jones became colonel of the regiment. Jones was a West Pointer who had proved himself in combat with the unit.

The regiment continued on outpost duty throughout the fall, but by December the picket lines were pulled back nearer to Centreville. Private Lee reported that the regiment "now extend[ed] from the Fredericksburg Railroad through below Fairfax Court House to Flint Hill Cemetery."[3] At that point, the First Virginia Cavalry connected with the First North Carolina Cavalry.

When not on duty, the Howard County Dragoons kept busy building log huts for winter quarters and shelter for their horses.

2.   WLU, Otho Scott Lee Collection
3.   Ibid.

Chapter II

1862

*"I have withdrawn from the First Virginia to fight
with the people of my native state."*

D uring the winter General Stuart rotated his companies on the picket
line. Because of the distance to the line from the camp near Centreville,
the troopers carried three days' rations and remained on post three or
four days. Private Lee wrote, "We had company headquarters in the rear of the
picket line some distance where we were required to be after being relieved
from duty. We had two hours on post, and four off. While on post we were not
allowed to dismount, but would sit on our horses in some secluded spot and
keep our eyes and ears open. . . . [W]hile picketing the men were not allowed
to unsaddle or unbridle their horses at night. During the day they were allowed
to unbridle them to feed, but not remove the saddles."[1]

While Lee was on picket near Fairfax Court House, General Stuart and his staff
staged a mock raid on the vedettes. The alarm spread, but the ruse was soon found
out. After the false alarm Stuart gathered some of the men and explained to them
that "his object was to teach us to be on the alert all the time; that as cavalry, we
were the eyes and ears of the army and that upon our vigilance depended the

1. WLU, Otho Scott Lee Collection

safety of the army."[2]

During March General Johnston, now in command of the Confederates, determined to withdraw his outnumbered army from Manassas. The sudden withdrawal caused the Confederates to burn mountains of supplies and soldiers' baggage. Lee recalled that at Gainesville Station, on the Manassas Gap Railroad,

> [O]ur regiment destroyed eight hundred barrels of flour stacked on the platform. This was done by knocking in the tops of the barrels and scattering the flour over the ground. I thought that this was a terrible waste and many of the men remarked that we would see the day when we would regret it. On the other hand, we had no way to take it with us and couldn't let it fall into the hands of the enemy. . . . [I]n a few months it became very scarce, and rations were cut down. Two years later our rations got down to one pint of corn meal and one-quarter pound of bacon per day.[3]

Stuart's troopers had only a few minor skirmishes with the Federal horsemen during the retreat. The First Virginia Cavalry fell back down the railroad to Warrenton Junction, destroying bridges and trestles as it went, and camped there for a week. Grumble Jones's troopers continued to scout and picket above the junction. Stuart reported to Johnston on March 26 that a column of Federal infantry was marching down the railroad seven miles from his position. "Captain Gaither says he counted six regiments without seeing either end of the column. . . . I immediately sent the First Virginia Cavalry (Jones) down to observe the enemy and report."[4]

The next day Jones reported that the Federals were encamped at Cedar Run, near Warrenton Junction. Later in the day the Federals occupied the junction, where they were harassed by Jones's troopers. The First fell back yet continued to delay the Union advance toward Bealton Station, thus enabling the evacuation of supplies and railroad stock southward.

On April 2 Stuart reported to Gen. James Longstreet that portions of the Union army were embarking aboard ships and preparing to destroy the bridges on the Rappahannock River, a sure sign of retreat. He was correct; Gen. George

2.   Ibid.

3.   Ibid.

4.   OR, Series I, Vol. II, Pt. 3, 402

B. McClellan, opting for the shorter river route to Richmond and the peninsula rather than a long overland effort, was moving his army. By mid-April Johnston had repositioned his army near Yorktown. Stuart left a small cavalry force along the Rappahannock and marched his troopers to the peninsula via Richmond. On April 21 the First camped near Bigler's Wharf on the York River.

The Howard County Dragoons and the other companies of the First Virginia Cavalry reenlisted for three years and reorganized on April 26. Thirty-one members of the company petitioned Col. Fitzhugh Lee, who was now commanding the First Virginia, for transfer to the newly organized Maryland Line. By April 28 the regiment had moved to a new bivouac site at Green's Wharf, closer to Williamsburg. On May 3 Johnston determined to evacuate his fortifications at Yorktown and retreat toward Richmond. The First served as rear guard during the move. Fitz Lee led his men into action against the enemy at Slatersville on May 9.

On May 13 the men who had petitioned for transfer got their wish. They received their discharges and rode out of camp toward Richmond.

Two days later eighteen former members of the Howard County Dragoons met in Richmond to organize a company of cavalry for the Maryland Line. One of the men told those who had gathered, "I have withdrawn from the First Virginia to fight with the people of my State, and if we do not form a company, I shall go into a Maryland command and shoulder a musket, if I cannot carry a sabre. It is a duty I owe her, and there are Marylanders enough here to represent her handsomely, if the proper steps are taken to assemble them."[5] All those present agreed, and the company was formed. Ridgely Brown was elected captain, with Frank A. Bond first lieutenant, Thomas Griffith of Montgomery County second lieutenant, and James A. V. Pue of Howard County third lieutenant. All of these original noncommissioned officers were veterans of the First Virginia.

Recruiting proceeded quickly, as Federal activities in Maryland put men with Southern sympathies who remained there at risk of imprisonment. Neither was leaving without its own peril: numerous Marylanders were arrested while attempting to cross the Potomac River or Chesapeake Bay on their way to join the Confederate army. Loss of property or imprisonment without trial was often the penalty. The Union army patrolled and picketed the roads, ferries, and likely crossing spots; the Federal navy blockaded the lower Potomac and Chesapeake Bay. Unionists reported suspicious activities by Confederate-leaning

5.   Author's Collection, no ascertainable publication facts

neighbors to authorities. Though the Potomac above Washington was fordable, few civilians in that area were Southern sympathizers. The Union army, which camped in southern Maryland in 1861–62, made it even more difficult to cross undetected. Still, thousands made the attempt. Overwhelmingly, Marylanders came to the aid of the Confederacy.

Edward R. "Ned" Rich, one of the new recruits, wrote that, while Maryland remained in the Union, not all of her people believed in its cause:

> [T]he hearts of many, true as steel, went out in loving sympathy for their southern brethren. There were alienation among friends, and families were broken up; spies were everywhere, and honest men and lovely women were torn from their homes and cast into prison, their only crime being sympathy with and fidelity to the Southern cause.
>
> No mere sentiment swayed them, but the same chivalrous honor, the same love of freedom that actuated their ancestors, who with self-sacrificing zeal and undaunted courage fought and won the battles of the Revolution. With this spirit many of Maryland's choicest sons crossed the Potomac and entered the armies of the Confederacy. Traveling under cover of night and through lanes and by-ways, stealing between pickets of Federal soldiers, wading and often swimming the upper Potomac, or running the blockading fleet on the deeper waters below; risking arrest and imprisonment, or perhaps death, they reached the Virginia shore and entered heartily into the service they so nobly espoused.[6]

Charles Kettlewell left merely a letter to be sent to his sister Olivia:

> Events have come upon me with such rapidity and force that I am scarcely able to master myself. This is my farewell. God bless you sister. I am now dressing to go South. Leave tonight on horseback and cannot write all I have or would like to say. May God in his mercy guard and guide you that we may once more meet. I remember with love your many prayers and kind guidance. Good bye.
>
>   With the love and prayers of your brother, Charlie
>   Monday evening—I will write soon.

6.   Rich 1907, 14

Pvt. Charles Kettlewell, Co. C, First Maryland Cavalry, and his messmates, Edmund C. Neale, Wilfred Neale, George C. Jenkins, Daniel G. Emory, and Lafayette Hause. The order is uncertain. (Maryland State Archives)

Kettlewell's father found the letter and added:

> The enclosed note will inform you of the great affliction that has been added to our already overflowing cup of sorrow. Our noble boy has gone—he has left us, and such a Home of desolation you can hardly conceive. He was of this earth to us our "all in all"—and the only Consolation we have, should we never see him again, is that he has offered himself a sacrifice to a Noble Cause— . . . I have a heart too full of grief to write you more. He was the joy of my heart—the prop of my old age—the pride of my life and he has gone . . .
>
> Yours, with regard, Jno Kettlewell
>
> [P.S.] Charley started on Monday night and I retained the enclosed until today, to give time of any notice of their or his Capture. The security of the orders in these cases, and the vigilance of the authorities made it an adventure of great risk.
>
> Up to this hour Friday 11 A.M. we have had no word of any such misfortune. On the Contrary, a reasonable hope that he is out of the state. He was accompanied by Wm. Howard (brother of the late Rev.d) Noel Nicholls, and young Mr. Dorsey.[7]

Kettlewell and his companions made it safely across the Potomac into Virginia.

Captain Brown and his lieutenants soon had sixty-four men enrolled in the company—twenty-six veterans and thirty-eight new recruits fresh from Maryland. As soon as the company was armed and equipped Brown was ordered to join the Maryland Line under Gen. George H. "Maryland" Steuart, who was operating in the Shenandoah Valley under Gen. Thomas J. "Stonewall" Jackson. Brown's Maryland cavalry joined Steuart at Martinsburg in time for the Confederate advance toward Harpers Ferry on May 29. Steuart camped his command beyond Charles Town following the day's march.

On May 30 the Maryland Line, supported by Capt. W. E. Cutshaw's Virginia battery, advanced on the enemy position on Bolivar Heights, overlooking Harpers Ferry. Bradley T. Johnson, now the colonel commanding the First Maryland Infantry, led the attack. Fire from Johnson's sharpshooters and Cutshaw's guns drove the Federals from their breastworks. Johnson then sent Brown's cavalrymen to occupy the position. The company captured the enemy's camp, including arms and supplies. Johnson's command meanwhile drove the Union forces into the town but was prevented by artillery fire from driving them out.

The supplies taken at Bolivar Heights and Harpers Ferry and turned over to Maj. Wells J. Hawks, Jackson's commissary officer, included about 156,000 pounds of hard bread; 1,315 pounds of salt pork; 1,545 pounds of salt beef; 19,267 pounds of bacon; and 4,930 pounds of coffee. Certainly Brown's troopers ate well for the next few days! Steuart ordered Johnson, after removing the captured stores, to fall back to near Charles Town.

Unbeknownst to Steuart, Johnson, and Brown, two Federal forces at that time were marching toward Jackson's flanks in an attempt to cut him off, and another force would soon be pressing the Confederates from Maryland. Gen. John C. Frémont's army was closing in from the west, Gen. James Shields's troops from the east, and Gen. Nathaniel P. Banks's command from the north. Jackson ordered a rapid retreat through Strasburg. Johnson, acting as rear guard for the army, marched seven miles beyond Winchester the first day. Brown's company kept stragglers on the move as they marched thirty-five miles through pouring rain. The next day, still acting as rear guard, Johnson marched his weary troops through Strasburg, having escaped the Federal trap.

Jackson retired his command slowly up the Valley toward Harrisonburg. Brown's company continued to act with the Maryland Line, which consisted of the First Maryland Infantry and the Baltimore Light Artillery during this period.

On June 2, again marching through a downpour, the Maryland Line fell back to Mount Jackson. Jackson retired to New Market the next day. Col. Thomas T. Munford's Second Virginia Cavalry burned the bridge at Mount Jackson before also falling back. The Union army brought up pontoons and was able to cross the river on June 5, forcing Jackson to retire to Harrisonburg. The Confederate cavalrymen meanwhile continued to keep their Federal counterparts at bay.

On June 6, with Jackson's forces camped along the Port Republic road, Federal cavalry attacked Turner Ashby's pickets and drove them back. Ashby brought up the rest of his brigade and in turn drove the Federals to within half a mile of Harrisonburg.

The Union cavalry came on again, this time backed by a brigade of infantry. Ashby determined to ambush the Federals. Gen. Richard S. "Old Baldy" Ewell sent Col. William C. Scott's Brigade, consisting of the Forty-fourth, Fifty-second, and Fifty-eighth Virginia and the First Maryland infantry regiments, to reinforce Ashby.

The brave but rash Ashby led the Fifty-eighth Virginia and First Maryland into the deep woods on the Port Republic road, hoping to attack the Federals' flank. Confederate cavalry commanded by Munford protected Ashby's flanks. Ashby's force ran head-on into the First Pennsylvania Rifles, an elite unit known for excellent marksmanship and nicknamed "the Bucktails." The Fifty-eighth Virginia and First Maryland were initially staggered by the Pennsylvanians' fire.

Ashby rode forward to lead the two regiments himself, and the men stormed through the woods after him. In the ensuing melee his horse was shot from under him. When the general leaped to his feet and ordered the men to follow him, he was shot and killed.

The Confederates kept up the attack, taking considerable casualties, and finally drove the Pennsylvanians from the woods, capturing their colonel and many other officers and men. Munford led a cavalry attack that drove the Federal troopers back before General Ewell arrived on the scene and ordered a withdrawal. He had Brown's and Munford's troopers bring the Confederate wounded off the field on their horses.

A few days later, during the battles of Cross Keys (June 8) and Port Republic (June 9), members of Brown's company supported the Baltimore Light Artillery and acted as couriers for the Maryland Line. After these battles, the men of the Line marched to the top of the Blue Ridge before going into camp without rations. June 10 was spent bringing in stragglers from many of the battle-worn units. Munford sent some of his dismounted men to Lynchburg in charge of Federal prisoners.

The next day Jackson sent Munford's troopers back down into the Valley. After recrossing the two forks of the Shenandoah, the Confederates, elated at having won three battles and in pursuit of the Federals, rode on to Mount Crawford, where they captured several Union pickets. As the Federals retired down the Valley the next day, Munford marched into Harrisonburg, where he captured two hundred prisoners, including many of the wounded from the battle of Cross Keys, numerous supplies, and two hundred Belgian muskets. Finding that the Union forces were in full retreat, Munford pushed on down the Valley toward New Market and Mount Jackson until relieved of command of the brigade by Gen. Beverly H. Robertson on June 13.

Brown's troops meanwhile had remained with the Maryland Line. After a few days of rest and ample rations near Weyer's Cave, all of the Marylanders were ordered to Staunton so the First Maryland Infantry could reorganize for the war.

A few days after his arrival in Staunton, Bradley Johnson met Stonewall Jackson on the street and was instructed to load his regiment on the railroad cars at the depot. Within an hour the First Maryland was loaded up and headed for Frederick's Hall on the Virginia Central Railroad. The Maryland cavalry and the Baltimore Light Artillery escorted the wagons eastward. On June 25 the First Maryland Infantry marched to Ashland, where Brown's company and the Baltimore cannoneers rejoined them.

Following the battles of Gaines's Mill and Frazier's Farm (June 27–30), Johnson ordered Brown's company to join Fitzhugh Lee's cavalry brigade. Lee, in turn, assigned the troopers to Munford's Second Virginia Cavalry. The Marylanders served as Company B in the regiment; the original Company B was acting as General Longstreet's escort. This assignment met with the approval of Brown and his men, as they were familiar with Munford's gallant regiment and would remain under Jackson's command.

As the Peninsula Campaign unfolded and Jackson advanced toward the Chickahominy River, Munford and his men led the way. On June 29 Jackson and Jeb Stuart reported that some of Munford's troopers had crossed the White Oak Swamp before being forced back by enemy artillery fire. The swampy, wooded terrain was certainly not favorable for cavalry operations. The difficulty of finding forage for the horses and rations and water for the men themselves was a serious problem. Scouting, patrolling, and picketing occupied much of the troopers' time. Conducting prisoners to the rear, bringing up stragglers, and gathering up the immense amount of arms, equipment, and supplies left by the retreating Federals also kept them busy. When the campaign was over, all of the Confederate soldiers were glad to leave the area, but none were happier than the cavalrymen.

During early July Gen. Robert E. Lee commenced moving Jackson's corps back into central Virginia, where the Confederates were facing a new threat from Gen. John Pope's Federal command. Munford's troopers again led the way and were in Gordonsville by mid-July. Union reports stated that on July 17 "Maryland and Virginia Cavalry made a reconnaissance six miles beyond Madison. It is reported Ewell is at Gordonsville with his division and Second Virginia Cavalry."[8]

The Second continued to act as the eyes and ears of Jackson's corps. Munford and his men took no active part in Jackson's victory at Cedar Mountain on August 9, but they picketed the flanks of the command.

8. OR, Series I, Vol. XII, Pt. 2, 828

General Lee next determined to drive Pope's army from the Rappahannock. Stuart's cavalry led the advance. While Stuart and two brigades pushed the Federal cavalry back from the fords on the Rappahannock, Munford, with a battery of horse artillery, protected Jackson's left wing as the infantry marched northward.

On August 23 the Second was engaged at Waterloo Bridge. The contest was an artillery duel, and Munford's regiment suffered casualties during the fight. In order to screen the movement of Jackson's infantry, Stuart was forced to use the combined strength of all his cavalry. When Munford moved forward on August 25, Ridgely Brown, in command of a squadron (two companies) of sharpshooters, was left behind to defend the crossing at the burned Waterloo Bridge. When Stuart's cavalry had cleared the area Brown led his squadron forward and rejoined the Second. By that time, on or about August 29, Munford's regiment had been placed in General Robertson's Brigade.

Robertson ordered the Second to take the advance on August 30. As the men marched forward they observed a Federal cavalry force on a hill overlooking Lewis's Ford on the south side of Bull Run. Robertson ordered the Second to charge the enemy, which appeared to be only a squadron in number. Munford sent Lt. Col. J. W. Watts to lead Brown's first squadron in a mounted charge on the Union troopers. Watts led the Marylanders and Virginians forward at a gallop and drove the enemy back. When he reached the crest of the hill he observed a large Union cavalry force stretching back to Lewis's Ford, so he halted his men and sent to Munford for reinforcements. Munford led the rest of the regiment forward and formed a line of battle, but seeing the size of the Federal force, he quickly determined to fall back to a better position. As soon as the Yankees saw the Confederates start to the rear, they advanced.

Munford wrote:

> We were then near enough to hear each other's commands. Hearing the command "Forward, trot," I wheeled my command to the right-about by fours and went at them with drawn sabers. The enemy was in column by regiment, composed of the First Michigan, Fourth New York and First Virginia (bogus) [West Virginia]. My regiment in line of battle going at a gallop, we went through the first line of the enemy and engaged part of the second. Here a terrible hand-to-hand fight ensued. The two commands were thoroughly intermingled, and the enemy overpowering us by numbers (being at least four to one), we were driven back; but as soon as the Seventh and Twelfth Cavalry re-enforced

me the whole of the enemy's command commenced a retreat. Had my regiment been promptly re-enforced my command would not have suffered so severely. My regiment went up in splendid order, and made as gallant a charge as was ever seen.

I did not pursue the enemy farther than Bull Run. . . . The Brigade captured some 300 prisoners, a large number of horses arms and accouterments.[9]

Among his casualties, Munford counted "John Lovely and F. R[awling] W. Nelson of Brown's mounted company, [who] were severely wounded and disabled."[10] Pvt. John Gill Jr. of Brown's troop recalled:

Colonel Munford and his regiment came up at a dashing gait, forming front into line, our company to the right.

Colonel Broadhead [Thornton F. Brodhead], commanding the Sixth [*sic*] Michigan Cavalry, moved out to take the same position in front of us. Here stood the two opposing regiments, within one hundred yards of each other, face to face. The excitement was intense. We were ordered to fight with sabres, and the command, "Draw sabres, forward, trot, gallop charge!" rang out from both commanders.

Colonel Broadhead [*sic*] was killed and Colonel Munford received a sabre cut over the head [and his horse was killed]. The two regiments locked sabers. Almost immediately support from both sides dashed into the fight. The dust and confusion became so great as to make it almost impossible to distinguish friend from foe.

I had joined the cavalry only a few weeks before, and it was my first cavalry fight. Unfortunately for me, my sabre, a poor specimen of Confederate iron, was soon bent and quite useless. I was attacked by three Yankees. I was fighting for my life, when kindly aid came from one of my comrades by the name of [F. Rawling W.] Nelson, who cut down two of my opponents, and at the third I made a right cut which missed him, and which nearly unhorsed me. Scarcely recovering my seat, I saw an officer coming straight at me tierce-point.

I had only a moment to gather my thoughts, and in that moment my pistol was levelled at him to surrender or die. He threw up his hands

9.   Ibid.
10.   Ibid.

and surrendered—horse, foot and dragoon. He was an officer of one of the Michigan cavalry regiments. During the remainder of the war I rode in his saddle.[11]

During the charge Pvt. Robert Goldsborough Keene was unseated; his horse ran away. Keene avoided capture by hiding in a hollow tree until dark and returned to camp that night minus his horse, sword, and hat.

The next day the Second rode with General Stuart on a scout to Chantilly, where the Confederates captured several hundred prisoners. On September 1, while the battle of Chantilly was being fought, Munford led the Second toward Leesburg. Scouts had reported that Samuel C. Means's Loudoun Rangers, Virginians loyal to the Union, occupied the town. The Confederates moved cross-country from the Dranesville Turnpike and approached the town on the Edwards's Ferry road, the Loudoun Rangers' direct line of retreat across the Potomac. Munford's troopers surprised the turncoat Virginians and drove them out of the town. As Means and his men fled Leesburg on the Point of Rocks road, they were reinforced by Maj. Henry A. Cole's Maryland Cavalry, U.S.A. Munford skirmished with the retreating Federals for seven miles, to Waterford, where he found himself with only about one hundred forty men; some of his units had not joined in the pursuit. Although Munford was disappointed not to have taken all of Means's men, he had succeeded in killing eleven, wounding nine, and capturing forty-seven, including two captains and three lieutenants.

Private Gill recalled:

> I was fortunate in capturing a live Yankee and a good horse, ridding myself of the old scrub which I had purchased a few months before while at Staunton, Va. I was now well mounted and well equipped with Yankee sabre, Yankee saddle, Yankee boots and Yankee horse, ready for the Maryland campaign.[12]

The next day Munford received orders to assist Maj. B. P. Noland of the commissary department in gathering cattle and other provisions for Lee's army from around Lovettsville. On September 4 Stuart ordered Munford to take command of Robertson's Brigade, the Seventh and Twelfth Virginia Cavalries, and join him in Maryland. Gill recalled, "We crossed the river at Edwards's Ferry,

11.   Gill 1904, 73–74
12.   Ibid., 75

marching in the direction of Frederick City, taking a position in a little town called Urbana." Munford reported joining Stuart at Urbana and receiving orders on September 8 to drive the enemy from Poolesville.[13]

Just as Munford's advance guard entered Poolesville, an enemy cavalry brigade supported by a four-gun battery was spotted. Munford moved his three regiments and battery, reduced to the size of large companies by details, casualties, and broken down horses, to some high ground to the left of the town, and his guns opened fire on the advancing Federal force. When the Union cannoneers returned the fire the Confederate gunners found themselves outgunned. The Federal cavalry charged their position, forcing Munford's troopers and guns back. The colonel pulled his men back to the key crossroads nearby where the sharpshooters of the Second Virginia Cavalry held the enemy in check. Despite constant attempts by the Federals to seize the road juncture and the detachment of the Seventh Virginia Cavalry for the next three days, Munford's troopers held onto the route that crosses Sugar Loaf Mountain.

On September 11 the Union infantry joined the fray, forcing Munford to give up the crossroads. The new brigade commander pulled his men back to within three miles of Frederick on the Buckeystown road. Private Gill noted: "We all enjoyed the kindly reception received from the citizens of Frederick. They were hospitable and liberal with their donations of good things."[14] Munford wrote, "In Maryland we lived on green corn, principally, for both men and horses."[15]

The next day Munford moved his brigade to Jefferson. September 13 was spent skirmishing with enemy cavalry. The Federal troopers were reinforced by infantry advancing on three roads toward Munford's small command, and he fell back to Burkittsville. The brigade's sharpshooters continued to hamper the progress of the enemy cavalry, and the Federals were kept in check as Munford's wagon train retreated up the mountain through Crampton's Gap. Using his artillery and sharpshooters, Munford repulsed the Union attempts to seize the gap.

The next morning Munford received orders from Stuart "to hold the gap at all hazards."[16] He found himself defending the position with two batteries and his dismounted cavalry. The troopers and cannoneers successfully fought off the first Union attack, but during the second Federal attempt Munford saw an entire

13.   Ibid.
14.   Ibid., 76
15.   OR, Series I, Vol. XII, Pt. 2, 828
16.   Ibid.

enemy division deploy and start up the mountainside. As the skirmishing began, Munford was reinforced by two small regiments of infantry. After three hours of fighting, Gen. Howell Cobb's Georgia Brigade came up. When Munford posted the first two Georgia regiments that arrived, his two Virginia infantry regiments, out of ammunition and believing they were being relieved, began to retire. As they fell back through the Georgians, the latter panicked and retreated in disorder. Munford's cannoneers were out of ammunition and had already withdrawn their guns; if they had not, they would have been captured. The two cavalry regiments acted as rear guard for the panic-stricken infantrymen, who fled down the Harpers Ferry road. Munford was then able to form his two regiments and move down the mountain to the Boonsboro road even as the enemy occupied it.

Later, he had high praise for his two regiments. "The cavalry (Second and Twelfth) behaved splendidly under the fire they were placed and did good service with their rifles."[17] General Stuart added, "In this hot engagement the Second and Twelfth Virginia Cavalry behaved with commendable coolness and gallantry, inflicting great injury with their long-range guns upon the enemy."[18]

Munford next retired toward the Potomac, guarding the extreme right of Lee's army. Gill wrote:

> [W]e witnessed a stubbornly contested struggle for two days [the battle of Antietam or Sharpsburg, September 17–18], we were not actively engaged ourselves. We could, however, see the desperate fighting going on on both sides, without being exposed to it.
>
> Our army retired across the Potomac without being further molested by the enemy. On this march our company brought up the rear.[19]

The return to Virginia was a sad one for the Marylanders, who had hoped to free their state of Union control, and disappointing for the Confederate leaders, who had hoped that the men of Maryland would rise up and enlist in their army in large numbers. Some recruits did join Brown's company, and some others took the opportunity to cross over into Virginia while Federal authorities were preoccupied with Lee's invasion. But overall, and although the army had occupied Frederick for more than a week, there were relatively few accessions.

17.   Ibid., 819
18.   Ibid., 819–20
19.   Gill 1904, 77–78

Bradley Johnson later blamed the low numbers on the fact that the First Maryland Infantry had been disbanded and the Second Maryland Infantry left behind to finish organizing. And, as was pointed out earlier, Baltimore and eastern Maryland were the strongholds of Confederate sympathy, not western Maryland.

Upon its return, the Second Virginia Cavalry was assigned to picket duty on the Shenandoah River. Brown's company was posted at Snickers's Ferry. "Here we were enabled to give our horses a much needed rest, and we amused ourselves, when not on picket duty, by shooting partridges and different kinds of game," Gill recalled. The regiment was later ordered to Leesburg, and Gill remembered that "the girls were delighted to see this splendid regiment of Virginians and Marylanders, and ran out of their houses to kiss our horses, but I will not say how many of the men kissed the girls."[20]

By October Brown's company had been detached from the Second Virginia Cavalry and ordered to Winchester, where the Maryland Line was reconstituted under General Steuart. On October 19 Captain Brown signed for 5,280 pounds of corn for his company. Two days later he received 6,160 pounds of hay. He continued to receipt for like amounts of hay and corn through the end of the month, signing the vouchers as captain of Company A, Maryland Cavalry.

Other companies of Maryland cavalry had been organized, but the Confederate War Department was slow to order them to join the Maryland Line. The challenge of obtaining horses, equipment, and arms also delayed the mobilization of these units.

Upon arrival at Winchester, Brown's company was placed on picket duty in a gap in the mountains on the Romney road, several miles west of the town. During early November the troop was relieved and ordered to Strasburg. There Brown's company met Capt. George M. Emack's newly formed troop of Marylanders, which had been organized at Charlottesville on September 16. The officers and men were a mixed group of veterans of the First Maryland Infantry and other organizations as well as new recruits. Emack, only about twenty years of age, had been a teenage messenger for the Confederacy when he was arrested in Prince George's County by Federal troops in 1861. While en route to Washington under guard Emack fatally stabbed the officer in charge and escaped across the Potomac. He was appointed a lieutenant of infantry and assigned to duty at Libby Prison in Richmond in October 1861. Tiring of prison duty and accused of mistreating Union prisoners, young Emack resigned with-

20.   Ibid., 78–79

Capt. Ignatius Dorsey, quartermaster, First Maryland Cavalry. (John Mattson)

in months. He immediately set about organizing his own troop of Maryland cavalry.

On November 12 the two companies elected Ridgely Brown major of the newly formed First Maryland Battalion of Cavalry; Emack's troop became Company B. The battalion returned to Winchester, and on November 25 the staff officers were named. George W. Booth, a veteran of the First Maryland Infantry, was appointed adjutant. Pvt. Ignatius W. Dorsey of Company A served as foragemaster until, when more companies joined, he was appointed quartermaster. Wilberforce R. McKnew, a recent graduate of the University of Maryland Medical School, was appointed assistant surgeon. Edward C. Johnson, another veteran of infantry service, was appointed sergeant major. Lt. Frank A. Bond was elected captain of Company A. Lieutenants Thomas Griffith and James Pue rose one rank, and Edward W. Beatty, one of the men who had transferred from the First Virginia Cavalry, was promoted to third lieutenant from corporal.

The other officers in Company B were 1st Lt. Mason E. McKnew, a veteran of the First Maryland Infantry; 2nd Lt. Adolphus Cooke, an 1861 graduate of Georgetown College; and 3rd Lt. Henry C. Blackistone of Kent County.

Pvt. Hobart Asquith wrote:

Company B was armed with Colt revolvers made at Hartford, Conn., and Chippapee sabers manufactured in Massachusetts, shipped to Nassau and reshipped by blockade runners to Wilmington, N.C., and paid for with money raised by our Maryland women, than whom no braver or more patriotic existed at that time.[21]

21. *Confederate Veteran*, Vol. XXVI, 431

On December 1 a strong force of Federal infantry, artillery, and cavalry under Gen. John W. Geary advanced toward Winchester from Bolivar Heights. The Winchester area was defended by Grumble Jones, who was commanding Confederate forces in the Valley consisting of his brigade of cavalry and the Maryland Line under General Steuart. The Confederates were forced to retire from Winchester on December 3, leaving a number of sick men of the First Maryland Cavalry and others to be captured by Geary's troops, which occupied the town the next day. Fortunately for the prisoners, a fear of smallpox caused the Union general to parole all of the captives. When Geary withdrew his command to Bolivar Heights, the Confederate cavalry reoccupied the town.

Brown pulled his battalion back to a position near Edinburg, but the Marylanders continued to picket the roads leading northward. At the end of December, Captain Bond reported that Company A had two officers and eighty-four men present and that the troopers were camped near New Market. Eighteen woolen overcoats were issued to the company near this time to protect the men from the frigid cold of the Valley winter. Troopers often shared their overcoats while on picket duty.

Company C, under Capt. Robert Carter Smith, joined the battalion at Edinburg. Although Smith, another veteran of the First Maryland Infantry, had begun organizing his company in Richmond in May 1862, it was not mustered into service until August. Like others in his position, Smith had found it difficult to arm and equip his men, who included reenlistees from the First Maryland Infantry and other organizations as well as new recruits fresh from Maryland. Smith's officers were 1st Lt. George W. Howard, who had served as an officer in Gaither's company, First Virginia Cavalry; 2nd Lt. Thomas Jefferson Smith, who had seen prior service with the Seventh Virginia Cavalry; and 3rd Lt. S. Graeme Turnbull, who had recently left his home in Baltimore to enlist.

Private Gill wrote, "[W]e went into permanent winter quarters. We had daily drills, and improvised a race track. We had many exciting races, at other times played cards, etc."[22]

During this period Company D also joined the battalion. Capt. Warner G. Welsh, a former officer in the Twelfth Virginia Cavalry, had brought enough recruits out of Frederick County, Maryland, during the recent invasion to organize his own company. In addition, a number of Frederick County men who had served in the First Maryland Infantry reenlisted in Welsh's troop. First Lt.

22.   Gill 1904, 80–81

Lt. William H. B. Dorsey (right), Co. D, First Maryland Cavalry, and an unidentified man. (Dave Marks)

William H. B. Dorsey was one of these. Both 2nd Lt. Stephen D. Lawrence and 3rd Lt. Milton Welsh, brother of the captain, were recruits. The company organized at Winchester on September 20 but was not assigned to the battalion until horses, arms, and equipment were obtained.

Upon learning that the Federals were reducing their strength in western Virginia, Robert E. Lee wanted Grumble Jones to drive them north of the Potomac and sever the important Baltimore and Ohio Railroad. Jones, now in command of the Valley District, attempted to drive the enemy from the Winchester area but found its forces too strong.

The First Maryland Battalion ended the year with increased strength and looked forward to greater accomplishments in 1863.

Chapter III

1863

"Some of my men actually fought with rocks; nor did
they give back an inch."

U nable to move the Federals in the Winchester area, Grumble Jones
determined to try in a different region. The cattle-rich surroundings of
the South Branch of the Potomac were his next prize. On January 2
Jones marched his cavalry brigade and the Maryland Line—infantry, cavalry,
and artillery—over the mountains to Moorefield. Private Gill described the
ordeal, on a bitterly cold day, as one of "marching night and day, crossing the
mountains. Many men were frost-bitten. Both of my heels were badly nipped,
but I soon recovered. . . . The suffering of the men was intense, and General
Jones became very unpopular for this movement."[1]

When Jones arrived before Moorefield the next day, he found it garrisoned by
the 116th Ohio Infantry, portions of the Third West Virginia Cavalry, and two
artillery pieces. The Confederates attempted to surround the town, but Col.
James Washburn of the Ohio regiment was able to send off his wagons before
the attack. Jones opened his artillery, hoping to force the enemy to surrender,
but the artillery shells proved defective and fell short. The Union cannoneers,

1.   Gill 1904, 81

with their superior guns and ammunition, played havoc with the Confederate cavalry. Finding the two wings of his command too far apart for mutual support and threatened by a Federal relief force, Jones withdrew his weary men back to the Valley. His half-frozen men returned to their camps around New Market and Edinburg. The Union troops at Moorefield were forced to burn a large amount of supplies to keep them from falling into Confederate hands. Jones reported his loss as one horse killed and two wounded. Robert E. Lee thanked Jones for his efforts and encouraged him to look for opportunities to drive the Federals out of the Valley.

Jones's raid did force the Union command to withdraw from Moorefield and the South Branch Valley a short time later. Lee kept prodding Jones to clear the Valley of all Federals, who were then concentrated at Winchester and Front Royal.

On January 31 General Steuart reported that the First Maryland Cavalry had 14 officers and 241 men present for duty, 273 aggregate present, 331 aggregate present and absent. This was an increase of 5 men during the month.

Jones took his command closer to the enemy on February 14 and 16, moving the men from their camps near New Market to one mile north of Edinburg. On February 23 Captain Bond, with overall command of his own Company A and Company D under Lt. William H. B. Dorsey, was placed on picket duty on Strawberry Hill, near Strasburg. Two days later Bond learned from one of Jones's scouts that a Federal picket post near Winchester could be captured. Bond, with forty of his men, and Dorsey, with twenty of his company, determined to make the attempt. Gill wrote: "[W]e started on a cold, chilly afternoon, reckoning to reach the outlying pickets about midnight."[2] Major Brown reported:

> They arrived within 1½ miles of Winchester, on the Cedar Creek road, at daybreak, charged through an infantry picket, receiving only a few random shots. At the junction of the Cedar Creek and Staunton roads they were met by a volley of musketry from a house, but it did not check them. They turned up the Staunton road toward home, riding down a third infantry picket. At Kernstown they found a cavalry picket of 15 men quietly warming themselves in a house. The house was instantly surrounded. They captured 7 men and 9 horses, and left several of the enemy dead or wounded in the house. They returned rapidly to

2.   Ibid., 82

Strasburg, bringing off their prisoners and captured horses with the loss of only 1 man missing.[3]

Gill recalled that Captain Bond then "dispatched two of his men to inform General Jones that one or two regiments were closing in on us, and to be ready to meet them when we came up. We were in no condition to fight after a gallop of nearly eighty-seven miles." Jones ordered out the Seventh and Eleventh Virginia, which advanced down the turnpike "nicely closed up and ready for the charge. This was fun for the Virginians," Gill noted.[4]

First the Eleventh Virginia struck the Thirteenth Pennsylvania Cavalry, which was strung out along the Valley Pike about a mile from Woodstock. Then the Eleventh, aided by the arrival of the Seventh, chased the Pennsylvanians and the First New York Cavalry all the way back to Cedar Creek, taking hundreds of prisoners, arms, and horses.

Major Brown, meanwhile, had sent Company B under Captain Emack and Company C, led by Lt. Thomas Jefferson Smith, to relieve Bond's men. They killed one man and captured seven men and five or six horses. These two companies chased the enemy to Middletown, losing one man wounded and one captured. Brown gathered the thirty men remaining in camp and joined in the pursuit but was not engaged.

Private Kettlewell wrote home about the action:

> [W]e took 290 prisoners. . . . It was one of the most exciting days I ever passed. [A]ll the excitement of a fox hunt. In the morning I as well as several others lost my hat and had to ride nearly all day without anything on my head. Toward evening I took up a Yankee's cap. . . . You would scarcely know me. I weigh 150 pounds, and so hardy that nothing affects me. Cold, rain, or snow. I was up two consecutive nights after the fight standing picket, while the rain was coming down as hard as it could pour.[5]

A week later he wrote:

3.   OR, Series I, Vol. XXV, Pt. 1, 38

4.   Gill 1904, 82

5.   MSA, Charles Kettlewell Letters

Capt. William I. Rasin, Co. E, First Maryland Cavalry. (Museum of the Confederacy)

This winter has been very severe, having 25 to 30 inches of snow storms. It now lies 8 inches deep. Yet I have passed very comfortable and pleasant time sleeping on the ground with 3 blankets over me. Scouting and picketing in all weathers, rain, hail or snow, and I have never been sick a day. It has made a man of me physically.[6]

On February 28 Companies B and C were attacked by the enemy at their picket posts near Strasburg. Companies A and D rode to their support, but the Federal cavalry withdrew. The Marylanders lost several men to capture. On March 28 Company A also skirmished with the enemy, near Kernstown.

During this period Company E, the "Winder Cavalry," joined the battalion. The company was led by Capt. William Independence Rasin of Kent County. Rasin was a merchant in Fort Leavenworth, Kansas, when the war started. He joined the Missouri State Guard under Gen. Sterling Price and served until 1862, when he returned to his family home in Kent County. In February he was arrested there by Union detectives who believed him to be a spy and thrown into Old Capitol Prison in Washington, D.C. Rasin escaped and again crossed the Potomac to reenter Confederate service. He determined to raise a company of cavalry and had little difficulty enlisting men; mounting them was more troublesome. Finally, he traveled to Salisbury, North Carolina, where he purchased forty horses for his men with his own funds. He also succeeded in obtaining thirty-two Colt army revolvers for his troopers. His company was sworn into Confederate service at Camp Lee in Richmond on January 20, 1863. The company's February muster rolls showed it still at Camp Lee, "Drilling and preparing to take the field." The "Winder Cavalry" joined the battalion by April 1863.

Rasin's officers were 1st Lt. John Sommersett B. Burroughs of Prince

6.   Ibid.

George's County; 2nd Lt. Nathaniel Chapman, a doctor of medicine who had served in Wade Hampton's South Carolina Legion Cavalry; and 3rd Lt. Joseph K. Roberts Jr., a young lawyer from Easton in Talbot County.

From Lacey Springs, Lieutenant Burroughs wrote to a friend:

> I arrived here sooner than I anticipated—via Charlottesville & Brown['s] Gap from Richmond. I am for the present in Comm[an]d of the Winder Cavalry. The Country here is rich and beautiful & reminds me very much of Salem [Maryland] & vicinity.[7]

Burroughs hinted to his correspondent that the command was expecting action soon.

Kettlewell wrote to his parents on April 6:

> Within the last week I have lost one of my truest friends and the Confed'y one of its noblest soldiers. Poor Graime [Graeme] Turnbull's is dead. After a sickness of only a week, and confined to bed but 4 days he died of deptheria [sic]. he is sadly missed by us all for his general [genial] companionship and soldier's qualities. He was our 3rd Liut., and had the respect and friendship of every man in the Co.[8]

Turnbull was the first officer in the battalion to die.

Robert E. Lee, having learned of major troop withdrawals by the Federals from the Kanawha Valley and other areas of western Virginia, determined to advance Gen. John D. Imboden's and Jones's commands into the region. He ordered Imboden to seize Beverly as a base of operations and, leaving his infantry to occupy the town, burn the bridges on the Baltimore and Ohio Railroad at Oakland and Rowlesburg. Jones was directed to threaten Romney, New Creek, and Cumberland, covering Imboden's movements. Lee hoped that the raid would draw Gen. Robert H. Milroy's command out of Winchester and clear the Valley to the Potomac. Jones and Imboden were also to destroy the railroad as far west as Grafton, and Lee wanted the two cavalry brigade commanders to bring out as many horses, cattle, and sheep as possible for his army. He believed that a large number of recruits could also be gotten from the area, as the oppressive tactics of the Federals had turned the people against them.

Jones was cautioned by Lee to conceal his departure from the enemy. Pickets

7.   Harvey Griff Collection, John S. B. Burroughs Letter
8.   MSA, Charles Kettlewell Letters

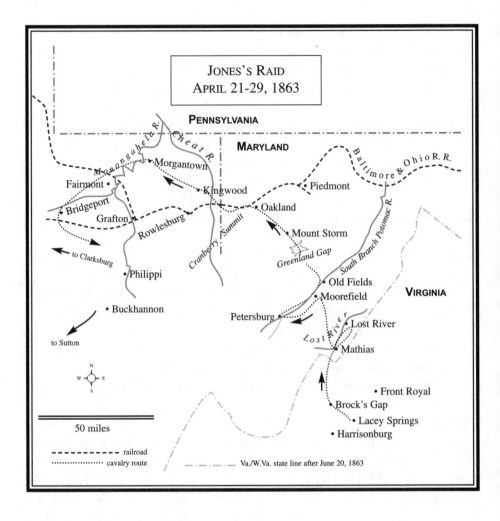

JONES'S RAID
APRIL 21-29, 1863

PENNSYLVANIA

MARYLAND

Cheat R.

Monongahela R.

Baltimore & Ohio R.R.

Morgantown

Fairmont

Kingwood

Piedmont

Bridgeport

Oakland

Grafton

South Branch Potomac R.

Rowlesburg

Cranberry Summit

Mount Storm

to Clarksburg

Greenland Gap

Philippi

Old Fields

Moorefield

VIRGINIA

Buckhannon

Petersburg

Lost River

to Sutton

Lost River

Mathias

N
W   E
S

Front Royal

Brock's Gap

Lacey Springs

50 miles

Harrisonburg

- - - - - - -   railroad
....   cavalry route   Va./W.Va. state line after June 20, 1863

were to remain in place. "An inspection should be made of every man, horse, and arm carried with you, and none must be allowed to go except those found every way competent for the hardships that may be incurred," admonished Lee.[9]

Jones, in coordination with Imboden, set out from Lacey Springs on April 21, taking all of his able-bodied cavalry, infantry, and artillery, including the Maryland Line. Major Brown led the 230 men of the First Maryland forward on their first raid. The first three days of the march were made in a pouring rain that rendered the mountain roads almost impassable. When the troops reached Moorefield, the South Branch of the Potomac was unfordable. Jones was forced to detour to Petersburg to find a crossing point, but even there "the ford was rough and dangerous from the swiftness of the stream," he reported. When one man and his horse drowned as the Sixth Virginia Cavalry crossed, the citizens of Petersburg came to the rescue of the Confederates, "recklessly plunging to the assistance of all in peril, and remaining for hours in the cold water until all were safe over."[10]

Pvt. John M. Heighe of Company A recalled:

[Lt. Col. John Sheshol] Witcher's Battalion of Cavalry from West Virginia, Mts., most of them riding ponies, were in advance. In starting to cross, several of the men and horses were washed down the river. General Jones halted the command and ordered the 1st. Md. Cavalry ahead. A farmer, riding a 17 hands high horse, went about 1/16 of a mile up the river and halted in the middle of the stream, and we were ordered to follow him.[11]

Captain Bond reported that "this was overcome without much delay, and all crossed safely with the exception of 5 men. Three of these men were not allowed to cross, owing to the weakness of their horses, and the other two attempted it, but were obliged to return after a thorough wetting."[12]

Jones was forced to leave his infantry and artillery behind.

Major Brown led the battalion onward, reaching Greenland Gap on April 25. Jones was surprised to find the gap occupied by the enemy and directed the

9.   OR, Series II, Vol. XXV, Pt. 2, 711

10. Ibid., Pt. 1, 114

11. Howard County Historical Society, Scrapbook of Company A, First Maryland Cavalry, 8

12. *Confederate Veteran,* Vol. XVII, 499–500; OR, Series II, Vol. XXV, Pt. 1, 124–27

Seventh Virginia Cavalry to attack the Federal picket force. The Virginians made a mounted attack on the enemy and succeeded in capturing several men, but the remainder of the two companies of Twenty-third Illinois Infantry, under command of Capt. Martin Wallace, was barricaded in a large log church and two log outbuildings. During the charge the Seventh became strung out along the rough, narrow road, and Captain Wallace and his riflemen were able to bring down horses and riders as the Confederates attacked piecemeal. Only part of the Seventh made it past the buildings, so the regiment was split further.

Unfortunately for Jones, the cannons, which could have driven the Federals out in short order, had been left behind because of the overflowing streams. He charged a captured noncommissioned officer with delivering to Captain Wallace a message instructing him to surrender and warning "that if he undertook to hold an indefensible position where he could kill many of us without danger to himself, and that if we succeeded, then according to the usages of war the garrison would forfeit their lives. Captain Wallace drove this man off and threatened him if he returned," Bond related.[13]

Before the flag of truce, Jones had dismounted Witcher's Battalion and Companies D, under Lieutenant Dorsey, and E, led by Captain Rasin, of the First Maryland battalion, all armed with long-range guns, and surrounded the position. These marksmen had pinned the enemy down. Believing the Yankees were surrendering, the two companies charged down the mountainsides toward the church. The Federals opened fire at close range, driving them back. Pvts. Frank Swomley and Charles Lambsden of Company D were wounded, Swomley mortally, and Pvt. John C. Spencer of Company E was killed. Pvt. Edward Rich recalled the sad story surrounding Spencer's death:

> [H]e left home a mere boy and against his father's consent. After his departure for the South became known his father, who was a strong sympathizer with the Union, was terribly incensed, and in his anger said to those who surrounded him, "May the first ball that strikes him bring death!" And his prayer was answered, for his gallant son no sooner entered this, his very first engagement, than he was struck full in the throat, uttered one groan, fell back into the stream and was dead.[14]

The Confederate sharpshooters kept the enemy pinned down until nightfall,

13. *Confederate Veteran*, Vol. XVII, 500
14. Rich 1907, 54–55

when Jones ordered Major Brown to attack the Federals. Brown dismounted Companies A and C and formed Bond's troopers in the road behind Captain Smith's company. Brown explained to Bond that his men were to proceed cautiously until fired upon and then charge the buildings. Major Brown and Adjutant Booth led the attack; they were followed by the colors and color guard. As he later noted, Bond thought it unnecessary to bring Company A's colors and guard at night. He estimated that seven officers and a hundred twenty men in the two companies made the assault. They were accompanied by two pioneers—men with axes and bundles of straw with which to fire the buildings. The Thirty-fifth Battalion Virginia Cavalry and elements of the Seventh Virginia Cavalry also joined in the attack.

"Forward! Double Quick," shouted Brown.

Booth reported:

> The moon shone out brightly and lit up the road so that it was almost as distinct and clear as under the noonday sun. With a wild rush and a loud yell, on went the devoted column, until it was soon under fire from the church, from the windows and doorways of which was poured the leaden hail. A winding stream crossed the road some several times in the distance of a hundred yards. Through this stream and under this deadly fire on rushed our brave boys. The weather was bitterly cold, and on emerging from the water their clothing soon stiffened in ice. But personal discomfort was not to be thought of at a time like this. One by one the men dropped, victims to the well directed fire; but onward pressed the column, and soon ranged itself around the house.
>
> If we had left off our sabers, we might have approached much nearer before drawing their fire, but stumbling about in the dark over logs and rocks soon attracted attention, and the houses blazed up with the flash from a hundred muskets. I remember distinctly noticing two lines of fire one above the other cut by a perpendicular black object which I guessed was a chimney, and I made this my objective, and was, I think, the first man to get there. Once there, I was safe, as the enemy, thrusting their guns out of the loopholes, could not reach us, and I was very soon closely pressed by a V-shaped body of men who could only in this way get out of range. We could not get in the house, but many of the men got close to the house to get below their line of fire.
>
> I remember distinctly hearing Major Brown call out in stentorian tones: "Where are those pioneers?" As we stood behind the chimney

Lt. Edward W. Beatty, Co. A, First Maryland Cavalry. (Dave Marks)

Sprigg Cockey, of my company, said: "Captain, I am wounded. What shall I do?" I suggested that he go to the rear; but he said "If I leave this chimney, I be killed sure." I then suggested that he remain where he was, but he said: "If I stay here, I will bleed to death." So I had to give it up.

Very shortly the pioneers came up with axes and bundles of straw and began a furious attack on the windows, and the one nearest me soon gave way. A large bundle of straw was ignited and thrown blazing into the building through this open window, and very soon the house was fully on fire. The inmates were for the most part exceedingly anxious to surrender, and the door was partly opened. Sergt. Maj. Edward [C.] Johnson immediately rushed in, but . . . the door was closed again and he was inside alone with the enemy. However, as by this time the enemy was even more anxious to get out than we had been to get in, the door was soon opened and Johnson came out with Captain Wallace as his prisoner.[15]

Bond described the defenders as "two companies of Chicago Irishmen well primed with whiskey." Wallace surrendered his Colt revolver to Bond, who carried it to the end of the war. "Under the circumstances [Wallace's failure to surrender and the ensuing Confederate casualties], our men were much incensed, and it was all I could do to protect the prisoners, and one I know was killed."

Bond later learned that some of the men from Company E, detailed as sharpshooters, had aided Companies A and C. "They were a gallant set of boys, many of them under fire for the first time: and when they found that we were assaulting the houses, they abandoned their position on the mountain side and joined in the attack."[16] Captain Rasin was wounded in this sortie.

15.   *Confederate Veteran,* Vol. XVII, 499–500; OR, Series II, Vol. XXV, Pt. 1, 124–27
16.   Ibid.

Major Brown received a wound in the leg but remained with the battalion. Adjutant Booth was also shot. Color Cpl. Robert W. Carvell of Company B was killed. In Bond's company, Pvt. Samuel A. Dorsey was killed and Lts. James A. V. Pue and Edward W. Beatty and three men were wounded. Capt. Robert Carter Smith of Company C, the only officer in his company present, was wounded, along with two of his men. Bond related:

> As we stood in the road before starting for the assault a man named [Kennedy] Grogan, who belonged to [Lt. Col. Elijah "Lige"] White's [Thirty-fifth Virginia Cavalry] Battalion, but who had a brother [Robert R. Grogan] in Company C of our battalion, came by. One of our boys asked him what he was doing away from his command. He was just opposite me, and I remember his answer well. He said: "I heard that General Jones had some Yankees up here in a box and you fellows were going to take the lid off, and I thought I would go along." He passed on and joined his brother, and this man was one of the killed and the brother was wounded.[17]

Sgt. Thomas J. Green commanded Company C until the raid was over. Bond reported, "I feel it my duty to say that, as far as I could see, the men generally behaved with great coolness and courage, going round the house and firing in wherever they could discover a crack large enough to admit the muzzle of a pistol."[18]

The losses and detachments reduced the battalion to 6 officers and 180 men. The number of unwounded Federals captured was 80, along with 6 or 8 wounded; several were killed. Four wagons and an ambulance, along with their horses, were taken, and a number of captured Enfield muskets were burned. Rich recalled that 5 dead Federals were carried from the house and buried beside the fallen Confederates. Asst. Surgeon Wilberforce McKnew of the First Maryland Cavalry and several men who were left behind to attend to the wounded of both sides were later captured.

The Irishmen's stubborn defense of the gap delayed Jones's advance so much that he missed capturing a train on the Baltimore and Ohio Railroad in which most of the officers of the Twenty-third Illinois were riding.

As it was, Jones pushed his command on to attack the Baltimore and Ohio

17. Ibid.
18. Ibid.

Railroad before Federal reinforcements could arrive. Speed was essential to the success of the operation. Col. Asher W. Harman, in charge of his own Twelfth Virginia Cavalry, Brown's Battalion, and Capt. John H. "Hanse" McNeill's company of Virginia partisan rangers, was sent toward the railroad. Rich described the ordeal: "[T]he weather was bitter cold, and as we rode along the water in our boots froze, and our clothes were a mass of ice. But we dared not halt, and on we pushed to Oakland, Maryland, which we reached at daylight."[19] Bond reported that "all who were in the fight at the house being wet to the waist, the suffering was intense."[20]

Harman wrote of the action of April 26:

> [D]estroyed the turnpike bridge over the North Branch of the Potomac, and reached Oakland at 11 A.M., surprised and captured a company of 57 men and 2 commissioned officers, and paroled them. Destroyed a railroad bridge east of the town and the railroad and turnpike bridges over the Youghlogheny River; also a train of cars.[21]

Bond noted that the Maryland battalion participated in the charge that captured the town without losing a man. Rich remembered that:

> [W]e captured a few home-guards, who were more frightened than hurt, and were ourselves captured by the citizens. And a noble and delightful capture it was. Every house was thrown open—warm fires and bright smiles caused the ice to melt and hearts to glow, and the inner man, which had known but three crackers and a bit of bacon since early Thursday morning [April 23], was regaled and strengthened with that feast that made that Sunday a memorable one.[22]

The respite was a short one. As soon as the prisoners were paroled, Harman led his command westward along the railroad. At Cranberry Summit he captured the guard of fifteen men and paroled them, along with twenty citizens, and destroyed the railroad property. The Confederate troopers rode on to the Cheat River before halting for the night.

19.   Rich 1907, 57
20.   *Confederate Veteran,* Vol. XVII, 500
21.   OR, Series I, Vol. XXV, Pt. 1, 134
22.   Rich 1907, 57

The next morning Harman sent Brown and his battalion in advance toward Kingwood and Morgantown. Once Harman's command had crossed the Cheat River, the suspension bridge was burned. Bond led Company A in advance as the battalion approached Kingwood. His troop charged through the small village but found that the enemy had fled. When Harman arrived he ordered Brown and his Marylanders on toward Morgantown; the rest of the command's troopers stopped to feed their horses.

Bond's company again took the van. As he approached the town, Bond learned that several hundred citizens had armed themselves and were preparing to defend it. When Major Brown arrived with the rest of the battalion, Bond offered to carry in a flag of truce and demand an unconditional surrender. Brown approved, and Bond rode boldly into the town. The citizens agreed to surrender, placed their arms in the courthouse, and returned to their homes.

The Maryland battalion occupied the town, found the weapons, and destroyed them. Rich reported the capture here of "a large train of cars laden with flour and meat for the Union troops."[23] The Marylanders stuffed their knapsacks and stomachs with the booty. After firing the railroad bridge, they ran the engine and nineteen cars into the river. Harman and the rest of the command arrived about two hours later. The entire unit marched immediately out again, and Harman bivouacked the troopers for the night about seven miles along the Independence road.

The weary riders were roused from their sleep at 2 A.M. and rode on until they met General Jones and the rest of the brigade. Jones led them back to Morgantown. Brown's battalion again led the command, and Bond's troopers again acted as the advance guard. During the ride the Marylanders were fired upon by bushwhackers, but the only damage they suffered was the death of Captain Rasin's horse. Bond's troopers chased the bushwhackers down a mountainside and captured three of them. The captain gave them a short trial and had them shot on the spot.

When the brigade reached Morgantown it camped on the west side of the suspension bridge over the Monongahela River. Jones rested his command and fed the horses from captured supplies. At dusk he started the brigade toward Fairmont. He halted about nine o'clock and rested the men and mounts until 1 A.M.

As he approached Fairmont, Jones learned from his scouts that the enemy had torn up the bridge over Buffalo Creek. Detouring via Barracksville, the

23. Ibid., 58

Confederates approached the town from the west, where Jones found the hills on either side of the road manned by Federal troops. He had Col. Lunsford L. Lomax dismount two companies of sharpshooters from his Eleventh Virginia Cavalry and Rasin's company of Brown's Battalion and advance toward the enemy on the Barracksville road. One company of the Eleventh advanced on the hill on the right of the road while Lomax led his other company and the Marylanders toward the hill on the left. Jones meanwhile directed Harman to take his regiment and White's Battalion of Virginia Cavalry to flank the enemy position from the right. Lomax reported:

> I entered the town on the left, the enemy giving way rapidly before our line of dismounted men, and pushing on to the bridge met Captain [M. D.] Ball, who had entered on the right, followed by Colonel Harman with the remaining regiments and battalions. . . . The enemy [in the town having] surrendered at this point, I moved my regiment to the hill opposite the railroad suspension bridge, covered by fences on the side of the road, without injury.[24]

The Federals defending the bridge crossing opened fire with a cannon, forcing the dismounted men to retire. Captain Rasin lost Pvt. W. Miles killed and two men wounded in the charge.

Meanwhile, the mounted charge of Harman's and White's commands gained the entrance to the suspension bridge, which was quickly repaired and crossed. The Confederates pushed the Federal defenders into a pocket near the bridge, where they were under fire from both sides of the river. A white flag soon went up, and the Union soldiers surrendered. Jones reported:

> Their arms were scarcely stacked before a train with artillery and infantry arrived from Grafton. The enemy at once commenced shelling our troops on the west bank of the river, and moved forward the infantry to recover the railroad bridge. These were promptly met by Colonel Harman on his side of the river. Lieutenant Colonel [Thomas] Marshall, with great presence of mind, moved his horses under shelter of a hill, and called on his men to dismount and take up the captured arms. The call was most gallantly answered by the ever-ready Seventh Virginia Cavalry, and the reception of the newcomers was soon too

24.   OR, Series I, Vol. XXV, Pt. 1, 132–33

warm for a long tarry.[25]

Of the destruction of the vital railroad structure, Jones wrote:

The bridge was of iron; three spans each 300 feet. This we destroyed
completely, throwing the whole magnificent structure into the river.
Two years were spent in its construction. . . . The fruits of this day's
work (April 29) were 4 railroad bridges destroyed, 1 piece of artillery,
300 small-arms, 260 prisoners and many fresh horses captured. At dark
we again marched for Clarksburg, resting a part of the night.[26]

The general was forced to leave his wounded behind.

Private Rich had captured a mounted Federal soldier and taken from him his
large gray horse, new sabre, and revolver. He carried the revolver throughout
the war.

The next day Jones advanced to within four miles of Clarksburg but learned
that the town was strongly occupied by the Federals. Crossing the Monongahela, he instead led his troopers up Simpson's Creek toward Bridgeport, where
he ordered the Maryland battalion to attack the village. Brown led the mounted
charge on the Federal garrison, capturing forty-seven prisoners with their arms
and a few horses. Pvt. Clinton Myers of Company C was killed in the charge.

"This work was done by the Maryland cavalry, under the gallant Major
Brown," wrote Jones. "A bridge on the left of town was destroyed and a cap-
tured train run into the stream. Tall trestling to the right of town was burned.
Marching until some time after dark we encamped."[27]

While the action at Bridgeport was taking place, Company B had been left
behind to picket the Clarksburg road, where it was attacked by a large Federal
force of mounted infantry. The Maryland troopers fell back behind a nearby
ford and engaged the enemy. Few men in the company were armed with long-
range guns, but they held the Union soldiers in check with the fire from their
revolvers.

The next day Jones marched his command to Philippi, gathering cattle and
horses as he went. Engineers were able to repair the damaged bridge in the
town, which enabled the general to send the captured animals, escorted by the

25.   Ibid., 118
26.   Ibid.
27.   Ibid., 118–19

Sixth Virginia Cavalry, to Beverly. The rest of the command trekked on toward Buckhannon.

When Jones's troopers reached the town they found General Imboden's command. Here Major Brown's wound forced him to leave the battalion. "If any one officer or man deserves especial mention," wrote Jones, "it is Major Ridgely Brown of the Maryland Cavalry. He was shot in the leg at Greenland Gap, there being two inches between the entrance and exit of the ball, yet he continued on duty, not even examining the wound until he arrived at Buckhannon, a distance of 168 miles, and then started home on the earnest solicitation of Dr. [R. P.] Johnson."[28]

Bond found himself in command of the battalion, which had been reduced to one hundred twenty men. He issued them four hundred rounds of Sharps carbine ammunition with caps, one hundred Colt army rounds, one hundred Colt navy rounds, and three hundred pistol caps.

From Buckhannon Jones and Imboden led their forces on to Weston, where the weary horsemen rested for two days. Here the main body of the Sixth Virginia Cavalry, stragglers, and the men who had been detailed to drive the animals to Beverly rejoined the brigades. The two leaders determined that the Federal force at Clarksburg was too strong to attack but that a raid on the Northwestern Railroad toward Parkersburg was feasible.

Jones sent Colonel Harman with part of the brigade toward West Union. He led the rest, including the Maryland battalion, in an attack on Cairo on May 7. As usual, the Marylanders led the assault. Bond dismounted Company E, equipped with long-range rifles, and directed its men to advance on the small Union force holding the village. He sent the rest of the men to the rear of the town. To make the Union leader believe he led a large force, Bond placed his men in a single skirmish line and moved toward the enemy. The Federal commander raised a white flag and surrendered his twenty men.

Bond's troopers then helped destroy the railroad bridge in Cairo. Jones also reported that two other bridges and a tunnel cribbed with wood were burned. "This work was done by hard marching, my command having traveled upward of eighty miles without unsaddling," he noted.[29]

On May 9 the Confederates reached Oiltown. "All of the oil, the tanks, barrels, engines for pumping, engine houses, and wagons—in a word, everything used for raising, holding, or sending it off was burned," Jones related.[30]

28.   Ibid., 121
29.   Ibid., 120
30.   Ibid.

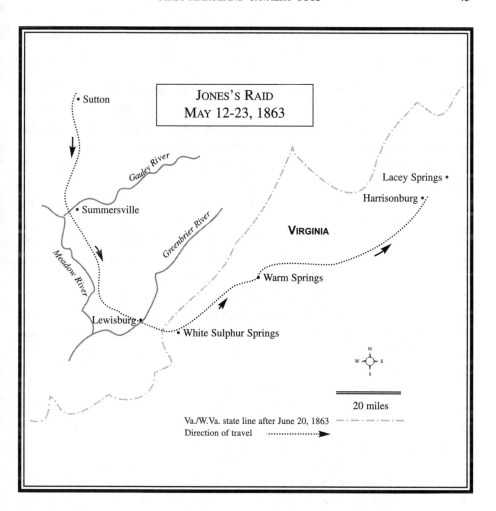

Rich described the scene:

We arrived there about one hour before sunset, and at once made preparations for such a display as is rarely witnessed by man. The oil wells
were scattered thickly between the railroad and the river, and tied up to
the wharf were several scows laden to the water's edge with barrels of
oil ready for shipment. It took but a short time to fire the vats containing thousands of gallons of oil, and as the flames roared and played
around them, the burning oil flowed out upon the river, and every wave

was capped with light. Up the river and down we gazed, fascinated with the weird sight.[31]

Rich and some comrades were so taken with the spectacle that they did not realize the bridge they were standing on was on fire until others warned them of the danger. "The bugle summoned us to mount, and hastily we sought our well-nigh maddened horses and the march was resumed. . . . Daylight found the command confronted by the enemy, who were soon put to flight," Rich concluded.[32]

Jones next led the brigade toward Glenville and a juncture with Imboden. The weary riders made easy marches through Glenville and Sutton and met Imboden's command at Summersville, where the Confederate leaders determined to return to the Shenandoah Valley. The units set off on various routes, the better to take advantage of the small amount of forage available in this mountainous region. Bond led his Marylanders on to Lewisburg. By May 23 the small band was back in the Valley after a seven-hundred-mile trek through western Virginia. In addition to the extensive damage done to the railroads and oil industry, the fruits of the foray included a thousand cattle and twelve hundred horses.

Bond's report of the campaign concluded, "I do not think the command is as well mounted as before starting out, even where the men are using captured horses, but they are in high spirits, with great confidence in themselves and their leaders, and anxious to be again led against the enemy."[33]

Upon their return to the Valley the Marylanders were detached from Jones's Brigade and returned to the Maryland Line. Back at the camp near New Market the riders rejoined the men left behind and found some new recruits who had been serving as pickets and scouts in the lower Valley. Captain Welsh and several men had been captured in minor actions during the First Maryland's absence. On May 30 the battalion marched northward to Fisher's Hill.

Jones's Brigade was meanwhile ordered to join General Stuart's cavalry at Culpeper, and Gen. Albert G. Jenkins's Brigade replaced it in the Valley. Gen. Isaac R. Trimble, a Marylander, was placed in command of the Valley District.

Once again Robert E. Lee determined to carry the war into the North. He directed Trimble to press Milroy's forces around Winchester with Jenkins's

31.   Rich 1907, 59–61
32.   Ibid., 61
33.   *Confederate Veteran,* Vol. XVII, 500

Brigade and the Maryland Line. Imboden was to threaten Romney and the Baltimore and Ohio Railroad to prevent Milroy from receiving reinforcements from the west.

General Ewell, commanding Jackson's old corps, joined Jenkins at Cedarville on June 12. He detached Gen. Robert E. Rodes's infantry division and most of Jenkins's cavalry to drive the enemy from Berryville. Ewell, with the rest of his command, advanced on Winchester.

Milroy was ordered to determine whether the Confederates were advancing down the Valley in force. The Southern cavalry had become bolder in the past two weeks and was constantly driving in his scouts and patrols and attacking his picket posts. He sent out a strong force on June 12 to investigate the Confederate intentions. Col. John W. Schall led this command, which consisted of his own Eighty-seventh Pennsylvania Infantry, the Thirteenth Pennsylvania Cavalry, and one section of Battery L, Fifth U.S. Artillery. Maj. Michael Kerwin led the advance with his

Maj. Harry W. Gilmor, Second Maryland Cavalry. (Daniel D. Hartzler)

Pennsylvania troopers. About two miles from Middletown Kerwin ran into Confederate cavalry, deployed in line of battle. He sent a courier to Schall with the news and proposed that the colonel ambush the Confederates as the mounted Pennsylvanians retired. Schall agreed and placed his regiment and the guns in position along the road.

Miss Kate Sperry, who lived in a house within sight of the action, wrote in her diary:

> In a few moments, 411 Yankee Infantry and two cannon came up—The Infantry were placed in a strip of woods about a hundred yards from the road toward Middletown—they were then divided into three squads— one staid in the woods—one laid down behind a tall rail fence this side of the woods. The third squad was held in reserve behind a small hill

in the same field, which had very tall orchard grass growing in it—the horses were unlimbered from the cannon and taken behind the hill and all was quiet.[34]

Kerwin retired his command slowly, skirmishing with the Confederates, who were led by part of the First Maryland Battalion. Captain Rasin, with about seventy men of his company, led the advance. Maj. Harry W. Gilmor of the Second Maryland Battalion of Cavalry, with a few of his men and some troopers from the Fourteenth Virginia Cavalry, joined in the pursuit. Gilmor consulted with Rasin and with eight of his men took the point. Gilmor wrote:

We followed the Yankees to within a mile and a quarter of Newtown when they wheeled about and faced us with drawn sabres, yelling and daring us to charge. Feeling quite certain now that an ambuscade was near, I waved my pistol back to hold up; but . . . he [Rasin] misunderstood the signal, and . . . I heard him give the order "Gallop—march—charge!" Just at that moment I caught a glimpse of blue uniform in the tall grass in a ravine on our left.[35]

Gilmor tried to warn his fellow Marylanders as they charged past, but their yells drowned him out. Realizing that he could not be heard, he attempted to reach Rasin at the head of the column.

Kate Sperry was watching the action. "Then all of a sudden, Captain Raison [*sic*] of 1st Maryland Cavalry with 63 men charged them—killed one and wounded several—say, then the Yanks ran and our noble 63 after them. . . . [O]ur men were coming on to certain death, for the clouds of dust made by the Yanks in running prevented our soldiers from seeing the Yankee Infantry 'til too late—brave souls, they came tearing on, cheering with all their might."[36]

Gilmor continued:

[F]our hundred infantry rose up in the grass, and discharged every gun into the flank of the column. At the same instant a small body of cavalry, about two hundred yards in front, opened to the left and right, unmasking two howitzers, that sent double charges of canister, ranking

34.   WFCHS, Kate Sperry Diary

35.   Gilmor 1866, 81

36.   WFCHS, Kate Sperry Diary

down the other side of our doomed men. Raisin [*sic*] rode by my side, but soon was knocked off his splendid black horse by a minié ball hitting him in the back of the head. He lay as if dead, and his horse ran to the enemy.[37]

Major Kerwin later wrote that he had brought Rasin down with a sabre cut when the two clashed in the road.
Kate Sperry continued:

When one half got past, the Infantry fired. . . . One half fell off their horses in the road and the rest retreated whilst the two cannon loaded with grape was poured into them—3 were instantly killed and one whose horse was shot fell almost before the door, the horse on him— he was finally brought in—never spoke, but died in ten minutes—his name was Sergeant Gimmel [Thomas H. Gemmill]—from Eastern Shore, Maryland. . . . [A]bout eight or ten of our men were wounded . . . and four killed. . . . Mr. Gimmel was shot in the stomach—and I forgot where Mr. Howard [Richard L. Harwood] received his death wound— he was only 19 years old and so handsome—the Yankees didn't get his body, for the pockets were full and the rest had their pockets rifled—the other man killed was Richard [Joseph] West. . . . [O]h, it was dreadful to bear the taunts, insults, and curses of the Yankees over our dead men—nearly every girl from Newton [Newtown] came out to see the dead and all the children from town also—they cried over them as though their hearts would break—it was too sad—I feel such an oppression I can write nothing more about it. The enemy didn't get a single horse from our men—they killed five or six horses but the rest ran back up the road.[38]

Gilmor recalled that five men were killed, including one of his own, nine wounded, and twenty-three captured. Col. James R. Herbert of the Second Maryland Infantry wrote in his diary on that date that Rasin lost four killed, thirteen wounded, and twenty captured. The muster rolls show that Pvt. Mordecai J. Ridgeway died of his wounds, Captain Rasin and one man were wounded and captured, and eighteen unwounded men were taken from

37. Gilmor 1866, 81
38. WFCHS, Kate Sperry Diary

Company E. Company C had three men captured and Company D one. The other men reported wounded apparently received only minor wounds. Despite the successful ambush of the Marylanders, Colonel Schall was unable to ascertain Ewell's movements. The next day the Maryland cavalry, operating as part of the Maryland Line, advanced on the enemy. The troopers occupied a ridge line between Bartonsville and Kernstown and skirmished with the Federals. Kate Sperry noted that "the Yanks were coming out to hunt up the company they whipped on yesterday—got nearly to Kernstown and the Maryland Line gave them fits—drove them back to Winchester."[39]

That evening the First Maryland Cavalry, under Captain Emack, was assigned to Jenkins's Brigade. Company A, under Captain Bond, was detached from the battalion and reported to General Ewell as his escort. Bond recalled that "there were 100 men for duty, perfectly equipped, splendidly mounted, well drilled, with perfect discipline, and an unbounded confidence in the officers and themselves. The average man was twenty-one years, and there was an unusual amount of intelligence pervading the whole."[40]

On June 14 came Confederate victory at Winchester. Ewell singled out the men of the Second Maryland Infantry for their gallantry, and Bond wrote:

[T]hey were materially assisted by the mounted men of Company A, who formed on their right and advanced with them, under a heavy artillery fire, and drove in the enemy's infantry behind their batteries and breastworks.[41]

Following the Federal defeat and rapid retreat, Bond's troopers led the chase. Their captain continued:

For two days after the defeat of Milroy the company, in squads, was actively engaged in pursuing and harassing the enemy, who were retreating in great disorder. Lieut. Pue, with six men, charged upon a body of infantry numbering nearly one hundred, who surrendered to him, but before he could disarm them a desultory firing began, and he was compelled to withdraw and allow them to proceed. After this experience we opened fire from ambush on similar bodies, and compelled

39.   Ibid.
40.   *Confederate Veteran,* Vol. VI, 78
41.   Ibid.

them to stack their arms before they discovered the weakness of the attacking party. A great many instances of personal daring was shown during this pursuit, and over five hundred prisoners of all arms were captured.[42]

Ewell's corps spent little time enjoying the supplies captured at Winchester. On June 15 Jenkins's cavalry—the lead element of Old Baldy's troops—forded the Potomac and marched into Maryland. While Company A moved into Maryland with Ewell, Emack and the rest of the battalion were placed under the command of Major Gilmor. Ewell ordered the Maryland battalion to destroy the iron railroad bridge at Monocacy, Maryland. Gilmor and the Marylanders set out, advancing through Boonsboro and on to Frederick before meeting any opposition. At Frederick a Federal cavalry brigade drove a scouting party under the command of Capt. Thomas Sturgis Davis out of town. Gilmor, with his two hundred men, responded by putting on a bold front and advancing on the Union troopers. The charge drove the Federals from the town. The only casualty was a new recruit who was wounded half an hour after his enlistment. Gilmor recalled:

> The people of Frederick turned out en masse, and never did I see so much enthusiasm. The ladies particularly crowded around us, and it was with difficulty we could move along. They gave the men all they wanted, invited us into their houses for refreshment, and manifested unmistakably their sympathy with the South; but, fearing the men might get too much scattered, I had the bugle sounded, and went toward the Monocacy to try the bridge, and found it impracticable for cavalry, there being a strong stockade at each end.[43]

The Marylanders retraced their steps through Frederick before moving to the top of South Mountain and then to Hagerstown. Here, wrote Private Gill, "they met old friends and relatives and were most royally treated."[44] Ewell then ordered Gilmor to join General Steuart's Brigade, which was marching on McConnellsburg. Joining Steuart at the top of the mountain, the Maryland cavalry took the advance on the descent to the town. As several cavalry and infantry occupied it, Gilmor charged through the darkness. Upon reaching the

42. Ibid.
43. Gilmor 1866, 93–94
44. Gill 1904, 86

Cpl. Edwin Selvage, Co. D, First Maryland Cavalry. (Mrs. William Albaugh III)

center of town he sent detachments to search the streets, but the enemy had fled. Gilmor set pickets to secure the approaches to the town, then sent a courier to Steuart reporting its capture. The troopers found a supply of corn and oats and were able to feed their animals.

For the next two days the Marylanders gathered in cattle and horses for the army from the surrounding area. Gilmor swept the area westward to Roxbury before rejoining Steuart at Shippensburg, Pennsylvania, on June 28. The next day the Maryland battalion began leading the advance to Carlisle, but before reaching its goal it was ordered to move to the York road. The unit marched through Papertown and Petersburg to Cashtown, where Gilmor received a dispatch from Col. Thomas H. Carter, who feared for the safety of his wagon train. The Marylanders trotted forward for two miles in the June heat but found no enemy.

Meanwhile, Bond was leading the advance of Ewell's Corps to Carlisle. Company A acted as provost guard over supplies the Federals had abandoned in the towns near their camps. Gill recalled that "[a]t Chambersburg and Carlisle, although in enemy's country, we received smiles from the girls peeping through the windows. No damage of any kind was done to property, and the citizens generally looked upon [us] as a rather civilized and well-behaved crowd."[45]

Bond's troopers also acted as couriers between Ewell and his divisions and General Lee's headquarters. Some of the men of Company A were captured performing this arduous duty.

On June 30 Ewell's corps marched on to Heidlersburg, leaving Bond and his men to hold Carlisle and guard about a thousand prisoners. When the citizens and prisoners learned that they were being held by fewer than a hundred men, the situation became perilous. Bond's firmness in dealing with the situation and the

45.   Ibid., 87

discipline of his men gave Ewell's infantry the full two-hour start it needed.

Cpl. Edwin Selvage of Company D was given a different mission that day. He and his detachment of eight men were to carry a dispatch to Jeb Stuart, who was believed to be near Carlisle. Selvage passed through Cashtown and had some close calls with Union pickets before he found Stuart's vedettes at about one o'clock in the morning. He and his men were taken to Stuart's adjutant to deliver their message. Selvage recalled:

> We were directed by the adjutant to stay there and rest. Some hour and a half later, Stuart himself rode up and inquired who was in command of the squad which had delivered the dispatch. I reported, and Stuart asked if I could lead his command to the place of the engagement [Gettysburg]. I replied that I could, and, toward daybreak, at the head of Stuart's column, I reported to Ewell, and was warmly commended for the service rendered the cause.[46]

Bond rejoined Ewell after his harrowing experience at Carlisle and was sent on a scout to within sight of Gettysburg. Having seen no sign of the enemy, Bond left Sgt. Hammond C. Dorsey with ten men on picket and reported back to Ewell. During the night Dorsey and his vedettes captured three Pennsylvania artillerists who had taken French leave from their battery. They were escorted to Ewell's headquarters, where they gave the Confederates their first information on the location of Gen. George G. Meade's army. Bond recalled:

> The next morning, July 1, was intensely hot and close. Our corps moved in the direction of Gettysburg, and I was sent with the full company to escort Col. Johnson [Capt. Elliott Johnston], of South Carolina, who had despatches for Gen. [A. P.] Hill, who was on our right, about ten miles away; but what might be between us no one knew. Col. Johnson set off at about three-quarter speed, and the company held their own pretty well for a couple of miles; but, as he never drew rein, when we struck Hill's pickets I alone was with him, and I was exceedingly glad to bid him good-by.
>
> Soon after returning and reassembling my men I heard heavy firing in the direction of Gettysburg, and determined to go directly toward it rather than back to Heidlersburg and follow the route of our corps. We

46. *Confederate Veteran*, Vol. XXX, 445

advanced with great caution, and found that we were in the rear of the extreme Federal left, [Union general John] Buford's Cavalry confronting them. Our situation was extremely perilous, but before we were fairly discovered the Federals were put to flight, and we advanced toward our infantry line of battle. By going alone, very slowly and bareheaded, I succeeded in reaching our lines without being fired upon, but it was a very unpleasant business.[47]

"Ewell had thrown his men against the Eleventh Army Corps," wrote Gill, "and by four o'clock the whole Confederate line was driving the enemy before it. . . . Captain Bond, leading his company, was among the first to charge into Gettysburg. General Ewell the next morning appointed Captain Bond Provost Marshal of the town."[48]

Harry Gilmor led the rest of the Marylanders to Gettysburg and reported to Ewell. Old Baldy ordered him to move to the extreme left of his line and support two artillery battalions. Placing the men and horses in a ravine, Gilmor and the recently exchanged Captain Welsh joined the gunners on the hill to watch the battle. Seeing Ewell's infantry charging across the open fields, with the Federals in full running retreat toward Gettysburg, was too much for Gilmor. He placed Captain Emack in command of the battalion and with Captain Welsh and Lt. William H. B. Dorsey dashed after the panicky Yankees. Gilmor wrote:

We dashed in among them, and had no difficulty in stopping just as many as we pleased. But few shots were fired at us, and those by the Feds, too much fluttered to take aim. Near the edge of town was a regiment, apparently in a very disorganized condition, but still holding on to their colors. In we dashed among them, slashing right and left. Most of them gave up, or, rather, threw down their arms, and continued on. A small squad of ten or more gathered round the colors. We dashed at them; two fired upon us, but so wildly that neither horse nor man was struck. They presented their bayonets, but, after knocking these aside and cutting down two or three of them, the rest surrendered. Welch [*sic*] could have taken the flag, but as the man lowered it, his horse, alarmed, shied off, and I grasped it before he could wheel. It belonged to the 149th New York [Infantry].

47.   *Confederate Veteran*, Vol. VI, 79
48.   Gill 1904, 89

By this time our right wing had gained the suburbs of Gettysburg, and were passing through the college yard. Dorsey had gone back with the prisoners, and Welch [*sic*] and I were the first two Confederate soldiers in the town of Gettysburg.

The next day I was ordered by General Ewell to act as provost-marshal of Gettysburg, and to search the town for prisoners, ammunition, and arms. Of the last a vast number was collected, and we stacked twenty-five hundred muskets in the public square; but they were not removed, and fell again in the hands of the enemy. On the afternoon of the 2nd of July Major Brown arrived, and I turned the battalion over to him.[49]

That day, Privates Rich and Henry W. Webb were acting as orderlies for Gen. Edward Johnson during the assault on Culp's Hill. Webb's arm was shattered, yet he refused to leave the field. Wrote Johnson, "His conduct entitles him to a commission."[50]

After the war, Bond wrote that he was the provost marshal of Gettysburg for three days. On July 3 he learned of the cavalry battle on the Confederate left flank and took it upon himself to withdraw his company from the town and join Stuart's troopers. "[I] had nearly reached there, passing under a heavy artillery fire for a considerable distance, when I was overtaken by one of Gen. Ewell's staff with preemptory orders to return immediately; and the way the old gentleman pitched into me when I got back was a caution!" Bond recalled.[51]

Brown led the rest of the battalion on a scout along the York road during the day of July 3, gathering up stragglers and returning them to their units along the way.

The following day Bond noted that:

On July 4 there was a pouring rain all day, and the army was quiet on the lines of battle. . . . Just at dark Gen. Ewell summoned me, and directed that at 10 P.M. I should stretch my company across the front of his entire corps and remain there until broad daylight, when I was to make a careful observation in the direction of the enemy's position, and then follow the army, to my great surprise, he told me was going to return to Virginia.[52]

49.   Gilmor 1866, 6–97
50.   OR, Series I, Vol. XXVII, Pt. 2, 505
51.   *Confederate Veteran*, Vol. VI, 79
52.   Ibid.

Private Gill wrote:

> [W]e were deployed in front of Ewell's lines as pickets to remain in our
> saddles until relieved. . . . The dead had been exposed to the broiling
> sun for more than twenty-four hours, and had already turned black.
>   To add to the horror of the scent and the cries and groans of dying
> men, in the midst of whom we stood, a terrible thunder and lightning
> storm broke over the battle-field. The rain fell in torrents, and as each
> of us stood at his post, with pistol in hand, the lightning flashed in our
> faces casting shadows on the dead strewn around us. Here we remained
> until day dawned. Who can forget that night! Our sergeant passed down
> the line, forming us into columns of fours, preparatory to marching off
> the battle-field.[53]

Bond rejoined Ewell about noon, reporting that the enemy had not advanced.
The general relieved Company A and directed Bond to move to the front of the
column and help guard the wagon train bound for Williamsport, Maryland, on
the Potomac. The company marched to the top of a mountain, about twenty
miles from Hagerstown, and camped for the night.

Ewell ordered Brown to escort the wagon train; the latter was forced to spread
his four companies thin to guard the myriad roads leading into the line of march
of miles of wagons. On July 4, as some Federal cavalry approached Monterey
Gap on the Emmittsburg road, it met Sgt. Samuel Spencer and six men of
Captain Emack's company. The rest of the troop, under Lts. Adolphus Cooke
and Henry C. Blackistone, was foraging for food for themselves and their horses. Spencer's vedettes had just taken their positions when they saw an
approaching Federal column. Emack was notified, and he immediately rode
back to halt the wagons to prevent their capture if the Yankee cavalry broke
through his pickets. He later reported:

> In doing this I came across a Lieutenant of a North Carolina battery
> who had but one gun and only two rounds of ammunition. With this he
> galloped up the road to my picket; and, placing him in position, I
> directed him to put both charges in his gun and await orders. Sergeant
> Spencer was placed in rear with five men, while I advanced down the

53.   Gill 1904, 90

road, accompanied by Private [Edwin] Thomas, until I met the head of the enemy's column. It was then dusk and raining; and as we wore our gum coats the Federal cavalry failed to recognize us. Without making any demonstration, we turned and retreated before them at a walk, shielding the gun as much as possible as we neared it. As soon as we passed the gun the Lieutenant fired into the head of the column. Taking advantage of the halt and confusion which followed this fire, I charged with my little party, in all only eight mounted men, and succeeded in driving them back for more than a mile, until they reached their artillery.

From the shouting and firing among the retreating enemy we concluded that they had become panic-stricken and were fighting among themselves.

The firing brought up Lieutenant Blackiston[e] with the rest of my company; and dismounting the men, we formed line in some undergrowth on one side of the road.

After fully an hour we heard the enemy advancing, this time with more caution and with dismounted skirmishers thrown out on each side of the road. Lying on the ground, we reserved our fire until they were within ten or fifteen paces of us, when we gave them a volley which caused another precipitate retreat. I now withdrew my men to another position, and formed them dismounted on either side of the road. Sergeant Spencer had charge of one squad and Sergeant [William A.] Wilson of the other. Lieutenant Blackiston[e] had charge of the horses and prisoners in the rear. [Gen. Judson] Kilpatrick now commanded a general advance with mounted and dismounted men and with artillery, firing at every step, which to us was rather amusing, as we were about a mile distant and lying snugly on the ground. About midnight he reached Monterey, and opened a tremendous fire on us with artillery and dismounted men, to which we made but little answer.[54]

Emack eventually learned that the wagons were again moving and rode back to find that Grumble Jones had ordered them to do so. When he explained the situation, the general implored him to hold his position until reinforcements could arrive. Emack wrote:

54.   McClellan 1885, 353–55

Pvt. Richard H. H. Key, Co. B, First Maryland Cavalry. (Private Collection)

I returned to my men and urged them not to yield an inch nor waste any ammunition (we had but little at the commencement). The enemy now increased their fire until it seemed as if nothing could stand before it. Still these men lay there under it coolly, awaiting an opportunity to strike another blow. The enemy's skirmishers at last walked into my line, and I was told that one of them actually trod on Private [Richard H. H.] Key, who killed him on the spot. The enemy was again driven back. My ammunition was entirely exhausted and some of my men actually fought with rocks; nor did they give back an inch.[55]

Jones was unable to get any assistance for the Marylanders, but Emack persuaded a lieutenant and ten men of the Fourth North Carolina Cavalry to dismount and come to his aid. The captain later wrote:

At about 3 o'clock A.M., finding that he had no force of consequence opposed to him, Kilpatrick advanced his cavalry to within twenty yards of my position and gave the order to charge. A running fight now ensued amid wagons and ambulances. As we passed down the mountain we met Captain Welsh's Company . . . at the junction of another road. Here the enemy was held in check for a moment, but they soon swept us aside, and on they went until they had captured all the wagons they found in the road.

In this fight about half the men I had engaged were captured, and I myself was wounded. According to the official report of General Kilpatrick, his loss was five killed, ten wounded and twenty-eight prisoners, in all forty-three men, or more than I had in the fight, including

55. Ibid.

horse holders.[56]

Jones praised the Marylanders: "This brave little band of heroes was encouraged with the hope of speedy reinforcements, reminded of the importance of their trust, and exhorted to fight to the bitter end rather than yield. . . . For more than two hours less than fifty men kept many thousands back."[57]

Emack's and Welsh's companies were both decimated. Lieutenant Cooke of Emack's B Company was wounded and captured and sat out the rest of the war in Federal prisons. One man was killed, at least two were wounded and captured, and twenty-six were taken prisoner. Many horses were killed in the melee. Welsh's D Company lost two men wounded and thirty-two captured. In addition, Company C lost one man killed, Pvt. Robert W. Cushing wounded, and thirteen captured during this period. Company E lost Pvt. Benjamin W. Cator, who was killed at Gettysburg, and had four wounded and five taken prisoner.

"By sunrise the next morning [July 5] we were on the march, and about noon reached the head of the column—miles and miles of wagons—which had halted on the outskirts of Hagerstown," Bond wrote. He also reported that his men were "spoiling for a fight."[58]

Finding other Confederate cavalry in and around Hagerstown, the Marylanders took an hour to find food for themselves and their horses. Before Bond could finish his meal he learned that a large Federal force was approaching. He quickly rallied 46 of his 109 men, formed a column of fours, and rode back into Hagerstown. He found Col. J. Lucius Davis and his Tenth Virginia Cavalry, the advance guard of Ewell's train, on the far edge of town, facing the enemy. Bond scouted toward the Federal position; when he returned he told Colonel Davis that he believed the Federals were about to charge the wagon train and suggested that they meet them with a countercharge. Unable to get Davis to agree, Bond started his command up a side street, hoping to reach the wagon train, but before the men had proceeded very far the Tenth Virginia fell back in confusion. As soon as most of the Virginians had cleared the main street, Bond ordered "fours right about charge!" and dashed toward the Federal cavalry. He later wrote:

56.   Ibid.
57.   OR, Series I, Vol. XXVII, Pt. 2, 753
58.   *Confederate Veteran,* Vol. XVII, 500

Immediately the enemy perceived there was a body of troops who did not intend to run, they checked their pursuit and halted in a confused mass in the street, except one, a sergeant on a bob-tailed horse, who came slap into us, and I shot him down. Sgt. Hammond Dorsey was the first man who dashed into the enemy's ranks and began to hew right and left. George Lechlider followed him closely, and almost immediately the enemy broke and ran, and were pursued to their main body by the entire company. Their loss was about twenty men killed and wounded. Five of them fell under Sergt. Dorsey's sword, and the last of them was a bugler, by this time in full flight. As he leaned over his horse's neck the bugle of brass, as thick as a man's arm, protected his head, and repeated blows were necessary to disable him. I examined this bugle later on, and it was cut nearly through in numerous places as clean as a carrot might be chopped with an ax.

Sergt. Dorsey, boiling in wrath, informed me that but for the bugle he would have gotten two or three more. The enemy made no counter-charge, and our wagon-train was saved. Our only loss was one man, Henry Stone, wounded by having a thumb shot off. Our men used their sabers entirely.[59]

Gill reported: "We drove them back on the road to Boonsboro."[60]
Bond wrote:

We were flushed with victory and retired to our side of town, where we were soon joined by reinforcements, and two pieces of artillery were added to my command. The enemy dismounted their sharpshooters and skirmished on the left of the town, and we mounted a few men and drove them back. In doing this [Nathan] Soper Childs and his brother Buck Childs, displayed conspicuous bravery.[61]

With the action over, Bond returned to town to find a meal. Before he could begin eating, however, an aide of General Stuart's interrupted with a request that he bring his company to the front. Bond wrote: "This was irresistible, and I hurried to the company, and at a trot went out the Williamsport pike about

59.   Ibid.
60.   Gill 1904, 91
61.   *Confederate Veteran*, Vol. VI, 80

three miles. I left the company in the road, and went on alone with an orderly (Lechlider), and found Gen. Stuart."[62]

When Bond reached him, the general was trying to get about two hundred reluctant, dismounted men to charge a Federal battery firing from the right of the pike. Bond described the event:

> "Bond, I want to see you," Stuart said, "but first help me here. We want to drive that battery off. Do you take one end of the line, and I will take the other." By a good deal of galloping up and down in front and by voice and action we induced the men to advance, at first slowly, and then at a run, and the Yankees limbered up and galloped away.
>
> By this time it was dark, and as we now occupied the same ground just abandoned by the enemy, our batteries were dropping shells right among us that had been going over our heads when we were in the hollow. I rode back to stop our firing, but did not go as far to the right as I should, and continued in the line of fire. A shell exploded immediately in front of me. One piece cut off the collar of my overcoat, which was rolled and strapped across the front of the saddle, and another piece passed between Lechlider and myself as we rode touching knees, slightly wounding him and very severely wounding me by carrying away five inches of fibula near the knee-joint. I rode on and stopped the firing, and then, by a special providence, was accosted by Dr. [Talcott] Eliason, who applied a tourniquet, that saved me from bleeding to death.[63]

Four of Bond's men carried him on their shoulders back to Hagerstown, where he was captured. He was later exchanged but was never able to return to duty with his company.

Company A rejoined Major Brown at Hagerstown, and on July 7 the major led the reunited battalion on to Williamsport. The Marylanders were immediately dispatched to picket the different roads leading into the town. Brown's weary troopers aided in the successful defense of the wagon trains parked around the village. Several men were captured.

Brown was ordered to rejoin Stuart on July 8. The battalion moved northward and skirmished with the enemy near Hagerstown before reaching the

62.   *Confederate Veteran*, Vol. VI, 80
63.   Ibid.

Confederate cavalry at Boonsboro. The Marylanders skirmished with the enemy cavalry again the next day, and on July 10 they scouted along the Pennsylvania state line. July 11–13 were spent on picket near Greencastle, Pennsylvania. On the 13th Brown led the battalion back to Williamsport. There the Marylanders acted with the rear guard as Lee's army recrossed the Potomac; several men were cut off and captured. Brown's exhausted troopers went into camp about five miles from the river.

On July 14 Brown moved the battalion between Martinsburg and Winchester and picketed the roads leading toward the latter. The next day the battalion moved to the Pughtown road. On July 16 Brown received orders to join Gen. Fitzhugh Lee's Brigade; the Marylanders found Lee's troopers camped at Leetown and joined them in a movement toward Culpeper, where Company A was placed on picket at Rappahannock Ford. The next day the battalion moved to Vediersville, and that night the Marylanders picketed Ely's Ford. On July 18 Company A picketed Morton's Ford; the battalion finally went into camp with the rest of the brigade the next day around Orange Court House. Here the Marylanders received a brief respite, broken only by picket duty along the Rapidan and drill.

The battalion received much needed reinforcements on July 29 when Company F, comprising Marylanders who had enlisted in Richmond on June 16, rode into camp. The new troop was led by Capt. Augustus F. Schwartz, a veteran of Company A; 1st Lt. Cyrus Irving Ditty, who had risen from a private in the Howard Dragoons; 2nd Lt. Fielder C. Slingluff, another who had risen through the ranks; and 3rd Lt. Samuel G. Bonn, a veteran of Company A. Some of the men had had prior service, but most were recruits who had come out of Maryland with Lee's army or had crossed the Potomac from the Eastern Shore.

Brown immediately set about rearming and reequipping his battle-worn men. On August 25 he receipted for 150 pairs of shoes, 200 pairs of pants, 350 pairs of drawers, 200 shirts, and 150 jackets. His request for 400 pairs of socks and 100 blankets went unfilled. On the requisition Brown noted, "The Command is in an Exceedingly destitute condition."[64] He also drew 30 skillets with lids, 12 camp kettles, 10 axes, and 7 fly tents. Some of these items were to replace those lost during the Gettysburg campaign; the others were for Companies E and F, which had never been issued them. Third Lt. Milton Welsh reported fifty-seven men with fifty-five horses present in Company D at this time.

Private Kettlewell wrote from camp near Fredericksburg on August 26, "Our

64.   Frederick D. Shroyer Collection, First Maryland Cavalry, Company C Muster Roll

Battalion has been attached to Gen'l Fitz Lee's Brigade and we have been stationed here, picketing the River, scouting, etc."[65]

Despite the battalion's move to near Fredericksburg, Company A was on picket at Ely's Ford on the Rappahannock until August 24. During the period of September 5–22 the company was again on outpost duty at Morton's Ford on the Rapidan. Company C, and perhaps others, helped thwart Kilpatrick's aborted raid on the Virginia Central Railroad. Lieutenant Howard wrote, "We succeeded in heading him off and drove him back across the Rapidan with the loss of many prisoners."[66] The other companies were rotating on picket with Company A, but their muster rolls give no specifics.

During this period the Maryland battalion was transferred to General Lomax's Brigade, and the Union cavalry became increasingly bolder. On the afternoon of October 10, Gen. John Buford's Division, spearheaded by the Eighth New York Cavalry, stormed across the Rapidan at Germanna Ford, capturing thirteen men of Company E. The Federals moved rapidly to Mitchell's Ford, where they took three more Marylanders prisoner. As they approached Morton's Ford the dismounted men of the Fifth Virginia Cavalry drove them back. Meanwhile, Lomax was gathering his command.

Brown rode out of camp toward Morton's Ford the next morning with 140 men of the Maryland battalion. One squadron, numbering 110 men less those captured, was still on picket near Mitchell's and Germanna fords. Lomax placed the Marylanders on the left flank of the Fifth Virginia, and Brown dismounted his men and led them forward. "We were exposed to a severe fire from the enemy's battery and sharpshooters, and lost 3 men killed and 8 wounded, but our fire told upon the enemy," he reported.[67] Lomax received infantry, cavalry, and artillery reinforcements. Once these units were in place, he ordered another assault on the Federals. "I advanced the whole line, and by a gallant charge of the sharpshooters drove the enemy across the river with considerable loss," he reported.[68] Lomax then crossed the river with his command and pursued the enemy toward Stevensburg. Brown wrote:

> We pushed him as he retreated, killing and wounding a number. When we came up with the enemy again at Stevensburg, I dismounted my

65. MSA, Charles Kettlewell Letters
66. Frederick D. Shroyer Collection, First Maryland Cavalry, Company C Muster Roll
67. OR, Series I, Vol. XXIX, Pt. 1, 466–67
68. Ibid., 465–66

men, and we followed the enemy almost at a double-quick at Brandy Station. My men were much exhausted by this, but they were always up with the advanced line of skirmishers, and used their long-rangers with good effect upon the enemy's cavalry. Though forced to retire several times, they contested every inch of ground, and once, when completely surrounded by the enemy's cavalry, fought hand to hand, using their pistols with effect.

I lost here 2 men wounded, a lieutenant [Edward W. Beatty] and 4 men captured. Captain Emack, with about a dozen mounted men, also charged several times with the other regiments of the brigade, capturing some prisoners, and having 1 man wounded.[69]

The Confederate pursuit continued the next day, with Lee's army following the cavalry's advance. Brown's Battalion marched across the Rappahannock and camped at Warrenton Springs. Lomax advanced to Auburn on October 13 and attempted to stop the Federals' retreat by that route. Brown wrote, "My men were dismounted and deployed in the edge of a woods. Our fire made the enemy move his battery, and held his cavalry in check until we were obliged to retire before a large force of infantry. Here I had one gallant fellow killed (Private [Samuel J.] Shipley, Company A)."[70] Lomax wrote, "The whole line was soon withdrawn by General Fitz. Lee's order, but not before my men had been exposed to a heavy fire of artillery and had contended most gallantly with the enemy's infantry."[71]

Lomax continued to move his brigade after the Federals. The next day Brown's battalion marched to Gainesville, where a squadron left behind on picket rejoined it.

On October 15 the Confederate cavalry kept up its harassment of the enemy. Lomax attacked the Federals as they crossed Bull Run at McLean's Ford. "We had a hot skirmish with the enemy for about an hour," reported Brown, "but finding it impossible to dislodge him we retired, without the loss of a man. Two horses were killed by a shell in moving off. The men immediately moved to the right. My men again dismounted and pushed a mile to the front to assist General [John B.] Gordon, but night coming on, we retired without being engaged."[72]

69.   Ibid., 466–67
70.   Ibid.
71.   Ibid., 465–66
72.   Ibid., 466–67

The next day's rain prevented much activity, and the battalion remained in bivouac near Manassas. Company A was on picket at Bull Run Bridge during the night.

Robert E. Lee, unable to induce a confrontation with the Union forces or to supply his troops adequately in the desolate area, decided to retire. On October 17 the First Maryland Cavalry fell back from Bull Run to Bristoe Station.

"On the 18th," Brown wrote, "the brigade being in position at Bristoe to resist the enemy, my command had position on the left of the railroad, and poured a volley into the enemy's ranks; but they retired so quickly we could not tell the effect of our fire."[73]

In Fauquier County the next day, during the "Buckland Races," as Stuart's men called their pursuit of Kilpatrick's Third Cavalry Division, Lomax's Brigade was in the rear when Stuart sprang his trap on the Union cavalry. "[W]e could not get up in time to do much," wrote Brown, "though my boys were as ever eager for fight, and double-quicked to the front in time to give the enemy a few farewell shots and capture a number of prisoners. My total loss in the campaign was 4 men killed, 11 wounded, a lieutenant and 4 men captured."[74] Brown's report did not cover the losses of two companies on picket at Germanna and Mitchell's fords.

On October 20 Brown and his men recrossed the Rappahannock at Beverly's Ford. The Marylanders received a few days' rest, and then Companies A and B were assigned to outpost duty at Waterloo Bridge on October 24–25. These two companies were relieved on October 28 and returned to camp on the John Botts farm, Auburn Plantation, near Brandy Station.

On October 31 the secretary of war ordered the Maryland Line to reassemble at Hanover Junction. Col. Bradley T. Johnson was placed in command. The First Maryland Cavalry, now on picket at Sommerville Ford, remained there until orders detaching it from Lomax's Brigade filtered down. Brown's Battalion rejoined the Maryland Line at Hanover Junction on November 7.

The battalion at this point was badly in need of refitting. Company E, for example, had lost eight men killed or died of wounds and had had a large number of men taken prisoner in the last ten months. Captain Rasin, recently exchanged, had all of his officers but only forty-two men present. During the recent campaign the company had lost nearly all of its horses; those remaining were, for the most part, unserviceable. Company A, under the command of Lt.

73.   Ibid.
74.   Ibid.

Adj. John Eager Howard Post, First Maryland Cavalry (as sergeant major). (Museum of the Confederacy)

Thomas Griffith, was probably similarly battered. Company C reported only three officers and seventy-two men present for duty at the end of November. Captain Welsh reported four officers and sixty-two men present—and only thirty-nine horses fit for duty. Captain Schwartz's Company F had dwindled to four officers and thirty-eight men present.

Brown had been promoted to lieutenant colonel with the addition of Company F. In Company C, Capt. Robert Carter Smith had been made a major, and George W. Howard had been elected captain; the lieutenants rose one rank. John Eager Howard Post had replaced Booth as adjutant of the battalion when Booth joined Johnson's staff, and Arthur W. Bond replaced Post as the battalion's sergeant major.

Brown's troopers were not idle. They picketed and scouted the peninsula as far as New Kent Court House and along the lower Pamunkey River at Dabney's Ferry. When not on duty the troopers were busy building huts for the winter. Brown inspected Company E and found its men in comfortable quarters at St. Mary's, as the Maryland Line's camp had been named. The muster rolls indicate that the camp was in good condition and its occupants quite healthy. The men's clothing was considered only "tolerable" because of the lack of overcoats and shoes, and their arms were rated "pretty good but insufficient." Discipline, instruction, and military appearance were deemed very good. The company was issued twenty-two rounds of .58-caliber ammunition with caps and fifteen hundred rounds of Sharps rifle ammunition, also with caps, near this time.

Company A was on picket at Jerico Ford on the North Anna in Hanover County from December 7 to 10. Once back at camp, Pvt. Elgar L. Tschiffely noted in his diary that the troopers kept busy drilling and building stables to protect their animals. Mounts suitable for cavalry service were in high demand and low supply in Virginia; dismounted men roamed to the Valley and into Hardy and Hampshire counties seeking horses, and some trekked as far as North Carolina. The more daring ventured behind Federal lines. Most came

back with horses, but a few ended up prisoners of war.

On the Sunday before Christmas the battalion held a dress parade. The men were
paid on December 23, so they were able to
eat well over the holidays. A few were
given passes to Richmond and bought
whatever was available. Tschiffely noted
on December 25 that he had "had a nice
dinner."[75] Pvt. Henry Clay Mettam of
Company E wrote:

> Our mess was composed of [John]
> Powell Cockey, Ned Rich, Skinner
> Quinn [John Henry Skinner Quynn],
> John Slingluff and your humble ser-
> vant, and we all got along nicely, each
> taking his share of the work. Our quar-
> ters was a log hut, built about 10 by 15
> feet, and with bunks for sleeping,
> good big open fireplace with plenty of
> chimney, and with cooking utensils
> such as pots, kettle and spider we
> could get up a pretty good meal, and

*Sgt. Maj. Arthur Webster Bond, First
Maryland Cavalry, in postwar uniform. (Bonney Grote)*

on Christmas Day we thought we would try our hands, so we waited
until several of our neighbors had finished with their cooking utensils
and we then borrowed them, one with roast pork and sweet potatoes,
one corn pone, one with oyster pot-pie, another biscuits, one mashed
potatoes and turnips, pot of coffee, etc., and I assure you we all had a
good, full meal and some left over; so we concluded to end with a
smoker and then rolled into our bunks for a snooze, thinking we would
eat the leavings for supper, but when we woke up found some one had
been in ahead of us and had eaten all up.[76]

On the last day of the year Company A was issued one hospital tent, two pairs

75.   Stephen R. Brockmiller Collection, Elgar L. Tschiffely Book
76.   *Maryland Historical Magazine,* Vol. 58, 151

*Pvt. Henry Clay Mettam, Co. E, First
Maryland Cavalry.* (Maryland Historical
Society)

of shoes, six pairs of drawers, and two caps. On Company E's muster roll, Captain Rasin wrote, "The men are generally in good health but much in need of overcoats, blankets &c [etc.]."[77]

77.   MHS, First Maryland Cavalry, Company E Muster Roll

Chapter IV

1864

"I have felt proud to belong to the Reg't."

The year 1864 began on a Friday with a cold wave that gripped both North and South. The cold abated the following Sunday, enabling the battalion to have an inspection and dress parade. Captain Griffith reported that Company A had two officers and eighty-seven men present for duty with one hundred horses on that day. Private Kettlewell wrote to his sister on January 14:

> Our Mess of 8 have the finest "residence," or log hut, in Camp with many of the conveniences of "civilized" life, being our own cooks, chamber maids, hostlers and performing other duties calculated to make us useful members of society. I pride myself in making bread. Our camp life is relieved by picketing, and as we go in a Country where but few troops have been stationed, and the people are truly generous & kind have a most delightful time. I have no less than three sweet hearts, so you see if the girls in Md. neglect us, we have a recourse.[1]

---

1.   MSA, Charles Kettlewell Letters

He added a footnote: "Poley [Adam Poley Jenkins] & Geo. Jenkins, sons of Thomas C. Jenkins, Willie [Wilfred Neale] & [Francis] C[onstantine] Neale, sons of Neale [of] N. Harris & Co., members of my mess are well. Tell their fathers."

The same day Private Tschiffely and the other troopers of Company A rode out of camp to Old Church and camped for the night. The next morning they trekked on to Garlick's Ferry on the Pamunkey. Company A remained on picket in New Kent County for eight days, during which Tschiffely ventured across the river into King William County for breakfast one morning. Also during their stay, the Marylanders stopped a suspicious boat and arrested the men in it. Otherwise the watch was uneventful, and Griffith's men moved back to Camp St. Mary's with little to report.

Back in camp, a revival was underway, and there were evening sermons for several weeks running. The men attended services in a chapel they had built. Drills, meanwhile, mounted and dismounted, continued when the weather permitted. Supplies being scant, details with wagons were sent farther and farther from camp to obtain forage for the hungry animals. Sometimes they returned empty-handed.

On January 28 the battalion was issued 111 bridles and 40 halters, 250 rounds of musket ammunition with caps, 1,500 rounds of pistol ammunition with caps, and 600 Colt army pistol rounds with caps.

On January 31 Kettlewell wrote:

> We are having a pleasant time in winter Qtrs., scouting & picketing. I attended a Ball about 3 weeks since, had a delightful time, a concert & several parties during the winter, so you see tho we are poor Confed's, there are many pleasures to relieve the arduous duties of a soldier's life. I have not been sick for 18 mos., never think of dyspepsia.[2]

Ridgely Brown reported that at the end of January the battalion had 17 officers and 275 men present for duty, 330 aggregate present, and 595 aggregate present and absent. Four officers and 100 men were prisoners of war.

On February 2 Company E was issued twenty military cavalry saddles and thirty-two .58-caliber carbines. A special report for February 10 shows the battalion with 16 officers and 282 enlisted men present for duty, 328 aggregate present, and 589 aggregate present and absent.

2.   Ibid.

First Maryland Cavalry camp near Hanover Junction, January 1864. (*Frederick D. Shroyer*)

Six days later, upon learning of a Federal raid toward Richmond, Brown ordered the men in camp to saddle up at 2 A.M. Tschiffely wrote: "Start after the yanks at day light. March to old ch [Old Church], feed. March from Old Ch to Cold Harbor . . . at night cloudy & cold."[3] Learning that the raiders had been turned back, Brown returned to Old Church. From there Company A marched on to Garlick's Ferry, where it relieved the company on duty, while Brown led the rest of the battalion back to camp. Company A's ten-day tour of duty saw

3.   Stephen R. Brockmiller Collection, Elgar L. Tschiffely Book

snow and the coldest temperatures of the season; gusting winds made the days and nights feel even colder. Company A was relieved on February 18 and returned to camp at Hanover Junction.

Griffith's company got only a brief respite; it returned to picket duty at Garlick's Ferry on February 27. On February 28 Kilpatrick's Federal cavalry began a raid on the railroads and threatened Richmond. On March 1, a miserably rainy day that gave way to a snowy night, Company A marched to Dabney's Ferry to picket. Instead, the company pursued the Federal cavalry and "skirmish[ed] with rear guard of Yanks all day," Tschiffely reported.[4] On March 3 the company trekked on toward Tunstall's Station after Kilpatrick's troopers.

Meanwhile, Bradley Johnson had responded to the enemy raid by deploying the Maryland Line to defend the vital bridges over the rivers. He had also ordered the pickets on the Pamunkey to destroy the boats on the river to prevent Kilpatrick from escaping across the stream. Johnson led sixty men of the First Maryland Cavalry and two guns of the Baltimore Light Artillery in pursuit. Near Taylorsville Johnson's scouts encountered the enemy's pickets, and the Maryland cavalrymen drove them in. The Marylanders pursued the Federals to Ashland Station, where they were able to keep them from burning the depot and destroying the railroad.

Johnson led his small command on to Yellow Tavern, where his troopers gained the flank of the enemy and captured five men carrying a dispatch from Col. Ulric Dahlgren to Kilpatrick. Although the message was verbal, Johnson was able to learn that Dahlgren, who had failed to cross the James River, was proposing an attack on the River road at dusk and asking for Kilpatrick's assistance. Johnson immediately attacked Kilpatrick's rear guard on the Brooke turnpike and drove it to the main body. Kilpatrick then broke off his attack on the Richmond defenses and moved off toward the Peninsula. He crossed the Chickahominy and camped his troops on the east side of the river. Johnson followed him down the west bank. During the night Gen. Wade Hampton's men attacked Kilpatrick's camp and drove the Federals off.

On March 2 the Confederates continued the pursuit until Kilpatrick met Federal infantry near Tunstall's Station. During the day, near Kilpatrick's camp of the previous night, the First Maryland captured a wagon with horses still hitched to it and a caisson loaded with ammunition. A number of prisoners and horses were also taken. Hampton wrote in his report:

4.   Ibid.

I cannot close my report without expressing my appreciation of the conduct of Colonel Bradley T. Johnson and his gallant command. With a mere handful of men he met the enemy at Beaver Dam and he never lost sight of them until they had passed Tunstall's Station, hanging on their rear, striking them constantly, and displaying throughout the very highest qualities of a soldier.[5]

Hampton urged Johnson's promotion. Gen. Arnold Elzey, commanding the Department of Richmond, also praised Johnson and the men of the First Maryland, who had captured twice their own number. He awarded Colonel Johnson a sword for his services.

During the fighting Captain Emack was slightly wounded, as were four of his men. Lieutenant Ditty was shot through the thigh.

Company C returned to picket duty on the Pamunkey; the rest of the battalion marched back to Camp St. Mary's. Once there, Kettlewell wrote of the recent engagements.

Two or three chases after Butler [Gen. Benjamin F. Butler, who commanded the Union forces on the Peninsula], the excitement of picket, but the most glorious sport was pushing Kilpatrick for 3 days at his rear, driving and scattering them. Of course killing & wounding some of the scoundrels. The Batt. behaved very well & recd. the most complimentary notices from the Comdg. Gen. [Robert E. Lee], Elz[e]y & the pres. [President Jefferson Davis]. no troops in this Country stand higher with the people and on hearing them talk I have felt proud to belong to the Reg't. We had but a handful of men, but with these annoyed their rear constantly and with so much vigor that the ranks thought a Brigade was fighting them. We captd. many horses, prisoners, etc. But for the disbanding [of] Fitz Lee's Division Kilpatrick would not have escaped. As it is, the raid was a failure. Many of his men & horses were captured. His troops demoralized and the damage done to Gov't property very slight, but your feelings would be aroused were I to mention some of their acts of actrocity [sic] to Citizens, which in their barbarism only a Yankee could be guilty of.[6]

5.   OR, Series I, Vol. XXX, Pt. 1, 201–2
6.   MSA, Charles Kettlewell Letters

The battalion was called out again on March 10, and after cooking three days' rations the men saddled up and rode through the night to Dabney's Ferry. The next day Brown led the Marylanders on to King William Court House. There they were ordered to the front in response to a Federal raid in King and Queen County. The Union cavalry was turned back, and the First Maryland returned to camp on March 13.

Two days later, while those in camp were snug in their huts, the company on picket had to endure a bitter storm of hail and snow. Another bad front came in on March 22, dropping fifteen inches of snow and leaving the battalion snow-bound for several days. Company C weathered picket duty along the Pamunkey from March 24 to 28.

Brown reported 16 officers and 309 men present for duty at the end of the month. Three hundred fifty was the aggregate present, with 597 aggregate present and absent. The slight increase in strength came from new recruits still filtering across the Potomac and the return of many recently exchanged prisoners. Four officers and 74 men still languished in Federal prisons.

Company A marched out of camp on March 31 to take up picket posts at Dabney's Ferry. On April 1 Captain Rasin reported that many of Company E's men were absent sick, wounded, or seeking horses and that the company needed clothing and shoes. Tschiffely noted on April 1 that the peach trees were in bloom; they suffered the next day, while he and the rest of Company A stood picket duty in another snowstorm. It rained for the rest of the tour of duty but cleared when the troop returned to camp on April 7. Back at Camp St. Mary's, the companies continued drilling and preparing for the spring campaign.

On April 20 the battalion numbered 18 officers and 294 men present for duty. The aggregate present was 338, and the aggregate present and absent was 591.

Company A returned to picket duty on the Pamunkey, this time at Bassett's Ferry, on April 28. The men continued on outpost until relieved at noon on May 2, when they rode back to camp through a severe mix of hail and driving rain.

On May 5, upon learning that Gen. Ulysses S. Grant's forces had crossed the Rappahannock, Brown put the battalion under marching orders, with rations cooked. The Marylanders remained at the ready until May 9, when they were ordered to defend Beaver Dam Station against Gen. Philip H. Sheridan's Union cavalry. Upon arrival the Maryland battalion found that the Federals had already captured the depot and were tearing up the railroad. Brown led 150 men in a dismounted midnight charge on Sheridan's camp. Although the Marylanders drove in the pickets and killed and wounded a number of the enemy horsemen, they could do little against 8,000 men.

The next morning Brown received a dispatch from Jeb Stuart directing him to harass and delay the enemy as long as possible; Stuart was in pursuit. Brown immediately attacked the Federal pickets and again drove them in. The Union troopers were reinforced and in turn drove the Marylanders back. Leaving Lieutenant Ditty with twenty men to watch the enemy, Brown withdrew a short distance to rest the men and permit them to graze their horses.

Ditty soon warned Brown that the Federals were moving to attack him. The colonel brought up the rest of the column and met the Yankee troopers head on, driving them back. The Marylanders repelled at least a dozen mounted charges in the same manner until flanked from their position by dismounted skirmishers. Brown and his men were driven out of the woods and into the open. No sooner were their small numbers exposed than the Federals charged them with overwhelming force. The Marylanders gave them a volley and then retreated. "Fighting until 12 o'clock fall back to Taylorsville, encamp at night," wrote Tschiffely.[7]

That daring action cost the battalion dearly. Company F's Captain Schwartz was wounded; he was later captured and carried by the Federals to Washington, D.C., where he died. Company A's Lt. James A. V. Pue was wounded a second time and later captured. Company A also lost Cpl. John E. " Bade" Harding and Pvt. David Clark killed and two men wounded. Company E lost one man captured, and Company F two men wounded.

On May 11 Brown retired to "new bridge," where some of the men began grazing their horses while scouting parties from the battalion continued to track the movements of Grant and Sheridan. Several skirmishes took place.

When Lee's army passed the Maryland Line's position he took some of the Marylanders with him, leaving Johnson only the First Maryland Cavalry and two guns of the Baltimore Light Artillery. With this force Johnson defended the bridges over various streams in the area until May 21. "Fight the Yanks at Wickham's. Stay all night at railroad bridge on southanna [sic]," Tschiffely wrote.[8]

On the 22nd, Johnson led the command across the river into Caroline County and marched cross-country to Polecat Station, where the Marylanders exchanged shots with some departing Federal cavalry. At Penola Station they discovered the Federals moving along the Telegraph road toward Richmond. Johnson was caught between Grant's infantry and

7.   Stephen R. Brockmiller Collection, Elgar L. Tschiffely Book
8.   Ibid.

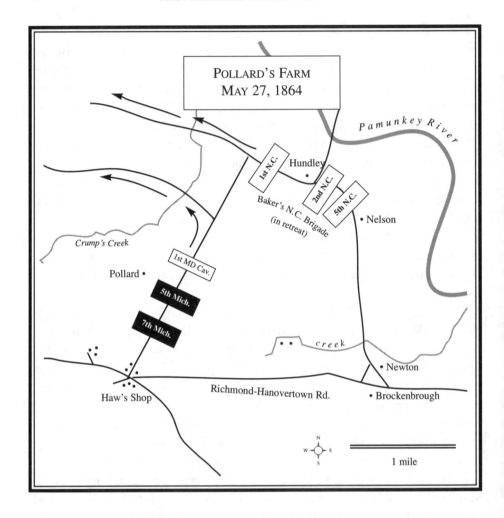

Sheridan's cavalry. He successfully extracted his command by cutting down the banks of the North Anna at Norman's Ferry and forcing a crossing. The Maryland troopers captured several Union couriers with dispatches indicating the movements of the enemy. This information was sent to General Lee, who complimented Johnson and the Maryland battalion for their efforts.

From May 24 to 26 the battalion rested in camp on Mrs. Winston's farm while a rainstorm raged. On May 27 Johnson was ordered to report to Gen. Fitzhugh Lee at Hanover Court House.

Lee assigned the Marylanders to General Lomax's Brigade. Lomax then sent them to reinforce a North Carolina brigade defending the Federally held crossing at Dabney's Ferry. Johnson reported to the brigade commander, Col. Laurence S. Baker, whose men were skirmishing with the enemy. Baker believed that the Union cavalry was a small force and might be captured. The two colonels devised a plan whereby Baker's Tar Heels would continue to skirmish with the enemy troopers, holding them in place, while Johnson attacked from their flank and captured them. Johnson took his command down a side road about a mile, where he met Baker's men falling back before the Federals. George W. Booth, Johnson's adjutant, recalled:

> We were in column in a rather narrow road, the left side of which bordered on a heavy, swampy piece of timber, while on the right was a ditch surmounted by a stout fence, beyond which were the open fields of a large farm. Colonel Johnson at once had the fence torn down and turned the head of the column into the field, while I rode back to the other squadrons and had them do likewise, it being important to get out of the road and effect some formation to meet the advancing enemy. . . . Before the regiment could complete the formation in the field, we were under heavy fire, but for some twenty minutes or more held our ground, suffering considerable loss.[9]

Booth joined Captain Rasin and his company on a small hill on the right of the line, which gave him a view of the battlefield.

> It did not take long to comprehend the situation; we had in front of us not less than a full brigade of Federal cavalry, who were now advancing on our devoted command, which was holding its position with great tenacity. Colonel Johnson, realizing the danger he was in, gave orders to withdraw, and sent me word to bring Rasin and come in. . . . At this time the enemy made a charge in line, and their dense masses came toward us as if to swallow up the little command. Colonels Johnson and Brown moved off in good order, but in passing through an opened gateway leading into an adjoining field, by some misfortune the gate was closed, leaving the rear troop in the field with the advancing enemy. Colonel Brown, with that gallantry and devotion for his men which ever marked him, took position endeavoring to open and so hold the gate, in order that the men might escape, and while thus engaged was

9.   Booth 1898, 114

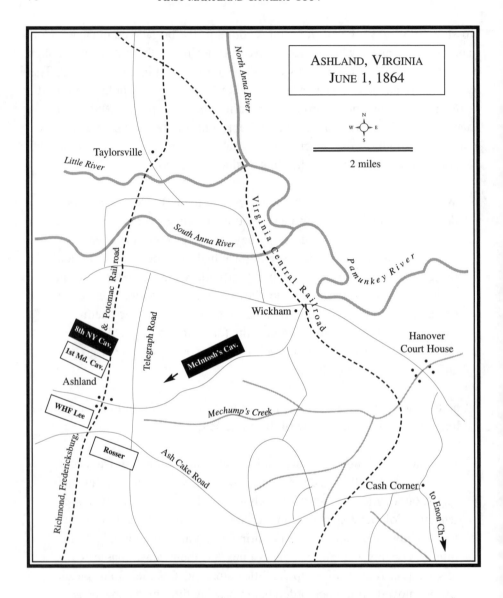

several times struck on the head by the sabres of the enemy, who were now among his men. The command then struck a gallop, and the retreat was made with all rapidity, the order being passed down the line to the men to scatter and take care of themselves, as there was little chance of making resistance, and by this course the pursuit would be broken. . . . We lost heavily in the encounter, about fifty men killed and wounded and prisoners, but we undoubtedly saved [James B.] Gordon's [North

Carolina] Brigade from destruction, as the enemy would have caught his horses in ten minutes' time and had his dismounted line at their mercy had we not made the fight.[10]

Henry Mettam recalled that his Company E had led the battalion into battle:

I saw Baker's pickets coming full tilt, with [Gen. George A.] Custer's men at their heels, pressing us so close that they knocked some of our men off their horses, and hardly giving us time to leave the narrow road and get into the open field, but tearing this wattling fence down we soon formed in line, and as Custer's men came up they had the brush fence to protect them, as the first volley they fired killed Colonel Johnson's horse and shot his sabre clean from his side. By this time a column of Federal cavalry was going by our left flank and into our rear, so we attempted to withdraw decently and in order, and as we found this impossible we were ordered to get out the best we could, and [Company E] lost some ten or more killed, wounded or missing.[11]

Maj. Alexander Walker of the Seventh Michigan Cavalry reported that in the charge his regiment killed four, wounded ten, and captured thirty-six members of the First Maryland Cavalry. Johnson later wrote that his loss was seventy killed, wounded, and missing of two hundred fifty engaged.

The muster rolls indicate that the fight at Pollard's Farm cost Company A 1st Lt. Edmund G. Duley; Duley, who had been taken prisoner at Gettyburg and only recently exchanged, was again captured. Pvt. Gustavus W. Dorsey was killed; another three men were wounded, and one was taken prisoner. Company B lost only two men to capture. Capt. George W. Howard of Company C and two of his men were taken prisoner, Pvt. William C. Cheseldine died of wounds, and one other man was wounded. Company D lost Pvt. Alexander A. Young killed, Pvt. Samuel B. Mercer mortally wounded, four others wounded, and nine taken prisoner. Rasin's troop suffered only one wounded but lost five to capture. Company F's losses included four men wounded and seven captured. Some of the wounded men of the battalion were also captured.

Johnson and Brown gathered up the badly shaken Marylanders and marched toward Ashland, where they found part of Fitzhugh Lee's command resting on

10. Ibid.
11. *Maryland Historical Magazine*, Vol. 58, 153

the roadside. Lee's men had just returned from an unsuccessful assault on a fort on the James River held by black troops.

When the officers reached Lee's headquarters, the general greeted them jocularly: "This is a pretty howdy-do for the Maryland cavalry—let the Yankees run you off the face of the earth." Booth, his arm in a sling from a wound to his shoulder, was in no mood for Lee's wit. He blurted out, "Well, General, one thing is certain, the people who have been after us were white men; we stayed long enough to find that out anyway." With the utmost good humor Lee laughed heartily at the rejoinder he had provoked.[12]

In his written account, Booth continued:

> For the next few days we occupied a position between Hanover Court House and the railroad at Wickham's. The enemy, however, were active and drove us out and back to the vicinity of the railroad bridge over the South An[n]a, not far from Taylorsville.
>
> In this position we were attacked on June 1st and compelled by force of numbers to retire, with little loss. . . . [T]owards the close of the afternoon we had taken position slightly in advance of the railroad crossing. The firing was not heavy, but persistent, and Colonel Johnson and myself rode back beyond the railroad to select a new position to which we could retire the command if occasion required. We were on our return to the front when one of the men rode up and announced that Colonel Brown had been shot, and presently his body was carried to the rear. We immediately galloped to the front and found the enemy making disposition for an advance which it was apparent we could not withstand with our small command. It became necessary to call in our skirmishers and retire in the direction of Ashland, which movement was made in good order, the Federals closely following and pressing our rear. On reaching the vicinity of Ashland we found they had already occupied the point, and we had to move with rapidity through the outskirts of the village until we reached a point where we were in communications with our troops. Notwithstanding the pressure under which the movement was made, I sought out the house to which Colonel Brown had been carried and found him unconscious, with but a few moments of life in his body. The ball had entered his brain, inflicting a mortal wound. In deep sorrow, I took the last leave of this

12.   Booth 1898, 116

dear friend, and stooped to kiss his brow, now covered with his life's blood. Ridgely Brown was one of the best-rounded and perfected characters I have ever known. He was as true as steel and as gallant as ever mounted a horse and drew blade.[13]

Henry Mettam described Brown's death:

[A]s no reinforcements came, at last Colonel Ridgely Brown determined to make an effort, and as he led us in one desperate charge, he was shot through the forehead and died without speaking a word. He was the bravest, the purest, the gentlest man from Maryland who died for liberty in that four years' war.[14]

Pvt. George S. Woolley of Company B, a hospital steward, recalled:

Colonel Brown sent a courier to me to send the two ambulances . . . to Richmond by way of Ashland at once, as he was going to fall back, which I did. . . . [I]n a few minutes . . . another courier came and said Colonel Brown was wounded and to send an ambulance at once.

I told the courier to go post haste and overtake the four-mule ambulance, tell the driver to cut the leaders loose and give them in charge of the other driver, as this was the best ambulance and had our medical supplies. I waited for the ambulance at the railroad crossing. In a short time I saw six men carrying Colonel Brown in a blanket. I rode down the road to meet them, and in a few minutes the ambulance returned.

We put him in as carefully as we could. I got in, he leaned his head on my shoulder. I soon saw that he was fatally wounded, the ball had entered the corner of his right eye in a line with the ear, and came out the back of his head. I gave him some whiskey, he raised up once and spoke, said "I am so sick."

Then Colonel [*sic*] Gus Dorsey came and asked me if he were seriously wounded.[15]

Wolley explained that the wound was mortal and that Brown could last no

13.   Ibid., 117–18

14.   *Maryland Historical Magazine*, Vol. 58, 154

15.   Author's Collection, no ascertainable publication facts

more than a few hours. He recommended that they stop at the nearest farm-house and send the ambulance on to Richmond, and Dorsey concurred. Wolley continued,

> In a short time we came to a house where there were a number of trees, we got out a stretcher and took the Colonel in the yard under the shade of the trees. The lady of the house gave me a pillow to put under his head. I took the effects of Colonel Brown, which consisted of his pistol, Bible, pen knife, pipe and tobacco pouch and hid them under the pig pen, expecting the enemy to arrive any minute, as some of them were in sight. The Colonel lingered until about six o'clock in the evening, and then passed away peacefully. The lady gave me a white shirt to put on him, I bathed him as well as I could. With the assistance of an old colored man, we carried him in the house and put him in an unoccupied room.
>
> I had heard that Mrs. Peters and daughter were living in Ashland, and knowing them to be friends of Colonel Brown, I questioned the colored man and found that he knew them. After dark I sent him to Ashland to tell them of the death of Colonel Brown and that I would bury him the next morning. I found some boards and with the aid of these old men, I made a box, put him in and fixed him as nicely as I could, with so little to do with. Mrs. Peters and her daughter got through the lines and came about 8 o'clock in the morning, and brought flowers, a neighbor, an old gentleman, and a colored man came over to help us bury him. The four men acted as bearers. Mrs. Peters, her daughter and I walked back of them. We buried him in an orchard. I cannot remember exactly, but I think Mrs. Peters read the burial service.[16]

Wolley gave Colonel Brown's personal effects to Mrs. Peters, who sent them to the colonel's sister.

The 150 Marylanders were fighting the Eighth New York Cavalry during the day of Brown's death. When Capt. Theodore S. Garnett, Gen. William H. F. "Rooney" Lee's aide-de-camp, arrived with a squadron of the Third North Carolina Cavalry, Johnson greeted him brusquely, exclaiming: "I don't want your squadron—Take it back,—Colonel Brown has been killed—I cannot stop

16.   Ibid. (Years after the war the sister visited Wolley in Baltimore to learn the particulars of Brown's death and burial. She gave Wolley her brother's tobacco pouch.)

the enemy here,—I am now falling back across the railroad."[17] The astonished Garnett and the Tar Heels returned to Ashland.

Colonel Johnson eulogized Brown with the following:

Headquarters Maryland Line, June 6, 1864—General Order No. 26.

Lieutenant-Colonel Ridgely Brown, commanding First Maryland Cavalry, fell in battle on the 1st instant, near the South Anna. He died, as a soldier prefers to die, leading his men in a victorious charge. As an officer, kind and careful; as a soldier, brave and true; as a gentleman, chivalrous; as a Christian, gentle and modest; no one in the Confederate Army surpassed him in the hold he had on the hearts of his men, and the place in the esteem of his superiors. Of the rich blood that Maryland has lavished on every battle-field, none is more precious than his, and that of our other brave comrades in arms who fell during the four days previous on the hillsides of Hanover. His command has lost a friend most steadfast, but his commanding officer is deprived of an assistant invaluable. To the first he was ever as careful as a father; to the latter as true as a brother.

In token of respect to his memory, the colors of the different regiments of this command will be draped, and the officers wear the usual badge of military mourning for thirty days.

By Order of Colonel Bradley T. Johnson, George W. Booth, A.A.G.[18]

Although Maj. Robert C. Smith, who had been wounded the year before at Greenland Gap, was still too disabled for field duty, he was promoted to lieutenant colonel of the battalion. Colonel Johnson was assigned command of the unit in the field with Captain Emack acting as major. Lieutenant Ditty was elected captain of Company F to replace the lamented Schwartz. The lieutenants in Ditty's company rose one rank, but no third lieutenant was elected. Ditty was issued sixteen captured Spencer rifles for his troopers near this time.

On June 3 Johnson led the battalion to Meadow Bridge and camped. The following day the campsite was moved to Mechanicsville, where the battle-weary troopers finally rested. The respite was short, however, as Johnson was soon ordered to march toward Louisa Court House. Sheridan was raiding along the Virginia Central Railroad.

17.   Garnett 1994, 77
18.   Goldsborough 1900, 200–1

The Maryland battalion and the Baltimore Light Artillery accompanied General Hampton on his ride to intercept the enemy cavalry. Booth recorded:

> [R]eached Trevillian's [sic] station just in time to oppose the head of Sheridan's force as it attempted to cross the line of the railroad. For two days the battle raged; at one time Custer, with his brigade, broke through our line and captured the horses of [Gen. Matthew C.] Butler's Brigade, the men being engaged at that time on foot. We had just reported to [Gen. Thomas L.] Rosser on our left, when the news of the mishap reached him. At once he started for the scene of difficulty, charging into Custer's column, now somewhat disordered by their success, and in a little time they were defeated and we had them on the run, recovering Butler's horses and making many captives of both men and horses from the enemy.[19]

Mettam wrote, "Our regiment captured over one hundred horses and men, completely armed and equipped, and my share was a fine pair of new cavalry boots, from one of Custer's lieutenants, what I was badly in need of."[20]

An unidentified newspaper account reported:

> For two days sabres flashed in a hand-to-hand conflict, and the carbine and pistol did their deadly work, strewing the plain with hundreds of dead and dying men. In those two dreadful days the little First Maryland was ever in the van, and their gallant bearing elicited the admiration of all. They fought as though to avenge the fall of their comrades at Pollard's farm, and their sabres drank deeply of the blood of the foremen. But Sheridan had met his match in Hampton, and suffered an unmistakeable [sic] defeat."[21]

Johnson now proposed to Hampton a plan, hatched at Hanover Junction, that called for Johnson to take two hundred well-mounted men, cross the Potomac, and capture President Lincoln at the Old Soldiers' Home in Washington, D.C. Johnson knew that Lincoln liked to spend the summer nights there, guarded by only a small detachment of cavalry. Hampton approved the plan, and Johnson

19.   Booth 1898, 120
20.   *Maryland Historical Magazine,* Vol. 58, 154
21.   Author's Collection, undated newspaper account

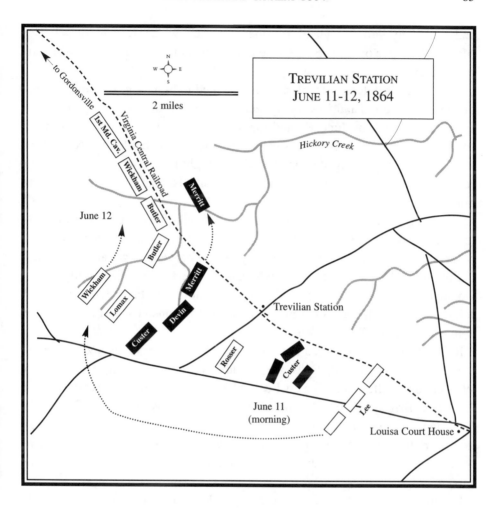

**TREVILIAN STATION
JUNE 11-12, 1864**

set his men to shoeing their horses and preparing for the raid.

While the preparations were being made, Gen. Jubal A. Early and his corps passed through the Gordonsville area on their way to oppose Gen. David Hunter's Federals, who were approaching Lynchburg. When Johnson made Early aware of his intentions, Old Jube prohibited the attempt. "I want to make that expedition myself, and I want you and your cavalry to assist me in it. You go to Waynesboro in the Valley and watch there, guarding my rear until I dispose of Mr. Hunter. As soon as I've smashed his little tea party, I'll come back and we'll go into Maryland together and see what we can do."[22] The Marylanders rode over the Blue Ridge as ordered and camped near Waynesboro for several days.

Following his defeat of Hunter, Early marched to Staunton, where his worn-out command rested and was resupplied. Johnson's promotion to brigadier general came through on June 18, and Early assigned him to command Grumble Jones's Brigade of cavalry. Jones had been killed in the battle of Piedmont on June 5. The cavalry brigade consisted of the Eighth and Twenty-first Virginia regiments and the Thirty-fourth, Thirty-sixth, and Thirty-seventh Virginia battalions of cavalry.

Johnson's promotion left the First Maryland under the command of the senior captain present, George M. Emack. Booth wrote that Emack "was not acceptable to the officers or men, not by reason of want of gallantry, but they did not prevail the confidence in his judgment or administrative ability which would have enabled him to hold the command in a state of efficiency."[23] Johnson and Booth persuaded Emack to serve on Johnson's staff and give the command to Capt. Warner Welsh.

Robert E. Lee next directed Early to proceed down the Valley and clear it of the enemy. If successful, Early was to advance into Maryland and threaten Washington itself. According to Lee's plan, Early would then send Bradley Johnson's Brigade to free the prisoners at Point Lookout Prison; Johnson's Brigade would be supported in the action by a naval and Marine Corps operation from the sea. Lee believed that this would have the added effect of drawing men from Grant's army away from Richmond, providing some relief for the capital.

During the last days of June the Marylanders advanced northward. Welsh marched his troopers through Port Republic, across Columbia Bridge, and through Luray to within four miles of Front Royal. On July 2 Johnson succeeded in having the Marylanders, including the Baltimore Light Artillery, assigned to his brigade officially. Tschiffely noted, "[M]arch all day & all night through Winchester & Smithfield &c very warm."[24] Of Johnson's fifteen hundred men, only eight hundred were mounted; the dismounted men followed along, waiting for a chance to remount.

On July 3 Johnson's Brigade fought with the Federals at Leetown. The

22. *Southern Historical Society Papers,* Vol. XXX, 216

23. Booth 1898, 122

24. Stephen R. Brockmiller Collection, Elgar L. Tschiffely Book

Confederates engaged Col. James A. Mulligan's Brigade of three thousand infantry and six guns, and the Marylanders and Virginians drove the Federals back to the Potomac at Shepherdstown. The fight lasted from morning to noon in the heat and dust; Mettam described the action as "hot and heavy." He and his companions went into the woods where the Union troops had camped. They "found fire burning and plenty of food of all descriptions, some sheep and hogs, all dressed and hanging up on the trees, some of the steaks cut off and in frying pans; so we all had a little lunch, and I opened one of the knapsacks and found some clean underclothes, which I needed, so proceeding to drop my dirty ones for clean ones."[25]

On Independence Day the Confederate cavalry drove the enemy across the Potomac at Shepherdstown. Pvt. J. Newman Johnson of Company A was killed in the skirmishing. The next day Johnson led his brigade across the river and around Sharpsburg and camped three miles from Boonsboro. The advance cost Company A another man mortally wounded and two men captured and Company D one wounded and one taken prisoner. Lt. George M. E. Shearer of Company D was captured near Hagerstown.

On July 6 Johnson moved the brigade on to Middletown, skirmishing all the way. The following day his troopers drove the Eighth Illinois Cavalry and a battery out of Boonsboro Gap and pushed on to Frederick, which was crammed with wagons abandoned by the Union forces retreating from Harpers Ferry. Johnson made disposition to attack the town, but he was stopped by Gen. Robert Ransom, Early's chief of cavalry, who believed that the Marylander was too eager to take his hometown. Ransom ordered Johnson's command back to Boonsboro Gap. Company A had lost one man wounded and another captured.

The brigade moved back to the gap just in time to defend it; the Federal cavalry attacked on July 8 but was driven off. This action cost the battalion one wounded and five taken prisoner.

That evening Johnson received the long-anticipated orders from Early directing him to march around Baltimore, burn the bridges on the railroads leading northward, and cut the telegraph wires. In circling the city he was to break up communications between Baltimore and Washington before moving on and attacking Point Lookout on July 12. Col. John Taylor Wood, with marines and sailors, was to launch a coordinated assault from the water. Johnson was then to march fifteen-thousand-odd newly freed prisoners to Bladensburg, where Early would be waiting, and across the Potomac. If Early proceeded to capture

25. *Maryland Historical Magazine*, Vol. 58, 155

Washington, he could arm the men from the capital's arsenals. The trek was 250 miles long and had to be made in three days and nights. Johnson told Early that he did not believe the condition of his horses would allow such an undertaking in the time allotted. Early ordered him to make the effort.

Harry Gilmor, with about 175 men of his Second Maryland Cavalry, had joined Johnson after crossing into Maryland. Gilmor reportedly was placed in command of both Maryland battalions.

On July 9, early in the morning, Johnson led the brigade eastward. The Confederates rode rapidly through Frederick, Liberty, New Windsor, and Westminster toward Reistertown. The weary riders rested on the Dover road at present-day Glyndon. Though exhausted, the Marylanders were not too tired to visit their nearby homes. Despite the presence of Federal troops in the area, many risked spending a night with family and friends.

When Mettam returned early the next morning he found the brigade along the road to Owings's Mills. The troopers went on to Cockeysville, where they burned a bridge. On a siding of the Western Maryland Railroad a car with freezers of ice cream was captured. The whole command shared the cold dessert. Mettam was amused by the troops from southwestern Virginia, who had never seen ice cream and "thought it was frozen mush and dipped it out into their hats and ate it riding along." Booth noted that the men used rubber blankets, buckets, old tin cans—anything, in fact, that would hold the refreshing treat. The Virginians were very satisfied with their new "frozen vittles."[26]

Gilmor, with his small battalion and part of the First totaling 175 men, was detached and ordered to raid the Philadelphia, Wilmington, and Baltimore Railroad. The Marylanders succeeded at burning the key Gunpowder River bridge and the Bush River bridge and capturing and destroying two trains. They also captured Maj. Gen. William B. Franklin and part of his staff, but due to the laxity of the guards, the prisoners escaped. Johnson had meanwhile led the rest of the brigade across the Green Springs Valley to Carroll's Caves.

A detachment of the First Maryland that had remained with Johnson under Lieutenant Blackistone burned Maryland governor Augustus W. Bradford's summer home in retaliation for General Hunter's burning of former governor John Letcher's home in Lexington, Virginia. Meanwhile, Confederate scouts sent into Baltimore returned with the news that the Federal Nineteenth Corps was debarking and en route to Washington. Johnson immediately sent an officer and five men to report this news to General Early.

26. Ibid., 157; Booth 1898, 124

On July 11 the brigade, still without Gilmor, passed around Baltimore and damaged the Baltimore and Ohio Railroad and the telegraph wires at Woodstock; it halted for the night at Tridelphia. Johnson had intended to break the Washington branch of the railroad at Laurel the next day, but scouts found that point to be heavily defended by infantry. Proceeding instead to Beltsville, Johnson drove off a large force of Federal cavalry and then destroyed the railroad and telegraph there. Several hundred government mules were captured in the course of the action and taken along for the Point Lookout prisoners to ride.

Just as Johnson was ready to ride eastward he received a message from Early, whose forces were not strong enough to capture Washington. Johnson was to abandon his attempt on Point Lookout and rejoin Early at once. He was directed to march to Silver Spring, where Early would hold his position at the Blair House, on the Rockville road, until nine o'clock that night. Johnson moved his column along the Washington Turnpike. Near the Maryland Agricultural College the Confederates engaged about five hundred Union cavalry, which they quickly drove back into the Washington defenses. Johnson then moved his brigade cross-country, using the Marylanders as scouts and guides. It was shortly after nine o'clock when Adjutant Booth, with the advance guard, reached Early and reported Johnson's arrival. Old Jube assigned the saddle-weary men to rearguard duty. The battalion had lost two men to capture during the day.

On July 13 the Marylanders stopped in Rockville to feed their horses and were attacked by the Second Massachusetts Cavalry. Capt. Wilson Carey "Bill" Nicholas, inspector of the Maryland Line and a member of Johnson's staff, asked Johnson for permission to take a squadron and charge the Federals. Johnson finally gave in. Mettam wrote:

> Captain Bill yelled and squadrons [Companies] E and F fell in line and away we went, about forty of us, after the Yanks. I remember well how we almost all of us dropped our bridles and with pistol in one hand, sabre in the other, and with our spurs into our horses' flanks, we followed them, yelling like Indians, and as they seemed to be satisfied to get away from us, we concluded to let them go.[27]

Company C lost Lt. Thomas J. Green wounded and captured and another man wounded in the day's fighting; Company A lost one man taken prisoner.

From Rockville Johnson's troopers, continuing to protect Early's long wagon

27. *Maryland Historical Magazine,* Vol. 58, 158

train and herds of captured horses and cattle, moved slowly to Poolesville. As the Confederates crossed the river, the pursuing Federal cavalry grew bolder, pressing the rear guard near the town. Johnson's men fought well in the action, which lasted for about an hour. During one of several charges and counter-charges Captain Nicholas was wounded and his horse killed, and he was taken prisoner. One of Company C's men was wounded, and Company A lost one man to capture.

Gilmor and his detachment rejoined Johnson's exhausted troopers and recrossed the Potomac that evening. They camped near Leesburg that night. Mettam recalled:

> This ride from July 9th to July 13th was probably the longest ride taken during the war. For one hundred and twenty hours we never dismount-ed except to unsaddle and feed once every twenty-four hours, and of course we ate what we could pick up on the roadside and slept in our saddles.[28]

The Marylanders brought a number of recruits out of their home state for the two battalions. In number these men more than made up for those lost during the campaign.

Frank L. Hering, one of the new recruits, wrote to his brother upon his safe arrival in Dixie:

> I came here from Maryland building no air castles consequently feel perfectly satisfied. I do not regret the step I have taken I expected to suffer many privations consequently am prepared for almost anything, and if the good Lord see fit to spare my life so that I may see my friends again.[29]

Joseph R. Stonebraker also slipped across the Potomac to enlist. One ragged veteran of Early's infantry, upon learning of young Stonebraker's purpose, told him, "You take the advice of an old soldier, and go back to your home." Stone-braker stuck with his decision.[30]

Following a day's rest Johnson marched the brigade toward the Shenandoah

28.   Ibid.
29.   Daniel D. Hartzler Collection, Frank L. Hering Letter
30.   Stonebraker 1899, 61–62

Valley, halting in Snickers's Gap. Gen. William W. Averell's Union cavalry harassed the Confederates as they retired, and Welsh lost one man wounded and four captured in the skirmishing.

From Snickers's Gap Johnson moved the brigade to Rippon, West Virginia, where two days were spent on picket duty. On July 19 the brigade engaged Federal cavalry near Charles Town, and the next day the Confederates fell back to the south, through Berryville and White Post, before bivouacking. On the 21st the Marylanders were forced to fall back even farther up the Valley, to Strasburg, in order to find feed for their horses. July 22 found the brigade in line of battle as Early advanced toward Winchester, and the next day the Marylanders engaged the Federals near Newtown before camping near Middletown. On July 24, Johnson led the brigade through pouring rain on an all-day-and-night march to Brucetown. All the while Early continued to maneuver, forcing the Union troops toward the Potomac between Williamsport and Harpers Ferry.

Early meanwhile determined to retaliate for the wanton burning of private homes and other property in the Valley by Gen. "Black Dave" Hunter, whose barbarous treatment of civilians, including his own relatives, had raised the ire of the Confederates. Early ordered Gen. John "John Tiger" McCausland and Johnson to raid Chambersburg, Pennsylvania.

On July 28 the First Maryland camped near Hedgesville. Harry Gilmor was once again in command of the two Maryland units, and the next night he led the Confederate advance to near McCoy's Ferry on the Potomac. Johnson ordered Gilmor to cross the river and seize the heights on the Maryland side. Two companies dismounted and acted as sharpshooters along the banks while Gilmor led his men across and captured his objective.

McCausland then ordered the Marylanders to picket the National Road in both directions. Lt. Thomas Jefferson Smith was posted with a detachment toward Hagerstown, and Captain Rasin was detailed in the direction of Cumberland. Both engaged the enemy; Rasin and his men captured a company of dismounted cavalry at Hancock, and Smith ran into the Fourteenth Pennsylvania Cavalry, ordered a charge despite his inferior numbers, and was driven back.

Gilmor's two hundred men, armed only with pistols and sabres, found themselves hotly engaged with both the Twelfth and Fourteenth Pennsylvania, whose men were armed with carbines. The Marylanders succeeded in driving the Federals back through the village of Clear Spring but were then ambushed in a mounted charge by the Pennsylvanians. Gilmor again rallied his troopers and drove the enemy off, afterward reporting the loss of seventeen men. In the First Maryland Pvts. Charles A. Warfield of Company A and Samuel B. Rogers of Company C were killed. Company C also lost one man wounded and three captured, and a man from Company D was wounded.

The Marylanders held the National Road while Johnson's and McCausland's brigades crossed the river and marched on toward Mercersburg, Pennsylvania. Gilmor withdrew his men after dark and caught up with the column about a mile beyond Mercersburg, where he learned from the two generals that their objective was Chambersburg.

The next morning the Confederate advance ran into a Federal ambush and was driven back. Gilmor and the Marylanders were summoned to the front. With the aid of Maj. James W. Sweeney's Thirty-sixth Battalion of Virginia Cavalry, they drove the Federals off and entered Chambersburg.

McCausland met the town's leading citizens and demanded one hundred thousand dollars in gold or five hundred thousand in currency as compensation for Hunter's acts or the city would be burned. The municipal authorities either were unable to come up with that amount or refused to comply. In response, Johnson directed Col. William E. Peters of the Twenty-first Virginia Cavalry to burn the town, but Peters refused. Gilmor and his command were then ordered to carry out the burning, and the Marylanders reluctantly complied.

In the afternoon Johnson led McCausland's column on to McConnellsburg, Maryland, where the two commands camped for the night. The next day, July 31, McCausland turned his command southward with Averell's Federal cavalry in pursuit. At Hancock, McCausland demanded thirty thousand dollars and five thousand cooked rations from the citizens, threatening to torch their town if they did not comply. When Johnson learned of this, he confronted McCausland. "Johnson was indignant," wrote Booth, "and told him Hancock was a Maryland town, with many southern residents whose relatives were in the confederate army, and intimating in most direct and positive language that the Maryland men of the brigade would submit to no such violent treatment."[31] Lt. Robert R. Zell recalled that "Johnson told him that if he did it would be over the dead bodies of the Maryland Brigade." Booth further reported that "[t]he angry interview was cut short by some rapid firing down the road and the report that Averill [*sic*] was driving in our pickets."[32]

McCausland abandoned his plan and directed Johnson to follow him toward Cumberland, destroying bridges and obstructing the road as he passed. The brigade carried out its mission, keeping the Federal cavalry at a safe distance.

31.   Booth 1898, 138
32.   *Confederate Veteran*, Vol. XXVIII, 261

When McCausland's advance approached Cumberland on August 1 his troopers were met by Federal cannon fire. Gen. Benjamin F. Kelly had posted most of his force on a commanding ridge line overlooking Evett's Creek. McCausland sent a squadron to flank the Union guns, but the unit ran into Yankee infantry posted in the woods. McCausland consulted with Johnson, and the two determined that the enemy position was too strong to be carried. McCausland then sent Gilmor to find a crossing on the Potomac. Gilmor arrested a citizen, placed him on a horse, and, with a pistol in his back, directed him to guide the command to the nearest ford. The fearful civilian led the Confederates to Old Town.

"We reached this point about daylight, . . . August 1," wrote Johnson, "and found the enemy, after burning the canal bridges, had posted himself on a hill between the canal and the Potomac." Johnson attacked from each flank with his Virginia units, "at the same time opening my two pieces of artillery vigorously on the enemy." The Confederate troopers meanwhile built bridges across the canal under the fire of the 153rd Ohio Infantry. "[The enemy] was driven across the Potomac at once, where he took position behind the railroad embankment, a strong block-house on his right and an iron-clad train of cars, a battery, three guns in each, covered with railroad iron at each end, and four cars iron-lined and musket-proof between the two. The first shot of my artillery drove through the engine-boiler." Johnson's horse was killed in the melee.[33]

Zell reported:

> This stopped the train. The second shot from the gun went inside a port-hole of one of the armored cars and exploded, killing three of the enemy; the rest of them crawled out on the opposite side. At the same time we sent two more shells into the cars containing the infantry, and they all left the train and took to the woods.
>
> We then gave our attention to the blockhouse on the opposite side at the ford in the river. General Johnson sent a flag of truce asking them to surrender, which they refused; After our shell hit the blockhouse twice they put out a white flag and surrendered.[34]

The colonel and eighty men of the 153rd Ohio surrendered their flag and their arms. The action had cost the First Maryland one killed and one wounded in

33.   OR, Series I, Vol. XLIII, Pt. 1, 5
34.   *Confederate Veteran,* Vol. XXVIII, 261

Company B and three men in Company C captured. Zell concluded, "We burned the blockhouse and the armored train by piling railroad ties under and around the cars and destroyed the track for some distance."[35]

The Confederates crossed the Potomac and rode to Springfield, West Virginia, along its south branch. Here McCausland decided to make another attempt on the railroad. On August 4 he moved the two brigades on New Creek. Upon arrival he found that the fortifications there, which had been reported to be unmanned, were in fact bristling with Federal infantry and artillery. Following an aborted assault by his brigade, McCausland withdrew his forces. The Marylanders were not engaged.

The weary cavalrymen rode on to Old Fields, north of Moorefield, and went into camp. Johnson's Brigade camped on the north side of the South Branch; McCausland's Brigade bivouacked on the other side of the stream, about three-quarters of a mile nearer Moorefield. Regiments and battalions spread out to enable the horses to graze on the available grass. Johnson was meanwhile directed to picket the Romney, Patterson's Creek, and Williamsport roads. Mettam reported that the pickets on the Romney road were twelve men from Companies E and F of the First Maryland commanded by Lt. Fielder Slingluff. During the night of August 6 McCausland received word that Averell's Federal cavalry was in pursuit and had reached Romney. He sent a courier to Johnson directing him to saddle up his command and send a scout out the Romney road.

Scouts from the Eighth Virginia Cavalry had no sooner passed through the picketing Marylanders than they were captured by Averell's advance, which was led by Jessie scouts—Union soldiers dressed as Confederates. The night was overcast and drizzling rain, which made the Federal approach an almost noiseless one in pitch-darkness. Henry Mettam and Carl Kauffmann were on post at about four o'clock that morning when the disguised Yankees approached and identified themselves as returning scouts. The three Jessie scouts rode between the two Marylanders and took them prisoner. Mettam and Kauffmann were taken before General Averell, who questioned them on the strength and disposition of their command. The Marylanders refused to answer and told Averell that he would have to find out for himself.

Meanwhile, Lieutenant Slingluff and the picket reserve were rudely awakened by kicks from angry Jessie scouts, who were pointing revolvers at their heads and shouting, "Get up, you —— Chambersburg-burning ——s!"[36]

35. Ibid.

36. *Confederate Veteran*, Vol. XVII, 559–61

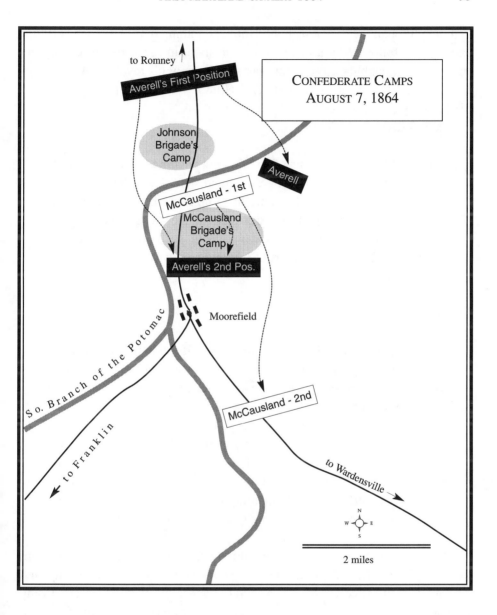

to Romney

Averell's First Position

CONFEDERATE CAMPS
AUGUST 7, 1864

Johnson
Brigade's
Camp

Averell

McCausland - 1st

McCausland
Brigade's
Camp

Averell's 2nd Pos.

Moorefield

So. Branch of the Potomac

to Franklin

McCausland - 2nd

to Wardensville

N
W ✦ E
S

2 miles

In the meantime, Gilmor had obeyed Johnson's orders to have the First and
Second battalions saddle their horses. When no further orders were received,
the Marylanders tied their steeds to a nearby fence and dozed under their blankets. Some time later, Gilmor heard several shots and the sound of horses

tramping through the darkness, but he thought nothing of it. A sudden "Get up, damn you!" followed by a pistol shot near his head succeeded in getting his attention. Although dazed, Gilmor was able to draw his revolver. After a second shot and the shout of "Surrender!" Gilmor shot the Federal trooper and tried to rally his command.[37]

Fielder Slingluff recalled:

> I saw the blue-black column of Averill [*sic*] winding down the road and breaking off into the fields where our men slept. I saw them . . . dashing in among the men and waking them up from their sleep. Some of our command who had heard the rush of the charge succeeded in mounting their horses and escaping. With such, some shots were exchanged, but the greater part of our regiment was caught asleep and captured without firing a shot.[38]

Johnson reported:

> About daylight a squadron in Confederate uniform moved by the camp of the First Maryland straight to my headquarters. Those who were up and saw them supposed them to be a returning scout or picket, and took no notice of them.
>
> They never fired a shot until they reached McNeill's house, where my camp was. Soon after them came a body of Federal cavalry, who rode at once through the camp of the First Maryland to that of the Second Maryland and dispersed both, they being very small, reduced by losses in battle and hard marching to an aggregate for both of not 130 men in camp, the First having twenty-eight men on picket duty.[39]

Johnson and most of his staff were able to escape on foot, and a lieutenant from the Second Maryland later let Johnson have his horse. The Twenty-first Virginia Cavalry tried to stop the Federal advance but was driven off, losing Colonel Peters wounded. Some of Johnson's scattered command fell back across the river and were pursued by the Yankees. McCausland's Brigade attempted to stop them at the ford but was driven back.

37. Gilmor 1866, 222–23
38. *Confederate Veteran,* Vol. XVII, 561
39. OR, Series I, Vol. XLIII, Pt. 1, 5

Johnson was able to rally about two hundred men from the brigade and slowly retired over the mountains to the Shenandoah Valley. Booth reported the loss of two hundred men in each brigade, and Johnson lost two guns of the Baltimore battery and all of his wagons and ambulances. Many of those who escaped lost their horses.

The First Maryland was decimated. Company A's Pvt. William Carter was killed; Captain Griffith and twenty-four men were captured. Company B had one man killed, one wounded, and sixteen captured. Company C lost Lt. Thomas Smith and another man wounded and fifteen captured. In Company D, one man was wounded, and Lieutenant Zell and seven men were captured. Company E lost one man killed, Lt. Joseph K. Roberts Jr. wounded, and ten captured. Company F lost one man killed; Lts. Slingluff and Samuel G. Bonn and four men were captured.

Pvt. Trusten Polk of Company A, who was one of those captured, later wrote: "We were marched on foot to New Creek Station, and next day sent to Wheeling, where we were quartered in the penitentiary for three days and then sent to Camp Chase, Ohio."[40]

Johnson led his battered remnants to Gen. Gilbert Meem's farm near Mount Jackson for a brief respite. He blamed McCausland for the debacle and pointed to the lax discipline shown by elements of the two brigades during and after the burning of Chambersburg as the cause of the defeat. McCausland blamed Johnson. It was Johnson's troops who were first overrun, even after being warned that Averell was en route. Johnson demanded a court of inquiry, but Early refused for the good of the service.

Booth recalled: "Unfortunately the innocent suffered, the reputations of others were called into question, and the cause sustained a serious loss in morale and in material from which this particular body of troops never entirely recovered. The hope of converting them into more efficient soldiers disappeared, and we were fearfully handicapped for the remainder of the campaign."[41]

• • •

Early now faced a new opponent in the Valley: General Sheridan and his growing force. Johnson rejoined Old Jube near Fisher's Hill on August 12. The brigade was placed on picket duty near Columbia Furnace on the Back road,

---

40.   Author's Collection, no ascertainable publication facts
41.   Booth 1898, 140

which ran along the foothills to the west and paralleled the Valley Turnpike to the east. Early continued to maneuver his troops as he sought an opportunity to strike Sheridan.

On August 6 the secretary of war had ordered the transfer of the Howard Dragoons, then Company K, First Virginia Cavalry, to the First Maryland Cavalry. The dragoons joined their fellow Marylanders about August 13. Capt. Gustavus W. "Gus" Dorsey led the new troop, and Lts. Nathan C. Hobbs, James R. Oliver, and Edward H. D. Pue were the other officers in the company.

On the day of Dorsey's arrival, the First Maryland, newly reattached to Lomax's Brigade, drove in the Federal pickets and their cavalry supports for several miles, taking thirty prisoners. Mission accomplished, the Confederate troopers had begun retiring when the the unit, still under Gilmor and now acting as rear guard, was suddenly attacked from the flank by several thousand Federal cavalry.

"One of the . . . columns would have struck us in flank," wrote Gilmor, "but for the coolness, presence of mind, and undaunted bravery of Captain Gus Dorsey."[42] Dorsey had been dressed in the manner of a Federal officer. Still later, Gilmor wrote:

Seeing the column about to cut off his whole company, [Dorsey] put spurs to his horse, leaped the fence, and, dashing alone right up to the advancing column, called out in a loud stern voice, "By fours, right about, wheel, march!" and the officer in charge, taking him to be one of his superiors, repeated the order to his command, and they wheeled. The enemy were now completely mixed up with us, all cutting, and slashing, and pistoling right and left. The race continued over three miles, and throughout the whole distance the scene of horror was going on.

When I got back to the wood whence we had first started, I saw the 1st Maryland drawn up ready for a charge. I made the men to break to right and left to let [the First Maryland] through. The enemy was right at my back, and the 1st Maryland doubtless thought all belonged to me, although I yelled out for them to charge. They did not move, however, until the column had fairly struck them full in front, when the whole battalion gave way and ran like mad—friend and foe all mixed together, cutting and slashing at each other right and left. Very few pistols

42.   Gilmor 1866, 240–41

were used, or our loss would have been twice as heavy. When a horse fell, a dozen or more would go blundering over him, and a sickening sight to behold many with broken necks.[43]

A member of the First remembered it differently.

At this juncture the head of the enemy's column, immediately in the rear of the First Maryland, had entered the stream before the rear of the battalion had reached the opposite bank. . . . At this critical moment, right in the midst of the stream, the battalion wheeled, and again charged, meeting the enemy midway, when a most desperate hand-to-hand fight ensued, the blood of both intermingling with the current. For a few minutes they held the enemy in check, expecting reinforcements, but none were available.[44]

Lomax ordered the artillery to fire into the struggling mass. Although one round landed among the Marylanders, the shelling helped, and they were able to fall back.

"After getting through the wood I turned into a field on the right, and, having rallied a few men, with Captain Welsh, checked the pursuit for a while, and even ran them back a little way, but it was only for a few minutes," Gilmor continued. Another wrote that the color-bearer of the First and Captains Ditty and Rasin were present. "There were two brigades after us, Custer's and [Gen. Thomas] Devin's, and the whole corps was in their rear to support them. We rallied and checked them twice more, and then had to run like mad, every one for himself, to keep from being taken,"[45] Gilmor concluded. He led the remnants over the Opequon. On the far side they dismounted to defend the crossing, and the enemy withdrew.

General Ransom reported Johnson's strength as 1,132 men on August 22. He recommended the consolidation of the two Maryland battalions into a regiment. The recommendation was not acted upon, but the remnants of Maj. Thomas Sturgis Davis's Maryland battalion were assigned to the First as Companies G, H, and I.

When Early moved his force against Sheridan on August 26 the First

43.   Ibid., 241–42
44.   Author's Collection, no ascertainable publication facts
45.   Gilmor 1866, 242–43

skirmished with the enemy near Smithfield, losing two men to capture. Gilmor, commanding about 175 men in the combined First and Second Maryland, reported the capture of more than 50 Federal prisoners. In the days that followed, the Confederate cavalry continued to push the Federals toward the Potomac. Company A's Pvt. Marcellus A. Price was killed in an action near Falling Waters on August 28. Dorsey's Company K had three men wounded and three captured there. The next day, in a skirmish near Duffield's Depot, Cpl. John Powell Cockey of Company E was killed, and Company C lost two men captured. The First continued to face the enemy between Bunker Hill and Winchester for several days more.

On September 2 Gen. John C. Vaughn's Tennessee Brigade was stampeded by overwhelming numbers of Federal cavalry near Bunker Hill. The enemy struck the flank of Johnson's Brigade and drove it back. The fire of the horse artillery batteries stopped any further Union advance.

The next day Lomax moved with three brigades to attack Averell's Federal cavalry near Bunker Hill. Despite his men being armed with single-shot weapons, Captain Rasin led the skirmishers of the Maryland battalions successfully against the seven-shot Spencers of the enemy, and the Confederates drove the Union pickets nearly to Darkesville. Five hundred yards beyond the town Gilmor ran into two regiments of Federal cavalry posted behind rail fences and armed with Spencers. With only forty carbines among them, Gilmor's men could not drive the enemy from its position; the major requested help, and Lomax sent the Eighteenth Virginia Cavalry to his assistance. Lomax placed the Virginians under Gilmor, who led a mounted charge on the Federal cavalrymen and, despite several casualties, drove them from the fence line. In the pursuit the Eighteenth captured more than forty prisoners.

Gilmor found Averell, with about thirty-five hundred men drawn up in line of battle, on a nearby ridgeline. Seeing an enemy regiment moving to flank him, he ordered the Virginians to withdraw. Encouraged by Federal artillery fire, Gilmor fell back until he met Lomax with the Maryland battalions. When Averell's troopers came at the Confederates with a strong skirmish line, Lomax dismounted Gen. William L. Jackson's Brigade to assist the Eighteenth Virginia and Gilmor's Marylanders.

"We had to fight every step of our way back to Bunker Hill," Gilmor recalled, "hard pressed by their heavy line of skirmishers making severe dashes upon our rear." The Confederates had to cross a narrow mill dam, and Gilmor sent the Virginians across while the First Maryland protected their rear. He led a mounted charge to cover the retreat but on returning found the crossing under fire and was forced to retreat across a marsh. Gilmor reported that two of the First were killed there and several wounded. To make matters worse, Lomax, believing that Gilmor had retired by a different route and that the Marylanders were Yankees, had his artillery open fire on them, bringing down men and horses.

After having the Confederate artillery adjust its fire, Gilmor ordered the Second Maryland to charge the Federals coming down the road. When enemy cavalry moved to encircle that small band, Gilmor ordered the First to charge to its relief and began to lead the way. Captain Rasin followed Gilmor but looked back and told him, "Major, there are not a dozen men following us."[46]

While trying to rally the battalion Gilmor was wounded in the shoulder, and Captain Welsh took command. The Marylanders did rally, and both battalions were able to extract themselves from their precarious situation. Lieutenant Blackistone was mortally wounded in the melee; another man was shot and still another captured.

In the battle's aftermath, Gilmor reported that Lomax seconded Ransom's earlier recommendation that the two Maryland battalions under Gilmor's command be consolidated. Generals John C. Breckinridge and Early endorsed the plan and sent it on to the War Department. Some of the officers in the First objected and threatened to resign, and the consolidation was disapproved. Captain Dorsey took command of the First and was promoted to major. Captain Ditty reported on September 6 that Company F was down to twenty-eight men present for duty with only twenty-five horses. The other companies were in similar condition.

Dorsey's Battalion continued on outpost duty, picketing and scouting near Bunker Hill. On September 10 his troopers marched through a hard rain to help drive the Federal cavalry from Darkesville and through Martinsburg. Later in the day the Confederate cavalry fell back to Darkesville. On September 18, during one of the numerous skirmishes with the Federal troopers, Pvt. Clement Glenn of Company C was killed at Bunker Hill.

General Sheridan, who had learned of the dispersed nature of Early's command, attacked him at Winchester on September 19. Johnson's Brigade was picketing along the Opequon that morning, with some of the units scattered around the area in order to graze their horses. Johnson led his nearest regiment to the support of the infantry pickets and drove back a Federal cavalry force attempting to gain the foot soldiers' rear and capture them. Within thirty minutes all of Johnson's units were in line of battle protecting the infantry's

46.   Ibid., 253–54

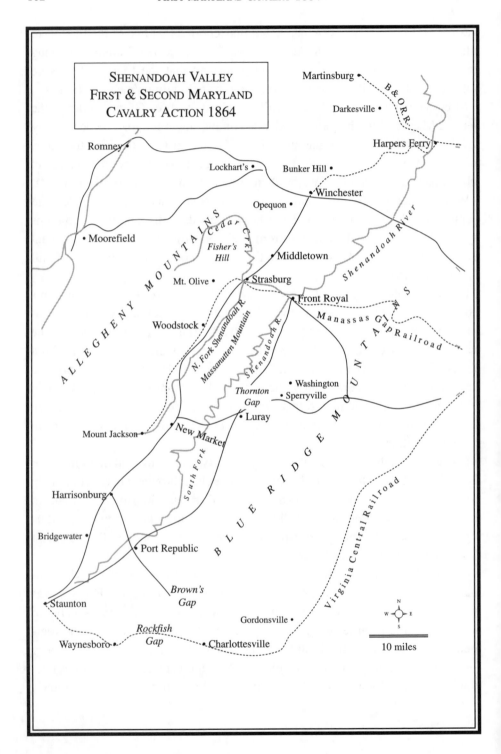

SHENANDOAH VALLEY
FIRST & SECOND MARYLAND
CAVALRY ACTION 1864

withdrawal. With only six hundred to eight hundred men present, Johnson charged the Federal infantry and drove it back as well, enabling the Confederate riflemen to reorganize and establish a strong line. He then took position on the flank of the foot soldiers, dismounted his men, and extended the infantry line. Early's troops held the Federals at bay until flanked by Union cavalry late in the day. Johnson extracted his brigade from the battle line and helped cover the retreat to Strasburg.

The fight was another costly one for the First. Harry W. Dorsey Jr., the assistant surgeon, left to tend to the wounded, was captured. One man in Company A was wounded. In Company B, Pvt. Edward "Ned" Waring was killed and Lt. Mason McKnew and another man were wounded. Sixteen-year-old private Robert E. Brown of Company C was killed. Company E had Lieutenant Roberts wounded and Pvt. Robert A. Browne killed. Pvt. James

Sgt. Nathan C. Hobbs, Co. K, First Virginia Cavalry, and captain, Co. K, First Maryland Cavalry. (Frederick D. Shroyer)

Meagher of Company F was killed. Company G lost one man to capture. In Company K, Pvt. Jarrett Hobbs was killed, and Lt. Nathan C. Hobbs and another man were wounded.

Early led his battered command to Fisher's Hill the next day. The First Maryland followed Johnson over Little North Mountain and up the Cedar Creek Valley to Mount Olive, where the troopers camped for the night. On September 21 Johnson's Brigade, including the First Maryland, was engaged with Sheridan's advance on the Middle road but could only slow their march.

Sheridan attacked Early the next day. While his infantry demonstrated in the direction of the Confederate front, he sent a large cavalry force to gain Early's flank. The Yankee troopers struck a thinly held line of dismounted cavalrymen and routed them. Many were captured before they reached their horses, a half mile distant. The First Maryland helped hold the road so the dismounted men could escape. Major Dorsey led a charge that drove the enemy back temporarily, enabling some captured Confederates to escape and reach their mounts.

During the fight he was shot in the neck and turned the command over to Captain Welsh. Tschiffely wrote that the battalion was "driven back in confusion."[47] In addition to Dorsey the battalion's casualties included Pvts. H. Bond of Company A and Benjamin Evans of Company K killed and three men captured.

Early's disorganized troops fell back to Mount Jackson with the cavalry protecting their rear near Woodstock. Sheridan continued his pursuit, forcing Early to retire all the way to Brown's Gap. Johnson's Brigade fell back along the Back road through Turleytown, then through Mount Solon and Staunton to Waynesboro. During the retreat six of the battalion's men were taken prisoner.

At Waynesboro, the First Maryland was assigned to General Jackson's Brigade, which was ordered east of the Blue Ridge to counter Union threats on Gordonsville and the Virginia Central Railroad. The First Maryland marched through Charlottesville, Gordonsville, Trevilian Station, Louisa Court House, Ashland, and on to their old camp at Hanover Junction. Lt. James D. Watters reported that Company C numbered seventy-two men with seventy horses at the end of the month. Lt. William H. B. Dorsey of Company D had forty-six men present but only thirty horses and four oxen.

The Federal threat having eased, the brigade rode back to the Valley through Rockfish Gap on October 7. Here the Marylanders and Virginians joined in the pursuit of Sheridan's retiring troops, which were burning mills, barns, and crops and capturing or killing livestock—in short, destroying anything that could be of use to the Confederates. Jackson's Brigade reached Bridgewater the next day.

Gilmor, who had recovered from his wound, rode northward with the Confederates and stopped to spend the night with a friend. He wrote:

> I found all the barns, stack-yards, and, in some places, the dwellings burned, and the people destitute of everything. We had to eat cakes of horse-feed chopped, for not a dust of meal or flour was to be had; all the mills were burned. We had not a cow, horse, or hog left, and most of the fencing had been destroyed. It was a sad thing to see the smoking ruins of so many splendid buildings, and to hear the horrible tales of outrages perpetrated. As it grew dark, the whole horizon in the line of Sheridan's retreat was one bright sheet of flame. Was that not enough to make the veriest coward fight to the death?[48]

47.   Stephen R. Brockmiller Collection, Elgar L. Tschiffely Book
48.   Gilmor 1866, 264–65

The next day he reported:

> In every direction were the visible marks of the firey ordeal. . . . The
> wretches engaged in this work did their ruthless errand in the most sav-
> age manner. After extorting from the citizens all their money and valu-
> ables under a promise of sparing their homes, they would hardly allow
> them time to get out before the torch was applied.[49]

Gilmor noted that Federal soldiers caught in the act were immediately put to
death.

Pvts. Churchill Crittenden and John J. Hartigan of Company C were foraging
for their troop in Page County during this period when they were surprised by
the Federals. The *Richmond Daily Examiner* reported that:

> Crittenden fought them to the last, emptying every load out of his pis-
> tol and wounding a Federal lieutenant very severely. The prisoners
> were brought through Luray in charge of a Captain Pendergast.
> Crittenden was slightly wounded before taken. These two men were
> taken out, by order of Colonel [William H.] Powell, and were shot
> dead. The reason assigned for shooting them was that some of their
> men were shot while burning barns. Powell has issued an order declar-
> ing that for every Union soldier shot by bushwhackers he will hang or
> shoot two Confederate soldiers now held by him as prisoners.[50]

"Henceforward . . . Powell's name was familiar and memories of the men of
the 1st Maryland Cavalry, and many were the vows there uttered over the dead
bodies of their comrades to avenge their death—and they were avenged, though
Powell escaped," recalled a member of the battalion.[51]

The Confederate cavalry could do little more than harass Sheridan's overwhelming force as it fell back to Cedar Creek. Early halted at Fisher's Hill, the
only available defensive position. Unable to draw Sheridan into a fight and
unable to supply his troops in this part of the Valley, he decided to mount a surprise attack. On October 19 his troops made a predawn assault on Sheridan's
fortified positions at Cedar Creek and routed the Federal troops. Later in the

49.   Ibid., 265
50.   *Richmond Daily Examiner,* October 20, 1864
51.   Author's Collection, no ascertainable publication facts

day Sheridan rallied his army and in turn drove the Confederates from the field. Captain Rasin was wounded near Middletown during the fighting.

Lomax moved his cavalry, including Jackson's Brigade, to Milford, a strong position in the Page Valley. Federal cavalrymen attacked Lomax there on October 26, but the Confederate troopers repulsed them. The next day Joseph Stonebraker joined Company C. He reported that the First Maryland, which had 650 men present in June 1863, "now . . . did not have over 90 in its ranks, and they were poorly mounted and badly equipped. They were doing picket duty on the south branch of the Shenandoah river, at Burner's Ford, just north of Milford." The youthful Stonebraker spent his first night of Confederate service in the rain, trying to keep the water from coming under his blanket. After midnight he huddled near the campfire to keep warm.

Jackson's Brigade had only 55 officers and 386 men present for duty, with an aggregate present of 528—out of 2,559 on the rolls. Of the absentees, 25 officers and 657 men were reported to be prisoners of war. During this period a number of the dismounted men of the First Maryland joined a large party of Virginians under Maj. Houston Hall of the Sixty-second Virginia Infantry seeking horses in western Virginia. On October 29 they attacked the camp of the Eighth Ohio Cavalry at Beverly but were driven off; this aborted attempt cost the First Maryland two wounded and thirteen captured.

The battalion remained camped at Milford and picketed Burner's Ford until November 10, when Gen. Henry B. Davidson took command of the wounded Jackson's Brigade. On November 11 Davidson led the brigade northward to Middletown, where it camped for the night. The next day the command rode through Front Royal and halted six miles north of the town. The brigade remained in line of battle during the day and in the evening retired below the town without having engaged the enemy. Two of Company C's men had been taken prisoner during the advance.

The Confederates returned to their old camps at Milford. In order to feed themselves and their horses, a third of the First Battalion was detailed to forage for supplies, yet the Marylanders returned with nothing for their efforts. Stonebraker recalled:

> Both men and horses have had little to eat for some days, in fact the horses are in starving condition. A small party from our company stole corn during the night. I am free to confess that I felt like a thief ought to feel when so engaged, but necessity knows no law; the Government can't feed our animals and it is steal or walk. Horses are selling from

five to eight hundred dollars apiece, and only those captured by a soldier can be had at any price. The next morning we went to the river and
did picket duty for two days; it rained and snowed the best part of the
time, with the mud knee deep.

The Federals having advanced against our position, we were hurried
to the front and formed in line of battle, mounted, just in the rear of our
breastworks, while the balance of the brigade were dismounted and
manned the works. The enemy came up, and after exchanging a few
shots with our outposts, fell back, but we remained in position until
long after dark, in case of an emergency.

We went back to camp both cold and hungry. To make matters worse,
neither men or horses got anything to eat, having fasted all day.[52]

On November 23 the brigade marched through Thornton's Gap in the Blue
Ridge to Sperryville. Stonebraker reported:

[W]e found snow two inches deep, the weather bitter cold, the men suffering because of their destitute condition. During the march we passed
many orchards full of frozen apples, which the men devoured raven-
ously, being the only thing they got to eat on the march.[53]

The Marylanders kept some of the frozen fruit to eat the next day.

Davidson led his command on to Little Washington on November 25; the
brigade camped here for several days. The half-starved troopers were finally
issued some flour and cornmeal, from which they made johnnycakes. Rappahannock County was full of corn and forage, but the people were reluctant to
part with it for Confederate money. This forced the Marylanders to forage in the
night. While hunting for apples the troopers discovered that the citizens had
made brandy from them. Stonebraker reported that "many of the men spreed for
a week."[54]

Sheridan, knowing Loudoun County to be a haven for Maj. John S. Mosby's
partisan rangers, now determined to make the area a barren wasteland. On
November 28 he sent Gen. Wesley Merritt's cavalry division on a mission of
destruction.

52.   Stonebraker 1899, 75–76
53.   Ibid., 76
54.   Ibid., 77

Davidson did not learn of the raid until two days later, on the last day of the month. He immediately marched the brigade toward Loudoun County. Lieutenant Ditty, with ten men of the Maryland battalion, acted as advance guard. According to Stonebraker, when Ditty and his squad returned to Davidson they found him drunk. Ditty and his men were ordered forward until they struck the enemy. After many adventures the detail returned to camp at Little Washington on December 3. Merritt had carried out his foray with little resistance from the Confederates.

Stonebraker reported:

> The weather continued very cold, greatly to the discomfort of the men, as they were without shelter of any kind, and being scantily fed, receiving one-half ration of corn meal to each man about every other day. The horses were worse off than the men and I determined not to let my horse starve as long as forage could be had, and from that time until the end of the war I raided hay and fodder stacks whenever the Government failed to furnish feed for my horse.[55]

On December 12 the brigade broke camp and marched to a position south of Sperryville. Without axes, the Marylanders were forced to burn fence rails to keep warm in the bitter cold. "Both men and horses went to sleep on empty stomachs," recalled Stonebraker. The next day the brigade marched through Criglersville and camped near the bridge over the Robinson River. Stonebraker wrote: "The weather was so cold that I dismounted and took hold of my horse's tail and walked the greater portion of the day to keep my feet from freezing." After another day's trek to Madison Court House the brigade returned to the Robinson River. The Marylanders remained in camp for the next several days but were issued only their half-pound ration of cornmeal each day. When the hungry soldiers called upon civilians for additional sustenance, the men turned the hungry soldiers from their doors. But "I can not recall a single instance of ever being turned away from a house empty handed by a woman, rich or poor," recalled Stonebraker.[56]

During this period General Jackson, recovered from his wounds, resumed command of the brigade. Lt. William H. B. Dorsey commanded the Marylanders.

55.   Ibid., 81
56.   Ibid., 82

Maryland Battalion on the Warpath, December 1864, *by Allen C. Redwood. (Stonebraker 1899)*

Sheridan sent his cavalry forces southward on December 19. Custer's Division advanced toward Harrisonburg before crossing the Blue Ridge and moving toward Charlottesville. Gen. Alfred T. A. Torbert led his division toward Gordonsville. When, on December 21, Jackson learned of the Federal advance, he marched his command through a storm of hail and sleet to challenge the enemy. The Confederates met Torbert's advance at the bridge over the Robinson River the next morning, and the fight continued until nine o'clock that night. Jackson's men removed the planking from the bridge and constructed makeshift breastworks for protection. The small brigade delayed the Federal advance, giving Lomax time to bring up McCausland's Brigade and maneuver his mounted force to confront the enemy. The large force of Union cavalry pushed the Confederates back through Madison Court House, but the Federals could make little headway. "The battle was closed by a charge of the First Maryland upon the left flank of the enemy, which flank was most advanced," recalled a member of the battalion. In spite of the fact that some of the horses stumbled into a wide, deep ditch in the darkness, the charge "had the effect to break and scatter [the enemy's] line in confusion, and keep him quiet for the balance of the night."[57]

57.   Author's Collection, no ascertainable publication facts

"We fell back some ten miles and encamped for the night at Jack's Shop," wrote Stonebraker. "The night was intensely cold, and we cleaned the snow from the ground and made a fire out of fence rails which we carried about a half mile. By daylight the next morning we were in the saddle, slowly falling back. We crossed the Rapidan river, burned the bridge, and formed in line of battle at Liberty Mills."[58]

Lomax dismounted most of Jackson's and McCausland's Brigades and had the men build breastworks protecting the bridge site and a nearby ford. This forced Torbert to find crossings above and below the ford, which could only be traversed in single file due to the rain-swollen river. His advance was again delayed until dark, when the Confederates retired toward Gordonsville.

On December 23 Torbert attacked Lomax again, driving the Confederates back to Southwest Mountain, about two miles from Gordonsville. Here Lomax again entrenched his men and fought off the enemy's assault. Torbert attempted to flank the position, but, upon hearing an engineer's whistle on the railroad, he concluded that the Southerners were receiving reinforcements and withdrew. Torbert's five thousand men had been turned back by fewer than fifteen hundred Confederates.

Soon after the battle the Maryland battalion began a two-day march to near Liberty Mills, where they camped. Stonebraker reported that the march was made through rain and mud that was knee-deep to the horses.

> We remained about four weeks, having intolerable weather. It rained and snowed for eight days, and between freezes and thaws our camp was in a wretched state, our little fly tents being our only shelter.
>
> Rations for the men and forage for the horses came at irregular intervals, compelling the men to exercise their wits to supply the deficiency.[59]

The paymaster and quartermaster finally caught up with the battalion at Liberty Mills, and the destitute men received their meager pay and, even more importantly, clothing and shoes. The dismounted men were given thirty-day furloughs to obtain horses, and those whose mounts were in bad condition were also given leave to secure another.

Major Dorsey returned during this period and resumed command of the battalion, which was much reduced in number. The end of the year found

58.   Stonebraker 1899, 84
59.   Ibid., 88

Company A, now under Lt. Otis Johnson, with forty-two men present. Lieutenant Watters had thirty-nine present in Company C, and Captain Rasin could muster only two officers and sixteen men in Company E. The rest of the command was in similar condition.

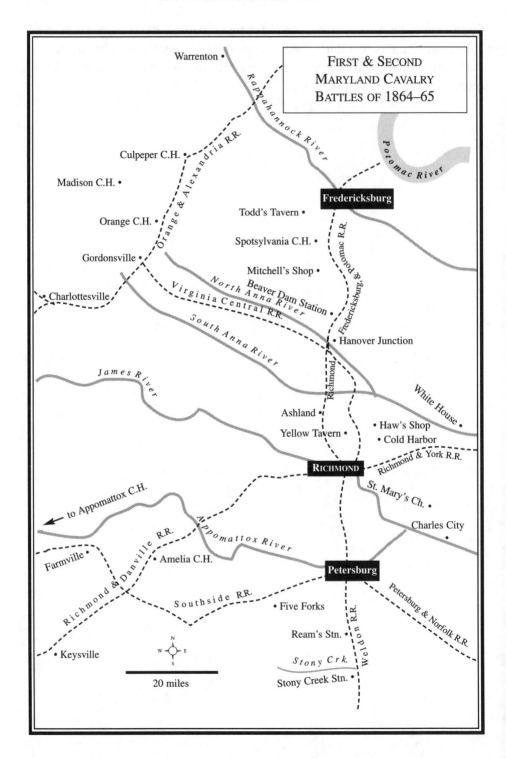

FIRST & SECOND
MARYLAND CAVALRY
BATTLES OF 1864–65

Chapter V

1865

"The fame you have won will be guarded by
Virginia with all the pride she feels in her own true
sons, and the ties that have linked us together
memory will preserve."

Pvt. Elgar Tschiffely penned a dismal entry in his diary to mark the start of 1865. "In camp, nothing to eat, rheumatism, very cold."[1] There was apparently little activity until the fourth week of the new year; Joseph Stonebraker reported that the battalion broke camp on January 26, marched to Orange Springs, some twenty miles east of Gordonsville, and bivouacked. The Marylanders finally went into winter quarters near Ellisville, where the troopers immediately began building log huts to protect themselves from the elements.

On February 6 Stonebraker returned to camp from a tour of duty as a courier. Eight inches of snow covered the ground, but the battalion was snug in cabins replete with fireplaces and chimneys. He noted:

We lived mainly on "black-eyed peas," which were boiled in an iron

1.   Stephen R. Brockmiller Collection, Elgar L. Tschiffely Book

kettle over a slow fire that took from early in the morning until three in the afternoon before they reached the proper consistency. Having but one spoon in the mess, the men sitting around the kettle used small [wood] chips to convey the beans to their mouths by scraping them up the side of the kettle as a miniature elevator. We scoured the country for books and spent most of my time reading.[2]

On February 27 Maj. "Gus" Dorsey received a long-awaited promotion to lieutenant colonel. The battalion was so depleted that no major was elected.

The Marylanders remained in camp until March 1, when Early ordered Dorsey to move the First Maryland to Charlottesville. Early's small command was defeated by Sheridan at Waynesboro on March 2, and he escaped to Charlottesville.

The Marylanders could do little but harass the large Federal cavalry force, which had pursued Early. As Sheridan's men continued to move eastward along the James River, however, Dorsey's men forced the Federals to stay closed up. As a result, the Marylanders cut off and captured Sheridan's scouts, stragglers, and marauding parties, taking prisoners in excess of three times their own numbers. As they pursued Sheridan to White House Landing on the York River, they were engaged at Hanover Court House on March 13 and two days later at Frederick's Hall. The chase cost the battalion at least one man wounded and fifteen taken prisoner.

Dorsey led his worn-out command back to Gordonsville. With the pressure mounting on the Confederate lines that began north of Richmond and stretched south of Petersburg, Robert E. Lee called in as many detached units as possible. Lomax's division of cavalry was ordered from the Valley, and on March 27 Dorsey received orders to join Gen. Fitzhugh Lee's cavalry south of Petersburg.

The Marylanders reached Richmond on April 2 and camped on the edge of the city. Dorsey had fewer than a hundred men with him. When the unit reached Petersburg the next day the men found the Army of Northern Virginia battling for its life. There were no orders from Fitz Lee, who had been last reported at Stony Creek, some twenty miles to the south. That night men and animals enjoyed an excellent meal; supplies had accumulated at Petersburg and were about to be destroyed. Because of the weakness of their horses, the troopers would be unable to carry away extra food or forage. With shot and shell passing overhead, the exhausted Marylanders slept through the din of battle.

2.   Stonebraker 1899, 90

After a few hours of rest Dorsey received orders to act as rear guard for Gen. William Mahone's infantry division, which in turn was the rear guard for Lee's army. While waiting for Mahone's command the Marylanders watched as the ordnance and quartermaster's stores were set on fire. Although Union cannoneers fired at the flames, the rounds did not reach the battalion. The explosion of Confederate ammunition added to the din. A member of the battalion recalled:

The First Maryland was drawn up along the roadside waiting to march, and coaxing their horses to eat as much oats as possible. Near by was a train of cars loaded with ammunition, and word was passed to look out, as it was about to be set on fire. For awhile every man stood to horse, but the explosion not ensuing as soon as

Pvt. Joseph R. Stonebraker, Co. C, First Maryland Cavalry. (Stonebraker 1899)

expected, attention was called off, and the caution forgotten. Bridles were let go, and some of the men walked toward the quartermaster's stores, near the ammunition train, to make further selections. Suddenly a tremendous shock was felt, which threw many to the ground, whilst the horses reared and plunged and broke from their riders, and for a time all was the wildest confusion. When matters had become a little calm, two men belonging to the quartermaster's department were found dead, and twenty horses of the First Maryland had run off at full speed toward Richmond, though fortunately none of the men were hurt beyond a few bruises. The runaway horses must have been terribly frightened, for in their poor condition they ran twenty miles without halting, and only thirteen of the twenty were recovered; and thus the battalion lost the services of seven men, who, being dismounted, had to remain with the wagons. The explosion took place two hundred yards distant, but the force was great enough to knock down those nearest to it, and greatly shock others.

Soon after this occurrence Mahone's Division came up at the quick-step and in fine order and spirits, which cheered the hearts of the little cavalry band beyond expression. Day had dawned before the rear passed, and just at that time, in the very gray light of morning, was seen a brilliant flash, and for a few moments the earth trembled under foot, and a tremendous explosion plainly told that the fortifications at Drury's [Drewry's] Bluff were no more. In ten minutes another flash, shock and explosion ensued, and the Confederate gunboats on the James had shared the fate of the batteries on shore. Other similar explosions followed as smaller magazines were destroyed, filling the atmosphere with sulphurous smoke, while the flames licked the sky from many a conflagration, and it was with sad hearts that the little battalion turned and followed in the footsteps of the infantry. . . . The roads were muddy and wretchedly cut up by the passage of the artillery and heavy wagons, and the army, though in constant motion, made slow progress.[3]

Tschiffely recorded that the march took the Marylanders through Chesterfield Court House and that portions of the battalion were on picket during the night.

"By the next afternoon (Monday, April 3) Amelia Court House was reached, when the enemy made a slight demonstration, but did not seriously attack," wrote a member of the battalion.[4]

The Marylanders spent the night on the banks of the Appomattox River. One man recalled:

Early on the morning of the 4th Colonel Dorsey, ascertaining the whereabouts of General Fitz Lee, joined his division, in pursuance of his original order, and was assigned to [Gen. W. H. F.] Payne's brigade. Before this the small supply of provisions and forage brought from Petersburg had been exhausted, and as none had been issued, men and horses were almost starving.

No rations having been issued, men and horses had been subsisting . . . on a scanty supply of hard corn, which the troops had not even time to parch, and ate raw from the cob as they marched. On one occasion someone of the battalion got hold of a raw ham, and generously divided it as far as it would go. Raw ham, and raw corn from the cob may

3.   Goldsborough 1900, 219–20
4.   Ibid., 220

not be very palatable to one unfasted, but to Colonel Dorsey and his men it seemed a luxury.[5]

On April 5 the Maryland battalion charged some Federal cavalry that had attacked a wagon train near Flat Creek. Wrote Stonebraker:

As we approached they began to retreat, when a running fight commenced. We pursued them for several miles, killed and wounded quite a number and took seventy prisoners. The road was strewn with guns, sabers, and knapsacks, which they threw away in their flight. We encamped for the night at Amelia Springs, being tired and hungry, the rain during the day adding very much to our discomfort.[6]

Another participant reported:

Here a small portion of flour was issued to each man, but which there was no time to cook, and the flour was tied up in bags, handkerchiefs, stockings, or anything else at hand that might serve the purpose; and so it remained for two days before opportunity to cook offered, the battalion being in the meantime constantly engaged.[7]

"Daylight the next morning [April 6] found us in the saddle moving westward," wrote Stonebraker. "Soon report reached us that the enemy was in our front trying to block General Lee's progress by burning bridges, when we pushed forward at a trot and found a body of infantry, supported by cavalry, within a mile of the South Side Railroad near Farmville."[8]

A Marylander recalled:

The brigade, which was now commanded by General Munford, General Payne having been disabled by wounds at Amelia Springs, was at once ordered to attack them, which it did with much gallantry, all being dismounted except the First Maryland, which was sent to the left to cut off the enemy's retreat. The enemy, which proved to be a brigade

5.   Ibid.
6.   Stonebraker 1899, 95-96
7.   Goldsborough 1900, 221
8.   Stonebraker 1899, 96

of infantry and about two hundred cavalry, behaved very gallantly, and at once met General Munford vigorously. His cavalry charged several times, but were repulsed with heavy loss, while their infantry and Munford's dismounted cavalry kept up a heavy fire, both sides suffering severely, without material advantage to either. At length [Gen. James Dearing's] Derings brigade came up and dismounted, and joined Munford, a general charge was made by the dismounted men in front and the First Maryland, mounted, in the rear and right flank of the enemy, which resulted in the defeat and capture of his entire force.[9]

"[I]n less than an hour we bagged the whole outfit, killed and wounded quite a number, capturing 780 prisoners, two stands of colors and a full brass band," boasted Stonebraker.[10]

A cavalryman of the First Maryland wrote:

At last it was impossible for human nature to hold out longer, and . . . it was determined to cook the flour. As soon, therefore, as night came on—which rendered the enemy's fire less accurate, and induced his cavalry to become less aggressive—the brigade, leaving a strong picket force still actively skirmishing, withdrew behind a neighboring hill and prepared to cook. There were no cooking utensils nor any convenience to bake, but soldiers who had gone through a four years' war had many devices at hand to meet exigencies. A detail with canteens was sent to the stream near by for water, and oil cloths were substituted for kneading trays. In this way the flour was hastily moistened into a paste, and as hastily parched in the embers of the very spare fires which proximity to the enemy reduced to the smallest possible dimensions that could be dignified with the name of fire. The skirmishers were then relieved by some who had eaten, to make similar provisions for their wants.

From this time until Lynchburg was reached, on the night of the ninth of April, . . . the First Maryland subsisted on corn and some rations taken from the captured enemy. It was hard to take food from prisoners, perhaps, but necessity knows no law, and between starving men the weakest must yield.[11]

---

9.   Goldsborough 1900, 221

10.   Stonebraker 1899, 96

11.   Goldsborough 1900, 221

"Our division having been ordered to cover the retreat, by 4 A.M. [April 7] we were in the saddle and in line of battle," reported Stonebraker. "At sunrise the enemy pressed steadily forward and we slowly fell back, stubbornly disputing every inch of ground as we moved." Near Farmville the weary troopers crossed a stream and came under enemy artillery fire. Trying to afford his men the protection of some woods, Munford moved his command closer to High Bridge. The Federal gunners found the range and knocked the timber to pieces but caused few casualties. Stonebraker continued:

Slowly we moved through Farmville, turning and showing our teeth when too hard pressed. We forded the Appomattox river, the bridge being in flames, exposed all the while to a galling fire from the enemy's guns. Our battalion was posted at the ford, which we held for hours, while the balance of the division passed on and took a position on our right.[12]

While the Marylanders held the ford, Munford and Rosser attacked a large force of Union cavalry that had crossed the river and drove it back, capturing its commander, Gen. J. Irving Gregg. Munford sent for Colonel Dorsey's command during the fighting. The Marylanders rode toward the sound of battle, but the smoke from six hundred burning wagons and the fierce fighting obscured the road and slowed their progress. Stonebraker noted:

[A]s we neared the point a mighty cheer went up, which told us the enemy had been repulsed.

When we reached the point of attack Gen. Munford took charge of the battalion, the men being formed into a column of fours, were stationed with drawn sabres in a road fringed with stunted pines. The smoke was so dense you could not see over ten yards in your front, and being so close to the enemy, the men were ordered not to speak above a whisper. We remained in this position for more than an hour, expecting the enemy to renew the attack at any moment.

As darkness set in the retreat was resumed and continued nearly the whole night. We passed through Prince Edward County, both men and horses showing signs of utter weariness from lack of rest and food. Some time in the after part of night we tied our horses to some trees and

12.   Stonebraker 1899, 98

laid down, but at daylight we were again in the saddle and on the move.[13]

Stonebraker found some corn during the day, and while the column halted to let some prisoners march by, the young Marylander was busy feeding his horse. He shared an ear with a Federal prisoner who begged for more. Stonebraker reported:

> We moved slowly over roads [on April 8], along which was scattered broken down wagons and ambulances, dead and worn-out mules and horses, and the remains of whole wagon trains that had been fired by our people.
>
> Just before sunset we had a slight brush with the enemy, but they seemed loath to press matters, and we were only too glad to be let alone. Soon we went into camp for the night, among some stunted oaks through which the road ran, and built our fires. I parched some corn and fell asleep while watching the thin, jaded, weary-looking lines of our infantry, as they silently trudged along.
>
> About midnight, being chilled to the marrow by the damp air, we mounted our horses and moved to Appomattox Court House. . . . [S]hortly before daylight on April the 9th, 1865, we formed into line of battle, to the right of the line, near the Village Church. As the sun made its appearance in the east the Federals, who occupied the Lynchburg road directly in our front, commenced to shell our positions.[14]

Having been relieved by infantry, Munford moved his division across the fields to escape the enemy fire. Elements of the division joined in a charge on the Union position and returned with prisoners and two cannons. The troops in the charge saw Federal infantry deployed in their front and the Federal cavalry regrouping.

There was a pause in the action for several hours as the Confederate leaders pondered their next action. The First Virginia Cavalry, on the picket line, was then attacked by the Federal cavalry. The Second Virginia Cavalry made a charge and drove the enemy back. The Union troopers came on again, and this time it was the Marylanders' turn to charge. Chaplain Randolph H. McKim of

13.   Ibid., 99
14.   Ibid., 100

Last Charge of the Maryland Battalion at Appomattox Court House, *by Allen C. Redwood.*
(Stonebraker 1899)

the Second Virginia Cavalry recalled:

> This was done handsomely by the First Maryland Cavalry, under the
> following circumstances: When the enemy, in full charge, was seen
> coming at them, not over a hundred yards distant, Captain W. J. Raisin
> [*sic*], commanding the first squadron and riding with Colonel Dorsey,
> at the head of the regiment, remarked, "Colonel, we must charge them,
> it is our only chance," and the words had not left his lips when Dorsey,
> who had perceived the necessity, gave the command, "Draw sabre!
> Gallop! Charge!"[15]

As the battalion charged down the Lynchburg road in a column of fours
Stonebraker looked back and saw the rest of the division moving up in supporting distance.

From a trot to a run soon brought us within easy range of the enemy,

15.   McKim 1910, 275

the bullets from their Spencers making that peculiar Zip! Zip! so familiar to an old veteran. The next moment down went my file leader
Private Price [Cpl. William C. Price], a member of Co. E, our horses
almost treading on his prostrate form.[16]

Pvt. John F. Hickey of Company B wrote that Price had been shot through the
heart "and his body received 7 or 8 bullets." Stonebraker continued:

Soon the battalion halted, the men began to waver, and some started
back, when Herman Heimiller of our Company shouted, "Come, boys,
rally around the flag."
    The next instant I was by his side, when we, with two others, whose
names I do not remember, overtook John Ridgely, our color-bearer,
who had pushed some distance ahead, stood waving our banner and
calling to the men to follow him.[17]

Pvt. J. R. Gibbons of the First Virginia Cavalry commented: "This regiment
[First Maryland] made no more gallant charge during the war than on this occasion, and seemed to be entirely enveloped by the Yankees."[18]
    When Stonebraker and the others reached Ridgely they were joined by the
color-bearer of the Seventh Virginia Cavalry. The Federals blazed away at the
brave troopers with the two flags from an elevated position to their front and
from their right flank. "The noise from their bullets sounded like a swarm of
bees, interspersed by the dull thud, as they hit the rails of the fence at our side,"
Stonebraker recalled. "The firing suddenly ceased, as an officer rode from their
ranks towards us with a white handkerchief on the point of his sabre."[19]
    Pvt. John M. Heighe of Company A believed the Yankees were surrendering.
"No doubt all of us were looking out for what we could get in the way of booty,
pocket books, etc.—we were a set of disappointed lads."[20]
    The Federal officer brought the news that General Lee had surrendered and
asked why the Confederate cavalry continued to fight. Munford's troopers had
cleared the Lynchburg road that morning but in doing so had become separated

16.   Stonebraker 1899, 101
17.   Ibid.
18.   *Richmond Times-Dispatch*, March 11, 1906
19.   Stonebraker 1899, 102
20.   Howard County Historical Society, Scrapbook of Company A, First Maryland Cavalry

from the rest of Lee's army. "Heimiller burst out crying as we slowly rode back," reported Stonebraker, "passing four men having our unfortunate comrade in a blanket, carrying him to the rear. . . . Many sun-burned faces were wet with tears."[21]

Gibbons later wrote:

> I have read frequently claims as to the last shot by the Army of Northern Virginia, but have always believed that the last shot was fired by a Maryland regiment, for when the regiment started to charge General [Clement A.] Evans['s infantry] had ceased firing, and the flag of truce had passed his line on the way to Fitz Lee.[22]

Pvt. Henry P. "Harry" Hayward, Co. C, First Maryland Cavalry. (Museum of the Confederacy)

Munford conferred with the other cavalry officers and determined not to surrender. Most of the Confederate cavalrymen, including the majority of the Maryland battalion, followed him around the Federal lines and on to Lynchburg.

The Marylanders who surrendered at Appomattox were Color Sgt. John T. Ridgely, Sgt. Hammond C. Dorsey, and Pvts. William M. Edelin, Reuben Riggs, and Dorsey G. Thompson of Company A; Pvts. Howard Bateman, Charles H. Elder Jr., Henry P. "Harry" Hayward, James N. Kinzay, Gustav W. Lüman, Samuel E. McAtee, Wilson C. N. Smith, and William F. Wharton of Company C; 2nd Lt. Samuel G. Bonn and Pvt. Isaac Chapman of Company F; and Lt. Andrew K. Shriver and Pvt. Leonard Giesendoffer of Company G. These officers and men were probably without horses or had been detailed to other duties and were not with the battalion.

"We reached Lynchburg in the early part of the evening," wrote Stonebraker, "where we found great confusion, and the Government warehouses, surrounded by crowds of men, women and children, both white and black, clamoring for

21.   Stonebraker 1899, 102

22.   *Richmond Times-Dispatch,* March 11, 1906

the supplies they contained."[23] Munford quickly restored order and had his famished troopers and their mounts fed from the depots. Dorsey led the Marylanders to the fairgrounds, where they ate their first full meal in a week. At midnight, after a brief rest, they marched across the James River and camped. Stonebraker reported:

> The next morning at daylight we were formed into line when Colonel Dorsey informed us that it had been determined at yesterday's conference to disband the Cavalry for a short time. Acting upon that agreement we were now free to go where we pleased until April the 15th, when he would expect every man to meet him at the Cattle Scales in Augusta County, Va.
>
> We broke ranks when Ridgely stripped our beloved Flag from its staff and put it in his haversack, the men scattering in every direction.[24]

Munford wanted time to find out the status of Gen. Joseph E. Johnston's army in North Carolina. He knew that his men and horses were worn out but that a week's respite could restore them to duty.

On the appointed date the Marylanders reassembled at the cattle scales. Stonebraker described their return.

> [N]early every member of the command was present when Colonel Dorsey formed us in line and said: "General Munford has ordered me to meet him at Salem, Roanoke County, with my Battalion. From there we expect to proceed south and join General Jos. E. Johnston's Army. I want every man to feel that he is at liberty to do as he pleases. Those who are willing to accompany me will ride to the right and form into line."
>
> Ridgely, in the meantime, had fastened our banner to a crude staff, under which every Marylander present rallied, and with Col. Dorsey at the end of the little band we moved forward, passing through Waynesboro, encamping for the night five miles south of the town.[25]

Frank Dorsey recalled:

23.   Stonebraker 1899, 102–3
24.   Ibid., 103
25.   Ibid., 105–6

At sunrise the march was resumed and proceeded southward for three days and a half, passing through Greenville, Midway, Fairfield, Lexington and Springfield, crossing the James River at Buchanan, and reaching Cloverdale about noon April 29, 1865, . . . when the command went into camp. Colonel Dorsey rode to the house to which General Munford was confined with sickness and returned with an address written by General Munford which he had read to the command, and gave them their discharge:

CLOVERDALE, BOTETOURT COUNTY, VIRGINIA, April 28th, 1865, Lieut.-Col. DORSEY, commanding First Maryland Cavalry:

I have just learned from Captain Emack that your gallant band was moving up the Valley in response to my call. I am deeply pained to say that our army cannot be reached, as I have learned that it has capitulated. It is sad, indeed, to think that our country is all shrouded in gloom. But for you and your command there is the consolation of having faithfully done your duty. Three years ago the chivalric Brown joined my old regiment with twenty-three Maryland volunteers, with light hearts and full of fight. I soon learned to admire, respect and love them for all those qualities which endear soldiers to their officers. They recruited rapidly, and as they increased in numbers, so did their reputation and friends increase, and they were soon able to form a command and take a position of their own. Need I say when I see that position so high and almost alone among soldiers, that my heart swells with pride to think that a record so bright and glorious is in some part linked with mine? Would that I could see the mothers and sisters of every member of your battalion, that I might tell them how nobly you have represented your State and maintained our cause. But you will not be forgotten. The fame you have won will be guarded by Virginia with all the pride she feels in her own true sons, and the ties which have linked us together memory will preserve. You who struck the first blow in Baltimore, and the last in Virginia, have done all that could be asked of you; and had the rest of our officers and men adhered to our cause with the same devotion, to-day we would have been free from Yankee thraldom. I have ordered the brigade to return to their homes, and it behooves me now to separate. With my warmest wishes for your welfare, and a hearty God bless you, I bid you farewell.

THOMAS T. MUNFORD, Brigadier-General Commanding Division[26]

26. *Confederate Veteran,* Vol. XXV, 254–55

"The Colonel now took each man by the hand, bidding them an affectionate farewell," wrote Stonebraker.[27]

The Marylanders rode northward, toward home. They scattered across Virginia in order to find food for themselves and their horses and were paroled at various points along the way. Many were not allowed to return home but were ordered north or south of Maryland. Even some who took the oath to the United States were forced from their home state. The valiant cavaliers could not hold public office nor, in some cases, practice their profession. Because of the intense bitterness of their Unionist neighbors, some of those who managed to return to Maryland had to leave the state again to find employment.

27.   Stonebraker 1899, 109

Chapter VI

Epilogue

In the first years following the war the former members of the First Maryland Cavalry, C.S.A., were concerned with rebuilding their lives and fortunes. Many settled in Virginia, the Northern states, and abroad. The younger soldiers returned to school to finish their education. Those who were able to remain in Baltimore found that they were luckier than those outside the city; employment opportunities abounded because so many of the influential people there had sympathized with the South. Those who met opposition or animosity elsewhere in the state because of their Confederate service seemed to migrate to Baltimore. Confederate service didn't disqualify First Marylanders from serving as officers in the Maryland National Guard or on the governor's staff, and many of them did so.

The Confederate Army and Navy Society of the Maryland Line Association drew nearly all the veterans into its ranks; even those who lived in parts of Maryland beyond Baltimore and in other states maintained their membership in this organization. Baltimore also had two Confederate Veterans camps. Other camps were located throughout the state and in Washington, D.C.

Gov. Edwin Warfield, who lost two brothers in the First Maryland Cavalry, hosted the 1899 reunion of Company A at his home, Oakdale, near Baltimore. More than sixty members attended. The highlight of the reunion came at noon, when the men were lined up in two ranks by Gen. Frank A. Bond. M. Warner Hewes of Baltimore, the secretary of the company, called the original roll. In the ranks stood two bank presidents, the general manager of a railroad, and

Point Lookout Prison, Maryland, May 8, 1865. The trooper at far left is Joseph E. Stone; C. E. Enloes is ninth from the left. Fourth from the right stands George E. Cooke. All are in the First Maryland Cavalry. (Confederate Veteran)

Pvt. Carlton B. Kelton, Co. E, Second Maryland Cavalry. (Private Collection)

Pvt. Eli Scott Dance, Co. C, First Maryland Cavalry. (Private Collection)

Reunion of Company A, First Maryland Cavalry, 1899. (Jack Kelbaugh)

several others of prominence.

Company B held a reunion at Upper Marlboro, in Prince George's County, in 1902. The members of the Washington Confederate Veterans Association were invited to attend.

Eight members of the regiment attended the Grand Reunion at Gettysburg in 1913 that brought together veterans of both Union and Confederate forces. The First Marylanders came from New York City; Philadelphia; Seattle, Washington; and Northland, Arizona, as well as from Virginia and Maryland. Adolphus Fearhake met Carlton B. Kelton of the Second Maryland Cavalry, C.S.A., for the first time since Kelton's escape from Point Lookout in 1864. Young Kelton had hidden himself on a coal barge on which one of the hands had smallpox; the Union guards did not inspect it for fear of catching the dreaded disease.

Many of the regiment's less fortunate members spent their remaining days in the Old Soldiers' Home in Pikesville, Maryland. Many of those who died there are buried in Baltimore's Loudon Park Cemetery.

When Eli Scott Dance died in Towson, Maryland, in 1945, he was the last member of the First Maryland Cavalry "to cross over the river and rest in the shade of the trees." He was also the last surviving Confederate veteran in Maryland.

Clockwise from top: Pvt. William T. Pope, Co. A, First Maryland Infantry, and Co. D, First Maryland Cavalry; Sgt. John F. Hayden, Baltimore Light Artillery; Lt. George W. Booth, Co. D, First Maryland Infantry, and adjutant, First Maryland Cavalry; Capt. John W. Torsch, Co. H, Forty-seventh Virginia Infantry, and Co. E, Second Maryland Infantry; unidentified; Pvt. James L. Aubrey, Co. E, Second Maryland Infantry; William H. Fitzgerald, Virginia Infantry and master's mate, Confederate Services Navy; Lt. A. C. Trippe, Co. A, Second Maryland Infantry.
(Booth 1894)

Clockwise from top: Pvt. Mark O. Shriver, Co. K (2nd), First Virginia Cavalry, and Co. K, First Maryland Cavalry; Pvt. August Simon, Co. D, First Maryland Infantry; Capt. George R. Gaither Jr., Co. K, First Virginia Cavalry, and Co. K (2nd), First Maryland Cavalry; Lt. Charles H. Claiborne, Co. G, First South Carolina Infantry; Pvt. Daniel L. Thomas, Co. C, First Maryland Infantry, Co. K (2nd), First Virginia Cavalry, and Mosby's Forty-third Battalion Virginia Cavalry; unidentified; R. James Stinson, Second Maryland Artillery. (Booth 1894)

Davis's Battalion of Maryland Cavalry

Chapter VII

Davis's Battalion of Maryland Cavalry

T he force behind Maryland's organized partisan rangers was Thomas Sturgis Davis. Although a native of Pennsylvania, Davis spent most of his life in Maryland. He was a schoolteacher before becoming a law clerk in Rockdale, Maryland. Davis entered Confederate service in 1861, enlisting in the Quartermaster Corps. On December 12, 1861, he was appointed adjutant of the Seventh Virginia Cavalry. His administrative abilities prompted Gen. Turner Ashby to appoint him captain and assistant adjutant general on his staff. Davis apparently also showed skill in handling troops in battle; he was recommended for promotion to colonel of cavalry on June 6, 1862. Ashby's death on that day, and the fact that Davis was a Marylander with no troops to command, may have stopped his promotion. He resigned his post as assistant adjutant general on September 13, 1862, and, encouraged by the new partisan ranger law that allowed recruitment in Federally occupied areas for the express purpose of operating behind enemy lines, began to raise a company.

By the spring of 1863 Davis's company, with men from Maryland and Virginia, had been formed. His officers were Lts. Thomas B. Gatch, George C. Merrick, and James P. Richey. The lack of muster rolls for the unit or other accounts of its actions severely hampers the recounting of its military record.

Davis led his company on Grumble Jones's raid into western Virginia in April and May 1863. Upon returning to the Shenandoah Valley, the company served on outpost duty near Winchester. When the Confederates advanced into Maryland, Davis's men operated with the First and Second Maryland as the

First Lt. Thomas B. Gatch, Co. A,
Davis's Battalion. (Daniel D. Hartzler)

advance guard for General Ewell's corps. Harry Gilmor, who commanded the Maryland units during the first part of the Gettysburg campaign, wrote that he was

ordered by General Ewell to go forward to Boonsboro, feel my way down to Frederick, and, if possible, destroy the Monocacy Bridge. I marched on to Boonsboro and camped there that evening [June 16], having sent Capt. T. Sturgis Davis, . . . on whose valor and management I placed great reliance, with some ten men, to Frederick on a scout. They went in, captured and paroled many prisoners, and were getting on quite smoothly, when a small force of cavalry dashed in and drove them out, wounding one of them severely, who was left behind in a hospital.[1]

Unfortunately the records do not indicate who the wounded man was or whether he survived.

From Frederick the company continued on to Gettysburg, where Davis and his men continued to serve with the Maryland battalions. Several men were captured on the retreat.

When the Marylanders returned to the Valley, Davis succeeded in raising five more companies from Marylanders who had come out of Maryland with the Confederates and Virginians. The Confederate War Department, which had become disenchanted with partisan ranger organizations in general, allowed the organization of Davis's battalion as cavalry on August 13, 1863. The department originally intended to assign the unit to the First Maryland Cavalry, but it never did so.

Davis was promoted to major the following month. Lieutenant Gatch was elected captain of Davis's old company, which had become Company A.

1.   Gilmor 1866, 92–93

Merrick and Richey rose one grade, and James P. Riley was elected third lieutenant. Company B was commanded by Capt. Charles E. Bishop; Lafayette Bowers, McPherson Kennedy, and John H. K. Uhlhorn were its lieutenants. Company C was led by Capt. John G. Phillips and Lts. Nicholas E. Edmunds and John M. Cooper. Company D elected George M. E. Shearer captain and George T. Snowden and William H. W. Reed lieutenants. Company E's officers were Capt. Wilson C. Nicholas and Lts. Henry Brooke and T. S. Bradshaw. Capt. A. D. Erwin commanded Company F; James A. Davis and Samuel A. Owings served as lieutenants. Irving S. Vallandingham was the battalion's assistant surgeon.

Davis appears to have been an excellent outpost officer. His troopers scouted the Union forces in the Shenandoah Valley during the fall and winter of 1863. Picket duty was hard on men and horses, but Davis seems to have kept them active and alert. In late 1863 Gen. John D. Imboden, commanding the Valley District, reported to Robert E. Lee that "Davis's cavalry company, Maryland Line," with the Forty-first Battalion Virginia Cavalry, part of Gilmor's Second Maryland Cavalry, and two guns of Capt. John H. McClanahan's Virginia battery, engaged the Twenty-first Pennsylvania Cavalry under Col. William H. Boyd at Rude's Hill on November 16. The Confederates were able to stop the advance of the Union column, and Boyd retired toward Charles Town. "Captain [sic] Davis with about 60 men pursued him 2 miles below Woodstock, where he halted to encamp; but Davis, dismounting a part of his men, approached near the camp and fired into it after dark when the retreat was hastily resumed, the enemy shooting a number of his broken down horses to prevent their falling into our hands," Imboden concluded.[2] The winter of 1863–64 was a severe one, yet Davis and his Marylanders continued on this important outpost duty until the spring campaign of 1864.

May 11, 1864, found Davis in command of a Confederate picket line that stretched twelve miles across the Valley, from Fort Mountain in the east to North Mountain in the west on a line between Edinburg and Mount Jackson. Davis's men and eighty-five of Gilmor's Battalion formed the first line of defense against Gen. Franz Sigel's Union column, which was advancing up the Valley from Winchester. On that day Davis reported to John C. Breckinridge, commander of the Confederate forces in the Valley, from Woodstock.

The enemy moved their main camp up to Cedar Creek yesterday evening. No other change. They are so located and the valley so narrow

2.   OR, Series I, Vol. XXIX, Pt. 1, 643-44

that it is impossible to penetrate their lines. They have large patrolling parties constantly in motion between their different posts. . . . [T]he condition of the atmosphere renders observation from the mountains impossible.

Later that day Davis wrote to Breckinridge from Mount Jackson:

The enemy drove in my pickets this morning at 10 o'clock. I had a slight skirmish with them, having 1 man wounded and two captured. They have, as far as came within my observation, 2,000 cavalry and six pieces of artillery. I heard from their rear to-day. They had the day before yesterday ten regiments of infantry. They have now twenty-eight pieces of artillery, all brass but four, and three mountain how-itzers—a very large proportion, but correct. The whole force is 6,000 men. Major Gilmor reports for duty this evening; his battalion was ordered by the Secretary of War to report to me. He says you ordered him to take his battalion and get to the enemy's rear. He has about 40 men for duty. In my own company I have twenty-six. If he takes his own men away I will be left with no men for picket. I am on outpost duty. The impression here is that he is still in arrest under another series of charges.[3]

Davis signed his report "Captain, Commanding Outpost." No orders have been found dismantling the battalion, but it had obviously occurred to Davis by this time that he ought to refer to himself as a captain.

What happened to Davis's Battalion? Captain Bishop's Company B became Company G, First Maryland Cavalry; it was later assigned to Gilmor's Second Maryland, and finally merged with Company E, Captain Nicholas's company, to become Company H, First Maryland Cavalry. Captain Phillips's Company C was assigned as Company G, Forty-first Battalion Virginia Cavalry. Captain Shearer's Company D became Company D of the Second Maryland Cavalry. Captain Erwin's Company F became Company I, First Maryland Cavalry. Still later Nicholas's and Erwin's companies were consolidated into Company G, First Maryland Cavalry. Davis was left with his original unit, Company A.

Pursuant to Breckinridge's orders, Gilmor proceeded to gather his men from picket duty. He heard gunfire and reported: "I heard sharp fire at a short

3.   OR, Series I, Vol. XXXVII, Pt. 1, 728–29

distance, and saw our pickets retreating, but fighting as they fell back." The major mounted his command in a column of fours and started toward the firing. He wrote:

> At this moment Major Davis rushed in, telling me it was useless to fight, as there were fully five hundred, and I should lose every man. I therefore merely charged the advance to give Davis time to form; drove them back on the main body; then wheeled and retreated under a heavy fire from a squadron of carbines, who were in front, with their bridles hooked up to their saddles, and peppering us at every jump.[4]

Gilmor and Davis continued to skirmish with the enemy as they fell back. Near Mount Jackson Gilmor was shot in the shoulder, and Davis again took command of the outposts. Gilmor's wound was not serious, however, and he led his men away on their assigned mission.

On May 12 Imboden reported that the "[e]nemy drove in my pickets on the pike, Middle and Back roads, and have since dashed into Mount Jackson."[5] Davis and his men fell back toward New Market. Imboden reported several men wounded and horses killed in the action, and Lt. James P. Riley was captured during the day.

Davis and his men continued to serve in the Valley. The captain served as chief of scouts for General Imboden, and he and his men were present at the battle of Piedmont on June 5. Lt. John N. Opie reported: "Col. [sic] Davis and I begged, swore at, and threatened them [the retreating Confederates], but so great was their terror that neither prayers, threats, nor even blows availed anything as they fled unglorishly [sic] to seek shelter in the Blue Ridge."[6] Davis and his men engaged the Twenty-first New York Cavalry at Buford's Gap on June 20.

Davis later was promoted to lieutenant colonel and served with Imboden until he was wounded and captured at Winchester on September 19, 1864. He spent the rest of the war a prisoner in Fort Delaware.

During the reorganization of the cavalry following the battles of Winchester and Fisher's Hill, Davis's original company was assigned to the Twenty-third Virginia Cavalry as Company M. Gatch was by then a prisoner of war, and Lieutenant Merrick was promoted captain of the troop.

4.   Gilmor 1866, 148–49
5.   OR, Series I, Vol. XXXVII, Pt. 1, 731
6.   Opie 1899, 222–23

After the war Davis practiced law in Towsonville (now known as Towson), Maryland, and from 1872 to 1876 he served in the Maryland senate. He died in Townsonville in 1883.

Second Maryland Cavalry

Chapter VIII

Second Maryland Cavalry

The history of the Second Maryland Cavalry begins and ends with Harry Gilmor. Gilmor enlisted in Ashby's Virginia Cavalry in 1861 and was soon promoted to sergeant major of the Twelfth Virginia Cavalry. In March 1862 Gilmor was elected captain of the Twelfth's Company F, in which Marylanders predominated. Gilmor gained a reputation as a staunch and sometimes reckless fighter who always led his men from the front, and his boldness and daring in action during Stonewall Jackson's Valley Campaign of 1862 brought him to the attention of the general.

During Robert E. Lee's first invasion of the North, in September 1862, Gilmor visited his family near Baltimore and was captured. Charged with spying, he languished in prison until he was exchanged in February 1863 and went to Richmond. From there he went to visit Jackson near Fredericksburg and was warmly greeted by his old commander. Following a brief leave he rejoined his regiment and was welcomed back enthusiastically. During a visit to Gen. J. E. B. Stuart's headquarters he participated in the battle of Kelly's Ford on March 17, 1863.

He again returned to the Twelfth for a brief period of time, serving with it until receiving a leave of absence to visit Richmond, where he sought authority to raise a battalion of partisan rangers. With Stuart's approval Gilmor was commissioned a major on May 27, 1863, and began organizing the Second Maryland Cavalry.

According to Gilmor, Capt. Nicholas Burke of Baltimore, an elderly Mexican War veteran, raised the first company by June 1, 1863. William W. McKaig Jr. of Cumberland, Maryland, was appointed first lieutenant. He had attended the Virginia Military Institute, served as a drillmaster in Richmond, and been an officer in the First Virginia Infantry and in the Twelfth Virginia Cavalry. Another Baltimorian, John B. Wells, who had seen service in the Thirteenth

Virginia Infantry, was appointed second lieutenant. Gilmor named one of his younger brothers, Meredith, third lieutenant. The company included many men from Richmond and Henrico County, Virginia.

Gilmor's troopers were armed with a mixed bag of weapons based on ordnance requisitions. The company drew 860 rounds for the Colt army revolver; 240 rounds for the Colt navy; 2,000 rounds for the Sharps carbine; 2,000 rounds for the Mississippi rifle (.59-caliber); 5,000 rounds for the Merrill carbine; and 200 rounds for the Burnside carbine, plus enough caps for all the weapons.

The War Department gave Gilmor little time to organize, mount, arm, and equip his new company; he was immediately ordered to join Gen. Albert G. Jenkins, who was then commanding the Valley District. Upon joining Jenkins at Fisher's Hill, Gilmor's new company was thrust into action scouting and picketing the Union forces in and around Winchester.

On June 12 Gilmor and his troopers were driven out of Middletown, south of Winchester, by a mixed force of Federals. In a brief skirmish the Marylanders captured five Union cavalrymen and lost one man wounded and another injured when his horse fell on him. Gilmor sensed from the conduct of the Federal troopers that some of them might be attempting to ambush the Confederates. His company fell back to a position near Middletown; here it was joined by Capt. William I. Rasin and some seventy men of the First Maryland Cavalry, who had heard the firing. Rasin, believing that Gilmor's raised hand was a signal for him to go on rather than stop, charged rashly down the road toward the Federals. The dust, noise, and confusion of the mounted charge carried Rasin and his men past Gilmor, who tried to gain the head of the column before it was ambushed. He arrived too late. The Federal infantry, hidden near the side of the road, fired a volley into the surprised Marylanders, bringing down men and horses. Gilmor tried to get some of the men still mounted to charge the enemy cavalry before the infantry had time to reload, but only two men followed him. One was killed. Gilmor escaped the scattered firing of the Federal infantrymen as some of them charged to the fence along the road and attempted to bayonet the downed Confederates. The Union cavalry pursued for only about a mile, picked up a few more prisoners, and then retired.

The next day Gen. Richard S. Ewell's corps advanced on Winchester. Gilmor's company and the First Maryland Cavalry accompanied the Second Maryland Infantry in the advance. The Marylanders rode through Newtown and Bartonsville to Kernstown without finding the enemy. As the column approached Hollingsworth's Mills, Col. James R. Herbert put the infantry in line of battle and advanced two guns of the Baltimore Light Artillery supported by the cavalry. The Maryland troopers advanced until they spotted a Federal cavalry force advancing rapidly down the turnpike toward them. As the Confederates fell back the Union troopers prepared to charge, forming a column of fours within half a mile of the battery. Gilmor and his troopers unmasked the battery, and its fire broke up the charge and drove the Federal cavalry back toward Winchester. As the Confederates closed in on the town, Gilmor and his men operated with skirmishers from Herbert's battalion.

Early on the morning of June 14 Gilmor led his company to the Millwood road, past the enemy dead at Swartz's Mill, and into the abandoned Federal camps, where the Marylanders looted the abandoned knapsacks and supplies. Gilmor had his men gather about one hundred gum cloths, which he left with a woman in a nearby house for future use.

When Ewell's corps charged into the suburbs of Winchester later that same day, Gilmor and Maj. William W. Goldsborough of the Second Maryland Infantry made a bet as to who would reach the town first. Both men charged ahead of their units amid the shouts and cries of joy of Winchester's women; both later claimed to have won the race. Gilmor met a mounted Federal who fired at him, shooting his horse through the leg. After treating the wound the major reported to General Ewell and was sent on a scout out the Berryville road. On his return he met a soldier he recognized as a Jessie scout, a Union soldier dressed as a Confederate. After gaining the Federal's confidence, Gilmor ran him through with his sword and took his fine gray horse and saddle. As he neared Ewell's headquarters on the Millwood road a chance shot from a Union skirmisher killed the gray horse. Gilmor saved the saddle but had to leave the bridle and halter behind. He exchanged his wounded horse for a mustang that belonged to the son of the owner of Swartz's Mill, and he rejoined Ewell in time to witness the bombardment of the Federal forts and the gallant assault by Gen. Jubal Early's troops.

Just before sunset the Confederates spotted Federal cavalry escorting wagons out the Pughtown road, and Ewell sent Gilmor, with his own men, the First Maryland Cavalry, and Capt. John H. McNeill's partisan rangers, after them. As the commands marched cross-country in the darkness they became scattered by the rough terrain, and Gilmor gave up the chase.

The next morning the Second Maryland Cavalry advanced into Winchester to find that the Federals had abandoned the forts and the town. Gilmor guided the Stonewall Brigade to a place where it could intercept the retreating enemy, and the brigade captured most of the Eighteenth Connecticut Infantry. Gilmor and his men marched the prisoners back to Winchester.

General Ewell next directed Gilmor to pursue Gen. Robert H. Milroy and the Union command. He could gather only about twenty men, and although the exhausted troopers rode through the night to Charles Town and beyond, Milroy and his escort escaped to Harpers Ferry.

After just a few days' rest, Gilmor's company joined Gen. Edward Johnson's command when it crossed the Potomac at Williamsport. When he learned that some of Milroy's headquarter's wagons were on the other side of the mountains, Gilmor got permission from Johnson to go after them. The Marylanders rejoined Johnson at Sharpsburg with eight wagons.

Shortly after this success, Ewell placed Gilmor in command of the First Maryland Cavalry; Maj. Ridgely Brown of the First was still absent because of wounds. Gilmor led his command, which included Capt. Thomas Sturgis Davis's Maryland troop, to Boonsboro. There were about two hundred men in the three Maryland commands. Their mission was to reach Frederick and destroy the vital Monocacy railroad bridge on the Baltimore and Ohio line. Upon reaching Boonsboro Gilmor sent Davis with about ten men into Frederick on a scout. Davis captured the town and a number of prisoners, which he paroled. Later in the day a Federal cavalry force drove the small band of Confederates out of Frederick.

The next day Gilmor led his entire force toward Frederick. As the column neared the town, the Federal cavalrymen opened fire with their carbines. Gilmor dismounted about twenty men armed with long-range weapons and advanced them along both sides of the road as skirmishers. When the advance unit reached the edge of town, the rest of the Marylanders charged down the road. The boldness of Gilmor's attack made the stronger Federal force believe that the Confederates' numbers were larger than theirs, and they retreated toward Harpers Ferry. Only one of the skirmishers was wounded.

Gilmor reported an enthusiastic welcome and warm hospitality from the residents of Frederick, who invited the Southerners into their homes for refreshment. Fearing the men would become scattered, he had the bugle sounded and moved them off toward the Monocacy. The destruction of the bridge proving to be impractical because of stockades, "I gave it up," he noted, "and returned through Frederick to the top of the South Mountain, near Boonsboro. From thence we went to Hagerstown, where I was ordered to join Gen. George H. St[e]uart, of Maryland, who was detached with his brigade to make a detour to the left as far as McConnellsburg, and rejoin the main army at Chambersburg."[1]

1.   Gilmor 1866, 94

The Maryland cavalrymen were fired upon as they descended the mountain into McConnellsburg, yet Gilmor kept on. Despite reports of Federal infantry and cavalry, he closed up his battalion and charged through the darkness into the town. The houses and other buildings were completely dark, and although Gilmor sent detachments down the side streets, he found no enemy soldiers. The bugler sounded assembly. Gilmor lined up his command in the center of town, assigned the necessary picket details to cover all the roads, and sent a courier to General Steuart with the good news. The weary troopers fed their horses with the corn and oats found in and around the town. The next two days were spent gathering horses, cattle, and other supplies from the surrounding area.

On June 28 Gilmor led his men through Roxbury and rejoined Jeb Stuart's cavalry at Shippensburg, Pennsylvania. The next day the general sent him on a scout toward Carlisle. When his command neared the town Gilmor received orders to move down the York road. After passing through Papertown and Petersburg to Cashtown, he received a request for assistance from Col. Thomas H. Carter, commanding Ewell's artillery, who believed he was threatened by an enemy force. Gilmor's troopers trotted forward about two and a half miles only to find that the threat was not serious. They went on to join General Ewell at Gettysburg.

At Gettysburg Gilmor was placed in support of Maj. William T. Poague's and Carter's battalions of artillery, both of which were already engaged with the enemy. The Federal cannon fire forced Gilmor to move some of his men to the rear and others to a nearby ravine. From his position Gilmor watched as Ewell's infantry drove the Federals off the field and into Gettysburg. He left his battalion in charge of Captain Emack of the First Maryland and, with Capt. Warner Welsh and Lt. William H. B. Dorsey of the First, joined the pursuit. Near the town the three officers captured the flag of the 149th New York Infantry from its color guard. A Federal soldier fired at Welsh and Gilmor as they rode into Gettysburg; he just missed hitting Gilmor, who dismounted, picked up a discarded rifle, and fired, killing his assailant.

The next day General Ewell made Gilmor the provost marshal of Gettysburg, charged with rounding up the Federals hiding in the town and gathering all the weapons and ammunition. Gilmor reported that his men stacked up twenty-five hundred arms in the town square, but the weapons were never removed and were later recaptured.

The First's Major Brown arrived on the afternoon of July 2 and resumed command of his battalion, thus relieving Gilmor, who joined Gen. Harry Hays

and his Louisiana brigade and observed their heroic but futile assault on the
entrenched Federals the next day. During the fighting a shell exploded under
Gilmor's horse, wounding it "in twenty places from shoulder to stifle."[2] The
horse recovered from its multiple wounds.

Gilmor had led his small band to Williamsport by July 6. General Lee's entire
wagon train was there, waiting to cross the rain-swollen Potomac. With the
approach of Federal cavalry, Gilmor turned his company over to Major Brown
and, with Gen. John D. Imboden's consent, organized 180 stragglers, teamsters,
and quartermaster personnel into a battalion and led them in an attack on the
Federal position in the nearby buildings of the White Hall estate. An infantry
lieutenant assisted, and the attack was successful. Gilmor explained:

> I could not say that I felt much confidence in the "crowd" I had now
> with me, however, I put them in line, and advanced directly up to the
> large barrack in which most of the Federals were stationed, passing
> through open fields under heavy fire. To my surprise and satisfaction,
> the men behaved handsomely, and, after a desperate conflict at the dif-
> ferent buildings, particularly the barracks, we drove them out, captur-
> ing twenty-eight. I lost thirty-four men; the enemy only five killed, nine
> wounded and the captured.[3]

Gilmor hardly had time to take stock of the situation and remove the prisoners before Federal artillery opened fire on the buildings. He concealed his men
behind a rick of wood between the house and barn, losing a few more wounded in the process. The Union cavalry charged several times but was driven back.
Gilmor sent to Imboden for reinforcements but was forced to fall back when it
became clear none were coming. Just after the retreat the Sixty-second Virginia
Infantry came up, charged, and retook the position, suffering fifty-nine casualties. Gilmor, now with about 120 men, charged the Federal artillery position.
Within a hundred yards of the guns the major lost consciousness, either from
exhaustion or from the shock of a shell exploding. He awoke to find himself a
prisoner of the Fifth U.S. Cavalry and the Federals ready to make an all-out
charge to take the wagon train. More firing broke out; Gen. Fitzhugh Lee had
arrived with his cavalry division. Lee attacked the enemy from the rear and
drove him off. During the night Gilmor's guards fell asleep, and he escaped,

2.   Ibid., 100
3.   Ibid., 101

recrossing the Potomac to rejoin Stuart. During the Gettysburg campaign he had lost one man killed and seven taken prisoner.

Stuart detailed Gilmor and his company for scouting duty between Harpers Ferry and the Opequon Creek. Gilmor made his headquarters at Shepherdstown. At one point during this period Stuart ordered Gilmor on a scout into Maryland to determine the location of the Federal army. Every crossing was heavily guarded, but Gilmor and ten men finally captured the Union pickets at Antietam Ford, below Harpers Ferry, bringing in a lieutenant and fourteen men with their arms. Acting on the information obtained from the prisoners, Stuart ordered Gilmor back to Shepherdstown while he and his command fell back to Berryville.

Upon the Second Maryland's return to camp Gilmor drew 11 Mississippi rifles (.54-caliber); 14 Enfields (.58-caliber); 5 musketoons (.69-caliber); 1,000 shotgun rounds and caps; 500 rounds for the Mississippi rifles; 560 rounds for the Enfields; 200 rounds for the musketoons; 600 rounds each for Colt army and navy revolvers; 22 cartridge boxes and belts; 20 waist belts; 9 cap pouches; 220 haversacks; and 300 canteens with straps. The men who were not issued cartridge boxes and cap pouches were forced to carry the ammunition and caps in their pockets.

Gilmor signed for 17,640 pounds of hay and 270 bushels of wheat on one occasion and 15,000 pounds of hay and 316 bushels of corn on another, which is an indication of the amount of food required by the horses.

The Federals soon advanced along the railroad from Harpers Ferry to Kearneysville, in Gilmor's rear, as he waited for Stuart's orders to fall back. On August 25 a Federal force crossed the Potomac at Burnt Mill, a mile and a half below Shepherdstown, and drove Gilmor and his men out of town. The Marylanders managed to avoid the Union troops along the railroad and reached Winchester safely.

Gilmor established his next camp near Mount Jackson; from here his command scouted to Martinsburg, Charles Town, and around Winchester. By the end of August Company B of the battalion had been formed under Capt. Eugene Digges of Charles County. A graduate of Georgetown University, Digges had served in the First Maryland Infantry and as a topographical engineer until appointed captain of the newly formed company. His first lieutenant was John S. Harrison of Queen Anne's County, and his second lieutenant was George W. Purnell of Worcester County. Purnell had attended both the University of Virginia and Princeton College before enlisting in T. Sturgis Davis's company as a private.

Company C had meanwhile been raised under Capt. Richard T. Gilmor, another of Harry Gilmor's brothers. This younger Gilmor had served in the First Maryland Infantry and joined his brother's company in the Twelfth Virginia Cavalry as second lieutenant. A transfer enabled him to organize Company C. David M. Ross of Kent County, who had also transferred from the Twelfth Virginia Cavalry, was the first lieutenant. George W. Forney was the second lieutenant, but he soon resigned to serve as a private in the Eleventh Virginia Cavalry. Julius C. Holmes of Baltimore, who had served in the Richmond Fayette Artillery and the Confederate States Navy, was the third lieutenant; he rose to second lieutenant upon Forney's resignation. William H. Kemp of Baltimore, who had served in the Twelfth Virginia Cavalry, would later become Company C's third lieutenant.

Lieutenant Ross signed for the following for his company: 90 .54-caliber Mississippi rifles with 2,100 rounds; 100 .58-caliber rounds for Enfields; 60 rounds for the Gallagher carbine; 100 rounds for the Sharps .53-caliber carbine; 600 rounds for the .44-caliber Colt army; and 72 rounds for the .33-caliber Colt navy, plus sufficient caps for all the ammunition.

Capt. George E. Shearer was appointed captain of Company D. He was captured at Winchester on August 8, 1863, and imprisoned in Fort McHenry until he escaped in May 1864; there is no record of his return to the unit. In Shearer's absence the company was temporarily commanded by John Redmond Burke. A native of Maryland, Burke had enlisted initially in the Second Virginia Infantry but soon transferred to the First Virginia Cavalry. Known as the "Potomac Scout" and attached to General Stuart's headquarters, Burke was officially appointed captain of the company in May 1864. From the company's inception, William J. McCarroll served as first lieutenant, and Francis W. "Polk" Burke of Harpers Ferry, who had served in the First Virginia Cavalry, was the second lieutenant. C. A. Rousselot was Company D's third lieutenant.

Capt. John E. Sudler of Kent County, who had transferred from the First Maryland Cavalry, led Company E. Henry W. Brewer of Georgetown, D.C., served as first lieutenant. Trained as a civil engineer, he had served for several years in the U.S. Navy and as an officer in the Seventh Virginia Infantry during 1861–62. He was then appointed to the engineer corps and served in that capacity until appointed to the Second Maryland Cavalry. George E. Ratcliffe of Baltimore, who had served in the Twenty-first Virginia Infantry, was named second lieutenant. Henry Marriott, who had served in the First Maryland Infantry, became Company E's third lieutenant.

Company F was captained by James L. Clark of Baltimore. Clark had attended the University of Virginia and had served with an infantry service and with the Twelfth Virginia Cavalry. William H. Richardson of Henrico County, another veteran of the Twelfth Virginia Cavalry, served as first lieutenant. James P. McAleese, who had transferred from the First Maryland Infantry, was the second lieutenant. William Dorsey of Howard County served as third lieutenant.

With six companies enrolled, Gilmor was able to name his staff. Herman F. Keidel of Baltimore was appointed adjutant; he had served in the Twelfth Virginia Cavalry. Norval W. Owens of Anne Arundel County was appointed quartermaster and was later succeeded by Nicholas W. Owings of Baltimore. Phillip D. Grove was the Second Maryland's original assistant surgeon; after his capture A. M. Woolfolk and Henry W. Turpin, both of Washington, D.C., served in that capacity. Edward "Ned" Williams of Georgetown, D.C., a veteran of the First Maryland Infantry and the Twelfth Virginia Calvary, was named sergeant major. William Allen of Frederick County, Maryland, the quartermaster sergeant, was later replaced by Nathan Gorsuch of Baltimore County. Eugene W. Field served as ordnance sergeant. The Second Maryland's bugler was Ferdinand Kline of New Orleans, Louisiana, and John S. Phipps of Anne Arundel County was the color-bearer.

On October 6 Gilmor, having learned that a herd of government horses and mules were grazing near Hagerstown, marched northward to the Potomac with about fifty men, but the river was too deep to be forded. Upon his return, Gilmor engaged Capt. George D. Summer's company of the Second Maryland Infantry, U.S.A., near Summit Point. Gilmor shot and killed Captain Summers. After a hand-to-hand fight the Confederates returned to camp with twenty-three prisoners and twenty-nine horses. The melee had cost them one killed, one wounded, and one captured.

On October 14 Gilmor led forty of his men northward toward Paw Paw Tunnel on the Baltimore and Ohio Railroad with the aim of destroying the railroad bridge near that point. The major stopped en route to visit some ladies at Carter Hall, near North Mountain; he stayed too long and could not catch up with his command, which had gone on. Capt. John C. Blackford, who had been left in charge, had meanwhile incautiously let his men straggle to some houses in the Back Creek Valley. An inhabitant reported the presence of the Confederates to the Federals, and they also were spotted by a Union lookout posted on a nearby mountaintop. Blackford, who had further failed to put out scouts or pickets, was unaware of these breaches. The men, feeling secure, went to sleep by their fires in a deep ravine in the mountains. While Company E of the 116th Ohio Infantry and Captain Moffett's company of the Twelfth West

Virginia Infantry blocked the mouth of the ravine, a company of Federal cavalry from the Twelfth Pennsylvania and another from the First New York surrounded the Confederate position. At dawn the infantry advanced and opened fire on the startled Marylanders, who fled for their lives. Captain Blackford and a few others were able to mount but were captured by the Union troopers as they tried to escape. Captain Digges and Adjutant Keidel were taken prisoner along with some twenty-five men and thirty horses; pistols, sabers, and other weapons were also lost. The Second Maryland's muster rolls show one man wounded and captured and eighteen others captured. Only five or six men escaped. One Federal report asserts thirty-seven prisoners, but some of the captured men may not have been from Gilmor's Battalion. Gilmor lamented that those lost "were the best men and horses in the command, and were selected for the occasion."[4]

The good news was that Captain Ross had meanwhile returned from a successful scout near Martinsburg. General Imboden, in command of the Valley District, had moved his brigade to White Post. Gilmor was now under his command.

On October 16 Gilmor led a scouting party of sixty men to Charles Town to determine the feasibility of capturing the Federal garrison there. He reported to Imboden, now at Berryville, that the garrison consisted of the Ninth Maryland Infantry and a battalion of cavalry and that it would require the general's whole force to capture it. Imboden held a council of war with the officers of his brigade and determined to make the attempt.

Gilmor led his unit around Charles Town, a distance of twelve miles, to a blocking position on the Harpers Ferry road. He had only sixty-five mounted men present, but thirty dismounted men kept up with the battalion, hoping to capture horses in the fight. The Eighteenth Virginia Cavalry accompanied them to block the Federal's logical retreat route.

Just after daylight on October 18 Imboden had the town surrounded. Gilmor sent his brother Richard with six men to capture the Union picket post on the turnpike on the outskirts of town. Harry Gilmor later wrote:

> In five minutes I heard them popping away at the pickets, and moved up close to support him, at the same time sending a courier to hurry up Colonel [George W.] Imboden [Eighteenth Virginia Cavalry] with his regiment. . . . Just as I got within sight of the turnpike, I saw about fifty cavalry coming out of town in column of fours. We drew sabres and

4.   Ibid., 113

charged them obliquely in flank, broke them without difficulty, and drove them across the fields. . . . We captured about twenty prisoners. We ran them farther than I intended, for I found it difficult to call in the men and reform them in time to meet a larger party that I felt sure would soon be upon us.

By the time I had accomplished this, the 18th, in line, were in the woods; my dismounted men, under Captain [Nicholas] Burke, were also there at a point near the turnpike. I was returning with my prisoners, and was within a quarter mile of the turnpike, when the remainder of the enemy's cavalry came out, charging in column with drawn sabres, seemingly determined to cut their way out through.

First, Burke opened on them with his Mississippi rifles, and, though several saddles were emptied, they kept on until they came opposite the 18th, when Captain Frank Imboden charged them with his squadron, while I struck them on the left flank at the head of their column. Only seven got by, and even these were captured farther down the road by our pickets. We captured thirty or forty more of them, and drove the rest back into town and across the country. I followed them for some distance, and then returned to wait for the infantry that I knew would next be coming forth.[5]

As this was going on, Gen. John Imboden charged into town and found the Ninth Maryland Infantry fortified in the courthouse. The Unionist Marylanders refused to surrender, and Imboden had McClanahan's Battery fire six shots into the building at a range of two hundred yards. Imboden reported that the "shells drove out the enemy into the streets, when he formed and fled towards Harper's Ferry."[6] Gilmor's account continues:

I recrossed the turnpike just as the enemy came out of town, and, having turned my prisoners over to the provost guard, I formed on the right of the 18th, about one hundred and fifty yards from the road, and waited impatiently for them to approach. As the column of infantry passed by Captain Burke gave them a volley, which threw the teams into some confusion; but, the regiment came on, and was passing our front, when

5.   Ibid., 114

6.   OR, Series I, Vol. XXIX, Pt. 1, 491

I rode up to our commanding officer and asked him if he was not going to charge, reminding him that General Imboden had ordered us to make a stubborn resistance. "Well," said the colonel, "my men have never charged infantry, and I do not know what to do." "Dismount, and charge them on foot," said I. Without giving any positive order, he turned round and said, "Men, I think you had better dismount, and make an attack on foot!" Some dismounted, but kept close to their horses' heads, popping away without taking aim, for not a man fell.

The enemy were by this time abreast of us, and we were in no little danger from our own shells. One of them cut a large limb from a tree, which fell on Dick Gilmor and Captain Ross, hurting them very much.

I ordered my men to draw pistols and prepare to charge. As we started out at a trot, we received a wild volley without much damage, though it was of buckshot and ball. Only myself and another were struck; and not till after the battle did I discover that I had buckshot in my leg.

In an instant we were among them; they broke, and made for a deep cut in the railroad. Had they been allowed to reach that we should have had some trouble in getting them out; but all surrendered except a part of the color company, and they made but a feeble stand. One of my lieutenants charged these with a few men, killing the color bearer with his own hand while he was in the act of tearing up his flag.[7]

One of the Federals waited to fire until Gilmor was near, but he missed. The man's thick felt hat saved him from the heavy saber blow that Gilmor gave him in return. Many of the Marylanders renewed old friendships among the prisoners. Gilmor wrote:

My command captured all the wagons and three flags—Dick Gilmor, Ned Williams and [Thomas E.] Dobbs each one. We also got all the swords, sashes, and side-arms of the officers. The prisoners, wagons, and ambulances were immediately started toward Berryville. Imboden brought off 434 prisoners.[8]

The Federal reaction was swift. A large force came out from Harpers Ferry and drove the Confederates from Charles Town. Gilmor's Marylanders and

7.   Gilmor 1866, 115–16
8.   Ibid., 116

Capt. John H. McNeill's Virginians, supported by several guns from Mc-Clanahan's battery, served as Imboden's rear guard during the retreat. The Union "cavalry fought hard to recover the prisoners,"[9] Gilmor noted. Gilmor had three horses wounded under him as the Confederates fell back to Berry-ville. He reported shooting and killing one Federal trooper while rescuing Pvt. Joseph W. Stansbury from capture. Company D lost five men taken prisoner during the day.

Imboden gave the Second Marylanders a break from the action. Because for-age was scarce in the Valley, Gilmor marched his battalion across Massanutten Mountain into the Page Valley and camped at Hawksbill, two miles north of Luray. He later moved his camp to Burner's Springs, a resort in Fort Valley, where there were cabins for his men and large barns for the horses.

A portion of Gilmor's Battalion aided in the repulse of a Federal cavalry expedition to Rude's Hill on November 16. Col. William H. Boyd of the Twenty-first Pennsylvania Cavalry reported the capture of at least four of the Second Maryland's horsemen.

On November 19 Ordnance Sergeant Field drew six hundred rounds each for the Colt army and navy revolvers; one thousand waterproof pistol caps; five hundred rounds each for the Gallagher and Smith carbines; and two hundred rounds for the Burnside carbines.

During December Gilmor led a night attack on a company of the First New York Cavalry camped at a bridge near Rude's Hill. Lieutenant Kemp com-manded on the left, Captain Burke on the right, and Gilmor in the center as the Marylanders approached the sleeping New Yorkers. When a Federal sergeant on duty discovered the Confederates, Gilmor fired a shot at him and ordered his men to charge the camp. The major later described the scene.

> The cry was "Surrender or be killed!" and the yelling and firing was quite lively. I must do them justice to say they fought desperately, fir-ing from their blankets as they lay behind their shelters, and it was with difficulty that any could be secured. We set fire to their shelters, but they fought their way into the log house, and opened fire upon us from the doors and windows. Up to this time we had taken about fifteen pris-oners, and several were killed and wounded. The fires around the house burned brightly and the soldiers within could see every one of us dis-tinctly. Three of our men were shot. To finish the business, we charged

9.   Ibid., 117

the house, hoping to take all prisoners, but the door was barricaded and could not be forced. My cousin Willie [Gilmor] was by my side nearly all the time. A bullet struck his right arm, and knocked the pistol from his hand. He cried out, "Major, I'm shot!" I asked him if he was much hurt. He replied, "No; but I'm bleeding." I told him to mount his horse, cross over to Doctor [A. Russell] Meem, and get the ladies to dress the wound. The brave boy looked up as if puzzled to know whether I was in earnest, and said, "But, major, I've got two loads left!" I told him to "blaze away," and I thought that his first shot took effect.[10]

Gilmor decided to burn the New Yorkers out and was wounded by a splinter in the nose when he attempted to throw fodder through a window. The Federal captain and one of his men escaped out the back door, and Gilmor tried to stop them. In the melee he grabbed the officer's revolver and diverted one shot, falling on some ice in doing so. The captain fired again, this time at Gilmor's head; he missed and fled into the night. Gilmor's face received a good splashing of mud and ice, yet he was none the worse for his close call. He attacked the house once more before calling off his men and leaving, taking the Federal captain's horse and twenty-five others.

Gilmor took one of his wounded men, Debril, to Dr. Meem while Captain Burke led the command toward its old camp. The Marylanders were able to cross the Shenandoah River at Bixler's Ferry on a flat boat, five men and five horses at a time. The next day they reached Luray, where Gilmor met Gen. Thomas L. Rosser of Stuart's cavalry and turned over the prisoners to Rosser's provost marshal.

Rosser ordered Gilmor back toward New Market to ascertain the position of Colonel Boyd, commanding the Federal cavalry expedition. Fifty men with horses were able to make the return to the Valley. They located the rear guard of Boyd's column camped at a bridge near Rude's Hill. In the dark, Gilmor advanced his skirmishers at a trot along the turnpike under the fire of the Federals at the bridge. Once the major was satisfied that there was no Union cavalry on his flanks, he and Lieutenant Kemp led the charge, with Dick Gilmor and the column right behind. The Union troops fired from the bluff on the other side of the stream. As Gilmor and several men approached the bridge they realized that the planks had been removed, so Kemp and Dick Gilmor led the men through the water and took off after the retreating Federals. The Confederates

10. Ibid., 126–27

kept up the chase until they were near Mount Jackson, but they had only two prisoners to show for their efforts.

The next morning Gilmor continued the pursuit through Edinburg and Woodstock and skirmished with Boyd's rear guard north of the latter town. The Confederates later engaged in a hand-to-hand fight with Maj. Henry Cole's Maryland Cavalry, U.S.A. Gilmor had seven men wounded. He reported that his men killed two, wounded nine, and captured thirteen of the enemy.

The Second Maryland continued to scout in the Valley until Boyd fell back to Winchester. Upon returning to their camp in the Page Valley, the Marylanders found that Federal cavalry had destroyed the camp and captured everything except two wagon loads, which the quartermaster had taken with him as he escaped into the mountains. The hard service in the Valley had reduced the battalion to seventy-five effective men. A number of Union prisoners of war had been allowed to enlist in the battalion, but most deserted at the first chance.

General Early, now commanding in the Valley, determined to make a cavalry raid into Hardy and Hampshire counties after badly needed supplies. Fitzhugh Lee was placed in command of the expedition, and Gilmor's small band was ordered to participate. Captain Ross led the battalion across the snow-covered mountains, while Gilmor traveled with Lee's and Rosser's staffs. When the officers tried to cross the mountains on January 1 they found the roads coated with sheets of ice and the ordnance wagons and artillery stalled on the mountainsides. Despite the intense cold, they made their way through the snow drifts to the Valley below. When Gilmor rejoined the battalion Rosser chastened him for not having been with his unit, which the general had relied upon to guide his brigade.

Gilmor's men and McNeill's rangers were detached to hold the gap on the Moorefield and Petersburg road until a Federal wagon train was captured. Once this was accomplished the rangers moved toward New Creek. The Federal garrison at Springfield fled when Gilmor made a feint toward its rear, leaving behind large stores of supplies. The battalion brought off twenty wagons loaded with three thousand pounds of bacon, crackers, sugar, salt, bread, horseshoes, nails, and leather. The remaining supplies were given to the civilians and the camp burned. Lee ordered Gilmor and McNeill on to Romney, but the intense cold and icy conditions forced the general to order the entire raiding party to return to the Valley. "Never have I witnessed so much suffering among troops as on that trip, and glad was I to camp again on Lost River, returning to the Valley," wrote Gilmor. "We returned to Mount Jackson on the 12th."[11]

Soon General Early ordered another attempt at gathering supplies on the other side of the mountains; this time the men would also try to break up the Baltimore and Ohio Railroad. Gilmor took one hundred men on this raid. The Marylanders were again assigned to Rosser, who marched across the mountains to Moorefield, arriving on January 29, and then moved the command to Petersburg, near the site where a large wagon train had recently been captured. Gilmor's men and McNeill's company were assigned the mission of gathering cattle along the eastern ridge of the Alleghenies; they brought off three hundred head. McNeill was then placed in charge of the Marylanders while Gilmor remained with Rosser. During an ensuing attack on the Federal position at New Creek, Gilmor was shot in the breast. The ball penetrated the two coats he wore and was stopped by a deck of playing cards in his breast pocket, at the ace of spades. From then on, Rosser frequently asked Gilmor if "spades were trumps."[12]

After the successes at Petersburg and New Creek, General Stuart directed Gilmor to cut the Baltimore and Ohio Railroad to prevent reinforcements from reaching the Army of the Potomac. He set out on a bitterly cold night with twenty-eight men. The first night's march brought them to the banks of the Opequon, where they camped among the pines during the day. On February 11 they approached the railroad near Duffield's Depot and found it heavily guarded. They chose an unguarded spot near Brown's Shop as the place to derail the next train and did not have long to wait. The engineer on the train, which was coming from Harpers Ferry, saw the logs on the track and was able to slow down the engine so that it barely left the tracks.

Lt. Henry W. Kearney of Company B led the boarding party. While looking for the mail car Gilmor mistakenly entered the smoking car, which was filled with Union soldiers, and he scuffled with a few of them. The safe eventually was found in the mail car, but the expressman had escaped, and the Confederates were unable to open it. Gilmor directed his men to knock down all of the stoves save one for the ladies and then burn the cars, but they were too busy robbing the passengers to carry out the order.

When a scout reported the approach of a train from the west, the major ordered his men to mount up. They took with them two captured officers but left behind some ninety others. The Marylanders rode beyond Winchester, and Gilmor concealed them in the pines while the Federals searched in vain. The

11.   Ibid., 126
12.   Ibid., 127

next day they returned safely to camp.

The Northern papers reported the robberies, and Robert E. Lee directed that Gilmor be tried by court-martial in Staunton. Col. Richard H. Dulany of the Seventh Virginia Cavalry presided over the deliberations. Gilmor was found not guilty; the court noted that the men had disobeyed his positive orders against looting and that the robberies had taken place without his knowledge. The results of the trial were sent to General Lee for his approval, but Lee was by then engaged with General Grant's army in the Wilderness, and it is not likely that he would have had time to review the record.

General Breckinridge, who had arrived in Staunton to take command in the Valley, did review the record of the trial, and he restored Gilmor to duty. By this time Gen. Arnold Elzey had arrived in Staunton to organize all of the Marylanders in the Confederate army into the Maryland Line.

Special Order No. 105. ADJUTANT AND INSPECTOR-GENERAL'S OFFICE, RICHMOND, VIRGINIA, 5 May 1864.

Major H. W. Gilmor's Battalion Partisan Rangers will be immediately mustered into the service of the Confederate States cavalry. Major Gilmor will then proceed by highway with his battalion of cavalry to Camp Maryland, Staunton, Virginia, and report to Major-General A. Elzey, commanding Maryland Line, for assignment. Citizens of other States who are enlisted in any company of this battalion may, if they desire it, be transferred to companies from their own State.

BY COMMAND OF SECRETARY OF WAR. John Withers, Acting Adjutant General[13]

Gilmor was not able to carry out this order; General Breckinridge directed him to rejoin his battalion and harass the rear of Gen. Franz Sigel's Union army, which was advancing up the Valley from Winchester. Gilmor found Imboden camped at Rude's Hill and learned that eighty-five of the Second Maryland's best-mounted men were on picket between Mount Jackson and Edinburg under the command of T. Sturgis Davis, in a picket line that ran from Fort Mountain in the east to North Mountain in the west, and about half of the battalion was at Staunton. Gilmor sent orders to his men directing them to meet him as soon as they were relieved.

About sixty Marylanders had arrived at the rendezvous by the time Davis

13. Goldsborough 1900, 244

rode up and reported that the pickets were being overrun by a column of Federal cavalry. Gilmor mounted his command and charged the advance guard of the Twenty-first New York Cavalry, driving it back to the main body and giving Davis time to form his company. The Union troopers came on in heavy force, firing their carbines at the now fleeing Marylanders. Gilmor retreated several miles to Hawkinstown, losing three men wounded.

Gilmor reported giving the order

> "By fours, right about wheel, march—charge," and we went at them with a yell. They were well mounted, well handled, and had evidently been selected for the occasion. When we wheeled their advance wheeled too, and retreated half a mile to a bridge, where the commanding officer, Major Charles Otis, of the 21st New York Cavalry, had formed his scattered column in a narrow way, no doubt expecting something of the kind. As we approached he gave us a volley from his carbines; and there being no room for sabres there, I had to beat a retreat, but in good order. Otis pushed forward in gallant style, at a gallop, but could not get near enough to do us in damage.[14]

About a mile past Hawkinstown Gilmor let his column pass and concealed himself behind a house. Three men stayed with him. When the Union advance guard approached he sprang out into the road and shot the lead man; his second shot brought down a horse. Gilmor retreated, firing as he went, rode about sixty yards, and turned to fire again. At this point he saw an officer dismount, grab a carbine, rest it on a post, and take deliberate aim at him. Gilmor wheeled and spurred his horse to full speed. He heard the carbine crack, and the bullet slammed into his back, two inches from the spine on the upper part of the right hip bone. The impact nearly knocked him out of the saddle. He became "deathly sick" and felt a paralysis of his spine, right hip, and leg. He managed to remain in the saddle, however, and when he regained his column he felt better and said nothing of his wound. Two of the men who had been with him were also wounded, and the third had fallen behind.

Near Mount Jackson Gilmor halted his men and determined to do battle. Major Otis and the New Yorkers rode near and then fell back, giving Gilmor time to examine his wound. The bullet had glanced upward and laid open the flesh. He remained in the saddle until reaching Dr. Meem.

14.   Gilmor 1866, 149

After his wound was dressed, Gilmor sent a telegram to Breckinridge revealing the location of Sigel's forces. He then attempted to carry out his mission of harassing Sigel's rear, but unfortunately his men came across a still and got drunk. Nevertheless, with Lieutenant Kemp and four others, Gilmor attacked a Federal cavalry detachment. He reported that two of the enemy were killed, nine drowned trying to escape, and eleven were captured; thirteen horses were captured and seven were killed. Three of his own men and four horses were wounded. Willie Gilmor, whose horse was wounded in the fight, was given one of the captured mounts. Gilmor continued to track Colonel Boyd's column of Union cavalry, which was leading Sigel's command.

Boyd and his men ran into Imboden's Brigade near New Market and were captured or scattered in the mountains trying to escape. On May 14 Gilmor crossed the mountain to Caroline Furnace. Breckinridge had sent word that he would fight Sigel at New Market and directed Gilmor to destroy the bridges over the North Fork of the Shenandoah River. The major received the message too late to act on it; Sigel, beaten by Breckinridge, was retreating down the Valley and burning the bridges himself.

On May 16 Breckinridge directed Gilmor to cross the Shenandoah River, which was running at the top of its banks, and press on after Sigel as a train of ambulances and wagons had been spotted. A squadron of Imboden's cavalry was assigned to aid him in this mission. After instructing the men to hold their arms and ammunition above their heads, Gilmor led them across the rain-swollen stream. He made it, but he emerged a hundred yards downstream from his starting point. All of the Marylanders made the crossing but three who were washed down to the burned bridge. Of Imboden's detachment, only one of the captains, some of the officers, and a few of the men could be persuaded to make the attempt. About sixty men rode on with Gilmor to Mount Jackson, where they were met with a flag of truce from General Sigel carried by Major Otis. Otis divulged that he was the one who had shot Gilmor, who now refused the flag of truce and continued down the Valley. The bridge at Edinburg had been destroyed, and the Confederates were forced to swim Stony Creek. They pushed on to Woodstock, picking up a few stragglers en route.

The next morning they advanced to Strasburg, where they ran into Sigel's outposts. Scouts reported that Sigel's whole command was just beyond Hupp's Hill. Gilmor fell back via Fisher's Hill to a safe place in a pine thicket near the Valley Turnpike. He sent a report of his actions to Breckinridge by courier; Imboden responded with the news that Breckinridge and all of the infantry had been ordered to Lee's army. Imboden was now in command in the Valley.

Gilmor remained near Strasburg for several days, scouting and skirmishing with the enemy. He learned that Gen. David Hunter, who had relieved Sigel, had received reinforcements. Imboden directed Gilmor to demonstrate in Hunter's rear so as to delay his movements southward as much as possible. Hunter picketed the Valley so thoroughly that the Marylanders were forced to detour east of the Blue Ridge below Front Royal and swim the Shenandoah River into Clarke County to gain his rear. Gilmor recalled:

> I operated between Middletown and Martinsburg, catching a good many couriers and parties of cavalry, causing him to guard his supply trains heavily.
>
> [Col. John S.] Mosby came over several times and attacked the trains, but found them too well guarded to do much damage.[15]

On May 29 Gilmor's scouts reported the approach of sixteen wagons escorted by eighty-three cavalrymen under Lt. Col. Augustus I. Root of the Fifteenth New York Cavalry. Gilmor waited until the wagon train was in Newtown and then attacked from the rear. He reported,

> As soon as the last of the rear guard had entered, I broke cover at a gallop, in column of fours, with my fifty-three men well closed up, but divided into two squads. I led the foremost, and Captain Burke the other, with orders to follow me steadily when I charged, and to act as a reserve in case I should be at first repulsed.
>
> I had my "best bower" Kemp with me. For a while they did not see us; not a word was spoken until they discovered us coming down at a charge. Then every man of us yelled as loud as possible, and kept on yelling, for it was the way to stampede the train, which by this time had got to the lower end of town.
>
> The officer in charge of their rear guard behaved coolly, but with no judgment, for he wheeled about, faced us, and formed in sections of eights, and, what is fatal to any body of cavalry, received us at a halt. They were all carbineers, and stood their ground manfully; but, though our numbers were smaller, in the street our front was as wide as theirs, and when we did get among them with our sabres, they gave way on every side, retreating across a deep muddy branch, and going to the rear

15.   Ibid., 162

of a large house of Dr. McLeod, at the extreme end of town. Two wagons had upset across the bridge, and the rest of them were going full speed toward Middletown.[16]

After many adventures, according to Gilmor, the wagon train was captured and burned. He reported the capture of forty prisoners, including six officers, and seventy horses. Root reported the loss of the train, one officer killed, nine men wounded, and Asst. Surgeon James C. Wall and nine men missing. He also stated that Gilmor had one hundred fifty men.

Hunter meanwhile had issued a circular to the citizens of the region stating that if any more wagon trains were attacked or pickets captured he would burn every house in the area. In the wake of Gilmor's attack, the townspeople believed they would be homeless by nightfall. Gilmor sent a letter to General Hunter telling him that he held thirty-five of his men prisoner in a secure place in the Blue Ridge and that if Hunter burned Newtown he would hang them all.

Three hundred Federal cavalry arrived the next day, read Gilmor's letter, and did not burn the town. When he was sure his message had had the desired effect, Gilmor sent Lieutenant Kemp to Staunton with the prisoners and horses. A number of Marylanders who had been serving in South Carolina units around Charleston, South Carolina, had been recently transferred to the Second Maryland and were awaiting mounts there.

Gilmor, left with only thirty mounted men, continued to harass Hunter's rear. He attempted to capture a small Federal cavalry camp near Duffield's Depot, but by the time he arrived, the enemy had changed camps.

At this point a dispatch was received from General Breckinridge. Gilmor summarized its contents: "Hunter had defeated [Gen. William E.] Jones and Imboden, killing the former, at New Hope [Piedmont]; . . . he had pushed on to Lexington, had no one to furnish him reliable information and wanted me to come immediately and operate on Hunter's flanks."[17]

Unbeknownst to Gilmor, part of his battalion had fought in the battle. The number killed and wounded was not reported, but Lts. Purnell and Harrison and twenty-nine men are known to have been captured. The Marylanders' participation had been brought about by the following order, issued by General Imboden on the eve of the battle.

16. Ibid., 163–64
17. Ibid., 165

Hd Qrs Valley Dist. June 2nd 64
  Sp Orders No. 1118
  I. With the view to the immediate organization of the various detachments of troops called to the field for the present emergency, Colonel Kenton Harper is charged with the formation of a Regiment to be composed of all unorganized companies and detachments in the vicinity of Mt. Crawford, or which may here after arrive till further orders, except the detachment from the Md. Line, and the detachment of the convalescents from Staunton. . . .
  II. The detachment from the Md. Line and the convalescent soldiers sent down from Staunton and dismounted men of Gilmor's Battalion will be immediately organized as a Battalion of four companies as nearly equal as may be. Capt. J. L. Smith of the Md. Line is charged with the organization of this temporary Battalion and assigned to its command.
  III. The Comdng. Officers of the Regt. and Battalion hereby formed will appoint and organize their respective staffs. . . .
  By order of Brig. Genl. Imboden[18]

After resting his men and mounts another day Gilmor had them march for New Market while he visited Dr. Meem. He found the physician's house ransacked from top to bottom and all of the animals killed, with the exception of a few chickens. The following day Gilmor rode on to Staunton, where he purchased a new horse. He rejoined his battalion at Waynesboro on May 24. Two days later he and his command arrived in Lynchburg and reported to General Breckinridge. Captain Ross and Lieutenant Kemp were there with sixty men, but all of the Second Maryland's horses, including those Gilmor and his band had ridden in on, were almost completely broken down.

Still, Gilmor and forty men made a scout around the rear of Hunter's army and reported back to Breckinridge that the enemy trains were moving westward. Early directed Gilmor to pursue the enemy despite the condition of the horses, and as Hunter fell back Gilmor skirmished with his rear guard near Liberty. He attempted to gain the enemy's flank but became hotly engaged. Nine men were wounded.

The next day, when he was again directed by Early to pursue Hunter toward the mountains, Gilmor protested, but to no avail. His men and horses were completely

18.   Dana Bible Collection, J. C. Vaughn Papers

worn out. They set out, however, and during the trek a Virginian in the command watched as his father's house and mill were burned. The home of his sister, who was ill, was also destroyed before his eyes. The soldier swore that he would take no prisoners during the rest of the pursuit of Hunter. Gilmor, Kemp, and the Virginian found a signal detachment and attacked; the Federals were ordered to halt, but two ran, and Kemp and the Virginian brought them down with one shot each. They captured five men, seven horses, and all of the signal apparatus, including rockets, flags, staves, and torches. Gilmor rested his men two miles from Bonsack's Depot for the night.

The next morning the Marylanders pushed on to Salem, where they attacked Gen. William W. Averell's rear guard, taking two prisoners. Imboden and his brigade arrived, and a considerable fight ensued. Gilmor rested his own troopers but led a battalion of dismounted men in an advance on the enemy. The Federal cavalrymen loosed a volley from their carbines at the mounted Gilmor; his horse was killed, but he was able to bring off his saddle and bridle. He reported to Imboden, who directed him and the dismounted men to flank the Union position, and then mounted a white horse that he had captured earlier in the day. The enemy was falling back, but the Confederates were able to cut off and capture the rear guard. Gilmor and his battalion pursued Hunter through Buford's Gap before giving up the chase.

The troopers rested near the Watts farm in Roanoke County, where Early made his headquarters. A few days after their arrival, the general briefed Gilmor on his plan to invade Maryland and capture or threaten Baltimore and Washington. Gilmor was directed to move down the Valley to Winchester, gathering in his men as he went, and cut off all communications north of that city to assure secrecy for the movement of Early's forces. Gilmor later claimed that even his own men did not know that Early's forces were moving down the Valley until the latter arrived near Winchester on July 2. On July 3 the Marylanders chased about one hundred Union cavalry away from the town.

The Second Maryland Cavalry, now assigned to Gen. Bradley T. Johnson's Brigade of Cavalry, joined its new command seven miles north of Winchester. Early was moving his forces toward the Potomac, and Gilmor, with one hundred men, was detached to act as the advance for Breckinridge's division, which was moving on Martinsburg with Gen. John B. Gordon's division. Gilmor later wrote:

> At daylight on the 4th of July we started, and on approaching
> Martinsburg, learned from a citizen that all was quiet there, and that my

command was all they supposed to be in the Valley. General Stahl [Julius Stahel] was there with about six hundred cavalry, the odds and ends of different regiments. Their pickets were easily driven in, but their reserve had a strong position, and fought stubbornly. I was some distance ahead of the infantry with my command, and was ordered to keep the enemy amused until a battalion of sharpshooters of the 9th Louisiana came to support me. We had no long-range guns, but were armed merely as light cavalry with sabre and pistol.[19]

Stahel, alerted by a citizen of the Confederate advance, brought out his whole force and took a strong position behind a rocky crest in a dense wood. When the Louisianans arrived Gilmor proposed flanking the enemy from its bastion. Their leader agreed and moved his sharpshooters toward the right flank of the Federals. At this point General Breckinridge arrived on the scene, learned what was happening, and directed the Louisianans instead to move down the road in column until they struck the enemy. The commander obeyed and started down the road. Several of the sharpshooters were wounded immediately, and Breckinridge's horse was killed by the Union fire. Gilmor and the Marylanders, supported by another infantry regiment, helped the sharpshooters gain Stahel's flank. The Federals fell back across several fields but reformed at the edge of a field near Darkesville. Gilmor's account continues:

We found two squadrons in reserve, drawn up in line in a wood, with the fence laid down in front. Our men were scattered about, picking up prisoners, when these two squadrons charged upon us, and forced us at first to retreat rapidly; but the charge was feeble, and soon came down to a walk; and, not being followed but across one field, when we reached the fence I called my color-bearer, [Frank] Pendleton, to me, and formed the line while under fire, the blue-coats being only about forty yards distant. Scarcely waiting for the line to dress, we made another dash, and easily put them to flight, driving them through Darkesville in the wildest confusion, and capturing a good many prisoners and horses. General Breckinridge then ran up a three-inch rifled gun, which kept them going for two miles. Afterward they made a more orderly retreat to Martinsburg. But we worried their rear guard every step of the way, and finally charged into Martinsburg, and there captured

19.   Gilmor 1866, 185

immense quantities of supplies of every description. They had made great preparation to celebrate the 4th of July.[20]

Gilmor and his men enjoyed the captured rations.

"We remained one day in Martinsburg," Gilmor wrote, "and then took up our line of march to Shepherdstown, part of our army having already crossed into Maryland. Here I had considerable accessions to my ranks, so that we now numbered one hundred and seventy-five men; but our horses were well tired from hard service."[21] On the evening of July 5 the Second Maryland Cavalry crossed the Potomac and rejoined the brigade near Boonsboro. Bradley Johnson placed Gilmor in command of both the First and Second Maryland.

On the afternoon of July 6 Gilmor was ordered to report to General Early at Sharpsburg. Some of the general's troops were demonstrating against a Federal force entrenched on Maryland Heights but were unable to drive it out. The next day Gilmor was ordered to advance cautiously toward Frederick but to remain within supporting distance of Johnson's Brigade. After passing through Middletown the Marylanders discovered a column of Federal cavalry crossing the Catoctin Mountain. Gilmor deployed his men near the base of the mountain to receive the Union troopers, and a hot skirmish ensued. Gilmor wrote:

At first the enemy seemed inclined to advance. I dismounted two squadrons of the 1st Maryland, who were nearly all armed with the Spencer rifle, and were most of them old infantry soldiers. We waited some time for an attack, but as they showed no disposition to make one, I advanced and opened on their skirmishers, with my mounted men well up, but did not bring them in sight, for they had with them two pieces of artillery in point-blank range. They shelled us until the dismounted men were obliged to lie down, when one of their squadrons ventured to try a charge, which, however, was very cautiously managed. As they came in range, one of my dismounted squadrons opened on them, and at the same time I ordered Captain Burke to bring up my own battalion, with which we made a counter-charge, and ran them back to within eight hundred yards of their guns; but we could go no farther, because there was a large stream between us, and they held the bridge.[22]

20. Ibid., 186–87
21. Ibid., 187
22. Ibid., 188

As the Marylanders fell back the Union cannoneers opened fire, wounding three or four men, including Capt. Richard Gilmor. He was left in charge of the wagons and lame horses.

Gilmor determined to flank the Federals out of their strong position. Before he could start, however, Early's chief of cavalry, Gen. Robert Ransom, countermanded the order. Ransom procrastinated for two or three hours before letting Gilmor carry out his original plan, and before the First and Second could get behind the Union troopers at the top of the mountain, the Federals had fled toward Frederick.

Johnson pushed the brigade on toward Frederick, where he engaged a large Federal force. The fight turned into a long-range artillery duel. Johnson wanted to turn the flanks of the enemy position and capture the town, but Ransom demurred. He instead ordered Johnson's Brigade to return to the Catoctin. Gilmor reported the loss of two men captured on picket duty during the night.

The Federals advanced against the Confederates the next day, and a hot skirmish took place. When the Eighth Illinois Cavalry got behind Johnson's headquarters the general ordered Gilmor to take the Marylanders and "clean them out." Gilmor later boasted:

> By a wood road I came upon them rather unexpectedly, and got them at a disadvantage, and, although they sustained their reputation, we whipped them handsomely, but ran them too far, for we found ourselves among a line of infantry, where we lost twelve horses, with four men wounded, but none killed. General Johnson witnessed the whole, and complimented us highly. Captain James L. Clark . . . behaved nobly. A bullet struck his jacket button, and made it concave, but inflicted no injury. His horse was killed by four or five bullets. He was one of my pets after that, for he was a perfect tiger in a fight. Kemp had his horse also shot under him.[23]

Early then sent Johnson and his brigade on an ambitious mission to release the prisoners at Point Lookout and destroy the railroads and communications leading into Baltimore. The brigade traveled as rapidly as possible before halting at New Windsor, where Johnson ordered Gilmor to take twenty men on fresh horses and cut the telegraph wires at Westminster. Gilmor wrote:

---

23.   Ibid., 189–90

It was near sunset when we approached and there learned there were one hundred and fifty men in the town.

Trusting to their supposing we were well backed, we drew sabres, closed up the column, and charged through the town at a fast gallop, with horses well in hand, and on the look-out for ambuscade in the cross streets. A few blue-coats were to be seen, and the boys gave an awful yell when they saw them, which brought every one to the doors and windows, and when a handkerchief was waved by a fair hand the yelling was louder than ever. The foe took two or three rapid looks, fired two or three shots, and then made for Baltimore.

The telegraph was seized, the wires cut, and the town picketed in less than fifteen minutes, and I shook hands with my friends, lots of whom I have there.[24]

Johnson later directed Gilmor to demand fifteen hundred suits of clothes, including boots and shoes, from the town's mayor. The mayor was unable assemble the city council to raise the necessary funds before the brigade arrived, however, and Gilmor persuaded the general to drop the demand.

The next day Johnson ordered Gilmor to take possession of the railroad at Cockeysville. This he did. The Marylanders also burned a bridge over the Gunpowder River and established picket posts within fifteen miles of Baltimore. Johnson soon arrived and had the other bridges burned.

Gilmor was next ordered to burn the bridges on the Philadelphia, Wilmington, and Baltimore Railroad. He pushed his band of 130 men on toward Baltimore but detoured briefly in the direction of Towsontown to destroy another bridge over the Gunpowder River. Gilmor also took time to visit Glen Ellen, his family home.

By this time the men were so exhausted that they were falling asleep on their horses, and a few were straggling from the command. Gilmor finally called a halt in Dulany's Valley, where the troopers rested until daylight.

At first light the Marylanders were on the move again, crossing the Bel Air and Harford roads and cutting telegraph wires. As they moved along Gilmor heard a shot up ahead. He rode rapidly forward and found his ordnance sergeant, Eugene W. Field, mortally wounded. Field had ridden up to the house of Ishmael Day and ordered him to take down his U.S. flag. Day refused, and when Field dismounted in order to do it himself, Day seized his shotgun and

24.   Ibid., 190

shot Field in the chest. Incensed, the Marylanders scoured the countryside for
Day, but to no avail; they had to settle for burning his house and outbuildings
to the ground. Gilmor continued:

> We pushed on, and, when within a mile and a half of the railroad
> bridge, where the Philadelphia, Wilmington, and Baltimore Road
> crosses the Gunpowder, I discovered a passenger train coming on from
> Baltimore, and ordered Captain Bailey [James R. Bayley], with twenty
> men, to charge ahead and capture it. The capture was soon effected.
> Guards were stationed all around, and I gave strict orders that no plun-
> dering should be done, threatening to shoot or cut down the first man I
> caught in any thing of the sort. . . . The engineer had made his escape,
> or I should have run up to Havre de Grace and made an effort to burn
> all the bridges, and likewise the large steamer there.
>
> Being informed that General [William B.] Franklin was on board, I
> went into the car pointed out to me, and asked some officers who were
> in it which was General Franklin. No reply. I then proceeded to exam-
> ine each one's papers, and presently I came to him. He acknowledged
> himself to be the man. . . . I put him under guard in the telegraph office,
> with several other officers that had been captured.
>
> Finding I could not run the train up to Havre de Grace, I burned it,
> and prepared to catch that which had left Baltimore forty minutes after
> this one. I had also sent a flag of truce to the drawbridge, where were
> two hundred infantry and the gunboat *Juniata,* sent to protect it,
> demanding a surrender, and was about ordering some sharpshooters to
> push them a little, when the second train of twelve passenger-cars came
> up and was easily captured. The engineer of this also escaped, but I
> took the engine in hand, ran it up to the station, and unloaded it in the
> manner of the first [allowing each passenger to have his baggage]. . . .
>
> While the train was being unloaded I kept up a good head of steam
> upon the engine, and, when every thing was clear, ordered Captain
> Bailey [*sic*] to move up his sharpshooters, and try to drive the infantry
> out of the bridge. He soon reported that they had fled to the gun-boat,
> and setting the train on fire, I backed the whole flaming mass down on
> the bridge, catching some of the infantry a little way from shore upon
> the structure, and compelling them to jump into the water. The train
> was running slowly, and stopped right on the draw, where it burned and
> fell through, communicating the fire and destroying the most important

part of the bridge. The wind was blowing directly toward the gun-boat, and she had to trip her anchor and get out of the way. . . .

I paroled most of the officers; first, because I had not horses enough to take them away; and secondly, because many of them were convalescents from field-hospitals. I think I started with five, including General Franklin, all in carriages.[25]

The whole affair had lasted six or seven hours. Gilmor had intended to threaten Baltimore but, upon learning that the streets were barricaded and manned by the militia, he turned off once again toward Towsontown. When he was within five or six miles of the town he learned that a force of Union cavalry had occupied it and was awaiting him. Disregarding this report, and leaving Captain Bayley and Lieutenant Dorsey in charge of the battalion, Gilmor and ten men rode into Townsontown. They arrived with pistols drawn. They found no Federal cavalrymen but were told that a force was on the way. When the rest of Gilmor's men arrived he formed them in the town square and sent out pickets.

Almost immediately the pickets reported a large force of cavalry approaching on the turnpike. Gilmor sent word to his cousin Hoffman Gilmor, who was on picket, instructing him to "let them advance, challenge, fire, and then retreat." He detailed ten men under Capt. Nicholas W. Owings to take off his prisoners. When it was dark he ordered Lieutenant Kemp to charge the enemy with fifteen men. Gilmor wrote:

Kemp's party advanced with pistols; my reserve drew sabres, and each man settled himself in the saddle, and I could see them pulling their hats down firmly on their heads. Just then I heard the pickets down the road fire on the advance, which was immediately answered from a dozen carbines. Kemp dashed on with a yell, and I told my reserve to join also in the yell, and keep it up, and it was done with a will. . . .

As I started down with the reserve at a steady trot I heard Kemp run into them, and I knew he was driving their advance; but soon I knew also that he was retreating rapidly, and, on advancing a little farther, saw a squad in the middle of the road, fired on them, [Kemp had been instructed to bring his men out through the fields on either side of the road], and ordered a charge, but, fortunately in time, recognized

25.   Ibid., 194–97

Kemp's voice; glad to say, no one was hurt.[26]

Gilmor then ordered his men to charge, which they did with a deafening yell. They chased the Federal troopers to Govansville, within four miles of Baltimore. The exhausted men and horses returned to Towsontown with only one horse wounded. During the night a number of recruits came out of Baltimore to enlist; they reported that the Federal picket line around the city had been broken by the fleeing Union cavalry.

Gilmor determined to push on and rejoin Captain Owings and the prisoners. "The whole command [was] completely broken down for want of sleep, and some of them snoring in their saddles before we had gone a mile. To prevent any of them being lost, I rode to the rear, for some of them would slide off and not wake up until well shaken and dragged roughly over the road."[27]

It was not long before Gilmor himself fell asleep in the saddle. He was startled to be awakened by a Federal sentry. He convinced the Union soldier that he was a Northerner and pursuaded him to get his captain. When the sentry left, Gilmor spotted the railroad and realized that he must be near the Relay House. He rode rapidly across the fields and regained the Towsontown road, where he found the man left to direct him—fast asleep. Gilmor rode on to Hunt's Meeting House; here he found all of his men stretched out asleep along the road. He had Captain Bayley awaken them, and they pushed on through the Green Springs Valley to a Mr. Craddock's, where Captain Owings had been directed to take the prisoners. Gilmor found Owings's entire party asleep and the carriage containing General Franklin and the other officers empty. An irate Gilmor sent twenty men to scour the countryside for the escapees, but they were nowhere to be found.

Gilmor gave his men several hours to rest, eat, and groom and feed their horses. Later in the day he moved his command near Pikesville, then sent a scouting party within four miles of Baltimore while he ventured to the Seven-Mile House on the Reistertown road. He was still so exhausted that he again fell asleep in the saddle en route; he dozed off for a third time while talking with two men at the house. The next morning he awoke in camp much refreshed. He wrote:

At sunrise we were all in the saddle, moving toward Rockville, where I expected to join General Early, Captain O[wings] acting as pilot, for

26.   Ibid., 198–99
27.   Ibid., 201

he knew the country thoroughly. Toward evening we learned that Early had fallen back to Poolesville, and that the enemy had possession of Rockville. This obliged us to take a direct course through Montgomery County for Poolesville, marching all night without halting.

We joined General Johnson's head-quarters at day-break [July 13], about two miles below Poolesville, and found him expecting an attack. He was delighted to see me safely back, saying that when he left me near Baltimore, he felt certain I would be captured.[28]

Gilmor had lost one man wounded and Asst. Surgeon A. M. Woolfolk and seven men captured.

When General Early withdrew across the Potomac the Second Maryland Cavalry bivouacked near his headquarters at Big Spring. Gilmor recalled:

We remained near Leesburg about two days, crossed the Blue Ridge at Snicker's Gap, and the Shenandoah at Berry's Ferry and encamped in the Valley near Rippon, between [Charles Town] and Berryville. . . . Our brigade (Johnson's) moved about the Lower Valley from point to point for some time, nothing of importance taking place. We had a few trifling skirmishes, but were chiefly employed in scouting.

No heavy fighting occurred in which our brigade was engaged, and about the 26th I crossed to Martinsburg, and camped about seven miles northwest of Hedgesville, having with me two battalions, namely, the 1st Maryland, and my own, the 2d. . . .

On the 29th I was ordered by General Johnson to move both my battalions near to McCoy's Ford, and hold them in readiness to march at a moment's warning; also to scout the river well, especially the fords, from Williamsport to Little Georgetown. [Gen. John] McCausland's brigade was with us, and he was the ranking officer.

In the evening I was ordered to move at 1 A.M., and take possession of the heights on the Maryland side, and hold them until the brigade came up. It was clear day-light when I reached the river, and found but a few pickets on the other side. I dismounted two squadrons of sharp-shooters, and, under cover of their fire, Kemp and I took over the advance, and got possession of the archway of the canal with but little trouble.[29]

28. Ibid., 203
29. Ibid., 205–6

The First Maryland Cavalry cleared the National Turnpike of enemy cavalry. "The village of Clear Spring is three miles to the east of where we struck the National Turnpike, and McCausland's plan was to march through that place and get on the road leading to Mercersburg," Gilmor noted. "I was ordered to attack the enemy's cavalry and drive them to the Conococheague, and there keep them until both [McCausland's and Johnson's] Brigades had passed through Clear Spring, when I was to follow." Bradley Johnson reported that Gilmor and his Marylanders, who numbered only two hundred, drove the Federal cavalry five miles toward Hagerstown, but that it was not easily done. The two small Maryland battalions faced the Twelfth and Fourteenth Pennsylvania regiments, which were armed with carbines. Gilmor believed they would take too long to flank. He later stated: "[A]fter we had driven them about a mile and a half, I took the first battalion and charged them on the main road, ordering Captain Burke to follow in support in case of a repulse."[30] Two charges were successful; the Marylanders drove the enemy back and took a few prisoners. The third charge met stiffer resistance, throwing the Confederates into confusion and causing them to fall back. At this point the Pennsylvanians had a strong position behind heavy fences and had two squadrons in ambush behind a stone fence that ran along the road. Gilmor continued:

> I sent a courier back for Captain Burke to hurry up; and when he came opposite to a barn where we were, I took the head of the column and dashed on, the men going in fine style. Most of the 1st joined my battalion, and eight or ten were in front of me. The dismounted squadron gave us a fierce volley as we came down, and, although at short range, did little harm. We then got in their rear, and made a dash at the cavalry farther on; but just as we got abreast of the wood, the two squadrons in ambush opened upon us with terrific effect, which obliged us to retreat in some disorder, but not until we had brought off all our wounded. They then charged our rear. We wheeled and repulsed them, and held our ground until out of range from their carbines.[31]

Gilmor lamented the loss of seventeen men killed and wounded in the action. Three of the Second had been killed, and at least four were wounded. The injured men were sent back to Virginia.

30.   Ibid., 206–7
31.   Ibid., 207–8

Thanks to the Marylanders, the two brigades passed through Clear Spring unmolested on their way to Mercersburg. Gilmor and the Marylanders did not catch up with Johnson's and McCausland's commands until they halted for the night about a mile beyond Mercersburg. When Gilmor reported to the generals, they informed him that they were going to march on to Chambersburg in order to be there at daybreak. The exhausted Marylanders were assigned to act as the rear guard. Gilmor himself had not slept in forty-six hours, and it was all he could do to keep the men in the saddle and moving.

Upon reaching Chambersburg McCausland sent Gilmor and the Marylanders to support Maj. James W. Sweeney's Thirty-sixth Virginia Battalion of Cavalry, which had dismounted and attacked the town. Sweeney's Virginians, armed with long-range rifles, had no trouble driving the enemy from the town without a casualty. The Marylanders rode through the village and beyond to make sure no Federals were in the area. When Gilmor returned he was ordered to arrest fifty of the most prominent citizens and put them under guard.

He had rounded up some forty by the time McCausland sent for him; General Averell's cavalry was approaching Chambersburg. General Early now ordered that the town be burned in retaliation for the destruction in Lexington and other acts of arson by Hunter in the Valley. He would desist only if the citizens met his demand for two hundred thousand dollars in gold or greenbacks. Gilmor reported that the citizens, who knew Averell was coming, positively refused to raise the money and laughed at the Marylanders when they threatened to burn the town. In the face of the refusal, McCausland ordered Gilmor to reduce the town to ashes. The major continued:

> I then directed my men to fire the town, but be kind to the women and children, and lend them all the assistance in their power. While I could remain in the streets, I did nothing but assist the people and see that no excesses were committed. Several times I received peremptory orders to make a thorough work of it, and was especially directed to destroy all fine dwellings.[32]

Gilmor regretted having to carry out the order but could only remember Hunter's wanton acts in the Valley. He refused to burn the home of Colonel Boyd of the Twenty-first Pennsylvania Cavalry. He reported that they left Chambersburg at noon and went into camp at McConnellsburg, where they

32.   Ibid., 210

found plenty of provender and rations.

On July 31 Averell attacked the Confederate pickets near McConnellsburg. While a Virginia regiment and battalion held the nearby hills, Gilmor and the Marylanders engaged the enemy in a lively skirmish in the town. McCausland and Johnson, meanwhile, started for Hancock. As the sun was going down the First and Second fell back, and Gilmor led them down the National Turnpike toward Cumberland before halting for the night.

Early on the morning of August 1 the Marylanders continued their trek toward Cumberland, where they found McCausland's Brigade engaged with the enemy some two miles from town. Gilmor reported to "John Tiger."

> *McCausland:* "Major Gilmor, do you know this country well?"
> *Gilmor:* "No, sir, I was never here before."
> *McCausland:* "Have you no guides?"
> *Gilmor:* "I have two, but both got drunk and went off."
> *McCausland:* "Unless we get out of this predicament soon, I fear it will
> be too late to save our guns and wagons, and we shall, besides, lose a
> good many men."[33]

McCausland ended by directing Gilmor to find a route across the Potomac into Virginia. After learning from a citizen that the river was seven or eight miles off, the major arrested a Union man and forced him to guide the Marylanders to a blind ford. It was dark when they neared the Potomac. The advance was fired upon by some Union cavalry vedettes, but a quick charge drove them away. Scouts were sent on to locate the ford, and Gilmor dispatched a courier to Johnson with a message to join him.

By dawn couriers had reported that Johnson was on his way, and scouts had returned with the news that eight hundred Federal infantry and ironclad railroad cars with cannon on board guarded the crossing. The Marylanders scouted along the river and discovered that the enemy was taking up the planking on the bridge across the canal on the road that led to the ford. A heavy fog covered the river bottom, limiting visibility. "This caused my advance, under Kemp, to run into an ambuscade, by which he lost one man ([Aristo] Gorman) killed and two wounded," Gilmor reported.[34]

When Johnson arrived the fog had partially lifted. He and Gilmor started their

33.   Ibid., 215

34.   Ibid., 217

commands toward Old Town and were fired upon by infantrymen three hundred yards distant. Fortunately their range was bad, and only three horses were hit before the Confederates turned into a ravine and took shelter behind a hill. Here Captain Welsh of the First Maryland built a new bridge across the canal. McCausland crossed the man-made waterway with three regiments, dismounted them, and engaged the Federal infantry, eventually driving it across the river. The Union soldiers took position in the ironclad railroad cars, and the train was then moved down the line until it was directly opposite the ford. Gilmor reported:

> One attempt was made to carry the ford with dismounted cavalry (8th Virginia Cavalry) and my second battalion. We gained the river, and charged across under a heavy fire of shells and musketry, but could not go out on the other side. I drew up my squadron in single rank under the Virginia shore, in water knee-deep. The dismounted men waded through, and lay down on the edge of the water. There was but one way out, and that was up the steep hill where the road went forth from the river, under an enfilading fire from the batteries.[35]

The Federal infantry also occupied a blockhouse 150 yards from the ford; there was an open gate in between. Gilmor and the dismounted force had lost about a dozen men, including five killed. He waited a while and then recrossed the stream to find Johnson and McCausland debating what to do. He tried to persuade them to bring down the horse artillery, but they were afraid that the horses would be killed before the guns could be positioned.

Gilmor rode back to Old Town and consulted with Lt. John R. McNulty of the Baltimore Light Artillery, who agreed to try it with two guns. The cannoneers loaded and primed their pieces before making the effort. The artillerymen crossed the bridge at a gallop, losing only two horses, and unlimbered on a ridge. Gilmor wrote:

> The gunner was a Baltimorean named [George W.] McElwee, and, though a brisk fire was opened on him, he coolly sighted his piece, and put a six-pound shell through the boiler, which exploded with a loud report. That was one of the best shots during the war, judging from its effect, for every man except those in the iron-clad stampeded. The third

35. Ibid., 218–19

or fourth shot entered the porthole of the iron-clad, dismounted the brass pivot-gun, whereupon both were evacuated.[36]

The gunners next turned their fire on the blockhouse, but with little effect. Johnson sent one of the Virginia regiments up the bank, but it was driven back, and several officers and men were lost. According to Gilmor, McCausland and Johnson could not decide how to proceed, so he suggested that they try to effect a surrender. He wrote:

> Johnson wrote the message, which I sent by two of my men, [Thomas J.] Kidd and McCaul. . . . They tied a white handkerchief to a cane, and advanced boldly to the block-house. The officer replied that his time was nearly out, and, if his men and officers were paroled, they would surrender. Most fortunate for us; it, no doubt, saved us many lives.
>
> After destroying the train we moved round to Springfield, nine miles on the Romney Road, camped two days to refresh our horses and on the 3rd of August went to Romney. Here all the wagons, dismounted men, and crippled horses were sent to the Valley.
>
> We marched in the direction of New Creek, which McCausland had determined to capture, and which I believe would have been done had there been proper concert of action; but we spent two days uselessly, and were foiled most signally in that expedition, although McCausland did assault and capture one fort. We lost forty or fifty men, gaining nothing by the trip. Most of the regiments were demoralized, principally because of the amount of plunder they were allowed to carry.[37]

The weary troopers returned to the Moorefield Valley and camped at Old Fields, north of Moorefield. The brigades were spread out, so there was plenty of grass for the horses. Johnson's Brigade was camped on the east side of the South Branch of the Potomac along the Romney road, about three-quarters of a mile from McCausland's bivouac on the west side of the stream. The Second Maryland was camped at the McNeill house, about five hundred yards from Johnson's headquarters.

It was here that General Averell's cavalry surprised the Confederates before dawn on August 7 (see pages 94–96). After shooting a Jessie scout who had

---

36. Ibid., 220
37. Ibid., 220–21

roused him from his sleep, Gilmor tried to rally his battalion.

> [M]any of my men mounted and came to me, for I too had mounted after killing the first man. The day was just dawning, and we could see that a large number of the enemy were upon us. We made a charge and drove them back, but then discovered that two squadrons had got round us to the west, while a whole regiment was making its way rapidly through the flats on the other side. By this time we were near the 1st Maryland camp, and heard the poor fellows call out to each other, "Stand firm, men; stand firm." And I saw the enemy riding them down, slashing right and left with their sabres, some crying, "Surrender, you house-burning scoundrels!"; others, "Kill every damned one of them."[38]

As Gilmor directed his men to dismount and pull down a fence, he noticed enemy troopers moving to his rear, determined to cut their way through to Johnson's headquarters. "[I]t was in doing so that we lost so many. . . . Lieutenant Richardson, dismounted, gave the general his horse, and was himself captured." Gilmor also lost Lieutenant Kemp, whose horse was shot from under him. He was immediately surrounded by the enemy. "He fought bravely and desperately, refusing to surrender. I saw him sink down in the corner of the fence while firing his last shot. I shot one, and he knocked down two before they killed him."[39]

Gilmor and five of his men escaped the melee. As they rode away toward Patterson Creek Mountain, Gilmor heard yelling near the ford across the river, followed by several volleys. Believing that McCausland's Brigade had turned the Federals back, he rode through the dense fog toward the sound of the firing—only to ride into a column of Union cavalrymen. Because he was dressed somewhat like a Federal officer, he was mistaken for one of their own and was able to return to his men. Near Moorefield the six Marylanders rejoined Johnson and about two hundred men who had escaped.

By Gilmor's tally, he had lost "forty-five men and six officers from my battalion."[40] From the incomplete records of the Second Maryland it appears that Company A lost seven men to capture and Company B one. Company C lost Lieutenant Kemp killed and ten men captured; in Company D two men were

38.   Ibid., 223
39.   Ibid., 223–24
40.   Ibid., 223

killed, one was wounded, and nine were captured. Company E's Capt. Henry W. Brewer and four other men were captured, and one was wounded. Company F lost its leader, Capt. James L. Clark, Lieutenant Richardson, and eight other men captured. One man in Company F was killed. The leadership of the battalion was decimated.

Gilmor led the remnants of his command over the mountains to the Valley, where they rested at Rude's Hill, near Mount Airy, for several days. The Marylanders had lost their flag in the last fight, but the ladies in Dr. Meem's household made a new one.

Johnson's Brigade rejoined General Early at Fisher's Hill on August 12. Early ordered the bulk of the command to picket the Back road; the Maryland battalions were detached and assigned to scouting duty. After reporting to Gen. Lunsford L. Lomax, Early's new chief of cavalry, Gilmor established two camps—one near Lomax's headquarters for the men who were ready for duty, and one at Newtown for the men with disabled horses.

Robert E. Lee, meanwhile, was sending reinforcements to Early to help combat the growing Federal force under Gen. Philip H. Sheridan, the new Union commander in the Valley. Fitzhugh Lee's division of cavalry moved up to Front Royal, which was on the flank of Sheridan's command, near Strasburg. Gen. Richard H. Anderson's corps moved to Culpeper, within supporting distance of Early.

At this point Sheridan fell back to Winchester, and Early followed the Federal retreat. Gilmor's Battalion was assigned to duty as the rear guard of the army and charged with keeping stragglers in the ranks. This was not the major's style; he had always led the advance in Confederate moves up and down the Valley. He sought and was granted permission to leave the Maryland battalions under the next senior officer and join the advance guard.

As the Confederate infantry drove the Federals back toward Winchester Gilmor observed two Southern brigades overlapping and firing upon each other in a cornfield. With Lt. Holmes Conrad of the Eleventh Virginia Cavalry, he rode forward to halt the firing. His horse was killed in the melee. Fortunately some Confederate skirmishers had brought in a captured Federal officer and his horse, which Gilmor appropriated for the moment.

Later in the day Gilmor and Conrad bluffed a company of the First New Jersey Cavalry into believing that they were trapped and about to be killed by Confederates concealed behind a stone wall. The entire company surrendered, and Gilmor was able to send forty-eight captured horses to his dismounted camp.

On August 21 Early advanced against Sheridan's forces at Charles Town. Lomax's cavalry led the advance down the Berryville road with Lee's cavalry on the right. The horsemen developed the surprised enemy, and the Confederate infantry drove the Federals back. Johnson's Brigade then advanced toward Leetown with instructions for Gilmor to charge the enemy's camp if he could surprise it. Gilmor, who had only the two small Maryland battalions, wanted Johnson to attack with his whole brigade, but by the time the regiments could be deployed the enemy had fled. The Federal cavalry came on in strong force, and Johnson sent the Nineteenth and Twentieth Virginia regiments to help hold the Leetown road. The major wrote:

Lt. Col. Gustavus W. "Gus" Dorsey.
(William W. Turner)

I had hardly dismounted the 19th regiment, and placed them in position in the wood, when we were charged in fine style by a regiment of cavalry in column. The 19th let them come quite near, and then opened upon them a steady fire, which threw them into some confusion, when I ordered Captain Welch [*sic*] to charge them with the 1st Maryland, and Captain [Gustavus W.] Dorsey and Burke to support him. The boys routed them handsomely, driving them back to their reserve, taking some prisoners, and killing and wounding a small number.

Lomax witnessed the whole affair, and came up exclaiming, "Well done, Gilmor—well done." At that moment my vedettes from the left and front reported a brigade moving around to attack me on the left flank. Lomax sung out, "For God's sake, Gilmor, don't let them turn your left; I am hard pressed myself by a heavy line of infantry skirmishers." "All right, sir; when they get round my flank there won't be many of my boys left."

A whole brigade was then plainly seen winding along. I moved the 19th and 20th to the left, and put them in a splendid position in a belt of wood within musket-shot of Mrs. McDaniel's house. Farther to the left was an extensive cornfield, next to this a meadow, and back of this another field. . . .

It was in this field that I drew up the two Maryland battalions, ready to assist the 19th and 20th, or repulse a charge on the flank. The Maryland battalions were hidden from the enemy by a small knoll in their front, on the top of which was a division fence. Two or three men quietly laid low the fence, and all was made clear for a charge.[41]

The morning was spent skirmishing with the Federals, who also shelled the woods in an effort to drive out the dismounted Confederates. After noon the enemy cavalry came on in strong force. Gilmor had the Nineteenth Virginia hold its fire until the Twelfth Pennsylvania Cavalry was within one hundred yards. When he gave the order to fire, the volley emptied many saddles among the Pennsylvanians, including that of their colonel, who was mortally wounded. In the confusion some of the Federals rode into the Confederate lines and were captured. The Federal cavalry came on again, this time more cautiously, and fell back when fired upon. The artillery then tried to blast the Confederates from the wood line, but with little effect. Gilmor continued:

After an hour's heavy shelling and some sharp skirmishing, I discovered another and a more formidable movement in front, and, giving instructions to the officers, I went over to the cavalry, put it in position to make a charge, and had but just got to the mounted men when a sudden and desperate charge was made on the wood in which the two Virginia regiments were lying. The charge was a bold and determined one, but the men had hastily thrown up a light barricade of rails, and would not give an inch. About fifty Federals cut their way through, but these we soon ran down and captured, with a squadron from the 1st Maryland, under Lieutenant William [H. B.] Dorsey and myself. It was a regular hunt, and some of them had to be chased half a mile before they were taken.[42]

Gilmor chased down the adjutant of the Twelfth Pennsylvania Cavalry, who was riding his colonel's horse, and only stopped him by wounding his mount.

41.   Ibid., 232–33
42.   Ibid., 234–35

He gave the fine horse to General Lomax. Gilmor concluded:

> While this was going on, Captain Welch [*sic*], with the rest of the
> mounted men, made a charge to take the enemy in flank, but as soon as
> he showed himself every gun opened upon him at short range. It would
> have been useless slaughter to have gone on, so I called it off.[43]

The men of the brigade slept on their arms during the night and at dawn found
that the Yankee cavalry had fallen back to a strong position near Charles Town.
Gilmor tried to flank the Federals from their breastworks, but they fell back,
again toward Charles Town, after a brief skirmish. The Marylanders followed
them closely, all the while harassing their rear guard. The Union cavalry fell
back still farther, to Duffield's Depot, and Gilmor followed it to Brown's Shop
on the Baltimore and Ohio Railroad. The Marylanders remained in the vicinity
for three days, keeping an eye on the Federal cavalry force and scouting toward
Shepherdstown and Martinsburg.

During this period Gilmor reported only 175 men present for duty in the two
Maryland battalions, and General Ransom recommended to Early that all of the
Marylanders be consolidated under Gilmor. The officers of the First Maryland
objected, however, and the proposal was not carried out.

On August 27 Gilmor led the Marylanders toward Falling Waters. Capt. Gus
Dorsey, with part of the First Maryland, was sent by a different road. Gilmor
reported:

> When I reached a high hill overlooking Falling Waters, we came upon
> a strong picket force. Captain Welch [*sic*] was ordered to charge with
> the first squadron.[44]

Warner Welsh and his men ran into a barricade across the road. With the river
bank on one side and a marshy pond on the other, they were forced back.
Gilmor described what ensued:

> I did not see the obstruction, and dashed on at the head of the next
> squadron, having previously sent thirty men to the left, around the hill,
> to strike them in flank. My boys, however, did not stop for the barricade,

43.   Ibid., 235
44.   Ibid., 238

but pushed through, and drove the enemy so fast that he left a good deal of plunder and some horses tied to the trees. I lost three good men at the barricade.[45]

Gilmor kept up the chase for several miles but learned from citizens that more Federal cavalrymen were nearby. Scouts confirmed these reports, and Gilmor withdrew to Falling Waters. Captain Dorsey, meanwhile, had engaged another Federal column across the river at Williamsport. Gilmor reported this to Lomax, who allowed the Marylanders to go into camp.

The next day Gilmor was ordered to take the two battalions near Leetown and replace the pickets of Gen. William E. Jackson's Brigade, which the enemy had been driving in all day. Just as the Marylanders were about to relieve the Virginians, the Federal cavalry attacked. The Virginians fell back in disorder. Gilmor ordered Capt. Richard Gilmor to take all of the men armed with long-range weapons—about forty in number—to his right, deploy them as skirmishers, and charge through the woods. The enemy cavalry came down the road four abreast, and the Marylanders brought down the leading Federals with their pistol fire, and Gilmor led his men in a countercharge. He wrote of the encounter:

> It was a severe shock when we did meet, but the enemy 6th [U.S.] Regulars gave way and a slashing race began. We had captured about thirty prisoners, and [were] still running them, . . . when suddenly a heavy column was seen charging down upon us in front, and a column [was] coming through the fields at us on each flank. . . . We wheeled and tried to get out of the trap, but the column in flank got among us and began playing the very devil.
>
> One of the other columns would have struck us in flank but for the coolness, presence of mind, and undaunted bravery of Captain Gus Dorsey.[46]

Gilmor, still dressed somewhat in the manner of a Federal officer, leaped his horse over a fence, dashed up to the advancing column, and ordered, "By fours, right about wheel, march!" The Union troopers obeyed.

"The enemy were now completely mixed up with us, all cutting, and slashing, and pistoling right and left," Gilmor recounted. "The race continued over

45.   Ibid., 238
46.   Ibid., 240–41

three miles, and throughout the whole distance this scene of horror was going on."[47]

The major, who was fighting in the rear of the column, was at one point charged by a Federal officer who pressed the muzzle of his revolver against him and fired. The pistol was empty, however, and Gilmor unhorsed his would-be killer with his saber. The melee continued to the point at which the action first began and where the First Maryland was drawn up. Gilmor shouted for its men to charge, but they could not distinguish friend from foe and hesitated. A Federal column then struck them, and the First was forced to fall back. The chase continued until the Confederates neared Smithfield, where Lomax had the horse artillery open fire on the enemy, which ended the pursuit.

"Officers and men behaved bravely in the fight," noted Gilmor, "among others, the color-bearer, John S. P[hipps], who was in the hottest places all the time. He held on to the colors, though there were two bullet-holes in the flag and several sabre-cuts on the staff. . . . I lost twenty-six of my brave boys."[48]

The battalion's scant records reveal that Capt. John D. Clarke and nine men were captured, and one man was wounded. Both Fitzhugh Lee and Lomax had had to fall back behind the Opequon before the powerful Federal cavalry force.

During early September the Marylanders clashed with their counterparts at Smithfield, Bunker Hill, and Darkesville. During the action on September 3 Gilmor was wounded, and Captain Burke took command of the battalion.

During the battle of Winchester on September 19 Gilmor, who was hospitalized in the town, was able to escape. His battalion fought against the First Maryland Cavalry, U.S.A., during the engagement, losing at least two men killed and three wounded—Lts. James M. Couborn and James M. Cooper, both of Company A, and Sgt. Maj. John McWilliams—and one man captured. The Marylanders acted as part of the rear guard as Early's battered forces fell back to Fisher's Hill. Maj. Gus Dorsey was wounded in the neck in a skirmish there on September 21, and command of the two battalions fell upon Captain Welsh.

Sheridan continued to pursue the dispirited Confederates, and Early fell back to Brown's Gap. Several members of the Second Maryland were captured during this retreat.

At Brown's Gap the two Maryland battalions were reassigned to Jackson's Brigade, which was ordered east of the Blue Ridge, and marched to Hanover Junction. The Union threat in that area had waned by October 7, and the

47. Ibid., 241
48. Ibid., 243

Marylanders returned to the Valley with Jackson. They were just in time to follow Sheridan's retirement toward Winchester. The Union cavalry spread across the Valley, burning everything of use to the Confederates as they went. The Federals who were captured in the act of burning barns, mills, or homes were executed immediately.

Early followed Sheridan to Fisher's Hill and determined to attack him. Little is known of the role of Jackson's Brigade during the battle of Cedar Creek on October 19, but Captain Sudler was wounded in the action. Early was defeated, and the Confederates fell back up the Valley to New Market.

Gilmor had returned to duty by this time and was involved in scouting for General Early. He seems not to have resumed command of the remnants of his battalion, however. After a leave of absence Gilmor reported to Early at Staunton in late December 1864. Early issued the following:

> Special Order No. 147
> Major H. Gilmor will take his battalion to Hardy County, for the purpose of operating in that and the adjoining counties. The companies of [Capts. John H.] McNeil [*sic*] and [Charles H. "Buck"] Woodson, already there, will report to Major Gilmor, and be permanently under his command.
> J. A. Early Lieut. Gen. commanding Army of Valley District.[49]

"To Hardy County I went, as directed, and began collecting the scattered men of my battalion, and had mustered about one hundred of my own, with two hundred of McNeil's [*sic*] and Woodson's when I was captured on Sunday morning, February 4th, 1865,"[50] Gilmor remembered.

General Sheridan, headquartered at Winchester, was well aware of Gilmor's orders, and Lt. Col. Edward W. Whitaker of the First Connecticut Cavalry was given the task of bringing him in. Whitaker chose three hundred men armed with sabers and pistols from his division of cavalry. Maj. Henry W. Young, Sheridan's chief of scouts, accompanied him. Young's Jessie scouts were dressed as Confederates and even carried authentic leave papers and passes taken from recently captured prisoners.

The expedition left its camp near Winchester on the evening of February 3 and marched rapidly to Wardensville, where the men halted briefly for coffee

49.   Ibid., 276
50.   Ibid.

and to feed their mounts. Major Young and his scouts led the rapid advance toward Moorefield with the goal of capturing it by midnight. The column was not able to travel as fast as anticipated, however, and it halted after midnight about four miles short of the town. Young's scouts, sent ahead into Moorefield, were not able to ascertain Gilmor's whereabouts. Whitaker and Young themselves entered Moorefield before dawn, but Gilmor was not there.

Leaving a detachment of the Second Ohio Cavalry behind to further search the town for concealed soldiers, Whitaker turned his column down the South Branch of the Potomac with Major Young and his scouts again in advance. After three miles they reached a Mr. Randolph's house and noticed a large number of horses in the stable. Major Young approached a female servant and asked, "What soldiers are in the house?" She replied, "Major Gilmor is upstairs." "Major Young immediately surrounded the house and seized the major and his young cousin [Hoffman] Gilmor, both in bed," reported Whitaker.[51] Gilmor recalled:

[T]he door suddenly opened, and five men entered with drawn pistols, and, although dressed as Confederates, I saw at a glance what they were. But it was too late for a fight, for they had seized my pistols, lying on a chair under my uniform. "Are you Colonel Gilmor?" said one of them. I did not answer at first; I was glancing around to see if there was any chance of escape. My attention was arrested by feeling the muzzle of a pistol against my head, and hearing the question repeated. "Yes; and who in the devil's name are you?" "Major Young, of General Sheridan's staff." "All right. I suppose you want me to go with you?" "I shall be happy to have your company to Winchester, as General Sheridan wishes to consult you about some important military matters."[52]

Gilmor was permitted to dress; he was then led to the stable and mounted on his horse. After crossing the stream he was introduced to Colonel Whitaker. At about this time three men of the Second Maryland dashed up to the other side of the river and opened fire. Gilmor shouted encouragement to his men although they caused but little confusion among the Yankees.

Whitaker turned his men back toward Moorefield. Young, sensing Gilmor

51. Ibid., 277
52. Ibid., 278

might attempt an escape, put him on a weaker horse. The column rode on toward Romney with Gilmor and other prisoners under guard in the center of the column. After passing Romney Whitaker took the Northwestern Turnpike toward Winchester; the command stopped only one hour for supper.

As they approached the Big Capon River, Major Young proposed to Whitaker that he take Gilmor and ride on to Winchester, but Whitaker refused. Major Young, in a huff, took his scouts and headed on toward Winchester, leaving Gilmor virtually unguarded. Before the Marylander could make a move, however, four of the scouts returned and continued to guard him, pistols drawn, to Young's camp on the river.

When the Union cavalry reached Winchester the next day, Gilmor was held in a hotel room guarded by two sentinels. The provost marshal had the Confederate handcuffed hand and foot by order of General Sheridan. Gilmor lay shackled on the floor of the unheated room for three days; had the lieutenant of the guard not given him two of his own blankets Gilmor would have had no covering at all. On the morning of the third day Major Young arrived with a detachment of twenty-five men, removed the irons, and guarded Gilmor to Stephenson's Depot, where they boarded a train for Harpers Ferry. Young and eight of his men escorted Gilmor to Fort Warren in Boston Harbor, where he remained a prisoner until the war was over.

What was left of the Second Maryland Cavalry operated with Capts. Jesse C. McNeill and Charles H. Woodson until the end of the war. Its men probably aided in the capture of Gens. George Crook and Benjamin F. Kelly at Cumberland, Maryland, on February 21, 1865. The majority of the officers and men were paroled at Winchester during April and May 1865.

Muster
Rolls

Introduction

The primary source for these muster rolls (the First, Second, and Davis's Battalions of Maryland Cavalry) is the Compiled Service Records in the National Archives, which consists of date and place of enlistment or conscription, rank, age, and, in some cases, occupation. Other data include presence or absence for specific periods, usually in sixty-day increments, and dates when the company was paid. Records of hospitalization, documentation of capture and exchange, clothing and equipment receipts, valuation of horses, and other miscellaneous material are included in each man's file. Compiled Service Records for the First Maryland Cavalry exist for certain periods for Companies A–F. No such muster rolls have been found for Company G, perhaps because most of the men who served in this company transferred from Davis's Battalion. Likewise, there are no known muster rolls for Davis's Battalion. Records for the Second Maryland Cavalry consist only of muster rolls for Companies D and F.

In the muster rolls that follow, the information in the Compiled Service Records has been supplemented by postwar rosters, pension applications, county histories, county marriage and death records, UDC and UCV records, cemetery listings, family genealogies and papers, family Bible records, newspaper accounts, and obituaries. Spelling is as found in these sources.

Each soldier's record of service is arranged chronologically from place and date of birth to place and date of death and burial site. Postwar careers have been included when available. Where the sources do not agree as to date of death, data from tombstone inscriptions are used.

Periods of confinement as a prisoner of war are not shown specifically but run from the date of capture until the prisoner was exchanged, released, took the oath of allegiance, or died. Transfer dates between Union prisons are not shown.

The term NO FURTHER RECORD (NFR) has been used to show when a man's service ended and no reason is stated. Periods of unauthorized absence are denoted as absent without leave (AWOL) or desertion based on the soldier's record. A lack of court-martial records usually indicates that the absence was excused upon return to duty.

Descriptive lists have been taken from enlistment, hospital, pay, discharge, leave, prisoner of war, parole, desertion, and death records. In a few cases, postwar descriptions have been included.

Although West Virginia did not become a state until Lincoln signed the statehood act on December 31, 1863, sites that fell within the new state are identified as being in West Virginia for the convenience of readers using contemporary maps.

Certain standard abbreviations have been used throughout the muster rolls:

Absent	Ab.	Judge Advocate	JA
Absent without leave	AWOL	Killed in action	KIA
Academy	Acad.	Lieutenant	Lt.
Adjutant	Adj.	Lieutenant Colonel	Lt. Col.
Army & Navy Soc., Md. Line Assoc.	ANS/MLA	Major	Maj.
Artillery	Arty.	Major General	MGen.
Assistant	Asst.	Missing in action	MIA
Assistant Adjutant General	AAG	Mount or Mountain.	Mt.
Assistant Inspector General	AIG	Mounted	Mt'd.
Assistant Judge Advocate	AJA	Obituary	Obit.
Battalion	Bn.	Ordnance.	Ord.
Battery	Bty.	Point	Pt.
Born	b.	Post Office	PO
Brigade	Brig.	Private	Pvt.
Brigadier General	BGen.	Provost Marshal	PM
Buried	Bur.	Quartermaster	QM
Captain	Capt.	Reenlisted	Reenl.
Cavalry	Cav.	Resident	Res.
Cemetery	Cem.	Returned to Duty	RTD
Church	Ch.	Second Lieutenant	2nd Lt.
College	Col.	Sergeant	Sgt.
Colonel	Col.	Sergeant Major	Sgt. Maj.
Commissary	Comm.	Squadron	Sqd.
Company	Co.	Third Lieutenant	3rd Lt.
Confederate States	CS	Transferred	Transf.
Confederate States Navy	CSN	United Confederate Veterans	UCV
Confederate States Ship	CSS	United Daughters of the Confederacy	UDC
Confederate Veterans	CV	University	U.
Corporal	Cpl.	Wounded in action	WIA
County	Co.		
Court House	CH		
Court-Martial	CM		

Deserted	Des.	Camp Chase	Camp Chase, Ohio
Died	d.	Camp Morton	Camp Morton, Indiana
Died in service	DIS	David's Island	David's Island, New York
Died of wounds	DOW	Elmira	Elmira, New York
District	Dist.	Ft. Columbus	Fort Columbus, New York
Division	Div.	Ft. Del.	Fort Delaware, Del.
Enlisted	Enl.	Ft. McHenry	Fort McHenry, Md.
First Lieutenant	1st Lt.	Ft. Monroe	Fort Monroe, Virginia
First Sergeant	1st Sgt.	Ft. Warren	Fort Warren, Massachusetts
Fort	Ft.	Johnson's Island	Johnson's Island, Ohio
General	Gen.	Newport News	Newport News, Virginia
General Court-Martial	GCM	Old Capitol Prison	Washington, D.C.
Graduated	Gd.	Pt. Lookout	Point Lookout, Md.
Hospital	Hosp.	Rock Island	Rock Island, Illinois
Infantry	Inf.	Wheeling	Wheeling, West Virginia

First Maryland Cavalry
and Davis's Battalion

ABBOTT, WILLIAM H.: Pvt., Co. B. b. Md. 1840. Res. Cedar Creek, Dorchester Co., Md. Captured St. Mary's Co., Md., 11/20/64; sent to Old Capitol; took oath, released, 11/23/64. Former res. of Baltimore. Sent to Baltimore. d. 1915. Bur. Greenlawn Cem., Dorchester Co.

ACKWORTH, WILLIAM WESLEY: Pvt., Co. B. Enl. Co. A, 47th Bn. Va. Cav., Richmond, 8/10/63. Transf. Co. B, 1st Md. Cav., 8/31/64; issued clothing 9/30/64; des. 1/4/65. NFR.

ADAMS, ANDREW: Pvt., Co. A, Davis's Bn. b. Baltimore circa 1827. Res. of Baltimore. Enl. Co. D, 1st Md. Inf., 2/26/62; discharged by order of Secretary of War 8/16/62. Age thirty-five, 5'8½", fair complexion, dark hair, blue eyes. Gunsmith. On postwar roster.

ADAMS, JOHN: Pvt., Co. A, Davis's Bn. Enl. Mt. Crawford, Va., 11/25/63; AWOL 1/1–10/31/64. Transf. to Co. M, 23rd Va. Cav. NFR.

ALBAUGH, IRA HALBROOK or HOLBROOK: 4th Sgt., Co. K. b. Howard Co., Md., circa 1841. Clerk, age nineteen, Freedom Dist., Carroll Co., Md., per 1860 census. Enl. as Pvt., Co. K (2nd), 1st Va. Cav., 5/1/61; discharged 5/14/62. Reenl. for the war 7–8/62; WIA Kelly's Ford, Va., 4/17/63; promoted 4th Sgt. WIA, captured, Gettysburg, Pa., 7/3/63; sent to Pt. Lookout. Transf. to Co. K, 1st Md. Cav., 8/64, while POW. Exchanged 2/26/65. Present Camp Lee, Richmond, 2/27/65. Paroled Winchester 4/23/65. Age twenty-six, 5'11", dark complexion, dark hair, green eyes. Brother of John W. Albaugh. (Photograph in Driver 1991)

ALBAUGH, JOHN WILLIAM: Pvt., Co. K. b. Howard Co., Md. Res. of Carroll Co., Md. Enl. Co. K (2nd), 1st Va. Cav., date unknown. Transf. to Co. K, 1st Md. Cav., 8/64; KIA Bunker Hill, W.Va., 10/12/64. Brother of Ira H. Albaugh. (Photograph in Driver 1991)

ALBERT, MARTIN: Pvt., Co. unknown. Captured, date, place unknown; received Pt. Lookout 11/29/64; took oath; transportation furnished to Philadelphia, Pa.

ALBERT, WILLIAM: Pvt., Co. B; issued clothing 11/9/64; ab. in Richmond hosp. 11/12–13/64. Captured, date, place unknown; received Pt. Lookout 11/23/64; took oath; transportation furnished to Baltimore.

ALLEN, J. C.: Lt., Co. unknown; present Greenland Gap, W.Va., 4/25/63. NFR.

ALLEN, WILLIAM N.: QM Sgt. b. Md. circa 1835. Farmhand, age twenty-five, Freedom Dist., Carroll Co., Md., per 1860 census. Captured Baltimore 11/3/64; sent to Ft. McHenry; took oath, released 1/15/65. 5'8½", dark complexion, black hair, black eyes. Transportation furnished to Preston Co., Va.

ANDERSON, JAMES: Pvt., Co. A, Davis's Bn. Enl. Richmond 6/16/63. Captured Newtown, Va., 1863; exchanged. Transf. to Co. M, 23rd Va. Cav. Captured Martinsburg, W.Va., 7/10/64; sent to Wheeling. Age thirty-three, 5' 8", dark complexion, dark hair, hazel eyes. Carpenter. Res. of Henrico Co., Va. Released 5/13/65.

ANDERSON, JOSEPH P.: Pvt., Co. G. b. Va. circa 1842. Farmer, age eighteen, High View PO, Allegany Co., Md., per 1860 census. Served in 1st Md. Arty. Enl. Richmond 5/1/63. Captured at Harpers Ferry, W.Va., 10/2/63; exchanged. Present through 12/31/64. Captured, date, place unknown; sent to Pt. Lookout; exchanged 2/10/65. In Richmond hosp. 2/14–15/65. Paroled, took oath, Harpers Ferry, W.Va, 5/29/65. Age twenty-two, 5'8", dark complexion, dark hair, dark eyes, res. of Cumberland, Md.

ANDERSON, OSCAR: Pvt., Co. C. Enl. New Market, Va., 2/1/62. Captured South Mt., Md., 7/4/63; sent to Ft. Del.; transf. to Ft. McHenry. Ab. as POW on rolls through 12/63. NFR.

ANDREWS, J.: Pvt., Co. G. Paroled Staunton, Va., 5/24/65.

ANNAN, ROGER PERRY: Pvt., Co. G. b. Cumberland, Md., 8/23/44. Att. Winchester Acad. Enl. Co. G, 7th Va. Cav., 5/1/62. Transf. to Co. G, 1st Md. Cav., 7/7/64. Captured Winchester 9/19/64; sent to Pt. Lookout; exchanged 3/15/65. Paroled Charles Town, W.Va., 5/5/65. 5'11", light complexion, brown hair, brown eyes. Postwar res. of Cumberland, Md.; moved to St. Louis, Mo., 1867. Broker and Commission Merchant, Webster Grove, Mo. d. St. Louis, Mo., 5/20/18. Bur. Bellefontaine Cem., St. Louis.

ARCHER, WILLIAM H.: Pvt., Co. B. In Richmond hosp. with dysentery 12/28/63–1/7/64. Paroled Brownsville, Tex., 6/25/65, res. of Howard Co., Md.; transportation furnished to Howard Co.

ARMSTRONG, JOSHUA: Pvt., Co. A. Res. of Howard Co., Md. Enl. Lacey Springs, Va., 4/10/63; present 7–8/63; ab. on duty 9–10/63; present 11–12/63 and 4/1/64; ab. on horse detail to Loudoun Co., Va., for seventeen days 4/9/64. Captured Hanover Junction, Va., 6/1/64; sent to Pt. Lookout; released 5/14/65. Farmer, res. of Baltimore Co., Md.

ARTERS, ROBERT: Pvt., Co. C, Davis's Bn. Captured, Webster Co., 2/8/64; sent to Wheeling. Age sixteen, 5'7", fair complexion, blond hair, blue eyes, Farmer, res. of Webster Co. Transf. to Camp Chase; d. there of diarrhea 12/16/64. Bur. Camp Chase Cem., Oh., grave #622.

ARTIS, JEREMIAH: Pvt., Co. A. b. St. Mary's Co., Md., 1838. "Gentleman" per 1860 census. Enl. Co. K (2nd), 1st Va. Cav., 10/1/61. Transf. to Co. A, 1st Md. Cav., 5/15/62; present 7–10/63; on rolls 11–12/63; ab. on duty 12/20/63; ab. on detached service 4/1/64. Transf. to 2nd Md. Inf. 5/14/64; des. to the enemy 9/1/64. Res. Smithersville, St. Mary's Co., Md.

ASHBY, R. W.: Pvt., Co. F. b. circa 1832. Enl. Richmond 7/6/63. Transf. to Co. E, 23rd Va. Cav., 10/24/63. Paroled Winchester 4/28/65. Age thirty-five, 5'11", dark complexion, dark hair, brown eyes. Res. of Newtown, Frederick Co., Va.

ASQUITH, HOBART: Pvt., Co. B. b. Md. circa 1845. Res. Anne Arundel Co., Md. Enl. Charlottesville 9/10/62; present Sharpsburg and Fredericksburg, Md., and Gettysburg, Pa.; present 7–12/63; horse died in camp 2/16/64; Scout for Gen. Wade Hampton; ab. sick with scabies in Charlottesville hosp. 8/31–12/31/64. NFR. Grocer, Baltimore. Entered Old Soldiers' Home, Pikesville, Md., 3/3/14, from Minneapolis, Minn. d. Baltimore 8/16/37. Bur. Loudon Park Cem., Baltimore.

ATKINSON, HENRY C.: Pvt., Co. C, Davis's Bn. Captured Harrisonburg, Va., 9/27/64; sent to Pt. Lookout; took oath, joined U.S. forces 10/14/64.

ATWATER, JOHN W.: Pvt., Co. F. Enl. Co. B, Md. Arty., 1861. In Richmond hosp. 5/28/62; discharged 7/12/62. Reenl. Co. D, 19th Bn. Va. Arty., 7/7/62. NFR. Enl. Co. F, 1st Md. Cav., 3/26/64; present 4/1/64; ab. on horse detail 4/20–31/64; ab. on horse detail to Hardy Co., W.Va., for a horse 5/1/64; ab. on horse detail 11–12/64, and "Unheard from since." NFR. Member ANS/MLA, 1894.

AUGUST, B.: Pvt., Co. F WIA (leg) Beaver Dam Station, Va., 5/9/64; on casualty list. NFR.

AULD, CHARLES S.: Pvt., Co. A. b. circa 1842. Res. of Baltimore. Enl. Wise Va. Arty. at Martinsburg, W.Va., 4/19/61. Transf. to Co. A, 1st Md. Cav., 6/5/62. Captured Martinsburg 10/1/62; sent to Ft. McHenry; exchanged 11/10/62. Captured Hampshire Co., W.Va., 5/9/63; sent to Wheeling. Age twenty-one, 5'8½", florid complexion, dark hair, dark eyes. Farmer. Transf. to

Camp Chase, Johnson's Island, and Ft. Del.; took oath, joined U.S. service 2/27/64.

AYERS, JOHN: Pvt., Co. C, Davis's Bn. Enl. Buffalo Gap, W.Va., 8/6/63. Transf. to Co. F, 23rd Va. Cav.; in arrest by civil authorities 10/31/64. NFR.

BADEN, JOHN HOLLIDAY: Pvt., Co. B. b. circa 1840. Res. of Prince George's Co., Md. Enl. Charlottesville 9/10/62; ab. sick with typhoid fever in Charlottesville hosp. 10/11/62. d. Charlottesville 10/30/62. Bur. Confederate Cem., U. of Va.; removed to Loudon Park Cem., Baltimore, 1874.

BADEN, JOSEPH N.: Pvt., Co. B. Res. of Nottingham, Prince George's Co., Md. Enl. Charlottesville 9/10/62; ab. on detached service in Signal Corps 1/63–4/1/64; detached in Secret Service 8/31–12/3/64. Paroled Richmond 4/28/65.

BADEN, WILLIAM ALBERT KERR: Pvt., Co. E. b. Prince George's Co., Md., 2/22/39. Enl. Richmond 1/7/63; horse died 5/23/63; present 7–8/63; WIA (scalp-skull fractured) at Morton's Ford, Va., 11/10/63; ab. wounded in Richmond hospitals until retired to Invalid Corps 10/19/64. Paroled Richmond 4/27/65. Farmer. d. 5/21/72. Bur. St. Paul's Episcopal Ch. Cem., Prince George's Co., Md.

BAILEY, _____: Pvt., Co. unknown. KIA Winchester 6/23/63. Bur. Stonewall Cem., Winchester.

BAKER, GEORGE W.: Pvt., Co. A, Davis's Bn. b. Va. 1/26/45. Enl. New Market, Va., 11/20/63. WIA near Woodstock, Va., 5/64. Transf. to Co. M, 23rd Va. Cav. Paroled Staunton, Va., 5/15/65. Age twenty, dark complexion, black hair, black eyes. d. Rockingham Co., Va., 4/14/28. Bur. Shady Grove Brethren Ch. Cem., Rockingham Co.

BAKER, HENRY W. (alias LEWIS): Pvt., Co. E. Res. of Baltimore. Enl. Co. G, 1st S.C. Inf., 7/63; discharged. Enl. Co. E, 1st Md. Cav., Earlysville, Va., 7/25/64. Captured at Moorefield, W.Va., 8/7/64; sent to Wheeling. Age seventeen, 5'8", light complexion, brown hair, blue eyes. Painter. Transf. to Camp Chase; exchanged 3/4/65. In Richmond hosp. 3/11–12/65; transf. to Camp Lee, Richmond, 3/17–18/65; ab. sick with "Feb. Int." in Gordonsville, Va., hosp. 3/23–24/65. Paroled Winchester 4/27/65. "Ordered north of Phila., Pa." Res. of Baltimore postwar. Member ANS/MLA, 1894.

BAKER, WILLIAM H.: Pvt., Co. A. Res. of Annapolis, Md. Paroled Harrisonburg, Va., 5/31/65. Age twenty-one, 5'9", dark complexion, light hair, blue eyes.

BARBER, CHRISTOPHER COLUMBUS: Pvt., Co. B. b. St. Mary's Co., Md., circa 1837. Res. of

Chaptico, St. Mary's Co. Enl. Hanover CH, Va., 8/4/62; detailed as Teamster 11/25–12/31/62; present 4/1–12/31/64. Captured Hanover Junction, Va., 3/13/65; sent to Pt. Lookout; released 6/10/65. 5'9¾", dark complexion, brown hair, blue eyes. Married St. Mary's Co. 6/19/77, age thirty. Res. of Charles Co., Md.

BARBOUR, OSCAR: Pvt., Co. C. b. circa 1829. Res. of Frederick Co., Md. Enl. Co. K (2nd), 1st Va. Cav., 8/4/61. Transf. to Co. C, 1st Md. Cav., 8/4/62. Captured near Winchester 9/28/62; sent to Ft. McHenry; exchanged 11/10/62; detailed as Teamster 12/62; present 7–9/63; ab. sick with dysentery in Richmond hosp. 10/10/63–4/1/64. Captured Moorefield, W.Va., 8/7/64; sent to Wheeling. Age thirty-five, 5'8", dark complexion, dark hair, dark eyes. Attorney. Transf. to Camp Chase; exchanged 3/4/65. NFR.

JAMES W.
BARR

(Ben Ritter)

BARHARD, EDWARD: Pvt., Co. G. Captured Strasburg, Va., 4/26/63; sent to Ft. McHenry; exchanged 5/14/63. NFR.

BARNES, JOHN: Pvt., Co. F. NFR.

BARNES, RICHARD MARION: Pvt., Co. C. b. Washington Co., Md., circa 1834. Enl. Co. B, 21st Va. Inf., 5/23/61. 6'1½", dark hair, dark eyes. Present 10–12/61. NFR. Enl. Co. C, 1st Md. Cav., Hanover CH, Va., 5/15/63. Captured South Mt., Md., 7/4/63; sent to Ft. McHenry; transf. to Ft. Del. and Pt. Lookout; exchanged 3/6/64. Present 6–12/64. Paroled Washington, D.C., 6/10/65. 6'2½", light complexion, brown hair, blue eyes. Res. Washington, D.C.

BARR, JAMES W. (photo): Pvt., Co. C. b. Winchester, Va., 8/14/37. Captured Winchester 8/13/62. NFR. Served later in Co. G, 25th Bn. Va., Local Defense Troops, Richmond. Manufacturer in Winchester postwar. Member Gen. Turner Ashby Camp, CV, Winchester. d. 9/4/99. Bur. Mt. Hebron Cem., Winchester.

BARRICK, WILLIAM T.: Pvt., Co. D. b. 9/9/33. Res. of Frederick Co., Md. Enl. Woodstock, Va. 7/5/62; ab. on horse detail to Shenandoah Co., Va., for ten days 4/1/64; des. 5/64; on rolls to 8/64. NFR. d. 7/11/86. Bur. Bethel Cem., Good Intent Rd., Frederick Co., Md.

BARRY, DANIEL R.: Pvt., Co. K. b. circa 1840. Res. of Baltimore. Enl. Co. C, 1st Md. Inf., 5/17/61; discharged 6/5/62. Age twenty-two, 5'10", light complexion, dark hair, blue eyes. Clerk. Enl. Co. K (2nd), 1st Va. Cav., 6/10/62. Transf. to Co. K, 1st Md. Cav., 8/64; present through 8/31/64; issued clothing 9/20 and 11/14/64; discharged 12/23/64. Paroled Richmond 4/20/65; took oath Ft. Monroe 4/24/65; transportation furnished to Baltimore.

BARRY, WILLIAM D.: Pvt., Co. D. b. Prince George's Co., Md., circa 1843. Res. of Prince George's Co. Enl. Charlottesville 9/10/62; present 7–8/63; ab. sick with dysentery in Richmond hosp. 10/14–11/15/63; present through 12/31/63 and 4/1/64; ab. on horse detail to Hardy Co., W.Va., for twenty days 4/7/64. Captured Moorefield, W.Va., 8/7/64; sent to Wheeling. Age twenty-two, 6'1", light complexion, brown hair, blue eyes. Farmer. Transf. to Camp Chase; exchanged 3/12/65. NFR. Member George Emack Camp, CV, Hyattsville, Md. Tobacconist, Baltimore, 1906.

BASKIN, JOHN: Pvt., Co. A, Davis's Bn. Enl. Waynesboro, Va. 9/1/64; present through 10/31/64. Transf. to Co. M, 23rd Va. Cav. NFR.

BASKINS, CHARLES N.: Pvt., Co. A, Davis's Bn. b. Va. 4/25/45. Student, N. Dist., Augusta Co., Va., per 1860 census. Enl. Waynesboro, Va., 9/1/64; present through 10/31/64. Transf. to Co. M, 23rd Va. Cav. Paroled Staunton, Va., 5/13/65. Age nineteen, 5'8", light complexion, light hair, blue eyes. d. Augusta Co., Va. 11/7/96. Bur. Tinkling Spring Presb. Ch. Cem., Augusta Co.

BATEMAN, HOWARD A.: Pvt., Co. C. Enl. Williamsport, Md., 7/6/63; present through 12/31/64. Paroled Appomattox CH, Va., 4/9/65. Took oath 5/20/65. Received Cross of Honor, Alaska, W.Va. 1905.

BATTE, ROBERT: Pvt., Co. C, Davis's Bn. On postwar roster.

BAUGHMAN, LOUIS VICTOR: Pvt., Co. D. b. Frederick, Md., 4/11/45. Att. Rock Hill Col. and St. Mary's Col., Md. Served in 2nd Md. Inf., but not on muster rolls. Transf. to Co. D, 1st Md. Cav., Frederick, Md., 7/1/64. Served as scout for Gen. Breckinridge. WIA, captured Moorefield, W.Va., 8/7/64, horse killed; sent to Wheeling. 5'5", fair complexion, black hair, brown eyes. Gentleman. Transf. to Camp Chase; exchanged 3/12/65. Ab. on leave at the surrender. Took oath

6/2/65. Went to Canada. Studied law in N.Y. Lawyer; moved back to Frederick, Md. Editor, *Frederick Citizen;* President, C&O Canal Co.; Md. State Comptroller; President, Frederick, Northern, and Gettysburg RR; Farmer and Journalist. d. Frederick, Md., 11/30/06. Bur. St. John's Catholic Ch. Cem., Frederick, Md. (Postwar photograph in Evans 1898, Maryland volume.)

BEALE, ALEXANDER "SANDY": Pvt., Co. B. b. St. Inigo's Dist., St. Mary's Co., Md., 6/24/39. Res. of St. Mary's Co. Enl. Charlottesville 10/9/62; ab. sick with "Febris Remitten" in Charlottesville hosp. through 10/18/62. Captured Monterey Springs, Pa.; 7/5/63; sent to Ft. Delaware; transf. to Pt. Lookout; exchanged 12/24/63. Paid 1/2/64; present 4/1/64; ab. sick in hosp. 8/31–12/31/64. Captured Frederick's Hall, Va., 3/13/65; sent to Ft. Monroe; transf. to Pt. Lookout; released 5/15/65; transportation furnished to Baltimore. Clerk. Purser for Weem's Steamboat Co. for thirty years. Member George Emack Camp, CV, Hyattsville, Md. Res. of Baltimore. d. 8/2/24. Bur. St. Michael's Catholic Cem., Ridge, St. Mary's Co., Md.

BEAN, THOMAS L.: Pvt., Co. B. b. St. Mary's Co., Md., circa 1841. Enl. Co. G, 13th Va. Inf., 5/28/61; discharged as nonresident 5/28/62. Ab. sick with "Febris Intermitt" in Charlottesville hosp. 10/17–11/11/62; present 7–12/63 and 3–12/64. Paroled Washington, D.C., 4/26/65. Shoe Merchant, Baltimore. Member Isaac Trimble Camp, CV. d. Baltimore 2/8/99, age fifty-seven. Bur. Greenmount Cem.

BEAN, WILLIAM N.: Pvt., Co. B. b. St. Mary's Co., Md., circa 1848. Student, age twelve, St. Mary's Co., per 1860 census. Enl. Charlottesville 9/10/62; ab. sick at Strasburg, Va., 12/20/62; present 7–9/63; ab. sick with scabies in Charlottesville hosp. 1/10–11/12/63; present 12/63; ab. on horse detail to Winchester for seventeen days 2/1/64; sick in camp 4/1/64; present through 12/64. Captured Hanover Junction, Va., 3/13/65; sent to Pt. Lookout; released 6/10/65. 5'10½", dark complexion, dark hair, dark eyes. Res. of Washington, D.C., postwar. Member George Emack Camp, CV, Hyattsville, Md., 1906.

BEASTON, GEORGE M.: Pvt., Co. F. b. Md. circa 1839. Res. of "Locust Grove," Kent Co., Md. Enl. CSN 10/1/62; discharged for disability 12/1/62. Enl. in Hosp. Service 12/6/62. NFR. Enl. Co. F, 1st Md. Cav., Richmond, 7/1/63; present through 12/63 and 4/1/64. Captured Pollard's Farm, Va., 5/27/64; sent to Pt. Lookout; transf. to Elmira; exchanged 3/19/65. Paroled Richmond 6/26/65; transportation furnished to Cecil Co., Md. Mem-

ber ANS/MLA. d. "Locust Grove," Kent Co., Md., 8/10/15, age seventy-six. Bur. Shrewsbury Ch. Cem.

BEATTY, EDWARD W.: 2nd Lt., Co. A. b. Montgomery Co., Md., 9/40. Res. of Baltimore. Enl. as Pvt., Co. K (2nd), 1st Va. Cav., 6/20/61. Transf. to Co. A, 1st Md. Cav., 5/15/62, and promoted Cpl.; elected 3rd Lt. 11/25/62. WIA (left shoulder) at Greenland Gap, W.Va., 4/25/63; promoted 2nd Lt. Captured Brandy Station, Va., 10/11/63; sent to Old Capitol; transf. to Johnson's Island; d. there of "chronic diarrhoea" 3/24/64, age twenty-three years and six months. Bur. Rockville Cem., Rockville, Md.

BECKHAM, HENRY: Pvt., Co. C, Davis's Bn. On postwar roster.

BECTELL, FREDERICK F.: Pvt., Co. F. Enl. Co. F, 1st Md. Inf., 5/22/61; present 9–12/61. NFR. Enl. Co. F, 1st Md. Cav., Richmond, 6/29/63; present through 8/31/63; des. to the enemy from outpost on the Rappahannock River 10/27/63; sent to Old Capitol; d. there 2/26/64.

BECTELL, JOHN M.: Pvt., Co. A. b. circa 1843. Res. of Washington Co., Md. Enl. Wise Va. Arty., Martinsburg, W.Va., 9/17/61. Transf. to Co. A, 1st Md. Cav., Charlottesville, 6/5/62; present 7–12/63 and 4/1/64. "Absent term of service expired—no discharge"; on rolls 11–12/64. Paroled Winchester 6/15/65. Age twenty-two, 5'11", light complexion, light hair, gray eyes.

BELL, HENRY C.: Pvt., Co. A. b. 1840. Res. of Hagerstown, Md. Enl. Hagerstown 7/1/63; present through 12/63; ab. on horse detail to Woodstock, Va., for eight days 1/9/64; present through 12/64. Paroled Winchester 5/14/65; destination Baltimore. Res. of Ellicott City, Md., postwar. d. 1927. Bur. Rose Hill Cem., Hagerstown, Md.

BENDER, FRANCIS T. "FRANK": Pvt., Co. A. Res. of Frederick or Washington Co., Md. Enl. Co. A, 1st Md. Inf., 5/21/61; ab. sick in Richmond hosp. 5/16/62. NFR. Enl. Co. A, 1st Md. Cav., Winchester, 11/1/62; present 7–12/63 and 4/1/64. "Term of service expired. Absent on detached service"; on rolls to 8/31/64. NFR.

BERNER, AUGUST: Pvt., Co. F. Enl. Richmond 7/6/63; present through 12/63 and 4/1/64. WIA (flesh wound right thigh and inside left knee) Beaver Dam Station, Va., 5/9/64; ab. wounded until furloughed to Mobile, Ala., for forty days 6/7/64; des. 6/29/64 on hosp. report; ab., wounded, through 12/64 on muster rolls. NFR.

BETTS, SAMUEL C.: Pvt., Co. K. b. Md. circa 1844. Age sixteen, Freedom Dist., Carroll Co., Md., per 1860 census. Enl. Co. K (2nd) 1st Va. Cav., 9/1/62. Captured Hartwood Ch., Va, 3/25/63; sent to Old Capitol; exchanged 3/63.

WIA Jerrell's Mill, Va., 5/9/64. Transf. to Co. K, 1st Md. Cav., 8/64. Paroled Winchester 4/18/65. Res. of Woodbine, Carroll Co., postwar.

BETTS, WILLIAM: Pvt., Co. unknown. Res. of Carroll Co., Md.

BEUNEFIELD, DANIEL: Pvt., Co. C, Davis's Bn. On postwar roster.

BIAYS, GEORGE: Pvt., Co. C. b. Washington Co., Md., 5/20/41. Enl. New Market, Va., 1/1/63; ab. sick with scabies in Gordonsville, Va., hosp. 3/30/63; present 7/63–12/64. Paroled Salisbury, N.C., 5/1/65. Hardware Manufacturer, Baltimore. Member ANS/MLA d. 5/28/13. Bur. Greenmont Cem., Baltimore.

BIDDLE, BENJAMIN S.: Pvt., Co. F. Captured Strasburg, Va., 9/22–23/64; sent to Pt. Lookout; released 4/30/65.

BIGGER, JOHN D.: Pvt., Co. K. Enl. Co. K (2nd), 1st Va. Cav., 6/10/62; present until captured at Gettysburg, Pa., 7/6/63; sent to Pt. Lookout. Transf. to Co. K, 1st Md. Cav., while POW; exchanged 9/10/64. Discharged 12/20/64. NFR.

BILLOPP, CHRISTOPHER: Pvt., Co. C. b. 11/2/36. Res. of Baltimore. Enl. New Market, Md., 9/1/62; recommended by Gen. Isaac Trimble for commission in Engineer Corps; present 9–12/63; horse died on scout 12/24/63; ab. on horse detail to Winchester for twelve days 1/9/64; AWOL 2/1–29/64; present 4/1/64. Captured Moorefield, W.Va., 8/7/64; sent to Wheeling. 5'8", dark complexion, dark hair, brown eyes. Engineer. Transf. to Camp Chase; exchanged 3/12/65. NFR. Member ANS/MLA d. 10/21/10. Bur. St. Barnabas's Episcopal Ch. Cem., Prince George's Co., Md.

BIRCH, J. A.: Pvt., Co. A. b. Charles Co., Md. circa 1845. Res. of St. Mary's Co., Md. On postwar roster.

BIRD, CHARLES DUPONT: Pvt., Co. B, Davis's Bn. b. circa 1837. Res. of Carroll Co., Md. Enl. Co. D, 1st Md. Inf., 6/1/61; discharged 8/17/62. Also claimed service in Co. C, 12th Va. Inf., and Co. G, 2nd Md. Cav. Entered Old Soldiers' Home, Pikesville, Md., from Philadelphia, Pa., 1/3/11, age seventy-four, Accountant. Member ANS/MLA. d. 10/3/12. Bur. Loudon Park Cem., Baltimore.

BISHOP, CHARLES E.: Capt., Co. B, Davis's Bn. Res. of Carroll Co., Md. Enl. Co. D, 1st Md. Inf., 6/1/61; present 9–12/61. NFR. In Petersburg, Va., hosp. 3/13/65 as Capt., Co. G, 2nd Md. Cav. NFR.

BLACKISTONE, HENRY CURTIS "HARRY": 2nd Lt., Co. B. b. Sassafras, Kent Co., Md., 6/8/38. Enl. as 3rd Lt., Winchester, 9/10/62; present through 12/62; presence or ab. not stated 7–8/63; present 9/63; ab. sick with "Feb Remit" in Charlottesville hosp. 10/10–11/63; present 12/63;

ab. on leave for fifteen days 1/23/64. Elected 2nd Lt.; ab. sick with "orchitis" in Richmond hosp. 3/8–4/17/64; present 7/64. "In charge of detail that burned the summer lodge of Maryland Governor Augustus W. Bradford near Elkridge in retaliation for the burning of Governor [John] Letcher's home in Lexington, Va." DOW received Bunker Hill, W.Va., 9/3/64. "Taken to the porch of Judge Boyd, where he died in a short time." Bur. Zion Episcopal Ch. Cem., Charleston, W.Va. Brother of Samuel H. Blackistone.

BLACKISTONE, SAMUEL HEPBRON: Pvt., Co. B. b. Kent Co., Md., 1836. Res. Sassafras, Kent Co. Enl. Charlottesville 10/1/62; present 7–12/63 and 4/1/64; ab. on horse detail 8/31/64; issued clothing 9/30/64; ab. sick with "Remittent Fever" in Charlottesville hosp. 10/5–17/64; ab. on horse detail through 11/3/64; present through 12/31/64. Paroled Richmond 5/15/65. Member ANS/MLA, Baltimore. d. 1887. Brother of Henry C. Blackistone.

BLAKELY, WILLIAM H.: Pvt., Co. K. b. circa 1844. Enl. Co. K (2nd), 1st Va. Cav., Martinsburg, W.Va., 9/10/62; present until transf. to Co. K, 1st Md. Cav., 8/64; ab. detailed as ambulance driver for Gen. Fitzhugh Lee 3/1–12/31/64. Paroled Winchester 4/23/65. Age twenty-one, 5'8", dark complexion, dark hair, hazel eyes. Res. Washington Co., Md.

BLAND, JOHN: Pvt., Co. D. Captured Brandy Station, Va., 10/11/63; sent to Pt. Lookout; exchanged 10/15/64. Res. Prince George's Co., Md. NFR.

BLAND, JOHN BOLLING: Pvt., Co. D. b. Va. circa 1845. Captured Prince George's Co., Md., 5/6/64; sent to Pt. Lookout; exchanged 3/14/65. NFR. Merchant, Baltimore. Member Baltimore City Council. d. Baltimore 11/16/95, age fifty. Bur. Hollywood Cem., Richmond.

BLODGETT, WILLIAM: Pvt., Co. A, Davis's Bn. Medical Doctor. Enl. Richmond 6/26/63. Transf. to Co. M, 23rd Va. Cav. Captured near Lacey Springs, Va., 12/21/64; sent to Pt. Lookout; released 6/5/65.

BOARMAN, JEROME N.: Pvt., Co. B. Gd. Georgetown U. 1836. Res. of Baltimore. Enl. Charlottesville 9/10/62; present 7/63–12/64. NFR. Res. Charles Co., Md., postwar.

BOARMAN, JOSEPH M.: Pvt., Co. B. Res. Charles Co., Md. Joined from Breathed's Battery Horse Arty. circa 1/64, but not on muster rolls of that unit; ab. on leave for twenty days to Hardy Co., W.Va., for a horse 4/9/64; issued clothing 9/30/64; ab. sick with scabies in Charlottesville hosp. 10/16/64; transf. to Lynchburg, Va., hosp. 10/26/64. NFR. d. by 1904.

BOGUE, FRANCIS: Pvt., Co. C. Captured near Washington, D.C., 7/10–12/64; sent to Old Capitol; transf. to Elmira; exchanged 2/24/65. NFR.

BOLDEN, DANIEL: Pvt., Co. G. Ab. sick in Richmond hosp. 11/19/64; furloughed for thirty days 11/20/64. NFR.

BOLLMAN, JOHN M.: Pvt., Co. K. b. circa 1842. Enl. Breathed's Battery Horse Arty., Petersburg, Va., 7/10/62. WIA Union 11/2/62. Transf. to Co. K (2nd), 1st Va. Cav., 8/14/64. Transf. to Co. K, 1st Md. Cav., 8/15/64; sent to Ft. McHenry; transf. to Pt. Lookout; exchanged 2/20/65. Paroled New Market, Va., 4/19/65. Age twenty-three, 5'7", dark complexion, dark hair, grey eyes. Machinist. Took oath 4/22/65, res. Baltimore, destination Baltimore. d. by 1903.

BOMAN, JOSEPH M.: Pvt., Co. B. Joined from Breathed's Battery Horse Arty. per postwar roster. Probably Joseph M. Boarman, above.

BOND, ARTHUR WEBSTER: Sgt. Maj. b. 1842. Res. Anne Arundel Co., Md. Served as Lt. and AAG, Md. Line, 6/25–7/1/62. Enl. as 3rd Cpl., Co. A, 1st Md. Cav., Charlottesville, 8/25/62; present 7–12/63; promoted Sgt. Maj. of the Regt. by 3/64; present 4/1/64; WIA (left thigh) 6/9/64; ab. wounded in Richmond hosp. until furloughed to Athens, Ga., for forty days; RTD 9/15/64; ab. sick with gonorrhea in Charlottesville hosp. 11/2–12/31/64; present when disbanded Cloverdale, Va., 4/28/65. Paroled Salisbury, N.C., 6/24/65. Took oath 6/29/65; transportation furnished to Anne Arundel Co., Md. Businessman, Baltimore. Member Francis Buchanan Camp, CV, Baltimore, and ANS/MLA. d. Millersville, Md., 4/11/31. Bur. St. Stephens Episcopal Ch. Cem., Millersville. Brother of Frank A. Bond.

BOND, BEVERLY WAUGH: Pvt., Co. A. b. "White House," Harford Co., Md., 9/5/43. On postwar roster Co. K (2nd), 1st Va. Cav. Enl. Co. A, 1st Md. Cav., date unknown. Took oath Harpers Ferry, W.Va., 5/10/65. Minister in postwar. d. Baltimore 1/22/20. Bur. Druid Ridge Cem., Pikesville.

BOND, FRANK AUGUSTUS: Capt., Co. A. b. Bel Air, Harford Co., Md., 2/6/38. Farmer, Bel Air. Capt., United Rifles, Md. State Guard. On postwar roster of Co. D, 1st Md. Inf. Served as Capt. and Drillmaster on staff of Gen. Thomas J. Jackson. Enl. as Pvt., Co. K (2nd), 1st Va. Cav., Leesburg, Va., 5/14/61; elected 2nd Lt.; present until not reelected 4/23/62; elected 1st Lt., Co. A, 1st Md. Cav., 5/15/62. Served as AAG on Gen. G. H. Steuart's staff at Cross Keys, Va., and Seven Days Campaign; WIA 2nd Manassas 8/30/62; present 10/62; elected Capt. 11/12/62; present until WIA (right knee—fractured head of tibia

followed by gangrene and anchylosis of knee joint) and captured Hagerstown, Md., 7/8/63; sent to Ft. McHenry; transf. to Pt. Lookout; exchanged 4/30/64. Furloughed to Athens, Ga., 7/28/64. Retired to Invalid Corps 10/64. Promoted Maj. on staff of Gen. Leventhorpe in N.C. Paroled Greensboro, N.C., 5/1/65. Took oath Baltimore 5/16/65. Farmer, Anne Arundel Co. Adj. Gen., Md. National Guard, 1874–81; Gen., Md. National Guard, 1899. Supt. of Md. House of Corrections until 1908. Member Confederate Veterans Association, Washington, D.C.; moved to N.C. d. on visit to his daughter in Philadelphia, Pa., 11/12/23. Bur. Loudon Park Cem., Baltimore. Brother of Arthur W. Bond. "His company was so thoroughly disciplined that it was chosen by Gen. Ewell to accompany him for special advance and other duties on the invasion of Pa."

BOND, H.: Pvt., Co. A. Enl. Winchester 8/1/64; present until reported captured Fisher's Hill, Va., 9/22/64. Not on Federal POW rolls; probably KIA.

BOND, JOHN W.: Pvt., Co. B. b. circa 1834. Res. Bel Air, Harford Co, Md. Enl. Charlottesville 9/10/62; present 7–10/63; ab. sick with scabies in Richmond hosp. 11/19–12/15/63; present 12/31/63; ab. on detail for twenty days to get a horse 3/15/64; present until ab. sick with syphilis in Petersburg, Va., hosp. 6/2/64; transf. to Kittrell, N.C., hosp. 6/18/64. Captured Harrisonburg, Va., 9/25/64; sent to Pt. Lookout; exchanged 3/17/65. Paroled Richmond 4/25/65. Arrested Baltimore 4/30/65; released to go to N.Y. 5/5/65.

BOND, WESLEY WILLIAM: Pvt., Co. A. b. circa 1841. Res. St. Mary's Co., Md. Enl. Hanover Junction, Va., 1/5/63; present 11/63–12/64. Paroled Winchester 5/2/65. Age twenty-four, 5'9", dark complexion, dark hair, blue eyes.

BOND, WILLIAM WESLEY: Pvt., Co. A. b. circa 1828. On postwar roster. Res. Howard Co. d. Baltimore 2/3/79, age fifty-one.

BONN, JOSEPH: 2nd Sgt., Co. F. b. circa 1842. Res. Ruxton, Baltimore Co., Md. Enl. Co. H, 1st Va. Inf., 5/4/61, age nineteen; discharged 6/5/62. Enl. as 2nd Sgt., Co. F, 1st Md. Cav., Richmond, 7/15/63; present through 8/31/63; WIA Morton's Ford, Va., 10/11/63; ab. wounded in Richmond hosp. until present 11–12/63 and 4/1/64; reduced to Pvt. 4/28/64. Captured Old Church, Va., 5/27/64; sent to Pt. Lookout; exchanged 2/18/65. Paroled Richmond 4/21/65. Took oath Richmond 4/22/65; transportation furnished to Baltimore.

BONN, SAMUEL G.: 2nd Lt., Co. F. b. circa 1838. Res. Baltimore. Enl. as Pvt., Co. A, Yorktown, 5/1/62; promoted 2nd Lt., Co. F, 7/16/63; present through 8/31/63; ab. sick with acute dysentery in Charlottesville hosp. 9/25–10/9/63; transf. to Richmond hosp. 10/10/63; RTD 10/16/63; presence or ab. not stated 11–12/63; ab. acting Ord. Officer— now ab. on leave 4/1/64. Captured Moorefield, W.Va., 8/7/64; sent to Wheeling. Age twenty-six, 5'11", light complexion, gray eyes, brown hair. Merchant. Transf. to Camp Chase; exchanged 3/12/65. Surrendered Appomattox CH, Va., 4/9/65. Paroled Richmond 4/22/65. Took oath Richmond 4/25/65. Former res. of N.Y., destination Baltimore.

BONNE, WILLIAM C. "BILLY": Pvt., Co. E. b. circa 1844. Enl. Camp Lee, Richmond, 12/22/62, age eighteen; ab. sick with "Erysipelas" in Charlottesville hosp. 3/17–4/27/63. Captured near Winchester 6/12/63; sent to Old Capitol; transf. to Ft. McHenry; exchanged 6/26/63. Age nineteen, fair complexion, gray eyes, light hair. Res. Washington, D.C. Horse killed at Winchester 6/2/63, paid $230. Captured at Raccoon or Germanna Ford, Va., 10/11/63; sent to Old Capitol; transf. to Pt. Lookout; exchanged 3/8/64. Captured Moorefield, W.Va., 8/7/64; sent to Wheeling, age twenty; transf. to Camp Chase; exchanged 3/12/65. Admitted Richmond hosp. with "Dyspepsia" 3/12/65; furloughed to Lynchburg, Va., for thirty days 3/16/65. Surrendered Greensboro, N.C., 5/8/65.

BOOKER, WILLIAM T.: Pvt., Co. E. b. circa 1843. Enl. Camp Lee 10/12/62, age nineteen; present through 9/30/63; ab. to get a fresh horse 10/28–31/63; present 11–12/63; ab. on leave for thirty days 3/24/64; ab. sick Dayton, Va., 8/1–31/64; AWOL 11–12/64. NFR.

BOOTH, GEORGE WILSON: Adj. b. Md. 7/29/44. Att. Baltimore City Col. Clerk. Enl. as Pvt., Co. D, 1st Md. Inf., 5/22/61; promoted Adj., 1st Md. Inf., 9–12/61; elected 1st Lt. 5/62; promoted AAG on Gen. Bradley Johnson's staff, Md. Line. WIA (thigh) 2nd Manassas 8/30/62. Transf. to 1st Md. Cav. as Adj. 1/20/63; WIA (thigh) Greenland Gap, W.Va., 4/23/63; present Gettysburg, Pa., and Brandy Station, Va. Transf. to Md. Line as AAG 11/63; present 2/6/64; WIA Pollard's Farm, Va., 5/27/64; present Trevilian Station, Va.; promoted Capt. and AAG, Johnson's Brigade, 6/64; present at Moorefield, W.Va., Winchester, and Fisher's Hill, Va.; accompanied Gen. Johnson to Salisbury, N.C., prison. Paroled Richmond 4/22/65 and Salisbury, N.C., 5/65. Businessman, Baltimore, 1865–66. Farmer, Essex Co., Va., twelve years. Auditor, B&O RR. Authored *Personal Reminiscences of a Maryland Soldier in the War between the States*, 1898. d. Baltimore 1/6/14. Bur. Loudon Park Cem., Baltimore.

BORDAREX, CHARLES A.: Pvt., Co. C, Davis's Bn. NFR.

BOUGHLON, _____: Lt., Co. unknown; present 9/7/62.

BOULDIN, DANIEL: Pvt., Co. A, Davis's Bn. b. Md. circa 1842. Res. of Baltimore. Enl. Co. D, 18th Bn. Va. Arty., Richmond, 5/3/61. Transf. to Co. A, Davis's Bn., 5/23/63. Captured at Middletown, Va., 9/20/63; sent to Ft. McHenry; transf. to Pt. Lookout; exchanged 2/4/65. Transf. to Co. M, 23rd Va. Cav., while POW. Paroled Winchester 4/26/65. Age twenty-three, 6', fair complexion, dark hair, dark eyes. Butcher.

BOURNE, JOSEPH B.: Pvt., Co. E. b. circa 1843. Res. Prince George's Co., Md. Enl. Camp Lee, Richmond, 11/5/62, age nineteen. Captured Winchester 6/12/63; sent to Old Capitol; exchanged 6/26/63; horse killed at Winchester 6/12/63, paid $230; ab. sick with neuralgia in Charlottesville hosp. 8/15–18/63. Captured at Germanna Ford, Va., 10/11/63; sent to Old Capitol; transf. to Pt. Lookout, Ft. McHenry, and Ft. Monroe; took oath and transportation furnished to Nottingham, Md., 3/5/64. NFR.

BOUVE, JOSEPH: Pvt., Co. F. Captured Hanover CH, Va., 5/27/64; sent to Pt. Lookout; exchanged 2/21/65. NFR.

BOWERS or BOWYERS, LAFAYETTE: 2nd Lt., Co. G. Res. Frederick Co., Md. Served as 2nd Lt., Co. B, Davis's Bn., and later Co. G, 1st Md. Cav; des. from 2nd Md. Cav.; arrested Piney Pt., Md., 12/25/64. Age thirty-two, destination Baltimore. NFR.

BOWIE, ALBERT: Pvt., Co. K. On postwar rosters of Co. K (2nd), 1st Va. Cav., and Co. K, 1st Md. Cav. Res. Prince George's Co., Md.

BOWIE, HENRY BRUNE "HARRY": 1st Sgt., Co. K. b. Prince George's Co., Md., 1/26/45. Enl. as Pvt., Co. K (2nd), 1st Va. Cav., 6/10/62; promoted 1st Sgt.; present until WIA (left arm) Spotsylvania CH, Va., 5/9/64; ab. wounded in Richmond hosp. until des. 5/23/64. Transf. to Co. K, 1st Md. Cav., 8/64. Captured near Sandy Springs, Md., with his brother Walter, who was mortally wounded, 10/7/64; sent to Old Capitol; transf. to Elmira and Ft. Warren as "guerrilla"; released 6/15/65. 5'9¾", fair complexion, light hair, gray eyes. Farmer. Lumber Dealer, Baltimore 1872–99. Member Ridgely Brown Camp, CV, Rockville, Md. d. Baltimore 4/6/08.

BOWIE, HENRY CLAY "HARRY": Pvt., Co. C. b. Prince George's Co., Md., 1844. Enl. Beltsville, Md., 7/10/64; present through 8/31/64 and 11–12/64. WIA twice on postwar roster. Paroled Conrad's Ferry, Md., 4/5/65. Merchant, Washington, D.C. d. 9/11/29. Bur. Union Cem., Rockville, Md. (no marker).

BOWLES, ROBERT: Sgt., Co. C, Davis's Bn. On

CHARLES
BRUCE BOYLE

*(Carroll County,
Md., Historical
Society)*

postwar roster.

BOWLING, ALEXANDER: Pvt., Co. B. b. circa 1839. Res. of Bryantown, Charles Co., Md. May have served in 1st Md. Arty. 1861–62. Enl. Charlottesville 9/10/62. Captured Greenland Gap, W.Va., 4/25/63; sent to Ft. McHenry; exchanged 5/4/63. Horse captured at Germanna Ford, Va., 10/11/63; ab. sick with "Remittent Fever" in Richmond hosp. 11/27/63–1/16/64; ab. on horse detail to Newtown, Va., for fifteen days 2/1/64; sick in camp 4/1/64; ab. detailed to Secret Service through 12/31/64; sent to Westmoreland Co., Va., to get a horse. Crossed Potomac, des. to the enemy; took oath Washington, D.C., 1/10/65. "Four horses shot from under him." d. 5/1/04, age sixty-five. Bur. Bryantown, Md.

BOWLING, DANIEL B.: Pvt., Co. B. Res. of Charles Co., Md. Not on muster rolls. KIA Beaver Dam Station, Va., 5/9/64; on casualty list.

BOWLING, NICHOLAS: Pvt., Co. B. b. circa 1840. Res. of Bryantown, Md. Enl. Charlottesville 9/10/62; ab. sick with debility in Charlottesville hosp. 11–12/62; WIA (right thigh) and captured South Mt., Md., 7/4/63; exchanged 9/27/63; ab. wounded in Richmond hosp. 9/28/63, age twenty-three, until furloughed for forty days 10/8/63 and 11–12/63; ab. in Richmond hosp. with "Erysipelas, Chronic" 4/1/64; ab. detailed as Clerk in Richmond hosp. 8/31–12/31/64. Paroled Richmond 4/20/65. Res. of Charles Co., Md.

BOYD, ANDREW G.: Pvt., Co. A. b. 4/20/25. Res. of Washington Co., Md. Enl. Lacey Springs, Va., 4/1/63; present 7/63–12/64; in Charlottesville hosp. 4/9–16/65. Paroled Winchester 5/3/65. 5'8", dark complexion, dark hair, hazel eyes. Took oath Harpers Ferry, W.Va., 5/15/65. Journalist. d. Hagerstown, Md., 10/2/85. Bur. Rose Hill Cem., Hagerstown.

BOYLE, CHARLES BRUCE (photo): Pvt., Co. D. b. Taneytown, Carroll Co., Md., 1841. Att. Calvert

Col. Farmer, age twenty-two, Westminster Dist., Carroll Co., per 1860 census. Enl. Boonsboro, Md., 6/15/63; present through 12/63 and 4/1/64; horse killed Pollard's Farm, Va., 5/27/64, paid $1,000; sorrel horse killed Moorefield, W.Va., 8/7/64, paid $1,900; present through 12/64. NFR. Gd. U. of Md. Medical School 1869. M.D., Hagerstown and Taneytown, Md. d. Hagerstown, 12/10/24. Bur. Rose Hill Cem., Hagerstown.

BRACCO, EDWARD L.: Pvt., Co. A. Res. of Talbot Co., Md. Enl. Yorktown, Va., 5/1/62; ab. sent to Staunton, Va., to get a horse 12/29/62; ab. sick 7/8–11/14/63; present 12/63; ab. sick with ulcer, left leg, in Richmond hosp. 2/22–5/6/64; present through 8/31/64; AWOL 12/31/64. NFR. Attended reunion 1899.

BRADLEY, ISAAC W.: Pvt., Co. B. b. circa 1841. Enl. Orange Co., Va., 9/15/63, age twenty-two years and seven months; present through 12/31/63 and 4/1–8/3/64; issued clothing 9/30/64. Captured Beverly, W.Va., 10/29/64; sent to Wheeling. Age twenty-three, 5'9", dark complexion, gray eyes, dark hair. Transf. to Camp Chase; released 6/12/65. Age twenty-four, 5'8", dark complexion, dark hair, hazel eyes. Farmer. Res. Sussex Co., Del.

BRADSHAW, T. S.: 1st Lt., Co. E, Davis's Bn., and Co. C, 1st Md. Cav. Paroled Harrisonburg, Va., 5/8/65.

BRADY, CHARLES H.: Pvt., Co. A, Davis's Bn. NFR. Paroled Augusta, Ga., 5/19/65, as Pvt., Co. C, 2nd Md. Inf.

BRADY, EUGENE W.: Pvt., Co. K. b. circa 1834. Enl. Co. K (2nd), 1st Va. Cav., Orange CH, 3/1/64. Transf. to Co. K, 1st Md. Cav, 8/64; present through 12/64. Paroled Winchester 4/17/65. Age thirty-one, 5'11½", dark complexion, dark hair, gray eyes. Bur. Petersville Catholic Cem., Frederick Co., Md., no dates.

BRAND, ALEXANDER J. S.: Pvt., Co. K. Res. of Baltimore. Enl. Co. K (2nd), 1st Va. Cav., Richmond, 7/10/62; AWOL 9–10/62; present until AWOL 10/23/63; present through 8/31/64. Transf. to Co. K, 1st Md. Cav., 8/64; ab. sick with scabies in Richmond hosp. 10/64; discharged at end of enlistment 12/20/64. Paroled Richmond 4/16/65. Res. Georgetown, D.C. Took oath 5/11/65; transportation furnished to Baltimore.

BRASHEAR, THOMAS PITTS: Pvt., Co. D. b. Frederick Co., Md., 7/3/39. Res. Merryland Tract, Frederick Co. Enl. Co. G, 7th Va. Cav., 6/21/61; discharged Orange CH, Va., 7/25/62. 6', fair complexion, dark hair, hazel eyes. Enl. Co. D, 1st Md. Cav., Winchester, 9/21/62; ab. sick at Newtown, Va., 11–12/62. Captured Strasburg, Va., 3/5/63; sent to Wheeling. 6'1", dark complexion, gray eyes, dark hair. Transf. to Camp Chase; exchanged 4/2/63. Captured at South Mt., Md., or Monterey Springs, Pa., 7/4/63, horse killed; sent to Ft. Del.; transf. to Pt. Lookout; exchanged 2/21/65. Paroled Harpers Ferry, W.Va., 5/5/65. Member ANS/MLA. d. Frederick, Md., 6/18/84. Bur. Mt. Olivet Cem., Frederick.

BRAWNER, THOMAS M.: Pvt., Co. E. b. circa 1843. Res. Port Tobacco, Charles Co., Md. Enl. Richmond 10/16/62. Age nineteen, 5'11½", fair complexion, blue eyes, light hair. Present through 12/62. Captured near Winchester 6/12/63; sent to Ft. McHenry; transf. to Ft. Monroe; exchanged 6/26/63. Horse captured Winchester, paid $230; present 7–8/63. Captured at Germanna Ford, Va., 10/11/63; sent to Old Capitol; transf. to Ft. McHenry and Pt. Lookout; exchanged 3/6/64. Horse captured at Beaver Dam Station, Va., 5/5/64, paid $1,800; present 7–12/64; went to Md. to buy a horse, was there when war ended. Received Cross of Honor, Prince William Co., Va., 1907.

BREED, LAWRENCE HENRY: Pvt., Co. F. b. circa 1846. Res. of Prince George's Co., Md. Enl. Richmond 7/11/63; present through 12/63 and 4/1/64; present through 8/31/64; lost horse 8/20/64; lost horse 9/2/64. Captured at Beverly, W.Va., 10/29/64; sent to Wheeling. Age twenty, 5'10", light complexion, auburn hair, blue eyes. Farmer. Transf. to Camp Chase; released 5/8/65. Took oath 5/19/65, age twenty-one. Member ANS/MLA. d. Baltimore 9/3/93, age fifty-two. Bur. Loudon Park Cem., Baltimore.

BREHM, JOHN PHILIP: Pvt., Co. C. b. Germany circa 1836. Res. of Baltimore. Captured attempting to cross the Potomac 8/61; sent to Ft. McHenry; transf. to Baltimore City Jail and Ft. Del.; exchanged 1/62. Enl. Richmond 8/4/62; present on western Virginia raid; present 7–12/63; present in arrest, CM'd, fined half of one month's pay 1–2/64; present 4/1–8/31/64; present Fisher's Hill, Va., 9/22/64; ab. sick in Gordonsville, Va., hosp. 11/10–12/31/64. Captured Frederick's Hall, Va., 3/13/65; sent to Ft. Monroe; transf. to Pt. Lookout; released 6/23/65. 5'6½", fair complexion, light brown hair, blue eyes. Iron Moulder, Baltimore. Entered Old Soldiers' Home, Pikesville, Md., 12/4/00, age sixty-four; d. there 1/18/02, age sixty-six. Bur. Loudon Park Cem., Baltimore.

BRENT, GEORGE T.: Pvt., Co. B. Res. of Picattaway, Prince George's Co., Md. Enl. Charlottesville 9/10/62; present 7–12/63; ab. sick with camp itch in Richmond hosp. 3/22–26/64; present 4/1/64; ab. sick in Richmond hosp. 4/20/64 until furloughed to Harrisonburg, Va., for thirty days 5/3/64; WIA and in Richmond hosp. 6/10/64. Applied for Clerkship in Bureau of Government in

Richmond 6/11/64; furloughed for sixty days 7/5/64; detailed in Richmond hosp. 9/20/64. NFR. Member ANS/MLA. Res. Brandywine, Prince George's Co., Md., 1906.

BRENT, WILLIAM C.: Pvt., Co. B. Res. of Baltimore. Issued clothing 3/30/64 and 9/30/64. Paroled Macon, Ga., 5/4/65. 5'5", fair complexion, gray eyes. Took oath 5/14/65. In Richmond hosp. 6/8–10/65. NFR.

BRISCOE, PHILIP T.: Pvt., Co. B. b. circa 1845. Res. Charles Co., Md. Enl. Co. D, 35th Bn. Va. Cav., Kernstown, Va., 12/25/62. Transf. to Co. B, 1st Md. Cav., 5/3/64; present through 12/64; ab. sick with debility in Richmond hosp. 3/4–5/65. Paroled Winchester 4/15/65. Age twenty-one, 5'9", dark complexion, brown hair, blue eyes; destination Charles Co.

BRITTIN or BRITTAN, FRANK: Pvt., Co. A, Davis's Bn. Enl. Edinburg,Va., 6/29/64. Transf. to Co. M, 23rd Va. Cav.; AWOL 10/31/64. NFR.

BROMWELL, HENRY HALL: Pvt., Co. D. Res. New Market, Frederick County, Md. Enl. Winchester 9/10/62; present 11–12/62. Captured Monterey Springs, Pa., 7/4/63; sent to Ft. McHenry; transf. to Ft. Del., Pt. Lookout, and Ft. Columbus; exchanged by 12/63; RTD 12/26/63 as paroled POW; present 4/1/64; present through 12/64; ab. sick with debility in Char-lottesville hosp. 4/7–8/65. NFR. Bur. Shipley Cem. on farm near New Market, no dates. Brother of Josiah R. and Thomas C. S. Bromwell.

BROMWELL, JOSIAH R.: Pvt., Co. D. Res. New Market, Md. Enl. Winchester 9/20/62; present 11–12/62, 7–12/63 and 4/1/64; ab. sick in Staunton, Va., hosp. through 12/64; ab. sick with debility in Charlottesville hosp. 3/1/65. Paroled Greensboro, N.C., 5/1/65. Bur. Washington, D.C., no dates. Brother of Henry H. and Thomas C. S. Bromwell.

BROMWELL, THOMAS C. S.: Pvt., Co. D. b. 1838. Res. New Market, Md. Enl. Winchester 9/20/62; present 11–12/62; present through 12/63; lost horse 9/30/63; present 4/1–12/31/64. NFR. d. 1892. Bur. Hall–Wood Cem., New Market. Brother of Henry H. and Josiah R. Bromwell.

BROOK, C. B.: Sgt., Co. H. b. circa 1834. Paroled Staunton, Va., 5/1/65. Age thirty-one, 5'11", dark complexion, light hair, blue eyes. Res. Stevenson, Md.

BROOKE, CLEMENT: Sgt., Co. E. b. circa 1839. Res. Prince George's Co., Md. Enl. as Pvt., Richmond, 10/31/62, age twenty-three; ab. sick in Winchester hosp. 2/13/63; transf. to Richmond hosp. 2/23/63; present until captured Winchester 6/12/63; sent to Ft. McHenry. Age twenty-four, 5'8½", dark complexion, dark eyes, brown hair. Exchanged 6/26/63. Horse captured Winchester, paid $230; promoted Sgt. Captured Germanna Ford, Va., 10/11/63; sent to Old Capitol; transf. to Pt. Lookout; took oath, released 1/22/64. Bur. St. Barbara's Episcopal Ch. Cem., Prince George's Co., no dates.

BROOKE, GEORGE WHITTAKER: Sgt., Co. E. b. 1844. Res. Prince George's Co., Md. Enl. Richmond 10/31/62, age eighteen. Captured Winchester 6/13/63; sent to Ft. McHenry. Age nineteen, 5'10½", dark complexion, dark eyes, dark hair. Transf. to Ft. Monroe; exchanged 6/26/63; present through 4/1/64. Captured Beaver Dam Station, Va., 5/10/64; sent to Ft. Monroe; transf. to Pt. Lookout; exchanged 3/15/65. Present Camp Lee, Richmond, 3/18–19/65. NFR. Member ANS/MLA. Res. of Leeland, Prince George's Co. d. 3/29/13. Bur. St. Barbara's Episcopal Ch. Cem., Prince George's Co.

BROOKE, HENRY: 1st Lt., Co. E, Davis's Bn. b. 2/12/39. Res. Upper Marboro, Prince George's Co., Md.; declined appointment. NFR. d. 2/19/79. Bur. Mt. Carmel Catholic Ch. Cem., Prince George's Co.

BROWN, CHARLES C.: Pvt., Co. A. b. Md. 1847. Res. Woodstock, Va., Howard Co., Md. Enl. Hanover CH, Va., 5/14/64. Captured King William CH. Va., 6/64; not on Federal POW rolls. NFR. Att. U. of Va. 1865–66. Lawyer, Annapolis. d. 1873.

BROWN, GEORGE E.: Pvt., Co. F. Enl. Richmond 7/13/63; des. to the enemy Culpeper, Va., 7/31/63; sent to Old Capitol; took oath, sent north 9/18/63. Age seventeen. Res. of Alexandria, Va. d. "Brooklandwood," Baltimore Co., 5/17/02, age fifty-six.

BROWN, GEORGE HENRY: Pvt., Co. K. b. circa 1842. Res. of Eldersburg, Carroll Co., Md. Enl. Co. K (2nd), 1st Va. Cav., 9/1/62; present until WIA Earlysville, Va., 1864; present through 8/31/64. Transf. to Co. K., 1st Md. Cav., 8/64; discharged at end of enlistment 12/26/64. Paroled Winchester 4/22/65. Age twenty-three, 5'10", fair complexion, black hair, gray eyes. Took oath 5/29/65.

BROWN, JAMES: Pvt., Co. A, Davis's Bn. On postwar roster. Possibly James A. Brown (6/11/35–5/31/11). Bur. Mt. Olivet Cem., Frederick, Md.

BROWN, JOHN RIGGS, JR.: Pvt., Co. A. b. 9/14/40. Res. of Woodstock, Howard Co., Md. Enl. Charlottesville 9/20/62; ab. sick in Richmond hosp. 11/12/62; transf. to Lynchburg, Va., hosp. NFR. Ab. sick with "chronic diarrhoea" in Richmond hosp. 7/5–12/31/63; present 4/1/64. Paroled New Creek 5/10/65. Took oath at Cumberland, Md., 5/16/65. Res. of Harford Co., Md.; destination Howard Co. Member ANS/MLA. Res. of Ellicott City, Md. d. 11/20/77. Bur. Brown–Garrett Cem., Howard Co.

BROWN, JOHN WESLEY: Pvt., Co. A. b. Md. circa 1835. Farmer, age twenty-five. Freedom Dist., Carroll Co., Md., per 1860 census. Enl. Co. A, 1st Md. Inf., 5/21/61; discharged 5/21/62. Enl. Co. A, 1st Md. Cav., date unknown. Paroled Harpers Ferry, W.Va., 5/19/65. Res. of Eldersburg, Carroll Co., Md.

BROWN, RIDGELY: Lt. Col. b. Montgomery Co., Md. 11/12/33. Farmer, Unity, Montgomery Co. Enl. as Pvt., Co. K (2nd), 1st Va. Cav., 5/14/61; elected 1st Lt. 8/1/61; not reelected 4/23/62. Elected Capt., Co. A, 1st Md. Cav., 5/12/62; present Leesburg, Va., 9/62; "served with credit and distinction." Present until promoted Maj. 11/12/62; present until WIA (leg) Greenland Gap, W.Va., 4/25/63; present through 8/20/63, promoted Lt. Col.; WIA (saber cut to hand) Pollard's Farm, Va., 5/27/64; present until KIA near Hanover Junction, Va., 6/1/64. "At the very last effort, a desperate charge, Ridgely Brown was shot through the forehead and died without speaking a word. He was the bravest, the purest, the gentlest man from Maryland who died for liberty in that four years' war." Bur. near Ashland, Va.; removed four days later to Hollywood Cem., Richmond; removed to the Brown family cem. at "Elton," near Unity, Montgomery Co., 12/65.

BROWN, ROBERT E.: Pvt., Co. C. b. circa 1848. Res. of Baltimore. Enl. Hagerstown, Md., 6/18/63; present through 8/31/64; KIA Winchester 9/19/64, age sixteen. Probably buried in Stonewall Cem., Winchester.

BROWN, SAMUEL THEOPOLUS: Pvt., Co. F. b. circa 1840. Enl. Richmond 7/31/63; des. near Culpeper, Va., 7/31/63; sent to Old Capitol. Age twenty-three. Res. of Alexandria, Va. Took oath, released 9/19/63.

BROWN, WILLIAM: Pvt., Co. unknown. Captured Darnestown, Md., 6/18/64; sent to Old Capitol; transf. to Pt. Lookout 2/25/65. NFR.

BROWNE, BENNETT BERNARD: Pvt., Co. E. b. "Wheatlands," Queen Anne Co., Md., 6/6/42; moved to Howard Co., Md. Att. Loyola Col., Baltimore. Enl. Co. K (2nd), 1st Va. Cav., 5/24/61. Transf. to Co. G, 7th Va. Cav.; detailed as Hosp. Steward, Ashby's Brigade, 7/9/61–2/62. Left with the wounded and captured at Greenland Gap, W.Va., 4/27/63; sent to Ft. Monroe; exchanged 5/23/63. Transf. to Co. E, 1st Md. Cav., 4/21/64; WIA (arm) and captured 5/15/64; sent to Old Capitol; exchanged 2/65. Paroled Charles Town, W.Va., 5/18/65. 6'1", light complexion, brown hair, blue eyes. Took oath 6/20/65. Res. of Howard Co., destination Baltimore. Gd. U. of Md. Medical School, 1867. M.D., Baltimore through 1879; M.D., Queen Anne's and Howard Cos.

Member ANS/MLA. d. 1922. Brother of Robert A. Browne.

BROWNE, ROBERT ALPHONSUS: Pvt., Co. E. Res. of Queen Anne's Co., Md. Enl. Co. G, 7th Va. Cav., 4/1/62. Transf. to Co. E, 1st Md. Cav., 4/21/64; KIA Winchester 9/19/64. Bur. Stonewall Cem., Winchester. Brother of Bennett B. Browne.

BROWNING, J. J.: Sgt., Co. A. On postwar roster.

BRUCE, ROBERT E.: 3rd Cpl., Co. K. Res. of Anne Arundel Co., Md. Enl. Co. K (2nd), 1st Va. Cav., 9/20/62; present through 8/64. Transf. to Co. K, 1st Md. Cav., 8/64; DOW (received Bunker Hill, W.Va., 8/13/64) in Winchester hosp. 9/22/64. Bur. Stonewall Cem., Winchester.

BRUN, JAMES: Pvt., Co. B. Paroled Richmond 4/22/65.

BRYAN, CHARLES A.: Pvt., Co. B. b. circa 1838. Res. of Chesapeake City, Cecil Co., Md. Enl. Hanover Junction, Va., 3/17/64; present through 4/1/64; ab. sick in Richmond hosp. 5/1–6/64. Captured Moorefield, W.Va., 8/7/64; sent to Wheeling. Age twenty-six, 5'10", fair complexion, light hair, gray eyes. Merchant. Transf. to Camp Chase; exchanged 3/12/65. Ab. sick with "chronic diarrhoea" in Richmond hosp. 3/13/65; furloughed for thirty days 3/26/65. Paroled Richmond 4/25/65.

BRYAN, WILLIAM: Pvt., Co. C, Davis's Bn. Res. of Baltimore. On postwar roster.

BRYAN, WILLIAM C.: Pvt., Co. E. Enl. Hagerstown, Md., 6/24/63. Captured Gettysburg, Pa., 7/2/63; sent to U.S. general hosp. 9/15/63; transf. to PM 9/26/63; took oath, released.

BRYAN, WRIGHTSON L.: Pvt., Co. B. Res. of Queenstown, Queen Anne's Co., Md. Enl. Charlottesville 9/10/62; present 7–11/63; ab. sick in Richmond hosp. 12/25/63–2/22/64; present through 12/31/64. NFR.

BRYANT, GEORGE N.: Pvt., Co. E. b. circa 1839. Res. of Havre-de-Grace, Harford Co., Md. Enl. Fredericksburg, Va., 8/22/63; present through 8/31/63; presence or ab. not stated 9–10/63; present 11–12/63; ab. on horse detail for twenty days 3/15/64; present 7–8/64; ab. on horse detail 11/25/64. Captured Baltimore 12/20/64; sent to Pt. Lookout; exchanged 2/20/65. Paroled Richmond 5/8/65. Lawyer, Harford Co. Entered Old Soldiers' Home, Pikesville, Md., 5/6/09, age seventy. d. Catonsville, Md., 9/12/15, age seventy-seven. Bur. Loudon Park Cem., Baltimore.

BRYNE, _____: Pvt., Co. C. On postwar roster.

BUCKINGHAM, GEORGE W.: 2nd Sgt., Co. K. Res. of Elk Landing, Cecil Co., Md. Enl. as Pvt., Co. K (2nd), 1st Va. Cav., 7/27/61; elected 4th Sgt. 4/26/62; present until WIA Kelly's Ford, Va., 3/17/63; RTD; present until ab. sick with variola

in Charlottesville hosp. 2/2–4/2/64; present until transf. to Co. K, 1st Md. Cav., 8/64; promoted 2nd Sgt. by 8/31/64; discharged at end of enlistment 12/14/64. Paroled Winchester 4/25/65. Took oath 5/20/65. Judge of Orphan's Court, Howard Co., Md., 1879.

BUCKLEY, JOHN: Pvt., Co. C, Davis's Bn. (See roster of 2nd Md. Cav.)

BULL, JOHN ELIJAH: Pvt., Co. C. b. Baltimore circa 1841. Enl. Co. D, 1st Md. Inf., 5/22/61; discharged 8/17/62. Age twenty-one, 5'8", fair complexion, brown hair, blue eyes. Clerk. Paid 9/2/62. Enl. Co. C, 1st Md. Cav., Hagerstown, Md., 7/11/63; present through 12/31/63; present sick 1–2/64; present 4/1/64; ab. on horse detail for twenty days to Hardy Co., W.Va., 4/9/64; ab. in Richmond hosp. 5/27–31/64; present through 12/31/64. Paroled Portsmouth 4/20/65. Took oath in Norfolk, Va., 5/10/65. Former res. of Harford Co.; destination Baltimore.

BULLEN, RHODERICK B.: Pvt., Co. B. b. circa 1841. Res. Broad Creek, Queen Anne's Co., Md. Enl. Charlottesville 9/10/62; ab. sick with "Febris Remitten" in Charlottesville hosp. 10/9–20/62; present 7–12/63; horse died New Castle Ferry, Va., 1/15/64; furloughed to Winchester for seventeen days for a horse 2/1/64; present 4/1–12/31/64; ab. sick with scabies in Richmond hosp. 2/12–3/27/65. Paroled New Market, Va., 4/19/65. Age twenty-four, 5'8", fair complexion, light hair, blue eyes. Took oath Harpers Ferry, W.Va., 4/29/65.

BUMP, GEORGE C.: Pvt., Co. K. Res. of Baltimore. Enl. Co. K (2nd), 1st Va. Cav., Richmond, 6/10/62; NFR until present 2/64–8/64. Transf. to Co. K, 1st Md. Cav., 8/64; ab. sick with "syphillis cons." in Charlottesville hosp. 10/24/64; transf. to Lynchburg, Va., hosp. 10/25/64. Paroled Ashland, Va., 5/2/65. Took oath Richmond 5/3/65. Butcher. Destination, Baltimore.

BUNION, R. W.: Pvt., Co. A, Davis's Bn. Enl. 5/1/63. Transf. to Co. M, 23rd Va. Cav.. Captured Winchester 9/19/64. On rolls to 10/31/64. NFR. May have been KIA.

BURCH, G. C.: Pvt., Co. unknown. Res. of Md. Enl. Co. B, 39th Bn. Va. Cav., 10/29/62. Transf. to 1st Md. Cav., 3/31/64; order cancelled 4/5/64. NFR.

BURCH, JAMES ALTON: Pvt., Co. B. Res. Charles Co., Md. Enl. Charlottesville 9/10/62; present 7–12/63; ab. sick in hosp. through 12/31/64. Sick in camp 4/1/65. Paroled Richmond 5/5/65. Res. of Baltimore 1903.

BURGESS, WILLIAM WALLACE: 1st Sgt., Co. K. b. 1841. Res. of Howard Co., Md. Att. U. of Va. 1861–62. Enl. as Pvt., Co. K (2nd), 1st Va.

Cav., Richmond, 5/23/62. Captured Manassas, Va., 8/27/62; sent to Old Capitol; exchanged 9/21/62. Present through 2/64, promoted 1st Sgt.; present until WIA Bunker Hill, W.Va., 8/13/64; present through 8/31/64. Transf. to Co. K, 1st Md. Cav., 8/64. Discharged at end of enlistment 12/4/64. NFR. M.D., Charlottesville, 1899; M.D., Orange CH, Va., 1908. d. 1913. Bur. Graham Cem., Orange Co., Va.

BURKE, THOMAS: Pvt., Co. A. WIA 5/10/64. NFR.

BURKE, THOMAS H.: Pvt., Co. K. WIA Taylorsville, Va., 5/13/64; on postwar roster.

BURLING, D.: Pvt., Co. B. On postwar roster.

BURMAN, JAMES: Pvt., Co. C, Davis's Bn. NFR.

BURNE, JOE: Pvt., Co. B. On postwar roster. Res. Lower Marlboro, Calvert Co., Md., 1903.

BURNS, JOHN: Pvt., Co. F. Enl. Richmond 5/27/63; des. near Culpeper, Va., 7/29/63. NFR.

BURRELL, JAMES: Cpl., Co. C, Davis's Bn. NFR.

BURROUGHS, JOHN SOMMERSETT B.: 1st Lt., Co. F. b. circa 1838. Res. Prince George's Co., Md. Enl. as Pvt., Richmond 12/16/62; age twenty-four; promoted 2nd Lt. 12/20/62; present 1/63; promoted 1st Lt. 2/1/63; presence or ab. not stated through 7/63; ab. sick with "Remitten Febris" in Charlottesville hosp. 8/15–9/10/63 and 10/26–12/8/63; furloughed for thirty days 12/9/63. Captured Potomac River 12/29/63; sent to Ft. McHenry; transf. to Pt. Lookout and Ft. Del.; released 6/8/65. 5'9½", dark complexion, black hair, brown eyes.

BURST, GEORGE T.: Pvt., Co. B. On postwar roster.

BUSK, JEROME: Pvt., Co. unknown. Res. of Baltimore. Enl. 1st Md. Arty. 8/17/61; present through 2/62. NFR. Enl. Co. F, 12th Va. Cav., date unknown. Transf. to 1st Md. Cav. by 11/62. Captured Pt. of Rocks, Md., 4/28/63. "Rebel soldier and spy." Sent to Ft. McHenry; took oath, released 5/7/63. NFR.

BUSSEY, C. F.: Pvt., Co. C. Paroled Edwards' Ferry, Md., 4/16/65. Took oath 4/18/65. Res. of Baltimore. "Ordered to leave the Department."

BUTLER, CYRUS SIDNEY: Pvt., Co. D. Res. of Frederick Co., Md. Enl. Co. A, 1st Md. Inf., 5/21/61; WIA 6/62; in Charlottesville hosp. 6/15–8/1962. Enl. Co. D, 1st Md. Cav., Lacey Springs, Va., 4/1/63; present 7–12/63; horse killed Buckland, W.Va., 10/18/63, paid $675; present 4/1/64; ab. on horse detail to Winchester for seventeen days 4/9/64; ab. sick in hosp. 8/31–12/31/64. NFR. d. age thirty-six years and two months, no dates. Bur. Mt. Olivet Cem., Frederick, Md.

BYRNE, ANDREW J.: Sgt., Co. G. b. circa 1828. Enl. 2nd Md. Arty. 8/15/61; present through 12/61. NFR. Enl. Co. A, Davis's Bn., date unknown. Captured Newtown, Va., 4/24/64; sent to Wheeling. Age thirty-six, 5'8", dark complexion, brown hair, black eyes. Farmer. Transf. to Camp Chase; exchanged 2/25/65. Paid $2,500 for horse killed at Columbia Furnace, Va., 5/10/64 (ridden by another man). NFR.

BYRNE, CHARLES K.: Pvt., Co. C. b. circa 1845. Res. of Frederick, Md. Enl. Leesburg, Va., 7/16/64. Captured Moorefield, W.Va., 8/7/64; sent to Wheeling. Age nineteen, 5'8½", sandy complexion, red hair, gray eyes. Student. Transf. to Camp Chase; exchanged 3/12/65. In Richmond hosp. 4/1–2/65. Paroled Richmond 4/28/65. Former res. of La.; destination La.

BYRNE, WILLIAM E.: Pvt., Co. G. Captured Monterey, Pa., 7/4/63; sent to Ft. Del.; transf. to Pt. Lookout; exchanged 12/26/63. NFR. Probably the man who served in Co. G, 7th Va. Cav. Res. of Maryland Heights, Washington Co., Md.

CADLE, JAMES RICHARD: Pvt., Co. E. b. Prince George's Co., Md., 1846. Res. of Anne Arundel Co., Md. Enl. Co. A, 17th Va. Inf., 8/29/61. Transf. to Co. C (Deas Md. Arty.), 19th Bn. Va. Arty., 4/14/62. Age twenty, 5'10", fair complexion, light hair, dark eyes. Transf. to Co. E, 1st Md. Cav., Richmond, 12/17/62, age twenty; present through 8/63; presence or absence not stated 9–10/63; present 11–12/63 and 4/1/64. Captured Moorefield, W.Va., 8/7/64; sent to Wheeling. Age twenty-one. Farmer. Transf. to Camp Chase; exchanged 3/12/65. Paroled New Market, Va., 4/19/65. Age twenty-two. 5'9", light complexion, light hair, brown or hazel eyes. Took oath Alexandria, Va., 5/9/65. d. 1881.

CAGITT, ROBERT: Pvt., Co. C. On postwar roster.

CALLAN, JOHN F.: Pvt., Co. F. Res. of Washington, D.C. Gd. Georgetown U. 1856. Enl. Co. A, 1st Md. Inf., 6/6/61; discharged 8/16/62. On postwar roster. Brother of Owen Callan.

CALLAN, OWEN: Pvt., Co. F. b. circa 1839. Res. of Baltimore. Enl. Co. F, 1st Md. Inf., 5/21/61; discharged 8/26/62. Age twenty-four, 5'8", light complexion, dark hair, dark eyes. Merchant. Enl. Co. F, 1st Md. Cav., Richmond, 7/15/63; present through 12/63 and 4/1/64. Captured Moorefield, W.Va., 8/7/64; sent to Wheeling. Age twenty-six, 5'7½", fair complexion, dark hair, light eyes. Silver Plater. Transf. to Camp Chase; released 6/10/65. Age twenty-four, 5'8", dark complexion, black hair, blue eyes.

CAMPBELL, JAMES: Pvt., Co. A, Davis's Bn. Enl. 6/25/63. Transf. to Co. M, 23rd Va. Cav. Took oath 8/7/65.

CAMPBELL, WILLIAM: Pvt., Co. K. Served in 2nd Md. Arty. Enl. Co. K (2nd), 1st Va. Cav., 4/1/64. Transf. to Co. K, 1st Md. Cav., 8/64; detailed as Teamster 10/31/64. NFR. Reported as captured on postwar roster.

CAMPION, JOHN: Pvt., Co. B., Davis's Bn. b. England circa 1835. Captured Beverly, W.Va., 10/29/64; sent to Wheeling. Age twenty-nine, 5'6", fair complexion, dark hair, blue eyes. Laborer. Res. of New Orleans, La. Transf. to Camp Chase; released 5/13/65.

CANBY, BENJAMIN DUVALL: Pvt., Co. A. b. near Colesville, Montgomery Co., Md., 1837. Res. of Rockville, Md. Enl. Leesburg, Va., 9/2/62; present, detailed in QM Dept., 7–10/63; present 11–12/63 and 4/1–8/31/64; WIA (right forearm shattered) Winchester 9/19/64; ab. wounded in Charlottesville hosp. 9/28/64; served as Scout. Paroled 1865. Farmer. Member Ridgely Brown Camp, CV, Rockville, Md. d. Colesville, Md., 10/31/18. Bur. St. John's Episcopal Ch. Cem., Olney, Md.

CANDEN, PAT: Pvt., Co. C, Davis's Bn. On postwar roster.

CANNON, JOHN GIBSON: Pvt., Co. A. Res. of Bridgetown, Carroll Co., Md. Asst. Principal, Rockville Acad., 1861. Enl. Co. A, 39th Bn. Va. Cav., 8/18/62. Captured 1863; sent to Old Capitol. NFR. Transf. to Co. A, 1st Md. Cav., 4/21/64; WIA and in Richmond hosp. 5/18–26/64; paid Richmond 5/30/64; present through 12/31/64. NFR. Res. Washington, D.C., 1909.

CAREY, MICHAEL: Pvt., Co. C. b. Albermarle Co., Va., circa 1844. Enl. Co. B, 1st Md. Inf., 5/21/61. Reenl. for two years 2/8/62. NFR. May have served as Gunner, CSN. Enl. Co. C, 1st Md. Cav., Lacey Springs, Va., 4/7/63; present through 12/64; horse killed. Paroled Greensboro, N.C., 5/1/65. d. Old Soldiers' Home, Richmond, 2/23/17, age seventy-three. Bur. Hollywood Cem., Richmond.

CARMAN, ROBERT: Pvt., Co. A. b. circa 1834. Res. of Baltimore. Captured Beverly, W.Va., 10/29/64; sent to Wheeling. Age thirty. Clerk. Res. of New Orleans, La. Transf. to Camp Chase; released 5/12/65. 5'7", florid complexion, dark hair, blue eyes. Res. of Orleans Parish, La.

CARMICK, PATRICK: Pvt., Co. I. Enl. Co. F, 5th Va. Cav., date unknown. Listed as des. from Co. I, 1st Md. Cav., 4/18/63, age twenty-four. Carpenter. Took oath 4/17/65.

CARROLL, ALBERT HENRY: 1st Lt., Co. unknown. Gd. Georgetown U. 1856. Res. of Ellicott City, Md. On postwar rosters. Appointed Signal Officer for Gen. Richard S. Ewell. KIA Bunker Hill, W.Va., 9/9/62. Brother of Robert G. H. Carroll.

CARROLL, EDMUND: Pvt., Co. unknown; des. Took oath, sent to Philadelphia, Pa., 6/7/64.

CARROLL, JOHN C.: Pvt., Co. F. b. circa 1846.

Res. of Baltimore. Enl. Brooke Va. Arty. 9/5/62, age under 18. Transf. to Co. F, 1st Md. Cav., 7/24/63; present through 12/63 and 4/1–7/31/64; ab. sick with neuralgia in Winchester hosp. 8/1/64; transf. to another hosp. 8/7/64; ab. sick in hosp. until 10/20/64; des. and captured Baltimore 12/25/64; took oath, sent north 12/31/64.

CARROLL, ROBERT GOODLOE HARPER: Pvt., Co. K. b. Baltimore 1838. Gd. Georgetown U. 1859. Enl. Co. K (2nd), 1st Va. Cav., 5/14/61; discharged at end of enlistment, 5/14/62. Age twenty-three, 5'7", fair complexion, dark hair, blue eyes. Gentleman. Res. of Ellicott City, Md. Fought as a civilian with the 1st Md. Cav. on the retreat from Gettysburg, Pa.; appointed 1st Lt. and ADC Gen. Richard S. Ewell 5/4/64. Cited for bravery at Spotsylvania CH, Va., where his horse was shot from under him; resigned 11/21/64. NFR. Member ANS/MLA. Res. of Baltimore 1905. d. "Homewood," Howard Co., Md., 1/20/15. Bur. New Cathedral Cem., Baltimore. Brother of Albert H. Carroll.

CARTER, GRAFTON: Pvt., Co. D. Res. Libertytown, Frederick Co., Md. Enl. Winchester 4/20/62 as substitute for C. H. Marriott; present 11–12/62. Captured Monterey Springs, Pa., 7/4/63; sent to Ft. Del.; transf. to Pt. Lookout and Ft. Columbus; exchanged 2/21/65; present Camp Lee 2/21/65. NFR. d. 8/8/78, age thirty-four years, eight months, and eleven days. Bur. Unionville Methodist Ch. Cem., Frederick Co.

CARTER, R.: Hosp. Steward. Captured Greenland Gap, W.Va., 4/27/63; sent to Ft. Monroe; exchanged 4/14/63. NFR.

CARTER, ROBERT W.: Pvt., Co. A. b. circa 1843. Res. Rockville, Montgomery Co., Md. Enl. Charlottesville 8/25/62; present 7–8/63; ab. on duty 10/28–31/63; present 11–12/63 and 4/1/64. Captured Moorefield, W.Va., 8/7/64; sent to Wheeling. Age twenty-one, 5'7½", fair complexion, black eyes, dark hair. Farmer. Transf. to Camp Chase. d. of pneumonia there 1/30/65. Bur. Camp Chase Natl. Cem., Oh.

CARTER, WILLIAM: Pvt., Co. A. Enl. Charlottesville 8/25/62; KIA Moorefield, W.Va., 8/7/64.

CARVELL, ROBERT W.: Color Corporal, Co. B. Res. Broad Creek, Queen Anne's Co., Md. KIA (shot in abdomen) Greenland Gap, W.Va., 4/25/63.

CARY, JOHN BRUNE: Pvt., Co. A. b. Baltimore Co., 4/18/40. Enl. Hanover Junction, Va., 5/15/64; present through 12/31/64. "Acting ADC Gen. John Pegram last five months of the war." Paroled Charlottesville 5/10/65. Took oath Charles Town, W.Va., 6/10/65, destination Baltimore. Secretary and Treasurer, Wilson Distilling Co., Baltimore 1899. Member ANS/MLA. Member Isaac

Trimble Camp, CV, Baltimore. Res. "Sherwood," Baltimore, 1914. d. 12/14/17. Bur. St. Thomas Ch. Cem., Garrison Forest, Baltimore Co., Md. Brother of Wilson M. Cary and Hetty Cary, "designer of the Confederate Battle Flag."

CARY, WILSON MILES "WILLIE": Pvt., Co. A. b. Harford Co., Md., 12/12/38. Res. of Baltimore. On postwar rosters. Served as volunteer ADC Gen. Joseph E. Johnston 1861. Promoted Capt. and QM on Gen. Robert E. Lee's staff. Promoted Maj. NFR. Deputy Clerk of Criminal Court, Baltimore. Member ANS/MLA. Member Isaac Trimble Camp, CV, Baltimore. d. Warrenton, Va., 8/28/14. Bur. St. Thomas Ch., Garrison, Md. Brother of John B. Cary.

CASHEL, JAMES: Pvt., Co. A. Des. New Market, Va., 12/26/62. NFR.

CASLON or CASLOW, JAMES: Pvt., Co. F. Enl. Richmond 7/20/63; des. near Newtown, Va., 7/23/63; present 9–10/63. Escaped from Brigade Guard House 12/25/63. NFR.

CASSELL, LIDE: Pvt., Co. A. On postwar roster.

CATHER, GEORGE ROBERT: 3rd Cpl., Co. D. Res. Kent Co., Md. Enl. as 3rd Cpl., Winchester, 9/20/62; present 11–12/62 as 4th Cpl.; present 7–8/63; ab. sick with hemorrhoids in Richmond hosp. 9/10/63–4/1/64; ab. on leave for twenty days to Hardy Co., W.Va., to get a horse 5/1/64. Captured Ellicott's Mills, Md., 7/12/64; sent to Old Capitol; transf. to Elmira; released 6/14/65. 5'7½", fair complexion, dark hair, blue eyes. Res. Newberne, Va.

CATOR, BENJAMIN FRANKLIN: Pvt., Co. E. Horse killed near Cairo on the B&O RR 5/9/63. Captured 5/13/63; exchanged by 12/63. Paid $230 for horse 12/30/63. NFR.

CATOR, BENJAMIN W.: Pvt., Co. E. b. Prince George's Co., Md., circa 1838. Res. Prince George's Co., Md. Enl. Richmond 11/15/62, age twenty-four; present 1/20/63; presence or ab. not stated through 2/28/63; KIA Gettysburg, Pa., 7/3/63.

CHAMBERS, G. W.: Pvt., Co. D, Davis's Bn. Paroled Winchester 4/26/65. Age thirty-seven, 6', fair complexion, brown hair, gray eyes.

CHAMBERS, ROBERT MARION, JR.: Pvt., Co. C. b. Baltimore 3/20/42. Res. of Baltimore. Enl. Co. G, 13th Va. Inf., 5/2/8/61. Plasterer. WIA Bull Run, Va., 7/21/61; discharged as nonresident 5/28/62. Enl. Co. C, 1st Md. Cav., New Market, Va., 2/6/62; present 7–10/63; AWOL 11/6/63. Captured near New Market 12/18/63; sent to Wheeling. 5'11", dark complexion, brown hair, gray eyes. Transf. to Camp Chase and Ft. Del.; exchanged 2/27/65. Contractor. Lynchburg, Va., 1865–85. Builder, Baltimore, 1895–98. Member

ANS/MLA. d. Baltimore 5/24/98. Bur. Loudon Park Cem., Baltimore.

CHAPIN, CHARLES: Pvt., Co. F. Res. of Baltimore. Enl. Co. F, 1st Md. Inf., 5/22/61; ab. sick in Lynchburg, Va., hosp. 3/21/62. NFR. Enl. Co. F, 1st Md. Cav., Richmond, 6/29/63; present 7–8/63; des. Orange Co. 9/29/63. NFR.

CHAPMAN, ISAAC N.: Pvt., Co. F. Res. of Baltimore. Enl. Richmond 7/8/63; present through 12/63 and 4/1–12/31/64. Paroled Appomattox CH, Va., 4/9/65. Took oath 4/18/65, destination Baltimore. Member George Emack Camp, CV, Hyattsville, Md., 1906.

CHAPMAN, NATHANIEL: 2nd Lt., Co. E. b. Charles Co., Md. 8/26/42. Att. Charlotte Hall Acad. and Jefferson Col., Pa. Res. of Perrymansville, Charles Co., Md. Enl. Hampton S.C. Legion 10/61 for one year. Requested clerkship in Bureaus, Richmond, 8/26/62. 5'6", light complexion, dark hair, blue eyes. Enl. as Pvt., Co. E, 1st Md. Cav., 11/12/62; present 1–2/63, promoted 2nd Lt. 2/1/63; present western Va. raid and 7–10/63; ab. sick with scabies in Richmond hosp. 11/10–12/31/63; present 4/1–9/30/64; ab. on detached service with Gen. Jones 10/25/64 for seventy-eight days; paid 3/2/65. Paroled Fredericksburg, Va., circa 5/65. Farmer, Fairfax Co., Va., two years. Gd. U. of Md. Medical School 1872. M.D., Charles Co., Md.; moved to Washington, D.C., 1892. Member Confederate Veterans Assoc., Washington, D.C., and ANS/MLA. d. Washington, 8/16/98. "A fearless and skillful officer." (Photograph in Pippenger 1990)

CHESELDINE, WILLIAM COLUMBUS: Pvt., Co. C. b. Md. circa 1843. Farmhand, age seventeen, St. Mary's Co., Md., per 1860 census. Res. of Chaptico, St. Mary's Co. On postwar roster Co. G, 1st Md. Inf. Enl. Co. C, 1st Md. Cav., Hanover CH, Va., 8/15/62; present 7–10/63; ab. detailed as Wagonmaster 11–12/63; present 1–2 and 4/1/64; WIA (right thigh) and captured Pollard's Farm, Va., 5/27/64; sent to Douglas Hosp., Washington, D.C.; leg amputated; DOW 6/8/64. Bur. Arlington Natl. Cem., Va.

CHESLEY, DANIEL SPRIGG: Pvt., Co. E. b. Prince George's Co., Md., circa 1840. Res. of Prince George's Co. Enl. Richmond 11/30/62, age twenty-two; presence or ab. not stated 1–2/63; present 7–8/63; presence or ab. not stated 9–10/63; present 11–12/63 and 4/1/64; present 7–9/64. Captured Beverly, W.Va., 10/29/64; sent to Wheeling. Age twenty-four, 6'4", dark complexion, dark hair, gray eyes. Farmer. Transf. to Camp Chase; released 5/11/65. Res. of Upperboro, Md.

CHILDERS, DANIEL: Pvt., Co. B, Davis's Bn. b.

1847. On postwar roster.

CHILDRESS, DANIEL: Pvt., Co. A. b. Richmond, circa 1847. Butcher. Enl. Richmond 1/25/64, age seventeen, one month, three days. Signed by mark; discharged as minor 10/25/64. NFR.

CHILDRESS, DAVID: Pvt., Co. A, Davis's Bn. Enl. Richmond 1/25/64. Transf. to Co. M, 23rd Va. Cav.; discharged from Richmond hosp. for "acute colitis" 10/25/64. Age fifteen, 5'3", light complexion, dark hair, blue eyes.

CHILDRESS, THADDEUS K.: Pvt., Co. B, Davis's Bn. b. 1846. Enl. Richmond 6/1/63. Captured Woodstock, Va., 5/17/64; sent to Wheeling. Age eighteen, dark complexion, dark hair, blue eyes. Printer. Transf. to Camp Chase; exchanged 2/25/65. Paroled Richmond 4/65.

CHILDS, NATHAN SOPER: Pvt., Co. A. b. 1834. Res. of Wells Cross Roads, Howard Co., Md. Enl. Martinsburg, W.Va., 7/15/63; present through 12/63 and 4/1/64; present 7–12/64. Took oath Washington, D.C., 1865. Elected School Commissioner, Howard Co., 1879. Received Cross of Honor, Millersville, Anne Arundel Co., 1927. d. 1931. Bur. Baldwin Memorial Cem., Anne Arundel Co. Brother of William H. Childs.

CHILDS, WILLIAM H. "BUCK": 3rd Sgt., Co. A. b. 1839. Res. of Olney, Montgomery Co., Md. Enl. as Pvt., Leesburg, Va., 9/2/62; ab. sick in Hanover Junction, Va., hosp. 7–9/63; present 9–12/63 and 4/1/64; present as 2nd Cpl. through 8/31/64; present as 3rd Sgt. 11–12/64. Paroled Winchester 5/16/65. Age twenty-six, 5'8", blond complexion, dark hair, dark eyes. Member Ridgely Brown Camp, CV, Rockville, 1900. Res. of Derwood, Montgomery Co. d. Anne Arundel Co. 1919. Brother of Nathan S. Childs.

CHRISMAN, WILLIAM J.: Capt., Davis's Bn. b. 6/11/34. Served in Co. H, 10th Va. Inf., 1861–62. Enl. McClanahan's Va. Arty. and served eighteen months. Raised Co. of Cav. and attached to Davis's Bn.; WIA (right hand) Piedmont, Va., 6/5/64. Promoted Maj. of Va. Reserves. Paroled Harrisonburg, Va., 6/15/65.

CHYZLER, HENRY C.: Pvt., Co. D. b. Baltimore circa 1843. Enl. Co. A, 1st Md. Inf., 5/21/61; reenl. 2/8/62. NFR. Enl. Co. D, 1st Md. Cav., Lacey Springs, Va., 4/1/63; present 7–12/63. In Richmond hosp. 3/8/64; present 4/1/64; WIA (left leg-splintering tibia) Darkesville, W.Va., 9/10/64. Captured Harrisonburg, Va., 9/25/64; sent to Pt. Lookout; exchanged 11/5/64; ab. wounded in Charlottesville hosp. 12/4/64. Retired to Invalid Corps 3/27/65, for "caries and necrosis" of the leg. Age twenty-two, 5'5½", fair complexion, light hair, hazel eyes. Clerk. Res. of Baltimore. Captured in Richmond hosp. 4/3/65; sent to

Newport News, Va., 4/23/65; released 6/15/65.

CLAGGETT, DAVID: Pvt., Co. K. Enl. Co. K (2nd), 1st Va. Cav., date unknown. Captured Shenandoah Co., Va., 11/19/63; sent to Ft. Del. Transf. to Co. K, 1st Md. Cav., 8/64 while POW. Released 6/6/65. 5'8½", dark complexion, dark hair, dark eyes. Farmer, Washington Co., Md.

CLAGGETT, HEZEKIAH H.: Pvt., Co. K. b. circa 1841. Res. Frederick City, Md. Enl. Co. K (2nd), 1st Va. Cav., Martinsburg, W.Va., 9/10/62; bay horse killed Rappahannock Bridge 8/11/63; present through 8/64. Transf. to Co. K, 1st Md. Cav., 8/64; discharged at end of enlistment 12/4/64. Res. Washington Co., Md. Paroled Winchester 6/2/65. Age twenty-four, 5'8", fair complexion, dark hair, dark eyes. Res. Jefferson Co., Va.

CLAGGETT, JOHN HENRY: Pvt., Co. A. b. Montgomery Co., Md., circa 1825. On postwar roster. Farmer. d. Gaithersburg, Md., 1/98. Bur. Briggs family cem. near Gaithersburg, Md.

CLAGGETT, JOHN W.: Pvt., Co. A. b. circa 1840. Res. of Montgomery Co., Md. Enl. Hagerstown, Md., 6/25/63; present through 12/63 and 4/1/64. Captured Strasburg, Va., 5/3/64; sent to Wheeling. Age twenty-four, 6', fair complexion, brown hair, blue eyes. Transf. to Camp Chase; exchanged 2/28/65. Admitted to Richmond hosp. with "debilitas" 3/7/65; furloughed for thirty days 3/9/65. NFR. Member George Emack Camp, CV, Hyattsville, Md., and Confederate Veterans Assoc., Washington, D.C., 1910. d. by 1917.

CLAGGETT, ROBERT G.: Pvt., Co. D. Res. of Md. Gd. U. of Md. Medical School 1863. Enl. Frederick, Md., 7/1/64; present through 8/31/64; detailed as Regimental Surgeon 9–10/64; ab. on detail to get a horse 11–12/64. NFR.

CLARK, BASIL CRAWFORD: 1st Sgt., Co. A. b. 4/14/41. Res. Clarksville, Montgomery Co., Md. Enl. as 2nd Cpl., Co. A, Davis's Bn. Urbana, Md., 10/9/62. Transf. to Co. A, 1st Md. Cav., 11–12/62; present 7–9/63. Captured Brandy Station, Va., 10/11/63; sent to Old Capitol; transf. to Pt. Lookout; exchanged 3/6/64. Ab. paroled POW 4/1/64. Promoted 1st Sgt.; WIA (right thighbone broken) Pollard's Farm, Va., 5/27/64; ab. wounded in Richmond hosp. until transf. to Lynchburg, Va., hosp. 10/4/64; ab., wounded, through 12/31/64. Surrendered Baltimore 6/10/65. Took oath 6/11/65. Clerk, Texas; Banker, Marlin, Texas. d. Marlin, Texas, 12/21/15. Bur. Clarksville, Md., Cem. Brother of David Clark.

CLARK(E), CHARLES D.: Pvt., Co. K. b. Md. 12/21/41. Enl. Co. K (2nd), 1st Va. Cav., date unknown. Transf. to Co. K, 1st Md. Cav., 8/64; WIA near Critzer's, Augusta Co., Va., 9/28/64; DOW 9/30/64. Bur. Riverview Cem., Waynesboro, Va.

CHARLES H.
H. CLARK

*(William W.
Wolfersberger)*

PVT. JAMES C.
CLARK, CO. A,
FIRST MD.
CAVALRY

*(Museum of the
Confederacy)*

CLARK, CHARLES H.: Pvt., Co. E. b. circa 1836. Res. of Baltimore Co. Enl. Winchester 9/10/62. Captured Winchester 12/24/62; sent to Wheeling. Age twenty-six, 5'5", dark complexion, dark eyes, dark hair. Moulder. Transf. to Camp Chase; took oath, released 3/27/63. NFR.

CLARK, CHARLES H. H. (photo): Pvt., Co. E. b. 1/16/42. May have served in Zarvona's Md. Zouaves. Enl. Winchester 9/20/62; present 11–12/62. Captured Monterey Springs, Pa., 7/4/63; sent to Ft. McHenry; transf. to Ft. Del. and Pt. Lookout; exchanged 2/21/65. Captured Hanover, Va., 3/13/65; sent to Ft. Monroe; transf. to Pt. Lookout; released 6/9/65. Arrived Wash-ington, D.C., 6/10/65; transportation furnished to Winchester. Member Gen. Turner Ashby Camp, CV, Winchester; d. there 10/28/05. Bur. Mt. Hebron Cem., Winchester.

CLARK, DAVID: Pvt., Co. A. b. Md. 1/11/42. Res. of Baltimore. Enl. Urbana, Md., 9/1/62; present 7–12/63 and 4/1/64; KIA Beaver Dam, Va., 5/9/64. Brother of Basil C. Clark.

CLARK, IGNATIUS: Pvt., Co. K. b. St. Mary's Co., Md., circa 1838. Enl. Co. K (2nd), 1st Va. Cav., Fairfax CH, Va., 10/3/61; present until captured near Upperville, Va., 5/20/63; sent to Ft. McHenry. Ex-changed 5/29/63; present through 2/64; ab. at Gen. Fitzhugh Lee's Headquarters 2–8/64. Trans. Co. K, 1st Md. Cav., 8/64; discharged at end of enlistment 12/4/64. NFR.

CLARK, JAMES C. (photo): Pvt., Co. A. b. Baltimore Co., Md., 6/18/40. Res. Ellicott City, Howard Co., Md. Enl. 3/62; served to 12/62 on postwar roster. President, Drovers and Mer-chants Bank, Baltimore, 1899. Member ANS/MLA. Bur. Loudon Park Cem., Baltimore, 6/26/09.

CLARKE, JOHN O.: Pvt., Co. A. b. "Locust Grove," Montgomery Co., Md., 2/7/41. Res. Matthews Store, Howard Co., Md. Served in Co. A, 1st Md. Inf., 1861–62, but not on muster rolls.

Enl. Co. K (2nd), 1st Va. Cav., 1862.; ab. sick with scabies in Richmond hosp. 3/2–4/30/62. Transf. to Co. A, 1st Md. Cav., 5/15/62. Transf. to Co. C, 2nd Md. Bn. Cav. Reenl. in Co. A, 1st Md. Cav., Urbana, Md., 9/14/63; present, sick in camp 7–8/63; present 9–12/63 and 4/1/64; ab. detached as Foragemaster 5–12/64. Paroled Spotsylvania CH, Va., 5/2/65. Took oath 5/18/65. Farmer, "Sunny Brook Farm," near Brookville, Montgomery Co. Member Ridgeley Brown Camp, CV, Rockville, Md. d. 11/3/19. Bur. St. John's Episcopal Ch. Cem., Olney, Montgomery Co.

CLARKE, JOSEPH: Pvt., Co. D. Gd. Georgetown U. 1832. Res. of Baltimore. Enl. Edinburg 2/28/63; present 7–8/63; ab. in arrest 9–12/63. Transf. to Co. E, 2nd Md. Inf., 4/1/64; present through 2/28/65. NFR.

CLARKE, WILLIAM J.: Pvt., Co. A. b. circa 1840. Res. Baltimore. Enl. Wise Va. Arty., Centreville, Va. VMI 1/17/62. Transf. to Co. A, 1st Md. Cav., 6/5/62; in Richmond hosp. with spinal injury 8/12–16/62. Joined Urbana, Md., 9/14/62; ab. Nurse in Winchester hosp. 11/8–12/62. Captured Winchester 12/28/62; sent to Wheeling. Age twenty-two, 5'7", ruddy complexion, blue eyes, black hair. Painter. Transf. to Camp Chase; exchanged 4/1/63; present through 12/63 and 4/1/64. "Ab. term of service expired—no discharge." On rolls to 12/31/64. Paroled New Market, Va., 4/19/65. Age twenty-three, 5'9", light complexion, dark hair, blue eyes.

CLARY, THADDEUS WILLIAM: Pvt., Co. G. b. 1840. Res. Frostburg, Md. Enl. Co. K, 13th Va. Inf., 6/13/61. Clerk. Discharged 6/13/62. Enl. McNeill's Rangers 4/63; present 11–12/63. Captured Harrisonburg, Va., 6/3/64; sent to Johnson's Island, where he claimed to be 1st Lt., Co. G, Davis's Bn. (Co. G, 1st Md. Cav.); released 6/14/65. Age twenty-four, 5'6", fair complexion, dark hair, gray eyes. Res. Frostburg, Md. (Photograph in Hartzler 1992)

CLARY, VACHEL T.: Pvt., Co. D. Enl. New Market, Va., 1/1/63; present 7–12/63 and 4/1/64; ab. on leave for twenty days to Hardy Co., W.Va., to get a horse 4/9/64; horse sold to dismounted man in Bn; present through 12/31/64. NFR.

CLAUDE, E. HAMMOND: Pvt., Co. C. b. circa 1837. Res. of Anne Arundel Co., Md. Enl. Edinburg, Va., 3/1/63; ab. sick in Hanover, Va., hosp. 8/5–31/63; ab. on horse detail 10/28–31/63; ab. sick with debility in Richmond hosp. 11/12/63 and 1/2–3/64; present 4/1/64; AWOL 7/5/64 until captured Howard Co., Md., 9/26/64; sent to Ft. McHenry. NFR until captured Baltimore 3/18/65; sent to Ft. McHenry; sentenced to be hanged as a spy; sentence was commuted on the intercession of his brother-in-law, Maj. Charles Howes, U.S. Army. NFR.

CLAYLAND, JAMES: Pvt., Co. D. Enl. Woodstock, Va., 7/5/62. NFR until paid 1/1/64; discharged at end of enlistment. On rolls to 8/31/64. NFR.

CLEARY, PAUL W.: Pvt., Co. E. b. circa 1842. Enl. Richmond 1/12/63; des. from Camp Lee, Richmond, 2/12/53. NFR.

CLEMENTS, WILLIAM J.: Pvt., Co. C. b. circa 1837. Res. Port Tobacco, Charles Co., Md. Enl. Hanover CH, Va., 8/4/62; present 1–8/63; present detailed as wagon driver for Gen. Fitzhugh Lee 9–12/63 and 1–12/64. Paroled Harrisonburg, Va., 8/5/65. Age twenty-eight, 6'4", light complexion, blue eyes, dark hair.

CLINTON, HENRY DEWITT: Pvt., Co. K. b. Va. circa 1836. Res. of Baltimore. Enl. Co. K (2nd), 1st Va. Cav., Martinsburg, W.Va., 9/10/62; present until WIA (right shoulder) and captured Westminster, Md., 6/28/63; sent to Ft. McHenry; transf. to Ft. Del.; exchanged 7/31/63; present until detailed in C.S. Laboratory (Arsenal), Richmond, 2/1–8/31/64. Transf. to Co. K, 1st Md. Cav., 8/64; ab. in Richmond hosp. with anchylosis of shoulder joint 11/17/64; discharged at end of enlistment 12/26/64 while in Richmond hosp. Released from Richmond hosp. 2/12/65. Served in Arsenal Guard, Richmond, to end of war. Member ANS/MLA. Bricklayer, Baltimore. Admitted to Old Soldiers' Home, Pikesville, Md., 7/21/88,

age fifty-three. d. 3/11/13. Bur. Loudon Park Cem., Baltimore.

CLOUGH, C. E.: Pvt., Co. G. Paroled Richmond 4/24/65.

COAKLEY, J.: Pvt., Co. E. Ab. in Richmond hosp. 10/4/64; transf. to Staunton, Va., hosp. NFR.

COBOURN, JOHN: Pvt., Co. A, Davis's Bn. Enl. Bentonsville, Va., 9/1/63. Transf. to Co. M, 23rd Va. Cav.; AWOL 12/5/64. NFR.

COBURN, _____: Pvt., Co. B. On postwar roster.

COBURN, JOSEPH: Pvt., Co. B, Davis's Bn. NFR.

COCKEY, CHARLES R.: 5th Sgt., Co. A. Res. of Baltimore. Enl. as Cpl., Leesburg, Va., 9/25/62; promoted 5th Sgt. 8/63; horse stolen Culpeper, Va., ab. on horse detail to New Market, Va., 11/63; present through 12/63 and 4/1/64; AWOL 11–12/64. NFR. Gd. U. of Md. Medical School 1866. M.D., Queenstown, Md., 1898.

COCKEY, JOHN POWELL: Cpl., Co. E. b. circa 1840. Res. Worthington's Valley, Baltimore Co., Md. Enl. as Pvt., Richmond, 11/27/62, age twenty-two; presence or ab. not stated 1–2/63; horse killed at Fairmont, W.Va., 4/30/63; paid $230; present 7–8/63; presence or ab. not stated 9–10/63; present 11–12/63 and 4/1/64; promoted Cpl.; "Shot in breast while serving with the infantry because he had no horse" at Smithfield, W.Va., 8/29/64; KIA. Bur. Cockey Cem., Worthington's Valley, Baltimore Co. "True as steel and brave as a lion, he never faltered in the discharge of duty, and whether in camp, on picket post, or in the field he was every inch a soldier."

COCKEY, SEBASTIAN SPRIGG: Pvt., Co. A. b. circa 1838. Res. Urbana, Frederick Co., Md. Enl. Rippon, W.Va., 9/20/62; WIA (shoulder) Greenland Gap, W.Va., 4/25/63; present 7–12/63 and 4/1/64; ab. sick in Gordonsville, Va., hosp. 8/31/64; present 11–12/64; ab. sick with "debilitas" in Charlottesville hosp. 2/8/65; transf. 2/9/65; paid $3,500 for horse killed 2/24/65. Age twenty-seven, 5'11½", dark complexion, gray eyes, brown hair. Paroled Fairfax CH, Va., 5/4/65. Member ANS/MLA. d. 9/22/92. Bur. New Market Meth. Ch. Cem., New Market, Md.

COCKRELL, JAMES DANIEL: Pvt., Co. D. b. 10/5/25. Res. of Doubs, Frederick Co., Md. On postwar roster. d. 12/13/25. Bur. Mt. Olivet Cem., Frederick, Md.

COLE, CHARLES EDWARD: Pvt., Co. D. On postwar roster. Merchant. d. Frederick, Md., 8/21/05, age fifty-eight.

COLE, CHARLES N.: Pvt., Co. D. b. circa 1841. Res. of Baltimore. Enl. Winchester 9/20/62; present 11–12/62 and 7–9/63; ab. sick with "Ointax Fever" in Richmond hosp. 10/31–12/8/63; present

12/31/63 and 4/1–12/64. Paroled New Market, Va., 4/19/65. Age twenty-four, 5'11", dark complexion, black hair, blue eyes. Took oath Stevenson's Depot, Va., 5/15/65; destination Baltimore.

COLLINS, H. E.: Pvt., Co. A. Paid Richmond for 1/1–2/64 on 4/14/64. Paroled Winchester 4/19/65.

CONDON, WILLIAM: Pvt., Co. C, Davis's Bn. Conscripted 3/64. Captured Summit Point, Va., 8/17/64; sent to Old Capitol. Age forty-six, 5'10", dark complexion, dark hair, blue eyes. Res. of Cincinnati, Oh. Transf. to Elmira; released 5/17/65.

CONLEY, MARTIN VAN BUREN: Pvt., Co. E. Enl. Morgantown, W.Va., 4/28/63; present 7–8/63; presence or ab. not stated 9–10/63; present 11–12/63, 4/1/64, and 7–12/64. NFR.

CONNELL, THOMAS: Pvt., Co. C, Davis's Bn. Res. of Baltimore. On postwar roster.

CONNELLY, PATRICK: Pvt., Co. C, Davis's Bn. Res. of Baltimore. May have served as Sgt., Co. E, 1st S.C. Inf. On postwar roster.

CONRAD, EPHRIAM: Pvt., Co. K. b. 10/6/34. d. Kamiah, Id., 11/14/07. Tombstone reads "Co. K, 1st Va. Cav." May also have served in Co. K, 1st Md. Cav.

CONRADT, CHRISTIAN J.: Pvt., Co K. b. Baltimore 2/37. Res. of Baltimore. Enl. Co. C, 1st Md. Inf., 5/17/61; discharged 5/23/62. Age twenty-five, 5'11½", light complexion, sandy hair, hazel eyes. Clerk. Enl. Co. K (2nd), 1st Va. Cav., 6/10/62; present until captured Cashtown, Pa., 7/5/63; sent to Ft. Del.; transf. to Pt. Lookout. Escaped; ab. escaped prison—on furlough on rolls 8/31/64. Transf. to Co. K, 1st Md. Cav., 8/64. Listed as exchanged 9/38/64; ab. on leave for thirty days 10/22/64; ab. sick with "debilitas" in Charlottesville hosp. 11/1/64; resumed furlough 11/4/64; discharged at end of enlistment 12/4/64; des. to the enemy Leonardtown, Md., 3/10/65; sent to Pt. Lookout; took oath, released 3/29/65. Former res. of Kent Co. Destination Kent Co. or Baltimore. Member ANS/MLA., and Frank Buchanan Camp, CV, Baltimore. Upholsterer. d. Baltimore, 4/22/15. Bur. Loudon Park Cem., Baltimore.

CONROY, John J.: Pvt., Co. unknown. b. Ireland 3/24/46. Arr. Baltimore 1846. Claimed service in 1st Md. Cav. Moved to Texas 1877. Blacksmith until 1910. Superintendent of Dallas waterworks eight years. Member Sterling Price Camp, CV, Dallas. d. Oak Cliff, Tex., 2/20/24. Bur. Oak Cliff Cem., Dallas Co., Tex.

COOK, THOMAS W.: Pvt., Co. C. Captured Leonardtown, Md., 11/14/64; sent to Old Capitol; transf. to Ft. Del.; released 5/11/65. 5'11", fair complexion, fair hair, gray eyes. Res. Baltimore.

COOKE, ADOLPHUS: 2nd Lt., Co. B. b. Prince George's Co., Md., circa 1840. Gd. Georgetown U. 1861. Res. of Prince George's Co. Enl. Winchester 9/10/62; present through 12/62. Commanding co., Greenland Gap, W.Va., 4/25/63; WIA Monterey, Pa., 7/4/63. Captured Williamsport, Md., 7/14/63; sent to Hagerstown, Md., hosp.; transf. to Cotton Factory hosp., Harrisburg, Pa., 8/10/63 with "Billous Fever"; transf. to West Buildings hosp., Baltimore; sent to Ft. McHenry 9/2/63. Age twenty-four, 5'11", light complexion, light hair, blue eyes. Trans. Johnson's Island; released 6/11/65; destination Prince George's Co. Member George Emack Camp, CV, Hyattsville, Md., and ANS/MLA. d. Stevenson, Baltimore Co., 7/30/05, age sixty-five. Bur. Druid Ridge Cem., Pikesville, Md.

COOKE, GEORGE E.: Pvt., Co. C. b. Md. circa 1838. Res. of Chaptico, St. Mary's Co., Md. Enl. Co. H, 1st Md. Inf., 6/18/61; discharged 6/18/62. Enl. Co. C, 1st Md. Cav., Richmond, 8/4/62; present 7–8/63; ab. on horse detail for twelve days 10/28/63; horse abandoned Manassas, Va., 10/15/63; present 11–12/63; ab. on leave for twenty days to Athens, Ga., to get a horse 2/26/64; present 4/1/64. Captured Green Spring Run, Md., 4/23/64; sent to Pt. Lookout; released 5/14/65. Clerk. Res. St. Mary's Co. Member George Emack Camp, CV, Hyattsville, Md., 1906.

COOPER, CHARLES E.: Pvt., Co. E. des. to the enemy in western Va. 1/64. Age twenty-six, 5'8", light complexion, light hair, hazel eyes. Laborer, Halifax Co., Va., Took oath, sent North 1/25/64.

COOPER, JOHN M.: 1st Lt., Co. C, Davis's Bn. Res. Annapolis Junction, Anne Arundel Co., Md. NFR.

COOPER, SAMUEL: Pvt., Co. unknown. Listed as POW 10/25/64. Possibly the Samuel Cooper who served in Co. C, 2nd Bn., Md. Cav. Res. St. Mary's Co., Md.

COOPER, WILLIAM T.: Pvt., Co. B. Res. Somerset Co., Md. Enl. Charlottesville 10/9/62; ab. sick with debility in Charlottesville hosp. 11/16/62 and with jaundice 12/2–24/62; bay horse killed Capon Springs, W.Va., 12/20/62, paid $300. Captured Romney, W.Va., 1/24/63; sent to Wheeling. Age thirty-three, 5'11", dark complexion, blue eyes, dark hair. Transf. to Camp Chase; exchanged 4/1/63. Captured Monterey Springs, Pa., 7/4/63; exchanged 7/63; present 9–12/63 and 4/1/64. Reported captured again, but not on Federal POW rolls; perhaps KIA.

CORCORAN, THOMAS W.: Pvt., Co. D. Res. Carroll Co., Md. Enl. Winchester 9/20/62; present 11–12/62. Captured Monterey Springs, Pa., 7/4/63; sent to Ft. McHenry; transf. to Ft. Del. and

Pt. Lookout; exchanged 2/21/65. Paid Camp Lee, Richmond, 3/2/65. NFR.

CORMICK, ROBERT E.: Pvt., Co. E. b. circa 1842. Enl. Richmond 11/14/62, age twenty; presence or ab. not stated 1–2/63; WIA (calf of leg) and captured near Winchester 6/12/63; sent to Ft. McHenry; exchanged 6–7/63; ab. sick with "Remit Fever" 8/15–9/8/63; present 11–12/63, 4/1/64 and 7–12/64; ab. sick with pneumonia in Charlottesville hosp. 1/11–2/2/65. Paroled Danville, Va., 6/17/65. Res. Aquasco, Prince George's Co., Md., 1903.

CORNELL, JAMES: Pvt., Co. unknown. Paroled Richmond 4/22/65.

CORNWELL, CHARLES C.: Pvt., Co. G. Served in Capt. Barry's Co., 1st Md. Inf.; paid 11/1/62. Enl. Co. G, 1st Md. Cav., 11/62. In Richmond hosp. 11/26–28/62. Captured Williamsport, Md., 7/14/63; sent to Ft. Del.; transf. to Pt. Lookout. Took oath, joined U.S. Service 1/28/65.

COUSINS, THOMAS J.: Pvt., Co. A. Paroled Winchester 4/19/65; signed by mark. Age eighteen, 5'9", florid complexion, dark hair, gray eyes. Res. Shelby Co., Mo. Probably a member of Capt. Woodson's Co. A, 1st Mo. Cav., which served in Va.

COVINGTON, JESSIE H.: Pvt., Co. A. Res. Howard Co., Md. Served in 1st Md. Arty. 7/23/61–2/62. Served in Hampton S.C. Legion Arty. Enl. Co. A, 1st Md. Cav., Leetown, W.Va., 9/1/62; present 7–9/63. Captured Brandy Station, Va., 10/11/63; sent to Old Capitol; transf. to Pt. Look-out; exchanged 3/6/64. Paid Richmond 4/12/64; ab. on leave 4/11/64; ab. POW on rolls to 12/64. NFR.

COX, JAMES B.: Pvt., Co. E. b. circa 1839. Enl. Richmond 10/20/62, age twenty-three; presence or ab. not stated 1–2/63; present 7–8/63; presence or ab. not stated 9–10/63; present 11–12/63, 4/1/64, and 7–12/64. NFR.

COYLE, JAMES: Pvt., Co. C, Davis's Bn. NFR.

CRAFT, JOHN B.: Pvt., Co. C, Davis's Bn. Res. Frederick Co., Md. NFR.

CRAIG, WILLIAM R.: Pvt., Co. A, Davis's Bn. Transf. to Co. M, 23rd Va. Cav. Paroled Winchester 4/15/65.

CRAIGVILLE, A. W.: Pvt., Co. D. Captured Monterey Springs, Pa., 7/6/63. Received Ft. Del. 7/7–12/63; died there, date unknown.

CRANE, ROBERT BRENT: Pvt., Co. A. b. St. Mary's Co., Md., 3/19/42. Att. St. Timothy's Hall, Baltimore Co. Res. Towson, Baltimore Co. Enl. Lacey Springs, Va., 4/1/63; WIA (lost eye) and captured Greenland Gap, W.Va., 4/25/63; exchanged 5/63. Ab. wounded until detailed with Medical Purveyor's Office, Charlotte, N.C., 10/1/63–4/1/64; present 7–12/63; ab. sick with scabies in Charlottesville hosp. 1/3–17/65. Paroled. Medical Purveyor's Office, Charlotte, N.C., 5/3/65. Teacher, St. Mary's Co., Md. Professor, Towson, Md. Member Arnold Elzey Camp, CV, Baltimore. d. Upper Falls, Md., 1/9/13. Bur. Loudon Park Cem., Baltimore.

CRANE, WILLIAM S., JR.: Ord. Sgt. b. 5/2/45. Res. St. Mary's Co., Md. Enl. as Pvt., Co. C, 1st Md. Cav., Hagerstown, Md., 7/12/63; present until Brandy Station, Va., 10/11/63, when bay horse was killed and he was captured; sent to Old Capitol; transf. to Pt. Lookout; exchanged 3/6/64. Paid $675 for horse killed; on parole, Richmond, 4/1/64; ab. sick with scabies in Richmond hosp. 6/9–13/64; furloughed for fifteen days; readmitted to Richmond hosp. 6/29–7/26/64; present through 8/31/64; present, detailed as Ord. Sgt. by Capt. Emack, commanding the regiment 10–12/64; ab. sick with scabies in Charlottesville hosp. 12/28/64; transf. to Richmond hosp. 1/6/65; RTD 2/2/65. NFR. d. 5/13/90. Bur. Ivy Hill Cem., Laurel, Md.

CRAWFORD, GEORGE J.: Pvt., Co. E. b. circa 1839. Res. Prince George's Co., Md. Enl. Co. F, 1st Va. Inf., 5/1/61. Transf. to Co. C, 1st Va. Arty.; discharged 11/13/61. Enl. Co. E, 1st Md. Cav., Richmond, 12/6/62, age twenty; presence or ab. not stated 1–2/63. Captured near Winchester 6/12/63, horse killed; sent to Ft. McHenry. Age twenty, 5'11", dark complexion, dark eyes, dark hair. Exchanged 6/63. Paid $650 for horse killed; ab. sick with "Pruringo" in Richmond hosp. 8/15/63; transf. to Lynchburg, Va., hosp.; ab. detailed in Richmond hosp. 11–12/63; RTD 4/6/64; ab. sick with "Fits" in Richmond hosp. 5/29/64; RTD 7/6/64; ab. sick in Charlottesville hosp. 7/7–12/31/64. Paroled Harrisonburg, Va., 5/7/65. Age twenty-two, 5'11", fair complexion, dark hair, hazel eyes. Member ANS/MLA. Admitted Old Soldiers' Home, Pikesville, Md., 7/30/88, age forty-nine, from Prince George's Co. Carpenter. Expelled. d. 9/20/99.

CRAWFORD, HENRY VAN BIBBER: Pvt., Co. B. b. Middletown, Del., 9/16/33. Res. Kent Co., Md. Enl. Charlottesville 10/1/62. Captured Monterey Springs, Pa., 7/4/63; sent to Ft. Del.; transf. to Pt. Lookout; exchanged 12/28/63; present 4/1/64. Captured Moorefield, W.Va., 8/7/64; sent to Wheeling. 5'10", fair complexion, gray eyes, brown hair. Farmer. Res. New Castle, Del. Transf. to Camp Chase and Pt. Lookout; exchanged 3/27/65. Paroled, took oath, Richmond 4/25/65. Res. Cecil Co., Md. Farmer. d. near Warwick, Cecil Co., Md., 1/14/97. Bur. St. Francis Xavier Ch. Cem.

CRAWFORD, JOHN THOMAS: Pvt., Co. A. Res.

Howard Co., Md. Captured Sugar Loaf Mt., Md., 1/4/65; sent to Old Capitol as "Guerilla"; transf. to Ft. Warren; released 6/13/65. 5'9¾", light complexion, brown hair, hazel eyes.

CRAWFORD, THOMAS W.: Pvt., Co. A. b. 12/4/36. Res. Howard Co. or Washington Co., Md. Enl. Sharpsburg, Md., 7/1/64; present through 12/64. NFR. d. 2/11/96. Bur. Urbana Methodist Ch. Cem, Montgomery Co., Md.

CRAY, WILLIAM R.: Pvt., Co. A, Davis's Bn. b. circa 1844. Enl. Mt. Crawford, Va., 11/25/63; present 1/1–12/31/64. Transf. to Co. M, 23rd Va. Cav. Paroled 4/16/65. Age nineteen, 5'5", light complexion, auburn hair, hazel eyes.

CRETIN, JOHN H.: Pvt., Co. C. b. circa 1825. Res. Washington Co., Md. Enl. Martinsburg, W.Va. 9/20/62; present 7–12/63, 1–2/64, 4/1/64, and 7–12/64. Paroled Winchester 5/3/65; took oath Kearneysville, W.Va., same day. Age forty, 5'10", dark complexion, brown hair, gray eyes. Res. near Shepherdstown, Jefferson Co., W.Va.

CRISSWELL, JOHN O.: Pvt., Co. D. Enl. Winchester 9/20/62. Captured near Martinsburg, W.Va. 11/62; exchanged 11/62; RTD 12/15/62; present, 7–8/63; horse killed Monterey Springs, Pa., 7/4/63, paid $860; present 9–12/63 and 4/1/64; AWOL 5/12/64. NFR.

CRIST, HENRY: Pvt., Co. G, Davis's Bn. Paroled Winchester 4/19/65. Age twenty, 5'9", fair complexion, light hair, blue eyes.

CRITTENDEN, CHURCHILL: Pvt., Co. C. b. Texas 1840; moved to Calif. 1851. Left Hobart College, Ind., in 1862 to enlist. Served as volunteer ADC to Gen. James J. Archer 6/62. Enl. Richmond 8/4/62; horse killed near Winchester 6/13/63, paid $450; present 7–8/63; ab. on horse detail to Newtown, Va., for fifteen days 2/1/64 and another fifteen days 2/16/64; ab. on four-month detail to go with H. H. Johnson and Col. Bradley to the Mississippi River by order Gen. Arnold Elzey to raise a company. On rolls 3/22–4/1/64; present 8/31/64. Captured with John J. Hartigan in Page Co. 10/27/64. Attempted escape, wounded, and recaptured. Executed by order of Col. William H. Powell of Gen. William W. Averell's Cav. "They were buried by the last farmer who had given them supplies, and he notified the command. When the graves were opened by the men of Co. C, and circumstances of the manner of their deaths verified, 'vows were uttered over the dead bodies of their comrades to avenge their deaths—and they were avenged, though Powell escaped.' " Bur. Shockoe Cem., Richmond, age twenty-four years.

CROMWELL, CHARLES: Pvt., Co. B, Davis's Bn. On postwar roster.

CROPPER, THOMAS EDWIN: Pvt., Co. B. b. Cecil Co., Md., circa 1840. Enl. Charlottesville 10/1/62; serving as Comm. Sgt. 12/1/62; present 7–11/63; ab. sick with camp itch in Richmond hosp. 12/28/63–3/17/64; present 4/1/64. Captured Kent Co., Md., 4/12/64; sent to Ft. Warren; released 6/10/65. 6', light complexion, brown hair, blue eyes. M.D. in Suffolk, Va., 1903; Surgeon and Dentist. d. Suffolk 1/13/15, age seventy-five.

CROSS, CHARLES LEWIS: 1st Sgt., Co. A, Davis's Bn. b. Govanstown, Md., 1/17/41. Res. of Baltimore. Enl. Co. C, 7th Va. Cav., 7/61. Clerk. Discharged 12/1/62. Enl. Davis's Bn. 1863; present Gettysburg, Pa.; captured Maj. of 1st N.Y. Regulars (Cav.) and Maj. of 151st Ohio Inf. at New Market, Va., 5/15/64; present at Monocacy and Winchester; WIA; present 1/1–10/31/64; served as Adj. of the Bn. to the end of the war (all on postwar account). Transf. to Co. M, 23rd Va. Cav. Took oath Baltimore 5/16/65. Recorder in Clerk's Office, Baltimore. Member ANS/MLA. d. Waverly, Md., 7/12/09. Bur. Govansville Presb. Ch. Cem.

CROTHERS, ILLINOIS: 1st Sgt., Co. C. Res. of Baltimore. Enl. Co. G, 13th Va. Inf., 7/16/61; discharged as nonresident 5/28/62. Enl. as 2nd Sgt., Co. C, 1st Md. Cav., Richmond, 8/4/62; appointed 1st Sgt. 7/15/63; present 7–12/63, 1–2, and 4/1/64; reduced to Pvt. 7/1/64. Courier for Gen. Bradley T. Johnson 9/10–12/64; des. to the enemy at Aquia Creek, Va., 12/4/64; sent to Ft. McHenry; released 5/21/65. 5'8", light complexion, dark hair, gray eyes.

CULBRETH, JOHN: Pvt., Co. K., b. circa 1838. Enl. Co. C, 1st Md. Inf., 12/27/61; discharged 6/19/62. Enl. Breathed's Bty., Petersburg, Va., 7/10/62. Transf. to Co. K (2nd), 1st Va. Cav., 8/14/64. Transf. to Co. K, 1st Md. Cav., 8/64; AWOL 11/12–12/31/64. NFR. d. Old Soldiers' Home, Pikesville, Md., 2/20/12, age seventy-four. Bur. Loudon Park Cem., Baltimore.

CUMMINS, GEORGE WILSON: Pvt., Co. C. b. 1845. Captured Darnestown, Md., 9/6/64; sent to Old Capitol; transf. to Ft. Warren; released 6/10/65. Res. Oak Vale, Fairfax Co., Va., postwar. d. 1922. Bur. Aaron Chapel, Fairfax Co. On postwar roster of Co. G, 43rd Bn. Va. Cav.

CUNNINGHAM, GEORGE W.: Pvt., Co. F. Res. of Oldtown, Allegany Co., Md. Enl. Richmond 7/8/63; present through 12/63; however, Enl. Co. C, 43rd Bn. Va. Cav., 12/1/63, and present in that unit through 2/64; present in Co. C, 1st Md. Cav., 4/1/64. Captured at Pollard's Farm, Va., 5/27/64; sent to Pt. Lookout; serving as Clerk in PM's Office, Pt. Lookout 11/12/64. Reported exchanged 11/15/64, however remained at Pt.

Lookout, took oath, and was released by order of President Lincoln 2/11/65.

CUNNINGHAM, ROBERT H.: Pvt., Co. K. b. Va. circa 1847. Student, age thirteen. Arcola PO, Loudoun Co., Va., per 1860 census. Enl. Co. K (2nd), 1st Va. Cav., 8/10/62; present through 8/64. Transf. to Co. K, 1st Md. Cav., 8/64; discharged at end of enlistment 12/14/64. NFR. Farmhand, age twenty-three, Arcola PO, Loudoun Co., 1870 census. Member ANS/MLA., 1894. Res. of Baltimore.

DADE, WILLIAM FRANKLIN: Pvt., Co. D. b. near Buck Lodge, Montgomery Co., Md., 1/29/28. Farmer, Old Medley's, Montgomery Co. Enl. Winchester 9/20/62; present 11–12/62. Captured at Monterey Springs, Pa., 7/4/63, horse killed; sent to Ft. McHenry; transf. to Ft. Del. and Pt. Lookout; exchanged 12/28/63. Paid $2,500 for horse; present 4/1–12/31/64. "Led in the front of the fight at Appomattox Courthouse." Paroled Louisa CH, Va., 5/10/65. 5'8", fair complexion, light hair, gray eyes. Took oath Washington, D.C., 7/6/65. d. near Beallsville, Md., 9/13/05. Bur. Monocacy Cem., Beallsville.

DALL, HORATIO McPHERSON: Pvt., Co. C. b. Washington Co., Md., 12/22/39; moved to Baltimore 1859. Clerk in Hardware Store. Enl. Co. B, 21st Va. Inf., 5/23/61; discharged 5/62. Enl. Co. C, 1st Md. Cav., Richmond, 8/4/62; present 7–12/63, 1–2/64, and 4/1–12/31/64. Captured Frederick's Hall, Va., 3/13/65; sent to Ft. Monroe; transf. to Pt. Lookout; released 6/20/65. 5'6", light hair, blue eyes. Res. of Frederick, Md.; destination Frederick. Employee of Adam Express Co. for three years; RR employee; Bookkeeper, Baltimore; Tax Collector; Bailiff in Tax Dept., Courts of Baltimore, 1900. Member ANS/MLA. d. Baltimore 5/24/03. Bur. St. John's Episcopal Ch. Cem., Hagerstown, Md.

DALL, RASH M.: Pvt., Co. K. Res. Williamsport, Md. On postwar rosters Co. K (2nd), 1st Va. Cav., and Co. K, 1st Md. Cav.

DANCE, ELI SCOTT: Pvt., Co. C. b. Delaney, near Loch Haven, Baltimore Co., 1/5/43. Res. of Baltimore. Enl. New Market, Va., 2/1/63; ab. sick in Hanover hosp. 8/25–31/63; ab. sick in Richmond hosp. 9/21–24/63; present 10–12/63, 1–2/64 and 4/1/64; ab. sick with gonorrhoea in Richmond hosp. 6/12–7/13/64. Captured Moore-field, W.Va., 8/7/64; sent to Wheeling. 5'4", dark complexion, dark hair, brown eyes. Farmer. Transf. to Camp Chase and Pt. Lookout; ex-changed 3/27/65; present Camp Lee, Richmond, 3/27/65. Paroled Winchester 4/22/65. Took oath Baltimore 5/4/65. Miller, Baltimore Co.; Bailiff of Orphan's Court, Baltimore, twenty-two years. d. Towson,

Md., 5/7/1945. Bur. Old School Bapt. Ch. Cem., Jarrettsville, Md. Last Confederate veteran in Md.

DARNELL, ALEXANDER: Pvt., Co. unknown, Davis's Bn. Captured; paroled 9/27/62. NFR.

DAVIDSON, J. E.: Pvt., Co. A, Davis's Bn. Enl. 1862 and served to 1865 per application to ANS/MLA. d. Baltimore 1/5/96. Bur. Loudon Park Cem., Baltimore.

DAVIDSON, JOSEPH G.: Pvt., Co. A, Davis's Bn. Res. of Georgetown, D.C. Enl. Richmond 1/1/64; present through 10/31/64. Transf. to Co. M, 23rd Va. Cav. Captured Woodstock, Va., 3/15/65; sent to Ft. McHenry, "not to be exchanged during the war." Released 5/9/65.

DAVIDSON, MARCELLUS: Pvt., Co. A, Davis's Bn. Enl. in Md. 7/12/64; present through 10/31/64. Transf. to Co. M, 23rd Va. Cav. NFR.

DAVIDSON, ROBERT: Pvt., Co. E. Res. of Baltimore. Enl. Cockeysville, Md., 7/25/64. Captured Moorefield, W.Va., 8/7/64; exchanged 3/65. Admitted to Richmond hosp. with "chronic diarrhoea" 3/28/65. Captured in Richmond hosp. 4/3/65; sent to Ft. Monroe. Took oath, transportation furnished to Baltimore, 4/23/65.

DAVIDSON, RUFUS C.: Pvt., Co. A, Davis's Bn. Res. of Prince George's Co., Md. Enl. Md. 7/12/64; present through 10/31/64. Transf. to Co. M, 23rd Va. Cav. NFR.

DAVIDSON, WILLIAM H.: Pvt., Co. A, Davis's Bn. b. 11/13/28. Res. of Georgetown, D.C. Transf. to Co. M, 23rd Va. Cav. Captured Woodstock, Va., 3/18/65; sent to Ft. McHenry, "not to be exchanged during the war." Released 5/9/65. 5'5", light complexion, brown hair, gray eyes. d. 1/3/02. Bur. Rock Oak Cem., Hardy Co., W.Va.

DAVIS, A.: Lt. , Co. F and I, Davis's Bn. Res. Carrollton Manor, Frederick Co., Md. On postwar rosters.

DAVIS, E. A.: Pvt., Co. D. Captured Waynesboro, Pa., 7/4/63; sent to Pt. Lookout; exchanged 2/21/65. NFR.

DAVIS, GEORGE: Pvt., Co. D. Captured Front Royal, Va., 5/16/63; sent to Ft. McHenry; exchanged 5/26/63. NFR.

DAVIS, HENRY B.: Pvt., Co. K. b. circa 1840. Enl. Co. K (2nd), 1st Va. Cav., 5/1/62 or 11/1/62; present until WIA (thigh) and captured Hartwood Ch., Va., 2/25/63; exchanged by 10/63; ab. wounded in hosp. through 1/64; present 2–8/64; ab. sick in hosp. 11–12/64. Paroled Heathsville, Va., 5/2/65. Age twenty-five, 5'10", dark complexion, dark brown hair, hazel eyes. Member ANS/MLA. Res. of Whaleyville, Worcester Co., Md. d. 7/18/02.

DAVIS, JAMES A.: Lt., Cos. F and B, Davis's Bn., and Co. G, 1st Md. Cav.; WIA, "Skull and over sacrum causing meclosis," 1/2/63; ab. wounded in

Richmond hosp. until furloughed for sixty days 11/26/63; in Richmond hosp. 8/5/64; furloughed for thirty days 8/7/65. Captured Front Royal, Va., 2/16/65 as Lt., Co. G, 1st Md. Cav.; sent to Ft. McHenry. "Guerilla not to be exchanged during the war by order of Maj. Gen. Sheridan." d. Ft. McHenry 3/3/65. Bur. Loudon Park Cem., Baltimore.

DAVIS, JAMES W.: Pvt., Co. unknown, Davis's Bn. b. 1837. Res. of Darnestown, Montgomery Co., Md. Enl. Co. G, 7th Va. Cav., 4/27/61. Captured Moorefield, W.Va., 9/11/63; sent to Ft. McHenry; escaped 11/16/63. Enl. Davis's Bn., Co. and date unknown. Captured on scout in Md. 10/20/64; sent to Ft. McHenry; transf. to Pt. Lookout; released 5/9/65. Res. of Cambridge, Md., postwar. (Photograph in Hartzler 1992)

DAVIS, PETER A.: Pvt., Co. B. Enl. Charlottesville 9/10/62. Captured Monterey Springs, Pa., 7/4/63; sent to Ft. Del.; d. there of typhoid fever 8/31/63. Bur. Finn's Pt., N.J., Natl. Cem.

DAVIS, PHINEAS JAMES: 1st Sgt., Co. D. b. Grant Co., Wis., 1839; moved to Baltimore as a child. Res. of Libertytown, Frederick Co., Md. Enl. Winchester 9/20/62; present through 12/62. Captured Strasburg, Va., 2/26/63; sent to Wheeling. Age twenty-three, 5'7¾", florid complexion, black hair, gray eyes. Student. Res. of Baltimore. Transf. to Camp Chase; exchanged 4/1/63. Captured Monterey, Pa., 7/4/63; sent to Ft. Del.; exchanged 7/63. Present through 12/63 and 4/1/64; horse killed at Moorefield, W.Va., 8/7/64, paid $2,000; issued clothing 9/30/64; paid 2/17/65. Paroled Winchester 4/65. Carpenter; moved to San Antonio, Tex., 1882. Member ANS/MLA. Entered Old Soldiers' Home, Austin, Tex., 7/15/16; d. there 2/16/19. Bur. Texas State Cem., Austin. Brother of William E. Davis.

DAVIS, ROBERT: Pvt., Co. E. b. circa 1847. Res. of Baltimore. Captured Moorefield, W.Va., 8/7/64; sent to Wheeling; transf. to Camp Chase and Pt. Lookout; exchanged 3/27/65. Captured in Richmond hosp. 4/3/65. Paroled from Libby Prison, Richmond, 4/22/65; transportation furnished to Baltimore. d. 2/2/70, age thirty-six. Bur. Loudon Park Cem., Baltimore.

DAVIS, THOMAS SAPPINGTON: Pvt., Co. D. b. 9/1/42. Res. of Libertytown, Frederick Co., Md. Enl. Winchester 9/20/62. Captured Monterey Springs, Pa., 7/4/63, horse killed; sent to Ft. McHenry; transf. to Ft. Del., Pt. Lookout, and Ft. Columbus; exchanged 2/18/65. Paid $3,000 for horse killed. Paroled Ashland, Va., 6/1/65; destination Baltimore. Took oath 8/25/65. M.D. in Frederick Co., Md. d. 11/25/20. Bur. St. Peter's Catholic Ch. Cem., Libertytown.

DAVIS, THOMAS STURGIS: Lt. Col., Davis's Bn. b. Johnstown, Pa., 1833; moved to Md. as a child. Teacher and Law Clerk, Rockdale, Md., 1861. Served in QM Corps, C.S.A. Enl. 7th Va. Cav., 2/1/62 as Adj.; appointed Capt. and AAG. on Gen. Turner Ashby's staff 6/62; present with Gen. William E. Jones on western Virginia raid 4–5/63. Organized Bn. for 1st Md. Cav. 8/13/63, but not assigned; raised six companies. Promoted Maj. of Bn. 9/63; commanding Bn. 11/16/63, 2/64, and 5/20/64. Assigned to 2nd Md. Bn. Cav. 5/5/64, but order disregarded. Served as Chief of Scouts for Gen. John D. Imboden; present at Piedmont, Va., 6/5/64; promoted Lt. Col.; WIA and captured Winchester 9/19/64 (horse shot, fell on his leg); sent to Ft. Del.; released 7/19/65. Lawyer, Towsonville, Md.; served in Md. Senate 1872–76. d. Towson, Md., 11/2/83. Bur. Black Rock Bapt. Ch. Cem., Reistertown, Md.

DAVIS, WILLIAM EVAN: Pvt., Co. D. b. Grant Co., Wis., 1841; moved to Md. as a child. Res. of Libertytown, Md. Enl. Winchester 9/20/62; present 11–12/62; ab. sick in hosp. 7–8/63; present 9–12/63 and 4/1/64; ab. on horse detail to Hardy Co., W.Va., for twenty days 4/9/64; ab. on detached duty with Co. A, Davis's Bn., through 12/64; horse killed Winchester 9/19/64, paid $3,500. NFR. Moved to Tex. 1878. Carpenter, San Antonio, Tex., 1879. Member ANS/MLA. d. Boerne, Kendall Co., Tex., 1/2/24. Bur. Boerne Cem. Brother of Phineas J. Davis.

DAVISON, GEORGE: Sgt., Co. A, Davis's Bn. On postwar roster.

DAVISON, ROSSER: Pvt., Co. A, Davis's Bn. On postwar roster.

DAVISSON, JOHN E.: Pvt., Co. D. b. circa 1840. Paroled Winchester 4/25/65. Age twenty-five, 5'9", dark complexion, black hair, brown eyes. Res. of Fairfax Co., Va.

DEAKINS, JAMES ROBERT H.: Cpl., Co. B. b. 7/26/40. Res. of Bladensburg, Prince George's Co., Md. Enl. Winchester 9/10/62. Captured Monterey Springs, Pa., 7/4/63, horse killed; sent to Ft. Del.; transf. to Pt. Lookout; exchanged 12/28/63. Paid $850 for horse; present 4/1/64 and 7/64; ab. sick with scabies in Charlottesville hosp. 10/7/64. Resumed furlough 10/21/64; present through 12/64; present Appomattox CH, Va., 4/9/65. Member George Emack Camp, CV, Hyattsville, Md., 1903. Res. of Hyattsville. d. 6/16/23. Bur. Deakins Cem., University Park, Md.

DEAVER, JOHN R.: Pvt., Co. F. b. circa 1836. Res. of Baltimore. Enl. Richmond 7/14/63; present through 9/63; WIA (right foot) and captured Brandy Station, Va., 10/11/63; sent to Old Capitol; exchanged 10/63; ab. wounded in

Richmond hosp. 10/14/63, age twenty-seven; transf. to Lynchburg, Va., hosp. Captured Potomac Run 5/30/64; sent to Old Capitol; transf. to Elmira and Pt. Lookout; exchanged 11/15/64. Admitted Richmond hosp. 3/9/65. NFR.

DECKER, LEE W.: Pvt., Co. A. b. circa 1844. Res. Frederick Co., Md. Captured Capon Springs, W.Va., 5/9/63; sent to Wheeling. Age nineteen, 6'¾", light complexion, blue eyes, brown hair. Gunsmith. Transf. to Camp Chase, Johnson's Island, and Pt. Lookout; exchanged 2/17/65; present Camp Lee, Richmond, 2/28–3/65. Paroled Burkeville Junction, Va., 4/14–17/65.

DELASHMUTT, WILLIAM G.: Pvt., Co. D. b. Frederick Co., Md., 1839. Res. Frederick City, Md. Enl. Winchester 9/10/62; present 11–12/62. Captured Monterey Springs, Pa., 7/4/63; sent to Ft. McHenry; transf. to Ft. Del.; exchanged 12/28/63. Present 4/1/64; WIA Pollard's Farm, Va., 5/27/64; present 7–12/64. Paroled Winchester 4/27/65. Age twenty-six, 5'11", dark complexion, dark hair, dark eyes. Member Alexander Young Camp, CV, Frederick, Md. d. Martinville, Ill., 12/16/15. Bur. Martinville.

DENNISON, JOHN E.: Pvt., Co. G. Also served in Co. B, Davis's Bn. Took oath Washington, D.C., 5/11/65.

DENT, JOHN MARSHALL: Pvt., Co. B. b. Md. 8/9/46. Student. Chaptico, St. Mary's Co., Md., per 1860 census. Enl. 1864; WIA (left hip) Winchester 9/19/64; ab. wounded in Charlottesville hosp. 9/22/64 until furloughed 9/27/65; detailed as Clerk in Richmond. Paroled Mechanicsville, Va., 4/28/65. Attorney, St. Mary's Co., Md., per 1870 census. d. 8/26/29. Bur. All Saints Cem., Oakley, Md.

DESPAIN, H. B.: Pvt., Co. A. Captured Atlanta, Ga., 7/21/64; sent to Camp Chase; released 5/13/65. Age twenty-one, 5'6", red complexion, blue eyes, light hair. Res. Webster Co., Md. [Mo.] Probably a member of Co. A, 1st Mo. Cav., with records misfiled.

DEVERIES, J. OCATVIUS: Pvt., Co. E. Res. Baltimore. Issued clothing 9/15/64; des. to the enemy at Annapolis, Md., 11/21/64. "Wishing to take oath, return to home in Baltimore." NFR. d. Westminster, Carroll Co., Md., 3/15/12, age seventy-four.

DICKINSON, LAURENCE THOMPSON: Pvt., Co. A. b. Cumberland, Md., 6/21/43. Res. of Allegany Co., Md. Enl. Charlottesville 8/25/62; present 7–9/63; WIA (hip) Morton's Ford, Va., 10/11/63. Captured at Brandy Station, Va., same day; sent to Old Capitol and Pt. Lookout; exchanged 3/29/64; WIA (right shoulder) Frederick, Md., 7/7/64. Captured in Hagerstown,

Md., hosp. 7/10/64; sent to West Buildings hosp., Baltimore; transf. to Ft. McHenry and Pt. Lookout; exchanged 12/30/64. In Richmond hosp. 1/10–2/15/65. Paroled Fairfax CH, Va., 5/4/65. 5'10", dark complexion, dark hair, blue eyes. Teacher and Leather Manufacturer, Chattanooga, Tenn., 1881–1914. Member N. B. Forrest Camp, CV, Chattanooga. d. Keokuk, Iowa 3/31/23. (Postwar photograph, Confederate Veteran magazine)

DIGGES, JOHN T.: Pvt., Co. D. Res. La Plata, Charles Co., Md. Served in 1st Md. Light Arty. 9/1/62–2/28/65. On postwar roster of Co. D, 1st Md. Cav. Gd. Georgetown U. 1869. M.D., New Market, Md. Member George Emack Camp, CV, Hyattsville, Md., 1903. Res. La Plata, Md., 1906.

DISHAROON, JOHN W.: Pvt., Co. E. b. circa 1840. Res. Somerset Co., Md. Enl. Richmond 11/10/62, age twenty-two; presence or ab. not stated 1–2/63. Captured near Winchester 5/12/63; sent to Ft. McHenry; transf. to Ft. Monroe; exchanged 6/30/63. Age twenty-two, fair complexion, dark eyes, dark hair; present 7–9/63. Captured Germanna Ford, Va., 10/11/63; sent to Old Capitol; transf. to Pt. Lookout; exchanged 3/6/64. WIA Pollard's Farm, Va., 5/27/64; present 7–8/64; issued clothing 9/30/64; AWOL 10–12/64. NFR.

DISNEY, A. J.: Pvt., Co. C. b. circa 1822. Res. of Baltimore. Issued clothing 9/30/64. Paroled Winchester 4/24/65. Age forty-three, 5'8½", fair complexion, black hair, hazel eyes.

DITMORE, J. C.: Pvt., Co. C, Davis's Bn. NFR.

DITTUS, JOHN FREDERICK: Pvt., Co. C. b. Baltimore 1/5/43. Res. of Baltimore. Enl. Richmond 8/4/62; ab. sick in Hanover hosp. 8/5–31/63; transf. to Lynchburg, Va., hosp. 9/63; ab. sick through 10/63; ab. on leave for a horse for six days to Winchester 11/14/63; ab. sick with a cold in Staunton, Va., hosp. 12/21–31/63; present 1–2/64 and 4/1/64; ab. dismounted service with 2nd Md. Inf. near Petersburg, Va., 8/31–12/31/64; des. to the enemy Bladensburg, Md., 4/5/65. Member ANS/MLA. Admitted Old Soldiers' Home, Pikesville, Md., 8/4/91, age forty-eight, from Baltimore. Butcher. d. Baltimore 4/17/07, age sixty-four. Bur. Loudon Park Cem., Baltimore.

DITTY, CYRUS IRVING: Capt., Cos. A and F. b. "Dryad Hill," Anne Arundel Co., Md., 9/26/38. Gd. Dickinson Col. 1857. Res. West River, Prince George's Co., Md. Lawyer, Baltimore, 1861. Enl. as Cpl., Co. K (2nd), 1st Va. Cav., Leesburg, Va., 5/14/61. Transf. to Co. A, 1st Md. Cav., 5/15/62, as 4th Sgt.; promoted 1st Lt., Co. F, 7/10/63; present through 10/63; ab. on leave 11–12/63; ab. 4/1/64; WIA (through thigh) Old Church, Va., 3/2/64; promoted Capt.; signed for sixteen Spencer rifles and sixteen carbines issued company 6/4/64; present 8/5–31/64. He and twenty-eight men with twenty-five horses present in Co. 9/6/64. AWOL for fifty-two days and in arrest 10/25/64; present 11–12/64; ab. on sick leave 12/27/64. Two officers and sixteen men present in Co. 12/31/64. Ordered to report to Capt. Avis, PM, Staunton, Va., 2/6/65. Escaped Appomattox CH, Va., 4/9/65. Started for Joseph E. Johnston's Army in N.C., then learned it had surrendered. Paroled Beaver Dam, Va., 5/3/65. Lawyer, Baltimore, 1875. d. Baltimore 10/30/87. Bur. Loudon Park Cem., Baltimore. Irvington, Md., is named in his honor.

DIX, WILLIAM T.: Pvt., Co. B. b. Fortress Monroe, Va., 6/26/39. Merchant, St. Mary's Co., Md., per 1860 census. Enl. Charlottesville 9/10/62; present 7–12/63; ab. on leave 3/22/64 for twenty-six days; present 7–12/64; left regiment 3/5/65. Captured Aquia Creek, Va., 4/23/65; sent to Old Capitol. Paroled Alexandria, Va., 4/27/65. Res. of Baltimore. Member George Emack Camp, CV, Hyattsville, Md., 1903; and ANS/MLA. Traveling Salesman and Bookkeeper. d. Fredericksburg, Va., 3/27/07. Bur. Masonic Cem., Fredericksburg.

DOLAND, PATRICK H.: Sgt., Co. C. On postwar roster. Served in Winder's Bty. one year. Member ANS/MLA., 1883. Res. of Baltimore.

DONLAN, THOMAS: Pvt., Co. C, Davis's Bn. NFR.

DOOLEY, THOMAS: Pvt., Co. F. Enl. Richmond 6/24/63; des. Richmond 7/16/63. NFR.

DORMODY, JOHN T.: Pvt., Co. D. Res. Cumberland, Allegany Co., Md. Enl. Co. G, 7th Va. Cav., 3/1/62. Transf. to Co. C, 1st Md. Cav., 4/29/64; bay horse KIA at Ashland, Va., 6/1/64, paid $1,250; sorrel mare KIA near Moorefield, W.Va., 8/7/64; discharged at end of enlistment. On rolls to 8/31/64, yet issued clothing 9/30/64. NFR. Member ANS/MLA., 1900. Res. Cumberland, Md.

DORSEY, ANDREW I.: Pvt., Co. A. b. 1834. Res. Howard Co., Md. Enl. Leesburg, Va., 9/1/62; present 7–12/63, 4/1/64, and 7–12/64. Paroled Winchester 5/18/65. Age twenty-three, 6', light complexion, light hair, blue eyes. Res. Randallstown, Baltimore Co., postwar. Member ANS/MLA. d. 10/7/06, age seventy-two. Bur. Loudon Park Cem., Baltimore.

DORSEY, AUGUSTUS: Pvt., Co. D. Transf. to Co. A, 1st Md. Cav., 11–12/62. NFR.

DORSEY, CASPER, or CASPER HENRY "HARRY": Pvt., Co. K, 1st Md. Cav. M.D. Res. of Md. (Photograph in Driver 1991)

DORSEY, CHARLES RIDGLEY: 3rd Sgt., Co. K. b. "Spring Hill," Howard Co., Md., 1/26/35. Gd. Princeton Col. Enl. Co. K (2nd), 1st Va. Cav.,

Leesburg, Va., 5/14/61. Captured at Haymarket, Va., 8/27/62; exchanged 9/62. Present until ab. sick with rheumatism in Richmond hosp. 7/31/63; RTD; ab. sick with fever in Richmond hosp. 8/5/63; RTD 10/26/63; reduced to Pvt., 11/1/63; present 2–8/64. Transf. to Co. K, 1st Md. Cav., 8/64; AWOL 10/14–12/31/64. Served with Mosby. Took oath Baltimore 4/24/65. Res. of Baltimore. Tried by Federal Court for burning bridge over the Patapsco River during the war; released to go South 5/6/65; sent to Cuba. Teacher and Lawyer, Penola, Va., postwar. Res. Howard Co. 1871. d. Bowling Green, Va., 7/10/34. Bur. "Hickory Grove," Todd–Collins Cem., Rt. 601, Caroline Co., Va. Brother of Samuel Worthington Dorsey.

DORSEY, CHARLES WORTHINGTON "DEVIL CHARLIE": Sgt., Co. A. b. "Linwood," Howard Co., Md., 6/4/31. Res. Howard Co. 1861. Enl. as Pvt., Co. G, 7th Va. Cav., 7/1/62 (as substitute for Samuel Driver). Transf. to Co. A, 1st Md. Cav., Urbana, Md., 10/1/62; promoted Sgt. by 10/10/62; present 7–12/63; horse stolen from camp 9/23/63; ab. on leave to Front Royal, Va., for a horse for twelve days 1/9/64; present 4/1/64; ab. on leave to Loudoun Co., Va., to get a horse 4/4/64; present on rolls through 8/31/64; term of service expired. Enl. Co. D, 43rd Bn. Va. Cav. (Mosby). Paroled Harpers Ferry, W.Va., as Sgt., Co. G, 7th Va. Cav., 5/19/65. Farmer, Howard Co., postwar. Member ANS/MLA. Entered Old Soldiers' Home, Pikesville, Md., 2/11/90; d. there 12/10/08. Bur. Loudon Park Cem., Baltimore.

DORSEY, FRANKLIN MOSS: Pvt., Co. unknown. b. circa 1842. On postwar roster. d. Ellicott City, Md., 4/3/01, age fifty-nine. Bur. Highland Cem., Carroll Co., Md.

DORSEY, GUSTAVUS W.: Pvt., Co. A. Res. of Howard Co., Md. Enl. Urbana, Md., 9/1/62; present 7–9/63. Captured Brandy Station, Va., 10/11/63; sent to Old Capitol; transf. to Pt. Lookout; exchanged 3/6/64. On rolls as paroled POW 4/1/64; KIA Pollard's Farm, Va., 5/27/64.

DORSEY, GUSTAVUS WARFIELD "GUS": Lt. Col. b. Md. circa 1841. Res. Brookfield, Montgomery Co., Md. Enl. as Pvt., Co. K (2nd), 1st Va. Cav., Leesburg, Va., 5/14/61; promoted 1st Sgt; present through 4/26/62; elected 1st Lt; present until WIA (side and arm) at Catlett's Station, Va., 8/22/62; RTD; present until WIA (arm broken) at Fredericksburg, Va., 11/9/62; RTD; present through 10/11/63; elected Capt; present until WIA (hip) at Buckland, W.Va., 10/19/63; RTD; present until WIA Bunker Hill, W.Va., 8/13/64, horse killed. Transf. to 1st Md. Cav. 8/64; commanding Regt. 9/1–22/64; WIA (neck) Fisher's Hill, Va.,

9/22/64; ab. wounded through 10/25/64; RTD 11/2–3/64; Commanding Regt. through 12/31/64; recommended for promotion to Lt. Col. for "valor and skill" by Gen. Lunsford Lomax; promoted Lt. Col. 2/17/65; recommended for promotion to Col. of Regiment, but the unit did not have the minimum ten companies. Commanded through 4/28/65, when he disbanded the unit at Salem, Va., with a hearty "God bless you" from General Munford. Farmer, Brookville, Md. Member Ridgely Brown Camp, CV, Rockville, Md. d. near Brookville, Md., 9/6/11. Bur. Owens Cem. near Brookville.

DORSEY, HAMMOND C. "HARRY": 2nd Sgt., Co. A. b. near Ellicott City, Md., 11/10/41. Enl. as Cpl., Co. K (2nd), 1st Va. Cav., Leesburg, Va., 5/14/61; present through 4/62. Transf. to Co. A, 1st Md. Cav., 5/14/62; ab. sick with "diarrhoea" and "hepitalis" 6/25/62; transf. to Scottsville, Va., hosp. 7/18/62; paid New Market, Va., 1/10/63; promoted 2nd Sgt; present 7–12/63 (postwar account credits him with killing five U.S. cavalrymen at Hagerstown, Md., 7/6/63); present 4/1/64; WIA, date and place unknown; on rolls as ab., term of service expired, 8/31–12/31/64. Reportedly served with Mosby. Surrendered Appomattox CH, Va., 4/9/65 as Sgt., Co. A, 1st Md. Cav., and at Relay House, Md., 4/23/65. Took oath Baltimore same day "to go South." Res. of Baltimore; destination Baltimore. d. Howard Co., Md. 1/9/98. Bur. Dorsey–Owings–Waters Cem., Howard Co., Md. (Photograph in Hartzler 1992)

DORSEY, HARRISON "HARRY": Pvt., Co. K. b. 8/4/40. Enl. Co. K (2nd), 1st Va. Cav., Richmond, 11/12/62. Age seventeen, 5'10½", light complexion, gray eyes, light hair. Student. Res. Howard Co., Md. Present through 12/63 and 4/1–8/31/64; ab. detailed as Courier for Gen. Lunsford Lomax 11–12/64. Paroled Darnestown, Md., 5/4/65. Took oath at Harpers Ferry, W.Va., 5/20/65. d. 9/12/17. Bur. Dorsey–Simpson Cem., Howard Co., Md.

DORSEY, HARRY WOODWARD, JR.: Asst. Surgeon. b. "Glenmount," near New Market, Frederick Co., Md., 1831. Gd. U. of Pa. Medical School 1857. M.D. in Howard Co., Md. Enl. as Pvt., Co. A, 1st Md. Cav., Winchester, 9/1/62; promoted Asst. Surgeon of Regt. Captured Winchester 9/19/64; sent to West Buildings hosp., Baltimore; transf. to Ft. Monroe; exchanged 1/6/65. Escaped Appomattox CH, Va., 4/9/65; went to Lynchburg, Va., in attempt to join Johnston's army in N.C. Paroled Frederick, Md., 8/65. M.D. in New Market and Hyattsville, Md. d. Urbana, Md., 1903. Brother of Ignatius W. Dorsey.

DORSEY, IGNATIUS G.: Pvt., Co. A. On postwar roster.

DORSEY, IGNATIUS WATERS: Capt. and QM. b. "Glenmount," near New Market, Md., 7/2/34. Enl. as Pvt., Co. A, 1st Md. Cav., Winchester, 9/1/62; promoted Forage Master of Regt. 12/62; promoted Capt. and QM 1863; helped Lt. Col. Ridgely Brown off the field 6/1/64; present Moorefield, W.Va., 8/7/64. Paroled Winchester 5/18/65. 6'1", dark complexion, gray eyes, auburn hair. Res. "Sedgely Farm," Frederick Co., Md., 1910. d. 10/18/15. Bur. Mt. Olivet Cem., Frederick Md. Brother of Harry W. Dorsey.

DORSEY, JAMES PEMBROKE: Capt. and QM. b. circa 1830. Res. of Howard Co., Md. Enl. as Pvt., Co. A, 1st Md. Cav., Leesburg, Va., 9/1/62; present, detailed as Comm. Sgt. of Regt., 6/10–12/31/63; horse died in camp 1/3/64; furloughed to Winchester for twelve days to get another 1/9/64; present as Pvt. 4/1/64; present detailed as Commissary Sgt. of Regt. through 12/31/64. Paroled Winchester 5/18/65 as Capt. and QM. Age thirty, 6'1", dark complexion, gray eyes, auburn hair. d. 12/19/93, age sixty-three. Bur. Green Hill Cem., Berryville, Va.

DORSEY, JESSIE W.: Pvt., Co. D. b. circa 1848. On postwar roster. Paroled Winchester 6/65 per UDC application. M.D. d. 6/25/10, age sixty-two. Bur. Urbana Cem., Montgomery Co., Md.

DORSEY, JOHN CUMMINGS: Pvt., Co. A. b. circa 1842. Farmer, Howard Co., Md. Enl. Co. K (2nd), 1st Va. Cav., Leesburg, Va., 5/14/61; present through 4/62. Transf. to Co. A, 1st Md. Cav., 5/15/62; present 7–8/63; present, detailed as Courier for Gen. Lunsford Lomax 9–10/63; present 11–12/63. Age twenty-two, 5'7", fair complexion, dark eyes, dark hair; present detailed 4/1/64; ab., term of service expired, on rolls 8/31–12/31/64. Paroled, took oath Harpers Ferry, W.Va., 5/19/65. Member ANS/MLA. Entered Old Soldiers' Home, Pikesville, Md., 6/7/98, age fifty-six, from Howard Co. d. 10/9/99. Bur. Loudon Park Cem, Baltimore.

DORSEY, JOHN W.: Pvt., Co. A. b. 9/4/31. Res. Howard Co., Md. Enl. Hanover Junction, Va., 3/3/64; present 4/1/64. May have served as Asst. Engineer, CSN on CSS Missouri. Paroled Appomattox 4/9/65 as Pvt., Co. A, 1st Md. Cav., and Staunton, Va., 5/9/65. 5'11", dark complexion, dark hair, blue eyes. Took oath Richmond 5/26/65; destination Howard Co., Md. d. 12/6/08. Bur. St. John's Episcopal Ch. Cem., Ellicott City, Md.

DORSEY, LLOYD EGBERT: Pvt., Co. A. b. 1840. Res. Annapolis Junction, Anne Arundel Co., Md. On postwar roster Co. K (2nd), 1st Va. Cav. Enl. Co. A, 1st Md. Cav., Charlottesville, 8/25/62; ab. sick in Hanover Junction, Va., hosp. 7–8/63,

UPTON L.
DORSEY

(Ben Ritter)

Richmond hosp. 9–10/63, and Farmville hosp. 11/63; RTD 11/4/63; present through 12/31/63 and 4/1/64. Captured at Moorefield, W.Va., 8/7/64; sent to Wheeling. Age twenty-four, 5'8½", fair complexion, gray eyes, dark hair. Farmer. Transf. to Camp Chase and Pt. Lookout; exchanged 3/27/65. Captured Leonardtown, Md., 4/20/65; sent to Old Capitol. Took oath Alexandria, Va., 5/3/65. Member George Emack Camp, CV, Hyattsville, Md. 1903. d. Annapolis Junction, Md., 1918.

DORSEY, PULASKI "PUE": 3rd Lt., Co. A. b. 8/18/33. Res. Simpsonville, Howard Co., Md. Enl. as Pvt., Co. K (2nd), 1st Va. Cav., Leesburg, Va., 5/14/61; elected 3rd Lt. 2/23/62. Transf. to Co. A, 1st Md. Cav., 5/15/62; ab. sick with "diarrhoea" and "Febris Cont" in Richmond hosp. 6/25/62; transf. to Scottsville, Va., hosp. 7/1/62. Captured 9/62; exchanged 9/21/62; ab. to buy a horse 11/62; paid 1/10/63; present 7–12/63 and 4/1/64; ab., term of service expired, on rolls 8/31/64. Enl. Co. D, 43rd Va. Bn. Cav. (Mosby). Paroled Edwards' Ferry, Md., 4/29/65. Took oath at Relay House, Md., 5/28/65. Judge, Howard Co. d. 1/12/12. Bur. Dorsey–Simpson private cem. at "Harper's Choice," Columbia, Howard Co.

DORSEY, SAMUEL A.: Pvt., Co. C. Res. of Howard Co., Md. Served in Co. H, 5th Ark. Inf. Enl. Co. C, 1st Md. Cav., date unknown; KIA (shot in chest) at Greenland Gap, W.Va., 4/25/63.

DORSEY, SAMUEL WORTHINGTON: 2d Lt., Co. K. b. Gloucester Co., Va., 7/8/38. Enl. Co. K, 1st Va. Cav., Leesburg, Va., 5/14/61; present until reduced to Pvt. 8/1/61; discharged at end of enlistment 5/19/62. 5' 9", fair complexion, light hair, blue eyes, law student, resident of Howard Co., Md. Served in Medical Purveyor's Office, Richmond. Member ANS/MLA. Res. of Baltimore. d. 3/17/09. Bur. St. John's Cem., Ellicott City, Md. Brother of Charles R. Dorsey.

DORSEY, UPTON LAWRENCE (photo): 2nd Sgt., Co. D. b. Frederick Co., Md., 1828. Farmer, Franklin Dist., Carroll Co., per 1860 census. Enl. Winchester 9/21/62; present 11–12/62, 7–12/63, and 4/1/64; ab. sick with debility in Richmond hosp. 2/17/64; RTD 3/31/64. Captured Pollard's Farm, Va., 5/27/64; sent to Pt. Lookout; exchanged 2/15/65. Paroled Winchester 5/5/65. Age twenty-seven, 6'1", dark complexion, black hair, hazel eyes. Took oath Harpers Ferry, W.Va., 5/11/65. Res. and destination Howard Co. Grain and fertilizer dealer, Winchester; manufacturer of phosphate. Member Gen. Turner Ashby Camp, CV, Winchester. d. Winchester 2/2/04, age seventy-seven. Bur. Mt. Hebron Cem., Winchester.

DORSEY, UPTON WALLACE: Pvt., Co. A. b. 1844. Res. Clarksville, Howard Co., Md. Enl. Urbana, Md., 9/1/62; present 7–12/63 and 4/1–9/64. Captured Woodstock, Va., 11/10/64; sent to Pt. Lookout; exchanged 2/21/65. Paroled Winchester 5/18/65. Age twenty-one, 5'10", dark complexion, black hair, hazel eyes. Took oath Harpers Ferry, W.Va., 5/19/65. Res. and destination Howard Co. d. Baltimore 8/4/07, age sixty-four. Bur. St. Louis Cem., Clarksville.

DORSEY, WILLIAM FREDERICK: 4th Sgt., Co. C. b. 11/11/25. Enl. as Pvt., Sharpsburg, Md., 9/17/62; appointed Cpl.; WIA (shoulder) at Fairmont, W.Va., 4/29/63. Captured there 5/8/63; sent to Ft. McHenry; exchanged 5/63. Appointed 4th Sgt. 7/25/63; present through 12/63; horse disabled, ab. on leave to Winchester for fifteen days to get another, 2/16/64; present 4/1–8/31/64; ab. as courier for Gen. Bradley T. Johnson 11–12/64. Paroled Salisbury, N.C., 5/1/65. d. 12/19/85. Bur. Dorsey–Owings–Warfield Cem., Howard Co., Md.

DORSEY, WILLIAM HEBY BUSARD: 1st Lt., Co. D. b. near Mt. Airy, Md., 8/23/41. Res. Mt. Airy, Frederick Co., Md. Enl. as 2nd Lt., Co. A, 1st Md. Inf., 5/21/61; present 6/28/62; discharged 1862. Enl. as 1st Lt., Co. D, 1st Md. Cav., Winchester, 9/20/62; present 11–12/62; commanding Co. 2/25–26/63 and 4/25/63; present 7–12/63 and 4/1/64; horse killed at Pollard's Farm, Va., 5/27/64, paid $2,000; WIA several times; present 6/4/64; present 8–9/64. Two officers and forty-six men with thirty horses, four mules and two oxen present 9/30/64. Ab. on detached service with Gen. Lunsford Lomax 10/25/64; commanding Regt. 11/30/64; present through 12/64. Took oath Frederick, Md., 9/18/65. Member ANS/MLA. d. Mt. Airy, Md., 12/4/79. Bur. St. John's Catholic Ch. Cem., Frederick, Md.

DOUGHERTY, JOSEPH: Pvt., Co. C. May have served in Co. C, 1st Md. Inf., 1861–62 (per postwar roster). Enl. Richmond 8/4/62; present 7–9/63; ab. sick in Richmond hosp. 10/11/63; present 11–12/63, 1–2/64, and 4/1/64; ab. sick with "debilitas" in Richmond hosp. 6/5–17/64; present through 8/31/64; ab. sick with dysentery in Charlottesville hosp. 10/29/64; d. there 12/30/64. Bur. Confederate Cem., U. of Va., Charlottesville; removed to Loudon Park Cem., Baltimore 1874.

DOWNEY, JESSE WRIGHT: Pvt., Co. D. b. 8/28/48. Res. New Market, Frederick Co., Md. On postwar roster. M.D., New Market. d. 6/25/10. Bur. New Market Episcopal Ch. Cem.

DUBROW, JOHN C.: Pvt., Co. A. b. circa 1847. Res. of Baltimore. Enl. Frederick, Md., 6/20/63; present through 12/63 and 4/1/64. Captured King William Co. 5/24/64; sent to Pt. Lookout; exchanged 11/15/4; ab. sick with "chronic diarrhoea" in Charlottesville hosp. 12/16/64–2/2/65; ab. sick with "chronic diarrhoea" in Gordonsville, Va., hosp. 3/30/65. Paroled Winchester 4/21/65. Age twenty-two, 5'11", fair complexion, dark hair, blue eyes. Took oath Harpers Ferry, W.Va., 5/19/65.

DUERSON, W. H.: Pvt., Co. K. Enl. Co. K (2nd), 1st Va. Cav., date unknown. Captured Gettysburg, Pa., 7/3/63; sent to Ft. Del.; transf. to Pt. Lookout. Transf. to Co. K, 1st. Md., Cav., 8/64, while POW; exchanged 9/18/64. Admitted Richmond hosp. 9/18/64; furloughed to Caroline Co., Va., 9/30/64. NFR.

DUFFY, MICHAEL: Pvt., Co. C, Davis's Bn. NFR. Merchant, Baltimore, postwar. d. 2/18/00, age seventy-two.

DUFRIEND, JAMES: Pvt., Co. A, Davis's Bn. Enl. Richmond, 8/8/63. Captured at Newtown, Va., 10/63. NFR. Storekeeper, Sandy Springs, Md.

DULEY, EDMUND GILMORE: 1st Lt., Co. A. b. near Germantown, Montgomery Co., Md., circa 1833. Res. of Montgomery Co. per 1860 census. Enl. date and place unknown. Captured Gettysburg 7/3/63; sent to Ft. McHenry; transf. to Ft. Del. and Ft. Pulaski, Ga. (one of the "Immortal 600"); exchanged 1863–64. Captured Hanover CH, Va., 5/26/64; sent to Ft. Del.; released 6/12/65. 5'11", ruddy complexion, light hair, blue eyes. d. Washington, D.C., 11/30/11. Bur. Union Cem., Rockville, Md.

DUNCAN, FRANK W.: Pvt., Co. D. Res. of Baltimore. Enl. date and place unknown. Captured Upper Potomac 6/30/64; sent to Old Capitol; transf. to Ft. Warren; released 6/10/65. 5'6½", light complexion, light hair, blue eyes.

DUNLOP, JOSEPH L.: Pvt., Co. A. Res. Baltimore. Enl. Leetown, W.Va., 9/1/62; WIA (elbow joint) at Fairmont, W.Va., 5/1/63; ab. wounded in Richmond hosp. until RTD 9/12/63; present

through 12/63 and 4/1/64; ab. on detached service—term of service expired on rolls 8/31–12/31/64. NFR.

DUNN, BENJAMIN F.: Pvt., Co. E. Res. Washington Co., Md. Enl. date and place unknown. Captured near Winchester 6/12/63; sent to Baltimore 6/14/63. Age twenty-six, 5'8", fair complexion, blue eyes, light hair. NFR.

DUNN, JAMES: Pvt., Co. C, Davis's Bn. On postwar roster. Probably James Dunn (1843–1932). Bur. Old Coney Cem., Allegany Co., Md.

DUNN, JOHN W. H.: Pvt., Co. F. Served in Co. G, 1st S.C. Inf. Enl. Co. F, 1st Md. Cav., Richmond, 7/15/63; des. near Richmond 7/16/63. NFR.

DURKIN, JOHN HENRY: Pvt., Co. K. b. Ireland circa 1838. Came to Baltimore as a child. Enl. Co. B, 1st Md. Inf., 5/21/61; discharged 8/62. Enl. Co. K (2nd), 1st Va. Cav., 8/10/62; present until WIA (left hand) at Haw's Shop 6/30/64; ab. wounded in Richmond hosp. until des. 6/18/64, age twenty. Farmer. Present through 8/31/64. Transf. to Co. K, 1st Md. Cav., 8/64; des. to the enemy at Annapolis 11/21/64; took oath, sent to Baltimore. Entered Old Soldiers' Home, Pikesville, Md., from Baltimore 12/3/95, age fifty-seven. Laborer. Dropped 1898. Moved to Cumberland, Md. Member ANS/MLA. d. 9/21/06. Bur. Cathedral Burial Ground, Baltimore.

DUSENBERRY, H. BOWIE: Pvt., Co. K. b. circa 1838. Res. of Annapolis, Md. Enl. Co. B, 21st Va. Inf., 5/23/61; discharged 3/1/62. Enl. Lee's Va. Arty. Transf. to 2nd Md. Arty. 6/27/62. Appointed Acting Master, CSN. 5/10½", dark hair, dark eyes. Enl. Breathed's Bty. 7/10/62. Transf. to Co. K (2nd), 1st Va. Cav., 8/14/64. Transf. to Co. K, 1st Md. Cav., 8/64; ab. sick in hosp. 10/1–12/31/64, yet listed as present in 2nd Md. Arty. 10/31/64. Paroled 5/13/65. Served in 2nd Md. Cav. per postwar roster.

DUTTON, JOHN T.: Pvt., Co. B. b. 1841. Res. of Charles Co., Md. Enl. Charlottesville 10/10/62; horse killed near Romney, W.Va., 11/23/62, paid $275; present 7–8/63; ab. sick with chronic rheumatism in Charlottesville hosp. 8/31/63; transf. to Lynchburg, Va., hosp. 9/21/63; RTD; ab. sick with chronic rheumatism in Charlottesville hosp. 11/1–17/63; present through 12/31/63 and 4/1/64. Captured Moorefield, W.Va., 8/7/64; sent to Wheeling. Age twenty-two, 5'4", fair complexion, light hair, light eyes. Farmer. Transf. to Camp Chase and Pt. Lookout; exchanged 3/27/65. NFR. Member ANS/MLA. and George Emack Camp, CV, Hyattsville, Md. Res. of Allen's Fresh, Charles Co., Md., 1903. Res. of Newburg, Charles Co., 1906. Member Confederate Veterans Assoc., Washington, D.C., 1910. d. 1920. Bur. Arlington

HENRY R.
DUVAL

*(Daniel D.
Hartzler)*

Natl. Cem., Va.; removed to Goodhope Bapt. Ch. Cem., Newburg, Md.

DUTTON, S. S.: Pvt., Co. B. On postwar roster.

DUTTON, W. JOSEPH: Pvt., Co. B. Res. of Charles Co., Md. WIA (elbow) western Va. raid 4/63. NFR.

DUVAL, HENRY REIMAN (photo): 2nd Lt., Co. C, Davis's Bn. b. Baltimore 1843. Served in Co. C, 1st Md. Inf., 1861–62. Served as Detective on Rappahannock River (until 10/29/62) and at Hedgesville, W.Va.; detailed Andersonville prison, Ga.,. Enl. McNeill's Va. Partisan Rangers; present 11– 12/63. NFR. Captured Harrisonburg, Va., 6/3/64 as 2nd Lt., Co. C, Davis's Bn; sent to Camp Morton. Age twenty-four, 5'10", light complexion, dark hair, gray eyes. Transf. to Johnson's Island; released 6/14/65. B&O RR Employee 1865–84; Erie RR Employee 1884–89; President, Fla. Central RR 1889–99; President of American Car and Foundry Co., Mutual Life Insurance Co., and American Sugar Beet Co., N.Y. City, 1912. Res. of East Islip, L.I., N.Y. d. St. Augustine, Fla., 3/18/24. Bur. Greenmont Cem., Baltimore.

DUVALL, JAMES E.: Pvt., Co. E. b. Prince William Co., Va., 4/11/38. Bricklayer. Enl. Co. E, 17th Va. Inf., 4/17/61; discharged as nonresident 7/26/62. 6'3", fair complexion, brown eyes, dark hair. Enl. Co. E, 1st Md. Cav., Richmond, 11/14/62; presence or ab. not stated 1–2/63; present 7–8/63; ab. sick with "Feb. Int Quo" in Charlottesville hosp. 8/15–18/63; ab. in charge of disabled horses 9–10/63; present 11–12/63; horse died in camp at Hanover Junction, Va., 2/15/64; ab. on horse detail to Winchester for twelve days 2/16/64; present 4/1/64. Captured near Washington, D.C., 7/25/64; sent to Old Capitol; exchanged 8/64; des. Harrisonburg, Va., 12/64. Captured Bladensburg, Md., 12/12/64; sent to Old Capitol; transf. to Elmira; took oath, released 2/13/65, "To

take care of his old, decrepit, and blind father." Res. Prince George's Co., Md. Member Confederate Veterans Assoc., Washington, D.C., 1894–1900. d. Belair Mills, Stafford Co., Va., 1/21/01. Bur. Cedar Run Cem., Prince William Co., Va.

DWYRA, JAMES: Pvt., Co. C, Davis's Bn. NFR.

DYER, AUSTIN MILES: Pvt., Co. B. b. Tenleytown, Prince George's Co., Md., 9/26/41. Res. Frederick, Md. Enl. Strasburg, Va., 12/1/62. Captured Monterey Springs, Pa., 7/4/63; sent to Ft. McHenry; transf. to Ft. Del. and Pt. Lookout; exchanged 3/1/65. Admitted Richmond hosp. 3/2/65; present Appomattox CH, Va., 4/9/65. Paroled Charlottesville 5/24/65. Gd. Worcester Polytechnic Inst., Mass. Member George Emack Camp, CV, Hyattsville, Md., 1903. Res. Dentsville, Charles Co., Md. d. 3/25/11. Bur. St. Mary's Catholic Ch. Cem., Bryanstown, Md.

EARECKSON, FREDERICK GOODHAND: Pvt., Co. B. b. Kent Island, Md., 1845. Res. Queen Anne's Co., Md. Joined by transfer from unknown unit, Richmond, 8/1/62. Captured Hampshire Co., W.Va., 2/16/63; sent to Camp Chase, age seventeen; exchanged 4/1/63; present 7–12/63; horse given to dismounted man in battalion; ab. on leave for seventeen days to Winchester to get another 2/1/64; sick in camp 4/1/64. Captured Moorefield, W.Va., 8/7/64; sent to Wheeling. Age eighteen, 5'10", fair complexion, gray eyes, red hair. Student. Transf. to Camp Chase and Pt. Lookout; exchanged 3/27/65. NFR. d. Baltimore 1914. Bur. Loudon Park Cem., Baltimore.

EARLE, JAMES TILGHMAN, JR.: Pvt., Co. B. b. circa 1840. Res. Centreville, Queen Anne's Co., Md. Enl. Charlottesville 9/10/62; present 7–9/63. Captured with horse at Brandy Station, Va., 10/11/63; sent to Wheeling. Age twenty-three, 5'6¼", fair complexion, gray eyes, black hair, sandy whiskers. Farmer. Transf. to Camp Chase; exchanged 10/63. Present 11–12/63; ab. on leave for fifteen days to Winchester to get a horse 2/16/64. In Charlottesville hosp. 3/3–5/64. d. 9/10/64, cause unknown. Probably bur. Confederate Cem., U. of Va., Charlottesville.

EBERT, CHARLES S.: Pvt., Co. B. b. 9/28/47. Res. of Frederick Co., Md. Enl. Frederick, Md., 6/20/63. Captured Monterey Springs, Pa., 7/4/63; sent to Ft. McHenry; transf. to Ft. Del. and Pt. Lookout; exchanged 12/28/63. Discharged as underage 4/1/64. NFR. d. 7/8/00. Bur. Mt. Airy Methodist Ch. Cem., Frederick Co.

ECKHERT, CHARLES H.: Pvt., Co. B. b. 1838. Res. Talbot Co., Md. Enl. Co. G, 1st Md. Inf., 5/2/61; discharged 7/8/62. Enl. Co. B, 1st Md. Cav., Lacey Springs, Va., 4/1/63; WIA Fairmont,

W.Va., 4/30/63; present 7–9/63. Captured at Raccoon Ford, Va., 10/10/63; sent to Old Capitol; transf. to Pt. Lookout; exchanged 3/4/64. WIA Port Republic 1864. Paroled Staunton, Va., 5/18/65. Age thirty-six, 5'6", dark complexion, dark hair, gray eyes. Member Stonewall Jackson Camp, CV, Portsmouth, Va., 8/19, age eighty. (Postwar photograph in *Confederate Veteran* magazine)

EDELIN, JESSE R.: Pvt., Co. E. b. Prince George's Co., Md., circa 1845. Enl. Richmond 1/29/63; present 7–8/63, however ab. sick with debility in Richmond hosp. 8/3–24/63; present until horse captured Brandy Station, Va., 10/11/63; ab. on leave to Hardy Co., W.Va., to get a horse through 10/31/63; present 11–12/63; ab. on leave for fifteen days to Winchester to get a fresh horse 2/16/64. Captured near Frederick, Md., 7/8/64; sent to Ft. McHenry; transf. to Pt. Lookout; exchanged 11/15/64; ab. sick in Richmond hosp. 11/21–22/64; furloughed for thirty days; ab. sick with "Icterus" in Charlottesville hosp. 11/26/64; furloughed 11/29/64; readmitted with debility 12/17/64. Went to Md. to obtain money to buy a horse. Paroled Washington, D.C., 5/20/65. d. 1/29/96. Bur. St. Mary's Catholic Ch. Cem., Prince George's Co.

EDELIN, WILLIAM MARSHALL "TIP": Pvt., Co. A. Res. of Baltimore. Enl. Leesburg, Va., 9/1/62; present 7–12/63 and 4/1–12/31/64. Paroled Appomattox CH, Va., 4/9/65. Took oath 6/23/65. Res. of Bel Air, Md., postwar. Killed in fall from second story window at Hyattsville, Md., 7/22, year unknown, age ninety-one. Bur. Mt. Olivet Cem., Frederick, Md.

EDMUNDS, NICHOLAS E.: 1st Lt. Co. C, Davis's Bn. On postwar roster.

EDWARDS, WILLIAM H.: Pvt., Co. C. b. Baltimore circa 1844. Res. of Baltimore. Enl. Co. G, 7th Va. Cav., 1/15/62. Captured Shepherd's Mill, Va., 5/3/63; sent to Wheeling. Age nineteen, 5'10¾", light complexion, light hair, dark eyes. Farmer, Jefferson Co., Va. Transf. to Camp Chase and Pt. Lookout; exchanged 5/8/63. Enl. Co. C, 1st Md. Cav., Richmond, 3/5/64; ab. on detail in hosp. 3/24–4/1/64. Captured 6/18/64; sent to Wheeling; transf. to Ft. McHenry; released 5/1/65. 6'1", dark complexion, brown hair, black eyes. Res. of W.Va. Member ANS/MLA. Entered Old Soldiers' Home, Richmond, 8/27/15, age seventy-two; discharged 7/16/16. Moved to Baltimore.

EICHELBERGER, DANIEL G.: Pvt., Co. B. Res. of Point of Rocks, Md.; issued clothing 9/30/64. Captured Fauquier Co., Va., 10/27/64; sent to Old Capitol; transf. to Elmira; released 6/14/65. 5'7",

fair complexion, auburn hair, hazel eyes.

EIGER, JOHN H.: Pvt., Co. F. Enl. Co. G, 26th Va. Inf., 6/2/62. Transf. to Co. F, 1st Md. Cav., 7/4/63; present through 9/63. Captured Brandy Station, Va., 10/11/63; sent to Old Capitol; took oath, was released 3/11/64.

ELDER, GEORGE HOWARD, JR.: Pvt., Co. C. b. Garrison, Baltimore Co., 8/41. Res. of Garrison, Md. Enl. Hagerstown, Md., 9/12/62; ab. on detail with Capt. Smith 7/21–8/31/63; WIA (arm, fractured humerus) Brandy Station, Va., 10/11/63; ab. wounded in Richmond hosp. 10/14–11/17/63; transf. to Charlottesville hosp. until furloughed to Albemarle Co. for sixty days 2/13/64, age twenty-two. Farmer. Ab. wounded in Charlottesville hosp. 1–2/64 and 4/1/64; RTD; WIA (side) Clear Spring, Md., 7/30/64; ab. wounded in Winchester hosp. through 8/2/64; transf. to another hosp.; RTD; present 11–12/64. Surrendered Appomattox CH, Va., 4/9/65. Took oath 6/8/65. Res. and destination Baltimore Co., Md. Member ANS/MLA. Res. of Pikesville, Md. d. Garrison, Md., 2/27/07. Bur. St. Thomas Ch. Cem., Garrison, Md.

ELDER, PHILLIP LAWRENCE: Pvt., Co. C. b. Baltimore circa 1838. Res. Baltimore. Enl. Co. B, 21st Va. Inf., 5/23/61. 5'10", brown hair, brown eyes. (Co. disbanded 1862.) Enl. Marion S.C. Arty. Transf. to Co. C, 1st Md. Cav., 11/23/63 (not yet reported on rolls 4/1/64); ab. on leave to Hertford, N.C., for ten days to get a horse 5/1/64; ab. sick with scabies in Richmond hosp. 6/14–30/64; WIA (left arm), captured near Washington, D.C., 7/14/64; sent to Old Capitol; transf. to Elmira and Pt. Lookout; exchanged 11/15/64. Paroled POW on leave 11–12/64. Captured Frederick's Hall, Va., 3/13/65; sent to Ft. Monroe; transf. to Pt. Lookout; released 7/3/65. Former res. of Baltimore; destination Baltimore.

ELLIOTT, GEORGE M.: Pvt., Co. B. Res. Eastern Shore of Md. Enl. Richmond 9/2/63; ab. detailed as Teamster for Gen. Bradley T. Johnson 3–12/64; present Salisbury, N.C., 1/5/65, enroute back to command. "Came down with horses of Gen. Johnson." NFR. Member ANS/MLA. Entered Old Soldiers' Home, Pikesville, Md., 4/29, age eighty-eight, from Delmar, Md. Farmer. d. 6/6/??, year unknown.

ELLIOTT, JAMES T.: Pvt., Co. B. May have served on gunboats CSS *General Sterling Price* and *General Van Dorn*. Paid New Orleans, La., 3/12/62. Enl. 9th Ga. Inf. 9/2/63. Transf. to Co. B, 1st Md. Cav., 7/1/64; present through 12/64; horse died of disease, paid $2,500 2/28/65. NFR.

ELLIS, B. F.: Pvt., Co. A. Paroled New Creek 5/8/65.

ELLIS, JOHN: Pvt., Co. D. Enl. Richmond 8/1/63;

present, detailed as Wagoner 2/25–12/31/64. NFR.

ELLIS, JOHN THOMAS: Pvt., Co. K (2nd), 1st Va. Cav., Richmond, 6/10/62; present until ab. on detached service 8/27/63. Captured 9/1 or 10/63. Not on Federal POW rolls; probably KIA. Transf. to Co. K, 1st Md. Cav., 8/64. Carried as ab. POW on rolls through 12/31/64. NFR.

EMACK, GEORGE MALCOLM: Capt., Co. B. b. "Locust Green," near Beltsville, Md., 1842. Res. Beltsville, Prince George's Co., Md. Fatally stabbed a Union officer sent to arrest him in 1861. Appointed 2nd Lt., C.S. Inf., 10/8/61; served in guard force at Libby Prison, Richmond; resigned. Enl. Co. B, 1st Md. Cav., Gordonsville, Va., 9/1/62; elected Capt. 9/12/62; ordered to report to Gen. Samuel Jones 9/15/62; present, sick in camp, Winchester 10/62; present 11–12/62 and 2/25–26/63; present 7/63; WIA Monterey Springs, Pa., 7/4/63; ab. wounded in Charlottesville hosp. 8/3/63; RTD 9/14/63; present through 12/63. Four officers and forty-five men present in Co. 12/31/63. WIA (thumb and forefinger) and bay horse captured in Hanover Co. during Dahlgren Raid 3/3/64; paid $2,000 for horse 4/1/64; WIA (right forearm) at Clear Spring, Md., 7/29/64, bay horse killed; ab. wounded in Charlottesville hosp. until transf. to Richmond hosp. 8/14/64; paid $950 for horse; ab. sick with diphtheria in Charlottesville hosp. 3/1/65; transf. to Richmond hosp. 3/9/65; RTD 4/2/65; present when regiment disbanded 4/28/65. Returned to Prince George's Co.; moved to New Orleans, La., for six years; moved to Versailles, Ky.; d. there 5/86. (Photograph in Hartzler 1992)

EMBERT, JOHN R. H.: Pvt., Co. B. b. Kent Island, Queen Anne's Co., Md., 3/13/38. Res. Queen Anne's Co. Joined by transf. from 4th Md. Arty., Heathsville, Md., 2/1/62; present 11/62. Captured near Winchester 5/19/63; sent to Ft. McHenry as "Bushwhacker"; exchanged 6/63; bay horse killed at Monterey Springs, Pa., 7/4/63, paid $850; present 7–12/63; ab. sick in Richmond hosp. 12/21/63–3/10/64; AWOL 3/29–4/1/64. Captured Dorchester Co., Md., 4/24/64; sent to Albany, N.Y., penitentiary, where he was placed in close confinement; exchanged 3/10/65. NFR. Farmer, Queenstown, Queen Anne Co., 1898. Member George Emack Camp, CV, Hyattsville, Md., 1903. Res. Wye Mills, Talbot Co., Md., 1906. Res. Forks, Md., 1920.

EMORY, DANIEL GRANT: Pvt., Co. C. b. circa 1828. Res. of Baltimore. Enl. Richmond 8/15/62; ab. sick Harrisonburg, Va., 11/1–12/31/62; ab. on leave for a horse for ten days 3/25/63; present sick 7–8/63; ab. sick with pneumonia 12/17/63–3/31/64, and 4/13–14/54; ab. sick in Harrison-

burg hosp. through 8/31/64; ab. on sick leave 11–12/64. Paroled Winchester 4/21/65. Age thirty-seven, 5'11", light complexion, brown hair, blue eyes. Took oath 8/10/65. Insurance man, Baltimore. Member ANS/MLA. d. Baltimore 2/14/86.

EMORY, GEORGE: Pvt., Co. B. On rolls. Transf. to Co. A, 2nd Md. Bn. Cav.

EMORY, JOHN H.: Pvt., Co. B. See Co. B, 2nd Md. Cav.

EMORY, WILLIAM T.: Pvt., Co. E. On postwar roster.

ENDUS, BENJAMIN: Pvt., Co. K. On postwar roster Co. K (2nd), 1st Va. Cav., and Co. K, 1st Md. Cav.

ENSOR, ZADOCK: Pvt., Co. D. Enl. Boonsboro, Md., 6/15/63; horse killed near Martinsburg, W.Va., 7/4/63, paid $2,100; present through 11/63; ab. sick with debility in Richmond hosp. 12/18/63–1/23/64; ab. on leave for ten days to New Market, Va., for a horse 2/1/64; ab. sick with debility in Richmond hosp. 2/14–25/64; present 4/1–12/31/64; paid 2/14/65. NFR.

ERICKSON, G. M. F. G.: Pvt., Co. B. Enl. Richmond 9/2/63; ab. detailed as a Teamster 11–12/64. NFR.

ERWIN, A. D.: Capt., Co. I; WIA (ankle) Cold Harbor 6/3/64. NFR.

EVANS, BENJAMIN: Pvt., Co. K. Enl. Co. K (2nd), 1st Va. Cav., date unknown. Transf. to Co. K, 1st Md. Cav., 8/64; KIA Fisher's Hill, Va., 9/22/64.

EVANS, W. B.: Pvt., Co. C, Davis's Bn. NFR.

EVANS, WILLIAM OLIVER: Pvt., Co. A, Davis's Bn. b. Md. circa 1840. Enl. Charles Town, W.Va., 8/8/64. Transf. to Co. M, 23rd Va. Cav. Paroled Staunton, Va., 5/15/65. Age twenty-five, 5'10", fair complexion, dark hair, blue eyes.

EVERGRAM, WILLIAM H.: Pvt., Co. B. b. circa 1828. Enl. date and place unknown. Captured South Mt., Md., 7/4/63; sent to Ft. McHenry; transf. to Ft. Del.; d. there of "chronic diarrhoea" 8/29/63, age thirty-five. Bur. Finn's Pt., N.J., National Cem.

EWING, HARVEY S.: Pvt., Co. D. Res. Cecil Co., Md. Enl. Winchester 9/30/62; present 11–12/62; paid New Market, Va., 1/10/63. Captured Monterey Springs, Pa., 7/4/63; sent to Ft. Del.; transf. to Pt. Lookout; exchanged 2/21/65; present Camp Lee, Richmond, 2/22/65. Captured Frederick's Hall, Va., 3/13/65; sent to Ft. Monroe; transf. to Pt. Lookout; released 6/11/65. 5'9", light complexion, brown hair, hazel eyes.

EWING, WILLIAM J.: Pvt., Co. D b. circa 1828. Enl. Winchester 9/20/62; present 11–12/62 and 7–8/63; roan horse killed South Mt., Md., 7/4/63, paid $450; ab. on horse detail 9–10/63; present

11–12/63 and 4/1/64; WIA Pollard's Farm, Va., 5/27/64; ab. wounded in Richmond hosp. through 12/14/64; transf. to Staunton, Va., hosp.; transf. to Richmond hosp.; RTD 3/25/65; again WIA and in Gordonsville, Va., hosp. 3/30/65. NFR. Merchant, Baltimore. d. 1/28/00, age seventy-two.

EWING, WILLIAM THOMAS: Pvt., Co. E. b. circa 1841. Res. Talbot Co., Md. Enl. Richmond 11/1/62, age twenty-one; presence or ab. not stated 1–2/63; present 7–12/63 and 4/1/64; WIA (right ankle) and admitted Richmond hosp. 4/1/64; transf. to Farmville, Va., hosp. 5/4/64; RTD 5/24/64; ab. sick in Richmond hosp. with debility 5/25/64; RTD; present through 12/31/64. Paroled Louisa CH, Va., 5/22/665.

FAIR, JOHN W.: Pvt., Co. C, Davis's Bn. NFR.

FALLIS, WILLIAM R.: Lt., Co. A. Res. of Baltimore. Enl. as Pvt., date and place unknown; commanding Co. as Lt. 9/29/63. Captured Frederick, Md., 7/7/64, as Sgt; sent to Old Capitol; transf. to Elmira; exchanged 2/28/65. Paroled Harrisonburg, Va., 5/8/65.

FAULTZ, JOHN H.: Pvt., Co. A. b. circa 1842. Res. Washington Co., Md. Enl. date and place unknown. Captured Hampshire Co., W.Va., 11/1/63; sent to Wheeling. Age twenty-one, 6', fair complexion, brown eyes, brown hair. Farmer. Transf. to Camp Chase and Ft. Del.; exchanged 3/1/65. NFR.

FEARHAKE, ADOLPHUS, JR.: Pvt., Co. D. b. Frederick, Md., 4/23/40. Att. Frederick Col. Res. Braddock Heights, Frederick Co., Md. Enl. Winchester 9/20/62; present 11/12/62. Captured Monterey Springs, Pa., 7/4/63; sent to Ft. McHenry; transf. to Ft. Del.; escaped. Exchanged Camp Lee, Richmond, 1/65. Paroled Winchester 4/28/65. Light complexion, black hair, hazel eyes. Lawyer, Frederick Co., Md., 1866. Surveyor of county, 1867; Deputy Clerk of Court through 1879; Clerk of Court, 1879–1907. d. Frederick, Md., 10/7/13. Bur. Mt. Olivet Cem.

FEARHAKE, W.: Pvt., Co. B. Captured Monterey Springs, Pa., 7/4/63; sent to Ft. Del.; transf. to Pt. Lookout; exchanged 2/21/65. NFR.

FENETER, D. C.: Pvt., Co. K. Captured Smithfield, W.Va., 8/28/64; sent to Camp Chase; transf. to Pt. Lookout; released 6/12/65.

FERGUSON, JOHN R.: Pvt., Co. E. b. Charles Co., Md. circa 1842. Res. of Port Tobacco, Charles Co., Md. Enl. Co. I, 1st Md. Inf., 6/15/61; discharged 8/17/62. Age twenty, 5'10", fair complexion, brown hair, blue eyes. Farmer. Captured on the Potomac River as Confederate Mail Carrier 10/4/62; sent to Ft. Monroe; exchanged 10/31/62. Enl. Co. E, 1st Md. Cav., Richmond, 11/11/62, age twenty; presence or ab. not stated 1–2/63; ab.

sick in Richmond hosp. 3/14/63. "Released from Castle Thunder in accordance with President's proclamation and supposed to have deserted" per rolls 7–8/63; present 3–8/64; ab. sick with scurvy and rheumatism in Richmond hosp. 8/28–9/9/64; ab. sick in hosp. 11–12/64. NFR.

FERRELL, JOHN THOMAS, JR.: Pvt., Co. B. b. circa 1842. Res. of Buena Vista, Prince George's Co., Md. Enl. Co. D, 1st Md. Inf., 6/1/61; discharged 8/62. Enl. Co. B, 1st Md. Cav., Charlottesville, 9/10/62. Captured on picket near Winchester, 11/23/62; sent to Wheeling. Age twenty, 6'1", fair complexion, dark hair, dark eyes. Exchanged 12/22/62. Captured Monterey Springs, Pa., 7/4/63; sent to Ft. McHenry; transf. to Del. and Pt. Lookout; exchanged, date unknown. Captured Moorefield, W.Va., 8/7/64; sent to Wheeling; transf. to Camp Chase and Pt. Lookout; exchanged 2/21/65. Paroled New Market, Va., 4/19/65. Age twenty-three, 6'1¼", fair complexion, light hair, brown eyes. Took oath Bladensburg, Md., 5/15/65. Member George Emack Camp, CV, Hyattsville, Md., and ANS/MLA. Entered Old Soldiers' Home, Pikesville, Md., 12/5/94, age fifty-three, from Loudons, Prince George's Co., Md. d. 2/18/19, age seventy-eight. Bur. Loudon Park Cem., Baltimore.

FERRIS, JOHN: Pvt., Co. G. Paroled Richmond 4/26/65.

FERRITER, TIMOTHY C.: Pvt., Co. G. Captured Smithfield, W.Va., 8/28/64; sent to Pt. Lookout; released 6/2/65. 5'8", fair complexion, gray hair, gray eyes. Res. of Martinsburg, W.Va. Took oath Washington, D.C., 6/13/65; transportation furnished to Martinsburg.

FIELDS, GEORGE W.: Pvt., Co. E. b. circa 1838. Enl. Co. C (Deas Md. Arty.), 19th Bn. Va. Heavy Arty., 4/13/62. Transf. to 2/7/62, age twenty-five; present in arrest 2/63. NFR.

FITZGERALD, THOMAS: Pvt., Co. D. b. circa 1841. Res. of Baltimore. Enl. Edinburg, Va., 2/28/63. Captured Moorefield, W.Va., 4/30/63; sent to Wheeling. Age eighteen, 5'8", fair complexion, sandy hair, blue eyes. Cooper. Transf. to Camp Chase, Johnson's Island, and Pt. Lookout; exchanged 2/21/65; present Camp Lee, Richmond, 2/27/65. ab. sick with "chronic diarrhoea" in Gordonsville, Va., hosp. 3/30/65. NFR. d. 6/24/82, age forty-one. Bur. Loudon Park Cem., Baltimore.

FITZGERALD, WILLIAM BOLTON: Pvt., Co. K. b. circa 1842. Gd. Georgetown U. 1859. Res. of Baltimore. Enl. Co. C (1st), 1st Md. Inf., 5/17/61; Co. disbanded. Enl. Co. K (2nd), 1st Va. Cav., 6/10/61. Captured Gettysburg, Pa., 7/3/63; exchanged 7/63. Captured Leesburg, Va., 10/31/63;

WILLIAM
HENRY
FORSYTHE

*(Museum of the
Confederacy)*

sent to Pt. Lookout; exchanged, date unknown. Captured Thompson's Cross Roads 5/4/64; sent to Ft. Del. Transf. to Co. K, 1st Md. Cav., while POW. Exchanged 2/7/65. Paroled Washington, D.C., 4/13/65; transportation furnished to Baltimore. Clerk, Baltimore. Member ANS/MLA. d. Baltimore 4/29/84, age forty-two.

FITZGERALD, WILLIAM H.: Pvt., Co. G, Davis's Bn.; des. to the enemy at Beverly, W.Va., 5/8/64; sent to Wheeling. Age twenty-four, 5'9", dark complexion, dark hair, blue eyes. Farmer. Res. of Nelson Co., Va.; took oath, released 5/13/64.

FITZHUGH, CLAGGETT DORSEY: Capt., Co. K. Enl. Co. K (2nd), 1st Va. Cav., date unknown. Captured Hagerstown, Md., 9/12/62; sent to Ft. Del. Transf. to Co. K, 1st Md. Cav., while POW. Exchanged 12/64. Paroled Lynchburg, Va., 4/13/65. Res. of Hagerstown. d. 7/30/17. Bur. St. John's Ch. Cem., Washington Co., Md.

FLANNIGAN, JOHN: Pvt., Co. C. b. circa 1841. Res. of Baltimore. Served in Co. H, 1st Md. Inf., 1861–62 per postwar roster. Enl. Co. H, 2nd Md. Inf., 7/27/63. NFR. Enl. Co. C, 1st Md. Cav., Culpeper CH, Va., 8/1/63; present, detailed as blacksmith 1–4/64. Captured Moorefield, W.Va., 8/7/64; sent to Wheeling. Age twenty-three, 5'6", fair complexion, light hair, blue eyes. Transf. to Camp Chase; released 5/8/65.

FLUHARTY, JOSHUA: 1st Sgt., Co. H; present 9/8/62. NFR.

FOLEY, DAVID R.: Pvt., Co. C. b. circa 1837. Res. of Baltimore. Enl. Co. G, 13th Va. Inf., 6/4/61. Machinist. Discharged as nonresident 5/28/62. Enl. Co. C, 1st Md. Cav., Richmond, 8/4/62, yet had horse killed Newtown, Va., 6/12/62, paid $500. Captured Monterey Springs, Pa., 7/4/63; sent to Ft. McHenry; transf. to Ft. Del. and Pt. Lookout; exchanged 2/21/64; ab. on horse detail 2/24–29/64 and 3/24–4/1/64; present through 12/64. NFR. Moulder, Baltimore. Member

ANS/MLA. Entered Old Soldiers' Home, Pikesville, Md., 4/11/94, age fifty-seven; d. there 11/27/97, age sixty. Bur. Loudon Park Cem., Baltimore.

FORD, BENJAMIN R.: Pvt., Co. B. Captured Monterey Springs, Pa., 7/4/63; sent to Ft. Del.; took oath, released 8/8/63.

FORD, JAMES: Pvt., Co. B, Davis's Bn. Captured Loudoun Co., Va., 7/16/64; sent to Old Capitol; transf. to Elmira; exchanged 3/10/65. NFR.

FORREST, ZACHARIAH G. D.: Pvt., Co. K. b. circa 1831. Res. of Baltimore. Enl. Co. G, 1st Md. Inf., 5/22/61; discharged 8/17/62. Age thirty, 5'8", light complexion, sandy hair, gray eyes. Engineer. Enl. Co. K (2nd), 1st Va. Cav., Richmond, 6/1/62 (so on muster rolls); present until captured at Berry's Ferry, Va., 5/16/63; sent to Rock Island. Transf. to Co. K, 1st Md. Cav., 8/64, while POW. Took oath, joined U.S. Army 11/17/64. Age thirty, 5'8", fair complexion, brown hair, gray eyes. Res. of York, Pa.

FORSYTHE, WILLIAM HENRY (photo): Pvt., Co. A. b. Howard Co., Md., 6/26/42. Res. of Sykesville, Md. Enl. Edinburg, Va., 2/1/63; present through 12/64. Paroled Edward's Ferry, Md., 5/18/65. Res. and destination Howard Co., Md. Farmer, Sykesville, Md., 1912. Member ANS/MLA. County Commissioner; Director of Patapsco National Bank for thirty years. d. Sykesville, Md., 10/24/21. Bur. Oak Grove Cem., Glenwood, Howard Co., Md.

FOSTER, MICHAEL: Pvt., Co. A. b. circa 1833. Enl. Co. D, 1st Md. Inf., Staunton, Va., 6/1/62; WIA (hand) Gaines' Mill, Va., 6/27/62. Reenl. Co. A, 1st Md. Cav; ab. sick with "diarrhoea" in Rich-mond hosp. 7/9–22/62; present as Wagoner 11–12/62 and 5–6/63; ab. detailed in Nitre Bureau 8/1/63–8/64. Captured at Port Republic, Va., 9/26/64; sent to Pt. Lookout; exchanged 2/15/65. Admitted to Richmond hosp. 2/16/65 with "frostbites"; furloughed for forty days 2/25/65. Took oath at Richmond 4/12/65, age thirty-two. Peddler. Res. of Belle Island, Va.

FRANCE, ROBERT LEE, JR.: Pvt., Co. H. b. Washington, D.C., 7/7/39. Reared and educated in Baltimore. Gd. Georgetown U. 1859. Served in Stafford Va. Arty. Promoted Ord. Sgt., Hughes Bn. Arty. Joined by transfer 8/5/64. Captured Loudoun Co., Va., 11/28/64, with Mosby's 43rd Bn. of Va. Cav; sent to Old Capitol; transf. to Elmira, Pt. Lookout, and Ft. McHenry; exchanged 2/19/65; ab. sick with debility in Wilmington, N.C., hosp. 2/19/85; furloughed to Rockville, N.C., 3/23/65. Paroled Charles Town, W.Va., 5/29/65. Lived in Va. 1865–80; moved to Chicago, Ill. Businessman. Commander, CV

Camp, Chicago, 1899.

FUNK, CHARLES DANIEL: Pvt., Co. D. b. Baltimore 4/18/44. Res. of Baltimore. Enl. Co. C, 5th Va. Cav., Culpeper CH, Va., 5/23/63; WIA (leg) Brandy Station, Va., 6/9/63. Transf. to Co. D, 1st Md. Cav., 7/30/64; WIA (lost thumb) in Valley 1864; present through 12/64. NFR. Clerk, Baltimore. Member ANS/MLA. Entered Old Soldiers' Home, Pikesville, Md., 9/22/92. Clerk. d. there 5/12/12. Bur. Loudon Park Cem., Baltimore.

FURGESON, A. JOHN: Pvt., Co. A; ab. on horse detail for thirty days 5/1/64. NFR.

FURRINGTON, JOHN: Pvt., Co. unknown, Davis's Bn. On postwar roster.

GALE, THOMAS McDONALD: Pvt., Co. unknown. KIA Farmville, Va., 4/9/65 per UDC application.

GAMBRILL, ALBERT A.: Pvt., Co. A. b. circa 1848. Paroled Harrisonburg, Va., 5/30/65. Age seventeen, 5'5", fair complexion, dark hair, hazel eyes. Manufacturer, Baltimore. d. 5/29/00.

GANTT, ALBERT W.: Pvt., Co. K. Gd. Georgetown U. 1843. Per postwar roster, Co. K (2nd), 1st Va. Cav. Paroled Columbia, Va., 5/6/65. Res. of Scottsville, Va.

GARDNER, J. J.: Pvt., Co. F. Enl. Richmond 7/1/63; des. 8/16/63. NFR.

GARDNER, JOHN W.: Pvt., Co. K. Enl. Breathed's Bty., Horse Arty., Petersburg, Va., 6/10/62. Transf. to Co. K (2nd), 1st Va. Cav., 8/14/64. Transf. to Co. K, 1st Md. Cav., 8/64. Captured at Fisher's Hill, Va., 9/22/64; sent to Pt. Lookout; released 6/12/65. 5'9", light complexion, black hair, hazel eyes. Res. and destination Baltimore.

GARGUS, SMITH: Pvt., Co. K. Enl. Co. K (2nd), 1st Va. Cav., Richmond, 5/1/62; present until detailed as ambulance driver 12/1/62; present until captured Gettysburg, Pa., 7/2/63; sent to Ft. Delaware; exchanged 9/2/63. NFR. Per postwar roster, Co. K, 1st Md. Cav.

GARNER, ROBERT: Pvt., Co. B. b. 11/24/36. Res. Friendship, Anne Arundel Co., Md. Enl. Mobile, Ala., 5/9/64; ab. detailed in Lynchburg, Va., hosp. because of "Phithissis pulmonutos" and "fistula" 1/26–2/19/65, age twenty-five; furloughed from Lynchburg, Va., hosp. for sixty days 3/17/65. Paroled Lynchburg, Va., 4/13/65. d. 8/15/82. Bur. St. James Episcopal Ch. Cem., Anne Arundel Co., Md.

GATCH, THOMAS BENTON: 1st Lt., Co. A, Davis's Bn. b. Lauraville, Baltimore Co., Md., 5/21/41. Gd. Va. Military Inst., Norfolk, Va., 1859. Att. Columbia Col. of Medicine, Washington, D.C. Enl. as 1st Sgt., Co. G, 7th Va. Cav., 6/21/61; WIA (one minié ball passing through his

shoulder, another through the thigh, and a third through his foot) at Gettysburg, Pa., 7/3/63. Transf. to Co. A, Davis's Bn., (later Co. G, 1st Md. Cav.) as 1st Lt. Transf. to Co. G, 2nd Bn. Md. Cav. Transf. back to Davis's Bn. (Co. transferred to 23rd Va. Cav. as Co. M.) Ordered back to 2nd Md. Bn. Cav. at Winchester, 9/64. Captured Harrisonburg, Va., 9/24/64; sent to Ft. Del.; released 6/9/65. 5'6", light complexion, light hair, blue eyes. Gd. Columbia Col. of Medicine, Washington, D.C. Maj., Md. National Guard, 1868; elected to Md. Legislature 1870; Farmer and Dairyman at "Bellview Dairy"; Clerk in Clerk's Office, Baltimore Co. 1892–1900; Farmer and Trucker for twenty-one years. Member ANS/MLA., and Harry Gilmor Camp, CV, Towson, Md. Owner of Quarry and Contracting Co. d. 8/2/33. Bur. Parkwood Cem., Baltimore.

GATCHELL, SAMUEL H.: Pvt., Co. K. b. Baltimore circa 1837. Enl. Co. K (2nd), 1st Va. Cav., date and place unknown. Captured Berry's Ferry, Va., 5/10/63; sent to Ft. McHenry; exchanged circa 5/63. Transf. to Co. K, 1st Md. Cav., 8/64; issued clothing 9/30/64. Captured at Beverly, W.Va., 10/29/64; sent to Wheeling. Age twenty-seven, 5'9", fair complexion, blue eyes, brown hair. Clerk. Transf. to Camp Chase; released 6/12/65. Res. and destination Baltimore.

GAUGING, MICHAEL: Pvt., Co. K. Enl. Breathed's Bty. Horse Arty., Petersburg, Va., 6/10/62. Transf. to Co. K (2nd), 1st Va. Cav., 8/14/64. Transf. to Co. K, 1st Md. Cav., 8/64; AWOL 11/12–12/31/64. NFR.

GEASEY, CHARLES E.: Pvt., Co. D. b. circa 1845. Res. Libertytown, Frederick Co., Md. Enl. Winchester 9/20/62; present 11–12/62, 7–12/63, and 4/1/64. Captured Moorefield, W.Va., 8/7/64. Age nineteen, 5'6", fair complexion, sandy hair, blue eyes. Student. Transf. to Camp Chase and Pt. Lookout; exchanged 3/27/65. Paroled New Market, Va., 4/19/65. Age nineteen, 5'6", fair complexion, light hair, blue eyes. Brother of James W. Geasey.

GEASEY, JAMES W.: Pvt., Co. D. b. circa 1835. Res. Libertytown, Frederick Co., Md. Enl. Co. A, 1st Md. Inf., 5/21/61; discharged 5/23/62. Captured and paroled Winchester, 6/62. Age twenty-seven, 5'8". Enl. Co. D, 1st Md. Cav., Winchester, 9/20/62; present 11–12/62. Captured at Monterey Springs, Pa., 7/4/63, horse killed; sent to Ft. McHenry; transf. to Ft. Del. and Pt. Lookout; exchanged 2/21/65; present Camp Lee, Richmond, 2/22/65; ab. sick with "Ulcus" in Gordonsville, Va., hosp. 3/30/65. Paroled New Market, Va., 4/19/65. Age thirty, 5'8", dark complexion, brown hair, blue eyes. Took oath Harpers

Ferry, W.Va., 4/22/65. Res. Frederick, Md., Bur. St. Peters Ch. Cem., Liberty, Md.; no dates. Brother of Charles E. Geasey.

GEIGER, JOHN D. G.: Pvt., Co. D. b. Md. circa 1837. Student, age twenty-three, Manchester Dist., Carroll Co., per 1860 census. Gd. U of Md. Medical School 1863. Res. Manchester, Carroll Co., Md. Enl. Frederick, Md., 7/1/64; present through 12/64. Paroled Richmond 5/20/65. Took oath Columbia, Va., 5/30/65. Res. and destination Carroll Co. Practiced as M.D. in Manchester, Md., postwar.

GEMMILL, THOMAS H.: 4th Sgt., Co. E. b. circa 1838. Res. Kent Co., Md. Enl. as Pvt., Richmond, 11/10/62, age twenty-four; promoted 4th Sgt. 1/20/63; ab. on detached service 2/28/63; horse killed Winchester 6/13/63, paid $350; KIA Winchester 9/3/64.

GEORGE, THOMAS J.: Pvt., Co. C. b. circa 1844. Enl. Fredericksburg, Va., 9/1/63; ab. detailed as Courier for Gen. Fitzhugh Lee through 12/63. Also listed as enlisting in Co. K (2nd), 1st Va. Cav., at Culpeper, Va., 11/1/63; detailed to Brigade Headquarters the same day; NFR. Ab. detailed as Courier for Gen. Fitzhugh Lee through 12/64. Took oath 6/21/65. Civil Engineer. d. Towson, Md., 9/4/98, age fifty-five.

GEPHARD, SOLOMON ARTHUR: Pvt., Co. A. b. Cumberland, Md., circa 1821; moved to Frederick, Md., as a child. Enl. Co. A, 1st Md. Inf., 4/21/61; discharged 5/21/62. Enl. Co. A, 1st Md. Cav., Charlottesville, 7/5/62; present through 12/63 and 4/1/64; ab. term of service expired and discharged on rolls 8/31–12/31/64; ab. sick with debility in Charlottesville hosp. 3/14–16/65. Paroled New Market, Va., 4/19/65. Age forty, 5'9½", light complexion, dark hair, brown eyes. Took oath at Harpers Ferry, W.Va., 4/25/65. Res. Frederick, Md. Shoemaker, Frederick, Md. Member ANS/MLA. Entered Old Soldiers' Home, Pikesville, Md., 6/19/88, age sixty-seven, from Frederick Co., Md.; d. there 3/14/04, age eighty-three. Bur. Loudon Park Cem., Baltimore.

GIBSON, E.: Pvt., Co. B. On postwar roster.

GIBSON, HENRY BOTELER: Pvt., Co. D. b. Baltimore circa 1842. Res. of Baltimore. Enl. as Sgt., Castle Pinckney Heavy Arty. of S.C., 1861. Enl. 1st Rockbridge Arty. 5/30/62. Transf. to Co. D, 1st Md. Cav., 11/1/63. Captured Frederick, Md., 12/3/63; sent to Wheeling. Age twenty-two, 5'6", light complexion, gray eyes, black hair. Res. Baltimore. Transf. to Camp Chase and Ft. Delaware; exchanged 3/17/65. Ab. sick in Richmond hosp. 3/21–22/65. Paroled Winchester 4/27/65, age twenty-three. Farmer and Surveyor. Entered Old Soldiers' Home, Pikesville, Md., 10/22/22,

age eighty-one. NFR. Admitted to Old Soldiers' Home, Richmond, from Baltimore, 1/20/27, age eighty-five; d. there 1/17/31. Bur. Hollywood Cem., Richmond.

GIBSON, JOHNATHAN E.: Pvt., Co. B. Res. Bladensburg, Prince George's Co., Md. Enl. Charlottesville 9/10/62; present 7–8/63; ab. sick with scabies in Richmond hosp. 9/25/63–10/63; transf. to Lynchburg, Va., hosp. 11–12/63; ab. sick with "Fistual" and "Chronic abcess posterior to sternum" in Richmond hosp. 4/1/64; RTD 11/16/64; detailed in QM Dept. through 12/64. NFR. Member George Emack Camp, CV, Hyattsville, Md., 1903. Res. Washington, D.C., 1904.

GIBSON, S.: Pvt., Co. B. Transf. to Co. E, 43rd Va. Bn. Cav. (Mosby), per postwar roster.

GIBSON, WILLIAM E.: Pvt., Co. A. Enl. date and place unknown. Captured Moorefield, W.Va., 8/7/64; sent to Pt. Lookout; released 6/6/65. Took oath Washington, D.C., 6/9/65; transportation furnished to St. Joseph Co., Mo.

GIESENDOFFER, LEONARD: Pvt., Co. G. Res. Prince George's Co., Md. Enl. Co B, Davis's Bn., date unknown. Surrendered Appomattox CH, Va., 5/9/65. Took oath Alexandria, Va., 5/17/65. 5'10", dark complexion, dark hair, hazel eyes.

GILES, WILLIAM FELL, JR.: Pvt., Co. C. Res. of Baltimore. Enl. Co. A, 13th Va. Inf., but not on muster rolls. Enl. Co. C, 1st Md. Cav., Bridgewater, Va., 5/17/63; present 7–9/63; ab. sick with scabies in Richmond hosp. 10/21–22/63; ab. on horse detail 10/28–31/63; present 11–12/63; ab. sick with scabies in Richmond hosp. 1/26–4/13/64; present through 8/31/64; ab. sick in Richmond hosp. 11/30–12/1/64; ab. detailed as Courier for Gen. Lunsford Lomax 12/23–31/64. Paroled, took oath, Winchester 5/25/65. Res. and destination Baltimore. Judge, Baltimore. Member ANS/MLA. d. 3/4/91.

GILL, GEORGE MURRAY, JR. (photo next page): Pvt., Co. K. b. 1/6/42. Gd. Princeton Col. Served in 1st Md. Inf. 1861–62 per postwar roster. Enl. Co. K (2nd), 1st Va. Cav., 8/1/62; WIA Stuart's Tavern, Va., 8/30/62; RTD; present until captured Williamsport, Md., 7/22/63; sent to Ft. Del.; transf. to Pt. Lookout; exchanged 12/24/63; present 2–8/64. Transf. to Co. K, 1st Md. Cav.; discharged at end of enlistment 12/14/64. Joined Mosby; WIA near Berryville, Va., 3/30/65; DOW 4/4/65. Bur. Blue Ridge Mts.; removed by his father to Greenmont Cem., Baltimore.

GILL, JOHN, JR.: Pvt., Co. A. b. Annapolis, Md., 8/15/41. Att. U. Va. 1860–61. Enl. Co. H, 1st Md. Inf., 5/1/61; WIA Cross Keys, Va., 6/8/62; paid 7/10/62; discharged when Co. disbanded. Enl. Co.

A, 1st Md. Cav., Charlottesville, 6/5/62, (so on muster roll); paid New Market, Va., 1/10/63; ab., detailed in Signal Corps, through 4/1/64; promoted Signal Sgt. of Division Signal Corps; ab. detailed as Courier for Gen. Fitzhugh Lee's Headquarters through 10/64; ab. commanding scouting party in Valley winter 1864–65. Attached to Mosby 3–4/65. Paroled Berryville, Va., 4/65, with about thirty others. Took oath at Relay House, Md., 4/22/65. Arrested in Baltimore and held ten days. Four horses killed under him. Went to Europe 9/65. Grain Merchant and Bank President, Baltimore, 1888. BGen., QM, and Chief of Arty., Md. National Guard. Member Isaac Trimble and Frank Buchanan Camps, CV, and ANS/MLA. Authored *Four Years as a Private Soldier,* 1904. d. Ventnor, N.J., 7/2/12. Bur. Greenmont Cem., Baltimore.

GEORGE M. GILL JR.

(Gary Smith)

GILL, WILLIAM H. "BILLIE": Pvt., Co. C. b. circa 1842. Res. of Baltimore. Enl. Richmond 8/15/62, age twenty; horse killed at Oakland, Md., 5/1/63, paid $500; WIA (foot) at Gettysburg, Pa., 7/3/63. Captured in hosp. at Hagerstown, Md., 7/14/63; sent to West Buildings hosp., Baltimore. Transf. to Ft. Del.; exchanged 8/63. On parole in Richmond 9–12/63; present 1–2/64; ab. sick with "gonorrhoa" and scabies in Richmond hosp. 3/2/64; RTD 5/7/64; present through 8/31/64 on muster rolls. Reportedly detailed as Clerk for Gen. Robert Ransom after Monocacy; ab. detailed as Courier for Gen. Lunsford Lomax 9–12/64; ab. sick in Richmond hosp. 12/25–27/64; ab. sick with "gonorrhoea" in Danville, Va., hosp. 4/5–8/65. Surrendered Greensboro, N.C., 5/1/65. Took oath at Eastville, Va., 5/15/65. Res. and destination Baltimore. Member ANS/MLA. Realtor, Baltimore; d. there 2/29/06, age sixty-four.

GILLAND, CHARLES: Pvt., Co. unknown. Paroled and took oath at Winchester 4/14/65. Res. of Baltimore. Ordered north of Philadelphia.

GILMAN, R. Y.: Pvt., Co. D. Admitted to Richmond hosp. 10/7/63; furloughed 10/8/63. NFR.

GILROY, THOMAS: Pvt., Co. E. b. circa 1846. Res. Charles Co., Md. Enl. Richmond 11/17/62, age eighteen; presence or ab. not stated 1–2/63; des. near Parkersburg, W.Va., 5/8/63; sent to Wheeling. Age eighteen, 5'10", florid complexion, blue eyes, light hair. Farmer. Transf. to Camp Chase; took oath, released 5/28/63. Age seventeen on oath.

GINNES, C. D.: Pvt., Co. D. Paroled Winchester 4/21/65.

GIVINS, CHARLES J.: Pvt., Co. C, Davis's Bn. Captured Harrisonburg, Va., 9/23/64; sent to West Building hosp., Baltimore, 10/13/64, age thirty. Took oath, released 2/7/65.

GIVINS, MARIAN: Pvt., Co. C, Davis's Bn. NFR.

GLENN, CLEMENT: Pvt., Co. C. Res. Harford Co., Md. Enl. Williamsport, Md., 7/6/63; present through 12/63, 1–2/64, and 4/1–8/31/64; KIA Bunker Hill 9/18/64. Bur. Edge Hill Cem., Charles Town, W.Va.

GLENN, EDWARD S.: Pvt., Co. E. Captured Germanna Ford, Va., 10/11/63. Not on Federal POW rolls; may have been KIA. NFR.

GLENN, ELIAS: Pvt., Co. B. b. 1840. Enl. Winchester 7/16/63; present through 12/63, 1–2/64, and 4/1–8/31/64; brown mare killed at Clear Spring, Md., 7/29/64, paid $2,500; ab., detailed as Courier for Gen. Lunsford Lomax, 11–12/64. Captured Shenandoah River 12/16/64; sent to Pt. Lookout; released 6/9/65. d. 1868.

GLENN, FRANCIS BUTLER "FRANK": Pvt., Co. C. b. Harford Co., Md., 1833. Res. Harford Co., Md. Enl. Williamsport, Md., 7/6/63. Captured at Martinsburg, W.Va., 7/18/63; sent to Wheeling. Age twenty-nine, 5'11", florid complexion, blue eyes, black hair. Hotel Keeper. Transf. to Camp Chase; took oath, released 12/22/64, age thirty. d. Baltimore 1911.

GLENN, JAMES SEWALL: Pvt., Co. E. b. circa 1836. Res. Baltimore. Enl. Richmond 11/10/62, age twenty-six; presence or ab. not stated 1–2/63. Captured near Winchester 4/12/63; sent to Ft. McHenry; exchanged 6/63; horse captured near Winchester 6/12/63, paid $230; present 7–9/63. Captured Germanna Ford, Va., 10/11/63; sent to Old Capitol; transf. to Pt. Lookout. Age twenty-six, 5'8", fair complexion, gray eyes, sandy hair; exchanged 3/6/64. Issued clothing 5/12/64. "Paroled and recaptured"; on rolls 11–12/64. NFR. d. circa 1916.

GLENN, JOSEPH P.: Pvt., Co. C. b. Ireland. Captured South Mt., Md., 7/4/63; sent to Ft. Delaware. Took oath, joined U.S. Navy 3/18/64.

GLENN, WALTER: Pvt., Co. A, Davis's Bn. NFR.

GOLDSBOROUGH, HARRISON G.: Pvt., Co. E. On postwar roster.

GOLDSMITH, GEORGE W.: Pvt., Co. A, Davis's Bn. Res. Baltimore. Enl. Md. 6/25/63. Captured at Newtown, Va., 1/6/64; sent to Wheeling. Age twenty-three, 5'10", dark complexion, dark hair, blue eyes. Druggist. Transf. to Camp Chase; released 5/11/65.

GOODLOE, WILLIAM: Pvt., Co. E. Enl. Culpeper, Va., 8/3/63; present until des. from camp near Orange CH, Va., 10/6/63. NFR.

GOODMAN, OTHO: Pvt., Co. C. Enl. Edinburg 3/1/63; present 7–10/63; horse stolen from camp near Culpeper, Va.; ab. on leave for a horse to Woodstock, Va., 11/14/63; horse captured in the Valley 12/20/63; ab. on leave for ten days to New Market, Va., to get a horse 2/1/64; AWOL 2/25–29/64. "Deserted—gone to Ohio" on rolls 4/1/64. NFR.

GOODMAN, ZACK: Pvt., Co. A, Davis's Bn. NFR.

GOREY, JOHN K.: Pvt., Co. C, Davis's Bn. Res. Golden Hill, Dorchester Co., Md. NFR.

GORGAS, MERIDITH: Pvt., Co. C, Davis's Bn. Enl. Richmond 11/1/63; present through 10/31/64. Transf. to Co. F, 23rd Va. Cav. NFR.

GOUGH, CHARLES EDWARD, SR.: Pvt., Co. B. b. St. Mary's Co., Md., 5/26/37. Gd. Georgetown U. 1860. Res. Leonardtown, Md. Enl. Charlottesville 9/10/62; present 7–8/63; ab. sick in Charlottesville hosp. 9–10/63; present 11–12/63; horse lost Heathsville, Va., 12/15/63; ab. on horse detail for ten days 2/1/64; present 4/1/64; WIA (flesh wounds in right arm), date and place unknown; ab. wounded in Richmond hosp. 8/31–12/31/64. Paroled 4/24/65. d. "Bloomsbury," St. Mary's Co., Md., 3/19/97. Pallbearers included John W. Williams of Co. B; T. Ed. Loker of Co. A; J. M. Dent of Co. B; and T. F. Yates of Co. K.

GOUGH, CHARLES EDWARD, JR.: Pvt., Co. C. b. Md. 4/30/42. Student, age sixteen, St. Mary's Co., Md., per 1860 census. Enl. Richmond 8/4/62; present 7–9/63; ab. sick with acute dysentery in Charlottesville hosp. 10/10–11/6/63; ab. sick with typhoid fever in Richmond hosp. 11/19/63–1/7/64; present 2/29/64 and 4/1–8/3/64; ab. sick with debility in Charlottesville hosp. 4/8–9/65. NFR. d. St. Mary's Co., Md., 1/17/69.

GOULDING, JOHN: Pvt., Co. unknown. In Libby Prison, Richmond, 4/10/65. NFR.

GRABILL, ABRAHAM W., JR.: Pvt., Co. D. b. 5/31/41. Res. of Johnsville, Frederick Co., Md. Enl. Winchester 9/20/62. Captured Monterey Springs, Pa., 7/4/63; sent to Ft. Del.; d. there of "cerebretis" 5/31/63. Bur. Finn's Pt., N.J., Natl. Cem.; removed to Grabill Cem. No. 1, Johnsville.

GRAHAM, ISRAEL J.: Pvt., Co. A. b. Loudoun Co., Va., 5/29/33. Res. of Burkittsville, Frederick Co., Md. Enl. Co. G, 7th Va. Cav., 3/1/62. Transf. to Co. A, 1st Md. Cav., Hanover Junction, Va., 5/1/64; WIA and captured Pollard's Farm, Va., 5/27/64; sent to Pt. Lookout; transf. to Elmira; released 6/16/65. 5'10½", florid complexion, black hair, blue eyes. Res. of Burton, Md. Salesman, Baltimore. Entered Old Soldiers' Home, Pikesville, Md. 10/4/04; d. there 12/1/08. Bur. Loudon Park Cem., Baltimore.

GRAHAM, JESSE W.: Pvt., Co. C. Enl. Co. F, 1st Md. Inf., 5/21/61; discharged 8/62. Enl. Co. D, Cobb's Ga. Legion. Transf. to Co. C, 1st Md. Cav., Staunton, Va., 3/31/63; ab. on horse detail to Staunton 2/9/64 and for seven days 3/27/64; ab. detailed in Provost Guard, Johnson's Brigade, 7/10–8/31/64; AWOL 9–12/64. NFR.

GRAVES, RICHARD: Pvt., Co. C, Davis's Bn. On postwar roster.

GRAY, HENRY S.: Pvt., Co., C. b. 1828. Enl. Richmond 8/10/62; paid near New Market, Va., 1/10/63; detailed as Teamster 5–7/63. Captured Williamsport, Md., 7/6/63; sent to Ft. McHenry; transf. to Ft. Del.; d. there of "chronic diarrhoea" 9/6/63. Bur. Finn's Pt. Natl. Cem., N.J.

GREEN, ALEXANDER: Pvt., Co. A, Davis's Bn. Enl. Co. E, 20th Bn. Va. Arty., 4/23/62. Transf. to Co. A, Davis's Bn., Richmond, 4/29/64. Captured Piedmont, Va., 6/5/64; sent to Camp Morton; exchanged 2/28/65. Took oath Washington, D.C., 5/1/65.

GREEN, HUGH T.: Pvt., Co. F. b. circa 1830. Res. of Baltimore. Enl. Co. D, 1st Md. Inf., 6/1/61; discharged 8/62. Enl. Co. F, 1st Md. Cav, Waynesboro, Va., 6/15/64; present through 12/64. Paroled, took oath, Winchester 4/20/65. Age thirty-five, 5' 8", dark complexion, black hair, gray eyes. Res. of and destination Baltimore.

GREEN, JOHN T.: Pvt., Co. A, Davis's Bn. b. 3/28/25. Enl. Co. G, 7th Va. Cav., date unknown; AWOL 8/1/62. NFR. Enl. Co. A, Davis's Bn, New Market, Va, 11/6/63. Transf. to Co. M, 23rd Va. Cav. Transf. to 2nd Md. Inf. NFR. d. 6/17/09. Bur. Mt. Olivet Cem., Frederick, Md.

GREEN, THOMAS J.: 2nd Lt., Co. C. Res. of Baltimore. Enl. Co. I, 1st Md. Inf., 6/15/61; discharged 6/15/62. Served as Lt. in Co. B., 61st Alabama Inf. Elected 3rd Lt. Co. C, 1st Md. Cav., 3/1/63; commanding Co. 4/25–5/63; promoted 2nd Lt. 6/1/63; ab. sick with "Mabicutis" in Richmond hosp. 11/22/63–1/3/64; present 1–2/64 and 4/1/64; WIA (right shoulder resulting in "debilitas" of right arm and partial paralysis) and captured at Rockville, Md., 7/13/64; paroled by 9/64; ab. in Richmond hosp. 2/22/65; present Camp Lee, Richmond, 3/65, as paroled POW. Assigned to duty there 3/24/65. NFR. Entered Old Soldiers' Home, Pikesville, Md., 12/6/98, from Baltimore, age sixty-two. Accountant. Dropped in 1900.

GREEN, WILLIAM: Pvt., Co. F. Enl. Richmond 7/15/63; des. near Culpeper, Va., 7/31/63. NFR.

GREEN, WILLIAM: Pvt., Co. G; ab. sick with dysentery in Richmond hosp. 7/4–25/64. NFR.

GREEN, WILLIAM: Pvt., Co. A, Davis's Bn. NFR.

GREEN, WILLIAM B.: Pvt., Co. E. b. circa 1841. Res. of Baltimore. Enl. Richmond 1/11/63, age twenty-one; des. from Camp Lee, Richmond, 2/12/63. NFR.

GREEN, WILLIAM OLIVER: Pvt., Co. B. b. Cecil Co., Md. 1837. Res. Cecil Co., Md. Served in Co. B, 2nd Va. Inf., but is not on muster rolls. Enl. Co. B, 1st Md. Cav., Charlottesville, 10/1/62. Captured at Old Church, Va., 3/2/64; sent to Pt. Lookout; exchanged 3/18/65; present at Camp Lee, Richmond, 3/19/65. Paroled Greensboro, N.C., 5/9/65. Took oath 5/13/65. Res. and destination Kent Co., Md. Member ANS/MLA. Farmer, Baltimore. Entered Old Soldiers' Home, Pikesville, Md., 2/5/07, age seventy; d. there 6/5/13. Bur. Loudon Park Cem., Baltimore.

GREENE, WILLIAM D.: Pvt., Co. E. Enl. at Winchester 7/20/63; present through 8/31/63; ab. on horse detail 9–10/63; des. 12/25/63 (escaped from Brigade Guard House); des. to the enemy at Yorktown, Va., 2/5/64; sent to Ft. Monroe; transf. to Pt. Lookout; took oath, released 4/18/64. Transportation furnished to Philadelphia, Pa. Arrested in Baltimore 7/22/64 for violation of oath. NFR.

GRAY, HUGH: Pvt., Co. K. Res. of Baltimore. Also on postwar roster Co. K (2nd), 1st Va. Cav.

GRAY, S. W. or L. M.: Pvt., Co. E. Captured Monterey Springs, Pa., 7/4/63; sent to Ft. Delaware. NFR.

GRIFFIN, GEORGE C.: Pvt., Co. A. Res. Harford Co., Md. On postwar roster of Co. K (2nd), 1st Va. Cav., as C. George Griffin. Enl. Co. A, 1st Md. Cav., Hagerstown, Md., 6/25/62; present 7–12/63 and 4/1–12/31/64. Served in Co. F, 43rd Bn. Va. Cav. (Mosby). Captured at Sugar Loaf Mt., Md., 1/4/65; sent to Old Capitol; transf. to Ft. Warren, as "guerilla." Released 6/13/65. 6'¼", light complexion, light hair, blue eyes. Postwar res. of Laurel, Md.

GRIFFIN, JOSEPH: Capt., Co. H. b. circa 1836. Res. of Baltimore. Enl. Co. B, 1st Md. Inf., 5/21/61; resigned 12/62. Enl. as 2nd Lt., Co. B, 24th Bn. Va. Partisan Rangers, 5/20/62; promoted Capt. 7/6/62; disbanded 1/15/63. Enl. Co. H, 1st Md. Cav., date unknown; listed as present 9/8/62. Served on staff of Gen. Fitzhugh Lee. Enl. 43rd Bn. Va. Cav. (Mosby); WIA (thigh) and captured at Hamilton, Va., 3/21/65; sent to Harpers Ferry,

W.Va., hosp.; transf. to Ft. McHenry. Released 6/10/65. Member John B. Strange Camp, CV, Charlottesville, 1895. d. 9/6/05.

GRIFFIN, RICHARD C.: Pvt., Co. G. Res. of Howard Co., Md. Captured Sugar Loaf Mt., Md., 9/16/64; sent to Old Capitol. Transf. to Ft. Warren; released 6/13/65.

GRIFFIN, WILLIAM: Pvt., Co. B, Davis's Bn. Captured Beverly, W.Va., 10/29/64; sent to Wheeling. Age twenty, 5'9", fair complexion, light hair, gray eyes. Carpenter. Res. of Alexandria, Va. Transf. to Camp Chase 11/22/64. NFR.

GRIFFITH, DAVID: Pvt., Co. A. b. Montgomery Co., Md., 4/9/37. Res. of Redland, Montgomery Co. Enl. Charlottesville 8/25/62; present as Forage Master 11/62 and as QM Sgt. 12/62; present 7–12/63 and 4/1/64. Captured King William Co. 5/9/64; sent to Pt. Lookout; exchanged 9/22/64. Admitted to Richmond hosp. with "diarrhoea" the same day; furloughed for forty days to Rockingham Co., Va., 9/26/64. Paroled Winchester 4/27/65. 5'11", dark complexion, brown hair, gray eyes. Farmer and Judge of Orphan's Court, Montgomery Co. Member Ridgely Brown Camp, CV, Rockville, Md. d. Montgomery Co. 12/28/14. Bur. Union Cem., Rockville. Brother of Francis and Thomas Griffith.

GRIFFITH, FRANCIS "FRANK": 3rd Lt., Co. A. b. "Edgehill," Montgomery Co., Md., 10/29/40. Enl. as Pvt., Co. K (2nd), 1st Va. Cav., 5/14/61; present until transf. to Co. A, 1st Md. Cav., 5/15/62, as 2nd Sgt; present 7–12/63 and 4/1/64; promoted 3rd Lt; present 6/27/64; commanding Co. 8/31/64; present 11–12/64. One officer and forty-two men present in Co. 12/1/64. NFR. d. 7/28/92. Bur. Griffith Cem., "Edgehill," near Unity, Montgomery Co., Md. Brother of David and Thomas Griffith.

GRIFFITH, JOHN JAMES: Pvt., Co. E. Enl. Co. G, 1st Md. Inf., 5/23/61; discharged 8/62. Enl. Co. E, 1st Md. Cav., date unknown. Captured at Port Republic, Va., 9/26/64; sent to Pt. Lookout; took oath, released 3/25/65.

GRIFFITH, LEONIDAS M. "LYDE": Pvt., Co. A. b. Montgomery Co., Md., 5/3/35. Enl. date unknown; des. near New Market, Va., 12/26/62. NFR. d. 4/14/06.

GRIFFITH, RICHARD: Pvt., Co. K. Res. of Carroll Co., Md. Enl. Co. K (2nd), 1st Va. Cav., 9/10/62; present until captured at Upperville, Va., 5/20/63; sent to Elmira. Transf. to Co. K, 1st Md. Cav., 8/64, while POW. Released 5/29/65. Res. Laurel, Prince George's Co., Md., postwar.

GRIFFITH, THOMAS: Capt., Co. A. b. Montgomery Co., Md., 4/29/31. Farmer, Olney, Montgomery Co. Enl. as Pvt., Co. K (2nd), 1st Va.

Cav., 5/14/61; present until elected 3rd Lt. 8/1/61; present until not reelected 4/23/62. Elected 2nd Lt., Co. A, 1st Md. Cav., 5/15/62; present at Sharpsburg, Md., 9/17/62; present 10–12/62 as acting QM of Bn.; promoted 1st Lt. 11/25/62; present 6/9/63 and at Gettysburg, Pa.; commanding Co. 9–10/63; present 11–12/63. Two officers and eighty-seven men with 100 horses present 1/64. Commanding Co. 4/1/64; promoted Capt. 1864 to rank from 7/63. Captured at Moorefield, W.Va., 8/7/64; sent to Wheeling. 5'11", fair complexion, dark hair, blue eyes. Transf. to Camp Chase; exchanged 3/14/65. Paroled at Richmond 4/29/65. Farmer, Olney, Montgomery Co., Md. Member Ridgely Brown Camp, CV, Rockville, Md. d. Olney, Md., 7/14/12. Bur. St. John's Episcopal Ch. Cem., Olney. Brother of David and Francis Griffith. "A gallant soldier, faithful in the execution of orders, and brave in the face of danger."

GRIMES, CORNELIUS D.: Pvt., Co. D. b. Md. 1841. Res. Baltimore. Served as Capt., Co. C, 1st Md. Inf., 1861–62, per postwar roster. Enl. Co. C (2nd), 2nd Md. Inf., Winchester, 9/20/62. Transf. to Co. D, 1st Md. Cav., 12/17/62; present through 12/31/62. Captured at Monterey Springs, Pa., 7/4/63, horse killed; sent to Ft. McHenry. Transf. to Ft. Del.; exchanged 7/31/63. Paid $400 for horse; ab. sick in Richmond hosp. 8/63; ab. on horse detail 9–10/63; present 11–12/63 and 4/1/64; ab. sick in hosp. 8/31/64; present 11–12/64. Paroled, took oath, Winchester 4/21/65. Age twenty-three, 5'10", light complexion, red hair, blue eyes. Res. Carroll Co., Md. Res. Front Royal, Va., postwar. Member William Richardson Camp, CV, Front Royal; d. there 9/30/09.

GRIMES, JOHN HENRY "HARRY": Pvt., Co. K. b. Carroll Co., Md., 9/16/42. Att. Calvert Col. (later New Windsor Col.), Md. Res. New Windsor, Carroll Co. Enl. Co. A, 1st Va. Cav., Berkeley Co., W.Va., 9/22/62; present until detailed as Courier for Col. Morgan 1–8/64. Transf. to Co. D, 1st Md. Cav., 10/18/64; ab. sick with scabies in Charlottesville hosp. 12/29/64. Not reported on rolls through 12/31/64; RTD 2/20/65. Paroled 4/25/65 at Winchester as Pvt., Co. A, 1st Va. Cav. Fair complexion, dark hair, blue eyes. Druggist, Shepherdstown, W.Va., 1865–66. Gd. U. of Md. Medical School 1868. M.D. in New Windsor, Carroll Co., Md. Merchant, Baltimore, 1894. Member ANS/MLA. and Isaac R. Trimble Camp, CV, Baltimore. d. Baltimore 11/7/14. Bur. Greenmount Cem., Baltimore.

GROGAN, JAMES J.: Pvt., Co. C. b. circa 1840. Res. of Baltimore. Enl. Co. B, 21st Va. Inf., 5/23/61. 5'9", dark hair, blue eyes; des. 9/61. NFR

until enl. Co. A, 2nd Md. Inf., Winchester 10/9/62. Transf. to Co. C, 1st Md. Cav., 5/23/64; present through 12/31/64. Captured in Fauquier Co., Va., 1/25/65; sent to Old Capitol; transf. to Ft. Warren as a "guerila"; released 6/16/65. 5'8½", dark complexion, brown hair, blue eyes. Member ANS/MLA, 1894. Res. of Stafford Co., Va., per 1910 census.

GROGAN, ROBERT RIDDLE: Pvt., Co. C. b. Baltimore 1829. Served in 5th La. Inf. and Tex. Arty. Enl. Co. C, 1st Md. Cav., Richmond, 8/10/62; WIA (lost thumb on left hand) Greenland Gap, W.Va., 4/25/63; present 1/64; left hand disabled through 4/1/64; ab., detailed as Color Sgt. by order Gen. B. T. Johnson, 5/25–11/64. Assigned to C.S. Prison, Danville, Va., by Medical Board 11/5/64. Paroled at Bunker Hill, W.Va., 5/27/65. Member ANS/MLA, 1885. Res. of McDounaugh, Baltimore. Res. Stafford Co., Va., 1888; moved to Mossy Creek, Va., 1891. Grocer. Joined Stonewall Jackson Camp, CV, Staunton, Va., 2/16/93, age fifty-five. d. Stafford Co. 7/6/14. Bur. Berryville, Va.

GROVE, FRANKLIN SAMUEL: Pvt., Co. C. b. Sharpsburg, Md., circa 1845. Enl. Winchester 8/15/64; present through 8/31 and 11–12/64. NFR. Merchant, Baltimore. Entered Old Soldiers' Home, Pikesville, Md., 8/4/08, age sixty-three. Left. Age sixty-seven, South River Dist., Augusta Co., Va., per 1910 census. Merchant, Mercer Co., W.VA. Transf. to from CV Camp #838 to Stonewall Jackson Camp, CV, Staunton, Va., 4/1/13. Res. of Basic City, Va. d. Charlottesville 5/12/15. Bur. Louisa, Va.

GROVE, JOHN: Pvt., Co. A. Res. Washington Co., Md. On postwar roster.

GROVE, THOMAS H.: Pvt., Co. C. b. circa 1845 Sharpsburg, Md. Enl. Hagerstown, Md., 6/18/63; present through 10/63; ab. sick with "Contin Fever" in Richmond hosp. 10/24/63 and with debility 11/19/63; RTD; horse given to dismounted man in Battalion; ab. on horse detail for ten days to Strasburg, Va., 2/1/64, and for fifteen days 2/18/64; present 4/1/64 through 12/64. Paroled Harrisonburg, Va., 5/7/65. Age twenty, 5'5¾", light complexion, light hair, blue eyes. d. circa 1/1/05, age sixty-two. (Postwar photograph in Stonebraker 1899)

GRUBER, BENJAMIN FRANKLIN: Pvt., Co. unknown. Enl. Charlottesville Arty. 4/21/62, age eighteen. Farmer. AWOL 7/10/62: "not formally transf. to from 1st Md. Cav."; Present 9/3/62; WIA (bruised by a shell) Chancellorsville, Va., 5/3/63; ab. wounded in Richmond hosp. 5/9/63; transf. to Danville, Va., hosp. 5/11–6/30/63. Admitted Richmond hosp. 7/20/63; des. 7/26/63. NFR.

GUAKLE, ALBERT: Pvt., Co. K. Paroled at New Market, Va., 4/19/65.

GUNBY, FRANCIS MARION "FRANK": Pvt., Co. unknown. b. Md. 7/14/44. On postwar roster. Enl. 1st Md. Arty. 7/21/61; discharged 10/31/64. NFR. Bur. Parsons Cem., Salisbury, Md., no dates. Brother of John W. Gunby.

GUNBY, JOHN W.: Pvt., Co. G. b. Md. 2/2/42. Res. of Worcester Co., Md. Enl. Co. I, 30th Va. Inf., 7/22/61, age sixteen; WIA Sharpsburg, Md., 9/17/62. Transf. to Co. G, 1st Md. Cav., 5/23/64; present 2/28/65. Took oath at Baltimore 5/11/65. Clerk, Salisbury, Md., per 1870 census. d. 10/7/79. Bur. Parsons Cem., Salisbury, Md. Brother of Francis M. Gunby.

GUYTHER, JOHN WILLIAM "JACK": Pvt., Co. B. b. Baltimore, 4/23/43; moved to Piney Point, St. Mary's Co., Md., as a child. Farmer, St. Mary's Co., per 1860 census. On postwar roster. Enl. 1st Md. Arty. 8/15/61; des. to the enemy at Washington, D.C., 3/6/65; took oath, released. Clerk, Baltimore postwar; moved to Brookville, Pa.; d. there 2/7/14.

GUYTHER, WILLIAM HENRY WAUGHOP: 3rd Sgt., Co. B, b. St. Mary's Co., Md., circa 1839. Farmer, Great Mills, St. Mary's Co., Md., per 1860 census. Enl. Co. B, 21st Va. Inf., 5/23/61. 6', light hair, blue eyes; present 11–12/61. NFR. Enl. Co. B, 1st Md. Cav., Charlottesville, 10/9/62. Captured Capon Springs, W.Va., 12/20/62; sent to Wheeling. Age twenty-three, 6'½", fair complexion, light hair, blue eyes, whiskers. Transf. to Camp Chase; exchanged 4/1/63. His horse was killed, and he was captured at Monterey Springs, Pa., 7/4/63; sent to Ft. McHenry; transf. to Ft. Delaware and Pt. Lookout; exchanged 12/28/63. AWOL 4/1/64; ab. sick with scabies in Richmond hosp. 6/13–30/64; ab. sick in Charlottesville hosp. 8/31/64 and again, with scabies, 11/29–12/19/64; present 12/31/64. Paroled Richmond 5/5/65. Farmer, Piney Point, St. Mary's Co.; d. there 1/31/71. Bur. St. George's Episcopal Ch. Cem., Poplar Hill, Md.; no marker.

GWYNN, JOHN M. S.: Pvt., Co. B. On postwar roster.

HACKMAN, BENJAMIN FRANKLIN: Pvt., Co. B. b. Lancaster, Pa., circa 1840. Enl. Co. D, 1st Va. Inf., 7/23/61; discharged for disability 11/6/61. Enl. Purcell Arty., Richmond, 2/27/62. Captured Williamsport, Md., 7/63; exchanged 5/3/64. Transf. to Co. B, 1st Md. Cav., 6/30/64; WIA at Moorefield, W.Va., 8/7/64; ab. wounded in Richmond hosp. 8/12–19/64; furloughed for thirty days. NFR. Member Confederate Veterans Assoc., Washington, D.C., 1894. Entered Old Soldiers' Home, Richmond, 10/13/03, age sixty-three, from Richmond. d. 3/18/04. Bur. Holly-

EDWARD HOWARD HALL

(*Museum of the Confederacy*)

wood Cem., Richmond.

HAGAN, JAMES A.: Pvt., Co. F. Res. Baltimore. Enl. date and place unknown; des. to the enemy at Martinsburg, W.Va., 9/4/64; sent to Ft. Mifflin, Pa.; took oath, released 9/26/64. 5'7", dark complexion, brown hair, hazel eyes. NFR. d. 2/28/65. Bur. Loudon Park Cem., Baltimore.

HAGER, JOHN H.: Cpl., Co. C. b. circa 1846. Res. Washington Co., Md. Enl. as Pvt., Hagerstown, Md., 6/18/63; present 7–8/63; present sick 9–10/63; present 11–12/63; horse died in camp 12/1/63; ab. sick with "Remit fever" in Richmond hosp. 12/25–28/63; ab. on leave for fifteen days to Strasburg, Va., to get another horse 2/1/64; present 4/1/64; promoted Cpl. 7/1/64; present through 12/64; present Appomattox CH, Va., 4/9/65. Paroled Harrisonburg, Va., 7/13/65. Age twenty-one, 5'5", light complexion, light hair, hazel eyes. Took oath at Kearneysville, W.Va., 5/20/65. Res. and destination Washington Co., Md. Member ANS/MLA. 1899. Res. Mandan, Dakota Territory. (Postwar photograph in Stonebraker 1899)

HAHN, REUBEN T. or H.: Pvt., Co. D. Enl. Co. A, 1st Md. Inf., 5/21/61; discharged 5/21/62. Enl. Co. F, 12th Va. Cav., 6/12/62; present 9–10/63; promoted 5th Sgt. by 3/31/64. Transf. to Co. D, 1st Md. Cav., 4/64, "without proper transfer—ordered back again." Issued clothing as member of Co. D, 1st Md. Cav., 9/30/64. NFR.

HALL, EDWARD HOWARD (photo): Pvt., Co. A. b. 1844. Res. Harford Co., Md. Enl. Co. A, Davis's Bn., Charlottesville, 7/15/62. Transf. to Co. A, 1st Md. Cav., 11–12/62; present 7–12/63 and 4/1/64. Captured at Pollard's Farm, Va., 5/27/64; sent to Pt. Lookout; exchanged 2/21/65. Present Camp Lee, Richmond, 2/27/65. Captured at Hanover CH, Va., 3/13/65; sent to Ft. Monroe; transf. to Pt. Lookout; released 4/20/65. Res. and destination Harford Co. d. 1917.

HALLMAN, P.: Pvt., Co. K. Enl. Co. K (2nd), 1st

Va. Cav., date and place unknown. Admitted to Richmond hosp. 6/1/64. NFR. On postwar roster of Co. K, 1st Md. Cav.

HAMBERTON, JAMES P.: Pvt., Co. B. b. circa 1841. M.D., Easton, Talbot Co., Md. Served as Sgt. in 35th Ga. Inf. Enl. Co. B, 1st Md. Cav., Charlottesville, 9/10/62. Captured Monterey Springs, Pa., 7/4/63; sent to Ft. McHenry. Transf. to Ft. Del. and West Buildings hosp., Baltimore; exchanged 11/17/63; ab. sick with "chronic diarrhoea" in Richmond hosp. 11/18–21/63; furloughed for thirty days; ab. on horse detail 3/16–4/1/64; present through 12/64; ab. sick in Richmond hosp. 1/21/65; furloughed for thirty-five days 1/22/65; ab. sick in Gordonsville, Va., hosp.; RTD 3/27/65. Paroled Winchester 4/22/65. Age twenty-four, 5'10½", dark complexion, dark hair, hazel eyes. Took oath at Baltimore 5/12/65. Res. and destination Talbot Co., Md.

HAMBERTON, THOMAS EDWARD: Pvt., Co. E. b. New Windsor, Carroll Co., Md., 5/16/29. Gd. St. Mary's Col. 1849. Manufacturer and dealer in agriculture implements. Enl. Camp Lee, Richmond, 2/24/63; hired John L. Slingluff as substitute and was discharged 2/28/63. Carried dispatches across the Potomac several times for the Confederate government. Purchased the blockade runner *Virginia Dare*. Served as blockade runner to end of war. NFR. Banker, Baltimore. Member, Isaac R. Trimble Camp, CV, Baltimore. d. "Hambledine," near Luthersville, Md., 9/21/06.

HAMMETT, JOHN M.: Pvt., Co. F. b. Md. circa 1836. Res. Great Mills, St. Mary's Co., Md., per 1860 census. Served in Co. I, 1st Md. Inf., 1861–62. Enl. Co. F, 1st Md. Cav., Richmond 7/11/63; present until KIA at Morton's Ford, Va., 10/11/63. Reburied Loudon Park Cem., Baltimore, 1874.

HAMMOND, CHARLES H.: Pvt., Co. A. b. 2/16/43. Res. Howard Co., Md. Enl. Co. A, 1st Md. Cav., Sharpsburg, Md., 7/1/64; present through 12/64. Paroled Staunton, Va., 5/1/65. Age twenty-four, 5'6½", dark complexion, brown hair, hazel eyes. Member ANS/MLA. d. 3/29/11. Bur. Lovettsville Cem., Loudoun Co., Va.

HAMMOND, CLAUDE: Pvt., Co. C. Res. Howard Co., Md. Enl. date and place unknown. Captured Howard Co., Md., 9/26/64; sent to Old Capitol and held in irons; transf. to Albany, N.Y., penitentiary and Ft. McHenry; released 5/24/65.

HAMMOND, DENTON: Pvt., Co. D. b. circa 1835. Res. New Market, Frederick Co., Md. Enl. Winchester 9/20/62; present 11–12/62. Captured Greenland Gap, W.Va., 4/25/63; sent to Ft. McHenry; exchanged 6/26/63; present 7–8/63; ab. on horse detail 9–10/63. Captured at Shepherdstown,

W.Va., 11/4/63; sent to Ft. Del.; released 7/24/65. 5'8", dark complexion, dark hair, gray eyes. d. 3/21/80, age fifty-five. Bur. Episcopal Ch. Cem., New Market. Bro. of Oliver B. Hammond.

HAMMOND, OLIVER BYRON: Pvt., Co. D. b. 11/12/36. Res. New Market, Frederick Co., Md. Enl. Winchester 9/20/62; ab. sick at Middle-town, Va., 11/62, and Staunton, Va., 12/62. Cap-tured Monterey Springs, Pa., 7/4/63; sent to Ft. Del.; d. there of typhoid fever 3/4/64. Bur. Finn's Pt. National Cem., N.J.; removed to Old Metho-dist Ch. Cem., New Market. Brother of Denton Ham-mond.

HAMPTON, THOMAS: Pvt., Co. F. Enl. Richmond 7/1/63; des. to the enemy near Fredericksburg, Va., 8/21/63; sent to Old Capitol; took oath, released 9/24/63. 5'6", light complexion, light hair, gray eyes. Res. of Philadelphia, Pa.

HANCE, JAMES J.: Pvt., Co. C. Res. Carroll Co., Md. Enl. Co. H (2nd), 1st Md. Inf., 6/18/61; dis-charged 6/18/62. Enl. Co. C, 1st Md. Cav., Richmond, 8/4/62; present 7–12/63 and 4/1/64; horse killed Pollard's Farm, Va., 5/27/64, paid $1,800; WIA at Clear Spring, Md., 7/29/64; ab. wounded in Winchester hosp. 7/30–8/2/64; ab. wounded in Harrisonburg, Va., hosp. through 8/31/64; issued clothing 9/30/64; present 11–12/64. Paroled New Market, Va., 4/20/65. Age forty-six, 5'10", dark complexion, dark hair, dark eyes. Took oath at Winchester 4/24/65. Res. Calvert Co., Md. Bur. Asbury Methodist Ch. Cem., Barton, Md., no dates.

HANNA, ALEXANDER B.: 1st Cpl., Co. C. b. circa 1838. Res. Baltimore. Enl. date and place unknown. Captured near Winchester 6/12/63; sent to Ft. McHenry; transf. to Ft. Monroe; exchanged 7/1/63, but never reported. Took oath Key West, Fla., 2/28/64. Age twenty-six, 5'10½", fair com-plexion, gray eyes, brown hair.

HANNIGAN, WILLIAM: Pvt., Co. F. Enl. Richmond 7/15/63; present through 8/31/63; in arrest Orange CH 10/30–12/31/63; des. 11/20/63; on rolls to 12/31/64 and 4/1/64. NFR.

HANWAY, WILLIAM H.: Pvt., Co. A. Res. Harford Co., Md. Enl. Hagerstown, Md., 6/25/63; present through 12/63; ab. on horse detail for fourteen days to Newtown, Va., 2/16/64; present 4/1/64. Captured Moorefield, W.Va., 8/7/64; sent to Wheeling. Age twenty-four, 5'11, fair complex-ion, blue eyes, light hair. Merchant. Transf. to Camp Chase; took oath, released 2/8/65.

HARBIN, THOMAS H.: Pvt., Co. B. Res. Prince George's Co., Md. Believed to have served in Secret Service. Paroled Ashland, Va., 4/28/65. Clerk, National Hotel, Washington, D.C., d. 11/18/85.

HARBY, ABRAHAM: Pvt., Co. A, Davis's Bn.; des.

at Lexington, Va., 8/29/64. Took oath at New Creek 10/25/64. Age forty-eight, 5'11", dark complexion, dark hair, gray eyes. Farmer, Augusta County, Va.

HARDING, JOHN EADE "BADE": 4th Cpl., Co. A. Res. Howard Co., Md. Enl. Co. K (2nd), 1st Va. Cav., Leesburg, Va., 5/14/61; present until transf. to Co. A, 1st Md. Cav., 5/15/62; promoted 4th Cpl. 8/1/63; present through 12/63 and 4/1/64; KIA at Beaver Dam, Va., 5/9/64.

HARDY, A. J.: Pvt., Co. G. Captured, date and place unknown; confined at Camp Hamilton, Va., 4/28/65; released 5/1/65.

HARGAVE, E. P.: Pvt., Co. C, Davis's Bn. NFR.

HARKER, ALOYSIS: Pvt., Ct. unknown. b. Md. circa 1847. Enl. 1863 and served to end of war per postwar account. Moved to Seattle, Wa., 1870. Member John B. Gordon Camp, CV, Seattle. Businessman. d. Seattle 1/6/29, age eighty-two.

HARKINS, JAMES L.: Pvt., Co. E. b. circa 1846. Enl. Richmond 11/4/62, age eighteen; presence or ab. not stated 1–2/63; present 7–12/63, 4/1/64, and 7–12/64; ab. sick with "Febris Remittens" in Charlottesville hosp. 12/7–29/64. NFR.

HARRIS, ELBERT E.: Pvt., Co. C. b. 2/1/38. Enl. Winchester 9/20/62; ab. sick at Winchester 10/15–12/31/62. NFR. d. 11/22/20. Bur. Urbana Episcopal Ch. Cem., Urbana, Md.

HARRISON, _____: Pvt., Co. A, Davis's Bn. NFR.

HARRISON, CHARLES H.: Pvt., Co. A. Enl. Co. A, 19th Va. Inf., 4/16/61. Requested transf. to Md. Line 5/23/64; WIA (right arm and shoulder) at Cold Harbor, Va., 6/3/64. Transf. to Co. A, 1st Md. Cav., 9/8/64. 5'5", light complexion, light hair, blue eyes. Engineer. Res. of Baltimore. Ab. wounded in hosp. 11–12/64. NFR.

HARRISON, EDWIN J.: Pvt., Co. A. Res. of Baltimore. Enl. date and place unknown. Captured Middletown, Md., 7/10/64; sent to West Building hosp., Baltimore; transf. to Ft. McHenry and Pt. Lookout; exchanged 11/15/64; ab. sick with debility in Charlottesville hosp. 4/7–8/65. Paroled Gordonsville, Va., 6/1/65, destination Baltimore.

HARRISON, JAMES E.: Pvt., Co. C, Davis's Bn. Res. Cambridge, Dorchester Co., Md. NFR. Probably James E. Harrison (1847–1926) bur. at St. Luke's Meth. Ch. Cem., Talbot Co., Md.

HARRISON, THOMAS: Pvt., Co. D. Enl. Edinburg, Va., 2/28/63. Captured near Romney, W.Va., 4/20/63. NFR. Not on Federal POW rolls; may have been KIA.

HARRISON, WILLIAM: Pvt., Co. C, Davis's Bn. NFR. d. 6/38/91, age sixty-six. Bur. Mt. Prospect Methodist Ch. Cem., Frederick Co., Md.

HARRISON, WILLIAM H.: Pvt., Co. D. b. circa 1840. Enl. Edinburg, Va., 2/28/63. Captured

Oakland, Md., 4/30/63; sent to Wheeling. Age twenty-three, 5'6½", dark complexion, gray eyes, black hair. Moulder. Res. Richmond. Transf. to Camp Chase, Johnson's Island, and Pt. Lookout; exchanged 11/15/64. Issued clothing 11/21/64; ab. on horse detail through 12/31/64. NFR. d. Baltimore 4/1/13, age seventy-two.

HARRY, ALBERT: Pvt., Co. C. b. circa 1842. Enl. Co. E, 39th Miss. Inf. Jackson, Miss., 3/15/62. Transf. to Co. C, 1st Md. Cav., 5/1/64; present through 12/64; ab. sick with scabies in Gordonsville, Va., hosp. 3/25–31/65. Paroled Winchester 4/18/65. Age twenty-three, 5'7½", fair complexion, brown hair, dark eyes.

HARRY, GEORGE: Pvt., Co. C. b. circa 1846. Res. Hagerstown, Washington Co., Md. Enl. Hagerstown 6/18/63; present through 9/30/63; ab. on horse detail 10/28–31/63. Captured near Winchester 11/10/63; sent to Wheeling. Age twenty, 5'10½", fair complexion, brown hair, brown eyes. Clerk. Transf. to Camp Chase and Ft. Del.; exchanged 3/1/65. Paroled Winchester 5/3/65. Age twenty-one, 5'9", dark complexion, dark hair, brown eyes. Destination near Shepherdstown, W.Va.

HARRY, JAMES P.: Pvt., Co. A. Enl. Front Royal , Va., 7/20/63; present through 12/31/63; ab. on leave 3/19– 4/1/64; des. 7/64; on rolls 8/31–12/31/64. NFR.

HARRY, JOHN T.: Pvt., Co. C. Res. Baltimore. On postwar rosters of Co. K, 30th N.C. Inf., and Co. C, 1st Md. Cav.

HARTIGAN, JOHN JAMES: Pvt., Co. C. Enl. Co. G, 13th Va. Inf., 7/10/61; WIA Munson's Hill, Va., 8/27/61; discharged 5/28/62 as nonresident. Enl. Co. C, 1st Md. Cav., New Market, Va., 9/1/62; present 7–9/63; ab. on horse detail 10/28–11/10/63; present through 12/63; ab. on horse detail to Augusta Co., Va., for seven days 2/16/64 and for twenty days 3/27/64; present through 8/31/64. Captured Page Co., Va., with Churchill Crittenden while gathering food for the Co.; attempted to escape, was wounded, and recaptured. Executed 10/27/64 by order Col. William H. Powell of Gen. W. W. Averell's Cav. (See Crittenden, Churchill). Bur. Lutheran Reformed Ch. Cem., New Market, Va., as "J. J. Hardigan."

HARTMYER, RICHARD J.: Pvt., Co. K. Res. of Baltimore. Enl. Co. C, 1st Md. Inf., Richmond 7/10/61; discharged. Enl. Co. K (2nd), 1st Va. Cav., Richmond, 6/10/62; present through 8/64. Transf. to Co. K, 1st Md. Cav., 8/64; ab. sick with scabies in Charlottesville hosp. 9/26–10/6/64; des. to the enemy 11/28/64, rank shown as Sgt. Arrested in Baltimore; took oath, released.

HARTZELL, JOHN C.: Sgt., Co. A, Davis's Bn.

Enl. Md. 6/25/63; present 1/1–10/31/64. Transf. to Co. M, 23rd Va. Cav. NFR.

HARWOOD, RICHARD LOOCKERMAN: Pvt., Co. E. b. 4/23/46. Res. Anne Arundel Co., Md. Enl. date and place unknown; KIA Winchester 6/13/63. Bur. St. Anne's Episcopal Ch. Cem., Annapolis, Md.

HAUSE, LAFAYETTE: 4th Cpl, Co. C. Clerk, Baltimore. Enl. date and place unknown; DOW received Williamsport, Md., 7/7/63.

HAYDEN, ALBERT: Pvt., Co. K. Res. of Md. Enl. Co. K (2nd), 1st Va. Cav., Richmond, 6/10/62; present through 2/64; AWOL 7/20–12/31/64. Transf. to Co. K, 1st Md. Cav., while AWOL 8/64. NFR.

HAYDEN, HORACE EDWIN: Pvt., Co. A. b. Catonsville, Md., 2/18/37. Att. St. Timothy's Hall. Gd. Kenyon Col., Ohio. School Teacher. Enl. Co. K (2nd), 1st Va. Cav., Leesburg, Va., 6/1/62; present until transf. to Co. A., 1st Md. Cav., 5/15/62; ab. sick with debility in Charlottesville hosp. 6/9–7/25/62. Ward Master, Charlottesville hosp. 12/62–3/27/63; ab. detailed as Clerk in Surgeon Gen.'s Office, Richmond, 7/27/64. Served as Hosp. Steward in Richmond hospitals. Served in Co. A, 3rd Bn., Local Defense Troops, Richmond, while on detail. Transf. to 3rd Va. Inf. 1864; not on muster rolls; discharged 12/31/64 to enter Theological Seminary, Staunton, Va.; ordained 1867. Presbyterian Minister, Charlottesville; in W.Va. and Pa. 1917. (His brother, Charles Hayden, served in U.S. Army.) d. Texas A&M Col. 8/28/17.

HAYDEN, RICHARD A.: Pvt., Co. K. b. Md. circa 1842. Age eighteen, 3rd Dist. St. Mary's Co., Md., per 1860 census. Served in Co. C, 1st Md. Inf., 1861–62. Enl. Co. K (2nd), 1st Va. Cav., date and place unknown. Captured Upperville, Va., 5/16/63; sent to Ft. McHenry; exchanged 5/26/63. NFR. On postwar roster Co. K, 1st Md. Cav. Married St. Mary's Co, 12/17/67, age twenty-five.

HAYDEN, WILLIAM: Pvt., Co. K. Res. of Md; WIA and captured. On postwar roster Co. K (2nd), 1st Va. Cav., and Co. K, 1st Md. Cav.

HAYES, JOHN F.: Pvt., Co. C, Davis's Bn. NFR.

HAYNES, MITCHELL: Pvt., Co. A, Davis's Bn. Enl. Woodstock, Va., 8/1/63; AWOL 10/31/64. Transf. to Co. M, 23rd Va. Cav; present 12/5/64. NFR.

HAYWARD, HENRY PEABODY "HARRY": Pvt., Co. C. b. 6/15/45. Res. of Baltimore. Enl. Hagerstown 6/18/63; present through 8/31/63; horse died 10/15/63; present sick 10/31/63; ab. sick with "Inter fever" in Richmond hosp. 11/30/63–1/29/64; ab. on leave for ten days to New Market, Va., for a horse 2/1/64; present 4/1–12/31/64. Surrendered Appomattox CH, Va., 4/9/65. Took oath Richmond 5/24/65; destination Baltimore. d. 11/15/67. Bur. St.

Thomas Ch. Cem., Garrison, Md.

HAYWARD, THOMAS B.: Pvt., Co. unknown. Enl. date and place unknown. Paroled Monrovia, Md., 4/20/65. Took oath Relay House, Md., 4/24/65. Res. and destination Frederick Co., Md.

HEARD, JOHN L.: Pvt., Co. F. Varnisher, Baltimore. Enl. Hanover Junction, Va., 3/10/64; ab. on horse detail 4/1/64. Captured Old Church, Hanover Junction, 5/27/64; sent to Pt. Lookout; released 5/15/65. Member ANS/MLA. d. Baltimore 12/2/97.

HEARNE, BENJAMIN G.: Pvt., Co. B. b. Somerset Co., Md. circa 1841. Res. of Somerset Co. Enl. Richmond 9/2/63; issued clothing 8/31 and 9/20/64; WIA and captured Beverly, W.Va., 10/29/64; sent to Wheeling. Age twenty-three, 5'10", dark complexion, blue eyes, light hair. Farmer. Transf. to Camp Chase; released 6/15/65. Res. Sussex Co., Del.

HEARNE, SAMUEL B.: Pvt., Co. B. b. Del. 1/28/41. Res. of Del. Crossed Chesapeake Bay with twelve others 8/22/62. Enl. Charlottesville 9/10/62; present 7–12/63 and 4/1/64. Captured Mouth of Straits, Del., while on leave 4/26/64; sent to Baltimore; sentenced to death as a spy; commuted; sent to Albany, N.Y., penitentiary and placed in solitary confinement by order of Gen. Lew Wallace; exchanged 3/15/65. Started to N.C. to join Johnston's Army. Returned to Richmond, paroled. Brothers served in U.S Army. Moved to "Hickory Hill" on Rappahannock River 1869. d. Port Royal, Va., 10/9/17.

HECK, ROBERT H.: Pvt., Co. D. b. Washington Co., Md., circa 1831. Carpenter, Boonsboro, Md. Enl. Co. A, 1st Md. Inf., 5/21/61; discharged by 8/62. Reenl. Co. C, 19th Bn. Va. Arty., Richmond, 8/31/62. Transf. to Co. D, 1st Md. Cav., 12/17/62; ab. detailed as Courier for Md. Line, Hanover Junction, Va., 11/2/63–2/28/65. Paroled New Market, Va., 4/19/65. Age thirty-four, 5'8", dark complexion, dark hair, brown eyes. Member ANS/MLA, 1894.

HEDIAN, THOMAS: Pvt., Co. C, Davis's Bn. On postwar roster. Merchant, Baltimore. d. 10/17/99, age sixty-four.

HEIGHE, JOHN M.: Pvt., Co. A. b. Baltimore 1/29/42. Res. of Baltimore. Enl. Manassas, Va., 9/11/62; present 7–12/63 and 4/1–8/31/64; issued clothing 9/30/64; ab. detailed as Courier for Gen. Davidson 11–12/64. Scout with Capt. Frank Stringfellow. Captured Leesburg, Va., 1865; exchanged by 3/65. Rejoined Co. A en route to Petersburg; present Appomattox CH, Va., 4/9/65. Took oath Richmond 5/20/65. Lawyer, Baltimore. Member ANS/MLA. d. Baltimore 3/22/28.

HEIMILLER, HERMAN: Pvt., Co. C. b. Germany 2/5/40. Res. of Baltimore. Enl. Co. B, 1st Md. Inf., 5/21/61; discharged 5/21/62. Enl. Co. C, 1st

Md. Cav., Richmond, 8/4/62; horse killed near Winchester 6/14/63, paid $650; present 7–12/63 and 4/1–8/31/64; issued clothing 9/30/64; present Appomattox CH, Va., 4/9/65. Paroled Salem, Va., 5/65. Took oath Baltimore 11/14/65. Policeman, Baltimore. Member ANS/MLA. d. 2/12/30. Bur. Loudon Park Cem., Baltimore. (Postwar photograph in Stonebraker 1899)

HEISKELL, JAMES MONROE: Pvt., Co. C. b. White House, Washington, D.C., 6/20/44 (grandson of Pres. James Monroe). Gd. Georgetown U. 1863. Res. Fauquier Co., Va. Enl. date unknown. Transf. to Co. D, 43rd Va. Bn. Cav. (Mosby), by 7/4/64. Captured Sugar Loaf Mt., Md., 1/4/65; sent to Old Capitol; transf. to Ft. Warren; released 6/13/65. 5'9", ruddy complexion, brown hair, hazel eyes. Private Secretary for Md. Gov. W. P. Wythe; Fire Marshal of Baltimore; Paymaster, U.S. Army, 1888. Moved to N.Y. 1889. d. N.Y. City 10/8/99. Bur. Mt. Hope Cem., Hastings-on-Hudson, N.Y. (Photograph in Hartzler 1992)

HELFRICK, JOHN A.: Pvt., Co. H. (originally in Co. B, Davis's Bn.) Captured Greencastle, Pa., 7/9/63; sent to Ft. Mifflin, Pa. Took oath, enl. in U.S. Marine Corps 12/2/63. 5'4", fair complexion, light hair, blue eyes. Res. of Franklin Co., Pa.

HELMUTH, A.: Pvt., Co. A; des. Mitchell's Ford 10/7/63; sent to Old Capitol. 5'10", light complexion, light hair, blue eyes. Res. of Mobile, Ala. Took oath, sent north 12/17/63.

HENDERSON, E. GAITHER W.: Pvt., Co. A. Res. Howard Co., Md. Enl. Sharpsburg, Md., 7/1/64; present through 8/31/64, AWOL 11–12/64. NFR. Attended reunion 1899.

HENDERSON, H. F.: Pvt., Co. B. Captured Greenville, S.C., 5/23/65. NFR.

HENSHAW, HOWARD: Cpl., Co. A, Davis's Bn. Enl. Richmond 8/8/63; present through 10/31/64. Transf. to Co. M, 23rd Va. Cav. NFR.

HERGESHEIMER, DAVID J.: Pvt., Co. D. b. circa 1819. Res. Frederick Co., Md. Enl. Boonsboro, Md., 6/15/63; present through 12/63 and 4/1–8/3/64, issued clothing 9/30/64; AWOL 12/15–31/64. NFR. d. Old Soldiers' Home, Pikesville, Md., 8/22/99, age eighty. Bur. Loudon Park Cem., Baltimore.

HERING, FRANCIS LOUIS "FRANK": Pvt., Co. D. b. Frederick Co., Md., 2/4/35. Miller, Finksburg, Carroll Co., Md. Enl. Frederick, Md., 7/1/64; present through 8/31/64 and 11–12/64. Paroled Staunton, Va., 5/1/65. Age thirty, 5'5¼", dark complexion, black hair, dark eyes. d. Finksburg, Carroll Co., 11/16/09. Bur. Finksburg Meth. Ch. Cem. (Photograph in Hartzler 1992)

HERNDON, THOMAS H.: Pvt., Co. A. b. circa 1837. Res. Harford Co., Md. Enl. Wise (Va.)

Arty., Harpers Ferry, W.Va., 5/23/61. Transf. to Co. A, 1st Md. Cav., 6/5/62; present through 12/62. Captured Strasburg, Va., 2/26/63; sent to Wheeling. Age twenty-six, 6', fair complexion, gray eyes, brown hair. Farmer. Transf. to Camp Chase; exchanged 4/1/63; present through 12/63 and 4/1/64. Captured Hagerstown, Md., 7/5/64, age twenty-seven; sent to Ft. Del.; exchanged 9/30/64; ab. sick in Richmond hosp. 10/6–7/64 and 11/20–21/64; issued clothing 11/20/64; term of service expired, discharged on rolls 12/31/64. Paroled New Market, Va., 4/20/65, age twenty-eight, 6', fair complexion, dark hair, blue eyes.

HERRON, GEORGE S.: Pvt., Co. C. b. circa 1841. Res. Harford Co., Md. Enl. Winchester 10/11/62; present 7–8/63; AWOL 10/24–31/63; present 11–12/63; ab. on horse detail 4/1/64; ab. on leave for fifteen days to Loudoun Co., Va., for a horse 5/1/64. Captured Moorefield, W.Va., 8/7/64; sent to Wheeling. Age twenty-three, 5'6½", fair complexion, brown eyes, brown hair. Clerk. Transf. to Camp Chase; released 4/17/65.

HEWES, MICHAEL WARNER: Pvt., Co. K. b. Baltimore, 11/22/46. Res. of Baltimore. Enl. Co. K (2nd), 1st Va. Cav., Leesburg, Va., 5/14/62. Transf. to Co. A, 1st Md. Cav., 5/15/62; discharged for ill health 12/1/62; paid 1/7/63. NFR. Member Isaac Trimble Camp, CV, and ANS/MLA. d. Baltimore 5/17.

HEWES, T. WARNER: Pvt., Co. A. Res. Baltimore. On postwar roster.

HEWES, WILLIAM: Pvt., Co. K. On postwar rosters of Co. K (2nd), 1st Va. Cav., and Co. K, 1st Md. Cav.

HICKEY, EDMUND PLOWDEN: Pvt., Co. B. Gd. Georgetown U. 1862. Son of Gen. William Joseph Hickey, U.S. Army. Res. Washington, D.C. Enl. Charlottesville 9/10/62; present 7–9/63; WIA and captured Raccoon Ford, Va., 10/11/63; sent to Old Capitol; transf. to Ft. Del. Reported exchanged 2/27/65, however, released to Washington, D.C., by order of President Lincoln, to report to his father, who was to be responsible for his behavior. Took oath Washington, D.C., 6/20/65. Secretary to U.S. Senate, Washington, D.C. Member George Emack Camp, CV, Hyattsville, Md. Res. of Hyattsville. d. 1898. Brother of John F. Hickey.

HICKEY, JOHN FRANCIS: Pvt., Co. B. b. 11/12/42. Son of Gen. William Joseph Hickey, U.S. Army. Res. Washington, D.C. Enl. Charlottesville 9/10/62; present 7–9/63; ab. sick with scabies in Charlottesville hosp. 10/10–11/13/63; present through 12/63; ab. on horse detail for twenty day 3/25/64; WIA (arm) Beaver Dam 5/9/64; WIA (seven wounds and left leg amputated) Williamsport, Md., 8/2/64. Captured Clear

Spring, Md., 9/12/64; sent to Wheeling. 5'6", dark complexion, brown hair, hazel eyes. Transf. to Camp Chase; released 3/6/65 by order of President Lincoln and placed in the charge of his father. Farmer, Washington, D.C. Clerk to Mayor and Common Council, Hyattsville, Md. Commander, George Emack Camp, CV, Hyattsville, Md., 1912. Member Confederate Veterans Assoc, Washington, D.C. d. 1922. Bro. of Edmund P. Hickey.

HICKS, CROWDER: Pvt., Co. A, Davis's Bn. Enl. Richmond 1/1/64; present through 10/31/64. Transf. to Co. M, 23rd Va. Cav. NFR.

HICKS, PATRICK: Pvt., Co. G; des. to the enemy 8/25/63; sent to Old Capitol; took oath, released 9/27/63. 5'8", dark complexion, brown hair, blue eyes. Res. of Lancaster, Pa.

HIGGINS, HENRY A.: Pvt., Co. A, Davis's Bn. b. Va., circa 1837. Res. of Little Orleans, Allegany Co., Md. Enl. Co. G, 7th Va. Cav., 2/10/62. Transf. to Co. A, Davis's Bn., 4/29/64; WIA (side) Wilderness, Va., 5/5/64. Captured Winchester 9/19/64; sent to Pt. Lookout; released 6/14/65. 5'10", light complexion, black hair, hazel eyes. Age thirty-three, Cumberland, Md., per 1870 census. Res. of Little Orleans postwar.

HIGGINS, JAMES R.: Pvt., Co. A, Davis's Bn. b. 1838. Res. of Allegany Co., Md. Enl. Co. G, 7th Va. Cav., 2/16/62. Transf. to Co. A, Davis's Bn. 4/29/64. Captured Winchester 9/19/64; sent to Pt. Lookout; released 6/14/65. 5'10¾", fair complexion, dark hair, hazel eyes. Res. of Little Orleans and Cumberland, Md., postwar. d. 1880. Bur. St. Patrick's Cem., Allegany Co., Md.

HIGGINS, T. E.: Pvt., Co. B, Davis's Bn. Paroled Staunton, Va., 5/23/65. Age eighteen, 5'5", light complexion, dark hair, gray eyes.

HILDT, JOHN: Pvt., Co. D. b. Frederick Co., Md., circa 1841. Enl. Co. A, 1st Md. Inf., 5/23/61; discharged for disability 11/15/61. Age twenty, 5'10", dark complexion, brown hair, brown eyes. Laborer. Enl. Co. D, 1st Md. Cav., date unknown; present as Wagoner 11–12/62. NFR.

HILIARD, R. E.: Pvt., Co. D. Returned to duty from Richmond hosp. 3/25/65. NFR.

HILL, EDWARD: Pvt., Co. C, Davis's Bn. On postwar roster.

HILL, JOHN BEALL: Pvt., Co. B. b. 1840. Res. of Prince George's Co., Md. Enl. Charlottesville 9/10/62; present 7–10/63. Captured Rapidan Station, Va., 11/7/63; sent to Old Capitol. Transf. to Pt. Lookout; exchanged 2/21/65; present Camp Lee, Richmond, 2/27/65. NFR. Member George Emack Camp, CV, Hyattsville, Md., 1903. Res. of Bennings, D.C. d. 1917.

HILL, WILLIAM MURDOCK: Pvt., Co. D. b. Balti-

more 6/28/38. Res. of Baltimore. Enl. Co. D, 1st Md. Cav., 6/1/61; discharged 8/17/62. 5'7", dark complexion, dark hair, dark eyes. Iron Moulder. Enl. Co. D, 1st Md. Inf., date unknown. Captured Frederick's Hall, Va., 3/13/65; sent to Ft. Monroe. Transf. to Pt. Lookout; released 6/14/65. 5'8", dark complexion, dark hair, dark eyes. Destination Baltimore. d. 7/20/70. Bur. Hill Cem., "Woodland," Prince George's Co., Md.

HILLEARY, THOMAS: Pvt., Co. D. b. Frederick Co., Md., 6/4/41. Res. of Petersville, Frederick Co. Enl. Co. G, 7th Va. Cav., 9/12/62. Transf. to Co. D., 1st Md. Cav., 8/9/64; present through 12/31/64. Paroled Winchester 5/3/65. 5'11", light complexion, brown hair, blue eyes. B&O RR employee, Petersville, Md. d. Zanesville, Oh., 9/30/15; bur. there.

HINKEY, JOHN M.: Pvt., Co. unknown, Davis's Bn. b. 1827. Res. of Annapolis, Md. On postwar roster. d. 1894. Bur. Taylorsville Cem., Anne Arundel Co., Md.

HIRST, JAMES P.: Pvt., Co. E; des. in western Va. 1/64. Age twenty-six, 5'10½", dark complexion, dark hair, hazel eyes. Laborer. Res. of Richmond. Took oath, sent north 1/25/64.

HISSANT, WILLIAM: Pvt., Co. unknown, Davis's Bn. d. 5/17/62. Bur. Hollywood Cem., Richmond.

HOBBS, JARRETT E.: Pvt., Co. K. b. Md. circa 1841. Res. of Howard Co., Md. Enl. Co. K (2nd), 1st Va. Cav., 6/28/62; present until WIA (thigh) Todd's Tavern, Va., 5/7/64; ab. wounded in Richmond hosp. 5/9/64 until des. from hosp. 6/14/64. Age twenty-five. Mason. RTD; present until transf. to Co. K, 1st Md. Cav., 8/64; KIA Smithfield, W.Va., 8/28/64, age twenty-five. Bur. Winchester; reburied Loudon Park Cem., Baltimore 1874. "Bravest of the brave."

HOBBS, NATHAN CHEW: 1st Lt., Co. K. b. circa 1837. Res. Cooksville, Howard Co., Md. Enl. as 2nd Sgt., Co. K (2nd), 1st Va. Cav., Leesburg, Va., 5/14/61; present through 2/8/62. reenl. and elected 2nd Lt; present until WIA and captured, Catlett's Station, Va., 8/22/62; exchanged; present until horse killed 9/29/62; paid $195; present until WIA (right thigh) and captured Hagerstown, Md., 7/10/63; sent to Pt. Lookout. Promoted 1st Lt. 10/1/63 while POW. Exchanged 3/24/64; present until WIA, Kennon's Landing, 5/24/64; RTD. Transf. to Co. K, 1st Md. Cav., 8/64; ab. wounded in Richmond hosp. 9/25/64; RTD; WIA (right forearm) circa 10/30/64; ab. wounded in Charlottesville hosp. 10/31–12/31/64. Paroled New Market, Va., 4/19/65, as 1st Lt. Age twenty-eight, 6'2", dark complexion, brown hair, gray eyes. Took oath Winchester 6/8/65. Res. and destination Howard Co. Member ANS/MLA. d. 2/26/95, age fifty-

eight. Bur. McKendree Cem., Howard Co., Md.
HOFFAR, DANIEL PAUL: Pvt., Co. B. Enl. date,
place unknown; issued clothing 8/1 and 11/19/64; in
Richmond hosp. 11/12/64; des. to the enemy
11/23/64; sent to Old Capitol; took oath, released;
transportation furnished to Philadelphia, Pa.
HOFFMAN, AUGUSTUS: Pvt., Co. D, Davis's Bn.
Captured Piedmont, Va., 6/5/64; sent to Camp
Morton; released 5/22/65. 5'10", florid complex-
ion, dark hair, blue eyes. Res. of Chicago, Ill.
HOFFMAN, JOHN: Pvt., Co. A, Davis's Bn. Enl.
Md. 1/25/63; present through 10/31/64. Transf. to
Co. M, 23rd Va. Cav. NFR. Probably the man who
served in the 43rd Bn. Va. Cav. (Mosby). Member
ANS/MLA. d. Old Soldiers' Home, Pikesville,
Md., before 1884.
HOLBROOK, JOHN F.: Pvt., Co. C. b. circa 1836.
Enl. Co. D, 1st Md. Inf., 6/1/61; discharged 8/62.
Enl. Co. C, 1st Md. Cav., Lacey Springs, Va.,
3/18/63. Captured South Mt., Md., 7/4/63, horse
killed; sent to Ft. Del. Transf. to Pt. Lookout;
exchanged 2/21/65. Paid Camp Lee, Richmond,
same day; paid $2,000 for horse 3/9/65. Paroled
Winchester 4/23/65. Age twenty-nine, 5'8", light
complexion, brown hair, hazel eyes. Took oath
5/27/65. Res. of Shepherdstown, W.Va.
HOLIDAY or HOLLYDAY, CLEMENT W.: Pvt.,
Co. B. b. Prince George's Co., Md., circa 1843.
Res. Nottingham, Prince George's Co. Enl.
Charlottesville 9/17/62; ab. sick with "Icterus" in
Charlottesville hosp. 10/19/62; RTD 11/11/62.
Captured on picket near Winchester 11/23/62;
sent to Wheeling. Age twenty, 5'10¾", fair com-
plexion, dark eyes, black hair. Farmer. Transf. to
Camp Chase; exchanged 12/22/62; ab. sick with
debility in Charlottesville hosp. 2/24/63 until furloughed 1/27/64; ab. sick with chronic nephritis in
Charlottesville hosp. until discharged for
"Chronic nephritis, general dropsy, cardiac disease." Age twenty-one, 5'11", light complexion,
dark eyes, dark hair. Released from hosp. 5/3/64.
NFR.
HOLLAND, JOHN J. J.: Pvt., Co. K. Enl. Co. K
(2nd), 1st Va. Cav., Richmond, 6/1/62; present
until captured Brandy Station, Va., 10/11/63; sent
to Pt. Lookout; exchanged 4/27/64; ab. sick with
"diarrhoea" 5/1/64; furloughed for thirty days
5/6/64; readmitted to Richmond hosp. 7/11/64;
RTD 8/1/64; present through 8/31/64. Transf. to
Co. K, 1st Md. Cav., 8/64; issued clothing
9/30/64; discharged at end of enlistment 12/4/64.
NFR. d. by 1904.
HOLLAND, JOHN R.: Pvt., Co. K. Enl. Co. K
(2nd), 1st Va. Cav., 9/1/62; present through 8/64.
Transf. to Co. K, 1st Md. Cav., 8/64; WIA Winchester 9/19/64; AWOL 12/12–31/64. NFR.

Member ANS/MLA. d. Old Soldiers' Home,
Pikesville, Md., 12/23/88.
HOLLAND, JOHN W.: Pvt., Co. K. AWOL
12/12–31/64. NFR. Montgomery Co., Md., 1908.
HOLLAND, JOSHUA: Pvt., Co. K. Captured and d.
of disease Pt. Lookout; on postwar rosters Co. K
(2nd), 1st Va. Cav., and 1st Md. Cav.
HOLLAND, PETER R.: Pvt., Co. K. Enl. Co. K
(2nd), 1st Va. Cav., 6/1/62; present until WIA
(thigh) Cold Harbor 6/1/64; ab. wounded in
Richmond hosp. 6/3–22/64; present 8/2–31/64.
Transf. to Co. K, 1st Md. Cav., 8/64; discharged at
end of enlistment 12/4/64. NFR.
HOLLAND, WILLIAM JAMES CANADY: Pvt.,
Co. K. b. Worcester Co., Md. circa 1833. Enl. Co.
K (2nd), 1st Va. Cav., Culpeper CH, Va., 2/62;
WIA (leg) and captured 2nd Manassas 8/62. Exchanged; WIA Hanover CH, Va., 5/64. Transf. to
Co. K, 1st Md. Cav., 8/64. Paroled Harpers Ferry,
W.Va., 4/65. Information from application for Old
Soldiers' Home, Pikesville, Md., 1/3/99, age seventy-six. Farmer, Worcester Co., Md.; d. there
3/2/00. Bur. Loudon Park Cem., Baltimore.
HOLLINGSWORTH, WILLIAM T.: Pvt., Co. E. b.
circa 1826. Enl. Richmond 10/18/62, age thirty-
six; presence or ab. not stated through 2/28/63 or
7–8/63; however, horse lost for lack of horseshoes
at Hagerstown, Md., 7/19/63, paid $230; ab. sick
in Richmond hosp. 8/21/63–3/22/64; present
4/1/64. NFR.
HOLLYDAY, GEORGE TILGHMAN: Pvt., Co. C.
b. Baltimore 3/14/46. Res. of Baltimore. Enl.
Hagerstown, Md., 6/16/63; present through 12/63
and 4/1–8/31/64; ab. sick in Richmond hosp.
9/26/64; furloughed for twenty days 9/27/64; ab.
detailed as scout for Gen. Lunsford Lomax
11/1–12/64; ab. sick with scabies in Charlottesville hosp. 12/21/64–2/4/65. NFR. Insurance
Agent, Baltimore. Member Isaac Trimble Camp,
CV. d. Baltimore 8/23/07. Bur. St. Thomas Ch.
Cem., Garrison, Md.
HOLLYDAY, GEORGE TILGHMAN: 4th Sgt., Co.
E. b. Baltimore circa 1834. Res. of Kent Co., Md.
Enl. as Pvt., Richmond, 11/25/62, age twenty-
eight; promoted 1st Cpl. 1/20/63; presence or ab.
not stated 1–2/63; promoted 4th Sgt.; horse dis-
abled 5/10/63, paid $230. Captured near Win-
chester 5/19/63; sent to Ft. McHenry; exchanged
10/24/63; ab. on horse detail 10/28–31/63; pre-
sent 11–12/63, 7–8/64, and 11–12/64. NFR. On
postwar roster Co. B, 35th Bn. Va. Cav. Member
Isaac Trimble Camp, CV, Baltimore, and ANS/
MLA. d. Baltimore 6/22/88.
HOLLYDAY, GEORGE GEIGER: Pvt., Co. C. b.
Washington Co., Md. 5/10/45. Enl. Hagerstown,
Md., 6/18/63; present through 12/63 and

GRESHAM
HOUGH

*(Museum of the
Confederacy)*

4/1–8/31/64; ab. sick in Richmond hosp. 9/26/64; furloughed for three days 9/27/64; ab. detailed as scout for Gen. Lunsford Lomax 11/1–12/31/64. Served with Mosby in 1865. Paroled 5/65. Moved to Baltimore 1866. Gd. U. of Medical School 1868. M.D., Baltimore 1868–1900. Member ANS/MLA. M.D., Point Comfort, Md. d. 3/15/12. Bur. Loudon Park Cem., Baltimore.

HOLMES, F. M.: Sgt., Co. unknown; WIA and captured in Hagerstown, Md., hosp., 7/63. NFR.

HOLT, WILLIAM: Pvt., Co. K; WIA, date and place unknown. On postwar roster Co. K (2nd), 1st Va. Cav., and Co. K, 1st Md. Cav.

HOPKINS, HENRY "HAL": Pvt., Co. K. b. Baltimore circa 1840. Res. of Baltimore. Enl. Co. C, 1st Md. Inf., 5/2/61; discharged 6/62. Enl. Breathed's Bty. 7/10/62; WIA Union, Va., 11/2/62; WIA Yellow Tavern, Va., 5/11/64. Transf. to Co. K, 1st Va. Cav., 8/14/64. Transf. to Co. K, 1st Md. Cav., 8/64; AWOL 11/1–12/31/64. However, enl. Co. F, 43rd Bn. Va. Cav. (Mosby), 10/10/64. Paroled Winchester 4/22/65. Age twenty-five, 5'10", fair complexion, light hair, gray eyes. Took oath at Winchester 6/6/65. d. by 1904.

HOPKINS, JOHN H., II: Pvt., Co. unknown, Davis's Bn. b. 3/2/45. Res. of Annapolis, Md. On postwar roster. d. 3/25/25. Bur. Christ Episcopal Ch. Cem., Owensville, Md.

HOPKINS, WILLIAM RIGBY: Pvt., Co. K. Res. of Talbot Co., Md. Enl. Breathed's Bty. 7/10/62; WIA, New Baltimore, Va. Transf. to Co. K (2nd), 1st Va. Cav., 8/14/64. Transf. to Co. K, 1st Md. Cav., 8/64; discharged at end of enlistment 12/4/64. NFR. d. by 1904.

HORNER, DAVID H.: Pvt., Co. F. Member Ridgley Brown Camp, CV, Rockville, Md., 1900 (only record of service). Res. Rockville, Md.

HORNER, FRANK B.: Pvt., Co. A. b. near Buffalo, N.Y., 1835. Miller, Brookville, Montgomery Co., Md. Enl. Charlottesville 6/4/64; present through

12/64. NFR. Member Ridgley Brown Camp, CV, Rockville, Md. d. near Rockville 8/29/20. Bur. Union Cem., Rockville.

HOUGH, GRESHAM (photo): Pvt., Co. A. b. 5/9/44. Res. of Baltimore. Att. Col. of Wm. & Mary 1860–61. Enl. Co. H (2nd), 1st Md. Inf., 6/18/61; discharged 6/18/62. Enl. Co. A, 1st Md. Cav., Charlottesville, 6/15/62. Tried to transf. to C.S. Marine Corps, spring 1863; present 7–12/63 and 4/1/64; ab. term of service expired and discharged; on rolls to 8/31/64. Enl. Co. D, 43rd Bn. Va. Cav. (Mosby), fall of 1864. Paroled Winchester 4/21/65. 5'10", fair complexion, dark hair, dark eyes. Took oath Harpers Ferry, W.Va., 4/25/65. Member ANS/MLA. d. Baltimore 10/14/94. Bur. Loudon Park Cem., Baltimore. Brother of Samuel J. Hough. (Photograph in Keen and Mewborn 1993)

HOUGH, SAMUEL JOHNSON: Pvt., Co. A. b. Baltimore 8/24/38. Res. Grad. Col. of Wm. & Mary 1855, Bachelor of Philosophy. Baltimore. Enl. Co. A, 8th Va. Inf., per postwar roster. Enl. Co. A, 1st Md. Cav., Hanover Junction, Va., 4/1/64; present through 8/31/64. Captured Harrisonburg, Va., 9/25/64; sent to Pt. Lookout; exchanged 2/27/65. Paroled Gordonsville, Va., 5/25/65. Took oath Richmond 5/27/65, destination Baltimore. Grad. Col. of Wm. & Mary, 1866, LLB. Lawyer, Baltimore. Member Franklin Buchanan Camp, CV, Baltimore; and ANS/MLA. d. Baltimore 1/7/11. Bur. Greenmount Cem., Baltimore. Brother of Gresham Hough.

HOWARD, CARVEL C.: Pvt., Co. C. b. circa 1846. Res. of Baltimore. Enl. Winchester 10/7/62; horse lost, Williamsport, Md., 7/6/63. Captured Hancock, Md., 7/19/63; sent to Wheeling. Age eighteen, 5/9", fair complexion, blue eyes, auburn hair. Transf. to Camp Chase; escaped 9/20/63. Present 11–12/63; ab. on leave for a horse to Winchester for fifteen days 2/16/64; horse stolen from camp at Hanover Junction, Va., 3/25/64; present 4/1/64; ab. on leave for ten days to Hardy Co., W.Va., for a horse 4/9/64. Captured Moorefield, W.Va., 8/7/64; sent to Wheeling. Age eighteen, 5'9", fair complexion, blue eyes, brown hair. Occupation: "Leisure." Transf. to Camp Chase and Pt. Lookout; exchanged 3/27/65; present Camp Lee, Richmond, 3/28/65. Surrendered Greensboro, N.C., 5/1/65. Took oath St. Mary's Co., Md., 5/15/65, destination Baltimore. Entered Old Soldiers' Home, Pikesville, Md., from Baltimore 9/6/10, age sixty-five; d. there 12/18/19, age seventy-three. Bur. Loudon Park Cem., Baltimore.

HOWARD, GEORGE WASHINGTON: Capt., Co. C. b. Ocracoke, Hyde Co., N.C., 9/18/33. Res. Howard Co., Md. Enl. Co. K (2nd), 1st Va. Cav.,

Leesburg, Va., 5/14/61; resigned as 1st Lt. 8/1/61. Captured Lewinsville, Va., 9/10/61; exchanged. NFR until elected 1st Lt., Co. C, 1st Md. Cav., 8/4/62; present 11/62; ab. as witness at CM 12/27–31/62; ab. Charlottesville 7–8/63; promoted Capt. 8/4 or 25/63; present through 12/63. Three officers and seventy-two men present in co. 12/31/63; ab. sick 1–2/64; ab. sick with scabies in Richmond hosp. 3/20–4/12/64. Captured Pollard's Farm, Va., 5/27/64; sent to Pt. Lookout. Transf. to Ft. Del. and Ft. Pulaski, Ga. (one of the "Immortal 600"); exchanged 12/2/64. Paroled Manchester, Va., 4/30/65. Took oath Baltimore 5/19/65. Farmer and Merchant, Florida, to 1880; moved to Washington Co., Md. Member ANS/MLA. d. 3/7/95. Bur. in N.C.

HOWARD, JOHN EAGER, JR.: Pvt., Co. C. b. circa 1837. Enl. Co. D, 1st Md. Inf., 5/22/61; discharged 8/17/62. Enl. Co. C, 1st Md. Cav., Richmond, 9/1/62; present 7–9/63; ab. sick with scabies in Charlottesville hosp. 10/11–11/16/63. Transf. to Richmond hosp. with dyspepsia through 12/31/63; horse given to dismounted man in Battalion; ab. on horse detail to Winchester for fifteen days to get another 2/16/64; present 4/1/64. Captured Snickers's Gap, Va., 7/16/64; sent to Old Capitol. Transf. to Elmira; exchanged 11/15/64. Ab. through 12/31/64; ab. sick with chronic bronchitis in Richmond hosp. 1/31/65 and 3/6–16/65. Paroled Greensboro, N.C., 5/1/65. Member ANS/MLA, 1894. Res. of Baltimore.

HOWARD, RICHARD: Pvt., Co. K. Res. Harford Co., Md. On postwar roster Co. K (2nd), 1st Va. Cav., and Co. K, 1st Md. Cav. Possibly Richard Henry Howard (8/20/39–12/8/99). Bur. Warrenton, Va. Cem.

HOWARD, RICHARD McGRAW: Pvt., Co. C. b. Manor, Baltimore Co., circa 1840. Res. of Monkton, Baltimore Co. Enl. Richmond 8/15/62. Captured South Mt., Md., 7/4/63; sent to Ft. McHenry. Transf. to Ft. Del. and Pt. Lookout; exchanged 9/18/64. Ab. sick with debility in Richmond hosp. 9/22/64; furloughed to Staunton, Va., for forty days 10/6/64; ab. sick with "Feb. Int. Quo." in Charlottesville hosp. 10/25/64. Resumed furlough 11/4/64; ab. through 12/31/64. Paroled New Market, Va., 4/20/65. Age twenty-five, 5'9", fair complexion, dark hair, blue eyes. Farmer, Monkton. Member ANS/MLA. d. Manor, Baltimore Co., 1/5/03, age sixty-two. Bur. St. James P. E. Ch. Cem., Monkton.

HOY, FABIUS G.: Pvt., Co. C, Davis's Bn. Enl. Avis's Provost Guard, Staunton, Va., 6/30/63. Turned over to another command as a doctor 11–12/63. Paroled Farmville, Va., 4/3/65, as Pvt., Co. B, 23rd Va. Cav.

HOYLE, GEORGE WASHINGTON: Pvt., Co. D. b. near Boyd's, Montgomery Co., Md., 11/23/37. Enl. 1862 per postwar roster and Cross of Honor application. Res. of Hyde, Md., 1910. Brother of Nathan L. S. Hoyle.

HOYLE, NATHAN LAWRENCE S.: Pvt., Co. D. Res. of Poolesville, Montgomery Co., Md. Enl. Winchester 9/20/62; ab. sick in Staunton, Va., hosp. 11/62; present 12/62; WIA (sabre cut left arm) and captured Monterey Springs, Pa., 7/4/63. In Frederick, Md., hosp. 7/6–7/63; sent to Ft. Del. Transf. to Pt. Lookout; exchanged 2/21/65; ab. sick with "Icterus" in Gordonsville, Va., hosp. 3/30/65. NFR. Farmer, Boyd's, Md. d. St. Louis, Mo., 7/17/92. Bur. Bellefontaine Cem. Brother of George W. Hoyle.

HUBBARD, ALEXANDER JAMES: Chief Musician. b. Dorchester Co., Md., 9/11/22. Jeweler, Baltimore; moved to Frederick Co., Md. Enl. Co. A, 1st Md. Inf., 8/8/61. Appointed Chief Musician; discharged 8/62. Enl. Co. A, 2nd Md. Inf., 1862. Enl. 1st Md. Cav. as Chief Musician, but not on muster rolls. Paroled Harpers Ferry, W.Va., 5/16/65, as Chief Musician, 1st Va. Cav. Member Isaac Trimble Camp, CV, Baltimore, and ANS/MLA. d. Baltimore 2/11/11. Bur. Loudon Park Cem., Baltimore.

HUCORN, JOHN F.: Pvt., Co. B. Res. of Broad Creek, Queen Anne's Co., Md. Enl. Charlottesville 9/10/62. Captured Monterey Springs, Pa., 7/4/63; sent to Ft. McHenry. Transf. to Ft. Delaware and Pt. Lookout; exchanged 11/21/64; ab. sick with "acute diarrhoea" in Charlottesville hosp. through 12/17/64; ab. sick with acute bronchitis in Charlottesville hosp. 1/2–12/65. NFR.

HUDDLE, JOHN: Pvt., Co. A, Davis's Bn. b. Va. circa 1846. Age fourteen, Northern Dist., Augusta Co., per 1860 census. Enl. New Market, Va., 11/20/63. Transf. to Co. M, 23rd Va. Cav. Paroled Staunton, Va., 5/16/65. Age eighteen, 5'11", light complexion, light hair, blue eyes.

HUDGINS, CHARLES H.: Co. C. b. circa 1835. Res. of Baltimore. Enl. Winchester 7/16/63; present through 12/63 and 4/1/64; ab. on horse detail to Hardy Co., W.Va., for twenty days 5/1/64. Captured Rockville, Md., 7/13/64; sent to Old Capitol. Transf. to Elmira; released 5/15/65. 5'7", fair complexion, dark hair, blue eyes. Plasterer, Baltimore. Entered Old Soldiers' Home, Pikesville, Md., 9/5/99, age sixty-four. NFR.

HUGHES, MAXEY: Pvt., Co. G. Res. of West River, Anne Arundel Co., Md; ab. sick with "debilitas" in Richmond hosp. 3/6/65; furloughed for thirty days 3/9/65. NFR.

HUME, CHARLES: Pvt., Co. unknown, Davis's Bn. On postwar roster. Served as Sgt. in 1st Md.

Inf. Captured Back River, Va., date unknown; sent to Ft. Monroe; escaped 7/62. NFR.

HUME, J. R. FRANK: Pvt., Co. C. b. Culpeper, Va., 7/21/43. Att. Bladensburg Acad. Clerk, Washington, D.C. Enl. Co. A, 21st Miss. Inf., 9/61; WIA (right hip) Gettysburg, Pa., 7/3/63. Transf. to Co. C, 1st Md. Cav., 4/3/64. Scout for Gen. J. E. B. Stuart; present through 8/31/64; AWOL 9/5–12/31/64. Paroled Washington, D.C., 6/65. Farmer, Orange Co., Va., 1865–70; member Va. legislature, 1889 and 1899. Wholesale Merchant, Washington, D.C., 1900. Res. of Alexandria, Va. d. Washington, D.C., 7/16/06. Bur. Ivy Hill Cem., Alexandria.

HUMMER, JOSEPH C.: Pvt., Co. F. b. circa 1841. Res. of Baltimore. Enl. Co. B, 1st Md. Inf., 5/21/61; discharged 8/15/62. Enl. Co. F, 1st Md. Cav., Richmond, 7/31/63; ab. sick with fractured head of the tibia and displacement of patella in Richmond hosp. 8/2/63–2/19/64; present 4/1/64; ab. sick with debility in Charlottesville hosp. 4/16–5/3/64; ab. on furlough with neuralgia 9/8–12/31/64; issued clothing in Staunton, Va., hosp. 10/7/64. Paroled Lynchburg, Va., 4/13/65. Took oath Washington, D.C., 5/13/65; transportation furnished to Baltimore. Clerk, Baltimore. Member ANS/MLA. Entered Old Soldiers' Home, Pikesville, Md., 2/11/90, age forty-nine, from Baltimore; d. there 12/2/97, age fifty-six. Bur. Loudon Park Cem., Baltimore.

HUMPHREY, JOHN T.: Pvt., Co. E. Enl. Richmond 11/4/62; presence or ab. not stated to 2/28/63. NFR.

HUMPHREYS, NELSON: Pvt., Co. unknown, Davis's Bn. Res. of Baltimore. NFR.

HUNT, CHARLES WILLIAM: Pvt., Co. E. Res. Friendship, Anne Arundel Co., Md. Enl. Richmond 10/7/62; presence or ab. not stated 1–2/63; present 7–8/63; horse died 10/10/63; presence or ab. not stated 9–10/63; present 11–12/63; ab. on leave for ten days to Westmoreland Co. to get a horse 2/1/64; present 4/1/64 and 7–8/64; issued clothing 9/30 and 11/9/64; AWOL 12/8–31/64. NFR.

HUNTER, THOMAS: Pvt., Co. A. b. Baltimore Co., Md. 8/26/37. Enl. Charlottesville 8/25/62; present western Va. raid and 7–8/63; ab. sick with "Feb. Remit" in Richmond hosp. 9/23/63; furloughed for thirty days 10/7/63; present 11–12/63; ab. on leave 3/15–4/1/64. Captured Moorefield, W.Va., 8/7/64; sent to Wheeling. 5'8½", dark complexion, dark hair, blue eyes. Farmer. Transf. to Camp Chase and Pt. Lookout; exchanged 3/27/65. Paroled Edward's Ferry, Md., 5/3/65. Took oath Rockville, Md., 5/29/65. Farmer, Wheaton, Montgomery Co., Md. Member ANS/MLA. Entered Old Soldiers' Home, Pikesville, Md., 5/6/90; d.

there 7/18/05. Bur. St. James Cem., Montgomery Co.

HUNTINGTON, JAMES W.: Pvt., Co. unknown, Davis's Bn. b. Fairfax Co., Va., 12/17/43. Enl. Alexandria Va. Arty. 7/12/61. Transf, Davis's Bn. 1863; WIA (above right eye) Forrestville, Va., 1864. Paroled Moorefield, W.Va., 4/65. Restaurant Owner, Grocer and Fish business, Alexandria. Member R. E. Lee Camp, CV, Alexandria, Va. d. 11/22/98. Bur. St. Paul's Episcopal Ch. Cem., Alexandria.

HURLEY, OTHO J.: Pvt., Co. K. Enl. Co. K (2nd), 1st Va. Cav., 6/1/62; present through 8/64. Transf. to Co. K, 1st Md. Cav., 8/64; present through 12/64. NFR.

HUTTON, CHARLES C.: Pvt., Co. A. b. near Brookeville, Montgomery Co., Md. 1844. Enl. Charlottesville 8/25/62; present as QM Sgt. 11/62; present as Forage Master 12/62; present 7–8/63; ab. in Charlottesville hosp. 9/5–10/31/63; present 11–12/63 and 4/1/64. Captured Moorefield, W.Va., 8/7/64; sent to Wheeling. 5'11", dark complexion, dark hair, hazel eyes. Farmer. Transf. to Camp Chase and Pt. Lookout; exchanged 3/27/65. Paroled Richmond 4/17/65. Took oath Washington, D.C., 6/6/65. 5'10", light complexion, brown hair, gray eyes. d. near Brookeville 4/11/92. Bur. St. John's Episcopal Ch. Cem., Olney, Md.

INGOLES, CHARLES E.: Pvt., Co. C. Res. of Baltimore. Enl. Co. H (2nd), 1st Md. Inf., 5/17/61; discharged 5/16/62. Enl. Co. C, 1st Md. Cav., Richmond, 8/4/63; present through 12/63; horse died, Hanover Junction, Va., 12/1/63; ab. to Petersburg, Va., on horse detail for five days 2/1/64; ab. on horse detail for fourten days 3/28/64; present through 12/64. Captured Frederick's Hall, Va., 3/13/65; sent to Pt. Lookout; released 6/12/65; destination Baltimore.

IRWIN, A. D.: Capt., Co. F, Davis's Bn. NFR. (See Erwin, A. D.)

ISAACS, JOSEPH WILLIAM: Pvt., Co. K. b. Elk Ridge, Howard Co., Md., 2/28/35. Postmaster, Fairfax Station, Va., 1861. Enl. Co. K (2nd), 1st Va. Cav., 9/1/62; present through 8/64. Transf. to Co. K, 1st Md. Cav., 8/64; AWOL 12/31/64; present Appomattox CH, Va., 4/9/65. Employee, Government Printing Office, Washington, D.C., during the Cleveland administration; and Locksmith for 52nd and 53rd Congresses. Res. Elk Ridge, Md., 1895. d. 2/27/04. Bur. Grace Episcopal Ch. Cem., Elk Ridge, Md.

JACKINS, WILLIAM H.: Pvt., Co. K. Enl. Co. K (2nd), 1st Va. Cav., 9/10/62; present through 8/64. Transf. to Co. K, 1st Md. Cav., 8/64; AWOL 9–12/64. NFR.

JACKSON, ANDREW J.: Pvt., Co. A. Enl. Co. F,

1st Md. Inf., date unknown. Captured Middletown, Va., 6/19/62; sent to Ft. Del.; exchanged 8/10/62. NFR. Enl. as Lt., Co. A, 39th Bn. Va. Cav., 2/9/63. Transf. to Co. A, 1st Md. Cav., 12/17/63, as Pvt; present through 12/31/63 and 4/1/64; WIA, captured, Frederick, Md., 7/8/64; sent to Ft. Mc-Henry; transf. to Pt. Lookout; exchanged 3/16/65. NFR.

JACKSON, ELIJAH: Pvt., Co. unknown, Davis's Bn. Res. of Millersville, Anne Arundel Co., Md. On postwar roster.

JAMES, GEORGE W. B. E. S.: Pvt., Co. G. b. circa 1841. Res. of Baltimore. Captured Winchester 9/20/63; sent to Ft. McHenry. Age twenty-three, 5'11", fair complexion, light hair, blue eyes. Mechanic. Transf. to Pt. Lookout; exchanged 1/21/65. NFR.

JAMES, JAMES P.: Pvt., Co. K. Res. of Md. Enl. Co. K (2nd), 1st Va. Cav., date unknown. Captured Champion's Hill, Miss., 5/17/63; sent to Elmira. Transf. to Co. K, 1st Md. Cav., while POW. Exchanged 11/15/64. NFR.

JAMES, R.: Pvt., Co. A. Captured Emmittsburg, Md., 7/3/63; sent to Ft. Del.; left at Ft. Delaware per POW rolls. NFR.

JAMISON, FRANCIS A. "FRANK": Pvt., Co. K. b. circa 1840. Enl. Co. I, 1st Md. Inf., 6/15/61; discharged 6/15/62. Enl. Co. K (2nd), 1st Va. Cav., 7/1/62; present until captured Upperville, Va., 5/16/63; exchanged 5/14/63. Present until WIA 12/63; admitted to Charlottesville hosp. wounded 12/13/63; RTD 12/29/63. Exchanged 5/24/63; present through 8/64. Transf. to Co. K, 1st Md. Cav., 8/64; discharged at end of enlistment 12/4/64. 5'9½", light complexion, light hair, hazel eyes. Res. of Md. Paroled Lewisburg, W.Va., 4/26/65. Age twenty-five, 5' 9", fair complexion, light hair, blue eyes. Farmer. Took oath, sent to Cumberland, Md., 4/27/65. NFR.

JARBOE, GEORGE BENEDICT: Pvt., Co. F b. Washington, D.C., 5/29/34. Carpenter, Carroll Co., Md. Enl. Co. E, 1st Va. Inf., 4/22/61; WIA Bull Run, Va., 7/21/61; discharged 5/9/62. Enl. Co. F, 1st Md. Cav., 1862 (not on muster rolls); WIA (head) Fredericksburg, Va.; WIA twice more. Captured and retaken. Served to end of war, All per postwar roster. On survey cruise with U.S. Navy 1865–67. Member ANS/MLA. Res. Carroll Co. 1900.

JARBOE, WILLIAM S.: Pvt., Co. E. b. circa 1845. Res. Prince George's Co., Md. Enl. Richmond 3/10/63; present 7–8/63; presence or ab. not stated 9–10/63, however, lost horse Brandy Station, Va., 10/11/63; present 11–12/63; ab. on horse detail for fifteen days to Winchester 2/16/64; present 4/1/64 and 7–9/64. Captured Beverly, W.Va.,

10/29/64; sent to Wheeling. Age nineteen, 5'6", dark complexion, dark eyes, dark hair. Student. Transf. to Camp Chase; released 6/12/65.

JARRETT, MARTIN LUTHER: Asst. Surgeon. b. circa 1840. Gd. U of Md. Medical School 1864. Res. of Jarrettsville, Harford Co., Md. Assigned 7/64. Age twenty-four, 5'6", light complexion, light hair, blue eyes. Captured Halltown, W.Va., or Martinsburg, W.Va., 10/4/64; sent to Old Capitol. Transf. to Ft. Del.; took oath, released 12/21/64; transportation furnished to Philadelphia, Pa. M.D. in Baltimore 1867–74. M.D., Jarrettsville, Md., through 1907.

JEFFERS, WILLIAM H.: Pvt., Co. B. b. circa 1837. Res. Kent Island, Queen Anne's Co., Md. Enl. Charlottesville 9/10/62; present 7–12/63; ab. sick with typhoid fever in Richmond hosp. 3/8/64; transf. to Lynchburg, Va., hosp. 7/9/64. Paroled Winchester and took oath Harpers Ferry, W.Va., 4/22/65. Age twenty-eight, 5'8", fair complexion, dark hair, gray eyes. Member ANS/MLA, 1885. Res. Renk Island, Queen Anne's Co., Md. d. by 1894.

JENKINS, ADAM POLAND "POLEY": Pvt., Co. C. b. Baltimore 8/19/35. Res. of Baltimore. Served in Dept. of Southwestern Va. 1861–62. Enl. Co. C, 1st Md. Cav., Culpeper, Va., 10/22/63; present through 12/63; ab. sick with scabies in Richmond hosp. 2/1–3/29/64; present through 8/31/64; AWOL 11–12/64. Res. Baltimore postwar. d. Old Sweet Springs, Va., 9/13/83. Brother of George C. and John C. Jenkins. (Photograph in Hartzler 1992)

JENKINS, EDWARD W.: Pvt., Co. E. Enl. date and place unknown. Captured Hagerstown, Md., 7/2/63. NFR. Merchant in Baltimore; d. there 9/20/04, age sixty-eight.

JENKINS, GEORGE CARROLL: Pvt., Co. C. b. Baltimore 10/15/36. Att. Mt. St. Mary's Col. Lawyer, Baltimore. Enl. Bridgewater, Va., 5/1/63; present 7–12/63, 4/1/64, and 7–8/64; ab. detailed as Courier for Gen. Lunsford Lomax 11–12/64; ab. sick with scabies in Richmond hosp. 1/16–2/28/65; promoted Capt. and QM on Lomax's staff; detailed with Col. Allen and ordered to report to Gen. John C. Breckenridge at Charlotte, N.C., after Appomattox. Surrendered Greensboro, N.C., 4/26/65. Took oath Richmond 5/26/65; transportation furnished to Baltimore. Businessman and Banker, Baltimore. Member Franklin Buchanan Camp, CV, and ANS/MLA. d. "Seven Oaks," Greenspring Valley, Baltimore Co., 6/5/30. Bur. New Cathedral Cem., Baltimore. Brother of Adam P. and John C. Jenkins. (Photograph in Hartzler 1992; postwar photograph in Angus 1923)

JAMES W.
JENKINS JR.

(Dave Marks)

JENKINS, JAMES WILCOX JR. (photo): Pvt., Co. E. b. 1844. Res. of Baltimore. Enl. Richmond 10/13/62, age nineteen; presence or ab. not stated 1–2/63. Captured Monterey Springs, Pa., 7/4/63; sent to Ft. McHenry; transf. to Ft. Del.; exchanged 2/18/65. Escaped Appo-mattox CH, Va.; surrendered Lynchburg, Va., 4/13/65. Took oath Richmond 6/12/65. Member ANS/ MLA. Res. Mt. Washington, Md. d. 12/12/10.

JENKINS, JOHN CARROLL: Pvt., Co. K. b. Baltimore 6/14/34. Enl. date and place unknown; KIA Front Royal, Va., 10/11/64. Bur. Oakwood Cem., Richmond; removed to Loudon Park Cem., Baltimore, 1874. Brother of Adam P. and George C. Jenkins.

JENKINS, SAMUEL: Pvt., Co. unknown, Davis's Bn. Res. Annapolis, Md. NFR.

JOHNSON, EDWARD C.: Adj. b. circa 1838. Att. Georgetown U., class of 1863. Res. Baltimore. Enl. Co. H, 1st Md. Inf., 6/18/61; discharged 7/16/62. Enl. Co. A, 1st Md. Cav., 11/62; Acting Sgt. Maj. of Bn. 11–12/62; promoted QM Sgt.; issued 660 Colt navy rounds and 2,000 pistol ammunition rounds 3/31/63; promoted Sgt. Maj.; horse killed 7/6/63, paid $900; horse stolen 8/10/63, paid $250; paid 9–10/63; promoted Ord. Sgt; present 11/30–12/31/63 and 1–2/64; issued clothing 3/30/64; promoted Adj. Paroled Winchester 6/21/65. Age twenty-seven, 5'8", light complexion, dark hair, dark eyes; destination Baltimore. Capt. and Comm. Officer, 5th Md. National Guard, 6/20/97–1899.

JOHNSON, GEORGE: Pvt., Co. F. Enl. Richmond 7/13/63; present through 12/63; des. 2/25/64; on rolls to 12/31/64. NFR.

JOHNSON, HENRY B.: Pvt., Co. F. Res. Baltimore. Served in Co. G, 1st S. C. Inf. Enl. Co. F, 1st Md. Cav., Richmond, 7/7/63; present through 12/63; ab. sick with debility in Richmond hosp. 3/26–5/2/64. Captured Boonsboro, Md.,

7/8/64; sent to Old Capitol; transf. to Elmira; took oath, released 11/4/64. 5'7½", light complexion, brown hair, dark eyes.

JOHNSON, J. NEWMAN: Pvt., Co. A. b. 12/27/39. Res. Urbana, Frederick Co., Md. Enl. Lacey Springs, Va., 4/1/63; present 7–12/63 and 4/1/64; KIA Shepherdstown, W.Va., 7/4/64. Bur. Elmwood Cem., Shepherdstown; removed to New Market Methodist Ch. Cem., Md. Brother of James T. Johnson Jr. and Otis Johnson.

JOHNSON, JAMES: Pvt., Co. A, Davis's Bn. b. circa 1841. Enl. Charles Town, W.Va., 8/8/64. Transf. to Co. M, 23rd Va. Cav; present through 10/31/64. Paroled Staunton, Va., 5/1/65. Age twenty-four, 5'6", light complexion, light hair, blue eyes. Res. of Albermarle Co.

JOHNSON, JAMES THOMAS, JR.: Pvt., Co. A. b. Charles Co., Md., 7/26/28. Gd. U of Md. Medical School 1848. M.D., New Market, Md. Appointed Asst. Surgeon, C.S.A., at Manassas, Va., 9/1/61. Served in hospitals Gordonsville, Farmville, and Lynchburg (all in Va.), and Salisbury, N.C., and as Medical Purveyor, Charlotte, N.C. Enl. Co. A, 1st Md. Cav. 1864, but not on muster rolls. Returned to Frederick, Md., 6/65. M.D. in Va. (1865–66), Urbana, Md. (several years), and Huntsville, Ala. d. there 8/9/99. Bur. Mt. Olivet Cem., Frederick, Md. Brother of J. Newman and Otis Johnson.

JOHNSON, JOHN: Pvt., Co. F. Enl. Richmond 7/13/63; present through 8/31/63; des. from camp in Orange Co., Va., 10/9/63. NFR.

JOHNSON, JOHN J.: Pvt., Co. F. b. 7/8/47. Enl. Co. E, 1st Md. Inf., 2/28/62; discharged 8/27/62; paid 11/3/62. Enl. Richmond 7/13/63; present through 8/31/63; des. from camp near Fredericksburg, Va., 9/10/63. NFR. d. 4/28/93. Bur. Mt. Olivet Cem., Frederick, Md.

JOHNSON, JOHN N.: Pvt., Co. A. b. Georgetown, D.C., circa 1825. Res. of Baltimore. Enl. Co. K (2nd), 1st Va. Cav., Leesburg, Va., 5/14/61; present until discharged at end of enlistment 5/14/62. Age thirty-seven, 5'10", fair complexion, dark hair, blue eyes. Druggist. Enl. Co. A, 1st Md. Cav., Chambersburg, Pa., 6/21/63; present through 12/63 and 4/1/–8/31/64; des. to the enemy Baltimore 12/7/64. Took oath, sent north of Philadelphia "not to return during the war."

JOHNSON, JOHN QUINCEY ADAMS: Pvt., Co. K. On postwar rosters Co. K (2nd), 1st Va. Cav., and Co. K, 1st Md. Cav.

JOHNSON, OTIS: 2nd Lt., Co. A. b. Frederick County, Md., circa 1842. Res. of Urbana, Frederick Co., Md. Enl. as Pvt., Urbana, Md., 9/12/62; paid 1/10/63; present 7–12/63 and 4/1/64; elected 2nd Lt. 6/18/64. Captured Moorefield, W.Va., 8/7/64; sent to Wheeling. Age twenty-two, 5'8½", dark complexion, dark hair, gray eyes. Transf. to Camp Chase and Ft. Del.; exchanged 3/12/65. Paroled Charlotte, N.C., 5/5/65. d. Cumberland, Md., 2/17/81. Bur. New Market Meth. Ch. Cem., Frederick Co., Md. Brother of J. Newman and James T. Johnson Jr.

JOHNSON, WILLIAM: Pvt., Co. E. b. Md. circa 1838. Age twenty-two, 4th Dist., St. Mary's Co., Md., per 1860 census. On postwar roster.

JOHNSON, WILLIAM E.: Pvt., Co. A, Davis's Bn. b. circa 1843. Enl. New Market, Va., 8/20/64. Captured Woodstock, Va., 5/13/64; sent to Wheeling. Age nineteen, 5'5", dark complexion, light hair, blue eyes. Transf. to Camp Chase; exchanged 2/25/65. NFR. Transf. to Co. M, 23rd Va. Cav., while POW. NFR.

JOHNSON WILLIAM E.: Pvt., Co. E. Farmer. Age twenty-two, St. Mary's Co., Md., per 1860 census. d. 1907. Bur. St. Joseph's Cem., Morganza, Md. Tombstone only record.

JOHNSON, WILLIAM P.: Pvt., Co. E. b. Md. circa 1842. Res. East New Market, Dorchester Co., Md. Enl. Richmond 1/13/63, age twenty; des. from Camp Lee, Richmond, 2/12/63. NFR.

JOHNSON, ROBERT W.: Sgt., Co. C, Davis's Bn. Res. of Frederick, Md. On postwar roster.

JONES, ALBERT, JR.: 4th Sgt., Co. D. b. Liberty, Frederick Co., Md., 3/8/42. Res. of Mt. Airy, Carroll Co., Md. Enl. Winchester 9/20/62, age twenty; present through 12/62 and 7–12/63; horse killed near Romney, W.Va., 12/14/63, paid $300; present 4/1/64. Captured Moorefield, W.Va., 8/7/64, horse killed. Escaped. Present Fisher's Hill, Va., 9/22/64 and 11–12/64; present Appomattox CH, Va., 4/9/65, "[H]e and his comrade, Wm. F. Dade of Montgomery county, led in the front of the fight." Paroled Winchester 4/28/65. 6', fair complexion, brown hair, hazel eyes. Took oath 6/19/65. Merchant, Jefferson Co., W.Va., 1865; moved to Baltimore, manufacturer of saddlery for thirteen years; moved to Mt. Airy, Md., 1887. Farmer and Banker there 1900. Member ANS/MLA. Res. of Baltimore 1912. d. 9/4/21. Bur. Loudon Park Cem., Baltimore.

JONES, E. C.: Pvt., Co. C, Davis's Bn. Captured Frederick, Md., 7/10/64; sent to Ft. McHenry; transf. to Pt. Lookout; exchanged 10/30/64. Present, Camp Lee, Richmond, 10/31/64. NFR.

JONES, EDWARD L.: Pvt., Co. D. b. circa 1843. Res. of Libertytown, Frederick Co., Md. Enl. Winchester 9/20/62; present 11/12/62. Captured Monterey Springs, Pa., 7/4/64, horse killed; sent to Ft. Del.; transf. to Pt. Lookout; exchanged 12/28/63. Present 4/1/64; WIA (thigh) Monocacy, Md., 7/8/64. Captured in Frederick, Md., hosp. 7/9/64; exchanged. Black horse killed Gordons-

JOHN JONES

(Frederick D. Shroyer)

ville, Va., 9/10/64; present through 12/64. Paroled Mt. Jackson, Va., 4/21/65. Age twenty-two, 5'7", fair complexion, light hair, blue eyes. Took oath Harpers Ferry, W.Va., 4/21/65. Businessman, Philadelphia, Pa., 1913. Member ANS/MLA. Entered Old Soldiers' Home, Pikesville, Md., from Philadelphia 6/8/14, age sixty-eight; d. there 3/30/15. Bur. Philadelphia.

JONES, GEORGE W.: Pvt., Co. C. b. 1830. Res. Friendship, Anne Arundel Co., Md. Claimed service in Co. H, 18th Va. Cav., but not on muster rolls. Enl. Co. C, 1st Md. Cav., Culpeper, Va., 8/1/63; present through 10/63; ab. on secret service 11–12/63; present 4/1/64. Captured Duffield Depot or Halltown, W.Va., 8/29/64; sent to Old Capitol; escaped; ab., escaped POW, on furlough 11/12/64. NFR. d. 1/3/99. Bur. Loudon Park Cem., Baltimore.

JONES, HENRY: Pvt., Co. A; des. Gordonsville, Va., 9/7/62. NFR.

JONES, HENRY W.: Pvt., Co. B, Davis's Bn. Res. Tobaccostick, Dorchester Co., Md. NFR.

JONES, JOHN (photo): Pvt., Co. B. b. circa 1831. Res. of Prince George's Co., Md. Enl. Charlottesville 9/10/62; Teamster for Brigade QM 12/62; paid 1/10/63; ab. on detached service 7–8/63. Captured Raccoon Ford, Va., 1/10/63; sent to Old Capitol; transf. to Pt. Lookout; exchanged 3/6/64. Ab. paroled POW 4/1/64. Captured Moorefield, W.Va., 8/7/64; sent to Wheeling. Age thirty-three, 5'6", dark complexion, dark hair, blue eyes. Blacksmith. Transf. to Camp Chase; released 5/13/65. 5'5", red complexion, gray hair, blue eyes.

JONES, JOHN WILLIAM: 4th Sgt., Co. A. b. New London, Md., 5/3/37. Enl. Co. K, 4th Va. Cav., 3/10/62; elected 2nd Lt. 8/19/62; resigned 8/9/62. Enl. as Pvt., Co. A, 1st Md. Cav., Leesburg, Va., 9/1/62; paid New Market, Va., 1/10/63; present 7–12/63 and 4/1/64; promoted 3rd Cpl; present

PVTS. JAMES C.
AND JOHN K.
KANE

*(Daniel D.
Hartzler)*

through 8/31/64; promoted 3rd Sgt; present 11–12/64. NFR. Member Alexander Young Camp, CV. d. 3/26/05. Bur. United Brethren Ch. Cem., Thurmont, Md.

JONES, JONES L.: Pvt. Co. unknown. Application to ANS/MLA is only record. Res. of Philadelphia, Pa., 1914.

JONES, PEMBROKE B.: 3rd Cpl., Co. B. Res. of Beltsville, Prince George's Co., Md. Enl. Charlottesville 9/10/62; ab. sick with syphilis in Charlottesville hosp. 10/25–12/15/62; present 7–12/63 and 4/1–12/31/64. NFR.

JONES, RICHARD T.: Pvt., Co. unknown, Davis's Bn. Res. Annapolis, Md. On postwar roster.

JONES, ROBERT H.: Pvt., Co. E. b. circa 1837. Res. of Somerset Co., Md. Enl. Richmond 11/10/62; presence or ab. not stated 1–2/63; present 7–8/63; presence or ab. not stated 9–10/63; present 11–12/63, 4/1/64, and 7–12/64. Paroled Ashland, Va., 5/14/65. d. Somerset Co., Md., 7/6/71, age thirty-four. Bur. St. Andrews Episcopal Ch. Cem., Princess Anne, Md.

JONES, SPENCER CONE: Pvt., Co. D. b. Rockville, Md., 7/3/36; moved to Frederick, Md., 1845. Att. Frederick Col.; Lawyer, Frederick, Md., 1860–62. Arrested 1862; jailed in Baltimore for eight months; released 12/62. Enl. Harrisonburg, Va., 5/1/63. Captured Monterey Springs, Pa., 7/4/63, horse killed; exchanged 7/63. Paid $1,000 for horse; ab. on detail 9–10/63; present 11–12/63, 4/1/64, and 8/31–12/31/64; present Appomattox, Va., 4/9/65. "Participated in the last gallant charge made by the cavalry before the sad event at Appomattox." Teacher, Huntsville, Tex., 1865–67. Lawyer, Rockville, Md., 1868–71; Attorney Gen. of Montgomery Co. 1871–79; Clerk of Md. Court of Appeals twelve years; Treasurer of Md. 1892–96; Mayor of Rockville 1898; Md. Senate 1901–07; President of Montgomery Co. Natl. Bank. Member Ridgely Brown

Camp, CV, Rockville, and George Emack Camp, CV, Hyattsville, Md.; ANS/MLA. d. 4/1/15. Bur. Mt. Olivet Cem., Frederick, Md. (Photograph in Angus 1923)

JONES, THOMAS A.: Pvt., Co. C, Davis's Bn. b. near Point Tobacco, Charles Co., Md., 10/2/20. On postwar roster. Served as Secret Service Agent. Helped John Wilkes Booth and David C. Herold cross the Potomac after the assassination of President Lincoln. Farmer, St. Mary's Co., Md. Member ANS/MLA. Entered Old Soldiers' Home, Pikesville, Md., 12/6/90, as former member of "Signal Service." d. La Plata, Charles Co., Md., 3/2/95. "Burial site not known."

JONES, W.: Cpl., Co. A, Davis's Bn; present 3/1–6/30/64. Transf. to Co. M, 23rd Va. Cav., NFR.

JONES WILLIAM G.: Pvt., Co. C. May have served in Co. B, 1st Md. Inf., 1861–62. Enl. Co. C, 1st Md. Cav., Martinsburg, W.Va., 9/20/62; present 7–10/63; AWOL 11/63; ab. detailed 12/4–31/63. Captured 4/1/64, but not on Federal POW rolls; may have been killed or des.

JUMP, CHARLES M.: Pvt., Co. E. b. circa 1843. Res. of Queen Anne's Co., Md. Enl. Richmond 10/18/62, age nineteen; presence or ab. not stated 1–2/63; WIA and captured near Winchester 6/13/63, horse killed; sent to Ft. McHenry; exchanged 6/26/63. Paid $230 for horse; present 7–8/63; presence or ab. not stated 9–10/63; present 11–12/63, 4/1/64, and 7–8/64; issued clothing 9/30/64. Captured Beverly, W.Va., 10/29/64; sent to Wheeling. Age twenty-two, 6'1", light complexion, light hair, blue eyes. Farmer. Transf. to Camp Chase; released 6/12/65. Age twenty-one, 6'1", fair complexion, light hair, blue eyes.

KANE, JAMES C. (photo): Pvt., Co. C. Res. of Baltimore. Enl. Co. C, 1st Md. Inf., 6/15/61; discharged 8/62. Enl. Co. C, 1st Md. Cav., date unknown. Captured Charlottesville 3/4/65; sent to Pt. Lookout; released 6/14/65. 5'7¾", light complexion, light hair, blue eyes; destination Baltimore.

KANE, JEREMIAH: Pvt., Co. unknown, Davis's Bn. On postwar roster. Served in 10th La. Inf.; enl. Co. D, 2nd Md. Inf., 9/11/62; returned to 10th La. Inf. as des. 6/17/63. NFR.

KANOUFF, GEORGE W.: Pvt., Co. D. Res. of Licksville, Frederick Co., Md. On postwar roster.

KATING, GEORGE P.: Pvt., Co. H. Captured Loudoun Co., Va., 11/28/64; sent to Old Capitol; transf. to Elmira; exchanged 3/15/65. NFR.

KAUFMANN, CARL: Pvt., Co. F. b. circa 1826. Res. of Frederick Co., Md. Enl. Co. B, 39th Bn. Va. Cav., 10/27/62. Transf. to Co. F, 1st Md. Cav., 4/21/64. Captured Moorefield, W.Va., 8/7/64; sent to Wheeling. Age thirty-eight, 5'7½", dark complexion, dark hair, brown eyes. Miller. Transf. to Camp Chase and Pt. Lookout; exchanged 3/27/65. NFR.

KEATING, EDWARD: Pvt., Co. E. b. circa 1834. Enl. 3rd Md. Arty; des. Enl. Co. E, 1st Md. Cav., Richmond, 11/29/62, age twenty-eight; presence or ab. not stated 1–2/63; present 7–8/63. Transf. to back to 3rd Md. Arty.; on rolls 9–10/63. NFR.

KEATS, JOHN THOMAS: Acting Asst. Surgeon. b. circa 1835. Res. of Queen Anne's Co., Md. Enl. as Pvt., Co. B, 1st Md. Cav., 4/1/63; present through 12/63; ab. to assist Asst. Surgeon Wilberforce McKnew 4/1/64. Captured Eastern Shore of Md. 4/8/64; sent to Ft. McHenry; released 5/12/65. Res. of Pacaniva, La. M.D., Talbott Co., Md. Member ANS/MLA. Entered Old Soldiers' Home, Pikesville, Md., from Queen Anne's Co. 4/5/92, age fifty-seven; discharged. d. 6/19/05, age seventy. Bur. Loudon Park Cem., Baltimore.

KECKBERGER, ALBERT: Pvt., Co. C. Enl. date unknown; ab. sick in Richmond hosp. 11/11/64; returned to horse detail 11/12/64; des. to the enemy Washington, D.C., 11/22/64. Took oath 11/23/64; transportation furnished to Philadelphia.

KEDGLEY, JOHN: Pvt., Co. D. Paroled New Market, Va., 4/28/65. Age twenty-two, 5'11½", dark complexion, dark hair, light eyes.

KEENE, ROBERT GOLDSBOROUGH "BOB": Pvt., Co. A. b. Baltimore, circa 1838. Res. of Baltimore. Enl. Co. K (2nd), 1st Va. Cav., 3/10/62; present until transf. to Co. A, 1st Md. Cav., 5/15/62; present 8/30/62, 7–12/63 and 4/1/64. Captured Moorefield, W.Va., 8/7/64; sent to Wheeling. Age twenty-seven, 5'7½", fair complexion, light hair, gray eyes. Lawyer. Transf. to Camp Chase and Pt. Lookout; exchanged 3/27/65. Paroled Richmond 4/26/65. Lawyer, Baltimore. Member Franklin Buchanan Camp, CV, Baltimore, and ANS/MLA. d. Baltimore 12/8/00, age sixty-two.

KEGLER, FRANCIS: Pvt., Co. A, Davis's Bn. Enl. Harrisonburg, Va., 1/4/64; present through 9/30/64. Transf. to Co. M, 23rd Va. Cav.; des. Luray, Va., 10/17/64. Took oath E. Tenn. 12/29/64. 5'11", light complexion, dark hair, blue eyes. Res. Washington Co., Va.

KELBAUGH, W.: Pvt., Co. K. Enl. Co. K (2nd), 1st Va. Cav., date unknown; ab. sick with fever in Gordonsville, Va., hosp. 10/7/63; transf. to Lynchburg, Va., hosp. 10/8/63. NFR. On postwar roster of Co. K, 1st Md. Cav.

KELLROY, _____: Pvt., Co. C. Killed by fall from horse in Luray, Va., 12/27/62.

KELLY, DANIEL B.: Pvt., Co. F. Enl. Richmond 7/13/62; present 7–12/63 and 4/1/64. Captured Old Church, Va., 5/27/64; sent to Pt. Lookout. Ex-

PVT. CHARLES W. KEMP

(James A. Knowles)

changed 2/21/65; present Camp Lee, Richmond, 2/27/65. Paroled Richmond 4/22/65. Took oath Washington, D.C., 5/22/65, to remain there. Member Confederate Veterans Assoc, Washington, D.C. d. by 1917.

KELLY, JOHN: Pvt., Co. A. Enl. date unknown. Paid 1/1–2/29/64. NFR.

KELLY, JOHN: Pvt., Co. F. Enl. Richmond 7/15/63; des. from camp near Fredericksburg, Va., 9/10/63. NFR.

KELLY, RICHARD: Pvt., Co. F. Enl. Richmond 7/15/63; present through 10/63; present, confined in brigade guard house, 11–12/63. NFR.

KELTON, C. V.: Pvt., Co. A, Davis's Bn. Enl. Woodstock, Va., 5/1/63. Captured in Md. 7/63. NFR.

KELTON, CARLTON BROWN: Pvt., Co. A, Davis's Bn. b. Baltimore 1838. Enl. Co. D, 1st Md. Inf., date unknown; ab. sick with "Int. Fever" in Charlottesville hosp. 10/17/61–1/16/62; discharged 8/17/62; paid 11/29/62. Enl. Co. A, Davis's Bn., date unknown. Captured 3/26/63; sent to Ft. Del.; transf. to Ft. Columbus and Pt. Lookout; exchanged 3/13/65. NFR. Also listed as serving in Co. E, 2nd Md. Bn. Cav. Went to Tombstone, Ariz., to prospect in 1879; sheriff of Cochise Co., Ariz.; member Ariz. legislature. Member ANS/MLA. d. Baltimore 5/04.

KEMP, CHARLES W. (photo): Pvt., Co. D. b. Baltimore Co. 7/14/30. Enl. Boonsboro, Md., 6/15/63. Captured Monterey Springs, Pa., 7/4/63; (on muster rolls, but not on Federal POW rolls); ab. as POW 4/1/64; des. 5/1/64; on rolls through 8/31/64. NFR. d. 11/19/76. Bur. Mt. Olivet Cem., Frederick, Md.

KEMP, FRED: Pvt., Co. unknown. Paroled Richmond 4/25/65.

KEMP, THEODORE: Pvt., Co. D. Res. of Baltimore. Enl. Boonsboro, Md., 6/15/63; present through 9/63; ab. sick in Richmond hosp. 10/6–7/63; present through 12/31/63 and 4/1/64; ab. on leave for twenty days to Hardy Co., W.Va., to get a horse 4/9/64. Captured Pollard's Farm, Va., 5/27/64; sent to Pt. Lookout; exchanged 11/15/64. Ab. sick in hosp. 11–12/64. Paroled, took oath, Richmond 4/25/65; destination Baltimore.

KENLEY, OLIVER GALLOP: Pvt., Co. K. b. Md. 11/38. Enl. Co. K (2nd), 1st Va. Cav., Leesburg, Va., 5/14/61; present through 4/62; ab. sick with fever in Danville, Va., hosp. 6/1/62. NFR until paroled Montgomery, Ala., 6/3/65. 5'9", fair complexion, light hair, blue eyes. Carpenter, Baltimore. Member ANS/MLA. Entered Old Soldiers' Home, Pikesville, Md., 6/7/10, age seventy-one; d. there 12/14/22. Bur. Holy Cross Cem., Baltimore.

KENLY, JOHN REESE: Pvt., Co. A. b. Baltimore 1/21/47. Res. of Howard Co., Md. Enl. Co. K (2nd), 1st Va. Cav., Martinsburg, W.Va., 7/10/63; present through 12/63 and 4/1–8/31/64. Transf. to Co. A, 1st Md. Cav., 8/15/64; present through 12/64. Paroled Winchester 5/2/65. 5'9½", light complexion, light hair, blue eyes. Took oath Richmond 6/28/65; destination Baltimore. Rodman, oil fields of W.Va.; employee, Richmond and Petersburg RR 1868; President of Atlantic Coast Line RR in 1913. Member R. E. Lee Camp, CV, Richmond. d. Wilmington, N.C. 3/1/28. Bur. Oakdale Cem., Baltimore. "Youngest member of troop."

KENNEDY, McPHERSON: Lt., Co. B, Davis Bn.; 1st Lt., Cos. A and G, 1st Md. Cav. Res. Frederick Co. Enl. as Pvt., Co. K (2nd), 1st Va. Cav., Richmond, 3/10/62; present until transf. to Co. A, 1st Md. Cav., 5/15/62; present 7–12/63; gray mare shot (contagious disease) 12/23/63, paid $300; ab. in hosp. 3/15–4/1/64; present through 8/31/64; ab. detailed as ADC on Gen. Bradley Johnson's staff 11–12/64. Paroled Salis-bury, N.C., 5/2/65 as 1st Lt., Co. G. Took oath Richmond 5/13/65. Res. and destination Balti-more. Res. of Hewletts, Long Island, N.Y., 1918.

KENNEDY, PRICE: Pvt., Co. A. b. circa 1836. Res. Hagerstown, Washington Co., Md. Enl. Winchester 10/25/62. Captured Falling Waters, Md., 7/14/63, age twenty-seven; sent to Old Capitol; took oath, released 9/24/63.

KENT, JOSEPH B.: Pvt., Co. E. Enl. Co. H, 9th Va. Cav., 7/10/61. Transf. to Co. E, 1st Md. Cav., 1/27/63. Paroled Ashland, Va., 4/26/65. Took oath Oak Grove, Va., 5/18/65. Former resident of Westmoreland Co., Va.; destination Annapolis, Md.

KEPLER, M. A.: Pvt., Co. B. b. circa 1833. Not on muster roll. Admitted Old Soldiers' Home, Pikesville, Md., 7/3/94, age sixty-one. d. 5/30/07. Bur. Loudon Park Cem., Baltimore.

KETTLEWELL, CHARLES S.: Sgt., Co. C. b. Baltimore circa 1842. Res. of Anne Arundel Co., Md. Enl. Co. I, 1st Va. Cav., 7/62. Transf. to Co. C, 1st Md. Cav., 8/10/62, as Pvt; present 7–8/63; WIA (saber cut) Gettysburg, Pa., 7/3/63; promoted 1st Cpl. 9/1/63; present through 12/63, 1–2/64, and 4/1/64; ab. sick with bronchitis in Richmond hospital 6/5–8/31/64; RTD 11/4/64; ab. on horse detail 12/25–31/64; promoted Sgt; present Appomattox CH, Va., 4/9/65. Paroled Richmond 5/8/65. Took oath Richmond 5/31/65; destination Baltimore. Salesman, Natl. White Lead Co. Vice-president ANS/MLA, 1900. d. 1/5/03, age sixty-one. Bur. Loudon Park Cem., Baltimore.

KETTLEWELL, EDWARD R.: Pvt., Co. A. b. circa 1843. Res. of Baltimore. Enl. Fredericksburg Arty. 5/31/61, age eighteen. Transf. to Co. A, 1st Md. Cav., 6/24/62; present 7–8/63; ab. detailed in Engineer Dept. 10/15/63–12/31/64. NFR.

KEY, HENRY J.: Pvt., Co. K. On postwar roster Co. K (2nd), 1st Va. Cav., and Co. K, 1st Md. Cav. Member Franklin Buchanan Camp, CV. Res. Baltimore 1900.

KEY, PHILIP: Pvt., Co. C. b. St. Mary's Co., Md. 2/15/41. Res. St. Mary's Co. Served in Co. A, 1st Md. Inf., 1861–62, per postwar roster. Enl. Co. C, 43rd Bn. Va. Cav. (Mosby), 1/8/64. Age twenty-one, 5'10½", florid complexion, brown hair, hazel eyes. Transf. to Co. C, 1st Md. Cav., date unknown. Captured Darnestown, Md., 6/9/64; sent to Old Capitol. Transf. to Ft. Warren; released 6/10/65. d. Salisbury, Md., 2/15/07.

KEY, RICHARD HENRY HAMMOND: Pvt., Co. B. Res. Prince George's Co., Md. Enl. Charlottesville 9/10/62; ab. sick with debility in Charlottesville hosp. 11/16–12/17/62; present 7–12/63; WIA (saber cuts) and captured Old Church, Va., 3/2/64, horse killed; sent to Pt. Lookout; exchanged 9/22/64. Admitted Chimborazo hosp., Richmond, with chronic dysentery 9/22/64; d. there 9/29/64. Bur. Hollywood Cem.; removed to Loudon Park Cem., Baltimore 1874.

KEY, WILLIAM WILFRED: Pvt., Co. C. b. 1846. Res. Anne Arundel Co., Md. Enl. Mt. Jackson, Va., 10/11/64; ab. Scout for Gen. Lunsford Lomax 11–12/64. Captured Myers Ford, Jefferson Co., W.Va., 2/17/65; sent to Old Capitol; d. there of congestion of the brain 2/24/65, age eighteen; no effects. Bur. St. Anne's Cem., Annapolis, Md.

KIBLER, CHARLES P.: Sgt., Co. I. Captured Charles Town, W.Va., 8/23/64; in U.S. Army; sent to Salisbury, N.C. "Deserted to the enemy (C.S. Army)" from POW camp to prevent starvation." Captured Salisbury, N.C., 4/65; sent to Nashville, Tenn., 5/16/65. NFR.

KIMBALL, HENRY C.: Pvt., Co. G. Res. of Baltimore. Enl. date and place unknown. Paroled, took oath, Greensboro, N.C., 5/2/65; destination Baltimore. Also served in Davis's Bn.

KIMBALL, LEWIS H.: Pvt., Co. F. Enl. Richmond 7/3/63. Captured near Gaines Cross Roads, Va., 7/23/63; sent to Old Capitol. Transf. to Pt. Lookout; d. there 2/21/64. Bur. Confederate Cem., Pt. Lookout, Md.

KIMBALL, ROBERT H.: Pvt., Co. C. Res. of Baltimore. Enl. Richmond 6/6/62. Captured Duffield Depot or Halltown, W.Va., 8/29/64; sent to Old Capitol; transf. to Camp Chase and Pt. Lookout; released 6/14/65. 5'8¾", dark complexion, dark brown hair, hazel eyes. Former resident of New Orleans, La.; transportation furnished to Baltimore.

KING, A. H.: Sgt., Co. B. Res. of Point of Rocks, Md. Enl. date unknown; issued clothing 9/30/64. Captured Fauquier Co., Va., 10/27/64; sent to Old Capitol; transf. to Elmira; released 6/19/65. 5'10", florid complexion, dark hair, blue eyes.

KING, R. K.: Pvt., Co. unknown; WIA (saber cuts over head and shoulders) Old Church, Va., 3/3/64. NFR.

KINSEY, HOWARD H.: 3rd Sgt., Co. F. b. Howard Co., Md., 7/4/42. Merchant, Montgomery Co., Md. Enl. Co. C, 18th Bn. Va. Arty., 6/3/61. Enl. as 3rd Sgt., Co. F, 1st Md. Cav., 7/15/63; present through 8/31/63. Returned to 18th Bn. Va. Arty. as des. on rolls 9–10/63; des. to the enemy Washington, D.C., 2/24/65. Took oath; sent to Baltimore 2/27/65. d. 7/11/17. Bur. Goshen Meth. Ch. Cem., Goshen, Md.

KITCHEN, JOSEPH GARRISON: Pvt., Co. unknown. b. near Shanghai, Berkeley Co., W.Va., 12/4/42. Served two-and-one-half years per post-war account; discharged for disability. Chief of Scouts and Enrolling Officer, Jefferson Co., Va. Farmer and Lumber Dealer, Jones Springs, W.Va. postwar; Member W.Va. House of Delegates 1889–91. d. 1/5/24. Bur. Calvary United Brethren Ch. Cem., Berkeley Co.

KNAFF, GEORGE W.: Pvt., Co. D. b. circa 1845. Res. of Baltimore. Enl. Co. B, 5th Va. Cav., New Market, Md., 9/1/62; WIA date and place unknown; WIA and in hosp. on rolls 2–12/64. Transf. to Co. D, 1st Md. Cav., 4/21/64; horse killed Darkesville, Md., 9/10/64, paid $2,500. Paroled Ashland, Va., 5/4/65. Butcher. Member ANS/MLA. d. 9/27/84, age thirty. Bur. Loudon Park Cem., Baltimore.

KNIGHT, J. M.: Pvt., Co. A. b. circa 1844. Paroled New Creek, Va., 5/8/65. Age nineteen, fair complexion, light hair, gray eyes.

KNOX, RICHARD T.: 2nd Cpl., Co. C. Res. of Baltimore. Enl. Co. D, 1st Md. Inf., 5/22/61; discharged 8/62. Enl. as Pvt., Co. C, 1st Md. Cav., Strasburg, Va., 12/9/62; present 7–12/63. Promoted 2nd Cpl. 8/1/63; ab. on leave for fifteen days

2/25/64; ab. on horse detail 3/24–4/1/64. NFR. Member Isaac Trimble and Franklin Buchanan Camps, CV; and ANS/MLA, 1900. d. Baltimore 1/20/10.

KONIG, HENRY S.: Pvt., Co. F. b. circa 1829. Res. of Baltimore. Enl. Richmond 7/10/63; present through 12/63 and 4/1–8/31/64; lost horse 8/20/64; issued clothing 9/20/64. Captured Beverly 10/29/64; sent to Wheeling. Age thirty-four, 5'10", fair complexion, blue eyes, dark hair. Painter. Transf. to Camp Chase; released 6/12/65. Age thirty-five, 5'10½", dark complexion, blue eyes, dark hair. d. 2/9/89, age sixty. Bur. Loudon Park Cem., Baltimore.

KRAUS, EDWARD: Pvt., Co. E; WIA (arm broken) near Winchester 6/12/63; on casualty list. NFR.

KRAUSE, CHARLES AUGUSTUS: Pvt., Co. E. b. Baltimore circa 1840. Res. Baltimore. Enl. Co. A, 7th Va. Cav., 5/61; WIA (wrist) Cross Keys, Va., 6/8/62. Transf. to Co. E, 1st Md. Cav., Richmond, 1/10/63, age twenty-four; presence or ab. not stated 1–2/63; present Western Va. Raid. Captured Front Royal, Va., 5/16/63; sent to Ft. McHenry; transf. to Ft. Monroe; exchanged 5/28/63; ab. sick with "sub Luxatio of right wrist and fractured left wrist" 8/15/63; transf. to Lynchburg, Va., hosp. 9/21/63; placed on disabled list 10/2/63; detailed 10/26/63; ab. on detail as Hosp. Guard, Lynchburg, Va., 11–12/64. Paroled Salisbury, N.C., 5/2/65. Member ANS/MLA, 1885. Res. of Salisbury, N.C. Entered Old Soldiers' Home, Pikesville, Md., from Baltimore 10/3/99, age fifty-nine. Painter. Discharged. d. Baltimore 6/23/13, age seventy-three. Bur. Loudon Park Cem., Baltimore.

KREBS, CHARLES T.: Pvt., Co. C. b. Baltimore circa 1842. Res. of Baltimore. Enl. Co. B, 21st Va. Inf., 5/23/61; discharged as nonresident 2/28/62. 5'10", light hair, blue eyes. Enl. Purcell Va. Arty. 8/6/62. Transf. to Co. C, 1st Md. Cav., 9/3/63; not reported on rolls 9–10/63; present 11–12/63; ab. sick with camp itch in Richmond hosp. 1/13/64 and with "sylphiuis" 2/2/64; sorrel mare killed Meadow Bridge 3/1/64, paid $850; ab. on horse detail 4/1/64; ab. sick with scabies in Richmond hosp. 4/20–6/9/64; ab. detailed in Provost Guard, Johnson's Brigade, 7/10–8/31/64; ab. sick with "sylphiuis" in Richmond hosp. 11–12/64. Paroled Greensboro, N.C., 4/26/65. Took oath Richmond 6/17/65; destination Baltimore. Bank Teller, Baltimore. 2nd Lt. Co. A, 5th Md. National Guard, 1867. d. Baltimore 7/11/93, age fifty-four.

KUHN, JOHN: Pvt., Co. K. Enl. Co. K (2nd), 1st Va. Cav 7/1/64; present dismounted through 8/31/64. Transf. to Co. K, 1st Md. Cav., 8/64; present 11–12/64. NFR. May have served in 2nd Md. Bn. Cav.

LAIRD, EDWARD: Pvt., Co. unknown, Davis's Bn. On postwar roster. Paroled Appomattox CH, Va., as Pvt., Co. D, 2nd Md. Inf.

LAIRD, SEVERN: Pvt., Co. unknown, Davis's Bn. Res. of South River, Anne Arundel Co., Md. On postwar roster.

LAM, BENJAMIN FRANKLIN: Pvt., Co. unknown. On postwar roster.

LAMDSDEN, CHARLES N.: Pvt., Co. D. b. Va. circa 1846. Age fourteen, Winchester PO, Frederick Co., Va., per 1860 census. On postwar rosters of Co. A, 1st Va. Cav., and Co. A, Davis's Bn. Enl. Co. D, 1st Md. Cav., Lacey Springs, Va., 4/1/63; WIA (leg fractured) Greenland Gap, W.Va., 4/25/63; ab. wounded until captured Winchester 10/63; exchanged; ab. wounded until captured near Newtown, Va., 5/3/64; sent to Wheeling. Age nineteen, 5'7", fair complexion, dark hair, gray eyes. Farmer. Transf. to Camp Chase; exchanged 2/28/65; ab. sick with debility in Richmond hosp. 3/7/65; furloughed for thirty days 3/9/65. Paroled Winchester 5/3/65. Age nineteen, 5'8", light complexion, dark hair, brown eyes. Res. of Winchester; d. there 6/17/07. Bur. Stonewall Cem.

LANCASTER, SAMUEL G.: Pvt., Co. E. b. Charles Co., Md., circa 1842. Enl. Co. I, 1st Md. Inf., 11/15/61; discharged 6/20/62. Age seventeen, 5'8", fair complexion, light hair, blue eyes. Student. Enl. Co. E, 1st Md. Cav., Richmond, 3/13/63; disabled horse abandoned 4/23/63; present 7–8/63; paid $230 for horse 8/22/63; presence or ab. not stated 9–10/63; paid 11/12/63. Age seventeen, 5'8", fair complexion, light hair, blue eyes. Student. Present 11–12/63 and 4/1/64. Captured Pollard's Farm, Va., 5/17/64; sent to Pt. Lookout; exchanged 1/21/65. Present Camp Lee, Richmond, 1/30/65; furloughed for thirty days. Was in Md. getting money to buy a horse when war ended. d. La Plata, Charles Co., Md., 5/22/01, age fifty-nine.

LANGLEY, THOMAS K.: Pvt., Co. A. b. St. Mary's Co., Md., 1836. Farmer, 1st Dist., St. Mary's Co., Md., per 1860 census. Enl. Co. K (2nd), 1st Va. Cav., Fairfax CH, 10/1/61; present until transf. to Co. A, 1st Md. Cav., 5/15/62; ab. sick in Hanover hosp. 7–8/63; ab. sick with chronic dysentery in Richmond and Charlottesville hospitals 8/23–12/31/63; present 4/1/64. Captured Moorefield, W.Va., 8/7/64; sent to Wheeling. Age twenty-seven, 5'7", dark complexion, blue eyes, dark hair. Farmer. Transf. to Camp Chase and Pt. Lookout; exchanged 3/27/65. Paroled, took oath, Richmond 5/26/65. Constable, St. Mary's Co., Md., 1870. Farmer, St. Mary's Co., per 1880 census.

LANIER, JOHN: Pvt., Co. G (originally Co. B, Davis's Bn.). Enl. date and place unknown; des. to the enemy 2/25/65. Took oath; sent north.

LANKFORD, FRANCIS L.: Pvt., Co. A, Davis's Bn. Captured New Market, Va., 5/15/64; sent to Camp Chase; released 5/8/65. Age twenty-five, 5'10", fair complexion, dark hair, blue eyes. Brick Mason. Res. of Somerset, Md.

LARKINSON, N.: Pvt., Co. E. Enl. Cockeysville, Md., 7/25/64. Captured Falling Waters, Md., 8/28/64. NFR; may have been KIA.

LATHAM, JOHN W.: Cpl., Co. F. On postwar roster. Member ANS/MLA. d. Baltimore 3/28/90. Bur. Loudon Park Cem., Baltimore. May be confused with Joseph W. Latham, below.

LATHAM, JOSEPH W.: 2nd Cpl., Co. F. b. circa 1841. Res. Frederick, Md. Enl. Co. C, 18th Bn. Va. Arty., 10/17/62. Transf. to Co. F, 1st Md. Cav., Richmond, 6/15/63 as 3rd Cpl; present 7–8/63; ab. sick in hosp. 9–10/63; promoted 2nd Cpl; present 11–12/63 and 4/1/64; WIA (gunshot wound left leg—flesh) Beaver Dam, Va., 5/9/64; admitted Richmond hosp. 4/14/64; RTD 6/16/64; paid 7/6/64. Captured Allegany Co., Md., 8/2/64; sent to Wheeling. Age twenty-three, 5'9", fair complexion, dark eyes, light hair. Clerk. Transf. to Camp Chase; exchanged 3/12/65. Ab. sick with "p. p." in Richmond hosp. 3/11–12/65. Paroled Staunton, Va., 5/12/65. Member ANS/MLA. d. Baltimore 3/29/90. Bur. Loudon Park Cem., Baltimore.

LATROBE, RICHARD STEUART: Pvt., Co. C. b. 1/17/45. Res. Baltimore. Enl. Hagerstown, Md., 6/18/63. Captured Smithtown, Pa., 7/4/63; sent to Ft. McHenry. Transf. to Pt. Lookout; exchanged 3/6/64. On parole in Richmond 4/1/64; WIA (left leg) Clear Spring, Md., 7/29/64; ab. wounded in Winchester hosp. 8/1/64; transf. to another hospital 8/4/64; present 8/31–12/31/64; horse killed near Liberty Mills, Va., 12/22/64, paid $2,500. NFR. Lawyer, Baltimore. Member Franklin Buchanan Camp, CV, and ANS/MLA. d. 3/14/00. Bur. Greenmount Cem.

LAWRENCE, STEPHEN DEMETT: 2nd Lt., Co. D. b. circa 1839. Res. Libertytown, Frederick Co., Md. Enl. Winchester 9/20/62; present 11–12/62 and 7–10/63; ab. on leave for ten days 12/31/63; resigned for ill health 1/29/64; paid 1/31/65. NFR. d. in Texas 6/15/29, age ninety.

LAWSON, C. D.: Pvt., Co. K. Enl. Co. K (2nd), 1st Va. Cav., date and place unknown; ab. sick with "catarrhous" in Richmond hosp. 1/28/64; sent to Castle Thunder (prison) 1/30/64. NFR.

LAWSON, JOHN H.: Pvt., Co. K. b. circa 1833. On postwar rosters of Co. K (2nd), 1st Va. Cav., and Co. K, 1st Md. Cav. d. 6/14/88, age fifty-five. Bur.

HAMILTON
LEFEVRE

*(Frederick D.
Shroyer)*

GEORGE W.
LEISHER

*(Frederick D.
Shroyer)*

Mt. Olivet Cem., Frederick, Md.

LECHLIDER, GEORGE P.: Pvt., Co. A. Res. Frederick Co., Md. Enl. Co. A, 1st Md. Inf., 9/22/61; discharged 5/21/62. Enl. Co. A, 1st Md. Cav., Staunton, Va., 6/15/62; WIA (leg) Hagerstown, Md., 7/8/63; sick in camp 8/31/63; WIA Brandy Station, Va., 10/11/63; ab. wounded through 4/1/64; term of service expired and discharged 8/31/64. NFR.

LEDLIN, NORMAN: Pvt., Co. unknown, Davis's Bn. Res. Annapolis, Md. NFR.

LEE, JOHN: Pvt., Co. A, Davis's Bn. b. Salisbury, Md., 9/15/32. Enl. Md. 7/12/64; present through 10/31/64. Transf. to Co. M, 23rd Va. Cav. NFR. Moved to Danville, Va., 1875. Lumber Dealer. d. Danville 4/8/11. Bur. Green Hill Cem., Berryville, Va.

LEFEVRE, HAMILTON (photo): 5th Sgt., Co. C. b. Harford Co., Md., 1840. Res. Harford Co. Enl. Co. K (2nd), 1st Va. Cav., date and place unknown. Transf. to Co. C, 1st Md. Cav., New Market, Va., 9/9/63; promoted 5th Sgt. to rank from 8/12/63; ab. on detail to get a horse for twenty-one days 10/30/63. Captured Frederick Co., Va., 11/17/63; sent to Wheeling. Age twenty-three, 5'9", dark complexion, hazel eyes, dark hair. Farmer. Transf. to Camp Chase and Ft. Delaware; had measles, typhoid fever, and pneumonia while in prison; was refused a pardon by President Lincoln, however, took oath and was released 7/25/64. Entered Old Soldiers' Home, Pikesville, Md., from Baltimore 5/2/13, age seventy-three. Accountant. d. Baltimore 5/30/17, age seventy-seven. Bur. St. James Cem., Baltimore Co., Md.

LEFFINGER, ISAAC: Pvt., Co. E. b. circa 1842. Enl. Richmond 11/17/62, age twenty; presence or ab. not stated 1–2/63; horse killed Winchester 6/13/63, paid $230; present 7–8/63; ab. on horse detail 9–10/63; present 11–12/63 and 4/1/64. Captured Moorefield, W.Va., 8/7/64; per muster

rolls. Not on Federal POW rolls; probably KIA.

LEGG, WILLIAM E.: Pvt., Co. K. b. circa 1837. Res. Broad Creek, Queen Anne's Co., Md. Paroled Winchester 4/27/65. Age twenty-eight, 5'9", fair complexion, dark brown hair, brown eyes.

LEISHER, GEORGE WASHINGTON (photo): Pvt., Co. A. Res. Cooksville, Howard Co., Md. Enl. Lacey Springs, Va., 4/1/63; present 7–12/63 and 4/1–12/31/64. Paroled, took oath, Conrad's Ferry, Va., 5/8/65; destination Howard Co. Attended reunion 1899.

LEITER, CHARLES W.: Pvt., Co. A. Enl. Wise (Va.) Arty., Martinsburg, W.Va., 9/17/61. Transf. to Co. A, 1st Md. Cav., 6/5/62; present 7–12/63 and 4/1/64; ab., term of service expired, no discharge 8/31–12/31/64. NFR.

LEMMON, WILLIAM SOUTHGATE: Pvt., Co. C. b. circa 1843. Res. of Baltimore. Enl. Co. H (2nd), 1st Md. Inf., 6/18/61; discharged 8/62. Enl. Co. C, 1st Md. Cav., Richmond, 8/4/62. Captured Monterey Springs, Pa., 7/4/63; sent to Ft. Delaware; exchanged 12/25/63. On parole Richmond 12/31/63; present 4/1/64; ab. on horse detail to Campbell Co., Va., for fifteen days 4/9/64 through 12/31/64. Paroled, took oath, Campbell CH, Va., 5/20/65. d. Baltimore 6/5/05, age sixty-two.

LEPPER, CHARLES V.: Pvt., Co. K. b. Baltimore 1838. Res. of Baltimore. Enl. Co. C, 1st Md. Inf., 11/9/61; discharged 6/9/62. Age twenty-two, 5'10", dark complexion, dark hair, gray eyes. Clerk. Enl. Co. K (2nd), 1st Va. Cav., 6/1/62; present until captured Monrovia Station, Md., 6/17/64; sent to Pt. Lookout. CM'd as a spy; acquitted. Transf. to Co. K, 1st Md. Cav., 8/64, while a POW. Exchanged 1865. Paroled Ashland, Va., 5/2/65, age twenty-six. Clerk. Salesman, Baltimore, postwar. Member ANS/MLA, 1894. Res. of Philadelphia, Pa. d. Baltimore 5/27/18, age eighty. Bur. Loudon Park Cem., Baltimore.

LESLIE, JOHN W.: Pvt., Co. F. Enl. Richmond 7/1/63; des. to the enemy Fredericksburg, Va., 8/20/63; sent to Old Capitol; took oath, released 9/28/63. 5'10", dark complexion, brown hair, hazel eyes. Res. of Rolla, Md. Sent to Philadelphia, Pa.

LEVERING, THOMAS HENRY: Pvt., Co. C. b. circa 1838. Res. of Baltimore. Enl. Co. H (2nd), 1st Md. Inf., 6/18/61; discharged 6/18/62. Age twenty-four, 5'11¾", light hair, light eyes. Clerk. Enl. Ward's Ala. Arty. 6/23/63. Transf. to Co. C, 1st Md. Cav., 6/11/64; paid 9/23/64; AWOL 11/1–12/31/64. Captured Port Tobacco, Md., 4/23/65; sent to Old Capitol; released 5/16/65.

LEWIS, SAMUEL: Pvt., Co. unknown, Davis's Bn. NFR.

LIAMBAUGH, WILLIAM C.: Pvt., Co. C. b. circa 1841. Res. Hagerstown, Md. Enl. Brucetown, Va., 10/1/62. Captured near Winchester 6/13/63, horse killed; sent to Ft. McHenry. Age twenty-two, 5'6", blue eyes, dark hair. Transf. to Ft. Monroe; exchanged 6/26/63. Paid $325 for horse; present 7–8/63; ab. detailed as Courier for Gen. Lunsford Lomax 9–10/63; present 11–12/63; ab. on leave for fifteen days 3/29/64; present 8/2–31/64; WIA Bunker Hill, W.Va., 9/9/64; ab. wounded through 12/31/64. Paroled New Market, Va., 4/19/65. Age twenty-four, 5'6", dark complexion, dark hair, blue eyes.

LICKLE, JOHN D.: Pvt., Co. D. b. Md. circa 1836. Res. New Market, Md. Enl. Winchester 9/20/62; present 11–12/62. Captured Monterey Springs, Pa., 7/4/63, horse killed; sent to Ft. McHenry; transf. to Ft. Del. and Pt. Lookout; exchanged 12/28/63. Paid $475 for horse; present 4/1/64; WIA date and place unknown; ab. wounded in Richmond hosp. through 8/31/64; WIA date and place unknown; ab. wounded in Richmond hosp. 9/16–11/22/64; present through 12/31/64. NFR. M.D., New Market; Teacher, Baltimore. Member ANS/MLA. d. Baltimore 3/20/00, age fifty-four. Bur. Loudon Park Cem., Baltimore.

LIGHTER: HENRY: Pvt., Co. F. Res. of Baltimore. Enl. date and place unknown; des. to the enemy 3/64; sent to Old Capitol; took oath, released 3/15/64. 5'7½", dark complexion, light hair, blue eyes.

LINCOLN, JAMES RUSH: 2nd Sgt., Co. A. Enl. as Pvt., Lacey Springs, Va., 4/1/63; present 7–12/63 and 4/1/64; promoted 2nd Sgt.; horse killed Kernstown, Va., 7/21/64, paid $3,500; ab. sick with "dysenteria" in Winchester hosp. 7/23–8/3/64; present through 8/31/64 and 11–12/64. Paroled Richmond 4/25/65.

LINDENBORN, JOHN: Pvt., Co. unknown,

Davis's Bn. b. 8/10/32. Bartender, Annapolis, Md., "who shot a Union officer." NFR. d. 5/71. Bur. St. Anne's Cem., Annapolis, Md.

LINTHICUM, EDWIN: 2nd Cpl., Co. A. b. 1840. Res. Howard Co., Md. Enl. as Pvt., Urbana, Md., 9/14/62; present 7–8/63; ab. on detached service 9–10/63; present 11–12/63 and 4/1/64; promoted 2nd Cpl. Captured Moorefield, W.Va., 8/7/64; sent to Wheeling. Age twenty-three, 5'7", fair complexion, gray eyes, black hair. Student. Transf. to Camp Chase and Pt. Lookout; exchanged 3/27/65. Paroled, took oath, Conrad's Ferry, Va., 5/18/65. Member ANS/MLA. d. 1888. Bur. St. John's Episcopal Ch. Cem., Ellicott City, Md.

LINTHICUM, JOHN: Pvt., Co. K. Paroled Winchester 5/6/65. Age forty-six, 5'8", dark complexion, gray hair, blue eyes. Res. Albermarle Co., Va.

LINTHICUM, JOHN WARREN: Pvt., Co. K. b. Thurston, Md., 11/15/36. Res. Clarksburg, Md. Enl. Co. K (2nd), 1st Va. Cav., Leesburg, Va., 9/1/62; present through 8/64. Transf. to Co. K, 1st Md. Cav., Leesburg, 9/1/62; present through 8/64. Transf. to Co. K, 1st Md. Cav., 8/64; discharged at end of enlistment 12/4/64. Captured Sugar Loaf Mt., Md., 1/4/65, while serving with Mosby; sent to Old Capitol; transf. to Ft. Warren; released 6/15/65. 5'8", light complexion, light hair, blue eyes. Res. Frederick Co., Md. Member George Emack Camp, CV, Hyattsville, Md. d. Kempstown, Md. 4/13/17. Bur. Urbana Methodist Ch. Cem., Urbana, Md. (no marker).

LINZAY, JAMES N.: Pvt., Co. C. b. circa 1842. Enl. Williamsport, Md., 7/6/63; present through 12/63 and 4/1–12/31/64. Surrendered Appomattox CH, Va., 4/9/65. Paroled Staunton, Va., 4/30/65. Age twenty-three, 5'8", fair complexion, light hair, gray eyes. Res. and destination Baltimore. Member ANS/MLA, 1894. Res. of Towson, Md.

LIPSCOMB, FRANCIS A. "FRANK": Pvt., Co. A. b. circa 1846. Enl. Bridgewater, Va., 6/1/63; present 7–9/63; ab. on detached duty 10/28–31/63; present 11–12/63 and 4/1/64; WIA near Falling Waters, Md., 8/64. Captured Moorefield, W.Va., 8/7/64; sent to Wheeling. 5'½", dark complexion, hazel eyes, dark hair. Res. Athens, Ga. Transf. to Camp Chase and Pt. Lookout; exchanged 3/27/65. NFR. Joined President Davis and his cabinet at Charlotte, N. C.; attempted to join Trans-Miss. Dept. Paroled Opelika, Ala., 6/21/65. Professor of "belles lettres," U. of Ga., 1900.

LITTLEPAGE, JAMES: Pvt., Co., unknown, Davis's Bn. NFR. Enl. Co. C, 2nd Md. Inf., 1862; paid bounty. NFR.

LITTLETON, R.: Pvt., Co. G. Enl. date and place unknown. d. of "acute diarrhoea" in C.S. Military hosp., Richmond, 1/23/64.

LLOYD, JOHN A.: Pvt., Co. A. Enl. Richmond 5/9/64. Captured near Washington, D.C., 7/12/64; sent to Old Capitol; transf. to Elmira; exchanged 3/13/65. Paroled Lynchburg, Va., 8/13/65. Took oath Richmond 6/29/65. Carpenter. Res. Washington, D.C.

LOGAN, ALEXANDER: Pvt., Co. K. b. circa 1832. Res. of Md. Enl. Co. K (2nd), 1st Va. Cav., Martinsburg, W.Va., 9/10/62; present until WIA Bunker Hill, W.Va., 8/13/64. Transf. to Co. K, 1st Md. Cav., 8/64; present through 8/31/64; discharged at end of enlistment 12/6/64. Paroled New Market, Va., 4/19/65. Age thirty-three, 6', dark complexion, dark hair, gray eyes.

LOKER, THOMAS EDWARD: Pvt., Co. A. b. Md. 11/1/40. Farm Manager, 1st Dist., St. Mary's Co., Md., per 1860 census. Served in 1st Md. Inf. 1861–62 per muster roll. Enl. Lacey Springs, Va., 4/1/63; horse killed near Rippon, Va., 6/15/63, paid $450; present sick in camp 7–8/63; ab. on duty 10/25–31/63; horse killed Blackburn's Ford, Va., 10/15/63, paid $675; present 11–12/63 and 4/1/64. Captured Moorefield, W.Va., 8/7/64; sent to Wheeling. Age twenty-two, 5'6", dark complexion, blue eyes. Farmer. Transf. to Camp Chase and Pt. Lookout; exchanged 3/27/65. NFR. d. "Valley Lee," St., Mary's Co., Md., 9/9/25. Bur. St. George Episcopal Ch. Cem., Poplar Hill, Md.

LOKER, WILLIAM ALEXANDER: Pvt., Co. A. b. Md. 10/19/29. On postwar roster. d. Leonardtown, Md., 10/31/02. Bur. Our Lady's Cem., Medley's Neck, Md.

LOKER, WILLIAM M.: Pvt. Co. A. b. 6/4/42. Res. of St. Mary's Co., Md. Enl. Lacey Springs, Va., 4/1/63; present 7–8/63; horse killed Blackburn's Ford, Va., 10/15/63, paid $750; ab. on duty 10/25–31/63; present 11–12/63 and 4/1/64. Captured Moorefield, W.Va., 8/7/64; sent to Wheeling. 5'4", light complexion, dark hair, blue eyes. Student. Transf. to Camp Chase. d. of pneumonia there 2/16/65. Bur. Camp Chase Natl. Cem., grave #1296.

LONG, ROBERT H.: Pvt., Co. K. b. Va. circa 1833. Farmer, age twenty-seven, Stephensburg PO, Frederick Co., Va., per 1860 census. Enl. Co. A, 1st Va. Cav., 4/19/61; appointed 1st Lt. 7/1/61; present through 4/23/62; not reelected. Enl. Co. K (2nd), 1st Va. Cav., date unknown. Transf. to Co. K, 1st Md. Cav., 8/64. Captured Smithfield, W.Va., 8/28/64; sent to Ft. Del. NFR.

LONG, WILLIAM H.: Pvt., Co. A, Davis's Bn. b. circa 1841. Transf. to Co. M, 23rd Va. Cav., Paroled Harrisonburg, Va., 5/8/65. Age twenty-four, 5'6", light complexion, brown hair, gray eyes.

LOTT, JAMES: Pvt., Co. C, Davis's Bn. On postwar roster.

LOVELY, JAMES E.: Pvt., Co. A; WIA, in hosp. 11/62. NFR.

LOVELY, JOHN EMANUEL: Pvt., Co. A. Res. of Frederick Co., Md. Enl. Co. A, 1st Md. Inf., 5/21/61; discharged 5/21/62. Enl. 1st Md. Arty. 5/30/62. Captured Winchester 12/2/62. Paroled 12/4/62. NFR. On postwar roster Co. A, 1st Md. Cav.

LOWE, DANIEL W.: Pvt., Co. unknown. b. circa 1834. Enl. Co. B, 1st Md. Inf., 5/21/61; discharged 5/15/62. Enl. Co. F, 43rd Bn., Va. Cav., 9/19/64; present through 12/64; des. from 1st Md. Cav. Landed Piney Point, Md., 12/25/64, age thirty-two. Took oath Baltimore 12/31/64. Res. of Charlottesville, Va.

LOYSDEN, N.: Pvt., Co. E. On postwar roster.

LUCAS, H. C.: Pvt., Co. F. On postwar roster.

LUM, BENJAMIN FRANKLIN: Pvt., Co. E. b. circa 1838. Res. Washington Co., Md. Enl. Richmond 11/17/62, age twenty-four; presence or ab. not stated 1–2/63. Captured near Winchester 6/12/63; sent to Ft. McHenry. Transf. to Ft. Monroe; exchanged 6/26/63. Present 7–8/63; horse abandoned near Hagerstown, Md., 7/12/63, paid $230; presence or ab. not stated 9–10/63; present 11–12/63 and 4/1/64. Captured Moorefield, W.Va., 8/7/64; sent to Wheeling. Age twenty-seven, 5'8", fair complexion, gray eyes, light hair. Clerk. Transf. to Camp Chase and Pt. Lookout; exchanged 3/27/65. Paroled Winchester 5/4/65. Age twenty-seven, 5'8", light complexion, light hair, blue eyes; destination Harrisonburg, Va.

LUMPKIN, JAMES T.: Pvt., Co. C. Res. of Baltimore. Enl. Co. H, 55th Va. Inf., 5/24/61; captured flag of 149th Pa. Inf. at Gettysburg, Pa., 7/3/63. Transf. to Co. C, 1st Md. Cav., 4/15/64; horse killed Old Church, Va., 3/3/64, paid $2,000. Captured Pollard's Farm, Va., 5/27/64; sent to Pt. Lookout; exchanged 11/15/64; present Camp Lee, Richmond, 12/1/64; ab. on leave 12/31/64. Paroled Richmond 5/3/65. Student. Minister, Richmond, 1896. Alive 1907.

LÜMAN, GUSTAV W.: Pvt., Co. C. Res. of Catonsville, Baltimore Co., Md. Enl. Richmond 9/1/62; ab. on leave 11/62; present through 12/62 and 7– 9/63; ab. on horse detail for twelve days 10/28/63; present 11–12/63 and 4/1/64; ab. sick with gonorrhoea in Richmond hosp. 4/18–20/64; present through 8/31/64; ab. sick with scabies in Charlottesville hosp. 11/7–12/20/64. Paroled Appomattox CH, Va., 4/9/65. Took oath Richmond 5/17/65; destination Baltimore. Member Isaac Trimble and Franklin Buchanan Camps, CV, Baltimore, 1900; and ANS/MLA. Res. of Catonsville. Bur. Greenmount Cem., Baltimore, no dates.

LUMAN, H. E.: Pvt., Co. F. Enl. Richmond 7/19/63; des. near Fredericksburg, Va., 8/6/63. NFR.

LUSBY, JAMES: Pvt., Co. F. b. Baltimore 1841. Res. of Baltimore. Enl. Co. E, 1st Md. Inf., 5/23/61; discharged 8/17/62. Age twenty-three, 5'6", fair complexion, light blue eyes, dark hair. Bricklayer. Reenl. in Breathed's Bty. 3/9/63. Transf. to Co. F, 1st Md. Cav., 5/14/64; present through 12/31/64. Paroled, took oath, Winchester 4/27/65. Hackman, Baltimore. Entered Old Soldiers' Home, Pikesville, Md., 4/1/90, age fifty-five; d. there 12/5/08, age seventy-three. Bur. Loudon Park Cem., Baltimore.

LYON, SAMUEL HALL: 3rd Cpl., Co. C. b. circa 1844. Res. Baltimore Co. Enl. as Pvt., Boonsboro, Md., 6/20/63; present 7–9/63; ab. sick with "Febris Intermitten" in Richmond hosp. 10/8–11/1/63; furloughed for thirty days; present 12/31/63 and 4/1/64; promoted 3rd Cpl. 7/1/64. Captured Moorefield, W.Va., 8/7/64; sent to Wheeling. Age twenty-nine, 5'8", dark complexion, blue eyes, black hair. Lawyer. Transf. to Camp Chase and Pt. Lookout; exchanged 3/27/65. Paroled in Europe 4/65. Took oath Paris, France, 7/65. Res. Baltimore. d. 12/19/17, age eighty-three. Bur. St. Thomas Ch. Cem., Garrison, Md.

LYONS, BRAXTON: Pvt., Co. B. Res. of Baltimore Co. Enl. date and place unknown. Captured Chesapeake Bay 4/26/64; sent to Old Capitol. Transf. to Albany, N.Y., penitentiary, and placed in close confinement; exchanged 2/5/65. NFR.

LYONS, BRINTON: Pvt., Co. B. Res. Baltimore Co. Enl. McConnellsburg, Pa., or Bedford, Pa., 6/24/63; present 7–12/63; sick in camp 4/1/64; ab. sick in Richmond hosp. 4/6–7/64. Captured Smithfield, W.Va., 8/26/64; sent to Old Capitol; transf. to Camp Chase and Pt. Lookout; released 6/14/65. 5'8", light complexion, brown eyes, dark hair.

MACATEE, HENRY: Pvt., Co. C. Enl. Williamsport, Md., 7/6/63; present through 9/63; ab. sick in hosp. 10/18–31/63; AWOL 11–12/63. Captured, "POW in hands of the enemy" on rolls 4/1/64;, W. "AWOL since 12/63" on rolls to 8/31/64. NFR. May have served in Co. D, 2nd Md. Inf. Res. of Harford Co., Md.

MAC GILL, DAVIDGE "PAT": Pvt., Co. C. b. circa 1837. Res. Hagerstown, Md. Enl. Martinsburg, W.Va., 9/20/62; ab. sick Leetown, W.Va., through 12/62; ab. on horse detail 8/25–31/63; ab. sick with "Int. Fever" in Richmond hosp. 10/30/63; RTD 12/15/63; ab. on horse detail 12/28–31/63; horse stolen in Valley on return from Md.; ab. on leave for ten days to New Market, Va., for another; present 4/1/64; WIA (left hand) 5/28/64; ab. wounded in Richmond hosp. 5/29–7/18/64; fur-

loughed to Woodstock, Va., for fifteen days; AWOL 9/1–12/31/64. Paroled New Market, Va., 4/20/65. Age twenty-eight, 5'6", fair complexion, dark hair, brown eyes. d. Leaksville, N.C., 7/10/97, age sixty. Bur. Hollywood Cem., Richmond. Brother of James and William D. MacGill.

MAC GILL, JAMES: Pvt., Co. C. b. Hagerstown, Md., 12/24/44. Res. of Hagerstown. Enl. C.S.A. 6/61 per postwar account; present Valley 1862, Gettysburg, Pa., Trevilian Station, Va., and Valley 1864; detailed in Topographical Engineers late 1864; ab. mapping Henrico, Chesterfield, Hanover, Amelia, and Dinwiddie Cos. when war ended. Returned to Baltimore, imprisoned 4/18–5/1/65; released, furnished transportation to Richmond. Res. Dublin Depot PO, Pulaski Co., Va., per 1870 census. Married the daughter of Gen. A. P. Hill 11/16/04. Res. Pulaski Co., Va., 1906. Res. of Ashland, Va., 1917. d. Pulaski, Va., 1/16/23. Bur. Hollywood Cem., Richmond. Brother of Davidge and William D. MacGill.

MAC GILL, WILLIAM D.: Pvt., Co. C. b. circa 1835. Res. of Hagerstown, Md. Enl. Shepherdstown, Md., 9/17/62; present sick 11/62. Captured Hagerstown 12/28/62; sent to Ft. McHenry; transf. to Ft. Monroe; exchanged 3/13/63; present 7–12/63 and 4/1/64. Captured Hagerstown 8/6/64; sent to Ft. Del.; exchanged 2/27/65. NFR. d. Baltimore 5/27/89, age fifty-four. Bur. Hollywood Cem., Richmond. Brother of Davidge and James MacGill.

MAC KALL, LEONARD COVINGTON: Pvt., Co. C. Res. of Baltimore. Served as Acting Master, Richmond Naval Station. Enl. Co. C, 1st Md. Cav., Hanover Junction, Va., 12/1/63; present through 12/31/63 and 4/1/64–11/64; ab. sick with scabies in Richmond hosp. 11/17/64–1/17/65. Transf. to Charlottesville hosp. with "Orchitis" through 2/7/65; transf. to Lynchburg, Va., hosp. Paroled Farmville, Va., 5/8/65. Took oath Richmond 5/23/65. Member ANS/MLA. Res. of Baltimore. d. Philadelphia, Pa., 5/6/90. Bur. Greenmount Cem., Baltimore.

MAC KALL, ROBERT MC GILL: Pvt., Co. K. b. 2/225/44. Res. Georgetown, D.C. Enl. Co. F, 1st Md. Inf.; discharged 10/31/61. Enl. Breathed's Battery of Horse Arty., Petersburg, Va., 6/10/62. Transf. to Co. K (2nd), 1st Va. Cav., 8/14/64. Transf. to Co. K, 1st Md. Cav., 8/64; AWOL 11/1–12/31/64. Enl. Co. D, 43rd Bn. Va. Cav. (Mosby), without authority 10/11/64; WIA (left leg below the knee), date and place unknown. Paroled Winchester 4/21/65. 5'6", dark complexion, dark eyes. Res. of Culpeper CH, Va., 1904. Member Confederate Veterans Assoc, Washington, D.C., 1922. d. Culpeper 6/21/34. Bur. Fairview Cem., Culpeper.

MAC KUBBIN, CLARENCE HENRY: Pvt., Co. K. b. Baltimore 4/17/37. Enl. Co. K (2nd), 1st Va. Cav., Culpeper, Va., 11/62; present Chancellorsville, Va., Gettysburg, Pa., and Cold Harbor, Va. Transf. to Co. K, 1st Md. Cav., 8/64. Captured near Harpers Ferry, W.Va., fall of 1864; sent to Elmira; released at the end of the war. All information is from application to Old Soldiers' Home, Pikesville, Md., circa 1900.

MAC KUBBIN, CLARENCE NELSON: Pvt., Co. K. b. circa 1834. Res. of Baltimore. on postwar rosters of Co. K (2nd), 1st Va. Cav., and Co. K, 1st Md. Cav. Member ANS/MLA. Entered Old Soldiers' Home, Pikesville, Md., 10/4/04, age sixty-seven; d. there 7/6/18. Bur. Loudon Park Cem., Baltimore.

MAC KUBBIN, EDMUND: Pvt., Co. K. Res. of Md. Enl. Co. B, 30th Va. Inf., 8/31/61. NFR. Enl. Co. K (2nd), 1st Va. Cav., 6/1/62; present until AWOL 6/1–8/31/63; present until captured Wheat-land, Loudoun Co., Va., 7/10/64; sent to Elmira. Transf. to Co. K, 1st Md. Cav., while POW. Released 5/17/65. 5'11", florid complexion, dark hair, blue eyes.

MAC KUBBIN, EDWARD: Pvt., Co. D. Enl. Boonsboro, Md., 6/15/63; ab. sick with "diarrhoea" in Richmond hosp. 7/31–8/25/63; present 11–12/63 and 4/1/64; horse died on picket 3/30/64; ab. on horse detail to Hardy Co., W.Va., for twenty days 4/9/64. Captured Winchester 9/19/64; sent to Pt. Lookout; released 6/12/65.

MAC KUBBIN, JAMES B.: Pvt., Co. D. b. 9/12/30. Enl. Boonsboro, Md., 6/15/63; detailed as Wagoner 7–10/63. NFR. d. 9/11/04. Bur. St. John's Episcopal Ch. Cem., Howard Co., Md.

MAC SHERRY, EDWARD COALE: Pvt., Co. D. b. 3/5/49. Res. of Frederick, Md. Enl. Frederick 7/1/64; present through 12/31/64. Paroled New Market, Va., 4/19/65. Age sixteen, 5'9", fair complexion, red hair, gray eyes. Took oath Harpers Ferry, W.Va., 4/22/65. M.D., Frederick; d. there 5/8/00. Bur. St. John's Catholic Ch. Cem., Frederick.

MAC SHERRY, RICHARD M.: Pvt., Co. K. b. Martinsburg, W.Va., 11/13/42. Att. Loyola Col., Baltimore. Gd. Georgetown U. 1860. Res. Frederick Co., Md. Enl. Co. K (2nd), 1st Va. Cav., 5/10/63; detailed in Brigade Signal Corps the same day; present 8/2–31/64. Transf. to Co. K, 1st Md. Cav., 8/64; WIA (left arm) Stony Creek Station, Va., 10/12/64; ab. wounded in Charlottesville hosp. 10/27/64; furloughed to Broadway, Brunswick Co., Va., for thirty days 11/24/64. Paroled Washington, D.C., 5/8/65. In business in Argentina 1865–67; att. U. of Va.; gd. U. of Md.

Medical School; Professor of Medicine, Baltimore, 1890. Lawyer. d. Baltimore 6/28/98.

MADIGAN, DENNIS T.: Pvt., Capt. Hayward's Co. b. N.Y. City 12/3/33. Enl. Richmond Howitzers 4/61; not on muster rolls. Enl. Capt. Hayward's Co., Col. Brown's Bn. of Cav. Served two years; WIA (hand) Yellow Tavern, Va., 5/11/64, horse killed; detailed as Courier Gen. G. W. C. Lee, Richmond Local Defense Troops. Surrendered Appomattox CH, Va., 4/9/65. Pa-roled Richmond 4/65. Member ANS/MLA. All information is from application to Old Soldiers' Home, Pikesville, Md., circa 1902.

MAGRUDER, EDWARD W.: Pvt., Co. E. b. 8/20/40. Gd. Georgetown U. 1861. Res. of Upper Marboro, Prince George's Co., Md. Enl. 1st Md. Arty. 7/23/61. Transf. to Co. E, 1st Md. Cav., 3/13/63. Captured near Winchester 6/12/63; sent to Ft. McHenry. 5'4", dark complexion, dark hair, dark eyes. Transf. to Ft. Monroe; exchanged 6/26/63. Paid $250 for captured horse; present 7–8/63; presence or ab. not stated 9–10/63; ab. on leave for twenty days 12/20/63; ab. on horse detail for twenty days 3/20/64; present 7–8/64. NFR. Member ANS/MLA. d. 7/31/86. Bur. Magruder Cem., "The Forest", Prince George's Co.

MAGRUDER, ZACHARIAH: Pvt., Co. A. b. Montgomery Co., Md. circa 1838. Res. of Goshen Hills, Montgomery Co. Enl. Charlottesville 8/25/63; present through 12/63 and 4/1–8/31/64; issued clothing 9/30/64; AWOL 11–12/64. NFR. Farmer. d. near Goshen, Md., 3/22/96. Bur. Goshen Meth. Ch. Cem., Goshen.

MAGUIRE, CHARLES E.: Pvt., Co. unknown. b. Baltimore circa 1830. Enl. Co. B, 21st Va. Inf., 5/23/61; WIA Kernstown, Va., 3/23/62. NFR. 5'10", dark hair, hazel eyes. On postwar roster.

MAGUIRE, HENRY A. W.: Pvt., Co. K. Res. of Baltimore. Enl. Co. K (2nd), 1st Va. Cav., 7/10/62; present until AWOL 2/8–28/63; present until ab. sick with scabies in Richmond hosp. 10/29–12/29/63; present until captured Leesburg, Va., 4/28/64; sent to Ft. Del.; sent to Washington, D.C., 7/20/64. NFR. On postwar roster of Co. K, 1st Md. Cav.

MAGUIRE, JOHN: Pvt., Co. C, Davis's Bn. On postwar roster. Possibly the John E. Maguire who d. Baltimore, 4/5/97, age fifty-six.

MAGUIRE, JOSEPH E.: Pvt., Co. D. Res. of Baltimore. Enl. Hanover Junction, Va., 5/30/64. Captured Boonsboro, Md., 7/8/64; sent to Old Capitol; transf. to Elmira; exchanged 2/28/65. Paroled Bedford, Va., 5/24/65. Took oath Bedford 5/28/65; destination Baltimore.

MAHOMER, MATHIAS: Pvt., Co. C. b. circa 1837. Enl. 3rd Ala. Inf., Mobile, Ala., 4/24/61. Transf. to

ALBERT
MAYNARD

*(Molly C.
Leonard)*

Co. C, 1st Md. Cav., 8/20/63; ab. detailed in Comm. Dept., Gen. R. E. Rodes's Div. 9–10/63; present 11–12/63; ab. on leave for forty-five days 2/15/64; ab. detailed as Comm. Sgt., Gen. Rodes's Div., through 12/31/64. Paroled Staunton, Va., 5/1/65. Age twenty-eight, 5'9", florid complexion, brown hair, blue eyes. Res. of Noxubee Co., Miss.

MALLON, WILLIAM B.: Pvt., Co. A. b. Baltimore Co., Md. circa 1845. Enl. Co. A, 1st Md. Inf., 5/61. Enl. Co. A, 1st Md. Cav. Captured Romney, W.Va., 9/64. All information from application to ANS/MLA. Machinist and Engineer, Baltimore. d. 1/19/90, age fifty-five. Bur. St. Mary's Cem., Govansville, Md.

MANNERY, THOMAS: Pvt., Co. B. Enl. date unknown. Captured Williamsport, Md., 7/4/63; sent to Ft. Del.; transf. to Pt. Lookout; discharged by order of the U.S. Secretary of War 9/22/63. NFR.

MARRIOTT, JOSEPH G. W.: Lt., 1st Md. Cav. Res. of Frederick Co., Md. Enl. Co. E, 1st Md. Inf., 5/22/61; promoted 1st Lt. 7/23/62. NFR. Applied for reinstatement in Md. Line 12/3/62, while serving in 1st Md. Cav. NFR.

MARSHALL, ROBERT: Pvt., Co. K. Enl. Breathed's Bty. 6/10/62. Transf. to Co. K (2nd), 1st Va. Cav., 8/14/64. Transf. to Co. K, 1st Md. Cav., 8/64. NFR.

MARTIN, CHARLES: Pvt., Co. unknown, Davis's Bn. Res. Annapolis, Md. On postwar roster.

MASON, RICHARD R.: Pvt., Co. A. Stable Master, Hanover Junction, Va., 7/1–12/31/63. Enl. Hanover Junction 2/10/64; present 4/1/64; ab. detailed as Wagoner 8/31–12/31/64. NFR. Res. of Orange Co., Va. postwar.

MATTHEWS, HENRY HAW: Pvt., Co. D. b. Washington, D.C., 1845. Res. of Georgetown, D.C. Enl. Co. F, 1st Va. Inf., 5/1/61, age nineteen. Student. Transf. to Co. C, 1st Va. Arty; discharged 10/14/61. Enl. Breathed's Bty. 3/16/62. Transf. to

Co. D, 1st Md. Cav., 8/64; paid 9/27/64; discharged at end of enlistment 12/1/64. Took oath Washington, D.C., 5/30/65; went to Georgetown, D.C. Member ANS/MLA, 1896. Res. of Higginsville, Mo. Entered Old Soldiers' Home, Pikesville, Md., from Baltimore, 6/2/96, age fifty-five; d. there 6/23/15, age seventy. Bur. Oak Hill Cem., Washington.

MAXEY, P. B.: Pvt., Co. C, Davis's Bn. On postwar roster.

MAYNADIER, JOHN HENRY: Pvt., Co. K. b. Harford Co., Md., 11/7/30. Enl. Co. K (2nd), 1st Va. Cav., 9/1/62; present until captured 5/1/63; sent to Ft. Del.; sentenced to be hanged as a spy; pardoned by President Lincoln; exchanged 5/63. Ab. detailed at Gen. Fitzhugh Lee's Headquarters 5/25–12/31/64. Transf. to Co. K, 1st Md. Cav., 8/64. Captured, date and place unknown; sent to Ft. Del.; released 6/16/65. Grain Merchant, Baltimore. Member Isaac Trimble Camp, CV, and ANS/MLA. d. Govans, Baltimore Co., Md., 4/15/06. Bur. Greenmont Cem., Baltimore.

MAYNADIER, JOHN MURRAY: 2nd Cpl., Co. K. b. Harford Co., Md., circa 1838. Enl. as Pvt., Co. K (2nd), 1st Va. Cav., Romney, W.Va., 7/1/61; present until wounded (jaw bone shattered) accidentally at Fairfax CH, Va., by a Mississippi soldier 10/13/61; RTD; present through 2/26/62, promoted 2nd Cpl; present until captured Pike Co., Ky., 5/10/63; released. Age twenty-five, 6', dark complexion, dark hair, dark eyes. Farmer. Present until ab. detailed in Brig. Signal Corps 7/10/63–2/64. Transf. to Co. K, 1st Md. Cav., 8/64; ab. on detail through 12/31/64. NFR. d. 1878.

MAYNARD, ALBERT (photo): Pvt., Co. D. b. Libertytown, Frederick, Md., 9/19/42. Res. Libertytown. Enl. Boonsboro, Md., 6/15/63; ab. sick in hosp. 7–8/63. Captured Woodstock, Va., 11/8/63; sent to Wheeling. Age twenty-one, 6'1", florid complexion, dark eyes, dark hair. Transf. to Camp Chase and Ft. Del.; exchanged 2/27/65. Paroled New Market, Va., 4/20/65. Age twenty-two, 6'1", florid complexion, dark hair, dark eyes. Took oath Harpers Ferry, W.Va., 5/13/65. Trunk maker, Baltimore. d. 2/14/25. Bur. Greenmont Cem., Baltimore.

MAYNARD, THOMAS B.: Pvt., Co. A. b. 7/20/31. Res. Libertytown, Frederick Co., Md. Enl. Leesburg, Va., 9/1/62; paid New Market, Va., 1/10/63; present sick in camp 7–8/63; present 9–12/63 and 4/1–12/31/64; horse killed, Forrestville, Va., 9/26/64, paid $3,000. Took oath Baltimore 4/24/65. Farmer. Member Alexander Young Camp, CV, Frederick, Md. d. Libertytown 12/12/24. Bur. Oak Grove Cem., Howard Co., Md.

McANTEE, JOSIAH J.: Pvt., Co. C. Enl.

Williamsport, Md., 7/6/63; present through 12/63 and 4/1/64; ab. on horse detail to Loudoun Co., Va., for fifteen days 5/1/64; horse killed Hanover Junction, Va., 6/1/64, paid $2,500; present through 12/31/64; horse killed Bunker Hill, W.Va., 9/3/64, paid $2,000. Parole lost. Took oath 5/20/65. d. date unknown. Bur. beside wife in unmarked grave, Christ Episcopal Ch. Cem., Rock Springs, Harford Co., Md.

McATEE, IGNATIUS J.: Pvt., Co. C. b. circa 1839. Res. of Harford Co., Md. On postwar roster. Member ANS/MLA. Entered Old Soldiers' Home, Pikesville, Md., from "The Rocks," Harford Co., Md., 1/7/96, age fifty-seven. Farmer. d. 6/16/97. Bur. Harford Co., Md.

McATEE, SAMUEL ECCLESTON.: Pvt., Co. C. b. circa 1843. Res. Harford Co., Md. Enl. Williamsport, Md. 7/6/63; ab. sick in Hanover hosp. 8/23–31/63 and 9–10/63; WIA (right foot) Hanover Junction, Va., 11/20/63; ab. wounded in Richmond hosp. through 2/17/64; RTD 3/25/64, age twenty-one. Farmer. Horse killed Hanover Junction, Va., 6/1/64, paid $1,500; WIA Milford, Va., 10/25/64; ab. wounded in Richmond hosp. through 12/31/64; RTD; WIA (right thigh—flesh) 3/9/65, horse killed; ab. wounded in Richmond hosp. through 3/20/65. Surrendered Appomattox CH, Va., 4/9/65. Took oath Harper's Ferry, W.Va., 5/20/65. d. 8/28/23. Bur. Prospect Hill Cem., Front Royal, Va.

McATEE, WILLIAM ARMSTEAD: Pvt., Co. K. b. Loudoun Co., Va., 1837. Enl. Co. H, 1st Va. Cav., 3/1/62; WIA ("sabred from back of skull to his back") 2nd Manassas 8/30/62; present through 8/64. Transf. to Co. K, 1st Md. Cav., 8/15/64; WIA (hand) and captured Smithfield, W.Va., 8/28/64. NFR. Served with Mosby. d. 1902. Bur. Stone's Chapel, near Berryville, Clarke Co., Va.

McBRIDE, EDWARD THOMAS: Pvt., Co. C. b. 12/6/40. Res. of Emmittsburg, Frederick Co., Md. Served in Co. D, 1st Md. Inf., but not on muster rolls. Enl. Co. C, 1st Md. Cav., Frederick, Md., 9/11/62; ab. sick near Strasburg, Va., 12/15–31/62; ab. sick in Hanover hosp. 8/5–31/63 and with scabies in Richmond hosp. 9/22–10/28/63; present 11–12/63 and 4/1/64; ab. sick with camp itch in Richmond hosp. 6/24–7/4/64. Captured Chambersburg, Pa., 8/1/64 (or Allegany Co., Md. 8/2/64); sent to Wheeling. 5'8", dark complexion, black hair, dark eyes. Transf. to Camp Chase; exchanged 3/12/65. In Richmond hosp. 3/11–12/65. Paroled Staunton, Va., 5/12/65. d. 2/14/04. Bur. Catholic Ch. Cem., Emmitsburg, Md.

McCABE, _____: Pvt., Co. B. On postwar roster.

McCABE, GEORGE WILLIAM E.: Pvt., Co. K. b. circa 1840. Res. of Baltimore. Enl. Co.C, 1st Md. Inf., 5/17/61; discharged 6/10/62. Age twenty-two, 5'11½", dark complexion, dark hair, gray eyes. Clerk. Enl. Breathed's Bty. 6/10/62. Transf. to Co. G, 2nd Md. Cav., date unknown; paid Charlottesville 4/15/64. Captured Frederick, Md., 7/10/64; sent to West Buildings hosp., Baltimore; transf. to Ft. McHenry and Pt. Lookout; exchanged 7/64. Transf. to Co. K (2nd), 1st Va. Cav., 8/14/64. Transf. to Co. K, 1st Md. Cav., 8/64; WIA (head) and captured Smithfield, W.Va., 8/27/64, age twenty-four; sent to Ft. McHenry. Transf. to Pt. Lookout; exchanged 3/18/65; present Camp Lee, Richmond, 3/19/65. NFR. d. by 1903.

McCALL, JOHN A.: Pvt., Co. D. Enl. date unknown. Captured Hampshire Co., W.Va., 10/30/64; sent to Old Capitol; transf. to Ft. Warren as "guerilla"; released 6/16/65. 5'6¼", light complexion, brown hair, hazel eyes. Res. Pulaski Co., Va.

McCALL, R.: Pvt., Co. B. Enl. Frederick, Md., 7/15/64. Captured on rolls through 12/31/64. Paroled Vicksburg, Miss., 5/26/65. Res. Donaldsonville, La.

McCAMPBELL, ANDREW W.: 2nd Lt., Co. A. b. circa 1841. Enl. date and place unknown. Captured Frederick, Md., 7/10/64, as Pvt; sent to Old Capitol; transf. to Elmira; exchanged 2/20/65. Paroled Winchester 4/17/65 as 2nd Lt. Age twenty-four, 6', fair complexion, dark hair, blue eyes.

McCLEERY, PETER HENRY: Pvt., Co. C. b. Allegany Co., Md., circa 1837. Res. Allegany Co., Md. Enl. Martinsburg, W.Va., 9/20/62; ab. on leave 11/62; present 7–10/63; horse died Fredericksburg, Va., 9/8/63; ab. sick with scabies in Richmond hosp. 11/8–19/63; present through 12/31/63; ab. on horse detail for fifteen days to Winchester 2/1/64; present 4/1–12/31/64. Paroled, took oath, Winchester 5/14/65. Res. and destination Washington Co., Md. Salesman, Baltimore postwar. Member ANS/MLA. Entered Old Soldiers' Home, Pikesville, Md., 12/4/00, age sixty-three; d. there 3/15/12, age seventy-five. Bur. Loudon Park Cem., Baltimore.

McCLEMMY, GEORGE T.: Pvt., Co. E. b. circa 1836. Enl. Richmond 1/16/63, age twenty-seven; presence or ab. not stated through 2/63; present 7–9/63. Captured Germanna or Raccoon Ford, Va., 10/10/63; sent to Old Capitol; transf. to Pt. Lookout; transf. to Ft. Monroe for exchange 3/2/64. NFR. May have died enroute.

McCLINTOCK, RICHARD: Pvt., Co. B. b. circa 1847. Res. Baltimore. Enl. date and place unknown. Captured Moorefield, W.Va., 8/7/64; sent to Wheeling. Age seventeen, 5'5½", fair complexion, gray eyes, light hair. Student. Transf. to Camp Chase and Pt. Lookout; exchanged

3/27/65. NFR.

McCLUSKY, J.: Pvt., Co. unknown; issued clothing 9/20/64. NFR.

McCLUSTER, JOHN: Pvt., Co. G. Enl. date and place unknown; des. to the enemy 1/16/64; sent to Old Capitol; took oath, released 3/14/64. 5'7", dark complexion, brown hair, gray eyes. Res. N.Y. City.

McCORMICK, VAN H.: Pvt., Co. B. Res. Prince George's Co., Md. On postwar roster Co.K (2nd), 1st Va. Cav. Enl. Co. B, 1st Md. Cav., Charlottesville, 9/10/62; present 7–10/63. Transf. to 1st Md. Arty. 10/17/63. Paroled Washington, D.C., 5/12/65. Res. Bennings, D.C., 1903.

McCOURT, JAMES R.: Pvt., Co. C. Enl. Richmond 8/4/62; present, detailed as Butcher for Bn. 7–8/63; present detailed as Butcher for Lomax's Brigade 9–10/63 and for Bn. 11–12/63 and 4/1/64; present through 12/64. Paroled Richmond 5/8/65.

McCULLOUGH, J.: Pvt., Co. C. b. circa 1835. Enl. date and place unknown; WIA and admitted to Richmond hosp. 1/7/65, age twenty-nine; sent to private quarters 2/5/65. NFR.

McDANIEL, JOHN THOMAS: Pvt., Co. D. b. Md. circa 1842. Res. Frederick, Md. Enl. Boonsboro, Md., 6/15/63; present through 8/31/63; ab. on horse detail 9–10/63; present 11–12/63 and 4/1/64. Captured Hagerstown, Md., 7/5/64, age twenty-two; sent to Ft. Del.; exchanged 2/27/65. Took oath Washington, D.C., 7/5/65; transportation furnished to Frederick Co., Md. d. Grayson Co., Tex. 8/3/12. Bur. Frederick, Md.

McDONNELL, _____: Capt., Co. unknown. Not on muster rolls; present 9/7/62. NFR.

McDOWELL, CHARLES W.: Pvt., Co.A. Enl. Hagerstown, Md., 7/10/63; present sick in camp 8/31/63; present 9–12/63 and 4/1/64. Captured Baltimore 4/64, while on horse detail; sent to Ft. McHenry; transf. to Albany, N.Y., penitentiary as a spy. NFR.

McFARLAND, WILLIAM HAMILTON "WILLIE": Pvt., Co. A. Enl. Co. E, 4th Va. Cav., 8/16/61; detailed in Signal Corps 1/64. Present Co. A, 1st Md. Cav., 6/64, but not on muster rolls. NFR. Enl. 43rd Bn. Va. Cav. (Mosby) 3/1/65; present with Mosby 4/8/65. Paroled Berryville, Va., 4/21/65. Res. of Richmond. Banker, Richmond. d. "Sherwood," Fluvanna Co., Va., 1/12/21, age seventy-six.

McGINNIS, JOHN B.: Pvt., Co. C. Res. Baltimore Co. On postwar roster. d. in Va. during the war; removed from Va. to Loudon Park Cem., Baltimore 1874.

McGINNIS, S. FRANK: Pvt., Co. K. Res. of Baltimore. Enl. Breathed's Bty. Horse Arty. Richmond

7/10/62. Transf. to Co. K (2nd), 1st Va. Cav., 8/14/64. Transf. to Co. K, 1st Md. Cav., 8/64; present through 8/31/64; ab. reason not stated 9/10–12/31/64. Enl. Co. D, 43rd Bn. Va. Cav.; issued clothing 4th qtr. 1864. Paroled Winchester 4/23/65. Took oath Harpers Ferry, W.Va., 4/25/65.

McINTYRE, WILLIAM H.: Pvt., Co. B. Enl. date and place unknown; issued clothing 9/30/64. Captured Fauquier Co., Va., 10/27/64; sent to Old Capitol; transf. to Elmira; exchanged 3/9/65. Ab. sick with "chronic diarrhoea" in Richmond hosp. 3/10/65; furloughed to Richmond for thirty days 3/18/65. Paroled Richmond 4/20/65.

McKEE, JAMES: Pvt., Co. C. b. circa 1833. Res. of Baltimore Co. Enl. New Market, Va., 1/28/63; present 7–12/63; ab. on horse detail for twelve days to Winchester 1/9/64. Captured Clarke Co., Va., 2/11/64; sent to Wheeling. Age twenty-seven, 5'11", fresh complexion, blue eyes, black hair. Plasterer. Transf. to Camp Chase and Ft. Delaware; exchanged 2/27/65. Paroled Winchester 4/16/65. Age twenty-nine, 5'10½", fair complexion, brown hair, gray eyes. Took oath Baltimore 4/27/65. Entered Old Soldiers' Home, Pikesville, Md., from Baltimore, 5/6/88, age fifty-seven; d. there 1/30/94, age sixty-one. Bur. Loudon Park Cem., Baltimore.

McKEEN, W. R.: Pvt., Co. G. Paroled Washington, D.C., 6/10/65.

McKEY, J. B. L.: Pvt., Co. G. Enl. date and place unknown. Captured Williamsport, Md., 7/5/63; sent to Ft. Del.; transf. to Pt. Lookout and Ft. Columbus; exchanged 5/3/64. NFR.

McKNEW, MASON EDWIN: 1st Lt., Co. B. b. 1836. Farmer, Beltsville, Prince George's Co., Md. Enl. Co. D, 1st Md. Inf., 5/61; served to 1862. Enl. as 1st Lt., Co. B, 1st Md. Cav., 9/10/62; present Winchester 10/62; ab. on horse detail 11/27–30/62; present New Market, Va., 12/62; WIA (left lung) and captured Potomac River 6/2/63; sent to Old Capitol; transf. to Pt. Lookout and Johnson's Island; exchanged 4/30/64. Ab. sick with "diarrhoea" in Richmond hosp. 5/1–5/64; furloughed for thirty days; ab. sick with "Bubo" in Charlottesville hosp. 6/8–13/64; ab. on leave 8/31/64; WIA (left side) Winchester 9/19/64 and admitted Charlottesville hosp. 9/27/64; RTD 10/17/64; AWOL 10/25/64; in arrest 10/31/64. Three officers and forty-six men present 10/31/64. Ab. on leave 12/15–31/64; paid 1/24/65. NFR. d. Baltimore 7/20/83. Bur. St. John's Episcopal Ch. Cem., Prince George's Co., Md.

McKNEW, WILBERFORCE RICHMOND: Asst. Surgeon. b. Prince George's Co., Md., 2/28/39. Att. Bladensburg Acad., St. John's Col., and Hobart Col., N.Y. Gd. U. of Md. Medical School

1861. Appointed Asst. Surgeon 10/13/62; assigned 11/12/62. Captured Greenland Gap, W.Va., 4/25/63; sent to Ft. Norfolk; exchanged 5/14/63. Assigned to Richmond hosp. through 1865. M.D. Prince George's Co., Md., 1865–69; moved to Baltimore. Surgeon, Md. National Guard. Member Isaac Trimble Camp, CV, Baltimore, and ANS/MLA. d. Baltimore 5/31/04. Bur. Loudon Park Cem., Baltimore.

McLANAHAN, WILLIAM H.: Pvt., Co. D. Res. of Frederick Co., Md. Enl. Co. A, 1st Md. Inf., 5/21/61; discharged 8/11/62. Enl. Co. D, 1st Md. Cav., Winchester, 9/20/62; present 11–12/62; des. at Leetown, W.Va., 8/8/63; returned to Winchester, on rolls 8/31/63; present 9–10/63; horse killed Brandy Station, Va., 10/11/63; present dismounted 11–12/63; ab. on horse detail to Woodstock, Va., 1/64. Transf. to 2nd Md. Inf.; on rolls 4/1/64, yet paroled Vicksburg, Miss., 5/31/65. Took oath Frederick, Md., 8/20/65. Member ANS/MLA, 1894. Res. of Philadelphia.

McLAUGHLIN, B. A.: Pvt., Co. C. d. in Richmond hosp. 10/23/63. Bur. Hollywood Cem.; removed to Loudon Park Cem., Baltimore, 1874.

McLEOD, WILFORD M.: Pvt. Co. B. b. Georgetown, D.C. Res. of Georgetown. Enl. Charlottesville 9/10/62. Captured Smithsburg, Md., 7/4/63; sent to Ft. Del.; escaped. Present 9–10/63 and 4/1/64; detailed as scout for Gen. Lunsford Lomax 5–12/64. NFR. Gd. Georgetown U. Medical School 1876. M. D., Georgetown, D.C., and Beallsville, Md. d. 2/11/97. Bur. Washington, D.C.

McMULLEN, CHARLES F.: Pvt., Co. F. b. circa 1840. Res. of Frederick Co., Md. Enl. Co. A, 1st Md. Inf., 5/12/61; discharged 8/11/62. Enl. Breathed's Bty. 6/16/63. Transf. to Co. F, 1st Md. Cav., 5/4/64; present through 8/31/64; issued clothing 9/30/64; ab. in hosp. 10/20–12/31/64. Took oath Richmond 4/11/65. Age twenty-five. Printer. Res. of Richmond.

McNULTY, JAMES: Pvt., Co. K. b. Baltimore 7/4/34. Res. of Baltimore. Enl. Co. D, 1st Md. Inf., 6/1/61; discharged 11/30/61 for disease of lungs and heart. Enl. Co. K (2nd), 1st Va. Cav., 9/1/62; present through 8/31/64. Transf. to Co. K, 1st Md. Cav., 8/64; present 11–12/64. Paroled Winchester 4/21/61. 5'10", dark complexion, brown hair, blue eyes. Coach maker. Destination Loudoun Co., Va. d. Old Soldiers' Home, Pikesville, Md., 8/4/15. Bur. St. Charles Cem., Baltimore.

McWILLIAMS, HUGH: Pvt., Co. C. b. Baltimore 11/10/40. Res. of Baltimore. Enl. Co. B., 9th Va. Inf., 6/5/61; Barkeeper; des. 9/25/61. NFR. Enl. Co. C, 1st Md. Cav., Richmond, 8/3/62. Captured Winchester 6/15/63; sent to Ft. McHenry; transf. to Ft. Del.; exchanged 6/26/63. Present 7–12/63; gave horse to dismounted man in Bn., ab. on horse detail to Newtown, Va., for twelve days 1/9/64. Captured Clarke Co., Va., 2/16/64; sent to Wheeling. Age twenty-four, 5'10", dark hair, blue eyes. Gentleman. Transf. to Camp Chase and Ft. Del.; released 6/10/65. 5'10", ruddy complexion, dark hair, gray eyes. Oyster Packer, Baltimore. Member ANS/MLA. d. 11/10/05. Bur. Loudon Park Cem., Baltimore.

MEAGHER, JAMES: Pvt., Co. F. Enl. Richmond 7/6/63; present through 12/63; present detailed as Blacksmith 4/1/64; KIA near Washington, D.C., 7/11/64.

MEISTER, CHARLES: Pvt., Co. F. Enl. Co. B, 10th Ga. Inf., 5/18/61. Transf. to Co. F, 1st Md. Cav., 7/10/63; present until captured Brandy Station, Va., 10/11/63; sent to Old Capitol. Took oath, sent to Philadelphia, Pa., 3/28/64.

MENTZER, SAMUEL: Pvt., Co. K. Enl. Breathed's Bty. 6/10/62. Transf. to Co. K (2nd), 1st Va. Cav., 8/14/64. Transf. to Co. K, 1st Md. Cav., 8/64; issued clothing 9/30/64; AWOL 11/1–12/31/64. Transf. to (or enlisted in) 2nd Md. Arty. by 10/31/64. Paroled Salisbury, N.C., 5/1/65.

MERCER, ELIHU WASHINGTON: Pvt., Co. K. b. Md. circa 1844. Res. of Point of Rocks, Md. Enl. Co. K (2nd), 1st Va. Cav., Leesburg, Va., 9/1/62; present until WIA (right thigh) Todd's Tavern, Va., 5/7/64; admitted to Richmond hosp. 5/9/64; furloughed for thirty days 6/6/64; admitted Charlottesville hosp. 6/8/64; furloughed for sixty days 6/12/64; ab. wounded through 8/64. Transf. to Co. K, 1st Md. Cav., 8/64; ab. wounded through 12/64. Captured near Petersburg, Va., 4/10/65; sent to Old Capitol; released 6/3/65. Farmer, age twenty-six, Farmwell Dist., Loudoun Co., Va., 1870 census.

MERCER, SAMUEL B.: Pvt., Co. D. b. circa 1845. Res. Unionville, Frederick Co., Md. Enl. Winchester 9/20/62; present 11–12/62, 7–12/63, and 4/1/64; WIA (right side and liver) and captured Pollard's Farm, Va., 5/27/64; sent to Stanton hosp., Washington, D.C.; DOW and "peritonitis" 6/11/64; no effects. Age nineteen. Bur. Dorsey Cem., Unionville, Md.

MERRICK, GEORGE CLARENCE: 1st Lt., Co. A, Davis's Bn., and Cos. E and G, 1st Md. Cav. b. 1839. Gd. Georgetown U. 1857. Res. Upper Marlboro, Md. Enl. as Pvt., Co. E, 1st Md. Cav., Richmond, 12/19/62, age twenty-three; presence or ab. not stated 1–2/63; promoted 1st Lt. Co. G. on rolls 7–8/63; later promoted Capt., Co. M, 23rd Va. Cav; present as 2nd Lt. 1/1–10/31/65. NFR. Judge, Prince George's Co., Md. d. 1915. Bur. Mt. Carmel Catholic Ch. Cem., Prince George's Co., Md.

MERRITT, SAMUEL: Pvt., Co. K. b. Frederick Co., Md., circa 1817. Seaman. Enl. Co. E, 1st Md.

Inf., 5/22/61; discharged 9/28/62. Enl. Co. K, 1st Md. Cav., Richmond, 5/20/62 (so on rolls); present until detailed as Nurse in Div. Hosp. 3–4/63; present until ab. detailed in Richmond 10/7/63; ab. sick with rheumatism in Gordonsville, Va., hosp. 10/8/63; transf. to Richmond hosp. with "phlebitis" 10/10/63; RTD 10/27/63; present through 8/64. Age fortysix, 5'8", florid complexion, auburn hair, blue eyes. Discharged at end of enlistment, 12/4/64. NFR.

MERRYMAN, JOSEPH R.: Pvt., Co. D. b. circa 1842. Res. Baltimore Co. Enl. New Market, Va., 2/1/63. Captured near Upperville, Va., 5/20/63; sent to Ft. McHenry; exchanged 5/29/63. Present 7–12/63; horse killed Gettysburg, Pa., 7/3/63, paid $550; ab. on detached service Richmond 4/1/64; ab. on furlough for another horse for twenty days to Hardy Co., W.Va., 4/9/64; WIA (left arm requiring exsection of left humerus) Hagerstown, Md., 7/5/64. Captured Sharpsburg, Md., 7/19/64; sent to West Buildings hosp., Baltimore; transf. to Ft. Monroe; exchanged 9/19/64, admitted to Richmond hosp. same day; furloughed to Trevilian, Va., for sixty days 10/18/64; admitted Richmond hosp., resection of left shoulder done 11/18/64; retired to Invalid Corps 1/4/65; admitted Richmond hosp. with "heamorrhage of lungs" 2/23/65. Captured in Richmond hosp. 4/3/65; sent to Newport News, Va.; released 7/18/65. 6', light complexion, dark hair, blue eyes. Destination Baltimore Co., Md. d. 1/16/66, age twenty-two. Bur. Vauxhall Cem., Baltimore Co., Md.

MERRYMAN, RICHARD S.: Pvt., Co. A. b. circa 1840. Res. of Md. Enl. Co. G, 7th Va. Cav., 9/25/62. Transf. to Co. A, 1st Md. Cav., 5/3/64. Took part in capture of Generals Crook and Kelly 2/21/65. Paroled Charles Town, W.Va., 5/15/65. Age twenty-four, 5'10", light complexion, black hair, hazel eyes. Postwar resident of Baltimore.

MESSICK, HIRAM ROSS: Pvt., Co. G. Served in Co. G, 2nd Md. Inf. Enl. Co. G, 1st Md. Cav., date and place unknown; paid 10/21/62. Captured Williamsport, Md., 7/14/63; sent to Pt. Lookout; transf. to Ft. Del.; took oath, released 4/2/64. 5'8", dark complexion, light hair, gray eyes. Res. of Teaford, Del.

METTAM, HENRY CLAY: Pvt., Co. E. b. Md. 10/2/43. Res. of Pikesville, Md. Enl. Richmond 1/2/63; presence or ab. not stated 1–2/63; horse abandoned 4/23/63, paid $230; presence or ab. not stated 7–8/63; ab. sick in Staunton, Va., hosp. 9–10/63; present 11–12/63 and 4/1/64. Captured Moorefield, W.Va., 8/7/64; sent to Wheeling. 5'9", dark complexion, brown hair, blue eyes. Clerk. Transf. to Camp Chase and Pt. Lookout;

exchanged 3/27/65. Ab. on leave to Md. to get a horse when war ended. Member ANS/MLA. Res. of Baltimore. d. 10/3/25. Bur. Loudon Park Cem., Baltimore.

METTEE, CHARLES H.: Pvt., Co. F. b. circa 1846. Res. of Baltimore. Served in 1st Md. Arty. Enl. Co. F, 1st Md. Cav., Richmond, 7/14/63; present through 10/63; present (in Brigade guard house) 12/31/63; present 4/1/64. Transf. to 3rd Md. Arty. 8/31/64; present 10–12/64; des. 2/22/65. NFR. Member ANS/MLA. d. 6/21/16, age seventy. Bur. Loudon Park Cem., Baltimore.

MEWSHAW, FRANK: Pvt., Co. unknown, Davis's Bn. Res. of East River Landing, Anne Arundel Co., Md. On postwar roster.

MICHAELS, HUGH: Pvt., Co. G. Enl. Co. A, Davis's Bn. New Market, Va., 8/8/63. Captured, date and place unknown. Transf. to Co. M, 23rd Va. Cav., while POW. Exchanged POW, Camp Lee, Richmond, 2/29/65, as member Co. G, 1st Md. Cav. NFR.

MIDDLETON, DE KALB: Pvt., Co. A, Davis's Bn. b. circa 1836. Captured near Harrisonburg, Va., 12/19/63; sent to Wheeling. Age twenty-seven, 5'8", dark complexion, dark hair, gray eyes. Res. Chesterfield Co., S.C. Transf. to Ft. Del.; exchanged 10/31/64. Transf. to Co. M, 23rd Va. Cav. Paroled Winchester 4/17/65.

MILES, GEORGE T.: Pvt., Co. D. b. 9/4/39. Res. of Frederick, Md. Enl. Co. A, 1st Md. Inf., 7/25/61; discharged 8/11/62. Enl. Co. D, 1st Md. Cav., Winchester, 9/20/62; present 11–12/62. Captured Strasburg, Va., 8/5/63; sent to Wheeling. 5'4", light complexion, light hair, blue eyes. Tailor. Transf. to Camp Chase; exchanged 4/1/63. Present 7–12/63 and 4/1/64. Captured Pollard's Farm, Va., 5/27/64; sent to Pt. Lookout; exchanged 3/16/65; ab. sick in Charlottesville hosp. 4/9–19/65. Paroled Winchester 4/24/65. Res. of Reading, Pa. d. 9/1/6? (tombstone eroded). Bur. Mt. Olivet Cem., Frederick, Md.

MILES, ROBERT: Pvt., Co. C. On postwar roster.

MILES, W.: Pvt., Co. C. Shot in head, killed, Fairmont, W.Va., 4/29/63.

MILLER, CHARLES: Pvt., Co. A, Davis's Bn. Enl. Front Royal, Va., 6/5/64; KIA Stephenson's Depot, Va., 9/64. NFR.

MILLER, GEORGE R.: Pvt., Co. A, Davis's Bn. On postwar roster.

MILLER, WILLIAM H.: Pvt., Co. A. b. 2/5/43. Res. of Clarksville, Howard Co., Md. Enl. Co. B, 1st Md. Cav., 5/21/61; discharged 8/11/62. Enl. Co. A, 1st Md. Cav., Sharpsburg, Md., 7/1/64; present detailed as Blacksmith through 8/31/64; present 11–12/64. NFR. d. 11/17/02. Bur. St. Louis Cem., Clarksville, Md.

MILLS, ROBERT M.: Pvt., Co. B; present sick 11/62. NFR.

MILNE, JOHN S.: Pvt., Co. F. Enl. Richmond 7/1/63; des. to the enemy near Fredericksburg, Va., 8/21/63; sent to Old Capitol. Took oath, sent to Philadelphia, Pa., 9/28/63. 5'11", light complexion, brown hair, hazel eyes. Res. of Philadelphia.

MILSTEAD, JOSEPH H.: Pvt., Co. B.; not on muster rolls. d. Washington, D.C., 6/1/24. Bur. Arlington Natl. Cem., Va.

MINNIHAN, THOMAS: Pvt., Co. F. Enl. Richmond 7/6/63; present through 12/63 and 4/1/64. Captured Moorefield, W.Va., 8/7/64; on rolls through 8/31/64. NFR. (May have been KIA.)

MITCHELL, JAMES: Pvt., Co. K; issued clothing La Grange, Ga., hosp. 6/29/64. NFR. Probably a member of Co. K, 1st Mo. Cav.

MITCHELL, JAMES M.: Pvt., Co. F and E. b. circa 1842. Res. Point of Rocks, Md. Enl. Co. B, 1st Md. Inf., 5/21/61; discharged 8/17/62. Served in Co. F, 12th Va. Cav. Enl. Co. F, 1st Md. Cav., Richmond, 7/1/63; AWOL 8/20–31/63; in arrest Richmond 9–10/63; ab. sick in Richmond hospital with rheumatism 9/7/63 and typhoid fever 9/14–28/63; returned to Castle Thunder prison; ab. sick in hosp. 11–12/63; ab. on horse detail 3/64; present detailed as Teamster 4/1/64. Transf. to Co. E 4/29/64; ab. sick with ulcer on right leg in Richmond hosp. 3/18/64–3/6/65. NFR. d. Baltimore 1/26/11, age sixty-nine. Bur. Loudon Park Cem., Baltimore.

MITCHELL, JAMES W.: Pvt., Co. F. b. circa 1841. Enl. Co. F, 12th Va. Cav., 5/10/62. Enl. Co. F, 1st Md. Cav., without proper authority and ordered back 12/62. Trans. Co. F, 2nd Md. Cav., 4/29/64; WIA (left side) date and place unknown; issued clothing 7/64; ab. sick with ulcer on left leg in Richmond hosp. 3/6/65; furloughed for sixty days 3/18/65. Paroled Richmond 4/65. Age twenty-four, 5'6", dark complexion, dark hair, dark eyes. Shoemaker. Res. of Baltimore. d. Baltimore 1/26/19. Bur. Loudon Park Cem., Baltimore.

MITCHELL, JOSEPH SHIPP: Pvt., Co. D. b. 1841. Enl. Bowen's Co., 7th Va. Cav., 6/18/61; des. 11/14/61. Enl. Co. I, 12th Va. Cav., 4/15/62. Enl. Co. D, 1st Md. Cav., without proper authority; ordered back 12/62. Captured Clarke Co., Va., 6/7/63; sent to Ft. McHenry; exchanged 6/26/63; AWOL 10/20/63–4/1/64. NFR. d. 1900. Bur. Sacred Heart Cem., Winchester.

MITCHELL, LEVIN: Pvt., Co. C. Enl. New Market, Va., 2/1/63; present 7–8/63; AWOL and in arrest Luray, Va., 9–10/63; AWOL 11–12/63; dropped as a des. NFR.

MITCHELL, OLIVER: Pvt., Co. C. b. Md. Res. of Dorchester Co., Md. Enl. date and place unknown.

ALBERT W. MOISE

(Confederate Veteran)

Captured Martinsburg, W.Va., 10/15/63; sent to Ft. Del. Took oath, joined U.S. Service 11/15/63, yet released from Ft. Del. 5/11/65. 5'7", ruddy complexion, dark hair, brown eyes.

MITCHELL, ROBERT: 1st Sgt., Co. A, Davis's Bn. Enl. New Market, Va., 10/20/63. Captured Woodstock, Va., 5/64. Transf. to Co. M, 23rd Va. Cav. NFR.

MITCHELL, ROBERT D. S.: 1st Sgt., Co. E and G. b. circa 1843. Enl. as Pvt., Co. E, Richmond, 11/29/62, age nineteen; promoted 4th Cpl. 1/30/63; presence or ab. not stated 1–2/63; transf. to Co. G 8/31/63; promoted 1st Sgt. Captured Shenandoah Co., Va., 5/13/64; sent to Wheeling. Age twenty-one, 5'11", florid complexion, brown eyes, dark hair. Farmer. Res. of Clarke Co., Va. Transf. to Camp Chase; released 5/10/65. 6', light complexion, dark hair, dark eyes. Res. of Md.

MOBBERLEY, J. BRADLEY: Pvt., Co. A. b. New Market, Md., 1848. On postwar roster Co. K (2nd), 1st Va. Cav. Enl. Co. A, 1st Md. Cav., Hanover Junction, Va., 4/15/64; present through 8/31/64; issued clothing 9/30/64; ab. on detail 11–12/64. Paroled Charlotte, N.C., 5/15/65 in Medical Purveying Dept. Took oath Frederick, Md., 8/17/65. M.D., Frederick, Md. d. New Market 7/13/74. Bur. Mt. Olivet Cem., Frederick, Md.

MOISE, ALBERT WELBORNE (photo): Pvt., Co. E. b. Memphis, Tenn., 12/11/46; moved to S.C. and Richmond. Att. Gonzaga Col., Washington, D.C.; Page in U.S. Congress. Enl. Richmond 1/12/63; presence or ab. not stated 1–2/63. Transf. to Co. B, 3rd Bn. Ga. Sharpshooters, as Pvt., 8/2/63. Promoted 2nd Lt., Co. H, 24th Ga. Inf., 8/63; present Knoxville, Tenn.; WIA Wilderness 5/64 while carrying the colors of his regiment; promoted 1st Lt. 12/1/64; surrendered Appomattox CH, Va., 4/9/65 commanding Co. D and H, 24th Ga. Inf. Gd. Gonzaga Col. Lawyer in Richmond, Kansas City and St. Louis, Mo. Wholesale Grocer. Member St.

Louis Camp, CV. d. St. Louis 12/1/20.

MONAHAN, JAMES J.: Sgt., Co. A, Davis's Bn. b. circa 1836. Res. of Carroll Co., Md. Enl. 1st Md. Arty. 8/5/61; present through 12/61. NFR. Enl. Md. 6/25/63; ab. sick 10/31/64. Transf. to Co. M, 23rd Va. Cav. NFR. Member ANS/MLA. Entered Old Soldiers' Home, Pikesville, Md., from Baltimore 6/5/06, age seventy. Painter. d. there 3/2/23. Bur. St. Charles Cem., Pikesville, Md.

MONK, CHRISTOPHER: Pvt., Co. E. On postwar roster; also claimed service in Co. E, 1st Md. Inf. Member ANS/MLA. Res. of Baltimore. d. Old Soldiers' Home, Pikesville, Md., by 1894.

MONROE, ROBERT: Pvt., Co. C. Enl. date and place unknown. Captured York, Pa., 7/21/64; des. from Co. B, 11th Vermont Heavy Arty; sent to Ft. Del.; sent to Regiment for trial 1/19/65. NFR.

MONTEREY, ANDREW: Pvt., Co. F. Enl. Richmond 7/31/63; present through 9/63; des. from outpost on Rappahannock River 10/29/63. NFR.

MONTIGNEY, HENRY: Pvt., Co. F. Enl. date and place unknown. Captured near Washington, D.C., 10/27/63; sent to Old Capitol; took oath, released 3/15/64. 5'5½", dark complexion, black hair, gray eyes. Res. New Orleans, La.

MOOG, JOHN J.: Pvt., Co. B. On postwar roster.

MOONEY, JOHN B.: Pvt., Co. A. Res. Harford Co. or Baltimore. Enl. Wise (Va.) Arty., Harpers Ferry, W.Va., 5/18/61. Transf. to Co. A, 1st Md. Cav., 6/5/62. Joined Staunton, Va., 6/15/62; present 7–12/63 and 4/1/64; ab. term of service expired, no discharge; on rolls 8/31–12/31/64. Paroled Winchester 5/29/65. Age twenty-one, 5'10½", florid complexion, light hair, gray eyes. Destination Shenandoah Co., Va.

MOORE, W. C.: Pvt., Co. C; not on muster rolls. Bur. Stonewall Cem., Winchester.

MORAN, EDWARD: Pvt., Co. C, Davis's Bn. NFR.

MORAN, WILLIAM: Pvt., Co. C, Davis's Bn. NFR.

MORGAN, BENJAMIN HAYDEN: 1st Lt., Co. K. b. St. Mary's Co., Md., circa 1840. Gd. Georgetown U. 1861. Res. Chaptico, St. Mary's Co. Enl. Co. C, 1st Md. Inf., 5/17/61; discharged 6/7/62. Enl. as Pvt., Co. K (2nd), 1st Va. Cav., Richmond, 6/7/62. Captured 8/22/62; sent to Old Capitol; exchanged. Present until detailed with Mosby 1/18/63; present through 12/63; elected 2nd Cpl; present through 8/64. Transf. to Co. K, 1st Md. Cav.; discharged at end of enlistment, 11/7/64. Paroled as 1st Lt., Lewisburg, W.Va., 4/26/65. Age twenty-five, 5'9", fair complexion, brown hair, hazel eyes. Carpenter. Moved to Urbanna, Va., 1865. Member ANS/MLA. Moved to Baltimore; d. there 1/8/95.

MORGAN, CHARLES H.: Pvt., Co. C, Davis's Bn.

NFR.

MORRIS, EDWIN T.: Pvt., Co. E. Enl. Hanover Junction, Va., 3/9/64; presence or ab. not stated 4/1/64. Captured Pollard's Farm, Va., 5/27/64; sent to Pt. Lookout. d. of disease there 8/9/64. Bur. Confederate Cem., Pt. Lookout, Md.

MORRIS, LEWIS: Pvt., Co. E. On postwar roster and O'Farrell's Bn. Va. Cav.

MORRIS, WILLIAM: Pvt., Co. E. Captured Pollard's Farm, Va., 5/27/64; on casualty list. d. Pt. Lookout, date unknown. Name deleted from monument at Pt. Lookout Cem.; his body may have been removed after the war.

MORTON, THOMAS: Pvt., Co. unknown. Enl. as 2nd Cpl., Co. B, 39th Bn. Va. Cav., Charlottesville, 8/18/62. Transf. to Md. Line 3/31/64. NFR.

MULL, JAMES M.: Pvt., Co. unknown. b. 12/28/44. Res. Frederick, Md. On postwar roster. Also served in Lucas's 15th S. C. Heavy Arty. d. 3/3/13. Bur. Mt. Olivet Cem., Frederick, Md.

MULLIN, CORNELIUS SAXTON: Pvt., Co. E. b. Baltimore 11/14/33. Res. of Howard Co., Md. Enl. Richmond 10/18/62, age nineteen (so on rolls); presence or ab. not stated 1–1/63; horse abandoned 5/15/63. Captured Front Royal, Va., 5/16/63; sent to Ft. McHenry; transf. to Ft. Monroe; exchanged 5/26/63. Paid $230 for horse; present 7–8/63; ab. on horse detail 9/10/63; present 11–12/63; ab. on horse detail for seventeen days 3/28/64; present 7–8/64; AWOL 12/8–31/64. Captured Charles Co., Md., 3/25/65; sent to Ft. McHenry; released 5/6/65. Res. of Baltimore. Member ANS/MLA, 1907. Res. of Chicago, Ill. Entered Old Soldiers' Home, Pikesville, Md., from Baltimore 2/5/08. Painter. d. there 4/19/28. Bur. Loudon Park Cem., Baltimore.

MURDOCH, AUGUSTUS: Pvt., Co. A. b. circa 1842. Res. of Urbana, Md. Enl. Urbana 9/15/62; WIA (shoulder) Greenland Gap, W.Va., 4/25/63; present through 12/63 and 4/1/64. Captured Montgomery Co., Md., 7/13/64; sent to Old Capitol; transf. to Elmira; exchanged 11/16/64. Paroled Mechanicsville, Va., 5/15/65. Took oath Richmond 6/28/65. d. Richmond 2/24/20, in 78th year. Bur. Riverview Cem., Richmond.

MURRAY, EDWARD C.: Pvt., Co. E. b. Baltimore circa 1833. Machinist, age twenty-seven. 1st Dist. St. Mary's Co., Md., per 1860 census. Enl. Co. C. (Deas Md. Arty.), 19th Bn. Va. Heavy Arty., 12/18/61. Transf. to Co. E, 1st Md. Cav., 12/17/62; presence or ab. not stated 1–2/63 and 7–8/63; ab. sick in Richmond hosp. 9–10/63; ab. detailed as Clerk in Adj.'s Office, Camp Lee, Richmond, 12/1/63–3/65. Paroled Ashland, Va., 4/28/65. Took oath Baltimore 8/2/65. Accountant, Baltimore. Member ANS/MLA. d. 9/20/92, age

fifty-two. Bur. Loudon Park Cem., Baltimore.
MURRAY, JOHN ALEXANDER: Pvt., Co. B. b.
circa 1832. Res. of Talbot Co., Md. On postwar
roster. d. Baltimore 9/29/01, age sixty-nine.
MURRAY, STERLING: Pvt., Co. K. b. Md.
10/11/33. Res. of Baltimore. Enl. Co. C, 1st Md.
Inf., 5/17/61; discharged 5/23/62. Enl. Stuart
Horse Arty. 6/25/62. Captured Westminster, Md.,
6/30/63; sent to Ft. Del. Transf. to Pt. Lookout;
exchanged 11/1/64. Transf. to Co. K, 1st Md.
Cav., 1/6/65. Paroled Winchester 4/22/65. Judge,
Orphan's Court, Baltimore. Member ANS/MLA
and Henry Hatcher Camp, CV, Leesburg, Va. d.
Leesburg 10/24/11. Bur. Union Cem., Leesburg.
MURRAY, W. A.: Pvt., Co. B. Captured 12/20/62.
NFR.
MYERS, CHARLES THOMAS: Pvt., Co. D. b.
circa 1846. Res. Frederick Co., Md. Enl. Boons-
boro, Md., 6/15/63. Captured Monterey Springs,
Pa., 7/4/63. Escaped; present 7–12/63 and 4/1/64.
Captured Moorefield, W.Va., 8/7/64; sent to
Wheeling. Age eighteen, 5'8½", dark complex-
ion, blue eyes, brown hair. Farmer. Transf. to
Camp Chase and Pt. Lookout; exchanged 3/27/65.
Paroled Glen Allen, Va., 4/28/65. Took oath Fred-
erick, Md., 7/10/65. Farmer and Businessman,
Jeannette, Pa., 1913.
MYERS, CLINTON: Pvt., Co. C. Res. of Frederick
Co., Md. KIA Bridgeport, W.Va., 4/63.
MYERS, P.: Pvt., Co. F. d. of "chronic diarrhoea" in
Danville, Va., hosp. 2/13/65. Probably bur.
Confederate Cem., Danville.
MYERS, THOMAS S.: Pvt., Co. D. Res. Frederick
Co., Md.; not on muster rolls. Captured, date and
place unknown. d. 1/16/63. Bur. Philadelphia, Pa.,
Natl. Cem.
NAYLOR, C.: Pvt., Co. B. Res. Prince George's
Co., Md. On postwar roster.
NAYLOR, J. M.: Pvt., Co. B. On postwar roster.
NAYLOR, N. J.: Pvt., Co. F. Enl. date and place
unknown; WIA (left leg) and captured Gettysburg,
Pa., 7/3/63; sent to General hosp. 7/14/63. NFR.
NAYLOR, THOMAS KREBS: Pvt., Co. B. b.
Prince George's Co., Md., 7/23/42. Res. West-
wood, Prince George's Co., Md. Enl. Charlottes-
ville 9/10/62; WIA Monterey Springs, Pa., 7/4/63;
horse killed, paid $800; ab. wounded in Rich-
mond hosp. 7/28/63–10/31/63; present 11–12/63;
ab. wounded in Richmond hosp. 4/1/64. Captured
Moorefield, W.Va., 8/7/64; sent to Wheeling. 5'9",
fair complexion, brown eyes, black hair. Student.
Transf. to Camp Chase and Pt. Lookout; exchanged 3/27/65. NFR. Member George Emack
Camp, CV, Hyattsville, Md. Farmer. d. Westwood
9/28/29. Bur. Naylor Cem. near Westwood.
NEALE, EDMUND CLARENCE (photo): 3rd Sgt.,

EDMUND
CLARENCE
NEALE

(Georgetown
University)

Co. C. b. Baltimore circa 1838. Gd. Georgetown
U. 1859. Res. of Baltimore. Enl. Co. B, 21st Va.
Inf., 5/23/61; ab. sick 11/21/61. 5'11½", brown
hair, brown eyes. NFR. Enl. as 3rd Sgt., Co. C, 1st
Md. Cav., Richmond, 8/15/62; present 7–12/63,
1/–/64 and 4/1/64; ab. on horse detail to
Winchester for twelve day 5/1/64; WIA (right foot
amputated) Pollard's Farm, Va., 5/27/64; ab.
wounded in Richmond hosp. until retired to
Invalid Corps 11/23/64; detailed as Clerk in
Comm. Dept., Richmond, 12/10/64. Paroled
Danville, Va., 4/28/65. Took oath Richmond
5/24/65; destination Baltimore. d. "Hillalee," St.
Mary's Co., Md., 4/6/75, age thirty-seven.
NEALE, FRANCIS CONSTANTINE "FRANK":
Pvt., Co. D. b. St. Mary's Co., Md., circa 1830.
Gd. Georgetown U. 1854. Gd. U. of Md. Medical
School, M.D., age thirty. Res. St. Mary's Co.,
Md., per 1860 census. Res. of Westminister,
Carroll Co., Md., 1861. Arrested and sent to Old
Capitol 1/28/62 for "helping the South;." released.
Enl. Breathed's Bty., date unknown. Transf. to Co.
D, 1st Md. Cav., Darkesville, Md., 9/25/62; pres-
ent 2/18–12/31/64. Transf. to 1st Md. Arty.
2/19/65. Paroled Lynchburg, Va., 4/13/65. M.D.
and Wine Merchant, N.Y. City, 1870s; d. there
1/7/95, age sixty. Res. of Wash-ington, D.C.
Brother of Henry S. and Wilfred Neale.
NEALE, HENRY S. "HARRY": Pvt., Co. D. b. Md.
circa 1844. Age sixteen, Westminster, Carroll Co.,
Md., per 1860 census. Enl. Breathed's Bty., date
unknown. Transf. to Co. D, 1st Md. Cav., Darkesville, Md., 9/25/62. Captured Muddy Branch,
Md., 10/22/63; exchanged by 1/64. Present
2/28–12/31/64. Transf. to 1st Md. Arty. 2/19/65.
Paroled Lynchburg, Va., 4/16/65. Res. of Balti-
more. Brother of Francis C. and Wilfred Neale.
NEALE, WILFRED "WILLIE": Pvt., Co. C. Gd.
Georgetown U. 1862. Res. of Baltimore. Enl.
Richmond 8/20/62; present 7–12/63; ab. sick with

GEORGE SMITH
NORRIS

*(Daniel D.
Hartzler)*

camp itch in Richmond hosp. 3/19–4/4/64; presence or ab. not stated 7–8/64; ab. sick with camp itch in Richmond hosp. 9/24–25/64; ab. scout for Gen. Lunsford Lomax 11–12/64. Captured Myers Ford, Jefferson Co., W.Va., 2/12/65; sent to Old Capitol; transf. to Elmira; exchanged 3/27/65. Paroled Danville, Va., 4/28/65. Took oath Richmond 5/24/65, destination Baltimore. Wine Merchant, N.Y. City. d. before 1895. Brother of Francis C. and Henry S. Neale.

NELSON, F. RAWLING W.: Pvt., Co. A. Enl. Richmond 5/8/62; WIA near Bull Run, Va., 8/30/62; ab. wounded and sick with debility in Charlottesville hosp. 9/8/62–1/3/63; presence or ab. not stated 7–8/63; present 9–12/63 and 4/1/64. Captured Chester Gap, W.Va., 10/23/64; sent to Old Capitol. Transf. to Elmira; exchanged 3/20/65; ab. sick with "p.p." in Richmond hosp. 2/27/65. NFR.

NELSON, ROBERT: Pvt., Co. G; des. to the Army of the Potomac at Bermuda Hundred, Va., 10/9/64; sent to Old Capitol. Took oath, sent to Baltimore 10/11/64.

NEWKIRK, JOSIAH V.: Pvt., Co. E. b. circa 1846. Res. of Baltimore. Enl. Cockeysville, Md., 7/24/64; present through 8/31/64; issued clothing 9/30/64; WIA (left thigh) and captured Beverly, W.Va., 10/29/64; sent to Wheeling. Age twenty, 5'11", fair complexion, dark hair, blue eyes. Painter. Transf. to Camp Chase; released 6/12/65. Age twenty-one, 5'5¾", dark complexion, dark hair, blue eyes. Res. of Baltimore Co., Md.

NEWMAN, GEORGE: Pvt., Co. C. Res. of Baltimore. Paroled Gordonsville, Va., 5/30/65.

NEWTON, JAMES W.: Sgt., Co. C, Davis's Bn. On postwar roster. Enl. 3rd Md. Arty. Vicksburg, Miss., 4/27/63. Captured Vicksburg 7/4/63. Paroled 7/10/63; AWOL 10/31/63. NFR.

NICHOLAS, WILSON CAREY "BILL": Capt., Co. H. b. N.Y. Naval Yard 9/3/36; moved to Baltimore

as a child. Gd. Oxford Col., Md. B&O RR employee, Reistertown, Md., 1861. Enl Co. G, 1st Md. Inf., 5/22/61; discharged 8/11/62. Appointed 1st Lt., C.S.A.; appointed Capt. and acting I.G. of Md. Line by 6/63; served until 6/64. Capt., Co. E, Davis's Bn., and assigned to 1st Md. Cav. 1864; WIA and captured Rockville, Md., 7/12/64. "Leading the charge of the first squadron, had his horse shot and was himself shot and taken prisoner." Exchanged 10/31/64. Assigned to 1st Md. Cav. 2/65 (promoted Maj. in postwar account.) Paroled Richmond as Capt. 4/18/65 and Charlottesville 5/10/65. Farmer, Owings Mill, Howard Co., Md., and "Attamsco," Caves Valley, Baltimore Co., Md. Member ANS/MLA. d. 12/25/43. Bur. St. Charles Cem., Pikesville, Md.

NICHOLSON, A. S.: Pvt., Co. C, Davis's Bn. On postwar roster.

NOEL, CHARLES EMILE: Pvt., Co. B. Res. of Canada. Enl. Frederick, Md. 7/15/64; ab. sick 11–12/64; WIA (left thigh) 1/65. Admitted Charlottesville hosp. 1/5/65; furloughed for thirty days 1/17/65. Captured in Richmond hosp. 4/3/65; sent to Pt. Lookout; released 5/15/65. Student.

NORRIS, ALEXANDER, JR.: Pvt., Co. C. b. 4/15/39. Res. of Harford Co., Md. Enl. Co. K (2nd), 1st Va. Cav., on postwar roster. Enl. Co. C, 1st Md. Cav., Richmond, 8/13/62. Captured Piedmont, Fauquier Co., Va., 5/16/63; sent to Ft. McHenry; transf. to Ft. Monroe; exchanged 5/19/63; present 7–12/63; ab. sick with camp itch in Richmond hosp. 12/18/63–3/28/64; present through 12/31/64. Paroled Harrisonburg, Va., 5/7/65. 5'8", light complexion, light hair, gray eyes. Res. of Harford Co., Md., 1873. d. 10/21/05. Bur. Cokesbury Meth. Ch. Cem., Abingdon, Md. Brother of George S. Norris.

NORRIS, GEORGE SMITH (photo): 1st Sgt., Co. C. b. 8/28/40. Res. Bel Air, Harford Co., Md. Enl. as Pvt., Richmond, 8/4/62; promoted 1st Cpl; ab. sick near Winchester 11/62; present 7–8/63 as 2nd Sgt; present sick 9–10/63; present 11–12/63, 1–2/64, and 4/1/64. Promoted 1st Sgt. 7/1/64; present until ab. sick with scabies in Charlottesville hosp. 9/30–10/11/64; present through 12/31/64; detailed in Signal Corps. Paroled New Market, Va., 4/20/65. 5'9", dark complexion, dark hair, dark eyes. d. Bel Air, Md. 6/2/12. Bur. St. Mark's Episcopal Ch. Cem., Emmonton, Harford Co., Md. Brother of Alexander Norris Jr.

NORRIS, LEWIS F.: Pvt., Co. E. b. circa 1846. Res. of Baltimore. Enl. Cockeysville, Md., 7/24/64; present through 8/31/64; issued clothing 9/30/64. Captured Beverly, W.Va., 10/29/64; sent to Wheeling. Age nineteen, 5'6", fair complexion, gray eyes, dark hair. Coppersmith. Transf. to

Camp Chase; released 5/11/65. Member Isaac Trimble Camp, CV, Baltimore, 1900.

NORRIS, RICHARD H.: 4th Cpl, Co. D. b. 1/26/42. Res. Libertytown, Frederick Co., Md. Enl. Winchester 9/20/62; present 11–12/62, 7–12/63, and 4/1/64. Captured Smithfield, W.Va., 8/28/64; sent to Wheeling; transf. to Camp Chase and Pt. Lookout; released 6/2/65. d. 3/11/96. Bur. Fairmont Cem., Libertytown, Md.

NORRIS, RICHARD JAMES, JR.: Pvt., Co. unknown. Res. of Baltimore. Enl. Co. G, 7th Va. Cav., 1/15/62. Transf. to Md. Line 8/9/64. NFR. Res. of Baltimore postwar.

OAKES, PATRICK HENRY: Pvt., Co. A, Davis's Bn. Enl. New Market, Va., 8/20/63. Transf. to Co. M, 23rd Va. Cav.; des. 10/31/64. NFR. Also listed as serving in Edelin's Co., Md. Heavy Arty.

OATES, JAMES F.: Pvt., Co. C. Enl. Hagerstown, Md., 6/18/63; present, detailed as Orderly for Maj. Brown 7–12/63; present 4/1/64; horse killed Ashland, Va., 6/1/64, paid $700; horse killed Middletown, Md., 7/7/64, paid $2,300; WIA Clear Spring, Md., 7/29/64; ab. wounded in Harrisonburg hosp. through 8/31/64; ab. wounded until captured Lacey Springs, Va., 12/2/64; sent to Pt. Lookout; exchanged 1/21/65. NFR.

OBENDERFER, JOHN LEONARD: Pvt., Co. D. b. 5/9/46. Res. Frederick, Md. Enl. Winchester 9/20/62; present 11/12/62. Captured near Winchester 5/19/63; sent to Ft. McHenry as "Bushwhacker"; exchanged 5/26/63; WIA Monterey Springs, Pa., 7/4/63; ab. on horse detail 9–10/63. Captured near Winchester 11/20/63; exchanged circa 7/64. Present Camp Lee, Richmond, 8/1/64; ab. on leave 10/16–31/64; ab. on horse detail 11–12/64. NFR. Member ANS/MLA. Entered Old Soldiers' Home, Pikesville, Md., from Baltimore, 1911, age sixty-five. d. 11/27/21. Bur. Mt. Olivet Cem., Frederick, Md.

O'BRIEN, EDWIN HARRISON: Pvt., Co. K. b. Baltimore 5/13/43. Res. of Carroll Co., Md. Enl. Co. D, 1st Md. Inf., 7/31/62; discharged 8/17/62. Enl. Stuart Horse Arty. 6/5/63; WIA Shady Grove Ch., Va., 5/9/64. Transf. to Co. K (2nd), 1st Va. Cav., 8/14/64. Transf. to Co. K, 1st Md. Cav., 8/64; issued clothing 9/30/64; AWOL 11–12/64. Enl. Co. D, 43rd Bn. Va. Cav. (Mosby), date unknown; WIA Lewinsville, Va., 3/12/65. Paroled Fairfax CH, Va., 5/6/65. 5'9", dark complexion, dark hair, hazel eyes. Wholesale Grocer and Lumber Dealer, Alexandria, Va. d. 10/20/29. Bur. Methodist Protestant Cem., Alexandria.

O'BRIEN, JEREMIAH WILLIAM PATRICK: Pvt., Co. K. b. Limerick Co., Ireland, 11/17/44. Arr. U.S. (New Orleans, La.) 1862. Enl. in U.S. Service; des. Enl. Co. K (2nd), 1st Va. Cav., by 5/64;

horse killed, Yellow Tavern, Va., 5/11/64; not on muster rolls. May have transf. to Co. K, 1st Md. Cav., 8/64, but not on muster rolls. Transf. to Capt. H. R. Garden's Palmetto Light Bty. of S.C. Paroled Appomattox CH, Va., 4/9/65. Information from pension application. Res. of Terrell, Tex. 1928. d. Kirbyville, Jasper Co., Tex., 6/27/50.

O'FARRAR, JAMES: Pvt., Co. H. Served in U.S. Army, captured near Dutch Gap, Va., 9/30/64; sent to Salisbury, N.C., prison. Enl. Co. H, 1st Md. Cav., date unknown. Captured Salisbury 4/65; sent to Nashville, Tenn. NFR.

O'LEARY, JEROME "JERRY": Pvt., Co. D. b. circa 1837. Res. of Frederick Co., Md. Enl. Winchester 9/20/62; present 11–12/62. Captured Strasburg, Va., 5/5/63; sent to Wheeling. Age twenty-six, 5'8", florid complexion, hazel eyes, dark hair. Clerk. Transf. to Camp Chase; exchanged 5/26/63. Captured Monterey Springs, Pa., 7/4/63; sent to Ft. McHenry; transf. to Ft. Del. and Pt. Lookout; exchanged 2/65. Present Camp Lee, Richmond, 2/17/65. NFR. Member ANS/MLA. d. Frederick Co., Md., 3/8/84. Bur. St. John's Cem., Frederick Co.

OLIVER, JAMES R.: 1st Lt., Co. K. b. circa 1840. Res. of Charles Co., Md. Enl. as Pvt., Co. K (2nd), 1st Va. Cav., Richmond, 4/20/62; present until captured Hartwood Ch., Va., 2/25/63; sent to Old Capitol; exchanged 2/26/63; present through 2/64; promoted 4th Cpl; present until WIA Meadow Bridge, Va., 5/12/64. Transf. to Co. K, 1st Md. Cav., 8/64; present 8/2–31/64; discharged at end of enlistment, 11/4/64. NFR until paroled Tallahassee, Fla., 5/12/65, as 1st Lt., Co. K, 1st Md. Cav. 5'10", fair complexion, dark hair, gray eyes. Res. of Baltimore 1911.

OLIVER, JOHN H. or D.: Pvt., Co. K. Res. of Md. Enl. Co. K (2nd), 1st Va. Cav., date unknown; present 5/11/64. Transf. to Co. K, 1st Md. Cav. Served as Courier for Gen. Fitzhugh Lee per postwar roster.

O'MALLEY, JAMES: Pvt., Co. A. On postwar roster.

ORMES, NATHAN: Pvt., Co. F. Enl. Richmond 7/13/63; des. near Richmond 7/16/63. NFR.

OTT, GEORGE MICHAEL: Pvt., Co. D. b. circa 1842. Res. Frederick, Md. Enl. Winchester 9/20/62; present 11–12/62, 7–12/63, and 4/1/64. Captured Pollard's Farm, Va., 5/27/64; sent to Pt. Lookout; exchanged 3/16/65. Paroled New Market, Va., 4/19/65. Age twenty-one, 5'8", fair complexion, light hair, gray eyes. Member ANS/MLA, 1904. d. 1912, age seventy-two. Bur. Mt. Olivet Cem., Frederick, Md., no dates.

OWINGS, JOHN HAMMOND: Pvt., Co. K. b. near Columbus, Howard Co., Md., 8/27/43. Res. Ellicott City, Md. Enl. Co. K (2nd), 1st Va. Cav.,

Leesburg, Va., 5/14/61; present until detailed as Courier for Gen. Fitzhugh Lee 5/1/62–4/63; present until captured Cooksville, Md., 6/27/63; sent to Ft. Del.; exchanged 7/31/63. Ab. detailed Gen. Fitzhugh Lee's HQ 2–8/64. Transf. to Co. K, 1st Md. Cav., 8/64; ab. on detail Lee's HQ 11–12/64; served as Ord. Officer on Lee's staff per postwar account. Paroled New Brunswick, Md., 4/10/65. Took oath Baltimore 6/15/65. Farmer near Oakland Mills, Howard County, Md., 1878. Clerk of Court, Howard Co., 1887, 1889, 1896–97. Res. "Hazelwood", Oakland Mills. d. 6/24/09. Bur. Dorsey–Owings–Waters Cem., Elk Horn, Md. (Photograph in Driver 1991)

OWINGS, SAMUEL A.: 2nd Lt., Co. F, Davis's Bn., and Co. I., 1st Md. Cav. b. Baltimore circa 1843. Res. Baltimore Co. Enl. Co. A, 1st Md. Inf., 5/23/61; accidentally wounded (left arm) Point of Rocks, Md. 5/24/61; discharged 8/17/61. Age nineteen, 5'8½", dark complexion, black eyes, black hair. Student. Appointed 2nd Lt. 1/31/61. Enl. date and place unknown. Took oath Nashville, Tenn., 5/9/65. 5'9", fair complexion, dark hair, hazel eyes. Res. Catonsville, Md., circa 1900.

PACA, EDWARD TILGHMAN: Pvt., Co. E. b. circa 1843. Res. Queen Anne's Co., Md. Enl. Richmond 9/29/62, age nineteen; presence or ab. not stated 1–2/63. Captured near Winchester 6/12/63; sent Ft. McHenry. Age twenty, 5'9", dark complexion. Transf. to Ft. Monroe; exchanged 6/26/63; present 7–9/63; WIA (left shoulder) Morton's Ford, Va., 10/11/63; ab. wounded in Richmond hosp. through 12/22/63; present 12/31/63; ab. sick with ulcerated leg in Richmond hosp. 1/26–2/5/64; furloughed to King William Co., Va., for thirty days 2/18/64; present 4/1/64. Captured Pollard's Farm, Va., 5/27/64; sent to Pt. Lookout; exchanged 2/15/65. Present Camp Lee, Richmond, 2/27/65. Paroled, took oath, Danville, Va., 4/65; destination Queen Anne's Co., Md. Member ANS/MLA, 1894. Res. Carmichael's, Queen Anne's Co., Md., d. 1922. (Postwar photograph in *Md. Historical Magazine,* Vol. 89, Winter 1994)

PALMER, ANDREW J.: Pvt., Co. C. b. Va. circa 1834. Enl. Co. C, 55th Va. Inf., 7/18/61. Age twenty-seven, 5'8", dark complexion, black hair, black eyes. Transf. to Co. C, 1st Md. Cav., 4/21/64; ab. on horse detail for twenty days 5/1/64; issued clothing 9/30/64; ab. sick with "Impetigo" in Richmond hosp. 10/4–12/15/64; present 12/31/64. Paroled Ashland, Va., 5/65. Merchant, Baltimore. Member Isaac Trimble Camp, CV, and ANS/MLA, 1904.

PANGLE, WATSON: Pvt., Co. A, Davis's Bn. Enl.

Mt. Jackson, Va., 11/20/63. Transf. to Co. M, 23rd Va. Cav.; AWOL 10/31/64. NFR.

PARKER, GEORGE SAMUEL: Pvt., Co. B. b. 12/10/41. Res. of Fishing Creek, Dorchester Co., Md. Enl. Charlottesville 9/10/62; present 7–12/63; WIA (saber cuts to head; right forefinger shot off) Old Church, Va., 3/3/64; ab. wounded in Richmond hosp. through 3/22/64; sick in camp 4/1/64; furloughed for twenty days. Captured Pollard's Farm, Va., 5/27/64; sent to Pt. Lookout; exchanged 1/21/65. Present Camp Lee, Richmond, 2/65. NFR. Farmer, Orange Co., Va. postwar. Member George Emack Camp, CV, Hyattsville, and ANS/MLA. Res. of Barboursville, Va., 1894. d. 9/24/14. Bur. Graham Cem., Orange Co., Va.

PARKINSON, THOMAS RICHARD: Pvt., Co. unknown, Davis's Bn. Res. of Annapolis, Md. On postwar roster.

PATRICK, CHARLES R.: Pvt., Co. A. b. circa 1840. Res. of Baltimore. Enl. Hanover Junction, Va., 12/1/62; present 9–12/63 and 4/1/64. Captured Moorefield, W.Va., 8/7/64; sent to Wheeling. Age twenty-five, 5'9", fair complexion, black hair, brown eyes. RR Ticket Agent. Res. of Chicago, Ill. Transf. to Camp Chase; took oath, released 3/7/65. Railroadman, Baltimore. Entered Old Soldiers' Home, Pikesville, Md., 6/29/99, age fifty-seven. Left.

PATRICK, JOHN H.: Pvt., Co. A. Enl. Co. H, 17th Va. Inf., 7/5/61. NFR. Enl. Co. B, 39th Bn. Va. Cav., 8/25/62; present 11/62–10/63. Transf. to A, 1st Md. Cav., 4/21/64; present through 8/64; issued clothing 9/30/64. Captured Ninevah, Va., 11/12/64; sent to Pt. Lookout; took oath, released 3/22/65; transportation furnished to Baltimore.

PATRICK, WASHINGTON: Pvt., Co. A. On postwar roster.

PATTEN, JAMES W.: Pvt., Co. F. Enl. Richmond 7/16/63; present through 9/63; ab. sick with pneumonia in Richmond hosp. 10/29/63–1/28/64; present 3/25/64; ab. on sick leave 4/1/64; issued clothing 4/7/64. Captured Loudoun Co., Va., 7/16/64; sent to Elmira; d. there of pneumonia 11/10/64; effects: one hat, one pair of shoes. Bur. Woodlawn Natl. Cem., Elmira, N. Y., grave #815 or #829.

PAYNE, JOSIAH THOMAS: Asst. Surgeon. b. Harford Co., Md., 1839. Gd. U. of Md. Medical School 1862. Also listed as serving in the 11th Bn. Va. Reserves and 4th Va. Reserves. Paroled Staunton, Va., 1865. M.D., Black Horse, Harford Co., and Corbett, Baltimore Co., Md.

PEARRE (see PERRIE)

PEARSON, WALTER H.: Pvt., Co. unknown. Enl. 1st Md. Arty. 6/27/61. Captured Md. 6/11/63; sent to Ft. McHenry as a spy; transf. to Ft. Del. NFR.

On postwar roster.

PEAY, AUGUSTUS: Pvt., Co. A, Davis's Bn. Enl. Richmond 6/20/63; present through 1/1/64. Transf. to Co. M, 23rd Va. Cav.; AWOL 10/31/64. Paroled New Market, Va., 4/19/65, and Ashland, Va., 4/25/65. Age seventeen, 5'6", dark complexion, light hair, gray eyes. Res. of Henrico Co.

PEAY, BENJAMIN: Pvt., Co. A, Davis's Bn. Enl. Richmond 8/15/63. Captured Piedmont, Va., 6/5/64; sent to Camp Morton. Transf. to Co. M, 23rd Va. Cav., while POW. d. of "chronic diarrhoea," Camp Morton, 6/5/65. Bur. Greenlawn Cem., Camp Morton, Ind., grave #1485.

PEAY, ROSSER: Pvt., Co. A, Davis's Bn. Enl. Richmond 9/17/63. Transf. to Co. M, 23rd Va. Cav. Trans. CSN. NFR.

PEDDICORD, BASCOMBE: Pvt., Co. A. b. circa 1847. Res. of Howard Co., Md. Enl. Md. 7/1/64. Captured Moorefield, W.Va., 8/7/64; sent to Wheeling. Age twenty-one, 5'11", dark complexion, dark hair, blue eyes. Clerk. Transf. to Camp Chase and Pt. Lookout; exchanged 3/27/65. Took oath Edwards' Ferry, Md., 4/18/65. Res. of Baltimore. Attended 1899 reunion.

PEELER, MALLARD T.: Pvt., Co. E. b. Montgomery Co., Md. circa 1848. Enl. Richmond 12/19/62, age seventeen; discharged (underage) by order Gen. C. S. Winder's office, 2/6/63. Age fifteen, 5', fair complexion, light hair, hazel eyes. Printer.

PEMEND, B. E.: Pvt., Co. G. Res. of Baltimore. Captured Moorefield, W.Va., 8/7/64. NFR until took oath Baltimore 5/15/65.

PEMBROKE, GEORGE W.: Pvt., Co. A. b. 4/5/44. Res. of Anne Arundel Co., Md. Enl. 2nd Md. Arty. 8/15/61; present 10/31/61. NFR. On postwar roster. M.D. d. Anne Arundel Co. 5/12/01. Bur. St. James Episcopal Ch. Cem., Anne Arundel Co.

PERDUE, JOHN: Pvt., Co. A. Res. of Monkton, Baltimore Co., Md. Enl. 7/15/64 and present Appomattox CH, Va., 4/9/65, per postwar roster. Member ANS/MLA. d. 7/19/96. Bur. St. James Ch. Cem., Monkton.

PEREGOY, LEWIS A.: 1st Sgt., Co. A, Davis's Bn. Enl. Md. 6/25/63; present through 1/1/64. Transf. to Co. M, 23rd Va. Cav. Captured Strasburg, Va., 10/19/64; sent to Pt. Lookout; released 6/16/65. 5'6", dark complexion, black hair, blue eyes. Res. of Baltimore; transportation furnished to Baltimore.

PERKINS, LEVI WROTH: Pvt., Co. B. Res. of Kent Co., Md. Enl. Charlottesville 9/10/62; ab. sick with "Frebris Intermittens" in Charlottesville hosp. 10/8–18/62; present 7–12/63 and 4/1/64; ab. on horse detail to Hardy Co., W.Va., for twenty days 5/1/64; KIA Sandy Springs, Md., 7/64 (or Winchester 9/3/64).

PERNEW, WILLIAM: Pvt., Co. G. Took oath Md. 5/1/65.

PERRIE (PEARRE on tombstone), AUBREY: Pvt., Co. D. b. 1838. Res. of Unionville, Frederick Co., Md. Enl. Winchester 9/20/62; promoted on Gen. Braxton Bragg's staff; on rolls 11–12/62; promoted 1st Lt. and Ord. Officer on Gen. Patrick Cleburne's staff. Paroled Greensboro, N.C., 4/26/65. Took oath Harpers Ferry, W.Va., 7/1/65. Dry Goods Merchant, Baltimore. d. 6/22/15. Bur. St. Thomas Ch. Cem., Garrison, Md. Brother of Oliver H. Perrie. (Photograph in Hartzler 1992)

PERRIE, JAMES WARFIELD: Pvt., Co. B. On postwar roster.

PERRIE, OLIVER HAGGARD: Lt., Co. B. b. 5/18/44. Res. of Prince George's Co., Md. Enl. Co. D, 1st Md. Inf., 6/1/61; discharged 8/11/62. Enl. as 5th Sgt., Co. B, 1st Md. Cav., Charlottesville, 9/20/62. Reportedly promoted on Gen. Braxton Bragg's staff 11–12/62; present 7–12/63; ab. on leave for twenty days 3/20/64; ab. in Charlottesville hosp. 8/31/64 and 11–12/64; promoted Lt; ab. sick with gonorrhoea in Charlottesville hosp. 2/28–3/30/65. NFR. Merchant, Baltimore; Lumber Dealer, Norfolk, Va. Member George Emack Camp, CV, Hyattsville, Md., 1903. Res. of Norfolk, Va. Member Pickett–Buchanan Camp, CV, Norfolk 1926. d. Old Soldiers' Home, Pikesville, Md., 6/3/32, age eighty-eight. Bur. Elmwood Cem., Norfolk, Va. Brother of Aubrey Perrie. May have changed name to Perry in postwar.

PERRIE, THOMAS H.: Pvt., Co. B. b. 3/12/39. Res. of Prince George's Co., Md. Enl. Charlottesville 9/10/62; detailed as Wagoner 9/16–12/31/62; ab. sick with scabies in Harrisonburg, Va., hosp. 4/13/63. Captured Monterey Springs, Pa., 7/4/63; sent to Ft. McHenry; transf. to Ft. Del. and Pt. Lookout; took oath, released 12/31/64. Member ANS/MLA. d. 1/23/92. Bur. St. Paul's Episcopal Ch. Cem., Prince George's Co., Md.

PERVIL(LE), LEIGHTON: Pvt., Co. F. Enl. Richmond 7/16/63; present through 10/31/63; AWOL 11/29–12/31/63; dropped as des. NFR.

PERVILLE, NATHAN: Pvt., Co. F. On postwar roster.

PHILLIPS, B. S.: Pvt., Co. C, Davis's Bn. Captured Strasburg, Va., 9/23/64; sent to Pt. Lookout; exchanged 3/17/65. NFR.

PHILLIPS, JOHN G.: Capt., Co. C, Davis's Bn. NFR. Enl. Buffalo Gap, W.Va., 8/1/63. Res. Cambridge, Dorchester Co., Md. NFR.

PICKELL, JOHN H.: Pvt., Co. G. Enl. Barry's Co., Md. Vols., 1861. Reenl. Co. A, 1st Md. Inf.; paid $50 bounty at Richmond 10/31/62; in Richmond hosp. 12/25/62. NFR. Enl. Co. G, 1st Md. Cav., date unknown; ab. sick with typhoid fever in Charlottesville hosp. 10/26/63; d. there 11/28/63. Bur. Confederate Cem., U. of Va., Charlottesville; removed to Loudon Park Cem., Baltimore, 1874.

PICKLE, J. L.: Pvt., Co. K. On postwar rosters of Co. K (2nd), 1st Va. Cav., and Co. K, 1st Md. Cav.

PIERCE, ALFRED A.: Pvt., Co. A. b. circa 1834. Res. of Baltimore. Enl. Co. E, 1st Md. Inf., 5/22/61; paid 5/8/62. NFR. Reenl. Co. A, 1st Md. Cav., Richmond, 7/16/63; present through 12/63 and 4/1/64. Captured Moorefield, W.Va., 8/7/64; sent to Wheeling. Age thirty, 5'11", dark complexion, dark hair, dark eyes. Printer. Transf. to Camp Chase and Pt. Lookout; exchanged 3/27/65. Paroled Staunton, Va., 5/12/65, age thirty-one. Took oath Winchester 5/15/65; destination Baltimore.

PINHORN, F.: Pvt., Co. B; des. to the enemy near Richmond 11/24/64; sent to Washington, D.C. Took oath 11/27/64; sent to N.Y. City.

PITT, WILLIAM: Pvt., Co. F. Enl. Richmond 7/8/63; present through 8/31/63; ab. in arrest Richmond 9–10/63; ab. undergoing sentence of CM, Richmond, 11–12/63 and 4/1–12/31/64. NFR.

PITTS, FREDERICK L.: Pvt., Co. K. b. Berlin, Md. circa 1843. Enl. Co. H, 1st Md. Inf., 6/11/61; discharged 6/18/62. Age nineteen, 5'8", fair complexion, light hair, light eyes. Student. Enl. Co. K (2nd), 1st Va. Cav., 5/25/62; present until WIA (shoulder) Cold Harbor, Va., 5/31/64; ab. wounded in Richmond hosp. 6/10–25/64; AWOL 7/20–8/31/64. Transf. to Co. K, 1st Md. Cav., 8/64; discharged at end of enlistment 12/10/64. Captured, escaped from Ft. McHenry, per postwar roster. Res. of Philadelphia, Pa., 1910.

PITTS, JOHN WILLIAM: Pvt., Co. K. b. Berlin, Worcester Co., Md., 11/5/42. Gd. Buckingham Acad., Md. Att. U. Va. 1861. Enl. Co. D, 1st Va. Inf., 5/13/61; promoted Cpl; present through 2/62. NFR. Enl. Co. K (2nd), 1st Va. Cav., Richmond, 5/25/62; present until captured Westminister, Md., 6/30/63; sent to Ft. Del.; exchanged 7/8/63. Present through 2/64; AWOL 7/20–8/31/64. Transf. to Co. K, 1st Md. Cav., 8/64; appointed Asst. Surgeon 8/64; served in Richmond hospitals to the end of the war. Gd. U. of Pa. Medical School 1867. M.D. in Berlin for forty years; Member of Co. School Board; first Mayor of Berlin; Capt. of Bond Light Horse, Md. National Guard; served in Md. legislature; banker; organized and President of Wicomico and Pocomoke RR. d. Berlin 12/27/10. (Photograph in Angus 1923)

PITTS, WILLIAM: Pvt., Co. K. Served in Lucas's 15th Bn. S.C. Arty. Enl. Co. K (2nd), 1st Va. Cav.,

Fredericksburg, Va., 11/1/62; present until captured Westminister, Md., 6/30/63; sent to Ft. McHenry; transf. to Ft. Del.; escaped 10/11/63; RTD; present through 2/64; AWOL 7/10–8/31/64. Transf. to Co. K, 1st Md. Cav., 8/64; AWOL 11–12/64. NFR.

PLACIDE, ROBERT E.: Pvt., Co. D. Res. of Baltimore. Enl. Lacey Springs, Va., 4/1/63. Captured Smithsburg, Md., 7/4/63; sent to Ft. Del.; transf. to Ft. Monroe; exchanged 12/28/63. Present 4/1/64. Captured Pollard's Farm, Va., 5/27/64; sent to Pt. Lookout; exchanged 3/15/65. Paroled, took oath, Harpers Ferry, W.Va., 4/20/65; destination Philadelphia.

PLUMMER, JOHN BOYLE: Pvt., Co. K. Res. Elk Landing, Anne Arundel Co., Md. Enl. Co. K (2nd), 1st Va. Cav., Richmond, 8/1/63, by transfer from unknown unit; present through 8/64. Transf. to Co. K, 1st Md. Cav., 8/64. Captured Strasburg, Va., 9/23/64; sent to Pt. Lookout; exchanged 2/15/65; present Camp Lee, Richmond, 2/20–27/65. NFR.

POACHAHUTAS, OSEOLA: Pvt., Co. C, Davis's Bn. Enl. Buffalo Gap, W.Va., 8/1/63. NFR.

POLK, SAMUEL: Pvt., Co. A. b. circa 1841. Res. Somerset Co., Md. Served in Co. F, 2nd Md. Inf., Enl. Hanover Junction, Va., 4/1/64; WIA (fractured left thigh) Pollard's Farm, Va., 5/27/64; ab. wounded in Richmond hosp. until furloughed to Columbia, Va., for thirty days 7/8/64; detailed in Auditor's Office, Richmond, 8/23/64 for sixty days; issued clothing 9/5/64. Took oath Baltimore 5/11/65. d. Somerset Co., Md., 9/6/66, age twenty-five. Bur. Manokin Presb. Ch. Cem., Princess Anne, Md.

POLK, TRUSTEN: Pvt., Co. A. b. Sussex Co., Del., 8/4/40; moved to Carroll Co., Md., 1852. Res. Sykesville, Carroll Co., Md. Enl. Co. K, 12th Va. Cav., 8/12/62. Transf. to Co. A, 1st Md. Cav., Lacey Springs, Va., 4/12/63; WIA Brandy Station, Va., 6/9/63; sick in camp 8/31/63; present 9–12/63 and 4/1/64. Captured Moorefield, W.Va., 8/7/64; sent to Wheeling. Age twenty-four, 5'11", dark complexion, gray eyes, dark hair. Farmer. Transf. to Camp Chase; exchanged 3/27/65. Paroled Winchester 4/20/65. Took oath Edwards' Ferry, Md., 5/16/65. Farmer, Carroll Co.; Member Md. legislature 1871; Deputy Register of Deeds, Howard Co., 1873–74; moved to Baltimore 1893; Gauger in U.S. Internal Revenue Service. Member ANS/MLA. d. Baltimore 7/12/02. Bur. Springfield Presb. Ch. Cem., Sykesville.

POLLITT, ALEXANDER A.: 4th Cpl., Co. E. b. circa 1838. Res. Princess Anne, Somerset Co., Md. Enl. as Pvt., Richmond, 11/10/62, age twenty-four; presence or ab. not stated 1–2/63; present

11–12/63 and 4/1/64; promoted 4th Cpl; ab. sick with "diarrhoea" Richmond hosp. 5/1–14/64 and 6/30–7/1/64; present through 12/31/64. Took oath Baltimore 5/11/65.

POOLE, THEODORE W.: Pvt., Co. C. b. circa 1843. Res. of Baltimore. Enl. Lacey Springs, Va., 4/1/63; present 7–12/63 and 4/1/64. Captured Moorefield, W.Va., 8/7/64; sent to Wheeling. Age twenty-one, 5'8", fair complexion, blue eyes, light hair. Druggist. Transf. to Camp Chase and Pt. Lookout; exchanged 3/27/65. Present Camp Lee, Richmond, 3/28/65. NFR.

POOLE, WILLIAM: Pvt., Co. C. Enl. Co. C, 19th Bn. Va. Arty., Richmond, 6/20/62; AWOL 10/31/62. NFR. On postwar roster. d. circa 2/25/15.

POOLE, WILLIAM C.: Sgt., Co. C. b. 1846. Enl. Co. C (2nd) 19th Bn. Va. Arty., Richmond, 6/20/62. Transf. to Co. C, 1st Md. Cav.; Enl. as Sgt., Richmond, 8/4/62; reduced to Pvt. 8/21/63; present through 9/63; ab. on horse detail 10/29–31/63; present through 12/63 and 4/1–8/3/64; ab. as scout for Gen. Lunsford Lomax 11/1–12/31/64; ab. sick with scabies in Richmond hosp. 3/23–29/65. Took oath Norfolk, Va., 6/15/65; destination N.C. Former res. of Elizabeth City, N.C. d. 1929. Bur. Springhill Cem., Easton, Md.

POOLE, WILLIAM H.: Pvt., Co. F. b. 4/13/42. Enl. Hanover Junction, Va., 2/17/64; present 4/1/64; des. 5/24/64 on rolls through 12/31/64. NFR. d. 7/17/99. Bur. Mt. Olivet Cem., Frederick, Md.

POOLE, WILLIAM HENRY: Pvt., Co. D. b. Frederick, Md., 2/14/43. Enl. Co. A, 1st Md. Inf., 7/25/61; WIA (lower left rib) Gaines' Mill, Va., 6/27/62; discharged 8/17/62. Enl. Co. D, 1st Md. Cav., Lacey Springs, Va., 4/1/63. Captured Monterey Springs, Pa., 7/4/63, horse killed; sent to Ft. McHenry; transf. to Ft. Del. and Pt. Lookout; exchanged 12/28/63. Present 4/1/64; present 4/1/64; ab. on horse detail for seventeen days to Winchester 4/9/64; WIA (left hand) Hagerstown, Md., 7/5/64; present through 12/31/64; present Appomattox CH, Va.; escaped. Paroled Mt. Jackson, Va., 4/23/65. 5'8", fair complexion, light hair, blue eyes. Took oath Harpers Ferry, W.Va., 5/23/65. "Served in 59 battles and skirmishes." Returned to Frederick, Md.; moved to Baltimore 1865. Tobacconist fifteen years; Merchant; Clerk of Lexington Market, Baltimore, 1880–88. Member, ANS/MLA. Supt., Old Soldiers' Home, Pikesville, Md., 1888–1900; d. there 12/6/04. Bur. Loudon Park Cem., Baltimore.

POPE, WILLIAM THOMAS: Pvt., Co. D, Davis's Bn. Res. Princeland, Anne Arundel Co., Md. On postwar roster.

PORTER, CHARLES EUGENE: Pvt., Co. unknown. b. Dover, Del., 8/10/42. Enl. CSN 5/24/61; discharged 4/62. Enl. 1st Md. Cav. 5/62. Transf. to Fluvanna Va. Arty. 9/62. Transf. to CSN 8/63. Paroled Greensboro, N.C., 4/26/65. Farmer and School Principal, Cumberland Co., Va.; Auditor, C&O RR, Lynchburg, Va. d. 3/3/08. Bur. Greenwood Cem., Richmond. Postwar account is the only record of service in 1st Md. Cav.

PORTER, JOHN J.: Pvt., Co. A. Res. of Rockville, Montgomery Co., Md. Enl. Md. 7/1/64; present through 12/31/64; ab. sick with debility in Richmond hosp. 1/31–2/5/65. Paroled Ashland, Va., 4/21/65. Also listed as having served in Co. F, 43rd Bn. Va. Cav. (Mosby).

POST, JOHN EAGER HOWARD: Adj. b. Baltimore circa 1840. Clerk, Baltimore. Enl. Co. H, 1st Md. Inf., 10/6/61; discharged 6/18/62. Enl. Co. C, 1st Md. Cav., date unknown; appointed Sgt. Maj. 7/1/63; present 7–8/63; ab. sick with scabies in Richmond hosp. 10/5–11/16/63; promoted 1st Lt. and Adj. for "valor and skill" 12/1/63; ab. sick with scabies in Richmond hosp. 12/29/64–1/11/65 and 3/8–4/2/65. Paroled Mechanicsville, Va., 5/5/65. Took oath Warsaw, Va., 5/20/65, destination Baltimore. Lived in Va. one year. Capt., Co. K, 5th Regt., Md. Natl. Guard 1867–70. d. Baltimore 2/14/76, in 36th year. Bur. Greenmont Cem., Baltimore.

POWELL, RANSOM L.: Pvt., Co. A. Captured Moorefield, W.Va., 8/7/64; sent to Wheeling. Age twenty-two, 5'11", fair complexion, red hair, blue eyes. Farmer, Adair Co., Md. [Mo.]. Transf. to Camp Chase; released 6/12/65. Age twenty-three, florid complexion, light hair, blue eyes. Res. Adair Co. Probably a member of Charles H. "Buck" Woodson's Co. A, 1st Mo. Cav.

PRETZMAN, DAVID R. P. C.: Pvt., Co. A. Res. of Carroll Co., Md. Enl. Gettysburg, Pa., 7/1/63; horse died on the march 11/1/63; present through 12/63; ab. on horse detail for ten days to Strasburg, Va., 1/9/64. Captured Hagerstown, Md., 2/9/64; sent to Old Capitol; transf. to Ft. Warren as guerilla; released 6/10/65. 5'7", light complexion, brown hair, hazel eyes. Res. of Hagerstown postwar.

PRICE, JAMES EDWARD: Pvt., Co. D. b. Baltimore Co., Md. 9/4/44. Enl. Winchester 9/20/62; present 11–12/62, 7/12–63, and 4/1/64; WIA (scalp) Haw's Shop, Va., 6/18/64; ab. wounded in Richmond hosp. 6/18/64. Farmer. Ab. sick in hosp. 7–8/64; AWOL 11–12/64. Captured near Strasburg, Va., 3/65; sent to Harpers Ferry, W.Va. "There paroled about two (2) weeks before Gen. Lee surrendered and came home to Md." Member ANS/MLA, 1907. Res. of Ottawa, Ill. Entered Old Soldiers' Home, Pikesville, Md., from Balti-more 1/7/08. Farmhand. d. there

8/11/16. Bur. Loudon Park Cem., Baltimore.

PRICE, JAMES HENRY: Pvt., Co. B. Res. Easton, Talbot Co., Md. Enl. Charlottesville 9/10/62. Captured Monterey Springs, Pa., 7/4/63; sent to Ft. McHenry; transf. to Ft. Del. and Pt. Lookout; exchanged 12/28/63. Admitted Richmond hosp. same day with "chronic diarrhoea"; furloughed for thirty days 1/6/64; ab. sick with "chronic diarrhoea" in Charlottesville hosp. 1/12–5/3/64; ab. sick with scabies in Charlottesville hosp. 10/9–29/64; present 11–12/64; ab. sick with "chronic diarrhoea" in Charlottesville hosp. 12/29/64–2/14/65. NFR. Employee, Western Md. RR, Baltimore, 1904. Member George Emack Camp, CV, Hyattsville, Md., and ANS/MLA.

PRICE, MARCELLUS A.: Pvt., Co. A. Enl. Charlottesville 8/25/62; detailed as Wagoner 5–6/63. Captured Williamsport, Md., 7/6/63, horse killed; sent to Ft. McHenry; transf. to Ft. Del. and Pt. Lookout; exchanged 12/28/63. Ab. on horse detail for fifteen days to Winchester 2/16/64; present 4/1/64; KIA Falling Waters, 8/28/64. Bur. Loudon Park Cem., Baltimore.

PRICE, WILLIAM COX: 3rd Cpl., Co. E. b. Kennedyville, Kent Co., Md. 1845. Res. of Kennedyville. Enl. as Pvt., 11/10/62, age eighteen; presence or ab. not stated 1–2/63; promoted 4th Cpl; present 7–8/63; horse killed near Williamsport, Md., 7/12/63, paid $230; promoted 3rd Cpl.; presence or ab. not stated 9–10/63; present 11–12/63 and 4/1/64. Captured Pollard's Farm, Va., 5/27/64, horse killed; sent to Pt. Lookout; exchanged 2/5/65. Present Camp Lee, Richmond, 2/20/65; paid $300 for horse; KIA Appomattox CH, Va., 4/9/65. "His was the last blood shed in the war in Virginia." Son of William Price, Executive Clerk of the U.S. Senate before the war.

PRUDEN, JOHN L.: Pvt., Co. K. Enl. Co. K (2nd), 1st Va. Cav. Age eighteen on postwar roster. Also on postwar roster Co. K, 1st Md. Cav.

PRUITT, JOHN C.: Pvt., Co. E. b. Worcester Co., Md., 1837. Enl. Richmond 11/10/62; presence or ab. not stated 1–2/62; WIA western Va. raid 4/63. Captured Germanna Ford, Va., 10/11/63; sent to Old Capitol; transf. to Pt. Lookout; exchanged 3/6/64. Present as Teamster 7–12/64. NFR. Moved to Highland Co., Va., circa 1866. Farmer. Member S. B. Gibbons Camp, CV, Harrisonburg, Va., 1896. Res. of Pinckney, Highland Co., Va., 1911. Bur. Hiner Cem., Highland Co., Va.; no dates.

PUE, ARTHUR: Pvt., Co. C. b. Harford Co., Md., 2/2/45. Res. of Harford Co. Enl. Hagerstown, Md., 7/28/64. Captured Moorefield, W.Va., 8/7/64; sent to Wheeling. 5'9", fair complexion, light hair, gray eyes. Farmer. Transf. to Camp Chase and Pt. Lookout; exchanged 3/27/65. Paroled Staunton,

Va., 4/30/65. 5'10", fair complexion, light hair, blue eyes. Entered Old Soldiers' Home, Pikesville, Md., from Baltimore, 11/3/03. Miner. NFR. Member ANS/MLA, 1908. Res. Townsend, Montgomery Co., Md.

PUE, EDWARD HILL DORSEY: 2nd Lt., Co. K. b. near Bel Air, Harford Co., Md., 4/27/40. Enl. Co. K (2nd), 1st Va. Cav., 5/4/61; WIA Gettysburg, Pa., 7/3/63; WIA and brown mare killed 1/24/64, paid $350 for horse; present until WIA Spotsylvania CH, Va., 5/8/64; present until WIA Reams Station, Va., 8/64. Transf. to Co. K, 1st Md. Cav., 8/64. Promoted 2nd Lt; WIA in Valley three times in 1864; present 11–12/64; paid 2/6/65. NFR. In 209 battles and skirmishes; received eleven wounds, including two saber cuts, one of which knocked out a couple of teeth. 6'1", fair complexion, light hair, blue eyes. Merchant, Rectortown, Va., seven years; Farmer, Bel Air. d. "Woodview," near Bel Air, 12/23/05. Bur. St. Mary's Ch. Cem., Emmonton, Md. (Photograph in Driver 1991).

PUE, FERDINAND CHATARD: Pvt., Co. A. b. Howard Co., Md., 6/16/43. Res. of Howard Co. Enl. Co. K (2nd), 1st Va. Cav., 5/14/61; present until transf. to Co. A, 1st Md. Cav., 5/15/62; present 9–12/63 and 4/1/64; ab. on detached service though 12/64; term of service expired. NFR. d. 4/7/09. Bur. St. Mark's Episcopal Ch. Cem., Howard Co. Brother of James A. V. Pue.

PUE, JAMES A. VENTRESS: 1st Lt., Co. A. Res. of Howard Co., Md. Enl. as 3rd Sgt., Co. K (2nd), 1st Va. Cav., 5/15/61; elected 3rd Lt., Co. A, 1st Md. Cav., 5/15/62; present 10–12/62; WIA (shoulder) Greenland Gap, W.Va., 4/25/63; presence or ab. not stated 7–8/63; present 9–12/63 and 4/1/64; promoted 1st Lt; WIA (right thigh) Beaver Dam Station, Va., 5/9/64. Captured Hanover Junction, Va., hosp. 5/24/64; sent to Old Capitol; transf. to Ft. Del., Ft. Pulaski, Ga., then back to Ft. Del. (one of the "Immortal 600"); released 6/16/65. 6'1", light complexion, light hair, blue eyes. Attended 1899 reunion. Brother of Ferdinand C. Pue.

PUE, WILLIAM H.: Pvt., Co. C. b. Howard Co., Md., circa 1840. Gd. U. of Md. Medical School 1860. Enl. Co. C, 1st Md. Inf., 8/19/61; discharged 6/11/62. Age twenty-two, 5'10½", light hair, blue eyes. On postwar roster; detailed Medical duty, Manassas, Va.; served in Richmond hosp. 12/62 until appointed Asst. Surgeon, 50th Ga. Inf., 6/1/64. NFR. Res. of Port Tobacco, Charles Co., Md.

PUMPHREY, GEORGE W.: Pvt., Co. E. b. circa 1842. Res. of Prince George's or Anne Arundel Co., Md. Enl. Richmond 11/27/62, age twenty; presence or ab. not stated 1–2/63; present 7–8/63;

horse killed Winchester 7/16/63; presence or ab. not stated 9–10/63; present 11–12/63 and 4/1/64; ab. sick with "chronic diarrhoea" in Charlottesville hosp. 6/13–26/64. Captured Moorefield, W.Va., 8/7/64; sent to Wheeling. Age twenty-two, 5'8", dark complexion, gray eyes, dark hair. Farmer, Prince George's Co., Md. Transf. to Camp Chase; d. there, heart disease, 3/17/65. Bur. Camp Chase National Cem., Oh., grave #565.

PUMPHREY, JOHN T.: Pvt., Co. E. b. circa 1844. Res. Princeland, Anne Arundel Co., Md. Enl. Richmond 11/14/62, age eighteen; presence or ab. not stated 1–2/63; horse killed Morgantown, W.Va., 4/27/63, paid $230; present 7–8/63; ab. on horse detail 10/28–31/63; present 11–12/63, 4/1/64, and 7–8/64; AWOL 9/1–12/31/64. NFR.

PURDUE, JOHN: Pvt., Co. A. Res. South River, Anne Arundel Co., Md. Enl. Md. 7/1/64; present through 12/31/64. NFR.

PURNELL, GEORGE WASHINGTON: Pvt., Co. A, Davis's Bn. and 1st Md. Cav. b. Snow Hill, Worcester Co., Md., 4/14/41. Gd. Snow Hill Acad.; att. U. Va. 1858–59; att. Princeton 1859–61. On postwar rosters of Co. A, Davis's Bn., and 1st Md. Cav. Promoted Adj., 2nd Bn. Md. Cav. Captured Piedmont, Va., 6/5/64; sent to Johnson's Island; released 6/15/65. Took oath Baltimore 8/12/65. Clerk and Merchant 1865–67. Gd. U. Va. Law School 1868. Lawyer, Snow Hill, 1868–99. Member ANS/MLA. d. Snow Hill 5/9/99. Bur. All Hallows Episcopal Ch. Cem., Snow Hill. (Photograph in Hartzler 1992)

PURNELL, WILLIAM S.: Pvt., Co. K. b. Worcester Co., Md. circa 1844. Res. of Worcester Co., Md. Enl. Co. H, 1st Md. Inf., 6/18/61; discharged 6/18/62. Age eighteen, 5'11", fair complexion, dark hair, dark eyes. Enl. Co. K (2nd), 1st Md. Cav., 7/1/62; present until captured 5/1/63; sent to Ft. McHenry as a spy; escaped 10/11/63. Present through 2/64; AWOL 7/20–8/31/64. Transf. to Co. K, 1st Md. Cav., 8/64; discharged at end of enlistment, 12/10/64. NFR.

PUSEY, AZARIAH C.: Pvt., Co. E. b. 12/29/42. Res. of Somerset Co., Md. Enl. Richmond 11/29/62; presence or ab. not stated 1–2/63. Captured near Winchester 6/12/63; sent to Ft. McHenry. 5'8", fair complexion, dark hair, dark eyes; exchanged 6/26/63; present 11–12/63; present, detailed as Teamster 4/1/64 and 7–12/64. Paroled Greensboro, N.C, 5/1/65. d. Worcester Co., Md., 5/24/24. Bur. Pusey–Maddux Cem., near Friendship Ch., Worcester Co., Md.

PYE, WILLIAM H.: Pvt., Co. C. Gd. Georgetown U. 1842. Farmer, Port Tobacco, Md. Enl. Fredericksburg, Va., 2/1/63 as substitute; present 7/10/63; paid 11/17/63; ab. on Secret Service

11–12/63; present 4/1–8/31/64; issued clothing 9/30/64; AWOL 11–12/64. Paroled Ashland, Va., 4/28/65.

QUIGLEY, G. W.: Pvt., Co. C, Davis's Bn. On postwar roster.

QUIGLEY, J. R.: Pvt., Co. C, Davis's Bn. On postwar roster.

QUIGLEY, R. S.: Pvt., Co. D, Davis's Bn. On postwar roster.

QUINN, JOHN P.: Lt., Co. K. Captured Winchester 6/5/63. On postwar roster Co. K (2nd), 1st Va. Cav. On postwar roster Co. K, 1st Md. Cav. Sheriff. d. Baltimore 12/6/99, age sixty-seven.

QUINN, MICHAEL J.: Pvt., Co. C. b. Ireland circa 1833. Porter, age twenty-seven, Eastern Dist., Henrico Co., Va., per 1860 census. Enl. Co. D (2nd), 10th Va. Cav., 6/25/62. Transf. to Co. C, 1st Md. Cav., 4/29/64; ab. sick in Richmond hosp. 10/31–12/15/64; transf. to Danville, Va., hosp. 12/22/64; paid in Richmond hosp. 2/15/65. NFR. Age thirty-eight, Fairfield Township, Henrico Co., Va., per 1870 census. d. Richmond, 11/25/14, age seventy-nine.

QUYNN, JOHN HENRY SKINNER: Pvt., Co. E. b. Nottingham, Prince George's Co., Md., 2/3/42. Res. of Baltimore. Enl. Richmond 1/26/63; presence or ab. not stated through 2/28/63; present Greenland Gap, W.Va., 4/23/63 and 7–8/63; ab. sick in Richmond hosp. 10/30–12/31/63; present 4/1–8/31–64. Captured Baltimore 12/4/64; tried as a spy and sentenced to be hanged; sentence was commuted. Member ANS/MLA, 1907. Res. of Pikesville, Md. d. 10/28/16. Bur. Loudon Park Cem., Baltimore.

RABORG, CHRISTOPHER E.: Pvt., Co. D. Enl. Winchester 9/20/62; ab. sick in Winchester hosp. 11–12/62. Captured Winchester 7/1/63; sent to Ft. McHenry; transf. to Ft. Del.; exchanged 12/28/63 per Federal POW rolls. d. of disease at Ft. Del. On muster rolls 9–10/63. NFR.

RABORG, WILLIAM R.: Pvt., Co. D. Enl. Bridgewater, Va., 6/1/63. Captured Monterey Springs, Pa., 7/4/63; sent to Ft. McHenry; d. Ft. McHenry. On rolls 9–10/63. d. Baltimore 8/3/63. On rolls 11–12/63.

RADCLIFFE, EDWARD B.: Pvt., Co. D. b. circa 1843. Enl. Richmond 10/25/62, age nineteen; present 11–12/62; presence or ab. not stated 1–2/63; present 7–12/63; brown horse killed Monterey Springs, Pa., 7/4/63, paid $900; brown horse killed Buckland, W.Va., 10/19/63, paid $600; wounded accidentally in head with his own Colt army pistol 3/8/64; DOW in Richmond hosp. 5/10/64. Effects: clothing valued at $40.

RAINS, K. P.: Pvt., Co. C, Davis's Bn. NFR.

RAITT, CHARLES H.: Pvt., Co. D. b. circa 1844.

ALLEN
CHRISTIAN
REDWOOD

*(Confederate
Veteran)*

Enl. Winchester 9/20/62; ab. to buy a horse 12/20–31/62. Captured Monterey Springs, Pa., 7/4/63, horse killed; sent to Ft. McHenry; trans. Ft. Del. and Pt. Lookout; exchanged 12/28/63; present 4/1/64; AWOL 8/31–12/31/64, yet issued clothing 9/13 and 9/30/64. Paroled Winchester 5/18/65. Age twenty-one, 5'8", light complexion, light hair, gray eyes. Res. Jefferson Co., W.Va.

RAPHAEL, EUGENE FRESSENJAT: Pvt., Co. C. Res. Baltimore Co. Enl. Baltimore Co. 7/10/64; present through 12/64. Captured Frederick's Hall, Va., 3/13/65; sent to Ft. Monroe; transf. to Pt. Lookout; released 6/17/65. 5'10½", dark complexion, brown hair, light hazel eyes. Res. of Harford Co., Md., 1905.

RASIN, WILLIAM INDEPENDENCE: Capt., Co. E. b. Still Pond, Kent Co., Md., 7/4/42; moved to St. Louis, Mo., age twelve, and Leavenworth, Kans., age fifteen. Served under Gen. Sterling Price in Mo. State Guard 1861–62. Returned to Md. Arrested 2/1/62; sent to Old Capitol; sentenced to Ft. Warren, for duration of the war 4/23/62; escaped to Va. Purchased forty horses for his Co. in Salisbury, N.C., 1/9/63, and enroute to Richmond. Enl. Richmond 1/20/63; Co. issued thirty-two Colt army revolvers; present 2/28/63; WIA (arm) Greenland Gap, W.Va., 4/25/63; continued with Co. to Oakland, Md., Morgantown, W.Va., and Fairmont, W.Va.; black mare killed Morgantown 4/28/63, paid $525; WIA (head) and captured near Winchester 6/10/63. Recaptured in Winchester hosp. 6/13/63; present 7–8/63; ab. sick with "Remit fever" in Charlottesville hosp. 9/23–10/13/63; present 1–12/63. Four officers and forty men present 11/1/63; Three officers and forty-two men present 12/31/63. Ab. sick with scabies in Richmond hosp. 2/3–4/4/64; issued one Colt army revolver 3/7/64; present Beaver Dam Station, Pollard's Farm, Wickham's Farm, and Trevilian Station (all in Va.), and Bunker Hill,

W.Va.; horse killed 9/5/64, paid $3,000; present Winchester and Fisher's Hill, Va.; ab. sick with scabies in Charlottesville hosp. 10/6–18/64; WIA (side of head) Cedar Creek, Va., 10/19/64; ab. sick with gonorrhoea in Charlottesville hosp. 11/10/64–2/28/65; present Appomattox CH, Va., 4/9/65, but escaped and started for Joseph E. Johnston's Army in N.C; present when regiment disbanded 4/28/65. Returned to Kent Co., Md.; merchant in Va., 1865; moved to Baltimore and engaged in Commission Business, 1873–76; Farmer, Kent Co., Md., 1876; Internal Revenue Cashier, Baltimore, 1876–1900, except for 1891–93. Member Franklin Buchanan Camp, CV, Baltimore, and ANS/MLA. d. Newport News, Va., 6/18/16. Bur. I. U. Ch. Cem., Worton, Md.

REAMER, JOHN C.: Pvt., Co. A. Paroled Harrisonburg, Va., 5/31/65. Age twenty, 5'9", fair complexion, light hair, blue eyes.

REDMOND, J. W.: Pvt., Co. C. Served in Co. H, 1st Md. Inf., 1861–62. On postwar rosters.

REDWOOD, ALLEN CHRISTIAN (photo): Pvt., Co. C. b. "Prospect Hill," Lancaster Co., Va., 6/9/44. Reared, educated in Baltimore; att. Polytechnic Inst., Brooklyn, N.Y., to train as an artist, 1860–61. Enl. Co. C, 55th Va. Inf., 7/24/61; WIA Mechanicsville, Va., 6/26/62; promoted Sgt. Maj. of Regt; WIA Chancellorsville, Va., 5/2/63; WIA (right elbow) Gettysburg, Pa., 7/3/63. Transf. to Co. C, 1st Md. Cav., 1/12/64; ab. on detail to get a horse for ten days to Warrenton, N.C., 2/1/64; present 4/1–8/31/64; horse killed Pollard's Farm, Va., 5/27/64. Captured near Somerton, Va., 4/7/65; sent to Newport News, Va.; released 7/3/65. 5'11", light complexion, dark hair, blue eyes. "Last man to leave prison." Went to Warren Co., N.C., and then to Baltimore. Artist and Writer, *Century* and *Harper's* magazines. Res. of Baltimore, Port Conway, Va., and N.Y. City. Res. Bergan Court, N.J., 1912. Member ANS/MLA. d. at the home of his brother Henry in Asheville, N.C., 12/24/22. Bur. Riverside Cem., N.Y. City. Brother of Henry Redwood. His jacket is in the Museum of the Confederacy, Richmond. His paintings appear on pages 109, 121.

REDWOOD, HENRY: Pvt., Co. F. Res. of Baltimore. On postwar roster; listed in 3rd Va. Bn. Local Defense Troops, Richmond. Res. of Asheville, N.C., 1922. His jacket and trousers are in the Museum of the Confederacy, Richmond. Brother of Allen C. Redwood.

REDWOOD, J. WILLIAM: Pvt., Co. C. Enl. Hanover CH, Va., 4/25/64; present through 12/31/64. NFR.

REED, JAMES: Pvt., Co. B. Captured Gettysburg, Pa., 7/4/63; sent to Ft. McHenry; transf. to Ft. Del. Remarks "Left at Ft. Del." NFR.

REED, MANUEL: Pvt., Co. B. Enl. McConnells-
burg, Pa., 6/24/63. Captured Monterey Springs,
Pa., 7/4/63. On rolls through 12/31/63. Not on
Federal POW rolls; may have been KIA.
REED, WILLIAM HENRY WATERS: 1st Lt., Co.
D, Davis's Bn. Res. of Baltimore. On roster.
REESE, G.: Pvt., Co. D. Aab. on leave to Staunton,
Va., 12/21–31/62. NFR.
REID, JOHN R.: Pvt., Co. C. Captured Sugar Loaf
Mt., Md., 1/6/65; sent to Old Capitol; transf. to Ft.
Warren as guerilla; released 6/15/65.
REILLY, JOHN H. F.: Pvt., Co. B. Res. of Prince
George's Co., Md. Enl. 1st S.C. Cav., 5/10/61.
Transf. to S.C. Heavy Arty. and stationed at Ft.
Pickens, S.C. Transf. to Co. B, 1st Md. Cav., date
unknown. All informatino from ANS/MLA appli-
cation, 1881. Res. of Baltimore. Alive 1894.
REILLY, JOHN T.: Pvt., Co. C. Res. of Baltimore.
Enl. 7/62 and served to end of war per application
to join ANS/MLA, 1904. Res. of Baltimore. Also
claimed service in 2nd Md. Arty.
REIN, EDWARD R.: Pvt., Co. E; ab. in Char-
lottesville hosp. 11–12/63. NFR.
REMY, LEON: Pvt., Co. F. b. circa 1842. Enl. Capt.
Gomez's Co., 22nd–23rd La. Inf., 9/10/61. NFR.
Enl. Co. F, 1st Md. Cav., Richmond, 7/3/63; present through 8/31/63; ab. sick in hosp. 9–10/63;
present 11–12/63 and 4/1–8/31/64; issued clothing 9/30/64. Captured Beverly, W.Va., 10/29/64;
sent to Wheeling. Age twenty-two, 5'9", dark
complexion, dark hair, dark eyes. Cook. Res. of
France. Transf. to Camp Chase; released 5/13/65.
Res. Orleans Co. (Parish), La.
RENCH, JOHN V.: Pvt., Co. K. b. circa 1831. Enl.
Co. K (2nd), 1st Va. Cav., 11/20/61; present until
captured Williamsport, Md., 9/15/62; exchanged
10/2/62; present until WIA (head) Aldie, Va.,
6/17/63; ab. wounded in Charlottesville hosp.
through 9/23/63; present through 2/64. Age thirty-
one. Clerk; WIA (leg) Todd's Tavern, Va., 5/7/64;
ab. wounded in Richmond hosp. through 8/2/64.
Transf. to Co. K, 1st Md. Cav., 8/64; present
through 8/31/64; WIA (forearm—flesh) and in
Richmond hosp. 10/2/64; furloughed to Albemarle Co. for forty days 10/8/64; discharged at
end of enlistment 12/4/64. NFR.
RHEAMS, JOSEPH VINCENT K.: Cpl., Co. A,
Davis's Bn. b. circa 1844. Enl. Woodstock, Va.,
8/14/63; present through 1/1/64. Captured
Frederick Co., Va. 4/24/64; sent to Camp Chase.
Age twenty, 5'10", florid complexion, brown hair,
blue eyes. Farmer. Res. Baton Rouge, La;
exchanged 2/25/65. Transf. to Co. M, 23rd Va.
Cav., while POW. NFR.
RIACH or REACH, JOHN: Pvt., Co. C. Enl.
Strasburg, Va., 6/1/63; present through 8/63; pres-

ent sick 9–10/63; present 11–12/63 and 4/1/64;
ab. sick in Harrisonburg, Va., hosp. 8/31/64; present 11–12/64. Paroled Richmond 4/20/65. Took
oath Richmond 5/20/65; destination Baltimore.
RICE, GEORGE RHODES: Pvt., Co. A. b. near
Darnestown, Md., 10/8/42. Res. of Montgomery
Co., Md. Served in 2nd Va. Inf. per postwar roster. Enl. Co. A, 1st Md. Cav, Charlottesville,
8/25/62; present South Mt. and Sharpsburg, Md.,
and Winchester. Captured Strasburg, Va., 2/26/63;
sent to Wheeling. 5'8", light complexion, brown
hair, gray eyes. Farmer. Transf. to Camp Chase;
exchanged 4/1/63; present 7–12/63 and 4/1/64.
Captured Moorefield, W.Va., 8/7/64; sent to
Wheeling. Brown hair, brown eyes, sandy
whiskers. Transf. to Camp Chase and Pt. Lookout;
exchanged 3/27/65. Paroled Washington, D.C.,
4/17/65. Took oath Edwards' Ferry, Md., 5/20/65.
Farmer, Travilah, Md., 1900. Member Ridgley
Brown Camp, CV, Rockville, Md. d. Darnestown
10/13/21. Bur. Darnestown Presb. Ch. Cem.
RICH, EDWIN ROBINS "NED": 2nd Cpl., Co. E.
b. 1/27/41. Student. Reistertown, Baltimore Co.,
Md. Served in Capt. Butler's Co., Hampton, S.C.
Legion Cav., 9/1/61–62, but not sworn in. Enl. as
Pvt., Co. E, 1st Md. Cav., Richmond, 11/27/62;
presence or ab. not stated 1–2/63; promoted 4th
Cpl; WIA (left arm broken just below the shoulder) Gettysburg, Pa., 7/3/63, while serving as
Orderly for Gen. Bradley T. Johnson; ab. wounded in Charlottesville hosp. 8/15/63–1/7/64; horse
captured Germanna Ford, Va., 10/10/63, while being ridden by another man; ab. on horse detail for
seventeen days 2/1/64; promoted 2nd Cpl; WIA
(right leg) Pollard's Farm, Va., 5/27/64; ab.
wounded in Richmond hosp. until transf. to
Charlottesville hosp. 9/10/64; RTD 11/3/64.
Captured Baltimore 12/7/64; tried and sentenced
to be hanged; sentence commuted; sent to Ft. Del.
"during the war" (not to be exchanged); released
6/7/65. Ordained an Episcopal Minister 1870;
Dean of Trinity Cathedral, Easton, Md., 1912.
Member ANS/MLA. d. 4/30/16. Bur. All Saints
Cem., Baltimore.
RICHARDSON, ALEXANDER: Pvt., Co. B. Res.
St. Mary's Co., Md. Served briefly in Co. A, 1st
Md. Inf. Enl. date, place unknown; issued clothing
11/9/64; des. to the enemy 11/22/64. Took oath
11/23/64; transportation furnished to Baltimore.
RICHARDSON, BEALE HOWARD, II: Pvt., Co.
A. Res. of Baltimore. Enl. Bridgewater, Va.,
6/1/63; present 7/8/63; ab. sick with "Int. Fever"
in Richmond hosp. 9/9–10/14/63; ab. on duty
10/28–31/63; present 11–12/63; present, serving
as a Scout, 4/1–8/64; ab. sick with "Hemarolspia"
in Richmond hosp.; furloughed to Montgomery,

Ala., for thirty days 8/14/64; ab. on leave from Richmond hosp. to Athens, Ga., 10/7/64. Appointed Capt. and Purchasing Officer, Mobile, Ala., 11/64. Paroled Meridian, Miss., 5/12/65.

RICHARDSON, BENJAMIN: Pvt., Co. A, Davis's Bn. Enl. Woodstock, Va., 6/1/63. Transf. to Co. M, 23rd Va. Cav; des. by 10/31/64. NFR.

RICHARDSON, GEORGE W.: Pvt., Co. G. b. 6/10/41. Res. Church Creek, Dorchester Co., Md. Enl. Co. A, Davis's Bn., Richmond, 9/14/63; present through 1/1/64. Captured near Woodstock, Va., 5/64; sent to Wheeling. 5'11", dark complexion, dark hair, blue eyes. Printer. Res. of Richmond. Transf. to Camp Chase; exchanged 2/25/65. Ab. sick with "debilitas" in Richmond hosp. 3/7/65; furloughed for thirty days 3/9/65. NFR. d. 3/28/19. Bur. Denton Cem., Denton, Md.

RICHARDSON, MONTAGUE L.: Pvt. or Capt., Co. D. b. circa 1830. Enl. date, place unknown. Enl. before Gettysburg, Pa. (7/1–3/63). Captured 7/10/63; sent to Ft. McHenry, "To be tried for treason"; escaped 8/63. Listed as Capt. on one report. Enl. as Pvt., Co. C, 43rd Va. Bn. Cav. (Mosby), 11/30/63. Captured Fauquier Co., Va., 5/19/64; sent to Old Capitol. Transf. to Ft. Del.; released 6/19/65. 5'10", fair complexion, brown hair, dark eyes. Destination Baltimore. Lawyer, Baltimore. Member ANS/MLA. Entered Old Soldiers' Home, Baltimore, 11/3/14, age seventy-four; d. there 1/21/19. Bur. Loudon Park Cem., Baltimore.

RICHEY, JAMES P.: 2nd Lt., Co. A, Davis's Bn. Captured Woodstock, Va., 5/64; on rolls to 10/31/64. Transf. to Co. M, 23rd Va. Cav. NFR.

RIDGELEY, SAMUEL: Color Sgt. b. circa 1839. Res. of Howard Co., Md. Enl. as Pvt., Co. K (2nd), 1st Va. Cav., 9/1/62; present through 8/31/64. Transf. to Co. K, 1st Md. Cav., 8/64; promoted Color Sgt. of Regt.; discharged at end of enlistment 12/4/64. Enl. Co. F, 43rd Bn. Va. Cav. (Mosby), date unknown. Paroled Winchester 4/22/65. Age twenty-five, 5'7", light complexion, light hair, blue eyes. Res. of Loudoun Co., Va. Baggage Master, Baltimore. Member ANS/MLA, 1885. Res. Cumberland, Md. Entered Old Soldiers' Home, Pikesville, Md., 7/2/95. d. Baltimore 7/17/97, age fifty-seven. Bur. Loudon Park Cem.

RIDGELY, JOHN: Pvt., Co. C. b. White Marsh, Baltimore Co., circa 1842. Enl. Richmond 8/4/62; present 7–9/63; ab. sick in Richmond hosp. 10/27–31/63; ab. sick with scabies and "erysipelas" in Richmond hosp. 11/17–12/29/63; present 12/31/63 and 4/1–12/31/64. NFR. Supervisor, Pennsylvania RR. Member ANS/MLA. Res. of Baltimore Co. 1872. d. Wilkes-Barre, Pa., 12/10/99 in 57th year. Bur. Greenmont Cem.,

Baltimore.

RIDGELY, JOHN THOMAS: Color Bearer. b. 1/25/42. Res. Sykesville or Crooksville, Howard Co., Md. Enl. as Pvt., Co. A, Sharpsburg, Md., 9/20/62; present 7–12/63 and 4/1–8/31/64; ab. detailed as Courier for Gen. Davidson 11–12/64. Surrendered Appomattox CH, Va., 4/9/65, as Color Sgt. of Regt. Took oath 4/10/65, destination Baltimore. 5'10", gray eyes. Member ANS/MLA. Res. of Sykesville 1927. d. 12/6/29. Bur. Bowling Green Farm Cem., Howard Co., Md. (Postwar photograph in Stonebraker 1899)

RIDGELY, THOMAS A.: Pvt., Co. A. b. 11/4/26. Res. Howard Co., Md. Enl. Meadow Bridge, Va., 7/1/64; ab. sick with "Fistula in arm" in Charlottesville hosp. 9/29/64–1/20/65. NFR. d. 8/7/02. Bur. Oak Grove Cem., Union Chapel, Howard Co.

RIDGEWAY, MORDECAI JEFFERSON: Pvt., Co. E. b. Prince George's Co., Md., 1/11/41. Served in 1st Md. Arty. 1861–62. Enl. Co. E, 1st Md. Cav., Richmond, 11/14/62; presence or ab. not stated 1–2/63; WIA (thigh) near Winchester 6/12/63; DOW Jordan Springs, Va., hosp. 9/21/63. Bur. Stonewall Cem., Winchester.

RIGGS, JOSHUA WARFIELD: 4th Sgt., Co. A. b. "Rockland," near Tridelphia, Montgomery Co., Md., 3/4/44. Res. Montgomery Co. Enl. as Pvt., Co. K (2nd), 1st Va. Cav., 5/14/61; present until transf. to Co. A, 1st Md. Cav., 5/15/62; promoted 4th Sgt; present 7–8/63; ab. on leave 9–10/63; present 11–12/63; issued clothing 3/30/64; WIA (arm) Beaver Dam Station, Va., 5/9/64; ab. detached service; term of service expired on rolls 8/2–31/64; discharged 12/27/64. Enl. Co. D, 43rd Bn. Va. Cav. (Mosby), date unknown. Paroled Winchester 4/21/65. 5'11", fair complexion, dark hair, gray eyes. Took oath Harpers Ferry, W.Va., 5/19/65. Grocer, Montgomery Co.; moved to Indianapolis, Ind.; moved to Baltimore; d. there 1/10/98. Bur. Loudon Park Cem., Baltimore.

RIGGS, REUBEN: Pvt., Co. A. b. Montgomery Co., Md., 11/29/39. Farmer, Goshen, Montgomery Co. Enl. Charlottesville 8/25/62; present through 12/63 and 4/1/64; brown horse killed Pollard's Farm, Va., 5/7/64, paid $1,800; present through 12/31/64; paroled Appomattox CH, Va., 4/9/65. Took oath 5/3/65. Member Ridgley Brown Camp, CV, Rockville, Md. d. near Laytonsville, Montgomery Co., 8/1/10. Bur. St. John's Cem., Montgomery Co.

RILEY, JAMES: Pvt., Co. C, Davis's Bn. On postwar roster.

RILEY, JAMES P.: 2nd Lt., Co. A and G. b. Va. 9/22/40. Deputy Clerk of Court, Winchester, Frederick Co., Va., per 1860 census. Enl. Co. D

(1st), 1st Va. Cav., 7/24/61; present until company transf. as Co. D, 6th Va. Cav., 9/61; AWOL 4–5/62. NFR. Enl. Co. A, 1st Md. Cav., 5/15/62; promoted 2nd Lt., Co. G. Captured Shenandoah Co., Va., 5/12/64; sent to Wheeling. 6'1¾", fair complexion, black hair, blue eyes. Lawyer. Transf. to Camp Chase; exchanged 2/28/65. Paroled Staunton, Va., 5/24/65. 6'2", dark complexion. Lawyer, Winchester, per 1870 census. d. Winchester 1/1/87. Bur. Mt. Hebron Cem. Brother of William B. Riley.

RILEY, JOHN: Sgt., Co. C. Not on muster rolls. d. Old Soldiers' Home, Pikesville, Md., 6/4/00. Bur. Loudon Park Cem., Baltimore.

RILEY, JOHN P.: Pvt., Co. C. b. circa 1840. Res. of Baltimore. Enl. Richmond 8/4/62; present 7–8/63; ab. on horse detail 8/28–31/63; paid Richmond 10/30/63. Captured Winchester 11/10/63; sent to Wheeling. Age twenty-three, 5'7½", light complexion, light hair, blue eyes. Farmer. Transf. to Camp Chase. Took oath, joined U.S. Navy 7/30/64.

RILEY, WILLIAM BRENT: Pvt., Co. G. b. Va. 1/12/43. Enl. Co. A, Davis's Bn., Strasburg, Va., 7/6/63. Captured Piedmont, Va., 6/5/64; sent to Camp Morton; exchanged 3/4/65. Paroled Winchester 4/157/65. 5'10", dark complexion, dark hair, blue eyes. Clerk, Winchester; d. there 11/13/73. Bur. Mt. Hebron Cem., Winchester. Brother of James P. Riley.

RILEY, THOMAS S.: Pvt., Co. A. Enl. Md. 7/1/64; present through 12/31/64. NFR.

RINEHART, A.: Pvt., Co. A, Davis's Bn. d. date unknown. Bur. Stonewall Cem., Winchester.

ROBERTS, JOHN KEPHART: Pvt., Co. K. Captured Sugar Loaf Mt., Md., 1/4/65; sent to Old Capitol; transf. to Ft. Warren as guerilla. NFR.

ROBERTS, JOSEPH KENT JR.: 2nd Lt., Co. E. b. Prince George's Co., Md., 3/13/41. Gd. Georgetown U. 1857. Lawyer, Easton, Talbot Co., and Bladensburg, Md. Enl. as Pvt., Richmond, 10/31/62; presence or ab. not stated 1–2/63; elected 3rd Lt. 2/1/63; paid 2/28/63. 5'5¼", light complexion, blue eyes, light hair. Promoted 2nd Lt. 3/20/63; horse abandoned near Chambersburg, Pa., 6/26/63, paid $600; present 7–9/63; ab. sick with "acute diarrhoea" in Charlottesville hosp. 9/30–10/27/63; paid 2/16/64; present 4/1/64; present 5–8/64; WIA Moorefield, W.Va., 8/7/64; WIA (right thigh) Winchester 9/64; ab. wounded in Charlottesville hosp. 9/19/64; transf. to Richmond hosp. 9/29/64; on leave from Richmond hosp. 10/10/64; present 11–12/64. NFR. Gd. U. of Va., LLD. Lawyer, Upper Marlboro, Md. Internal Revenue Service Collector. Member ANS/MLA. d. Upper Marlboro, Md., 10/31/88. Bur. Holy

Trinity Episcopal Ch. Cem., Prince George's Co.

ROBERTS, RICHARD: Pvt., Co. E. Att. Georgetown U. class of 1864. Res. of Bladensburg, Md. Enl. Richmond 2/7/63; presence or ab. not stated through 2/28/63. d. of pneumonia circa 4/63. Bur. Lacey Springs Cem., Rockingham Co., Va.

ROBERTSON, GEORGE W.: Pvt., Co. C, Davis's Bn. Res. of Washington Co., Md. NFR.

ROBERTSON, JAMES F.: Pvt., Co. C, Davis's Bn. NFR. Possibly J. E. Robinson (b. 1846). Enl. Bradley Johnson's Brigade 1863; served two years. Member Greenville Camp, CV, Uvalde, Tex., 1912.

ROBEY, TOWNLEY, JR.: 1st Sgt., Co. E. b. Charles Co., Md., circa 1835. Res. of Baltimore. Enl. as Pvt., Co. K (2nd), 1st Va. Cav., Leesburg, Va., 6/14/61; promoted 4th Sgt; present until discharged 5/14/62. Age twenty-seven, 6'2", fair complexion, brown hair, blue eyes. Merchant. Enl. as Pvt., Co. E, 1st Md. Cav., Richmond, 12/6/62, age twenty-eight; promoted 1st Sgt. 1/20/63; presence or ab. not stated 1–2/63; WIA (face) Winchester 6/13/63; present 7–9/63; ab. sick with scabies in Charlottesville hosp. 10/27–11/17/63; present through 12/63; ab. on leave for fifteen days 3/25/64; present until ab. sick with typhoid fever in Charlottesville hosp. 7/20/64; furloughed for thirty days 7/21/64; present 8–12/64; horse killed Strasburg, Va., 9/4/64, paid $3,000; in Richmond hosp. 2/15/65. Reenl. as Sgt., Co. F, 24th Va. Cav.; surrendered Appomattox CH, Va., 4/9/65. Took oath Alexandria, Va., 5/9/65. Clerk, Baltimore. Member ANS/MLA. Res. of Bryantown, Charles Co., Md. d. 9/7/90, age fifty-six. Bur. Old Field Episcopal Ch. Cem., Hughesville, Charles Co.

ROBINSON, EDWARD W.: Pvt., Co. C. Captured Sugar Loaf Mt., Md., 1/4/65; sent to Old Capitol; transf. to Ft. Warren as guerilla; released 5/22/65.

ROBINSON, WILLIAM H.: Pvt., Co. C. b. circa 1841. Res. of Baltimore. Enl. Co. D, 1st Md. Inf., 6/1/61; discharged 8/11/62. Enl. Co. C, 1st Md. Cav., Lacey Springs, Va., 4/19/63. Captured New Creek, W.Va., 1/8/64; sent to Wheeling. Age twenty-three, 5'10½", light complexion, brown hair, hazel eyes. Clerk. Transf. to Camp Chase; took oath, released 3/26/64. Also listed as exchanged; present Camp Lee, Richmond, 2/27/65. NFR.

RODGERS, GEORGE: Pvt., Co. C. b. circa 1832. Res. of Baltimore. Enl. Hanover Junction, Va., 5/20/64; WIA (left breast—flesh wound) Clear Spring, Md., 7/29/64; ab. wounded in Winchester 8/1–4/64; transf. to Charlottesville hosp.; RTD 8/22/64; issued clothing 9/30/64; present 11–12/64. Paroled Winchester 4/23/65. Age thirty-three, 5'7½", light complexion, brown hair, hazel eyes.

RODGERS, JOSEPH: Pvt., Co. K. Enl. Co. K (2nd), 1st Va. Cav., date and place unknown. Captured, date and place unknown; sent to Elmira. Transf. to Co. K, 1st Md. Cav., 8/64, while POW. d. of disease Elmira 9/21/64. Bur. Woodlawn National Cem., Elmira, N.Y., grave #492.

RODGERS, PHILIP: Pvt., Co. C. b. Baltimore Co. circa 1836. Res. of Baltimore. Enl. Winchester 7/16/63; present through 12/63; ab. on horse detail for twenty days to Asheville, N.C., 2/16/64; present 4/1–8/31/64; bay horse killed Rockville, Md., 7/13/64, paid $2,500; issued clothing 9/14/64; paid 9/26/64; ab. detailed as scout for Gen. Lunsford Lomax 11–12/64. Paroled Winchester 5/4/65. Age twenty-nine, 5'9", light complexion, light hair, blue eyes. Took oath Winchester 5/16/65, destination Baltimore. Druggist, Baltimore, postwar; d. there 1/7/89, age fifty-three. Bur. Greenmont Cem., Baltimore.

ROE, SAMUEL: Sgt., Co. E. b. circa 1838. Farmer, Centreville, Queen Anne's Co., Md. Enl. Richmond 10/18/62, age twenty-four; presence or ab. not stated 1–2/63; present 7–9/63; ab. sick with acute dysentery in Charlottesville hosp. 10/1–11/6/63; present 11–12/63 and 4/1/64; promoted 3rd Cpl. by 7–8/64; horse killed Bunker Hill, W.Va., 9/3/64, paid $3,000; present through 12/64. Paroled as Sgt., Ashland, Va., 5/10/65. Member ANS/MLA, 1904. Res. Centreville. d. 1/8/18.

ROGERS, JAMES P.: Pvt., Co. C. b. Baltimore circa 1836. Gd. Georgetown U. Res. of Brooklandville, Baltimore Co. Enl. Co. B, 21st Va. Inf., 5/23/61. 6'2¾", fair complexion, brown hair, blue eyes. Discharged as nonresident 5/24/62. Enl. Co. C, 1st Md. Cav., Richmond, 9/1/62; ab. 11/62; present 7–9/63; ab. on leave for eight days 10/23/63; present 11–12/63; ab. on leave for fifteen days 3/27/64; WIA Boonsboro, Md., 7/5/64; ab. wounded through 12/64. Paroled, took oath, Winchester 4/21/65. Age twenty-seven, 6'2", light complexion, brown hair, blue eyes. Farmer, "Eutaw Place," near Buckley, Md. d. 1/2/92. Bur. St. Joseph's Cem., Carrollton Manor, Md.

ROGERS, SAMUEL B.: Pvt., Co. C. b. circa 1844. Res. of Brooklandville, Baltimore Co. Enl. Co. H, 1st Md. Inf., Fairfax Station, Va., 10/6/61; discharged when regiment disbanded 8/11/62. Enl. Co. C, 1st Md. Cav., Richmond, 9/1/62. Captured near Newtown, Va., 6/12/63, horse killed; sent to Ft. McHenry. Age nineteen, 5'10½", fair complexion, blue eyes, auburn hair; exchanged 6/26/63. Paid $450 for horse; present 7–9/63; ab. sick in hosp. 10/29–12/31/63; ab. on horse detail

for fifteen days 3/27/64; KIA Clear Spring, Md., 7/29/64.

ROLLEY, THOMAS H.: Pvt., Co. D. Enl. Hanover Junction, Va., 2/28/64; present 4/1/64; des. 8/5/64; on rolls to 8/31/64. NFR.

ROLPH, GEORGE W.: Pvt., Co. E. b. circa 1843. Res. of Kent Co., Md. Enl. Richmond 10/25/62, age nineteen; presence or ab. not stated 1–2/63; WIA (saber cut to head), captured near Winchester 6/12/63; sent to Ft. McHenry. Age twenty-one, 5'8", fair complexion, blue eyes, light hair; exchanged 6/26/63. Paid $230 for horse 6/12/63; present 7–9/63; ab. on horse detail 10/28/63; present 11–12/63; ab. sick with camp itch in Richmond hosp. 1/7–8/64 and 3/27–4/6/64. Captured Moorefield, W.Va., 8/7/64; sent to Wheeling. Age twenty-three, 5'8", florid complexion, blue eyes, red hair. Clerk. Transf. to Camp Chase and Pt. Lookout; exchanged 3/27/65. Admitted Richmond hosp. same day with "chronic diarrhoea." Captured in Richmond hosp. 4/3/65. Paroled 4/26/65. Res. of Baltimore postwar. Member Franklin Buchanan Camp, CV, and ANS/MLA. d. 7/12/11, age seventy-five. Bur. Loudon Park Cem., Baltimore.

ROLPH, WILBUR FISKE: Sgt., Co. F. Enl. as 1st Cpl., Richmond, 7/1/63; present through 9/63; WIA (left wrist) Morton's Ford, Va., 10/11/63; ab. wounded in Richmond hosp. 10/15–11/19/63; present through 12/63 and 4/1/64. Captured Pollard's Farm, Va., 5/27/64; sent to Pt. Lookout; exchanged 2/15/65; ab. sick in Richmond hosp. 2/23–24/65; furloughed from Camp Lee, Richmond, for forty days 2/27/65. Paroled as Sgt., Richmond 5/2/65. d. Gloucester Co., Va., 2/11/15.

ROSAN, CHARLES W.: Pvt., Co. D. b. circa 1841. Res. of Baltimore. Enl. Richmond 5/26/64; horse killed Smithfield, W.Va., 8/28/64, paid $2,000; present through 12/31/64. Paroled Staunton, Va., 5/15/65. Age twenty-four, 6' dark complexion, dark hair, dark eyes. Took oath Winchester 5/20/65; destination Baltimore.

ROSAN, STERLING L.: Pvt., Co. F. b. Baltimore, circa 1842. Enl. Winchester 7/15/63; present through 8/31/63; ab. sick in Richmond hosp. 9–12/63; paid 10/3/63. Age twenty-one, 6', dark complexion, hazel eyes, black hair. Applied for transfer from Capt. Thomas Kevitt's "United Arty." 3/30/64, but not on muster rolls of that unit. Returned to Smith's Bn. Heavy Arty. as des.; on rolls 4/1/64. Transf. officially 5/27/64. NFR.

ROSE, AUGUSTUS PORTER: Pvt., Co. C. b. circa 1840. Enl. Lacey Springs, Va., 3/26/63. Captured Hughes River, W.Va., 5/9/63; sent to Wheeling. Age twenty-three, 5'8½", light complexion, gray eyes, brown hair. Student. Res. McClelland, Tex.

Transf. to Camp Chase; released 6/5/65; destination, Detroit, Mich.

ROSE, L. JESSE: Pvt., Co. F. b. 11/16/23. Enl. Breathed's Bty. Horse Arty. 6/5/62. Transf. to Co. F, 1st Md. Cav., 4/21/64; present through 8/31/64; horse lost 8/28/64; issued clothing 9/30/64. NFR. d. 3/27/05. Bur. Mt. Hope Cem., Woodsboro, Md.

ROSS, PICKNEY J.: Pvt., Co. F. b. circa 1843. Enl. date and place unknown. Captured Beverly, W.Va., 10/29/64; sent to Wheeling. Age twenty-one, 5'8", dark complexion, gray eyes, light hair. Laborer. Res. of New Orleans, La. Transf. to Camp Chase; d. there of pneumonia 2/2/65. Bur. Camp Chase Natl. Cem., Oh., grave #1004.

ROWLEY, WILLIAM: Pvt., Co. unknown, Davis's Bn. Res. of Johnson's Store, Anne Arundel Co., Md. NFR.

ROWLAND, H. R.: Pvt., Co. A. Enl. Richmond 9/1/62; horse killed Smithfield, W.Va., 8/28/64, paid $2,000; issued clothing 9/30/64. Captured Mt. Crawford, Va., 10/3/64; sent to Pt. Lookout; exchanged 2/15/65. Present Camp Lee, Richmond, 2/27/65. NFR.

ROZIER, CHARLES B.: Pvt., Co. A. b. Charles Co., Md. 1834. Res. of Montgomery Co., Md. Enl. Strasburg, Va., 11/29/62; present 7–12/63; ab. sick with debility in Richmond hosp. 1/6–3/25/64; present 4/1–8/31/64; issued clothing 9/30/64; ab. on detail 11–12/64. NFR. Farmer. d. Washington, D.C., 12/10/13. Bur. Union Cem., Rockville, Md.

RUDDLE, JOHN T.: Pvt., Co. A, Davis's Bn. b. circa 1842. Enl. Co. H, 5th Va. Inf., 6/1/61, age twenty; AWOL 11/18/63 to join cavalry. Enl. Mt. Crawford, Va., 1/1/64; ab. sick 8/1–10/31/64. Transf. to Co. M, 23rd Va. Cav. Paroled Staunton, Va., 5/13/65. Age twenty-three, 5'8", light complexion, light hair, blue eyes. Farmer.

RUSHING, JOHN D.: Pvt., Co. F. Enl. Richmond 7/8/63; present through 9/63. Captured Brandy Station, Va., 10/11/63; sent to Old Capitol; transf. to Pt. Lookout. Took oath, joined U.S. Army 2/12/64. NFR.

RUSK, JOHN ROBERT: Pvt., Co. D. b. Warren Co., Va., 6/14/40. Enl. as Lt., Co. I, 12th Va. Cav., 4/17/62. Joined from 12th Va. Cav. without transfer, ordered back on rolls to 12/62. Captured Beverly Ford, Va., 6/9/63; exchanged circa 8/63. Commanding Co. I, 12th Va. Cav., 9–10/63 and 3–4/64. Captured Warren Co. 2/18/65; sent to Ft. McHenry; exchanged 2/24/65. Paroled 5/1/65. d. Haymarket, Va., 6/1/19. Bur. St. Paul's Episcopal Ch. Cem., Haymarket.

RUSSELL, JAMES A. or S.: Pvt., Co. E. Enl. date and place unknown. Captured Prince George's Co., Md., 4/3/64; sent to Old Capitol. Transf. to

Pt. Lookout; exchanged 2/27/65. NFR.

SAGER, SAMUEL: Pvt., Co. A, Davis's Bn. Enl. New Market, Va., 9/14/64. Transf. to Co. M, 23rd Va. Cav.; AWOL 10/31/64. NFR.

SAKERS, JOHN T.: Pvt., Co. K. b. 1/25/38. Res. of Laurel, Prince George's Co., Md. Enl. Co. K (2nd), 1st Va. Cav., Leesburg, Va., 9/1/62; present through 8/64. Transf. to Co. K, 1st Md. Cav., 8/64; issued clothing 9/30/64; discharged at end of enlistment 12/4/64. Paroled Winchester 5/25/65. Took oath Baltimore 8/24/65. Res. of Howard Co., Md. Member ANS/MLA. d. Laurel 5/6/18. Bur. Ivy Hill Cem., Laurel.

SAKERS, SAMUEL: Pvt., Co. G. b. circa 1835. Enl. Co. G, 7th Va. Cav., 4/1/62. Transf. to Co. G, 1st Md. Cav., 7–8/64. Paroled Staunton, Va., 5/1/65 as member Co. G, 7th Va. Cav. Age thirty, 5'9", light hair, gray eyes. Res. of Berkeley Co., Va. Res. of Md. in postwar.

SANDERS, D.: Pvt., Co. A, Davis's Bn. NFR.

SANDERS, EDWARD: Pvt., Co. A, Davis's Bn. Enl. Richmond 6/26/63; present through 10/31/64. Transf. to Co. M, 23rd Va. Cav. NFR. Member George Emack Camp, CV, Hyattsville, Md., 1906. Res. near LaPlata, Charles Co., Md.

SANDERS, JOSEPH: Pvt., Co. A, Davis's Bn. Enl. Co. I, 1st Md. Inf., 7/1/61; discharged 8/15/62. Enl. Richmond 6/26/63; present through 1/1/64. Transf. to Co. M, 23rd Va. Cav.; AWOL 10/31/64. NFR.

SANDERS, M.: Pvt., Co. A, Davis's Bn. NFR.

SANDERS, T. HILLEN: 4th Cpl., Co. C. b. 8/15/45. On postwar roster Co. D (2nd), 1st Va. Cav. Enl. as Pvt., Co. C, 1st Md. Cav., Richmond, 8/4/62. Captured, sent to Ft. McHenry 10/16/62; exchanged 11/16/62. Present 7–9/63; ab. on horse detail for twelve days 10/28/63; present 11–12/63 and 4/1/64; promoted 4th Cpl., 7/64; present 7–8 and 11–12/64. NFR. Commanding Co. at Appomattox on postwar accounts. Member ANS/MLA, 1889. Res. of N.Y. City. d. 1903. Bur. Mt. Hope Cem., Hastings-on-Hudson, N.Y.

SARTIN, JOHN: Pvt., Co. C, Davis's Bn. NFR.

SAUNDERS, JOHN O.: Pvt., Co. C, Davis's Bn. NFR.

SAVAGE, GEORGE F.: Pvt., Co. unknown. Enl. Co. A, 39th Va. Inf., 6/8/61. Captured Northampton Co., Va., 11/61. NFR. Reenl. 1st Md. Cav., date unknown. Bur. Johnson's Ch. Cem., Northampton Co.; no dates.

SAVAGE, JOHN H.: 2nd Sgt., Co. D. b. Charles Co., Md., circa 1841. Farmer, Charles Co. Enl. Co. A, 17th Va. Inf., 8/29/61. Transf. to Dea's Md. Bty. (Co. C, 19th Bn. Va. Heavy Arty.) 4/29/62. Age twenty-three, 5'7", fair complexion, blue eyes, light hair. Promoted Cpl. Trans. Co. D, 1st

JOHN POOLE
SELLMAN

*(Daniel D.
Hartzler)*

Md. Cav., Richmond, 12/17/62, age twenty-four, as Pvt.; presence or ab. not stated 1–2/63, yet promoted 2nd Sgt. 1/20/63; WIA (side) and captured near Winchester 6/12/63; sent to Old Capitol as "spy"; transf. to Pt. Lookout; d. there of "chronic diarrhoea," 11/5/63. Bur. Pt. Lookout Confederate Cem. Name deleted from monument; his body may have been removed after the war.

SCAGGS, EDWARD OLIVER: Pvt., Co. B. b. Fairland, Montgomery Co., Md., circa 1845. Res. of Prince George's Co., Md. Enl. Charlottesville 9/10/62; present 7–9/63. Captured Raccoon Ford, Va., 10/10/63, horse killed; sent to Old Capitol; trans. Pt. Lookout; exchanged 2/15/65. Paid $2,000 for horse; present Camp Lee, Richmond, 2/27/65. Paroled Winchester 5/4/65. Age twenty, 5'9", light complexion, dark hair, hazel eyes. Res. of Washington, D.C. Wood and Coal Dealer, Washington. Member George Emack Camp, CV, Hyattsville, Md., and Confederate Veterans Assoc., Washington. d. Washington 4/27/33. Bur. Arlington Natl. Cem., Va.

SCAGGS, GEORGE A.: Pvt., Co. K. b. 9/23/34. On postwar rosters Co. K (2nd), 1st Va. Cav., and Co. K, 1st Md. Cav. d. 3/28/15. Bur. Mt. Zion Cem., Howard Co., Md.

SCAGGS, JOSEPH A.: Pvt., Co. B. b. Fairland, Montgomery Co., Md., 10/44. Farmer, Montgomery Co., Md. Enl. Beltsville, Md., 7/15/64. Captured Moorefield, W.Va., 8/7/64; sent to Wheeling. Age twenty, 5'11½", dark complexion, dark hair, dark eyes. Transf. to Camp Chase and Pt. Lookout; exchanged 3/27/65. NFR. Member George Emack Camp, CV, Hyattsville, Md. d. 1912. Bur. St. John's Episcopal Ch. Cem., Beltsville, Md.

SCAGGS, ROBERT RIDGLEY: Pvt., Co. K. Res. of Clarksville, Howard Co., Md. Enl. Co. K (2nd), 1st Va. Cav., Leesburg, Va., 9/1/62; present through 8/64. Transf. to Co. K, 1st Md. Cav., 8/64.

Discharged 12/4/64, at end of enlistment. NFR. d. Washington, D.C., 5/8/31. Bur. Arlington Natl. Cem., Va.

SCHOLL, JOHN H.: 1st Sgt., Co. A. b. New Market Dist., Montgomery Co., Md., 1838. Res. of Monocacy, Montgomery Co., Md. Enl. Co. K (2nd), 1st Va. Cav., 6/14/61; present until transf. to Co. A, 1st Md. Cav., 5/15/62, as 1st Sgt; present 7–12/63; ab. on horse detail for fifteen days to Winchester 2/16/64; present 4/1/64; ab. term of service expired—no discharge on rolls 8/31–12/31/64. Enl. as Pvt., Co. B, 35th Bn. Va. Cav. Paroled Conrad's Ferry, Md., 4/65.

SCHULTZ, WILLIAM S.: Pvt., Co. D. b. 3/16/43. Enl. Co. B, 1st Md. Inf., 5/21/61; discharged 8/11/62. Enl. Co. D, 1st Md. Cav., New Market, Va., 6/1/63. Captured Monterey Springs, Pa., 7/4/63, horse killed; sent to Ft. McHenry; transf. to Ft. Del. and Pt. Lookout; exchanged 2/21/65. Paid $2,400 for horse; present Camp Lee, Richmond, 2/27/65; paid Richmond 3/25/65. Paroled Richmond 4/17/65. 5'11", fair complexion, dark hair, blue eyes. d. 5/20/76. Bur. Central Cem., north of New Market, Md.

SCHWARTZ, AUGUSTUS F.: Capt., Co. F. b. circa 1841. Res. of Baltimore. Enl. as Pvt., Co. A, 1st Md. Cav., Manassas, Va., 8/31/62; promoted Capt. of Co. F, 1st Md. Cav., 7/16/63; present with fifty-three horses 10/31/63; present through 12/63. Four officers and thirty-eight men present 11/30/63. Present Hanover Junction, Va., with thirty-four horses 12/31/63; present 2/6/64 and 4/1/64; WIA (hip) Beaver Dam Station, Va., 5/9/64. Captured Hanover Junction, Va., hosp. 5/24/64; sent to Lincoln General Hosp., Washington, D.C.; DOW there 6/12/64, age twenty-five. Bur. "Soldiers burial grounds"; removed to Loudon Park Cem., Baltimore, postwar.

SCOTT, GEORGE W.: Pvt., Co. A. b. circa 1842. Res. of Howard Co., Md. Served in Rhett's 1st S.C. Heavy Arty. Enl. Co. A, 1st Md. Cav., Charlottesville, 6/15/64. Captured Moorefield, W.Va., 8/7/64; sent to Wheeling. Age twenty-two, 5'5½", fair complexion, blue eyes, light hair. Farmer, Baltimore. Transf. to Camp Chase and Pt. Lookout; exchanged 3/27/65. Admitted to Richmond hosp. with pneumonia 3/28/65; transf. to another hosp. NFR.

SCOTT, JOHN EMORY: Pvt., Co. C. Res. of Baltimore. Enl. Co. E, 12th Va. Inf., 5/4/61. Captured 5/2/63; sent to Old Capitol; exchanged 6/63. Captured 7/5/63; sent to Ft. Del.; exchanged circa 1/64. Transf. to Co. C, 1st Md. Cav., 8/16/64; AWOL through 12/31/64. NFR.

SELLMAN, JOHN POOLE (photo): Pvt., Co. A. b. Comus, Montgomery Co., Md., 12/11/40. Res. of

Barnesville, Montgomery Co. Ran away from Brookville Acad., Md., and enlisted Co. K (2nd), 1st Va. Cav., Fairfax CH, Va., 9/1/61; present until transf. to Co. A, 1st Md. Cav., 5/15/62; present 7–12/63 and 4/1–8/3/64. Captured on picket in Loudon Co., Va., 9/6/64; sent to Old Capitol; transf. to Pt. Lookout; exchanged 2/25/65. Term of service expired—no discharge; on rolls to 12/64. Enl. Co. D, 35th Bn. Va. Cav. Captured, held at Old Capitol to end of war. Stockraiser, Loudoun Co. and Montgomery Co.; County Commissioner, 1888, served two terms; Member Md. legislature 1902. Member Ridgely Brown Camp, CV, Rockville, Md. d. Barnesville, Md., 7/22/08. Bur. Old Monocacy Cem., Beallsville, Md. (Additional photograph in Driver 1991)

WALLACE
SELLMAN

(Museum of the Confederacy)

SELLMAN, WALLACE (photo): Pvt., Co. A., but not on muster rolls. Also listed as having served in 35th Bn. Va. Cav., but not on muster rolls. b. 11/12/42. Res. Old Medley's, Montgomery Co., Md. Served as Courier for Capt. Philip Henry Lee. d. of typhoid fever in Montgomery Co., Md., 5/22/64. Bur. Old Monocacy Cem., Beallsville, Md.

SELVAGE, EDWIN: 2nd Cpl., Co. D. b. Baltimore, 10/23/39. Telegrapher. Res. of Frederick Co., Md. Enl. Co. D, 1st Md. Inf., 5/22/61; WIA (head) Malvern Hill, Va., 7/1/62; released from Richmond hosp. 7/20/62; discharged when regt. disbanded 8/11/62; served briefly as ADC to Gen. George H. Steuart. Enl. Co. D, 1st Md. Cav., Winchester, 9/20/62, as 2nd Cpl; present 11–12/62; WIA Woodstock, Va.; present Kernstown, Va., Greenland Gap, W.Va., Oakland, Md., Morgantown and Cairo Station, W.Va.; and Middletown, Va.; WIA, captured South Mt., Md., 7/4/63, horse killed; sent to Ft. McHenry; exchanged 12/28/63. Paid $600 for horse; present Old Church, Va., 3/3/64 and 4/1/64. Captured Pollard's Farm, Va., 5/27/64; sent to Pt. Lookout; exchanged 2/15/65. WIA near Lynchburg, Va., 4/9/65; carried dispatches to Danville, Va., for President Davis; ordered by Gen. John C. Breckinridge to Salisbury and Charlotte, N.C.; met President Davis, delivered dispatches; carried dispatch from Davis to Gen. Kirby Smith in Tex.; rode through N.C., S.C., Ga., Ala., and Miss.; in Sunflower, Miss., when he learned of Gen. Smith's surrender. Paroled, took oath, White River, Ark., 6/5/65. Returned to Baltimore; went west as RR worker for a time; cotton broker for Lane and Co., N.Y. City, 12/65–1926; member N.Y. Produce Exchange for fifty-three years. Member ANS/MLA. Killed by taxicab, Brooklyn, N.Y., 10/15/30. Bur. Mt. Hope Cem., Hastings-on-Hudson, N.Y. "Captured 5 times, escaped

twice and was recaptured by McNeill's Rangers once. Escaped from Pt. Lookout twice, once by bribing a guard and another time with the aid of his brother." Brothers served in Federal army.

SERPALL, GOLDSBOROUGH McDOWELL: 1st Sgt., Co. B. b. circa 1838. Farmer, Prince George's Co, Md. Enl. as 1st Cpl., Charlottesville, 9/10/62; ab. sick with "secondary syphilis" in Charlottesville hosp. 4/18–5/18/63. Captured near Matlock's Creek, Md., 6/2/63; sent to Old Capitol; trans. Pt. Lookout; exchanged 6/26/63. Present 11–12/63; ab. sick with scabies in Richmond hosp. 1/14–2/23/64; present 4/1/64; ab. on horse detail for ten days to Shenandoah Co., Va., 5/1/64; promoted 1st Sgt. Captured Moorefield, W.Va., 8/7/64; sent to Wheeling. Age twenty-six, 6', light complexion, brown eyes, light hair. Transf. to Camp Chase and Pt. Lookout; exchanged 3/27/65. Admitted to Richmond hosp. with "chronic diarrhoea" same day. NFR. Member George B. Emack Camp, CV, Hyattsville, Md. President, Atlantic Coast RR. d. Norfolk, Va., 1/13/12, age seventy-four.

SHAFER, CORNELIUS L.: Pvt., Co. D. Res. Cooksville, Howard Co., Md. Enl. Winchester 9/20/62; present 11–12/62, 7–12/63, and 4/1–12/31/64; horse killed Chambersburg, Pa., paid $3,000. NFR. Member George Emack Camp, CV, Hyattsville, Md. Employee, Atlantic Coast Line RR, Norfolk, Va., 1906.

SHAFER, JOHN W.: Pvt., Co. B. Enl. date and place unknown. Captured Williamsport, Md., 7/11/63; sent to Ft. Del.; sent for exchange 2/27/65. NFR. May have died enroute.

SHAFFER, THOMAS HAMNER: Pvt., Co. D. Enl. Frederick, Md., 7/1/64; present through 12/31/64. Paroled, took oath, Harpers Ferry, W.Va., 5/20/65. d. 4/7/99, no age. Bur. Mt. Airy Methodist Ch. Cem., Frederick Co., Md.

SHANLEY, T. E.: Pvt., Pvt., Co. A; ab. sick with

THOMAS
SHERWIN

*(Stonebraker
1899)*

"debilitas" in Richmond hosp. 8/31–9/19/63.
NFR.

SHANLEY, TIMOTHY: Pvt., Co. B. Enl. date and
place unknown. Captured Falling Waters, Md.,
7/14/63; sent to Old Capitol. Took oath, sent to
Philadelphia, Pa., 12/13/63. 5'5½", light complexion, light hair, blue eyes. Res. of Philadelphia.

SHAW, JAMES C.: Sgt., Co. G. Enl. date unknown.
Captured Kearnesyville, W.Va., 11/21/63; sent to
Ft. Del.; exchanged 2/7/65. Paroled Winchester
4/17/65. Age twenty-eight, 5'7½", brown hair,
blue eyes. Arrested Baltimore 4/28/65; took oath,
released to go South.

SHAW, JOHN: Cpl., Co. A, Davis's Bn. Enl.
Woodstock, Va., 8/14/63; present through 1/1/64.
Transf. to Co. M, 23rd Va. Cav; des.

SHEARER, GEORGE M. E.: 1st Lt. and Drillmaster, 1st Md. Cav., and Capt., Co. D, Davis's Bn. b.
circa 1841. Res. of Frederick Co., Md. Enl. as 2nd
Lt., Co. A, 1st Md. Inf., 5/21/61; not reelected
4/29/62. Captured Hancock, Md., 7/25/62; sent to
Ft. McHenry; transf. to Ft. Del.; exchanged
11/10/62. Appointed 1st Lt. and Drillmaster, 1st
Md. Cav., 12/5/63; recommended by Col. Bradley
T. Johnson for "singular daring"; paid 1/1/64 and
3/28/64. Captured Hagerstown, Md., 7/5/64. Age
twenty-three; res. of Calif., serving on staff of
Gen. Bradley T. Johnson. Sent to Old Capitol;
transf. to Ft. Del. and Ft. McHenry; released
6/7/65. 6'2", fair complexion, light hair, blue
eyes. Res. of Nevada Co., Calif. Member ANS/
MLA. d. Mt. Idaho, Idaho Territory, 1/2/90.

SHELL, HORACE E.: Pvt., Co. D. b. circa 1845.
Res. Frederick, Md. Enl. 1862; present 11–12/62.
Captured Strasburg, Va., 2/26/63; sent to Wheeling. Age eighteen, 5'4", dark complexion, brown
eyes, black hair. Transf. to Camp Chase;
exchanged 4/1/63. NFR. Bur. Mt. Olivet Cem.,
Frederick, no dates.

SHERRY, CHARLES T.: Pvt., Co. F. Res. of

Washington, D.C. Enl. Co. C, 19th Bn. Va. Arty.,
Richmond, 3/31/62; des. 2/28/63. Enl. Co. F, 1st
Md. Cav., Richmond, 7/13/63; present through
12/63 and 4/1/64. Captured near Washington,
D.C., 7/12/64; sent to Old Capitol; transf. to
Elmira; released 5/29/65. 5'8½", fair complexion,
auburn hair, blue eyes. Member ANS/MLA,
1916. Res. of Pikesville, Md. d. circa 1916. Bur.
Loudon Park Cem., Baltimore.

SHERWIN, THOMAS (photo): Pvt., Co. K. b.
1839. Enl. Co. K (2nd), 1st Va. Cav., Martinsburg,
W.Va., 9/10/62; present through 8/64. Transf. to
Co. K, 1st Md. Cav., 8/64; horse killed Fisher's
Hill, Va., 9/21/64, paid $3,000; issued clothing
9/30/64; discharged at end of enlistment 12/12/64.
Paroled Staunton, Va., 5/13/65. Age twenty-four,
6', dark complexion, black hair, hazel eyes.

SHESSLER, HENRY: Pvt., Co. D. Served in
Holbrook's Md. Arty. Enl. date and place unknown. Captured in Richmond hosp. 4/3/65; sent
to Newport News, Va. NFR.

SHICKELS, EZRA R. W.: Pvt., Co. unknown.
Davis's Bn. Res. Annapolis, Anne Arundel Co.,
Md. NFR.

SHIPLETT, PLEASANT: Pvt., Co. C. Conscript,
enrolled Hanover Junction, Va., 3/1/64; detailed
as Wagoner 4/1/64. Captured near Silver Spring,
Md., 7/14/64; sent to Old Capitol. transf. to
Elmira; released 5/29/65. 5'9", dark complexion,
dark hair, hazel eyes. Res. of Waynesboro, Va.

SHIPLEY, ALBERT E.: Pvt., Co. A. b. 1840. Res.
of Howard Co., Md. Paroled Edwards' Ferry,
Md., 4/25/65. Took oath Edwards' Ferry 5/25/65.
d. 1906. Bur. Ivy Hill Cem., Laurel, Md.

SHIPLEY, E. A.: Pvt., Co. B. b. Howard Co., Md.,
circa 1836. Enl. Hanover, Va., 8/29/62. Captured
Darkesville, Md., 9/6/62; exchanged 11/18/62.
Paid Richmond 11/26/62. Age twenty-six,
5'11½", fair complexion, gray eyes, light hair.
Merchant. NFR.

SHIPLEY, SAMUEL J.: Pvt., Co. A. Res. of
Howard Co., Md. Enl. Leesburg, Va., 9/1/62;
present 7–9/63; KIA Auburn, Va., 10/13/63.

SHOCKLEY, HANDY B.: Pvt., Co. E. b. 4/8/37.
Res. Worcester Co., Md. Enl. Richmond 11/29/62,
age twenty-four; presence or ab. not stated
1–2/63; ab. sick in hosp. 7–10/63; present 11–
12/63 and 4/1–12/31/64. Paroled Alexandria, Va.,
4/19/65. Took oath Washington, D.C., 4/21/65. d.
Worcester Co., Md., 7/16/05. Bur. Methodist
Episcopal Cem., Snow Hill, Md.

SHOOKS, JUSTICE J.: Pvt., Co. C. Res. of
McPherson's Landing, Anne Arundel Co., Md.
Enl. Barry's Co. Md. Vols. 1861; discharged
1862. Enl. Co. C, 1st Md. Cav., date unknown.
Captured Gettysburg, Pa., 7/4/63; sent to Ft. Del.;

exchanged 8/1/63. Admitted to Petersburg, Va., hosp. the same day with "Feb. cont" and "chronic diarrhoea"; d. there 9/15/63. Effects $2. Probably buried in Blanford Cem., Petersburg.

SHORB, DONALD McNEAL: Pvt., Co. C. b. circa 1842. Res. of Frederick Co., Md. Enl. Winchester 10/15/62; present 7–12/63; ab. on horse detail for ten days to Bridgewater, Va., 2/1/64; present 4/1–8/31/64; ab. detailed as Courier for Gen. Lunsford Lomax 11–12/64. Took oath Washington, D.C., 4/65. d. Clairvoix, Md., 7/10/66, age twenty-eight.

SHORB, JOSEPH COSMAS: 4th Cpl., Co. F. b. Emmittsburg, Frederick Co., Md., 4/30/43. Res. of Emmittsburg. Enl. Co. C, 18th Bn. Va. Arty. 10/17/62. Transf. to Co. F, 1st Md. Cav., Richmond, 6/15/63, as 4th Cpl; present through 10/63; ab. sick with debility in Richmond hosp. 11/25/63–2/8/65. Paroled Columbia, Va., 5/2/65. Admitted Old Soldiers' Home, Pikesville, Md., circa 1900; d. there 2/27/02. Bur. Westminster, Md.

SHOW, JOSEPH: Pvt., Co. K. Res. of Md. Enl. Co. K (2nd), 1st Va. Cav., 7/1/64; present dismounted through 8/64. Transf. to Co. K, 1st Md. Cav., 8/64; present 11–12/64. NFR.

SHOWERS, GEORGE THEODORE: Pvt., Co. D. b. Manchester, Md., 8/20/41. Gd. Marshall Col. 1860, A.B. Farmhand, Manchester Dist., Carroll Co., Md., per 1860 census. Enl. Frederick, Md. 7/1/64; present through 12/64. Paroled Winchester 4/30/65. 5'11½", light complexion, light hair, blue eyes. Res. of Carroll Co., Md. RR Contractor. Gd. Hahnemann Medical Col., Philadelphia, Pa., 1882. M.D., Hampden, Md.; Professor, Homeopathic Medical Col., Baltimore, 1892–1908. d. Baltimore 2/2/23. Bur. Greenmont Cem., Baltimore.

SHRIVER, ANDREW KAISER: Lt., Co. G. b. 3/21/36. Res. of Baltimore. Served in Medical Dept., Richmond. Surrendered Appomattox CH, Va., 4/9/65 as Lt., Co. G, 1st Md. Cav. Took oath Baltimore 5/15/65; destination Carroll Co., Md. Member ANS/MLA, 1894. Res. of Baltimore. d. 5/21/97.

SHRIVER, MARK OWINGS (photo): Pvt., Co. K. b. Union Mills, Carroll Co., Md., 3/3/42. Laborer, Myers Dist., Carroll Co., per 1860 census. Enl. Co. K (2nd), 1st Va. Cav., Union Mills, 7/1/63; present Gettysburg, Pa. Transf. to Co. K, 1st Md. Cav., 8/64; present Berry's Ford, Va., Bunker Hill, W.Va., Winchester, Fisher's Hill, Brown's Gap, and Cedar Creek (all in Va.). Paroled Staunton, Va., 5/22/65. 5'11", fair complexion, dark hair, gray eyes. Took oath Charles Town, W.Va., 5/31/65. Res. of Baltimore. Returned to Balti-

MARK OWINGS SHRIVER

(Carroll County, Md., Historical Society)

more. Arrested, sent to Carroll Co. for trial; acquitted. Oyster and Fruit business, Baltimore. Member ANS/MLA. d. 3/28/24. Bur. New Cathedral Cem., Baltimore. Brother of Thomas H. Shriver.

SHRIVER, THOMAS HERBERT: Pvt., Co. A. b. Union Mills, Carroll Co., Md., 2/14/46. Enl. Co. K (2nd), 1st Va. Cav., Union Mills, 6/27/63. Served as guide for Gen. J. E. B. Stuart during the Gettysburg Campaign; discharged to enter VMI 9/1/63; New Market Cadet. Enl. Co. A, 1st Md. Cav.; on the retreat to Appomattox CH, Va.; tried to join Gen. Joseph E. Johnston in N.C. Took oath Baltimore 6/28/65. Merchant, Bank Teller, Salesman, and in canning business, Baltimore; Member Md. Legislature 1878 and 1880 and Senate 1884; Deputy Collector, Port of Baltimore 1886; BGen. and Comm. Gen. on Governor of Md.'s staff; Vice President, President, and Director of banks in Baltimore. Member ANS/MLA. d. Union Mills 12/31/16. Bur. St. John's Catholic Ch. Cem., Westminister, Md. Brother of Mark O. Shriver. (Postwar photograph in Angus 1923)

SHROFF, PETER FRANKLIN: Pvt., Co. C. b. 10/3/38. Res. of Fallston, Harford Co., Md. On postwar roster Co. K (2nd), 1st Va. Cav. Enl. Co. C, 1st Md. Cav., Richmond, 8/13/62; ab. sick near Harrisonburg, Va., 7/20–10/31/63; present 11–12/63 and 4/1–8/31/64. Captured Sugar Loaf Mt., Md., 1/4/65; sent to Old Capitol. Transf. to Ft. Warren as guerilla; released 6/15/65. 5'9¾", dark complexion, brown hair, hazel eyes. Member ANS/MLA. Entered Old Soldiers' Home, Pikesville, Md., 3/10/17; d. there 6/18/23. Bur. Christ Episcopal Ch. Cem., Rock Springs, Harford Co.

SHYROCK, JAMES FREDERICK: Pvt., Co. K. b. Frederick Co., Va. Res. of White Post, Clarke Co., Va. Mexican War Veteran. Enl. Co. A, 1st Va. Cav., 7/10/63; AWOL through 2/64; CM'd and in Lynchburg, Va., C.S. Military Prison 7/64; RTD.

HENRY B.
SLATER

*(Georgetown
University)*

Transf. to Co. K, 1st Md. Cav., 1/10/65. NFR.

SIMMONS, ALBERT: Pvt., Co. D. b. circa 1844. Res. of Baltimore. Enl. Co. E, 1st Md. Inf., 5/22/61; discharged for "Scrofolo" 1/25/62. Age seventeen, 5'11", dark complexion, light hair, blue eyes. Enl. Co. D. 1st Md. Cav., Bridgewater, Va., 6/1/63. Captured Monterey Springs, Pa., 7/4/63, horse killed; sent to Ft. McHenry; transf. to Ft. Del.; exchanged 1/21/65. Paid $2,000 for horse; present Camp Lee, Richmond, 1/25/65. Paroled, took oath, Richmond 4/19/65; destination Baltimore.

SIMPSON, GEORGE R.: 1st Cpl., Co. D. b. circa 1847. Res. of Libertytown, Frederick Co., Md. Enl. as Pvt., Winchester, 9/20/62; promoted 2nd Cpl; present 10–12/62. Promoted 1st Cpl; present 7–12/63 and 4/1/64. Captured Pollard's Farm, Va., 5/27/64; sent to Pt. Lookout; transf. to Elmira; exchanged 2/65. Paroled New Market, Va. 4/20/65. Age twenty-two, 5'11", dark complexion, dark hair, blue eyes. Took oath Harpers Ferry, W.Va., 5/13/65. d. 1927, age eighty-five. Bur. Kansas City, Mo.

SIMPSON, JOHN T.: Pvt., Co. E. b. circa 1843. Farmer, Prince George's Co., Md. Enl. Richmond 11/18/62, age nineteen; presence or ab. not stated 1–2/63; ab. sick with "diarrhoea" in Richmond hosp. 4/14/63; present 7–8/63; presence or ab. not stated 9–10/63; present 11–12/63 and 4/1/64. Captured Moorefield, W.Va., 8/7/64; sent to Wheeling. Age twenty, 6', dark complexion, light hair, gray eyes. Transf. to Camp Chase and Pt. Lookout; exchanged 3/27/65. Paroled New Market, Va., 4/19/65. Age twenty-one, 5'9", light complexion, light hair, blue eyes. Took oath Alexandria, Va., 4/29/65.

SISSON, CHRISTOPHER R. "KIT": Pvt., Co. D. b. Lynchburg, Va., circa 1847. Res. of Baltimore. Enl. Breathed's Bty. Horse Arty., Richmond, 6/13/63. Transf. to Co. D, 1st Md. Cav., 4/64; "not

reported" on rolls to 8/31/64. Captured Beverly, W.Va., 10/29/64; sent to Wheeling. Age twenty-one, 5'10", dark complexion, dark hair, dark eyes. Student. Transf. to Camp Chase; released 6/12/65. Age twenty-two, 5'10½". d. by 1903.

SISSON, OSCAR B.: Pvt., Co. K. b. Lynchburg, Va., circa 1839. Res. of Baltimore. Enl. Co. C, 1st Md. Inf., 5/17/61; discharged 6/27/62. Age twenty-three, 5'9", dark complexion, dark hair, dark eyes. Clerk. Enl. Co. K (2nd), 1st Va. Cav., 2/25/63. Captured Loudoun Co., Va., 5/16/63; sent to Ft. McHenry; exchanged 5/26/63. AWOL 6/1–30/63; present dismounted 7–8/63; present 9–10/63; AWOL 11/63–2/64; issued clothing in Richmond hosp. 3/25/64; present through 8/31/64. Transf. to Co. K, 1st Md. Cav., 8/64; AWOL 12/1–31/64. Paroled Richmond 4/22/65; transportation furnished to New Orleans, La.

SLATER, GEORGE MEACHAM, JR.: Pvt., Co. K. b. "Rose Hill," Frederick Co., Md., 12/25/40. Res. of Baltimore. Enl. Co. C (2nd), 1st Md. Inf., 5/17/61; WIA (forehead) Bull Run, Va., 7/21/61; discharged 6/9/62. 5'8", light complexion, brown hair, gray eyes. Clerk. Enl. Co. K (2nd), 1st Va. Cav., 6/1/2; present until WIA and captured Catlett's Station, Va., 8/22/62; sent to Old Capitol; exchanged 9/21/62. Present until detailed with Mosby, 1/18–3/19/63 at least; present until WIA 1–2/64; detailed with another comrade to bring Gen. J. E. B. Stuart from the field after he was wounded at Yellow Tavern, Va., 5/11/64, help him from his horse and into an ambulance. Transf. to Co. E, 43rd Bn. Va. Cav., 7/28/64 (also transf. to Co. K, 1st Md. Cav., 8/64; listed as AWOL through 12/64); WIA near Fairfax Station, Va., 8/9/64; present 10/17/64 and 3/21/65. Paroled Winchester 6/16/65. Farmer, Rose Hill Farm, near Paris, Loudoun Co., Va. d. Paris, Va., 1/2/23. Bur. Ivy Hill Cem., Upperville, Va. (Photograph in Driver 1991)

SLATER, HENRY B. (photo): Pvt., Co. B. Att. Georgetown U. Res. of Baltimore. Served in Co. D, 43rd Bn. Va. Cav. (Mosby). Enl. Co. B, 1st Md. Cav., date and place unknown. Captured Sugar Loaf Mt., Md., 1/4/65; sent to Old Capitol; transf. to Ft. Warren, as guerilla; released 6/15/65. 5'8", ruddy complexion, brown hair, gray eyes. Res. of Baltimore.

SLATER, WILLIAM J.: Pvt., Co. C. b. circa 1832. Enl. 1st Md. Arty. 6/27/61; present through 2/62. NFR. Enl. Co. C, 1st Md. Cav., Brucetown, Va., 9/27/62; present 7–12/63; horse died in camp 3/20/64; present 4/1/64; ab. on horse detail for seventeen days to Winchester 4/9/64; AWOL 7/15–12/31/64. Paroled Winchester 4/23/65. Age thirty-three, 5'7½", fair complexion, dark hair, gray eyes. Res. near Martinsburg, W.Va.

SLAVEN, JOHN W.: 4th Cpl., Co. E. b. circa 1841. Enl. as Pvt., Richmond, 11/26/62, age twenty-one; promoted 4th Cpl. 1/20/63. d. of congestive chill, Camp Lee, Richmond, 1/29/63. Bur. Hollywood Cem., Richmond.

SLAYTER, BENJAMIN F.: Pvt., Co. F. Res. of Baltimore. Enl. Brooke Va. Arty. 8/10/63. Transf. to Co. F, 1st Md. Cav., 4/21/64; ab. sick with paralysis of left arm in Richmond hosp. 5/26–7/27/64. Captured Harpers Ferry, W.Va., 9/24/64; on rolls to 12/31/64. Not on Federal POW rolls; may have been KIA.

SLINGLUFF, FIELDER CROSS: 1st Lt., Co. F. b. Baltimore Co., Md., 6/16/42. Res. of Baltimore Co. Gd. Yale U. 1861. "Before leaving Yale he ran up the stars and bars of the Confederacy to the top of the Yale Chapel flagpole and securely locked the door leading to the flagpole before leaving for his Md. home." Enl. as Pvt., 2nd Va. Cav., 8/61. Enl. as Pvt., Co. A, 1st Md. Cav., Manassas, Va., 8/31/62; elected 3rd Lt., Co. F, 7/16/63; present through 12/31/63; served as Adj. of Regt. 12/63–1/15/64; ab. sick with gonorrhoea in Richmond hosp. 2/25–4/1/64; promoted 2nd Lt. and 1st Lt. Captured Moorefield, W.Va., 8/7/64; sent to Wheeling. 6', light complexion, gray eyes, brown hair. Student. Transf. to Camp Chase; exchanged 2/12/65. Present 3/13/65; present Appomattox CH, Va., 4/9/65. Paroled Richmond 4/29/65; took oath Richmond 5/11/65; destination Baltimore. Studied law 1865–67. Lawyer, Baltimore 1867–1900. Merchant, Banker, and Financier. Member Franklin Buchanan Camp, CV, and ANS/MLA. d. Baltimore 5/20/18. Bur. Greenmont Cem., Baltimore.

SLINGLUFF, JOHN L.: Pvt., Co. E. b. circa 1844. Res. of Baltimore Co. Enl. Co. I, 4th Va. Cav., date and place unknown. Captured Emmittsburg, Md., 9/13/62; exchanged 10/6/62. Enl. Co. E, 1st Md. Cav., Richmond, 2/24/63; WIA near Winchester 6/12/63; paid $250; ab. sick with scabies in Charlottesville hosp. 8/17–9/13/63; present 11–12/63 and 4/1–8/31/64; AWOL 11/5–12/31/64. Paroled Petersburg, Va., 5/3/65. Took oath Richmond 6/19/65. Member ANS/MLA. Entered Old Soldiers' Home, Pikesville, Md., from Baltimore 11/4/06, age sixty-two. Laborer. Bur. Greenhill Cem., Berkeley Co., W.Va., no dates.

SLINGLUFF, JOSIAH H.: 1st Sgt., Co. F. b. Baltimore 3/11/36. Merchant, Baltimore. Enl. as 1st Sgt., Richmond, 7/10/63; present through 12/63 and 4/1/64. Captured Moorefield, W.Va., 8/7/64; sent to Wheeling. Age twenty-eight, 5'10½", fair complexion, brown eyes, light hair.

Transf. to Camp Chase and Pt. Lookout; exchanged 3/27/65. Present Camp Lee, Richmond, 3/28/65. Paroled Richmond 4/20/65. Merchant, Baltimore. d. Baltimore 1/31/95. Bur. Greenmont Cem., Baltimore.

SLINGLUFF, TRUEMAN CROSS: Pvt., Co. C. b. 7/19/44. Res. of Baltimore Co., Md. Enl. date and place unknown. Captured Boonsboro, Md., 7/8/64; sent to Old Capitol; transf. to Elmira; exchanged 3/21/65. Paroled Salisbury, N.C., 5/2/65. Took oath Baltimore 6/23/65. Member George Emack Camp, CV, Hyattsville, Md. Res. Woodmore, Prince George's Co., Md. d. 9/1/06. Bur. Holy Trinity Episcopal Ch. Cem., Prince George's Co.

SLOAN, JOHN A.: Pvt., Co. C, Davis's Bn. NFR.

SMALL, GEORGE, JR: Pvt., Co. K. Res. of Md. Enl. Co. K (2nd), 1st Va. Cav., Richmond, 8/1/62; present until detailed in Brig. Signal Corps 5/10/63–2/64. Transf. to Co. K, 1st Md. Cav., 8/64; ab. detailed at Gen. Fitzhugh Lee's Hqtrs. 8/2–31/64; discharged at end of enlistment 12/14/64. NFR.

SMITH, CHARLES W.: Pvt., Co. K. b. Boonsboro, Md., 8/14/43. Res. Prince George's Co., Md. Enl. Co. K (2nd), 1st Va. Cav., Richmond, 7/1/64. Transf. to Co. K, 1st Md. Cav., 8/64. Captured and confined in Chambersburg, Pa., jail 8/10–12/64; exchanged. Present through 12/31/64. NFR. d. 3/28/18. Bur. St. Peter's Rocky Hill Lutheran Ch. Cem., Woodsboro, Frederick Co., Md. Brother of William J. Smith.

SMITH, DANIEL: Pvt., Co. A. b. 5/15/35. Res. Downsville, Washington Co., Md. Enl. Urbana, Md., 9/15/62; present 7–10/63; ab. on duty 12/12–31/63 and 4/1/64; ab. on leave in Richmond 8/31/64; AWOL 11–12/64. NFR. Attended reunion 1899. d. 11/19/07. Bur. Welty Ch. Cem., near Greensburg, Md.

SMITH, HENRY E.: Pvt., Co. A, Davis's Bn. b. 10/12/37. NFR. d. 4/11/14. Bur. Mt. Olivet Cem., Frederick, Md.

SMITH, JAMES: Pvt., Co. G. d. of "chronic diarrhoea," Danville, Va., hosp., 12/3/64.

SMITH, JAMES J.: Pvt., Co. B. b. circa 1841. Res. Queen Anne's Co., Md. Enl. Charlottesville 9/10/62; present 7–9/63. Captured Raccoon Ford, Va., 10/10/63; sent to Old Capitol; trans. to Pt. Lookout; exchanged 3/6/64. Paroled POW 4/1/64. Captured Moorefield, W.Va., 8/7/64; sent to Wheeling. Age twenty-three, 5'7½", fair complexion, blue eyes, brown hair. Transf. to Camp Chase and Pt. Lookout; exchanged 3/27/65. NFR.

SMITH, JAMES T.: Pvt., Co. G. b. circa 1846. Res. of Baltimore. Enl. date and place unknown. Captured Newtown, Va., 1/6/64; sent to Wheeling.

Age eighteen, 5'9", florid complexion, gray eyes, dark hair. Carpenter. Transf. to Camp Chase and Ft. Del.; exchanged 2/27/65. NFR.

SMITH, JOHN FRANK: Pvt., Co. A, Davis's Bn. b. 1840. Enl. New Market, Va., 8/8/63. Captured Newtown, Va., 2/64. Transf. to Co. M, 23rd Va. Cav. NFR. Sheriff of St. Mary's Co., Md., 1/17/69. d. 1921.

SMITH, JOHN F.: Pvt., Co. A. Att. Georgetown U. Res. of Prince George's Co., Md. Enl. Co. K (2nd), 1st Va. Cav., Richmond, 7/20/62; present until transf. to Co. A, 1st Md. Cav., 8/6/64; detailed as ambulance driver; AWOL 8/31/64. NFR.

SMITH, JOHN H.: Pvt., Co. C, Davis's Bn. b. 12/22/32. NFR. d. 11/27/05. Bur. St. Peter's Rocky Hill Lutheran Ch. Cem., Woodsboro, Frederick Co., Md.

SMITH, JOHN P.: Pvt., Co. K. b. 1/3/42. Res. Prince George's Co., Md. Enl. Co. K (2nd), 1st Va. Cav., Richmond, 7/20/62; present until detailed as ambulance driver 5–10/63; present until detailed in Provost Guard 1–8/64. Transf. to Co. K, 1st Md. Cav., 8/64; ab. detailed in Provost Guard through 12/31/64. NFR. d. 1/10/39. Bur. Mt. Olivet Cem., Frederick, Md.

SMITH, PETER: Pvt., Co. C. Enl. 6/20/61 in unknown unit. Enl. Co. C, 1st Md. Cav., date and place unknown. Captured Leonardtown, Md., 4/25/65; sent to Old Capitol. Trans. Elmira; released 7/7/65. 5'5½", fair complexion, dark hair, blue eyes. Res. of N.Y. City.

SMITH, RICHARD C.: 3rd Cpl., Co. C. Enl. as Pvt., Richmond, 8/15/62; promoted 3rd Cpl. 8/12/63; present 7–12/63, 1–2/64, and 4/1/64. Captured Rockville, Md., 7/12/64, horse killed; sent to Old Capitol; transf. to Elmira; exchanged 3/15/65. Paid $2,500 for horse; paid Richmond 3/24/65. Paroled Salisbury, N.C., 5/1/65, as Pvt.

SMITH, ROBERT CARTER: Lt. Col. b. Baltimore Co., Md., 1828. Gd. Episcopal HS, Alexandria, Va., and Georgetown U. 1855. Merchant and Coffee Importer, Baltimore. Enl. as 2nd Lt., Co. C, 1st Md. Inf., 5/19/61; present Bull Run, Va.; elected Capt. 7/21/61; present 9–12/61. NFR. Elected Capt., Co. C, 1st Md. Cav., 5/19/62; present Brandy Station, Catlett's Station, and 2nd Manassas (all in Va.), and Sharpsburg, Md.; present 11–12/62. Ninety men in co. 11/62: eighty-five mounted, six or eight absent as POWs, and others ab. sick and on detail; WIA (right arm) Greenland Gap, W.Va., 4/25/63; ab. wounded in hosp. 7–8/63; promoted Maj. of Regt. 9/2/63 to rank from 8/20/63. Three officers and seventy-two men present in Co. C 11/63. Promoted Lt. Col. 6/1/64; detailed to command military prison, Danville,

Va., 6/1/64; ab. sick with "fracture of humerus" in Charlottesville hosp. 9/21/64; transf. to another hosp. 9/22/64; commanding Camp of Md. Line near Richmond 10/8/64; assigned to command military prison, Danville, 10/26/64; retired to Invalid Corps for disability 12/2/64. Paroled Salisbury, N.C., 5/1/65. Took oath Danville, Va., 5/5/65. Officer of the Courts, Baltimore, postwar. Member Isaac R. Trimble Camp, CV, Franklin Buchanan Camp, CV, Baltimore, and ANS/MLA. d. Catonsville, Md., 2/13/00. Bur. Loudon Park Cem., Baltimore. Brother of Thomas J. and Wilson C. M. Smith.

SMITH, SAMUEL D.: Pvt., Co. G. b. 2/10/33. Captured date and place unknown; sent to Hampton, Va., 4/25/65; released 5/1/65. d. 4/20/05. Bur. Mt. Hope Cem., Woodsboro, Frederick Co., Md.

SMITH, THOMAS: Pvt., Co. A. b. circa 1838. Paroled New Market, Va., 4/19/65. Age twenty-seven, 5'6", dark complexion, black hair, black eyes.

SMITH, THOMAS JEFFERSON: 1st Lt., Co. C. b. circa 1824. Res. of Baltimore. Enl. Co. G, 7th Va. Cav., 8/4/62; leg broken Sharpsburg, Md., 9/16/62; ab. in Charlottesville hosp. until furloughed for ninety days 12/23/62; Commanding Co. 2/24–25/63; present 7–12/63; promoted 1st Lt. 8/25/63; ab. on leave for fifteen days 1/8/64; present 2/64 and 4/1/64. Captured Moorefield, W.Va., 8/7/64; sent to Wheeling. Age forty, 5'9", dark complexion, gray eyes, dark hair. Farmer. Transf. to Camp Chase; exchanged 3/12/65. Member ANS/MLA, 1894. Brother of Robert C. and Wilson C. M. Smith.

SMITH, THOMAS T.: Pvt., Co. F. Res. of Baltimore. Enl. Richmond 7/14/63; present through 8/31/63; ab. in arrest Richmond 9–10/63; ab. undergoing sentence of CM, Richmond, 11–12/63 and 4/1/64; present through 8/31/64; ab. as Courier for Gen. Lunsford Lomax 9/8–12/31/64. Paroled Greensboro, N.C., 5/1/65. Took oath Richmond 5/15/65. In Old Soldiers' Home, Pikesville, Md., 1894.

SMITH, WILLIAM: Pvt., Co. K. Enl. Co. K (2nd), 1st Va. Cav., Richmond, 7/26/62; present until transf. to Co. K, 1st Md. Cav., 8/64; present until captured Rockville, Md., 10/2/64; sent to Elmira; released 5/19/65. 5'5", fair complexion, auburn hair, blue eyes. Res. of St. Louis, Mo.

SMITH, WILLIAM JACOB: Pvt., Co. K. b. Boonsboro, Md. 3/31/45. Res. Queen Anne, Anne Arundel Co., Md. Enl. Co. K (2nd), 1st Va. Cav., Richmond, 8/1/62; present until transf. to Co. K, 1st Md. Cav., 8/64. Captured Rockville, Md., 10/2/64; sent to Elmira; released 5/19/65. Printer, Shepherdstown, W.Va. Att. Roanoke Col. Lutheran Minister. d. near Mt. Falls, Frederick Co., Va., 2/19/11, age sixty-six. Bur. Mt. Hebron Cem., Winchester. Brother of Charles W. Smith.

SMITH, WILSON CARY NICHOLAS: Pvt., Co. C. Res. of Baltimore. Enl. New Market, Va., 2/1/63; present 7–12/63 and 4/1/64–8/31/64; horse killed Kernstown,Va., 7/23/64, paid $1,800; present 9–12/64. Surrendered Appomattox CH, Va., 4/9/65; took oath there 4/10/65; destination Baltimore. Brother of Robert C. and Thomas J. Smith.

SMOOT, JOSEPH R.: Pvt., Co. K. Enl. Co. K (2nd), 1st Va. Cav., Richmond, 4/8/62; present until AWOL 3–4/63. Captured with Mosby 5/23/63; exchanged. Present through 2/64. Transf. to Co. K, 1st Md. Cav., 8/64; AWOL 7/30–12/31/64, however, enl. Co. F, 43rd Va. Bn. Cav. (Mosby) 9/13/64; issued clothing 4th Qtr. NFR. d. 5/3/07.

SNOOK, JEROME A.: Pvt., Co. D. Res. of Frederick Co., Md. Enl. Co. A, 39th Bn. Va. Cav., Gettysburg, Pa., 7/3/63. Transf. to Co. D, 1st Md. Cav., 12/27/63; present 4/1–8/64; ab. sick with scabies in Richmond hosp. 8/3–15/64; present 9–12/64; WIA (amputation of left forearm middle third in consequence of a childhood accident) 3/65; admitted Richmond hosp. 3/5/65. Captured in Richmond hosp. 4/3/65. In Petersburg, Va., hosp. 4/9/65; sent to Pt. Lookout; released 7/19/65. 5'8", dark complexion, black hair, black eyes. d. 5/25/81, no age given. Bur. Mt. Olivet Cem., Frederick, Md.

SNOWDEN, GEORGE T.: Capt., Co. D, Davis's Bn. Res. of Howard Co., Md. NFR.

SNOWDEN, JOHN CAPRON: Pvt., Co. C. b. Prince George's Co., Md., 6/29/43. Farmer, Prince George's Co. Enl. Bridgewater, Va., 5/24/63; present 7–12/63 and 4/1/64. Captured Moorefield, W.Va., 8/7/64; sent to Wheeling. Age twenty-one, 5'6", dark complexion, blue eyes, light hair. Transf. to Camp Chase and Pt. Lookout; exchanged 3/27/65. Present Camp Lee, Richmond, 3/28/65. Paroled Burkeville, Va., 4/26/65. Clerk, Baltimore, postwar. Member ANS/MLA. Entered Old Soldiers' Home, Pikesville, Md., 7/5/04, age sixty-one; discharged. d. 12/2/10. Bur. St. Philip's P. E. Ch. Cem., Laurel, Md.

SOLLERS, WILLIAM OWENS: Pvt., Co. D. b. 8/1/36. Res. of Baltimore. Enl. Boonsboro, Md., 6/15/63; present through 8/31/63; ab. on horse detail 10/31/63. Captured Williamsport, Md., 11/7/63; sent to Ft. Del.; exchanged 2/27/65. Paroled Winchester 4/26/65. 5'7½", fair complexion, dark hair, blue eyes. Clerk, Baltimore, postwar. Member ANS/MLA. Entered Old Soldiers' Home, Pikesville, Md., 12/7/03. d. 6/2/24. Bur. Loudon Park Cem., Baltimore.

SPEAR, DEWITT CLINTON: Pvt., Co. B. b. circa 1829. Farmer, Queen Anne's Co., Md. Enl. Charlottesville 10/1/62. Captured on picket near Winchester 11/23/62; sent to Cumberland, Md., and Wheeling. Age thirty-four, 5'7", light complexion, gray eyes, brown hair. Transf. to Camp Chase; exchanged 12/22/62. Present 7–8/63; ab. on detached service 9–10/63; horse captured Germanna Ford, Va., 10/11/63; present 11–12/63; ab. on horse detail for fifteen days to Botetourt Co., Va., 2/16/64; present 4/1/64; gray horse killed Beaver Dam Station, Va., 5/10/64, paid $1,175; ab. on horse detail for twenty days to Hardy Co., W.Va., 5/21/64. Captured Beltsville, Md., 7/12/64; sent to Old Capitol. Transf. to Elmira; exchanged 3/15/65. Paroled New Market, Va., 4/19/65. Age thirty-six, 5'8", fair complexion, light hair, gray eyes. Took oath Harpers Ferry, W.Va., 5/2/65.

SPEAR, EDWIN WALLACE: Pvt., Co. B. b. 8/15/41. Res. Kent Co., Md. Enl. Charlottesville 11/1/62; present through 11/30/62 and 7–9/63. Captured Germanna or Raccoon Ford, Va., 10/10/63; sent to Old Capitol. Transf. to Pt. Lookout; exchanged 3/6/64. Present as paroled POW 4/1/64; WIA, captured Pollard's Farm, Va., 5/27/64, horse killed; sent to Pt. Lookout; exchanged 1/21/65. Admitted Richmond hosp. same day; furloughed for thirty days 1/31/65; paid $2,500 for horse. Paroled Winchester 4/22/65. 5'6", light complexion, light hair, blue eyes. Took oath Harpers Ferry, W.Va., 5/4/65. Member George Emack Camp, CV, Hyattsville, Md. Res. of Sudlersville, Queen Anne's Co., Md., 1903. d. "Greenwood Farm," Kent Co., Md., 9/5/16. Bur. Millington Cem. Brother of James J. Spear.

SPEAR, JAMES JACKSON: 2nd Cpl., Co. B. b. circa 1837. Res. Kent Co., Md. Enl. Charlottesville 9/10/62; ab. sick with "syphilis" in Charlottesville hosp. 10/25–12/18/62; present 7–12/63 and 4/1/64. Captured Kent Co., Md., 4/12/64, age thirty-one; sent to Old Capitol. Transf. to Ft. Warren, as guerilla; released 6/10/65. 5'8¼", dark complexion, brown hair, hazel eyes. Res. "Queen Anne Farm," Kent Co., postwar. Brother of Edwin W. Spear.

SPENCER, JERVIS, JR.: Pvt., Co. C. b. Md. 3/2/43. Res. of Baltimore. Enl. Hagerstown, Md., 9/12/62; present 7–12/63; ab. on horse detail for twelve days to Winchester 1/9/64; present 4/1/64; ab. sick with acute dysentery in Richmond hosp. 6/5–27/64. Captured Moorefield, W.Va., 8/7/64, horse killed; sent to Wheeling. Age nineteen, 5'9", fair complexion, blue eyes, light hair. Teacher. Transf. to Camp Chase and Pt. Lookout; exchanged 3/27/65. Paid $3,000 for horse; present Camp Lee, Richmond, 3/28/65. NFR. Lawyer, Baltimore postwar. Member ANS/MLA. Entered

Old Soldiers' Home, Pikesville, Md., 9/3/01, age fifty-six; dropped. d. Garrison, Baltimore Co. 6/29/10. Bur. St. Thomas Ch. Cem., Garrison, Md.

SPENCER, JOHN CHAPMAN: Pvt., Co. E. b. 11/44. Res. Snow Hill, Worcester Co., Md. Enl. Richmond, 11/10/62, age eighteen; presence or ab. not stated 1–2/63; shot through lungs, KIA Greenland Gap, W.Va., 4/25/63. Bur. near Chestertown, Kent Co., Md.

SPENCER, SAMUEL B.: 1st Sgt., Co. B. b. circa 1837. Clerk, Washington, D.C. Enl. Co. E, 1st Va. Inf., 4/22/61, age twenty-four. Transf. to Co. F, 6th Va. Cav., 2/1/62; discharged 6/23/62. Enl. Co. B, 1st Md. Cav., Charlottesville, 9/10/62; present 7–12/63 and 4/1/64; WIA (right shoulder and neck) Clear Spring, Md., 7/12/64. Captured Chambersburg, Pa., 7/29/64; sent to Ft. Del. Transf. to Pt. Lookout; exchanged 11/15/64. Admitted Charlottesville hosp. 11/19/64. Captured Hanover, Va., 3/13/65; sent to Ft. Monroe. Transf. to Pt. Lookout; released 6/12/65. 5'11", freckle complexion, light brown hair, gray eyes. Destination Washington, D.C.

STACLE, JOHN: Pvt., Co. D. On postwar roster.

STAIMAN, J. F.: Pvt., Co. A. Captured and paroled Winchester 6/12/62. Age twenty-two, 5'8". NFR.

STALLINGS, CHARLES L.: Pvt., Co. E. b. circa 1840. Enl. Richmond, 11/10/62, age twenty-two; presence or ab. not stated 1–2/63. WIA and captured Winchester 7/25/63; exchanged. Ab. wounded in Richmond hosp. 8/31–10/31/63, age twenty-three; ab. sick with "scrofula" in Richmond hosp. 1/30–3/31/64; ab. on horse detail for twenty days to Hardy Co., W.Va., 4/9/64; des.— went home and took oath; on rolls 7–8/64. NFR.

STALLINGS, CLARENCE L.: Pvt., Co. C. Res. of Anne Arundel Co., Md. On postwar roster.

STANLEY, CHARLES H.: Pvt., Co. B. b. Connecticut 11/20/42. Farmer, Collington, Prince George's Co., Md. Served in Co. B, 1st Md. Inf., 1861–62. Enl. Co. B, 1st Md. Cav., Charlottesville, 9/10/62; WIA and captured Romney, W.Va., 2/16/63; sent to Wheeling. 5'10", light complexion, light hair, gray eyes. Transf. to Camp Chase; exchanged 4/1/63; WIA and captured Monterey Springs, Pa., 7/4/63; sent to Ft. McHenry. Transf. to Ft. Del.; exchanged 8/64. Present Camp Lee, Richmond, 8/31/64; present Winchester 9/19/64; ab. sick in Richmond hosp. 10/6–7/64; transf. to Staunton, Va., hosp. 11/20–21/64; present 12/64; present Manchester and High Bridge. Escaped at Appomattox CH, Va., and went to Danville, Va., en route to Gen. Joseph E. Johnston's Army in N.C. Paroled Charlottesville 5/6/65. Teacher, Prince George's Co., 1865–68; studied law; lawyer, Laurel, Md., 1868, and later in Balti-

more; served in Md. Legislature 1882; Mayor of Laurel two terms; State Director of the B&O RR for five years; President of Citizens Bank of Laurel; and Attorney for Penn. RR. Member George Emack Camp, CV, Hyattsville, Md., and ANS/MLA. d. Laurel 12/20/13. Bur. Ivy Hill Cem., Laurel.

STANLEY, E. H.: Pvt., Co. B. Res. of Baltimore. On postwar roster. Member ANS/MLA, 1894. Res. of Baltimore.

STANSBURY, J. W.: Pvt., Co. C; present sick 11/62. NFR.

STEELE, JOHN H.: Pvt., Co. D. b. Md. circa 1821. Farmer, age thirty-nine, Freedom Dist., Carroll Co., Md., per 1860 census. Enl. Co. A, 1st Md. Inf., 5/21/61; discharged 5/21/62. Captured Cross Keys, Va., 6/8/62. Age forty-six, 5'10"; sent to Ft. McHenry; exchanged 4/12/62. Enl. Co. D, 1st Md. Cav., Lacey Springs, Va., 4/1/63; present 7–12/63 and 4/1/64; ab. detailed Gen. Bradley Johnson's Hqtrs. through 12/64; present Salisbury, N.C., 1/9/65. "Brought Gen. Johnson's horses down and will return to command." Captured Salisbury, N.C., 4/12/65; sent to Louisville, Ky.; transf. to Camp Chase; released 6/12/65. Age fifty, 5'6", dark complexion, dark hair, blue eyes. Res. of Frederick Co., Md. Member ANS/MLA. Entered Old Soldiers' Home, Pikesville, Md., from Carroll Co. 9/23/88, age seventy; d. there 12/16/90, age seventy-two. Bur. Loudon Park Cem., Baltimore.

STERMIS, JOSEPH: Pvt., Co. B. On postwar roster.

STETSON, W. H.: Pvt., Co. G. Captured, date and place unknown; sent to Camp Hamilton, Newport News, Va., 4/27/65; released 5/1/65.

STEVENS, JAMES C.: Pvt., Co. B. Res. of Broad Creek, Queen Anne's Co., Md. Enl. Charlottesville 9/10/62; horse killed South Mt., Md., 7/4/63; present 7–12/63; ab. on horse detail for fifteen days to Warrenton, N.C., 2/16/64; present 4/1/64. "Missing since 8/1/64, supposed to be killed"; on rolls 8/31–12/31/64. NFR.

STEVENSON, DAWSON H.: Pvt., Co. D. b. Baltimore circa 1842. Res. Frederick Co., Md. Enl. Lacey Springs, Va., 4/1/63. Captured Monterey Springs, Pa., 7/4/63, horse killed; sent to Ft. McHenry; transf. to Ft. Del. and Pt. Lookout; exchanged 12/28/63. Paid $500 for horse; ab. sick with pneumonia in Richmond hosp. 1/27–3/31/64; horse killed Smithfield, W.Va., 8/28/64, paid $2,500; present through 12/31/64. Paroled New Market, Va., 4/28/65. Age twenty-three, 5'6", light complexion, light eyes, light hair. Took oath Frederick Co., Md., 6/26/65; destination Baltimore. Member ANS/MLA. Merchant, Baltimore; d. there 11/16/00, age sixty. Bur. Loudon

Park Cem., Baltimore.

STEVENSON, THOMAS H.: Pvt., Co. D. b. circa 1840. Enl. Winchester 9/25/62; present 11–12/62. Captured Monterey Springs, Pa., 7/4/63, horse killed; sent to Ft. McHenry; transf. to Ft. Del. and Pt. Lookout; exchanged 12/28/63. Present 4/1–12/31/64; ab. sick with "debilitas" in Charlottesville hosp. 3/1/65. Paroled Winchester 4/23/65. Age twenty-five, 5'10", fair complexion, sandy hair, blue eyes. Res. of Charles Town, W.Va.

STEVES, CHRISTOPHER P.: Pvt., Co. D. b. 12/8/43. Res. of Frederick, Md. Enl. Winchester 9/20/62; present 11–12/62; paid New Market, Va., 1/10/63. Captured near Winchester 5/19/63; sent to Ft. McHenry; transf. to Ft. Monroe; exchanged 6/26/63. Present 7–9/63; ab. sick with debility in Richmond hosp. 10/4/63; present 10–12/63 and 4/1/64; WIA (left thumb) Pollard's Farm, Va., 5/27/64; ab. wounded in Richmond hosp. 5/28/64 until furloughed for thirty days 7/11/64; present 8/31/64; KIA Liberty Mills, Orange Co., Va., 12/22/64. Bur. St. John's Catholic Ch. Cem., Frederick, Md.

STEWART, JOHN ALLEN: Pvt., Co. D. Res. of Davidsonville, Anne Arundel Co., Md. Claimed that he "was conscripted 11/63" upon capture near Harpers Ferry, W.Va., 7/16/64; sent to Old Capitol; transf. to Elmira; released 5/15/65. 5'8", fair complexion, light hair, blue eyes. Res. of Calia Co. [sic], Ohio.

STEWART, SEPTIMUS HUNTER: Pvt., Co. C. Att. U.S.M.A. Bookkeeper, Baltimore, per 1860 census. Enl. as 1st Lt., Co. C, 1st Md. Inf., 5/17/61. Captured Sangster's Station, Va., 3/9/62; exchanged 8/5/62. Promoted Asst. QM, Md. Line, 4/16/62, while POW; dropped 8/30/62. Enl. as Pvt., Co. C, 1st Md. Cav., date unknown. Captured Monterey Springs, Pa., 7/4/63; sent to Ft. McHenry; transf. to Ft. Del., Ft. Columbus, and Pt. Lookout; exchanged 12/38/63. Appointed Capt., 2nd Va. Reserves. Surrendered Appomattox CH, Va., 4/9/65. Took oath Washington, D.C., 4/22/63. d. 1/6/93. Bur. Loudon Park Cem., Baltimore.

STINE, ISAAC: Pvt., Co. E. b. circa 1847. Sailor. Res. of Baltimore. Captured Moorefield, W.Va., 8/7/64; sent to Wheeling. Age twenty-one, 5'7", light complexion, dark hair, gray eyes. Transf. to Camp Chase and Pt. Lookout; exchanged 3/27/65. NFR.

STINE, JOSEPH A.: Pvt., Co. D. Enl. 1st Md. Arty. 8/16/61; present through 2/62. NFR. Joined without proper transfer from 12th Va. Cav.; returned to that unit, on rolls 12/62. NFR. Transf. to Co. F, 2nd Md. Bn. Cav. and promoted 1st Sgt. Member ANS/MLA, 1894. Res. of Baltimore.

STINSON, CHARLES R.: Pvt., Co. C. b. circa 1842. Res. of Baltimore. Served previously in Co. B, 43rd Bn. Va. Cav. (Mosby). Enl. Co. C, 1st Md. Cav., date unknown. WIA (left hip fractured) and captured Rectortown 10/4/64; sent to U.S. hosp., Alexandria, Va.; DOW there 10/13/64, age twenty-two. His father, Richard Stinson, came to hosp., had body shipped to Baltimore for burial. Effects: one jacket, one pair of trousers, and one book.

STOCKDALE, F. G.: Pvt., Co. C. Application to ANS/MLA, 1894, is only record of service. Res. of Baltimore. Also claimed service in 2nd Md. Bn. Cav.

STODDARD, JOHN: Pvt., Co. A, Davis's Bn. Enl. Mt. Jackson, Va., 11/10/63; present through 1/1/64. Captured near Martinsburg, W.Va., 8/64. On rolls to 10/31/64. Transf. to Co. M, 23rd Va. Cav. NFR.

STODDARD, JOHN T.: Pvt., Co. B. b. circa 1844 Student, Charles Co., Md. Captured Moorefield, W.Va., 8/7/64; sent to Wheeling. Age eighteen, 5'5", dark complexion, black hair, black eyes. Transf. to Camp Chase and Pt. Lookout; exchanged 3/27/65. Paroled Richmond 4/24/65.

STONE, CARTER: Pvt., Co. A. Enl. Hanover Junction, Va., 2/1/64; present 4/1–12/31/64. NFR.

STONE, F. E.: Pvt., Co. C. Enl. date and place unknown. Captured Monterey Springs, Pa., 7/4/63; sent to Ft. Del.; released by order of the Secretary of War, 8/31/63. NFR.

STONE, HENRY P.: Pvt., Co. A. b. near Potomac, Md., 1844. Res. Rockville, Montgomery Co., Md. Enl. Winchester 10/21/62; WIA (thumb shot off) Hagerstown, Md., 7/6/63; ab. wounded in Charlottesville hosp. 8/15/63 until transf. to Lynchburg, Va., hosp. 9/21/63; ab. detailed as Wardmaster in Charlottesville hosp. 11/23/63–1/16/64; present 4/1–12/31/64; ab. sick with catarrhous in Charlottesville hosp. 1/9–13/65. Took oath Edwards' Ferry, Md., 5/24/65; destination Rockville, Md; moved to Tennessee by 1898.

STONE, JOHN: Pvt., Co. D; des. 11/62. NFR.

STONE, JOHN A. C.: Pvt., Co. A. b. Haw Bottom, Frederick Co., Md., 2/14/46. Enl. Richmond 5/29/64; issued clothing 9/30/64. Took oath Edwards' Ferry, Md., 5/2/65. Farmer, Middletown, Frederick Co., Md. d. 1927. Bur. Reformed Ch. Cem., Middletown.

STONE, JOSEPH FORD: Pvt., Co. C. b. Leonardtown, St. Mary's Co., Md., 1840. Att. West Point Military Acad., N.Y. Gd. Georgetown U. 1861. Res. Leonardtown. Enl. Richmond 8/4/62. Captured South Mt., Md., 7/4/63; sent to Ft. McHenry; transf. to Ft. Del., Pt. Lookout, and Ft. Columbus; exchanged 12/28/63. Present 4/1/64. Captured near Charlotte Hall, Md.,

5/23/64. Accused of spying but not convicted; sent to Pt. Lookout; released 5/14/65. Clerk. Enl. Co. M, 3rd U.S. Cav., Baltimore, 1/13/66, as Farrier. Discharged Ft. Wingate, N.M., 10/13/68. d. Globe City, Ariz., 11/9/79, age thirty-nine.

STONE, ROBERT C.: Pvt., Co. A. On postwar roster.

STONEBRAKER, JOSEPH L.: Pvt., Co. C. b. LaGrange, Mo., 2/1/40. Res. of Funkstown, Washington Co., Md. Arrested as Southern sympathizer, sent to Ft. McHenry without a trial, 8/9/62; held three months; released. Joined his uncle, who was the QM of the Stonewall Brigade, and served as a Courier. Enl. Co. C, 1st Md. Cav., 10/64; present Appomattox CH, Va., 4/9/65, but escaped. Paroled Harrisonburg, Va., 5/7/65. 5'11½", light complexion, brown hair, blue eyes. Moved to Baltimore 5/66. Wholesale liquor dealer; Vice President, Fidelity and Deposit Co., and Director, Continental Bank, Baltimore; Financier. Member ANS/MLA. Author of *A Rebel of '61*, 1899. d. Baltimore 10/25/03. Bur. Loudon Park Cem., Baltimore. Tombstone inscription reads, "The bearer, Joseph R. Stonebraker, Co. C, 1st Md. Cavalry, having done his duty faithfully to the present time, is permitted to go where he pleases until called for. C. W. Dorsey, Lt. Co. Commander, 1st Md. Cavalry, C.S.A." Brother of Edward L. Stonebraker, 2nd Md. Cav.

STONER, JOHN: Pvt., Co. D; des. 9/29/62; on rolls to 12/31/62. Possibly the J. D. Stoner who died in Va. during the war and was reburied in Loudon Park Cem., Baltimore, in 1874.

STREET, JAMES POLK: Pvt., Co. C. b. circa 1846. Farmer, Harford Co., Md. Enl. Williamsport, Md., 7/6/63; present through 12/63 and 4/1/64. Captured Moorefield, W.Va., 8/7/64; sent to Wheeling. Age sixteen, 5'10", fair complexion, light hair, blue eyes. Transf. to Camp Chase; took oath, released 2/11/65. Alive in 1927.

STRONG, W. R.: Pvt., Co. B. b. circa 1846. Res. of Canada. Enl. Hanover Junction, Va., 3/17/64; present 4/1/64. Captured Moorefield, W.Va., 8/7/64; sent to Wheeling. Age twenty, 5'8", fair complexion, black hair, brown eyes. Student. Res. of Jacksonville, Fla. Transf. to Camp Chase and Pt. Lookout; exchanged 3/27/65. NFR.

SUDLER, JOHN EMORY: Pvt., Co. unknown. b. Kent Co., Md., 3/4/39. Farmer, Still Pond, Kent Co., per 1860 census. On postwar roster. Promoted Capt., Co. E, 2nd Bn. Md. Cav; WIA (ankle) Chancellorsville, Va., 5/3/63; WIA Cedar Creek, Va., 10/19/64. Paroled Mechanicsville, Va., 4/28/65. Member Isaac Trimble Camp, CV, Baltimore. d. 1910. Bur. St. James Episcopal Ch. Cem., Anne Arundel Co., Md.

SULLIVAN, FRANK: Pvt., Co. C. b. Md. circa

1845. Clerk, Baltimore. Enl. Richmond 9/1/62; present 7–12/63; requested furlough to Greensboro, N.C., 1/15/64. Age nineteen, 5'10", dark complexion, black hair, black eyes; present 4/1–12/31/64; surrendered Appomattox CH, Va., 4/9/65. Took oath 4/10/65. Member ANS/ MLA, 1884. Res. of Cincinnati, Oh. Res. of Baltimore 1894. Possibly Francis E. Sullivan (12/24/44–11/30/20). Bur. Springhill Cem., Easton, Md.

SULLIVAN, M. H.: Pvt., Co. C, Davis's Bn. On postwar roster.

SULLIVAN, THOMAS: Pvt., Co. A, Davis's Bn. Enl. New Market, Va., 6/15/64. Transf. to Co. M, 23rd Va. Cav; present through 10/31/64. NFR.

SUNTON, G. F.: Pvt., Co. F. Paroled Greensboro, N.C., 5/1/65.

SWANEY, G. F.: Pvt., Co. unknown; issued clothing 9/30/64. NFR.

SWEENEY, GEORGE W. H.: Pvt., Co. E. Enl. Richmond 4/1/63; present through 8/31/63; presence or ab. not stated 9–10/63; present 11–12/63 and 4/1/64. Captured Moorefield, W.Va., 8/7/64; listed as POW, Camp Chase, on muster rolls to 12/31/64. Not on Federal POW rolls, however; may have been KIA.

SWEETING, BENJAMIN HARRISON "HARRY": Pvt., Co. F. b. circa 1843. Res. of Baltimore. Enl. Co. F, 1st Md. Inf., 5/22/61; discharged 8/11/62. Application to ANS/MLA is only record of service. Served in 43rd Bn. Va. Cav., 1863–65; WIA Dranesville, Md., 2/22/64. M.D., Baltimore and The Rocks, Harford Co., Md., 1893. Entered Old Soldiers' Home, Pikesville, Md., from Harford Co., 3/20/93, age fifty. Farmer. d. Old Soldiers' Home 1/6/96.

SWITZER, JOHN A.: Pvt., Co. I. b circa 1841. Res. of Mt. Airy, Carroll Co., Md. Paroled Staunton, Va., 5/26/65. Age twenty-six, 5'5", light complexion, auburn hair, gray eyes.

SWOMLEY, FRANK: Pvt., Co. D. Res. of New Market, Md. Enl. date unknown; ab. on leave to Staunton, Va., 12/20–31/62; WIA (chest and hip) Greenland Gap, W.Va., 4/23/63; DOW's 4/25/63.

SWOMLEY, THOMAS: Pvt., Co. D. On postwar roster.

SYMINGTON, WILLIAM STUART: Pvt., Co. A. b. Baltimore 1/6/39. Res. of Baltimore. Enl. as Lt., Co. B, 1st Va. Inf., 5/23/61; present Kernstown, Va.; not reelected 5/23/62. 5'10½", high color, dark hair, dark eyes. Enl. as Pvt., Co. A, 1st Md. Cav., date and place unknown; detailed on recruiting duty Richmond. Served as volunteer ADC to Col. John B. Strange at Frazier's Farm,Va., and ". . . acted with a bravery seldom equalled. His horse was shot down early in the action, but still he exposed himself to every danger, rallying retreating troops, stragglers, &c., and in every way rendering the most efficient service." Appointed Lt. and ADC on Gen. George Pickett's staff 10/10/62; promoted Capt; present Gettysburg, Pa., and Drewry's Bluff, Petersburg, and Five Forks (all Va.); surrendered Appomattox CH, Va., 4/9/65. Refused to take the oath. Went to Germany for a year; returned to Baltimore. Manuacturing Chemist 1866–81; Life Insurance business 1888–90; Chief of Department of City Lighting, Baltimore. Member ANS/MLA. Mayor of Baltimore. d. Baltimore 6/9/12. Bur. Greenmont Cem., Baltimore. (Photograph in Hartzler 1992)

TACEY, HILLARY: Pvt., Co. G. b. circa 1846. Res. of Frederick Co., Md. Enl. date and place unknown; issued clothing 7/1/63. Captured Frederick Co., Va. 1/6/64; sent to Wheeling. Age eighteen, 5'5", dark complexion, brown eyes, dark hair. Paper Hanger; res. of Alexandria, Va. Transf. to Camp Chase and Ft. Del.; exchanged 2/27/65. NFR.

TAYLOR, CHARLES J.: Pvt., Co. D. b. circa 1846. Student, "Arcadia," Frederick Co., Md. Enl. Winchester 9/20/62; present 11–12/62. Captured Strasburg, Va., 3/5/63; sent to Wheeling. Age seventeen, 5'11", fair complexion, gray eyes, auburn hair. Transf. to Camp Chase; exchanged 4/1/63; sent to Wheeling; transf. to Camp Chase and Ft. Del.; exchanged 2/27/65. Ab. sick in Richmond hosp. 3/2–3/65. Paroled Staunton, Va., 5/1/65. Age nineteen, 6', dark complexion, light hair, gray eyes. d. 9/6/74, age twenty-six. Bur. Mt. Olivet Cem., Frederick, Md.

TAYLOR, J. H.: Pvt., Co. B. Captured Richmond hosp. 4/3/65. In Jackson hosp., Richmond 5/28/65. NFR.

TAYLOR, ROBERT: Pvt., Co. C, Davis's Bn. NFR. Possibly Robert H. Taylor (6/4/42–11/22/90). Bur. Greensboro Cem., Greensboro, Md.

TENNANT, THOMAS M.: Pvt., Co. C. b. Baltimore circa 1838. Res. of Baltimore. Enl. Co. B, 21st Va. Inf., 5/23/61, age twenty-three, 5'6", black hair, black eyes; present 11–12/61. NFR. Enl. Co. C, 1st Md. Cav., Culpeper, Va., 8/1/63; present through 8/31/63; present sick 9–10/63; present 11–12/63 and 4/1/64. Captured Pollard's Farm, Va., 5/27/64; sent to Pt. Lookout; exchanged 2/15/65. Present Camp Lee, Richmond, 2/20/65. Paroled Hanovertown, Va., 5/24/65. Took oath Amherst CH, Va., 5/25/65.

THACKER, ALBERT: Pvt., Co. F. On postwar roster.

THOMAS, DANIEL LEVIN, JR.: Pvt., Co. K. b. Baltimore, 1842. Res. of Baltimore. Enl. Co. C, 1st Md. Inf., 5/17/61; discharged 5/17/62. Enl. Co. K (2nd), 1st Va. Cav., Richmond, 6/10/62; ab. detailed with Mosby 1/18/63. Captured Gettys-

burg, Pa., 7/5/63; sent to Pt. Lookout; exchanged 12/25/63. AWOL 4/10–8/64. Transf. to Co. K, 1st Md. Cav., 8/64; AWOL through 12/31/64, however, enl. Co. F, 43rd Bn. Va. Cav. (Mosby), 9/3/64. Paroled Winchester 4/22/65. 5'9", fair complexion, dark hair, gray eyes. Bookkeeper, Baltimore, 1869–1900. Member John S. Mosby Camp, CV, Baltimore, and ANS/MLA. d. 10/23/18. Bur. Loudon Park Cem., Baltimore.

THOMAS, EDWIN: Pvt., Co. B. b. St. Mary's Co., Md., 2/28/43. Res. of St. Mary's Co. Enl. Co. H, 1st Md. Inf., 9/27/61; discharged 6/18/62. Enl. Co. B, 1st Md. Cav., Charlottesville, 9/10/62; WIA near Winchester 11/62; present 7–9/63; ab. sick with "debilitas" in Charlottesville hosp. 9/20/63; transf. to Lynchburg, Va., hosp. 9/21/63; RTD; present 11–12/63 and 4/9/64; ab. in Lynchburg, Va., hosp. 9/30/64; present 10–12/64. Paroled Burkeville Junction, Va., 4/27/65. Clerk and Banker, Baltimore. Capt., Co. A, 5th Rgt., Md. National Guard, 1878. Member ANS/MLA. d. Baltimore 10/18/88. Bur. All Faiths Cem., Charlotte Hall, Md.

THOMAS, JAMES E.: Pvt., Co. G. b. circa 1839. Farmer, Charles Co., Md. Enl. Co. G, 7th Va. Cav., 4/1/62. Captured Charles Town, W.Va., 8/30/62; sent to Ft. McHenry; transf. to Ft. Monroe; exchanged 12/10/62. Transf. to Co. G, 1st Md. Cav., 4/14/64. Captured Winchester 7/20/64; sent to Wheeling. Age twenty-five, 5'8", dark complexion, dark hair, blue eyes. Took oath, released 4/3/65.

THOMAS, JOHN H.: Pvt., Co. B. b. Fairfax Co., Va., circa 1843. Enl. Co. A, 4th Va. Cav., 4/18/62. Age nineteen, 6', fair complexion, dark hair, blue eyes. Discharged 5/23/63. On postwar roster. Enl. Co. A, 43rd Bn. Va. Cav. (Mosby), 9/1/63. Paroled Winchester 4/21/65. Res. of Richmond. Took oath Alexandria, Va., 5/9/65. d. Baltimore 4/24/98. Bur. near Valley Mills, Augusta Co., Va.

THOMAS, JOHN HANSON, JR.: Pvt., Co. B. b. 1844. Res. of Prince George's Co., Md. Enl. Charlottesville 9/10/62; ab. sick with "Febris" in Charlottesville hosp. 10/1–18/62. Captured Monterey Springs, Pa., 7/4/63; sent to Ft. McHenry; transf. to Ft. Del.; released 6/8/65. 5'10½", light complexion, dark hair, blue eyes. Lawyer, Baltimore postwar. Capt., Co. A, 5th Regt. Md. National Guard, 7/1/67; resigned. RR treasurer. d. 1902. Bur. St. Thomas's Episcopal Ch. Cem., Croom, Md. Brother of Raleigh C. Thomas.

THOMAS, RALEIGH COLSTON: Pvt., Co. C. b. Baltimore 10/8/44. Res. of Baltimore. Enl. Fredericksburg, Va., 9/1/63; present through 12/63 and

CHARLES R.
THOMPSON

*(Frederick D.
Shroyer)*

4/1–8/31/64; ab. detailed as Courier for Gen. Lunsford Lomax 11–12/64. Paroled Greensboro, N.C., 5/5/65. Member ANS/MLA, 1884. Res. of Baltimore. d. 1887. Brother of John H. Thomas Jr.

THOMAS, WILLIAM: Pvt., Co. E. Enl. Harpers Ferry, W.Va., 4/1/64; des. 6/15/64. NFR.

THOMPSON, BENJAMIN WILSON: Pvt., Co. A. Took oath Washington, D.C., 5/5/65. 6'1½", fair complexion, brown hair, hazel eyes.

THOMPSON, CHARLES R. (photo): Pvt., Co. E. b. 1845. Res. of Charles Co., Md. Att. school in Baltimore 1861. Enl. Richmond 10/30/62, age eighteen; presence or ab. not stated 1–2/63; present 7–8/63; horse wounded Gettys-burg, Pa., and abandoned Hagerstown, Md., 7/8/63; presence or ab. not stated 9–10/63; present 11–12/63 and 4/1/64. Captured Moorefield, W.Va., 8/7/64; sent to Wheeling. Age twenty, 5'4½", fair complexion, blue eyes, sandy hair. Farmer. Transf. to Camp Chase; d. there of "erysipelas" 1/23/65. Bur. Camp Chase National Cem., grave #851.

THOMPSON, DORSEY G.: Pvt., Co. A. b. 1/8/40. Res. of Ellicott City, Md. Enl. Charles Town, W.Va., 9/20/62; ab. on leave 7–8/63; ab. sick with "Sub-Lux." in Richmond hosp. 10/9–12/14/63; present 12/31/63 and 4/1/64; WIA (right hip) Beaver Dam Station, Va., 5/9/64; ab. wounded in Richmond hosp. until furloughed for thirty days to New Market, Va. 7/15/64; present 9–12/64; surrendered Appomattox CH, Va., 4/9/65. Took oath Richmond 6/7/65. Two horses killed under him during the war. d. 10/4/24. Bur. St. John's Episcopal Ch. Cem., Ellicott City, Md.

THOMPSON, EDWARD LIVINGSTON "NED": Pvt., Co. A. b. Md. circa 1832. Farmer, age twenty-eight, St. Mary's Co., Md., per 1860 census. Enl. Charles Town, W.Va., 9/10/62; present 7–12/63 and 4/1–12/31/64. Paroled Charlottesville 5/26/65. Took oath Darnestown, Md., 6/13/65. Listed as serving in Co. A, 43rd Va. Bn. Cav.

(Mosby), but not on muster rolls. Attended reunion 1899. d. 1935. Bur. St. John's Cem., Ellicott City, Md.

THOMPSON, GILBERT LIVINGSTONE: Pvt., Co. A. b. 8/9/41. Res. of Ellicott City, Md. Enl. Charles Town, W.Va., 9/20/62; present 7–12/63 and 4/1/64. Captured Pollard's Farm, Va., 5/27/64; sent to Pt. Lookout; exchanged 2/15/65. Paroled Charlottesville 5/26/65. Took oath Darnestown, Md., 6/13/65. d. 10/18/76. Bur. St. John's Episcopal Ch. Cem., Ellicott City, Md.

THOMPSON, HENRY: Pvt., Co. C. Res. of Baltimore. Enl. 5/22/61, unit unknown. Enl. Co. C, 1st Md. Cav., date and place unknown. Captured Leonardtown, Md., 4/25/65; sent to Old Capitol; transf. to Elmira; released 7/7/65. 5'7", fair complexion, dark hair, blue eyes.

THOMPSON, JAMES HAMNER: Pvt., Co. unknown, Davis's Bn. Gd. Hampden–Sydney Col. 1857. Res. of Baltimore. Served as Clerk for Gen. Thomas J. Jackson. NFR. Member ANS/MLA. d. Baltimore 1/26/08.

THOMPSON, JOHN: Pvt., Co. E. Enl. date and place unknown. Captured Charles Town, W.Va., 3/30/63; sent to Ft. McHenry; transf. to Ft. Monroe; exchanged 4/2/63. NFR.

THOMPSON, JOSEPH: Pvt., Co. D, Davis's Bn. Res. of Frederick Co., Md. NFR.

THOMPSON, ROBERT: Pvt., Co. A, Davis's Bn. b. circa 1843. Enl. Co. D, 18th Bn. Va. Arty., 5/3/61. Transf. to Co. A, Davis's Bn. 6/26/63. Captured Piedmont, Va., 6/5/64; sent to Camp Morton. Transf. to Co. M, 23rd Va. Cav., while POW. Exchanged 3/10/65. Paroled New Market, Va., 4/19/65. Age twenty-two, 5'8", light complexion, light hair, blue eyes.

THOMPSON, WILLIAM B.: Pvt., Co. E. Enl. Richmond 2/12/63; horse abandoned 6/26/63, paid $230; present 7–9/63; ab. sick with "typhoid pneumonia" in Richmond hosp. 10/28/63–3/22/64; present 4/1–12/31/64. Paroled Greensboro, N.C., 5/1/65.

TILGHMAN, JAMES: Pvt., Co. B. b. circa 1820. Res. of Queen Anne's Co., Md. Enl. date and place unknown; issued clothing 9/20/64. Paroled Mt. Jackson, Va., 4/20/65. Age forty-five, 6'1", fair complexion, dark hair, gray eyes. Took oath Winchester 4/21/65.

TIPPETT, MAXIMILLIAN ALAWAY KEPLER: Pvt., Co. B. b. St. Mary's Co., Md., 12/11/35. Farmer, St. Mary's Co., per 1860 census. Served in Co. H, 1st Md. Inf., 1861–62, but not on muster rolls. Enl. Charlottesville 9/10/62; present 7–10/63; horse captured Germanna Ford, Va., 10/10/63; present 11–12/63 and 4/1/64; ab. on horse detail for twenty days to Hardy Co., W.Va.,

4/9/64. Captured Moorefield, W.Va., 8/7/64; sent to Wheeling. Age twenty-nine, 5'9", fair complexion, brown eyes, dark hair. Transf. to Camp Chase and Pt. Lookout; exchanged 3/27/65. Paroled Mechanicsville, Va., 4/28/65. Farmer, St. Clements Bay, St. Mary's Co., postwar. Member ANS/MLA. Entered Old Soldiers' Home, Pikesville, Md., 7/3/94, age sixty-one; dropped 1/9/04; readmitted 12/6/05; d. there 5/30/07. Bur. Loudon Park Cem., Baltimore.

TOLBY, GEORGE W.: Pvt., Co. A. b. 1842. Nailcutter, Baltimore. Enl. Co. I, 6th Va. Inf., 5/9/61; des. 6/20/62. Enl. Co. A, 1st Md. Cav., Staunton, Va., 6/15/62; present 7–12/63 and 4/1/64; ab. on detached service through 8/31/64; ab. term of service expired and discharged on rolls 11–12/64. Took oath Richmond 4/12/65, age twenty-two. Nailor. Res. of Belle Isle. Entered Old Soldiers' Home, Pikesville, Md., from Baltimore, 1/3/93, age fifty. Member ANS/MLA. d. 6/13/93. Bur. Loudon Park Cem., Baltimore.

TOLBY, JOSEPH: Pvt., Co. B. Res. of Harford Co., Md. On postwar roster.

TOLLY, E. GEORGE: Pvt., Co. A. Res. of Cambridge, Dorchester Co., Md. Enl. Md. 7/1/64; present through 8/31/64; ab. on leave 11–12/64. NFR.

TOLSON, ALFRED CLIFTON: Pvt., Co. B. b. Prince George's Co., Md., 1844. Res. of Old Fields, Prince George's Co. Enl. Charlottes-ville 9/10/62. Captured Monterey Springs, Pa., 7/4/63, horse killed; sent to Ft. McHenry. Transf. to Ft. Del. and Pt. Lookout; exchanged 12/28/63. Paid $650 for horse; ab. on horse detail for fifteen days to Winchester 2/16/64; ab. sick in Char-lottesville hosp. 3/3–5/64; present 4/1–12/31/64. Paroled Washington, D.C., 6/2/65. Judge, Colesville, Md., 1903. Member George Emack Camp, CV, Hyattsville, Md., Ridgley Brown Camp, CV, Rockville, Md., and ANS/MLA. d. 4/28. Bur. St. John's Catholic Ch. Cem., Forest Glen, Montgomery Co., Md.

TOLSON, CHARLES E.: Pvt., Co. B. b. circa 1842. Res. of Broad Creek, Queen Anne's Co., Md. Enl. Charlottesville 9/10/62. Captured Monterey Springs, Pa., 7/4/63, horse killed; sent to Ft. Mc-Henry; transf. to Ft. Del., Ft. Columbus and Pt. Lookout; exchanged 21/5/65. Present Camp Lee, Richmond, 2/27/65. Paroled Winchester 4/23/65. Age twenty-three, 5'11", light complexion, brown hair, blue eyes. B&O RR employee, postwar. Member George Emack Camp, CV, Hyattsville, Md. Res. of Kent Island, Queen Anne's Co., Md. d. by 1903.

TONGE, RICHARD H.: Pvt., Co. K. b. Baltimore circa 1844. Res. of Baltimore. Enl. Co. C, 1st Md.

Inf., 11/29/61; discharged 8/1/62. Enl. Breathed's Bty. Horse Arty., Richmond, 6/27/62; promoted 3rd Cpl. and Sgt. Transf. to Co. K (2nd), 1st Va. Cav., 8/14/64. Transf. to Co. K, 1st Md. Cav., 8/64. Captured Bunker Hill 9/3/64; exchanged by 11/64. Ab. on leave 11/14/64. Paroled Guyandotte, W.Va., 4/65, as Sgt. Age nineteen, 5'8", dark complexion, black eyes, dark hair. d. by 1904.

TONGE, WILLIAM G. D.: Pvt., Co. K. b. Baltimore 1843. Res. of Baltimore. Enl. Co. G, 13th Va. Inf., 5/28/61; discharged as nonresident 5/28/62. Went to Bainbridge, Ga., and worked in father's cotton factory. Enl. 1st Md. Cav., Richmond, 9/25/63, age twenty. Clerk. Not on muster rolls. Enl. Stuart Horse Arty. 1864. NFR. Living Bainbridge, Ga., 1895.

TOUMAY, SYLVESTER CHARLES: Pvt., Co. K. Res. of Towson, Baltimore Co. Enl. Co. E, 1st Md. Inf., 5/22/61; discharged 8/11/62. Served in Ord. Dept. and CSN. Enl. Co. K, 1st Md. Cav., date unknown. Paroled Richmond 4/16/65. Clerk, Baltimore Sun, 1865; Insurance business, 1875; Asst. Editor, Md. Journal, Towson, Md., 1875–1900. Member ANS/MLA. d. 1/31/01.

TOWLES, JOHN CHOWNING: Pvt., Co. C. b. 11/26/34. Farmer and Oysterman. Enl. Co. D, 9th Va. Cav., 12/23/61. Transf. to Co. C, 1st Md. Cav., 5/3/64; present through 8/31/64; issued clothing 9/30/64; ab. in Charlottesville hosp. 11–12/64. NFR. d. Lancaster, Va., 4/9/21. Bur. White Marsh Episcopal Ch. Cem.

TOYSEY, JAMES: Pvt., Co. A, Davis's Bn. Enl. Richmond 6/21/63. Captured near Newtown, Va., 2/64. Transf. to Co. M, 23rd Va. Cav. NFR.

TRACY, _____: Pvt., Co. A, Davis's Bn. NFR. Probably Joseph F. Tracy who attended reunion of 1st Md. Cav., 7/8/99.

TRAIL, LOUIS WILLIAM: 5th Sgt., Co. D. b. Baltimore 2/10/43. Res. of Prospect Hill, Frederick Co., Md. Enl. as Pvt., Winchester, 9/20/62; present as 1st Cpl. 10–12/31/62; present as 5th Sgt. 7–12/63 and 4/1/64; WIA Clear Spring, Md., 7/29/64; present through 12/64. Paroled Winchester 5/3/65. 5'10", dark complexion, dark hair, hazel eyes. Grain Exporter, Baltimore, postwar; retired 1881; moved to Talbot Co., Md.; moved to Easton, Md., 1898. Member Charles S. Winder Camp, CV, Easton. d. Easton 2/28/23. Bur. Christ Ch. Cem., Cambridge, Md.

TRAPNELL, JOSEPH H.: Pvt., Co. D. b. 9/1/42. Res. of Merryland Tract, Frederick Co., Md. Enl. Co. G, 7th Va. Cav., Knoxville, Md., 9/12/62. Transf. to Co. D, 1st Md. Cav., 8/9/64; present through 12/31/64. NFR. Res. of Charles Town, W.Va., postwar. d. 3/16/12. Bur. Zion Episcopal

Ch. Cem., Charles Town.

TRAPPLETTE, PAYNE: Pvt., Co. K. b. 1841. d. 1914. Bur. Old Norborne Ch. Cem., Berkeley Co., W.Va. Tombstone states Co. K, 1st Va. Cav.; may have also served in Co. K, 1st Md. Cav.

TREAKLE, ALBERT C.: Pvt., Co. K,. b. 2/9/38. Res. of Howard Co., Md. Enl. Co. K, 1st Md. Cav., 8/64; discharged at end of enlistment 12/4/64. Paroled New Market, Va., 4/19/65. 5'9", dark complexion, dark hair, brown eyes. Took oath Harpers Ferry, W.Va., 5/19/65. d. 11/10/02. Bur. Treakle Cem., Sheppards Lane, Clarksville, Md.

TREAKLE, EMMETT S.: Pvt., Co. A. b. 5/20/41. Res. of Cooksville, Howard Co., Md. Enl. Urbana, Md., 9/15/62; present 7–12/63 and 4/1–12/31/64. Paroled Winchester 5/2/65. 5'8¾", dark complexion, dark hair, hazel eyes. d. Howard Co. 8/15/06. Bur. Treakle Cem., Sheppards Lane, Clarksville, Md.

TREGNER, CHARLES I.: QM Sgt. On postwar roster.

TSCHIFFELY, ELGAR LAURIE: Pvt., Co. A. b. Washington, D.C., 11/5/42; moved to Montgomery Co., Md. 1852. Res. Hunting Hill, Montgomery Co. Enl. Hagerstown, Md., 6/25/63; present through 12/63 and 4/1–12/31/64; present Appomattox CH, Va.; attempted to join Gen. Joseph E. Johnston's army. Paroled Staunton, Va., 5/11/65. Age twenty-two, 5'4", dark complexion, dark hair, blue eyes. Took oath Edwards' Ferry, Md., 5/25/65. Farmhand, Montgomery Co., Md., 1865; Insurance Business 1895–1930; Planter, Hunting Hill, Montgomery Co. Member Ridgely Brown Camp, CV, Rockville, Md. d. 6/4/30. Bur. Darnestown Presb. Ch. Cem., Darnestown, Md. He was the last survivor of Co. A.

TUBMAN, RICHARD W.: Pvt., Co. G. b. 9/4/37. Res. of Howard Co., Md. Enl. date and place unknown. Captured Cashtown, Pa., 7/5/63; sent to Ft. McHenry; transf. to Pt. Lookout. d. there of disease 11/14/63. Bur. Trinity Episcopal Ch. Cem., Howard Co.

TUCKER, ALBERT J.: Pvt., Co. F. Enl. Co. C, 19th Bn. Va. Arty., Richmond, 5/5/62. Transf. to Co. F, 1st Md. Cav., 12/17/62; present through 12/63 and 4/1/64; WIA Pollard's Farm, Va., 6/27/64; MIA on muster rolls through 12/64. Member ANS/MLA, 1894. Res. of Baltimore.

TUNIS, JOHN OLIVER: Pvt., Co. B. b. 10/3/43. Res. of Broad Creek, Queen Anne's Co., Md. Enl. Charlottesville 9/10/62; ab. sick with typhoid fever in Charlottesville hosp. through 10/18/62 and with debility 10/21–11/7/62; present 7–9/63. Captured Raccoon Ford, Va., 10/10/63; sent to Old Capitol; transf. to Pt. Lookout; exchanged 3/6/64. Captured Fairview, Md., 8/2/64; sent to

Wheeling. Age twenty-one, 5'9", dark complexion, gray eyes, dark hair. Farmer. Transf. to Camp Chase and Pt. Lookout; exchanged 3/27/65. NFR. d. 9/22/83. Bur. Cem. at "Maple Hall," Tilghman's Creek, Talbot Co., Md. Brother of Theophilus Tunis.

TUNIS, THEOPHILUS: Pvt., Co. B. b. Talbot Co., Md., 1842. Res. of Talbot Co. or Broad Creek, Queen Anne's Co., Md. Enl. Charlottesville 9/10/62, age twenty; present 7–12/63; horse captured 12/25/63; ab. on horse detail for twenty days to Newnan, Ga., 2/1/64; present 4/1–12/31/64; horse killed Criglersville, Va., 12/21/64, paid $3,000; ab. sick with "dyspepia" in Charlottesville hosp. 3/22–30/65; present when Co. B. disbanded Charlottesville. Sawmill Operator, Talbot Co., postwar; Member Md. Senate 1886–88; President of Tunis Lumber Co. 1889–1903. Member, Isaac Trimble Camp, CV, Baltimore, George Emack Camp, CV, Hyattsville, Md., and ANS/MLA. Moved to Norfolk, Va., circa 1903. Entered Old Soldiers' Home, Pikesville, Md., date unknown; d. there 9/16/32, age ninety. Bur. Cem. at "Maple Hall," on Tilghman's Creek, Talbot Co. Brother of John O. Tunis.

TURNBULL, S. GRAEME: 2nd Lt., Co. C. b. Md. 3/14/39. Res. of Baltimore Co., Md. Enl. as 3rd Lt., Richmond, 8/4/62; ab. on detail to get clothing for the co. in Richmond 11/18–30/62; present New Market, Va., 12/62; promoted 2nd Lt. d. of diphtheria Lacey Springs, Va., 3/30/63. Bur. Woodbine Cem., Harrisonburg, Va.

TURNBULL, WILLIAM S.: 2nd Lt., Co. C. On postwar roster. Bur. Central Chapel Methodist Ch. Cem., New London, Frederick Co., Md. Stone sunken; dates are below the ground.

TURNER, ALFRED: Pvt., Co. C, Davis's Bn. NFR.

TURNER, DUNCAN MANRO: 4th Sgt., Co. B. b. St. Mary's Co., Md., 2/8/34. Farmer, Bachelor's Hope, St. Mary's Co., per 1860 census. Claimed service in Co. H, 1st Md. Inf., 1861–62. Charlottesville 9/10/62; ab. to buy a horse 11/62; present 7–12/63 and 4/1/64; ab. sick with scabies in Charlottesville hosp. 8/31/64–3/30/65. Paroled Washington, D.C., 4/28/65. Res. of Leonardtown, Md., 1903; d. there 11/13/12. Bur. St. Aloysius Catholic Ch. Cem., Leonardtown.

TURRELL, BARRON: Pvt., Co. D. b. circa 1846. Enl. date and place unknown; issued clothing 9/30/64. Captured Beverly, W.Va., 10/29/64; sent to Wheeling. Age eighteen, 5'10", fair complexion, gray eyes, light hair. Farmer, res. of Hanover Co., Va. Transf. to Camp Chase; received 11/4/64. NFR.

TURTON, BENJAMIN FRANKLIN: 5th Sgt., Co. E. b. Prince George's Co., Md., circa 1830. Enl. as

Pvt., Richmond, 11/14/62, age thirty-two; promoted 2nd Cpl. 1/20/63; presence or ab. not stated 1–2/63; promoted 5th Sgt.; horse captured 5/9/63, paid $230; WIA (left arm—severing the "Ulsan & Median nemo"—and side) Winchester 6/12/63; ab. wounded in Charlottesville hosp. until discharged for disability 12/21/63. Age thirty-five, 6'½", dark complexion, dark eyes, black hair. Farmer. Detailed as Clerk under Maj. C. D. Hill in QM Dept., Richmond; paid Richmond 3/28/64. NFR.

TURTON, MORTIMER W.: Cpl., Co. E. b. 1839. Res. of Prince George's Co., Md. Enl. as Pvt., Richmond, 11/14/62, age twenty-three; presence or ab. not stated 1–2/63; ab. sick with chronic rheumatism in Charlottesville hosp. 8/15/63; transf. to Lynchburg, Va., hosp. 9/21/63; transf. back to Charlottesville hosp. 10/1/63; RTD 2/9/64; ab. sick with chronic pneumonia in Charlottesville hosp. 2/14–7/9/64; RTD; promoted Cpl; ab. sick with chronic pneumonia in Charlottesville hosp. 10/17–29/64; RTD; furloughed 4/5/65; ab. sick with chronic rheumatism in Charlottesville hosp. 4/11–15/65. Paroled Ashland, Va., 4/23/65. Took oath Nottingham, Prince George's Co., 1865. d. 1889. Bur. St. Thomas's Episcopal Ch. Cem., Crooms, Md.

TUTWILER, WILLIAM: Pvt., Co. A. Res. of Hyattsville, Prince George's Co., Md. Paroled as member of Capt. Woodson's Co. A., 1st Mo. Cav., Staunton, Va., 5/23/65. Age twenty-eight, 5'8", fair complexion, dark hair, blue eyes.

TYLER, GEORGE: Pvt., Co. D. b. circa 1846. Student, Frederick, Md. Enl. Co. A, 1st Md. Inf., 5/21/61; discharged by 8/11/62, when regiment disbanded. Clerk for PM, Winchester, 9/23–11/62; Clerk, Military CM, 1/8–3/8/63. Enl. Co. D, 1st Md. Cav., Boonsboro, Md., 6/15/63; ab. sick in Richmond hosp. 8/31/63; present 9–12/63; ab. on leave 1/1–2/29/64; present 4/1/64; paid 4/13/64. Captured Moorefield, W.Va., 8/7/64; sent to Wheeling. Age twenty, 5'9", dark complexion, gray eyes, dark hair. Transf. to Camp Chase and Pt. Lookout; exchanged 3/27/65. NFR. Brother of John B. and Samuel A. Tyler.

TYLER, JOHN BAXTER or BAILEY: Pvt., Co. D. b. Frederick, Md., 1849. Laborer, Frederick. Reportedly served as Drummer Boy in Co., A, 1st Md. Inf., age twelve. Enl. Co. D, 1st Md. Cav., Winchester, 9/20/62; present 11–12/62. Captured Strasburg, Va., 3/5/63; sent to Wheeling. Age seventeen, 5'7", light complexion, hazel eyes, brown hair. Transf. to Camp Chase; exchanged 4/1/63; present 7–9/63. Captured Raccoon Ford, Va., 10/10/63; sent to Old Capitol; transf. to Pt. Lookout; exchanged 3/6/64. Captured Pollard's Farm, Va., 5/27/64; sent to Pt. Lookout; exchanged 3/16/65. Paroled New Market, Va., 4/19/65. Age nineteen, 5'6", fair complexion, brown hair, hazel eyes. Destination Martinsburg, W.Va. Brother of George and Samuel A. Tyler. d. Chicago, Ill. circa 1904.

TYLER, SAMUEL ALBERT: Pvt., Co. D. Enl. Boonsboro, Md., 6/15/63 or Bloomsburg, Pa., 7/1/63. Captured Monterey Springs, Pa., 7/4/63; sent to Ft. Mifflin, Pa.; escaped 1/15/64. NFR. Bur. Mt. Olivet Cem., Frederick, Md., no dates. Brother of George and John B. Tyler.

TYLER, WINFIELD SCOTT: Pvt., Co. F. Res. of Md. Enl. Brooke Va. Arty. 9/30/62. Transf. to Co. F, 1st Md. Cav., 4/21/64; ab. on horse detail for seventeen days to Winchester 5/1/64. Captured Chambersburg, Pa., 7/11/64; sent to Ft. Del.; exchanged 2/27/65. In Richmond hosp. 3/2–3/65. Paroled Lynchburg, Va., 4/15/65. Member John Q. Marr Camp, CV, Fairfax CH, Va. d. age forty-seven. Bur. Fairfax Cem.

UHLHORN, JOHN H. K.: Lt., Co. G. Res. of Baltimore. Enl. Co. C, 1st Md. Inf., 5/21/61; discharged 6/9/62. Enl. Co. G, 1st Md. Cav., date unknown. Captured Ft. Harrison, Va., 9/30/64; sent to Pt. Lookout; exchanged 2/15/65. Paroled, took oath, Richmond, 4/29/65; transportation furnished to Baltimore 8/5/65.

UPSHUR, LEVIN: Sgt., Co. unknown, Davis's Bn. and 2nd Md. Cav. (Also see entry page 338.) Res. of Worcester Co., Md. On postwar rosters. Member ANS/MLA, 1880. Res. of Baltimore.

VALENTINE, GEORGE S.: Pvt., Co. C. b. Frederick Co., Va., 10/14/34. Res. of Baltimore. Enl. Richmond 8/4/62; present 7–10/63; AWOL 11/20/63 until captured at Mt. Jackson, Va., 12/18/63; sent to Wheeling. 5'4½", dark complexion, dark hair, blue eyes. Transf. to Camp Chase and Ft. Del.; escaped 7/64. Present 8/31/64 and 11–12/64. Paroled New Market, Va., 4/19/65. 5'7", dark complexion, dark hair, gray eyes. d. 12/2/64. Bur. Mt. View Luth. Ch. Cem., Harvey, Frederick Co., Md.

VALLANDINGHAM, IRVING S.: Asst. Surgeon. b. Ohio. Reared on eastern shore of Md. Gd. U. of Md. Medical School 1862. Res. of Del. Enl. Co. B, 1st Md. Cav., 4/64; appointed Asst. Surgeon 8/22/64 and assigned to 3rd Corps, ANV. Assigned to Davis's Bn. 11/3/64. Assigned to McIntosh's Bn. of Arty. Surrendered Appomattox CH, Va., 4/9/65. M.D., New Castle Co., Del., postwar. Member ANS/MLA. 1904.

VALLANDINGHAM, JOHN LAWSON: Pvt., Co. B. b. circa 1847. Res. of Cecil or St. Mary's Co., Md. Enl. date unknown; issued clothing 3/31/64; presence or ab. not stated on rolls 4/1–8/16/64.

NFR. "Received four flesh wounds." Married St. Mary's Co., 12/26/76, age twenty-nine. Res. of St. Clement Bay, St. Mary's Co., per 1890 census.

VAN AMSBURG, CHARLES: Pvt., Co. A, Davis's Bn. Enl. Woodstock, Va., 8/1/63; present through 1/1/64. Transf. to Co. M, 23rd Va. Cav; des. by 10/31/64. NFR.

VAN AMSBURG, JESSE: Pvt., Co. A, Davis's Bn. On postwar roster.

VANDIVER, GEORGE T.: Pvt., Co. E. b. circa 1839. Res. of Havre-de-Grace, Harford Co., Md. Enl. Fredericksburg, Va., 8/22/63; present through 8/3/63; presence or ab. not stated 9–10/63; present 11–12/63 and 4/1/64. Captured Pollard's Farm, Va., 5/27/64; sent to Pt. Lookout; exchanged 2/15/65. Present Camp Lee, Richmond, 2/27/65. Paroled Winchester 4/22/65. Age twenty-six, 5'7", light complexion, light hair, blue eyes. Res. of Frederick Co., Md. Took oath Harpers Ferry, W.Va., 5/9/65. "Died a few years after the war"; on postwar roster.

VAN METRE, ROBERT BEALL: Pvt., Co. F. b. Berkeley Co., Va., 9/1/43. On postwar roster and Co. F, 1st Va. Cav. Member ANS/MLA, 1894. Res. of Baltimore.

VANNOY, HENRY S.: Pvt., Co. D. Enl. date unknown. Captured Bunker Hill, W.Va., 7/25/63; sent to Ft. Del.; took oath, released 3/11/65. 5'9", fair complexion, auburn hair, gray eyes. Res. of Wilkes Co., N.C.

VAUGHAN, JAMES G.: Pvt., Co. D. Paroled Gordonsville, Va., 5/20/65.

VERMILLION, W. H.: Pvt., Co. C. Res. of Frederick Co., Va. d. 11/10/02. Bur. Stonewall Cem., Winchester. Obituary only record of service.

VESTLE, DENIS A.: Pvt., Co. A. Enl. date unknown; WIA (left shoulder) and captured; in 24th Corps hosp., Army of the James, 4/11/65; sent to General Hosp. 4/13/65. NFR.

VIA, JAMES T.: Pvt., Co. G. Enl. Co. A, Davis's Bn., Woodstock, Va., 1/1/64. Captured Strasburg, Va., 10/19/64; sent to Pt. Lookout; exchanged 2/15/65. Present Camp Lee, Richmond, 2/20/65. NFR.

WADDELL, JOHN: Pvt., Co. C, Davis's Bn. On postwar roster.

WADE, R. OSCAR: 1st Cpl., Co. A, Davis's Bn. Enl. Richmond 6/27/63; present through 1/1/64. Transf. to Co. M, 23rd Va. Cav; present through 10/31/64; issued clothing 11/28/64. NFR.

WAGNER, CHARLES VALENTINE: 1st Lt., Co. unknown. b. Baltimore 5/6/43. Res. of Baltimore. Enl. as 1st Lt., Co. G, 7th Va. Cav., before 12/2/61. WIA (thigh) and captured Fairfield, Pa., 7/3/63; sent to DeCamp General Hosp., David's Island; exchanged 8/23/63. Present sick 3–4/64.

Transf. to Md. Line 4/29/64. Captured Leesburg, Va., 12/11/64; sent to Ft. Del.; released 6/14/65. 5'10", fair complexion, dark hair, dark eyes. (Postwar roster says WIA and captured at Cedar Creek, Va., 10/19/64). Merchant, Baltimore and N.Y. City. Member ANS/MLA. d. N.Y. City 1/28/15. Bur. Mt. Hope Cem., Has-tings-on-Hudson, N.Y.

WAGNER, HENRY. "HARRY": Pvt., Co. K. Enl. Breathed's Bty. Horse Arty., Petersburg, Va., 7/10/62; WIA Beverly Ford, Va., 6/9/63. Transf. to Co. K, 1st Va. Cav., 8/14/64. Transf. to Co. K, 1st Md. Cav., 8/15/64. In Old Soldiers' Home, Pikesville, Md., 1894.

WAGNER, RICHARD C.: Pvt., Co. A. WIA, Gettysburg, Pa., 7/3/63; DOW 7/12/63, age twenty-two. Bur. St. Peters Cem., Liberty, Md.

WAKENIGHT, JOHN THOMAS: Pvt., Co. G. b. Boonsboro, Md., 8/7/44. Res. of Funkstown, Washington Co., Md. Enl. Co. G, 7th Va. Cav., 4/1/62. Transf. to Co. G, 1st Md. Cav., 5/3/64. Transf. to Co. A, Davis's Bn. 7/6/64. Transf. to Co. M, 23rd Va. Cav. Captured Waynesboro, Va., 3/2/65; sent to Ft. Del.; released 8/12/65. Postwar Shoemaker, Harrisonburg, Va., Boonsboro, and Washington Co. Member S. B. Gibbons Camp, CV, Harrisonburg, 1905. Entered Old Soldiers' Home, Richmond, 7/13/1927. d. 8/6/27. Bur. Woodbine Cem., Harrisonburg.

WAKENIGHT, WILLIAM B.: Pvt., Co. G. b. 2/4/31. On postwar rosters Co. G, 7th Va. Cav., and Co. A, 1st Md. Cav; WIA. Res. of Funkstown, Md., and Harrisonburg, Va., postwar. d. 2/6/91. Bur. Funkstown Public Cem.

WALLIS, HENRY CRAYTON: 4th Sgt., Co. E. b. circa 1838. Res. of Kent Co., Md. Enl. as Pvt., Richmond, 11/10/62, age twenty-four; promoted 3rd Cpl. 1/20/63; presence or ab. not stated 1–2/63; promoted 1st Cpl. Captured near Winchester 6/12/63, horse killed; sent to Ft. McHenry. Age twenty-five, 5'8", dark complexion, brown eyes, brown hair; exchanged 6/26/63. Present 11–12/63 and 4/1/64; in Richmond hosp. 4/30/64; WIA (toes) Beaver Dam Station, Va., 5/9/64, horse killed, paid $2,500; WIA Pollard's Farm, Va., 5/27/64; ab. wounded in Charlottesville hosp. 6/9/64; RTD 7/8/64; promoted 4th Sgt; present through 12/31/64. NFR. Teacher postwar. Entered Old Soldiers' Home, Pikesville, Md., from Still Pond, Kent Co., 11/5/89, age forty-eight; discharged date unknown. Member ANS/MLA, 1894.

WALLIS, WILLIAM THOMAS: Pvt., Co. B. b. Kent Co., Md., 8/30/31. Farmer, Kent Co. Enl. Co. E, 1st Md. Inf., 5/23/61; WIA (abdomen) Harrisonburg 6/6/62; discharged 1/16/63. Enl. Co. B,

1st Md. Cav., date unknown. Captured Moorefield, W.Va., 8/7/64; sent to Wheeling. 5'10½", florid complexion, blue eyes, light hair. Transf. to Camp Chase; released 5/13/65. d. 9/29/09. Bur. St. Thomas's Episcopal Ch. Cem., Prince George's Co., Md.

WALSH, THOMAS R.: Pvt., Co. K. Res. of Baltimore. Enl. Co. K (2nd), 1st Va. Cav., Richmond, 6/20/62; present until ab. sick with syphilis in Richmond hosp. 2/27/63; des. from hosp. 4/5/63; RTD; present until ab. sick with scabies in Richmond hosp. 9/23/63; RTD 10/17/63; present until detailed in Provost Guard 1–2/64; WIA date and place unknown; present through 8/64. Transf. to Co. K, 1st Md. Cav., 8/64; discharged at end of enlistment 12/26/64. Captured Charlottesville 3/5/65; sent to Ft. Monroe; transf. to Pt. Lookout; released 6/21/65. 5'10", fair complexion, dark brown hair, blue eyes. Transportation furnished to Baltimore.

WALTERS, JOHN: Pvt., Co. A, Davis's Bn. Enl. Woodstock, Va., 8/14/63; KIA Piedmont, Va., 6/5/64.

WALTERS, JOHN H.: Pvt., Co. E. Res. of Piney Point, Md. Enl. 11/11/62. Not on muster rolls. Captured Moorefield, W.Va., 8/7/64; sent to Camp Chase; exchanged 3/18/65. Paroled 5/8/65. Gd. Georgetown U. 1869.

WALTERS, JOHN W.: Pvt., Co. G. Enl. Co. C, 19th Bn. Va. Arty. Richmond 3/26/62. Transf. to Co. G, 1st Md. Cav., 12/17/62; des. to the enemy, Bermuda Hundred, 10/9/64; sent to City Pt.; transf. to Old Capitol; took oath and released 10/12/64; transportation furnished to Baltimore. Member ANS/MLA, 1894.

WALTHEN or WATHEN, DANIEL: Pvt., Co. K. b. St. Mary's Co., Md., circa 1844. Enl. Co. C, 1st Md. Inf., Centreville, Va., 11/5/61; discharged 5/23/62. Age eighteen, 5'9", light complexion, light hair, gray eyes. Student. Reenl. Co. K (2nd), 1st Va. Cav., 6/10/62; des. 12/10/63. NFR. Claimed service in Co. K, 1st Md. Cav., on pension application. Res. of Vienna, Va., 1917.

WARD, ARCHER: Pvt., Co. E. Enl. Richmond 9/7/64; present 11–12/64. Paroled Lynchburg, Va., 4/13/65.

WARD, JOSEPH: Pvt., Co. F. On postwar roster. Possibly Josephus C. Ward who died at Hagerstown, Md., 2/25/13.

WARD, WILLIAM W.: Pvt., Co. K. Enl. Breathed's Bty. Horse Arty., Richmond, 6/1/62. Transf. to Co. K, 1st Va. Cav., 8/14/64. Transf. to Co. K, 1st Md. Cav., 8/15/64; des. to enemy 3/8/65; transportation furnished to Washington, D.C.

WARFIELD, ALBERT GALLATIN, JR.: Pvt., Co. A. b. Oaksdale, Howard Co., Md., 10/5/42. Att.

Stanmore Acad. Res. of Lisbon, Howard Co. Enl. Urbana, Md., 9/15/62; ab. sick with typhoid fever in Winchester hosp. 10/29–12/62. Captured Winchester 12/27/62; sent to Wheeling. 5'10", dark complexion, blue eyes, auburn hair, dark whiskers. Transf. to Camp Chase and Ft. McHenry; exchanged 4/1/63. Captured on scout near Winchester 5/19/63; sent to Pt. Lookout. Escaped and WIA (scalp) when recaptured 9/13/63; exchanged 2/15/65. Acted as part of escort for President Davis to Washington, Ga. Paroled there 5/9/65. Took oath Baltimore 5/20/65. Civil Engineer for Howard Co. and engaged in railroad building postwar. Went to Japan in 1872 as member of American Scientific Commission; returned in 1875. Civil Engineer, Southern Pacific RR, B&O RR, and W.Va. Central and Pittsburgh RR. d. Howard Co., 12/25/83. Bur. Governor Warfield Cem. on Jennings Chapel Rd., near Florence, Howard Co. Brother of Gassaway W. Warfield.

WARFIELD, CHARLES ALEXANDER: Pvt., Co. A. b. 10/29/35. Enl. Charlottesville 6/15/64; KIA Green Springs, Md., 7/28/64. Reburied Loudon Park Cem., Baltimore, 1874.

WARFIELD, DENNIS F.: Pvt., Co. D. Res. of Johnstown, Frederick Co., Md. Enl. circa 9/62; present 11/62. Captured Martinsburg, W.Va., 12/15/62. NFR. Not on Federal POW rolls; may have been KIA.

WARFIELD, EVAN WILLIAM: Pvt., Co. D. Res. of Johnstown, Frederick Co., Md. Enl. circa 9/62; present 11/62. Captured Martinsburg, W.Va., 12/15/62. NFR. Not on Federal POW rolls; may have been KIA.

WARFIELD, GASSAWAY WATKINS: Pvt., Co. A. b. Oakdale, Howard Co., Md. 11/29/46. Att. Rock Hill Col. 1861–5/64. Res. of Ellicott City, Md. Enl. Tridelphia, Md., 6/1/64; present Bladensburg, Md., and Chambersburg, Pa. Captured Moorefield, W.Va., 8/7/64; sent to Wheeling. 5'9", light complexion, gray eyes, light hair. Transf. to Camp Chase; d. there of typhoid fever and pneumonia 1/4/65. Bur. Camp Chase National Cem., Oh., grave #773; reburied Governor Warfield Cem. on Jennings Chapel Rd., near Florence, Howard Co. Brother of Albert G. Warfield Jr.

WARFIELD, THOMAS WALLACE F.: Pvt., Co. D. Enl. circa 9/62; present 11–12/62. NFR. d. Montgomery Co., Md., 12/25/77.

WARFIELD, WILLIAM R., JR.: Pvt., Co. D. b. circa 1830. Enl. Frederick, Md., 7/1/64; ab. on detail in 2nd Md. Arty. through 8/31/64; issued clothing 9/30/64; ab. sick in hosp. 11–12/64. Paroled Staunton, Va., 5/23/65. Age thirty-five, 5'5½", light complexion, dark hair, blue eyes. d.

circa 1897, age sixty-seven. Bur. Governor Warfield Cem. on Jennings Chapel Rd., near Florence, Howard Co., Md.

WARING, C. B.: Pvt., Co. B. Res. of St. Mary's Co., Md. On postwar roster.

WARING, EDWARD "NED": Pvt., Co. B. b. Md. 2/13/43. Res. of Chaptico, St. Mary's Co., Md. Enl. Charlottesville 9/10/62; ab. sick with debility in Charlottesville hosp. 11/16–12/12/62; horse captured Capon Springs, W.Va., 12/20/62, paid $120. Captured Monterey Springs, Pa., 7/4/63; ab. on horse detail for twenty days to Hardy Co., W.Va., 2/16/64; present 4/1/64; ab. on horse detail for twenty days to Hardy Co., W.Va., 4/9/64; ab. sick with debility in Charlottesville hosp. 4/30–5/1/64; present through 8/31/64; KIA Winchester 9/19/64. Bur. Stonewall Cem., Winchester. Brother of Henry William and James H. Waring Jr.

WARING, HENRY BASIL: Pvt., Co. A. b. Middlebrook, Montgomery Co., Md., 2/3/42. On postwar roster. Farmer. d. Montgomery Co. 3/6/04. Bur. St. Rose of Lima Catholic Ch. Cem., Cloppers, Montgomery Co.

WARING, HENRY W., JR.: Pvt., Co. A. Gd. Georgetown U. 1861. Res. of Middlebrook, Montgomery Co., Md. Enl. Co. B, 35th Bn. Va. Cav.; on postwar roster. Enl. Co. A, 1st Md. Cav., Charlottesville, 8/25/62; present 7–12/63 and 4/1–12/31/64. Paroled Potomac River 4/20/65. Member ANS/MLA. d. Baltimore 9/5/93.

WARING, HENRY WILLIAM: Pvt., Co. B. b. Md. 3/3/45. Res. of St. Mary's Co., Md. On postwar roster. Brother of Edward and James H. Waring Jr.

WARING, JAMES H., JR.: Pvt., Co. B. b. Md. 3/26/41. Att. Georgetown U. Res. of Chaptico, St. Mary's Co., Md. Served in Co. B, 21st Va. Inf., Enl. Co. B, 1st Md. Cav., Charlottesville, 9/10/62; his horse was shot and he was captured, Monterey Springs, Pa., 7/4/63; sent to Ft. McHenry. Transf. to Ft. Del. and Pt. Lookout; exchanged 12/28/63. Paid $700 for horse; ab. on horse detail for fifteen days to Winchester 2/16/64; present 4/1/64; ab. on horse detail 3/31/64 and 11–12/64. Paroled Mechanicsville, Va., 4/28/65. Maj. of Cav., Md. Natl. Guard, postwar. Member Bradley T. Johnson Camp, CV, Leonardtown, Md. d. 9/25/78. Bur. Christ Ch. Cem., Chaptico. (Photograph in Hartzler 1992)

WARING, ROBERT BOWIE: Pvt., Co. B. Res. of Bald Eagle, Prince George's Co., Md. Enl. Winchester circa 9/62; ab. sick Strasburg, Va., 12/20–31/62. NFR. d. Strasburg 12/28/62, per UDC application. Brother of William W. Waring.

WARING, THOMAS G.: Pvt., Co. E. b. Prince George's Co., Md., circa 1838. Enl. Richmond 11/14/62, age twenty-three; presence or ab. not stated 1–2/63; horse abandoned Morgantown, W.Va., 5/1/63, paid $230; present 7–8/63; presence or ab. not stated 9–10/63; present 11–12/63 and 4/1/64. Captured Pollard's Farm, Va., 5/27/64; sent to Pt. Lookout; exchanged 3/16/65. Paroled Macon, Ga., 5/9/65. Took oath Baltimore 5/23/65. Moved to Va. Teacher. Moved to Miss. 1874. Farmer, Pike and Marion Cos., Miss. d. 12/15/09, in 71st year.

WARING, WILLIAM WORTHINGTON: Pvt., Co. B. b. Prince George's Co., Md., 1845. Res. of Prince George's Co. Enl. Charlottesville 9/10/62; served as Recruiting Sgt.; discharged for underage 3/30/63. Age seventeen, 5'9", fair complexion, blue eyes, dark hair. Student. Paid Richmond 4/14/63. Captured, date and place unknown; sent to Pt. Lookout; exchanged, date unknown. Paroled Greensboro, N.C., 5/8/65. Took oath Baltimore 5/13/65. Gd. U. of Md. Medical School 1869. M.D., Upper Marlboro, Md. d. by 1894. Brother of Robert B. Waring.

WARREN, JAMES: Pvt., Co. B. Res. of St. Mary's Co. On postwar roster.

WARRING, WILLIAM H.: Pvt., Co. A. On postwar roster.

WARRO, JOSEPH: Pvt., Co. F. b. circa 1833. Enl. as 2nd Lt., Co. B, 11th La. Inf., 8/19/61; present through 10/31/61. NFR. Enl. Breathed's Bty. of Horse Arty., Richmond, 6/27/62. Transf. to Co. F, 1st Md. Cav., 7/26/64; present 11–12/64; in Richmond hosp. 1/29–30/65. Age thirty-two. 5'9", dark complexion, black hair, blue eyes. Res. of Plaquemine, La. d. by 1903.

WATERS, GREENBERRY GRIFFITH: Pvt., Co. K. b. 9/13/41. Res. of New Market, Frederick Co., Md. Enl. Co. K (2nd), 1st Va. Cav., Leesburg, Va., 9/1/62; present until captured Monrovia Station, Md., 6/17/64; sent to Ft. McHenry. Transf. to Co. K, 1st Md. Cav., while POW 8/64. d. of typhoid fever at Ft. McHenry 12/15/64; bur. there; removed to Loudon Park Cem., Baltimore, 6/1/65. No marker.

WATERS, JOHN H.: Pvt., Co. E. b. 1841. Res. of St. Mary's Co., Md. Enl. Richmond 11/16/62, age twenty-one; presence or ab. not stated 1–2/63; horse lost near Warm Springs 5/10/63, paid $230; detailed as teamster 5–6/63. Apparently captured or left with wounded at Gettysburg, Pa., 7/3/63; "Ab. in hosp. Gettysburg 4 months"; on rolls 7–10/63, but not on Federal POW rolls; present 11/63–4/1/64. Captured Moorefield, W.Va., 8/7//64; sent to Wheeling. Age twenty-three, 5'6½", light complexion, blue eyes, light hair. Farmer, Charles Co., Md. Transf. to Camp Chase and Pt. Lookout; exchanged 3/27/65. In Richmond hosp. 4/8/65. Paroled 5/8/65. Member

ANS/MLA. Entered Old Soldiers' Home, Pikesville, Md., 7/1/31, age ninety. Sailor. Res. of Baltimore. d. at his son's house in Baltimore 12/19/31. Bur. Loudon Park Cem., Baltimore.

WATERS, THOMAS JACKSON: Pvt., Co. K. b. Washington, D.C., 6/25/43. Att. Georgetown U. Res. of St. Mary's Co., Md. Enl. Co. K (2nd), 1st Va. Cav., 7/1/62; present until captured Gettysburg, Pa., 7/3/63; sent to Pt. Lookout; escaped. RTD; WIA, date and place unknown; present until ab. sick with scabies in Charlottesville hosp. 12/7/63; RTD 1/13/64; present through 2/64; present Yellow Tavern, Va., 5/11/64. Transf. to Co. K, 1st Md. Cav., 8/64; ab. detailed at Gen. Bradley T. Johnson's Hqtrs. through 8/31/64 and 11–12/64. NFR. d. N.Y. City 2/14/19.

WATKINS, LOUIS J.: Pvt., Co. A. Res. of Clarksville, Howard Co., Md. Enl. Urbana, Md., 9/15/62; present 7–10/63; ab. sick with "Bubo simplex" in Richmond hosp. 11/25–12/31/63 and with "syphilas" 2/18/64; present 4/1–8/31/64. Paroled Lawrencetown, Md., 4/28/65. Took oath Harpers Ferry, W.Va., 5/20/65. Clerk of Court, Howard Co. Res. Ellicott City, Md. Member ANS/MLA. d. 11/18/88. Bur. Loudon Park Cem., Baltimore.

WATKINS, NICHOLAS W.: Pvt., Co. B. b. circa 1842. Res. of Baltimore. Served in Co. A, 9th Ga. Inf., Enl. 2nd Md. Arty. 9/12/62. NFR. Enl. Co. B, 1st Md. Cav., 7/63; issued clothing 9/30/64; ab. sick in hosp. through 12/64 on rolls dated 1/5/65; surrendered Appomattox CH, Va., 4/9/65 with 2nd Md. Arty. Lawyer, Baltimore. Member ANS/MLA. Entered Old Soldiers' Home, Pikesville, Md., 5/5/96, age fifty-four; d. there 2/7/05, age sixty-two. Bur. Mt. Olivet Cem., Frederick, Md.

WATSON, OLIVER: Pvt., Co. D. Served in Barry's Co., Md. Volunteers, 1861–62. Reenl. Co. D, 1st Md. Cav., date unknown. Captured Hampshire Co., W.Va., 1/8/63; sent to Wheeling. Age twenty-one, 5'6", florid complexion, blue eyes, sandy hair, sandy whiskers. Res. of Md. Transf. to Camp Chase; took oath, released 2/23/63 as Oliver Birkhead, res. of Anne Arundel Co., Md.

WATSON, P. S.: Pvt., Co. C, Davis's Bn. On postwar roster.

WATTERS, JAMES D.: 2nd Lt., Co. C. b. Thomas Run, Harford Co., Md., 1/11/34. Gd. Dickinson Col., Pa., 1856. Tutor, Teacher, and Law Student, St. Louis, Mo. On postwar roster of Co. K (2nd), 1st Va. Cav. Enl. as Pvt., Co. C, 1st Md. Cav., Richmond, 9/7/62; present 7–8/63; promoted 1st Cpl. 8/1/63; present sick 9–10/63; present 11–12/63 and 4/1/64; ab. on horse detail for ten days to Murfreesboro, N.C., 4/9/64; elected 2nd

Lt. 6/18/64; Commanding Co. 8/31 and 10/28/64. One officer and thirty-nine men with seventy horses present 9/30/64; ab. sick with scabies in Richmond hosp. 2/24–3/11/65. Paroled, took oath, Staunton, Va., 5/15/65. 6', light complexion, red hair, blue eyes. Res. of Harford Co. Member ANS/MLA, 1891. Res. of Bel Air, Harford Co. d. 3/29/08. Bur. Watters Memorial Ch. Cem., Thomas Run, Harford Co.

WATTERS, JESSE: Pvt., Co. G. Res. of Baltimore. Enl. Co. G, 2nd Md. Inf., 1862. Captured Peebles Farm, Va., 9/30/64; exchanged. Transf. to Co. G, 1st Md. Cav., date unknown; KIA Appomattox CH, Va., 4/9/65.

WEAVER, HIRAM S.: Pvt., Co. D. Res. of Funkstown, Washington Co., Md. Enl. Co. A, 1st Md. Inf., 6/2/61; discharged 5/21/62. Enl. Co. C, 2nd Md. Cav., date unknown. Captured and sent to Ft. McHenry; transf. to Ft. Monroe 12/29/62; exchanged. NFR. Enl. Co. D, 1st Md. Cav., Lacey Springs, Va., 4/1/63. Captured Monterey Springs, Pa., 7/4/63; escaped; des. Winchester 7/30/63; on rolls 7–8/63. NFR. Businessman, Seattle, Washington, 1913. (Also see entry page 336.)

WEBB, HENRY W.: Pvt., Co. E. b. Baltimore circa 1823. Res. of Carroll Co., Md. Enl. date unknown; WIA (arm broken) Gettysburg, Pa., 7/2/63, while serving as Orderly for Col. Bradley T. Johnson. NFR. Also listed as serving in Co. E, 15th Va. Cav. Hardware Merchant, Baltimore. d. 12/17/81, age fifty-eight. Bur. Greenmont Cem., Baltimore.

WEBB, WILLIAM ABNER: Pvt., Co. A. b. circa 1840. Res. of Lisbon, Howard Co., Md. Enl. Co. B, 9th Va. Inf., 6/5/61; des. 6/10/61. NFR. Enl. Co. D, Davis's Bn. Leesburg, Va., 9/1/62. Transf. to Co. A, 1st Md. Cav., 11–12/62; present sick in camp 8/31/63; present 9–12/63; ab. on leave 3/15–4/1/64. Captured Moorefield, W.Va., 8/7/64; sent to Wheeling. Age twenty-four, 5'11", dark complexion, dark hair, gray eyes. Farmer. Transf. to Camp Chase and Pt. Lookout; exchanged 3/27/65. Paroled Winchester 5/2/65. Age twenty-five, 5'10", dark complexion, dark hair, blue eyes. Took oath Winchester 5/16/65. Sheriff of Howard Co. 1867–69.

WEBER, EDWARD: Pvt., Co. C. b. circa 1847. Res. of Baltimore. Enl. Co. E, 1st Md. Inf., 5/22/61; discharged 8/11/62. Enl. Co. C, 1st Md. Cav., Culpeper CH, Va., 8/1/63; detailed as Blacksmith through 12/31/64. Paroled Winchester 4/30/65. Age twenty-two, 5'6½", florid complexion, dark hair, blue eyes. Member ANS/MLA. d. Old Soldiers' Home, Pikesville, Md., 11/20/91.

WEBER, PHILIP: Pvt., Co. F. Enl. Richmond 7/1/63; des. near Fredericksburg, Va., 8/6/63;

returned 10/31/63; ab. in arrest in Castle Thunder prison, Richmond, through 12/31/63; ab. sick with scabies in Richmond hosp. 11/18–12/16/63. Returned to Castle Thunder. CM'd 2/1/64. NFR.

WEBSTER, WILLIAM H.: Pvt., Co. A. Enl. Co. I, 1st Md. Inf., 6/15/61; discharged 6/15/62. On postwar roster. d. 5/15/13, age seventy-eight and six months. Bur. Lutheran Ch. Cem., Middletown, Frederick Co., Md.

WEBSTER, WILLIAM SAMUEL: Pvt., Co. A. b. Harford Co., Md., 6/18/38. Farmhand, Harford Co. Enl. Co. K (2nd), 1st Va. Cav., 5/14/61; present until transf. to Co. A, 1st Md. Cav., 5/15/62. Captured Hagerstown, Md., 7/13/63; sent to Pt. Lookout; exchanged 3/20/64. Present as paroled POW 4/1/64. Captured Pollard's Farm, Va., 5/27/64; sent to Pt. Lookout; exchanged 2/21/65. Present Camp Lee, Richmond, 2/27/65. Apprentice Carpenter, Philadelphia, Pa.; Carpenter and Farmer, Harford Co. 1866–97. Attended reunion 1899.

WEEKS, HENRY CRABTREE: Pvt., Co. K. b. Annapolis, Md., 9/15/34. Res. of Baltimore. Enl. Co. D, 1st Md. Inf., 6/1/61; discharged 7/62. Enl. Stuart Horse Arty. 7/12/62. Captured Hagerstown, Md., 7/12/63; exchanged 3/16/64. Transf. to Co. K (2nd), 1st Va. Cav., 8/14/64. Transf. to Co. K, 1st Md. Cav., 8/64; issued clothing 9/10 and 15/64; discharged at end of enlistment 12/4/64, however, issued clothing 12/31/64. NFR. Auctioneer, Baltimore. Member ANS/MLA. d. Baltimore 6/16/14. Bur. St. Vincent's Cem.

WEGNER, CHARLES J.: QM Sgt. Res. of Baltimore. Enl. Co. D, 1st Md. Inf., 5/22/61; discharged 8/11/62. Enl. Co. A, 2nd Md. Inf.; transf. to Co. A, 1st Md. Cav., date unknown; promoted QM Sgt, Davis's Bn.; paid 12/31/62. Transf. to 1st Md. Cav; present 1–12/64. Paroled, took oath, Fredericksburg, Va., 5/9/65.

WEGNER, HENRY FREDERICK "HARRY": Pvt., Co. K. b. Baltimore 1827. Res. of Baltimore. Enl. Co. D, 1st Md. Inf., 5/22/61; discharged 7/62. Enl. Breathed's Bty. 7/10/62. Transf. to Co. K (2nd), 1st Va. Cav., 8/14/64. Transf. to Co. K, 1st Md. Cav., 8/64; discharged at end of enlistment 12/4/64. Paroled Point of Rocks, Md., 5/13/65. Took oath Harpers Ferry, W.Va., 5/16/65; destination Baltimore. Clerk, Baltimore. d. Old Soldiers' Home, Pikesville, Md., 10/5/09. Bur. Greenmont Cem., Baltimore.

WEISHER, MICHAEL: Pvt., Co. F. Res. of Uniontown, Carroll Co., Md. Enl. Co. B, 39th Bn. Va. Cav., Staunton, Va., 10/29/62. Transf. to Co. F, 1st Md. Cav., 4/21/64; WIA (left shoulder) Pollard's Farm, Va., 5/27/64; ab. wounded in Charlottesville hosp. until furloughed 10/6/64. NFR.

WELCH, ANDREW J.: Pvt., Co. E. b. circa 1842.

Enl. Richmond 10/30/62, age twenty; presence or ab. not stated 1–2/63; present 7–8/63; presence or ab. not stated 9–10/63; present 11–12/63 and 1/4/64. NFR.

WELCH, C. JOSEPH: Pvt., Co. C. Res. of Baltimore. Enl. Martinsburg, W.Va., 9/30/62; present 7–8/63; AWOL 10/3–31/63; present 11–12/63 and 4/1/64; ab. on horse detail for ten days to Westmoreland Co. 4/9/64; AWOL 6/15–12/31/64; des. Captured Leonardtown, Md. 3/6/65; sent to Washington, D.C.: "Wishes to take oath." NFR.

WELCH, JAMES: Pvt., Co. C, Davis's Bn. Enl. Co. B, 1st Md. Inf., 5/21/61; discharged 8/11/62. On postwar roster.

WELLER, F. F.: Pvt., Co. A. Captured Gettysburg, Pa., 7/5/63; sent to Ft. Del. NFR.

WELLS, A. H.: Pvt., Co. D. Served in Co. G, Davis's Bn. Captured on Potomac 6/3/63 as Lt; sent to Old Capitol; exchanged date and place unknown. Transf. to State Line Troops 12/31/63. Transf. to Co. D, 1st Md. Cav; WIA (left hand), in Richmond hosp., 9/21/64; furloughed to Staunton, Va., for forty days 10/4/64. NFR.

WELLS, WILLIAM: Pvt., Co. F. b. St. Louis, Mo., circa 1840. Prior service in 3rd Md. Light Arty. On postwar roster. Bank Cashier, Baltimore; d. there 1/4/92, age fifty-two. Bur. Greenmont Cem., Baltimore.

WELSH, LUTHER BROOKE, JR.: Pvt., Co. D. b. circa 1839. Res. of Libertytown, Frederick Co., Md. Enl. Boonsboro, Md., 6/15/63; present 7–12/63 and 4/1–12/31/64. Paroled New Market, Va., 4/28/65. Age twenty-six, 6'1", dark complexion, dark hair, blue eyes. Brother of Milton and Warner G. Welsh.

WELSH, MILTON: 2nd Lt., Co. D. b. circa 1843. Res. of Libertytown, Frederick Co., Md. Enl. as 3rd Lt., Winchester, 9/20/62; present 11–12/62 and 7–12/63; horse killed South Mountain, Md., 7/4/63, paid $875; Commanding Co. 8/31/63, one officer and fifty-seven men with fifty-five horses present; promoted 2nd Lt. 12/63 or 2/29/64; present 2/16/64, 4/1, and 4/9/64; ab. on detached service in Shenandoah Co., Va., 8/31/64; present 3/13/65. Paroled Winchester 4/28/65. Age twenty-two, 5'11", fair complexion, brown hair, gray eyes. Brother of Luther B. and Warner G. Welsh. Living Kansas City, Mo., 1912.

WELSH, WARNER GRIFFITH: Capt., Co. D. b. Poplar Springs, Howard Co., Md., 1835. Res. of Libertytown, Frederick Co., Md. Enl. as 1st Lt., Co. F, 12th Va. Cav., 4/10/62. Transf. to Co. D, 1st Md. Cav., and elected Capt., 9/20/62; present 11–12/62; in arrest 12/31/62; in Richmond hosp. 3/13/63. Captured near Winchester 5/20/63; sent to Ft. McHenry; escaped 6/10/63; present 7–12/63. Four officers and forty-two men present with thirty-nine horses 12/1/63; present 2/6/64 and 4/1/64; Commanding Regt. 7/30/64; bay horse killed Moorefield, W.Va., 8/7/64, paid $2,700; ab. sick in hosp. 8/31–12/31/64, yet horse killed Winchester 9/19/64, paid $3,500. Paroled Salisbury, N.C., 5/1/65; WIA on postwar roster. Farmer, Libertytown, 1865–87; Sugar Inspector, State of La., 1894. Member ANS/MLA. d. "Capsylia," near Libertytown, 3/9/95. Bur. St. Peter's Catholic Ch. Cem., Libertytown. Brother of Luther B. and Milton Walsh.

WEST, JOSEPH, JR.: Pvt., Co. E. b. circa 1835. Res. of New Castle, Del. Enl. Richmond 12/18/62, age twenty-seven; presence or ab. not stated 1–2/63; KIA Newtown, Va., 6/12/63. Probably buried Newtown (now Stephens City), Va.

WHALEN, JOHN WESLEY: Pvt., Co. A. b. Howard Co., Md., 1844. Res. of Cooksville, Howard Co. On postwar roster Co. B, 35th Bn. Va. Cav. Enl. Co. A, 1st Md. Cav., Winchester, 11/8/62; present 7–11/63; ab. sick with chronic rheumatism in Richmond hosp. 11/30/63–1/12/64; present 4/1–8/31/64; issued clothing 9/30/64. Captured Strasburg, Va., 10/10/64; sent to Pt. Lookout; exchanged 2/21/65. Present Camp Lee, Richmond, 2/28/65. Paroled New Market, Va., 4/19/65. Age twenty-five, 5'8", light complexion, light hair, blue eyes. Took oath Harpers Ferry, W.Va., 5/27/65. d. Frederick Co., Md. 3/8/86, age forty-six. Bur. Mt. Olivet Cem., Frederick, Md.

WHARTON, WILLIAM FITZHUGH: Pvt., Co. C. b. Washington Co., Md. Res. of Prince George's Co., Md. Enl. Hagerstown, Md., 6/11/63; present through 12/31/63 and 4/1–12/31/64. Paroled, took oath, Appomattox CH, Va., 4/9/65. Attorney, Baltimore. Member ANS/MLA, 1871. Res. of Towsonton, Md. d. Baltimore 10/27/89. Bur. Rose Hill Cem., Hagerstown, Md. (Postwar photograph in Stonebraker 1899)

WHEATLEY, CHARLES: Pvt., Co. K. Enl. Co. K (2nd), 1st Va. Cav., 7/20/62; present until detailed with Mosby 1/18/63; present until transf. to Co. K, 1st Md. Cav., 8/64; discharged at end of enlistment 12/4/64. Paroled 4/27/65. Took oath 5/12/65. Res. of Georgetown, D.C. Member ANS/ MLA, and Confederate Veterans Assoc., Washington, D.C. d. 1898.

WHEATLEY, JOHN WALTER: Pvt., Co. K. Res. of Georgetown, D.C. On postwar roster. Enl. 43rd Bn. Va. Cav. (Mosby), 10/3/64; present through 12/64. NFR.

WHEELER, _____: Pvt., Co. H; present 10/8/62. NFR.

WHEELER, JAMES RUSSELL: Pvt., Co. E. b.

Cheltenham, Oxfordshire, England, 5/21/43. Arr. U.S. 1849. Res. of Havre-de-Grace, Harford Co., Md. Newspaper compositer, Baltimore Exchange 1861. Enl. Richmond 1/16/63; presence or ab. not stated 1–2/63. Captured near Winchester 6/12/63; sent to Ft. McHenry; transf. to Ft. Monroe; exchanged 6/26/63. Present 7–9/63. Captured Raccoon Ford, Va., 10/11/63; sent to Old Capitol; transf. to Pt. Lookout; exchanged 2/15/65. Paid $750 for bay mare captured; present Camp Lee, Richmond, 2/27/65. Paroled Winchester 4/22/65. 5'7", dark complexion, dark hair, hazel eyes. Res. of Frederick Co., Md. Contractor, Baltimore 1865–70; Manager, Md. White Lead Co., 1870–90; Manager, Md. Veneer Co., 1890–94; Banker, Baltimore, 1894–1912. Member ANS/MLA. d. Baltimore 1/24/25. Bur. New Cathedral Cem., Baltimore. (Postwar photograph in Angus 1923)

WHITE, STEPHEN: Pvt., Co. C. Enl. date unknown; ab. 7–8/63. "Supposed to be with Maj. _____ in Valley." NFR.

WHITELEY, ROBERT M. "BOB": Pvt., Co. C. Res. of Baltimore. Enl. Co. D, 1st Md. Inf., 5/21/61; discharged 8/11/62. Enl. Co. C, 1st Md. Cav., date unknown; KIA (shot in chest) Bridgeport, W.Va., 4/30/63.

WHITTEN, ALEXANDER: Pvt., Co. I. Paroled Winchester 6/62. NFR. Also listed in Co. B, Davis's Bn.

WICKES, HARRY: Pvt., Co. K. Res. of Md. Enl. Stuart Horse Arty. 1863; WIA Brandy Station, Va., 6/9/63. Transf. to Co. K (2nd), 1st Va. Cav., 8/14/64. Transf. to Co. K, 1st Md. Cav., 8/64. NFR. Res. of Baltimore postwar.

WIEL, GEORGE: Pvt., Co. C. b. Europe circa 1832. Res. of Baltimore. Enl. Co. B, 1st Md. Inf., 5/21/61; discharged 8/11/62. Enl. Cobb's Ga. Legion 11/24/62. Transf. to Co. C, 1st Md. Cav., 2/29/64. Captured Moorefield, W.Va., 8/7/64; sent to Wheeling. Age twenty-six, 5'3½", fair complexion, dark hair, brown eyes. Butcher. Transf. to Camp Chase. Took oath, enl. in U.S. Army, 4/22/65. Dairyman, Baltimore, postwar. Member ANS/MLA. Entered Old Soldiers' Home, Pikesville, Md., 12/3/95, age sixty-three. Ordered off by the Board of Directors. d. Baltimore, 7/9/96, age sixty-three. Bur. Fells Point Cem., Baltimore.

WIESNER, JOHN D.: Pvt., Co. A. Enl. Hagerstown, Md., 7/10/63; present through 8/31/63. Served as teamster 8/15–31/63; present 11–12/63 and 4/1–12/31/64. NFR.

WILCOX, JAMES: Pvt., Co. unknown, Davis's Bn. Res. of Forge, Anne Arundel Co., Md. NFR.

WILDS, LUTHER: Pvt., Co. K. b. circa 1845. Res. of Frederick, Md. Served in Co. B, Davis's Bn. Enl. Co. K, 1st Md. Cav., date and place un-

THOMAS P.
WILLIAMS

(Dave Marks)

known; issued clothing 9/30/64. Paroled, took oath, New Market, Va., 4/20/65. Age twenty, 5'8", dark complexion, dark hair, blue eyes. Res. of Baltimore 1905. d. 1/27/29. Bur. Mt. Olivet Cem., Frederick.

WILE, DANIEL LUTHER: Pvt., Co. K. b. circa 1845. Res. of Frederick, Md. Served in Co. B, Davis's Bn. Enl. Breathed's Bty. Horse Arty., Richmond, 1/9/63. Transf. to Co. K, 1st Va. Cav., 8/14/64. Transf. to Co. K, 1st Md. Cav., 8/15/64; issued clothing 9/30/64. Paroled, took oath, New Market, Va., 4/20/65. Age twenty, 5'8", dark complexion, dark hair, blue eyes. Res. of Baltimore 1905. d. 1/27/29. Bur. Mt. Olivet Cem., Frederick.

WILE, HENRY A.: 4th Sgt., Co. F. Enl. Co. C, 18th Bn. Va. Arty., 10/17/62. Transf. to Co. F, 1st Md. Cav., Richmond, 6/15/63; present through 9/63; KIA Morton's Ford, Va., 10/11/63.

WILKERS, G. W.: Pvt., Co. C, Davis's Bn. NFR.

WILKS, THOMAS M.: Pvt., Co. B. Res. of Centreville, Queen Anne's Co., Md. On postwar roster. Served as Midshipman, Richmond Naval Yard.

WILLIAMS, AUGUSTUS A.: Pvt., Co. C. Res. of Baltimore. Enl. Co. H, 1st Md. Inf., 5/15/61; discharged 5/16/62. Enl. Co. C, 1st Md. Cav., 8/4/62; present 7–8/63; ab. sick with scabies in Richmond hosp. 9/23–11/17/63; present through 12/31/63; ab. sick with scabies in Richmond hosp. 3/2–3/64 and 4/1/64. Captured Baltimore 4/12/65; sent to Ft. Warren as a spy; released 6/12/65. 5'4", dark complexion, brown hair, hazel eyes.

WILLIAMS, DAVIS H. S.: Pvt., Co. F. Enl. Richmond 7/6/63; present through 8/31/63; des. from camp in Orange Co., Va., 9/29/63. NFR.

WILLIAMS, GEORGE W.: Pvt., Co. B. "See 1st Mo. Cav." on card. Possibly George W. Williams, who d. 2/28/02, age fifty-six, one month, twenty-five days. Bur. U. B. Ch. Cem., Wolftown, Md.

WILLIAMS, JAMES H.: Pvt., Co. C. Paroled

Winchester 4/21/65. Age twenty-seven, 5'8", dark complexion, dark hair, gray eyes. Res. near Salem, Md.

WILLIAMS, JOHN H.: Pvt., Co. C. b. 1836. Arrested Leonardtown, Md., 5/2/65; sent to Old Capitol; took oath, released 5/19/65. d. 1918. Bur. St. Paul's Episcopal Ch. Cem., Prince George's Co., Md.

WILLIAMS, JOHN W.: Pvt., Co. B. b. Md. circa 1845. Res. of Aquaster, Prince George's Co., Md. Enl. Charlottesville 9/10/62; present 7–12/63 and 4/1–12/31/64; horse killed Bunker Hill, W.Va., 9/3/64, paid $2,750. Paroled Richmond 4/21/65. Age thirty-five. Sixth Dist., St. Mary's Co., Md., per 1880 census; res. of Laurel, Md., 1903. Member George Emack Camp, CV, Hyattsville, Md. d. "Cedarcroft," Baltimore Co., Md., 10/5/26. Bur. Woodlawn Cem., Baltimore. "In camp, on the march, and in battle he was ever inch a soldier, as brave as the bravest and co[n]cientious in the discharge of every duty."

WILLIAMS, THOMAS: Pvt., Co. C. Enl. date unknown. "Left company on or about July 20/63. Not heard from since"; on rolls 7–8/63. Captured Shepherdstown, W.Va., 7/27/63; sent to Ft. McHenry; transf. to Ft. Del.; left in hosp., Ft. Del., 9/26/63. May have died of disease. NFR.

WILLIAMS, THOMAS J.: Pvt., Co. C. b. circa 1841. Enl. date and place unknown. Captured Strasburg, Va., 12/20/62. Res. of Caroline Co., Md; sent to Wheeling. Age twenty-one, 5'7", ruddy complexion, gray eyes, black hair. Sailor. Transf. to Camp Chase; exchanged 4/1/63. NFR.

WILLIAMS, THOMAS P., JR. (photo): Pvt., Co. C. b. Charleston, S.C., 5/4/40. Sailor, Caroline Co., Md.; moved to Baltimore. Enl. Co. B, 21st Va. Inf., 5/1/61; present 11–12/61. NFR. Enl. Marion, S.C., Light Arty. 2/23/62. Transf. to Co. C, 1st Md. Cav., 3/24/64; not reported on rolls 4/1/64. ab. on horse detail for ten days to Hertford Co., N.C., 5/1/64. Captured Moorefield, W.Va., 8/7/64; sent to Wheeling. Age twenty-four, 5'7½", fair complexion, blue eyes, light hair. Merchant, Baltimore. Transf. to Camp Chase and Pt. Lookout; exchanged 3/27/65. Present Camp Lee, Richmond, 3/28/65. Paroled Burkeville, Va., 4/20/65. Took oath Eastville, Va., 5/15/65. Clerk, Baltimore. Member ANS/MLA. d. Baltimore 4/8/91. Bur. Greenmount Cem., Baltimore.

WILLIAMSON, JOHN B.: Pvt., Co. I. b 5/24/43. Res. of Allegany Co., Md. Served in Jacob's Mounted Riflemen from Md. Enl. McNeill's Rangers; discharged. Enl. Co. I per postwar roster. "WIA several times by sabre and ball." Member James Breathed Camp, CV, Cumberland, Md., and ANS/MLA. d. Baltimore 7/17/93. Bur.

Loudon Park Cem. (Photograph in Hartzler 1992)
WILLIS, CHARLES N.: Pvt., Co. C. b. Easton, Md. 7/4/44. Res. of Carroll Co., Md. Enl. Winchester 10/25/62; paid New Market, Va., 1/7/63; WIA (thigh) and captured Greenland Gap, W.Va., 4/25/63; sent to Ft. McHenry; transf. to Ft. Monroe; exchanged 5/26/63. Present 7–12/63 and 4/1/64; ab. on horse detail for fifteen days to Loudoun Co., Va., 5/1/64; present through 8/31/64; ab. as Courier for Gen. Lunsford Lomax 11–12/64; served as scout; WIA several times. NFR. Moved to Kans. 1889. Lumberman. Moved to St. Joseph, Mo., 1904. President of Willis-Lucas Lumber Co. and Willis-Lucas Cadillac Co. d. St. Joseph 2/9/20.

WILLIS, R. M.: Pvt., Co. C; ab. sick in Richmond hosp. 11/5–12/31/62. NFR.

WILLIS, THOMAS E.: Pvt., Co. B. Served as Bugler in Breathed's Bty. Transf., date unknown; WIA; captured in Hagerstown, Md., hosp. 7/12/63. NFR.

WILLIS, THOMAS N.: Pvt., Co. D. b. circa 1842. Res. of Queen Anne's Co., Md. Enl. Richmond 7/28/64. Captured Moorefield, W.Va., 8/7/64; sent to Wheeling. Age twenty-two, 5'9", dark complexion, gray eyes, dark hair. Farmer, Talbot Co., Md. Transf. to Camp Chase and Pt. Lookout; exchanged 3/27/65. NFR.

WILLIS, THOMAS W.: Pvt., Co. B. b. 2/12/37. Res. of Centreville, Queen Anne's Co., Md. Enl. Charlottesville 9/10/62; ab. sick with "Icterus" in Charlottesville hosp. 11–12/62. Captured Chambersburg, Pa., 7/3/63; sent to Ft. Del. Transf. to Ft. Columbus and Pt. Lookout; exchanged 2/15/65; present Camp Lee, Richmond, 2/22/65. Paroled Winchester 4/22/65. Age twenty-seven, 5'8", dark complexion, dark hair, gray eyes. Res. of Frederick Co., Md. Member George Emack Camp, CV, Hyattsville, Md., 1903. Farmer, Lacey Springs, Va., 1906. d. 1/5/19. Bur. Lacey Springs Cem.

WILLIS, WILLIAM: Pvt., Co. F. Enl. Richmond 7/10/63; present through 9/63; WIA (thigh and scrotum) Morton's Ford, Va., 10/11/63; ab. wounded in Richmond hosp. until furloughed to Wilmington, N.C., for forty days 10/16/63. Express Agent. In Richmond hosp. 12/16–28/63; present 4/1–12/31/64; horse killed Moorefield, W.Va., 8/7/64, paid $2,200. Captured Frederick's Hall, Va., 3/13/65; sent to Pt. Lookout; released 6/3/65. Claimed prior service in Co. I, 1st Va. Cav., but not on muster rolls. Member George Emack Camp, CV, Hyattsville, Md., 1903.

WILLS, F. LEO: 1st Cpl., Co. K. b. Charles Co., Md., circa 1828. Enl. as Pvt., Co. K (2nd), 1st Va. Cav., Leesburg, Va., 5/14/61; present until dis-

FREDERICK
S. WILLSON

(Frederick D. Shroyer)

charged 5/14/62. Age thirty-four, 5'8", brown complexion, black hair, gray eyes. Farmer near Pomfret, Charles Co. Later Reenl; present until appointed 3rd Cpl. 7–8/62; present through 12/63. Promoted 2nd Cpl; present until transf. to Co. K, 1st Md. Cav., 8/64. Promoted 1st Cpl; present through 8/31/64; issued clothing 9/30/64; AWOL 12/1–31/64; present Appomattox CH, Va., 4/9/65. NFR.

WILLSON, FREDERICK S. (photo): Pvt., Co. D. b. 1847. Att. Georgetown U. class of 1864. Res. of Frederick Co., Md. Enl. Boonsboro, Md., 6/15/63; present through 11/63; ab. sick with camp itch in Richmond hosp., 12/28/63, until furloughed for thirty days, 1/15/64; present 4/1–12/31/64; ab. sick with camp itch in Richmond hosp. 2/28–3/5/65. Paroled Winchester 4/19/65. Age eighteen, 5'6", fair complexion, brown hair, gray eyes. Took oath Harpers Ferry, W.Va., 4/22/65, and Frederick, Md., 7/6/65. Capt., Co. K, 5th Regt., Md. Natl. Guard, 8/19/76; resigned 2/10/77.

WILLSON, JAMES HENRY: Pvt., Co. B. b. Queen Anne's Co., Md., 9/18/40. On postwar roster. Farmer. d. Old Soldiers' Home, Pikesville, Md., 5/18/23. Bur. Loudon Park Cem., Baltimore.

WILNE, J. S.: Pvt., Co. F. On Postwar roster.

WILSON, ALGERNON SIDNEY: Pvt., Co. K. Enl. Breathed's Bty. 7/10/62. Transf. to Co. K (2nd), 1st Va. Cav., 8/14/64. Transf. to Co. K, 1st Md. Cav., 8/64, however, AWOL 6/20–12/31/64. Captured Port Tobacco, Md., 4/23/65; sent to Old Capitol; took oath, released 5/19/65. Member George Emack Camp, CV, Hyattsville, Md., 1906. Res. of Accokeek, Prince George's Co., Md.

WILSON, AQUILA HENRY: Pvt., Co. B. b. 5/22/32. Res. of Nottingham, Prince George's Co., Md. Enl. 1862; horse killed Romney, W.Va., 11/23/62. Captured Capon Springs, W.Va., 12/20/62; sent to Wheeling. 5'8¾", dark complexion, dark eyes, black hair. Farmer. Transf. to Camp Chase; took oath, released 2/23/63. d. 5/9/01. Bur. St. Thomas's Episcopal Ch. Cem., Croom, Md.

WILSON, CHARLES, JR.: Pvt., Co. K. b. Frederick Co., Md., circa 1840. Civil Engineer, Baltimore. Enl. Co. F, 1st Va. Inf., 6/16/61; discharged 9/20/61, age twenty-one. Enl. Breathed's Bty. Horse Arty., Richmond, 8/1/63. Transf. to Co. K (2nd), 1st Va. Cav., 8/14/64. Transf. to Co. K, 1st Md. Cav., 8/64; present through 8/31/64; paid 9/24/64; discharged at end of enlistment 12/4/64. Paroled, took oath, Harpers Ferry, W.Va., 5/16/65. d. by 1903.

WILSON, CHARLES ALEXANDER, JR.: Pvt., Co. E. b. circa 1842. Enl. Md. 7/25/64; present through 12/64; horse killed Oldtown, Md., 8/22/64, paid $3,000. Paroled, took oath, Washington, D.C., 5/19/65. Carpenter, Baltimore. Entered Old Soldiers' Home, Pikesville, Md., 5/2/11, age sixty-nine; d. there 8/30/11. Bur. Loudon Park Cem., Baltimore.

WILSON, EDWARD F.: Pvt., Co. D. Res. of Baltimore Co; ab. sick with "orchitis" in Gordonsville, Va., hosp. 3/30/65. NFR.

WILSON, GEORGE W.: Pvt., Co. B. b. 6/18/43. Res. of Forest Home, Anne Arundel Co., Md. On postwar roster. Also listed in Davis's Bn. Member ANS/MLA and George Emack Camp, CV, Hyattsville, Md. Res. of Marlboro, Md., 1903. d. 3/15/07. Bur. Trinity Episcopal Ch. Cem., Prince George's Co., Md.

WILSON, JOSEPH KENT: Pvt., Co. B. b. circa 1842. Res. of Prince George's Co., Md. Enl. Charlottesville 9/10/62. Captured Monterey Springs, Pa., 7/4/63; sent to Ft. McHenry. Transf. to Ft. Del., Ft. Columbus and Pt. Lookout; exchanged 12/28/63. Present 4/1/64; WIA (right hand: "1st & 2nd meta carp bones fractured") and captured Beverly, W.Va., 10/29/64; sent to Wheeling. Age twenty-two, 5'6½", fair complexion, blue eyes, dark hair. Farmer. Transf. to Camp Chase and Pt. Lookout; released 6/21/65. Farmer, Seat Pleasant, Prince George's Co., 1903. Member George Emack Camp, CV, Hyattsville, Md. Entered Old Soldiers' Home, Pikesville, Md., 10/6/08, age seventy, from Brightseat, Md. d. 10/23/15. Bur. Greenmount Cem., Baltimore.

WILSON, ROBERT E.: Pvt., Co. D. b. Prince George's Co., Md., 3/17/46. Att. Georgetown U. Res. of Georgetown, D.C. Enl. Frederick, Md., 7/1/64; present through 12/31/64; present Appomattox CH, Va., 4/9/65. Took oath Washington, D.C., 6/9/65. Member Confederate Veterans Assoc., Washington. d. Prince George's Co. 2/27/39. Bur. Arlington Natl. Cem., Va.

WILSON, ROBERT RICHARD: Pvt., Co. A. Enl. date unknown. Captured Frederick, Md., 7/10/64;

sent to Old Capitol; transf. to Elmira; d. there of "Variola" 2/11/65. Bur. Woodlawn Natl. Cem., Elmira, N.Y., grave #2001 or #2082.

WILSON, WILLIAM: 1st Cpl., Co. A. Res. of Harford Co., Md. Enl. Richmond 5/14/62; present 7–12/63; ab. on leave 3/30/64; present through 12/31/64. NFR.

WILSON, WILLIAM ALEXANDER: 2nd Sgt., Co. B. b. Calvert Co., Md., circa 1842. Res. of Prince George's Co., Md. Enl. Co. D, 1st Md. Inf., 6/1/61; discharged 8/11/62. Enl. Co. B, 1st Md. Cav., Charlottesville, 9/10/62. Captured Monterey Springs, Pa., 7/4/63, horse killed; sent to Ft. Del.; transf. to Pt. Lookout; exchanged 12/28/63. Ab. sick with gonorrhoea in Charlottesville hospital 1/22–5/3/64; WIA (right side) Clear Spring, Md., 7/29/64. "Carried ball in his side twenty years." Captured Chambersburg, Pa., 8/19/64; sent to Ft. Del.; exchanged 11/15/64. Issued clothing 11/17/64; ab. wounded in Charlottesville hosp. 11/19/64–1/11/65. NFR. RR Builder. Member ANS/MLA. Entered Old Soldiers' Home, Pikesville, Md., from Prince George's Co., 2/7/93, age fifty-one; discharged. d. 10/20/09. Bur. Beltsville, Prince George's Co.

WILSON, WILLIAM BOWLEY: Pvt., Co. K. b. Baltimore, 12/6/39. Res. of Baltimore. Reported himself to the U.S. Embassy, London, England 10/19/65 and took oath before U.S. Minister to Great Britain as member of Co. K, 1st Va. Cav. Res. of Baltimore postwar. Member ANS/MLA, 1904. Res. of Annapolis, Md. d. Baltimore 2/14/15. Bur. Greenmount Cem., Baltimore.

WILSON, WILLIAM S.: Cpl., Co. A. Enl. Co. K (2nd), 1st Va. Cav., date and place unknown. Transf. to Co. A, 1st Md. Cav., 5/15/62, as Cpl. NFR.

WILSON, WILLIAM W.: Pvt., Co. B. Gd. Georgetown U. 1854. Res. of Bladensburg, Prince George's Co., Md. Enl. 1st Md. Arty. 10/26/62. Transf. to Co. B, 1st Md. Cav., 3/64; present 2/28/65. NFR.

WINTER, HENRY S. "HARRY": Pvt., Co. D. Enl. Co. F, 12th Va. Cav., before 11/62. Transf. to Co. D, 1st Md. Cav., 11/62. Returned to Co. F, 12th Va. Cav., 11/62. NFR. d. 1/05. Bur. St. John's Episcopal Ch. Cem., Ellicott City, Md.

WISE, FELIX J.: 2nd Cpl., Co. F. b. circa 1841. Res. of Emmittsburg, Frederick Co., Md. Enl. Co C, 18th Bn. Va. Arty., 12/14/62. Transf. to Co. F, 1st Md. Cav., Richmond, 6/15/63 as 2nd Cpl; present through 10/63; present as Pvt. 11–12/63 and 4/1/64. Captured Pollard's Farm, Va., 5/27/64; sent to Pt. Lookout; exchanged 2/15/65. Present Camp Lee, Richmond, 2/17/65. Paroled New Market, Va., 4/19/65. Age twenty-four, 6', light complexion, light hair, brown eyes. Took oath Winchester 4/28/65, dark hair, hazel eyes.

WISE, HENRY ALEXANDER: Sgt. Co. F. b. "Green Holly," St. Mary's Co., Md., 10/4/42. Res. of 2nd Dist., St. Mary's Co., per 1860 census. Attended St. Thomas Col. On postwar roster. Served as Lt. in 1st Md. Arty. and Co. B, 2nd Md. Inf. Employee, Weems Steamboat Co.; Merchant, Chester, Pa., and Baltimore. Member ANS/MLA. d. Baltimore 5/29/99. Bur. St. Nicholas Ch. Cem., St. Mary's Co.

WISHER or WISNER, M.: Pvt., Co. F. Enl. date and place unknown; WIA (left shoulder) Pollard's Farm, Va., 5/27/64. Admitted Richmond hosp. same day; furloughed for thirty days 6/13/64; in Charlottesville hosp. 8/9/64, furloughed for sixty days the same day; in Richmond hosp. 9/12/64. NFR.

WISSMAN, LOUIS ORVILLE: Pvt., Co. B. b. 2/17/39. Res. of Baltimore, Prince George's Co., Md. Enl. Charlottesville 9/10/62. Captured Monterey Springs, Pa., 7/4/63; sent to Ft. McHenry; transf. to Ft. Del., Ft. Columbus, and Pt. Lookout; exchanged 12/28/63; present Camp Lee, Richmond, 10/31/64; issued clothing 12/9/64; present Appomattox CH, Va. Member ANS/ MLA and George Emack Camp, CV, Hyattsville, Md., 1903. Res. of Baltimore; res. of Hyattsville, 1912.

WITZLEBEN, THEODORE ALFRED: Pvt., Co. K. b. circa 1822. Enl. Co. E, 1st Va. Inf., 4/22/61, age thirty-nine. Clerk. Transf. to Co. K (2nd), 1st Va. Cav., 6/1/62; present through 12/63; detailed in Provost Guard 2–8/64. Transf. to Co. K, 1st Md. Cav., 8/64; AWOL 12/1–31/64. NFR.

WOLFE, J. R. K. P.: Pvt., Co. D; ab. sick Strasburg, Va., 11–12/62. NFR. Possibly Johnathan Wolfe (3/10/43–5/7/18). Bur. Reformed Ch. Cem., Wolfsville, Md.

WOOD, FRANCIS M.: Pvt., Co. E. b. circa 1836. Enl. Co. C (2nd), 19th Bn. Va. Arty. 3/26/62 Richmond. Transf. to Co. E, 1st Md. Cav., Richmond, 12/17/62, age twenty-six; presence or ab. not stated 1–2/63. Transf. to Co. C (3rd), 19th Bn. Va. Arty. 2/15/65. Des. to the enemy 2/8/65. Took oath Washington, D.C., 2/16/65. Member ANS/MLA. d. 1/27/12, age seventy. Bur. Galesville Meth. Ch. Cem., Anne Arundel Co., Md.

WOOD, JOHN J.: Pvt., Co. C. Enl. Winchester 10/1/62; ab. on leave 11/62; ab. sick near Strasburg, Va., 12/15–31/62; ab. sick with debility in Charlottesville hosp. 2/23–8/5/63; present 8/31/63. NFR.

WOODIS, ALEXANDER: Pvt., Co. E. Arrested for stealing a horse and sent to Castle Thunder Prison, Richmond, circa 11/20/63. NFR.

WOODWARD, ARCH: Pvt., Co. A, Davis's Bn. Enl. New Market, Va., 9/14/63; des. near Wood-

stock, Va., 5/64. On rolls to 10/31/64. Transf. to Co. M, 23rd Va. Cav. NFR.

WOODWARD, COLUMBUS O.: Pvt., Co. D. b. circa 1837. Res. of Howard Co., Md. Enl. Co. F, 1st Md. Inf., 5/21/61; discharged 8/11/62. Enl. Co. D, 1st Md. Cav., Winchester, 9/20/62; present 11–12/62 and 7–8/63; WIA and lost horse 9/30/63; ab. wounded in Staunton, Va., hosp. through 10/31/63; present 11–12/63 and 4/1/64; ab. on horse detail for seventeen days to Winchester 4/9/64. Captured Moorefield, W.Va., 8/7/64; sent to Wheeling. Age twenty-seven, 5'8", dark complexion, dark hair, dark eyes. Farmer. Transf. to Camp Chase; exchanged 3/27/65. NFR. Member Confederate Veterans Assoc, Washington, D.C., 1910. d. Washington 2/23/20. Bur. Arlington Natl. Cem., Va.

WOOLFORD, ARTHUR GEORGE: Pvt., Co. A. b. circa 1842. Res. Princess Anne, Somerset Co., Md. Joined by transf. from Co. F, 2nd Md. Inf., in exchange for Jeremiah Artis, 5/1/64. Captured Moorefield, W.Va., 8/7/64; sent to Wheeling. Age twenty-two, 5'9", light complexion, blue eyes, light hair. Farmer. Transf. to Camp Chase; took oath, released 3/23/65, age twenty-three.

WOOLLEY, GEORGE SIDNEY: Pvt., Co. B. b. 10/42. Res. of Centreville, Queen Anne's Co., Md. Enl. Charlottesville 10/10/62; present as Hosp. Steward 11/1/62–10/1/63; ab. sick with typhoid fever in Charlottesville hosp. 10/2–11/25/63; present through 12/31/63; ab. on horse detail for ten days to New Market, Va., 2/1/64; present through 12/31/64. NFR. Member George Emack Camp, CV, Hyattsville, Md., 1903. Res. of Chesapeake City, Md. d. 11/16.

WOOTEN, HENRY EDGAR: Pvt., Co. A. b. 9/21/37. Gd. Yale U. 1856. Res. of Howard Co., Md. Enl. Urbana, Md., 9/15/62; present 7–12/63 and 4/1/64. Captured Hanover CH, Va., 6/1/64; sent to Pt. Lookout; exchanged 2/21/65. Paroled New Market, Va., 4/19/65. 6', light complexion, red hair, gray eyes. Took oath Winchester 7/26/65. Lawyer. State Attorney, Howard Co. 1867–83. d. 4/13/94. Bur. St. John's Episcopal Ch. Cem., Ellicott City, Md.

WOOTERS, ALEXANDER: Pvt., Co. E. b. circa 1837. Enl. Richmond 11/18/62, age twenty-five; presence or ab. not stated 1–2/63; present 7–8/63; present in arrest, accused of stealing a horse at Orange CH, Va., 9–10/63, and ab. in arrest Richmond 11–12/63. d. of typhoid pneumonia in Richmond hosp. 1/12/64. Effects: $5.

WORTHINGTON, CHARLES ALEXANDER WARFIELD: Pvt., Co. A. b. Frederick Co., Md. 9/27/28. Res. of Anne Arundel Co., Md. Enl. Co. C, 1st Md. Inf., 1861; discharged 1862. Enl. Co.

A, 1st Md. Cav., Charlottesville, 6/15/64; present through 11/64; WIA (right thigh) 12/64; ab. wounded in Richmond hosp. 12/13/64–3/15/65. NFR. Farmer, Louisa Co., Va., and Rivanna, Albemarle Co., Va. d. Lynchburg, Va., 10/1/06. Bur. Rivanna.

WORTHINGTON, GEORGE E.: Pvt., Co. D. Enl. Winchester 9/20/62; present 11–12/62; ab. sick in Staunton, Va., hosp. 7/19–12/31/63. d. near New Market, Va., 1/20/64.

WORTHINGTON, HENRY T.: Pvt., Co. E. b. circa 1830. Enl. Richmond 11/8/62, age thirty-one; presence or ab. not stated 1–2/63; horse killed Williamsport, Md., 7/12/63, paid $230; ab. sick with acute dysentery in Charlottesville hosp. 8/15/63; transf. to Lynchburg, Va., hosp. 9/21/63; present 11–12/63 and 4/1/64; horse given to dismounted man; ab. on horse detail for twenty days to Hardy Co., W.Va., 4/9/64. NFR.

WORTHINGTON, JOSHUA E.: Pvt., Co. A. Res. of Frederick Co., Md. Enl. Urbana, Md., 9/15/62. Captured Harpers Ferry, W.Va., 9/23/63; sent to Ft. McHenry; transf. to Ft. Del. and Pt. Lookout; exchanged 12/28/63. Paid Richmond 12/31/63. NFR.

WORTHINGTON, REZIN H.: Pvt., Co. A. b. 12/13/39. On postwar roster. d. 3/22/72. Bur. family cem., Baltimore Co., Md.

WORTHINGTON, THOMAS G.: 3rd Sgt., Co. D. b. circa 1838. Res. of New Market, Md. Enl. Winchester 9/20/62; present through 12/62. Captured, horse killed, Monterey Springs, Pa., 7/4/63; sent to Ft. Del.; exchanged 10/5/64. Ab. sick with "Lumbago" in Richmond hosp. 10/6–22/64; furloughed for forty days; present 12/31/64. Paroled Winchester 4/23/65. Age twenty-seven, 6'½", fair complexion, gray hair, blue eyes.

WRIGHT, CLINTON: Pvt., Co. E. Farmer, Queen Anne's Co., Md. Enl. 9/3/64; present through 12/31/64; WIA, date and place unknown. Paroled Ashland, Va., 5/14/65.

WRIGHT, LEWIS: Pvt., Co. C, Davis's Bn. NFR.

WRIGHT, RICHARD B.: Pvt., Co. B. b. circa 1842. Res. of Washington, D.C. Enl. Charlottesville 9/10/62. Captured near Moorefield, W.Va., 2/23/63; sent to Wheeling. Age twenty-one, 5'11", dark complexion, dark eyes, gray hair. Druggist. Transf. to Camp Chase; exchanged 4/1/63. Paid 4/6/63; des. Williamsport, Md., 7/1/63. NFR.

WRIGHT, SOLOMON: 3rd Sgt., Co. E. b. near Centreville, Md., 7/22/38. Business-man, St. Louis, Mo. Enl. as Pvt., Richmond, 11/10/62; presence or ab. not stated 1–2/63, however, promoted 3rd Sgt. 1/20/63; present 7–8/63; presence or ab. not stated 9–10/63; present 11–12/63 and

4/1–12/31/64. NFR. Conductor, B&O RR; employee, Chester River Steamboat Co. Member ANS/MLA; Isaac Trimble Camp, CV, Hyattsville, Md.; and Franklin Buchanan Camp, CV, Baltimore. d. Baltimore 11/21/14. Bur. St. Paul's Cem., Kent Co.

WRIGHT, WILLIAM HOLMES: 1st Sgt., Co. K. b. Md. 1839. Res. of Cooksville, Howard Co., Md. Enl. as 1st Cpl., Co. K (2nd), 1st Va. Cav., Leesburg, Va., 5/14/61; present until ab. sick with rheumatism in Richmond hosp. 2/11–4/19/62. Promoted 2nd Sgt; present through 5/1/63, promoted 1st Sgt; present through 8/64. Transf. to Co. K, 1st Md. Cav., 8/64; AWOL 9/22–12/31/64. NFR. Served in Co. A, 43rd Bn. Va. Cav. (Mosby). Paroled Paris, Va., 4/27/65. Farmer, Baltimore. Member ANS/MLA. Entered Old Soldiers' Home, Pikesville, Md., 5/2/99, age sixty-one; d. there 3/19/01, age sixty-three. Bur. Loudon Park Cem., Baltimore.

WURSTEN, HENRY: Pvt., Co. C. b. circa 1827. Enl. Co. G, 13th Va. Inf., 6/30/61; discharged as non-resident 5/28/62. Enl. Co. C, 1st Md. Cav., Winchester, 10/23/62. Captured Monterey Springs, Pa., 7/4/63, horse killed; sent to Ft. McHenry; transf. to Ft. Del. and Pt. Lookout; exchanged 1/21/65. Paroled Winchester 4/19/65. Age thirty-eight, 5'6", dark complexion, light hair, gray eyes. Took oath Harpers Ferry, W.Va., 4/22/65. Ordered North of Philadelphia, Pa.

WYNN, A. JOSEPH: Pvt., Co. E. Enl. Co. C, 19th Bn. Va. Arty., Richmond, 5/14/62. Transf. to Co. E, 1st Md. Cav., 12/17/62; presence or ab. not stated 7–8/63; ab. sick with "Insipent phthisis" 8/7–10/2/63; ab. in hosp. 4/1/64. NFR.

WYNN, JAMES A.: Pvt., Co. E. b. circa 1842. Res. of Baltimore. Enl. Co. C, 19th Bn. Va. Heavy Arty., Richmond, 3/18/62. Transf. to Co. E, 1st Md. Cav., Richmond, 2/14/63; presence or ab. not stated through 2/28/63. Captured near Winchester 6/12/63, horse killed; sent to Ft. McHenry. Age twenty-five, 5'8½", dark complexion, blue eyes, dark hair. Transf. to Ft. Monroe; exchanged 6/26/63. Paid $500 for horse; present 7–8/63; ab. on horse detail 10/28/63; present 11–12/63; ab. on detail 3/25/64. Captured Hagerstown, Md., 4/2/64; sent to Baltimore as a spy. NFR.

YATES, THOMAS FRANKLIN: Pvt., Co. K. b. Leonardtown, St. Mary's Co., Md., circa 1843. Enl. Stuart Horse Arty., 8/10/62; WIA (nose) Carlisle, Pa., 7/1/63. Transf. to Co. K (2nd), 1st Va. Cav., 8/14/64. Transf. to Co. K, 1st Md. Cav., 8/64; issued clothing 9/30/64. Captured in Md; sent to Old Capitol 3/65. NFR. Member ANS/MLA. Res. of Leonardtown, 1903; res. of Chestertown, Kent Co., Md., 1908, age seventy. d.

5/7/14, age seventy-six. Bur. Our Lady's Cem., Medley's Neck, Md.

YERBY, ALBERT FRANCIS: Pvt., Co. C. b. near Upperville, Va., 1820. Res. of Md. On postwar roster. Enl. Co. G, 43rd Bn. Va. Cav. (Mosby) 12/1/64. NFR. d. Baltimore 11/1/89.

YOUNG, ALEXANDER H.: Pvt., Co. D. b. Washington, D.C. Res. of Frederick Co., Md. Enl. as Sgt., Co. B, Hampton Legion Arty. of S.C. Transf. to Chesapeake Md. Arty. Promoted Sgt. Maj. of Parker's Va. Bty. Transf. to Co. D, 1st Md. Cav., 4/12/64; KIA Pollard's Farm, Va., 5/27/64. Bur. Ch. Cem., Hanover CH, Va. "Son of a former comptroller of the treasury of the United States under Buchanan's administration, was a model of manly beauty, of chivalry and grace, of courage and accomplishment! Beautiful as he was brave, refined as highly educated; intelligually, physically and morally he was a pattern gentleman. He died in his tracks, dismounted on the skirmish line, holding his place against a charge of mounted cavalry." The CV Camp in Frederick, Md., was named in his honor.

YOUNG, W. WASHINGTON: Pvt., Co. C. b. Md. circa 1836. Enl. as Pvt., Co. C, 8th La. Inf., 3/15/62, age twenty-six. Res. of Frederick Co.,

Md. Transf. to Co. C, 1st Md. Cav., 2/64. Paroled Ashland, Va., 4/26/65. Res. of Washington, D.C.

ZELL, ROBERT ROSS: Lt., Co. D. b. circa 1845. Res. of Baltimore. Enl. Co. F, 7th Va. Cav., 12/1/63. Transf. to Co. D, 1st Md. Cav., 5/3/64; mare KIA, Wilderness, 5/5/64. Captured Moorefield, W.Va., 8/7/64; sent to Pt. Lookout; exchanged 2/15/65. Present Camp Lee, Richmond, 2/17/65. Paroled New Creek 4/26/65. Age twenty, 5'7", dark complexion, dark hair, black eyes. Took oath Cumberland, Md., same day. Res. of Baltimore. Mechanical Engineer, Birmingham, Ala. Member ANS/MLA, 1894. Res. of Baltimore. Admitted Old Soldiers' Home, Pikesville, Md. d. 11/12/18.

ZEPP, CHARLES T.: Pvt., Co. A. b. circa 1846. Res. of Howard Co., Md. Enl. Urbana, Md., 9/10/62; present 7–12/63 and 4/1/64. Captured Moorefield, W.Va., 8/7/64; sent to Wheeling. Age eighteen, 5'6½", dark complexion, gray eyes, dark hair. Farmer. Transf. to Camp Chase and Pt. Lookout; exchanged 3/27/65. Paroled Berryville, Va., 4/19/65. Took oath Harpers Ferry, W.Va., 4/20/65. Attended reunion 1899. Bur. St. Louis Catholic Ch. Cem., Clarksville, Howard Co., no dates.

Second Maryland Cavalry

ACRCE, THOMAS L.: Pvt., Co. A. b. Richmond circa 1848. Enl. Richmond 2/6/64. Age sixteen, 4'10½", light complexion, gray eyes, light hair. Paid Richmond 6/28/64, age sixteen and nine months; signed by mark. NFR.

AINSWORTH, THOMAS: Pvt., Co. A. Captured Staunton, Va., 6/7/64; sent to Camp Morton. NFR.

ALBAND, W. H.: Pvt., Co. D. Removed from Va., reburied Loudon Park Cem., Baltimore, 1874.

ALCHER, FRANCIS G.: Pvt., Co. A. b. circa 1843. Also listed Co. D, 18th Va. Cav. Des. New Market, Va., 11/6/63; des. to the enemy Paw Paw Tunnel, W.Va., 11/11/63. Age twenty-one, 5'2½", fair complexion, dark eyes, dark hair. Res. Henrico Co., Va. Transf. to Ft. Del.; took oath, released 12/31/64. NFR.

ALCOCK, WILLIAM C.: Pvt., Co. C. Issued clothing in Staunton, Va., hosp. 10/14/64. Paroled Winchester 5/10/65. Took oath Winchester 6/9/65. Age twenty-one, 5'10", dark complexion, dark hair, gray eyes. Res. of Baltimore; destination Shenandoah Co., Va.

ALL, S. D.: Pvt., Co. unknown. Body removed from Va., reburied Loudon Park Cem., Baltimore, 1874.

ALLEN, JOHN: Pvt., Co. F. b. Va. circa 1819. Enl. Co. A, 1st Md. Inf., 3/25/62; discharged 8/18/62. Age forty-two, 6', dark complexion, brown eyes, dark hair. Sawyer. Signed by mark. Enl. Co. F, 2nd Md. Cav., Big Spring, Va., 7/27/64; horse killed Bunker Hill, W.Va., 8/21/64; paid $3,000 3/30/65. NFR.

ALLEN, WILLIAM: QM Sgt. On roster. NFR. Probably William Allen who d. 2/20/10, age seventy-two. Bur. Petersville Catholic Ch. Cem., Frederick Co., Md.

ALLHARN, JOSEPH: Pvt., Co. A. Des. sent from Baltimore to Ft. McHenry 8/25/63. NFR.

ALMOND, J. W.: Pvt., Co. A. Captured Moorefield, W.Va., 1/2/65; sent to Wheeling, "Charged with murder." Age twenty-two, 5'6", florid complexion, gray eyes, dark hair. Merchant. Res. of Orange Co., Va. Escaped 7/18/65.

AMABLE, JAMES: Pvt., Co. D. Enl. Richmond 10/1/63. Captured 10/18/63; on rolls 12/31/63–8/31/64. NFR. Not on Federal POW rolls.

ANDRE, JOHN A.: 2nd Cpl., Co. F. Enl. Co. A, 1st Md. Inf., 7/25/61; reenl. 2/8/62. NFR. Enl. Co. F, 12th Va. Cav., Martinsburg, W.Va., 8/23/62. Transf. to Co. F, 2nd Md. Cav., 4/29/64. NFR.

ARIGONI, GUISEPPIE: Pvt., Co. D. Enl. Richmond 10/1/63; des. near Winchester 10/15/63; des. to the enemy Harrisburg, Pa., 10/18/63; sent to Ft. Mifflin, Pa.; took oath, released. 5'7", dark complexion, dark hair, hazel eyes. Res. of Richmond.

ARGONE, WILLIAM: Pvt., Co. D. On postwar roster. Res. West River, Anne Arundel Co., Md.

ARVIN, THOMAS E.: Pvt., Co. D. Enl. Richmond 7/1/63; detailed in Armory, Richmond, 12/31/63–8/31/64. NFR. Res. Carroll Co., Md.

BAILEY, _____: Pvt., Co. unknown; present 1/64. NFR.

BAIRD, HENRY: Pvt., Co. D. Enl. Winchester 7/1/64; present 8/31/64; issued clothing 9/30/64. Paroled Charles Town, W.Va., 4/21/65. Age seventeen, 5'8", light complexion, dark hair, blue eyes.

BAKER, FREDERICK D.: 1st Sgt., Co. C. Captured Moorefield, W.Va., 8/7/64; sent to Wheeling. Age twenty, 6'1", florid complexion, blue eyes, sandy hair. Farmer. Res. Kent Co., Md. Transf. to Camp Chase; exchanged 3/12/65. Paroled Winchester 4/19/65, age twenty-two.

BAKER, GEORGE H.: Pvt., Co. B. Des. to the enemy 4/20/64; sent to Old Capitol; transf. to Pt. Lookout; took oath, released 1/10/64.

BAKER, JAMES: Pvt., Co. B. Captured Falling Waters, Md., 7/14/63; sent to Old Capitol; transf. to Pt. Lookout; took oath, released 1/1/0/64.

BAKER, LEWIS H.: Pvt., Co. C. Captured Frederick Co., Va., 3/26/65; sent to Wheeling. Age twenty-four, 5'10½", dark complexion, hazel eyes, dark hair. Clerk. Res. of Madison Parish, La. Transf. to Camp Chase. Took oath, joined U.S. Army 4/22/65.

BAKER, SAMUEL B.: Pvt., Co. D. Enl. Richmond

10/1/63; des. to the enemy Charles Town, W.Va., 10/18/63; sent to Wheeling. Age thirty, 5'5", fair complexion, blue eyes, light hair. Carpenter. Res. Richmond. Transf. to Camp Chase; took oath, released 3/15/65.

BAMBERGER, H.: Pvt., Co. B. Enl. Richmond 10/1/63; ab. sick with fever in Staunton, Va., hosp. 2/24/64; issued clothing 12/5/64 and 12/7/64. NFR.

BARNES, PLOWDEN: Pvt., Co. C; ab. sick with "debilitas" in Richmond hosp. 3/6/65; furloughed for thirty days 3/8/65. NFR. d. 5/5/71, age twenty-five. Bur. Old St. Joseph's Cath. Ch. Cem., Morgantown, W.Va.

BARNETT, WILLIAM H.: Pvt., Co. B. Captured Piedmont, Va., 6/5/64; sent to Camp Morton; released 5/28/65. 5'4½", dark complexion, dark hair, blue eyes. Res. of Baltimore.

BAYLEY, JAMES R.: Capt., Co. B. b. Fauquier Co., Va., 1831. Enl. Co. H, 21st Va. Inf., Richmond, 5/23/61; discharged 11/2/61. 5'8½", sallow complexion, light hair, light beard, gray eyes. Farmer. Enl. Co. B, 2nd Md. Cav., date unknown; issued clothing for co., Lynchburg, Va., 7/31/64; signed requisition for forage 8/31/64. NFR.

BEALL, WILLIAM B.: Pvt., Co. F. Enl. Co. I, 1st Md. Inf., 6/15/61; discharged 6/15/62, age thirty-four. On postwar roster Co. F, 2nd Md. Cav. In Old Soldiers' Home, Richmond, 1934.

BELLESON, WILLIAM K.: Pvt., Co. E. b. Carroll Co., Md., circa 1833. Enl. Richmond 1/6/64. Age thirty-one, 5'10", light complexion, hazel eyes, brown hair. Blacksmith; ab. sick with chronic pneumonia in Richmond hosp. 3/6/65; furloughed for thirty days to Hanover Junction, Va., 3/18/65. Took oath Winchester 4/19/65. Age thirty-one, 5'10", dark complexion, black hair, gray eyes. Former res. of Baltimore or Howard Co., Md.

BENNETT, JAMES: Pvt., Co. unknown. Des., captured, Franklin, Pa., 5/18/64; sent to Ft. Del.; transf. to Washington, D.C., for trial; des. from Co. C, 93rd N.Y. Inf.

BENNETT, WILLIAM: Pvt., Co. F. Enl. Big Spring, Va., 7/27/64. NFR. Res. of Princeland, Anne Arundel Co., Md.

BENNETT, WILLIAM H.: Pvt., Co. B. b. 1/21/42. Captured Falling Waters, Md., 7/14/63; sent to Old Capitol; transf. to Pt. Lookout and Elmira; exchanged 3/15/65. Paroled Montgomery, Ala., 5/13/65. 5'7", dark complexion, dark hair, hazel eyes. Res. of Baltimore. M.D., Anne Arundel Co., Md., postwar. d. 11/13/99. Bur. Galesville Meth. Ch. Cem., Anne Arundel Co.

BERRETT, JOSEPH W.: Pvt., Co. F; issued clothing 9/30/64; des. to the enemy Washington, D.C., 3/13/65. Took oath, transportation furnished to

Carroll Co., Md.

BERRETT, J. T.: Pvt., Co. F. Enl. Big Spring, Va., 7/27/64. NFR.

BIAYS, P. A.: Pvt., Co. D. Enl. Richmond 7/7/63; present 12/31/63–8/31/64; issued clothing 9/30/64. Paroled Mt. Jackson, Va., 4/21/65. Age twenty-nine, 6'3", light complexion, light hair, blue eyes. Former res. of Baltimore; destination Baltimore.

BIAS, PHILIP: Pvt., Co. C; issued clothing 9/10/64. NFR.

BIGGS, BENJAMIN J.: Pvt., Co. C. Captured Loudoun Co., Va., 2/2/65; sent to Ft. McHenry: "Guerilla not to be exchanged during the war." Released 5/1/65. Res. Patuxent Forge, Anne Arundel Co., Md.

BIGGS, JOSEPH: Pvt., Co. C. Bay mare killed Bunker Hill, W.Va., 9/4/64, paid $3,000. Captured Loudoun Co., Va., 2/3/65; sent to Ft. McHenry; released 5/2/65. 5'10", light complexion, brown hair, gray eyes. Res. Rappahannock Co., Va. Signed by mark.

BILLINGS, HENRY: Lt., Co. D; present 5/64. NFR.

BIRD, CHARLES DUPONT: Pvt., Co. G. See 1st Md. Cav.

BISHOP, CHARLES: (See page 201.)

BLACKFORD, JOHN CORBIN: Pvt., Co. A. b. 1/1/39. Res. Frederick Co., Va. Enl. as Pvt., Co. A., 12th Va. Cav., Charles Town, W.Va., 6/26/61, for one year; present 11–12/61. NFR. Reenl. Co. A, 2nd Md. Cav.; present 9/63; WIA (knee) 9/15/63. Captured Martinsburg, W.Va., 10/15/63; sent to Ft. McHenry; escaped 10/20/63. "Supposed to be Capt. Blackford the Guerilla." In Newtown, Va., 10/63; KIA near Newtown 1/6/64; bur. near Newtown; removed to family cem., Jefferson Co., W.Va.

BODELL, GEORGE M.: Pvt., Co. C. Captured Winchester or Middletown, Va., 9/20/63; sent to Ft. McHenry. Age seventeen, 5'10", fair complexion, blue eyes, dark hair. Mechanic. Res. New Market, Va.. Transf. to Pt. Lookout; exchanged 2/15/65. Present Camp Lee, Richmond, 2/18/65. Paroled Winchester 4/19/65. Age twenty, 5'10", fair complexion, brown hair, blue eyes.

BOHN, J.: Pvt., Co. unknown; present 8/64. NFR.

BOND, WILLIAM: Pvt., Co. A. Res. of Howard Co., Md. On postwar roster.

BOSLEY, JOHN R.: Sgt., Co. C. Res. of Baltimore; WIA (calf of leg) Charles Town, W.Va., 10/18/63. Enl. Big Spring, Va., 7/27/64; on roster. NFR. Res. Cockeysville, Md., postwar.

BOWYERS or BOWERS, LAFAYETTE: (See page 203.)

BOYD, WILLIAM: Pvt., Co. D. b. Auburn, Ireland. Captured Harrisonburg, Va., 12/20/63; sent to

Wheeling. Age twenty-seven, 5'7", florid complexion, hazel eyes, dark hair. Transf. to Camp Chase; took oath, released 6/10/64.

BOYLE, PHILIP: Pvt., Co. F. On postwar roster.

BRADFORD, DANIEL: Pvt., Co. B. Paid Richmond 5/5/64 for 1–2/64. Paroled Winchester 4/29/65. Age eighteen, 5'11", fair complexion, light hair, gray eyes. Res. Richmond.

BRADLEY, JAMES: Pvt., Co. B. Des., captured Front Royal, Va., 8/4/63; sent to Wheeling. Age twenty-two, 5'6", light complexion, auburn hair, gray eyes. Laborer. Res. of La. Transf. to Camp Chase. Took oath 9/3/64. Res. of Roanoke, Va.

BRADY, JOHN H.: Pvt., Co. unknown. b. Baltimore circa 1841. Enl. Co. B, 21st Va. Inf., 5/23/61, age twenty-two, 5'7½", black hair, blue eyes. NFR. On postwar roster 2nd Md. Cav., Rosser's, and Mosby's commands.

BRADY, S. H.: Pvt., Co. B. Enl. New Market, Va., 8/63; present 9–10/63; WIA date and place unknown. Admitted Staunton, Va., hosp. 1/28/64; RTD 2/29/64; horse killed Woodstock, Va., 9/21/64, paid $500. NFR.

BRADY, WILLIAM: Pvt., Co. B. Des. and arrested Franklin Co., Pa., 5/18/64; sent to Ft. Del.; transf. to Washington, D.C., for trial as des. from Co. A, 125th N.Y. Inf.

BRANDENBURG, JESSE W.: Pvt., Co. C. b. 12/19/38. Res. Winfield, Carroll Co., Md. Served as 1st Lt., Lee's Md. Cav., 1862; enl. date, place unknown. Paroled Winchester 4/25/65. Age twenty-five, 5'10", dark complexion, black hair, gray eyes. d. 1/9/79. Bur. Eldersburg Methodist Ch. Cem., Frederick Co., Md. (Photograph in Hartzler 1992)

BRAITH, AUGUSTINE: Pvt., Co. B. Captured Chambersburg, Pa., circa 11/12/63; sent to Ft. Del. 11/17/63. NFR.

BREWER, HENRY WILMOT: Capt., Co. E. b. Georgetown, D.C., 1834. Civil Engineer. Master's Mate, U.S. Coastal Survey, U.S. Navy, 1859–61. Clerk, U.S. Treasury Dept. Enl. as 2nd Lt., Co. H, 7th Va. Inf., 4/22/61; promoted 1st Lt. 4/26/62. Co. disbanded 5/16/62. Asst. Engineer, Richmond defenses and in Mississippi, 1862–63; recruiting for Md. Line summer 1863–2/64; served as 1st Lt. and Capt. Co. E, 2nd Md. Cav.; signed for clothing for co. 8/15/63 and 8/29/63, with twenty-four men present; signed for clothing 9/5/63 and 9/12/63, thirty-six men present. Commanding Camp Md. at Camp Lee, Richmond, 9/14/63; signed for clothing and equipment 11/12/63, 12/18/63, and 2/15/64; in Lynchburg, Va., 6/16–17/64; horse killed, Clear Spring, Md., 7/29/64. Captured Moorefield, W.Va., 8/7/64; sent to Wheeling. Age twenty-nine, 5'11", fair complex-

ion, brown hair, gray eyes. Res. Georgetown, D.C. Transf. to Camp Chase; exchanged 3/12/65. Paid $4,000 for horse killed Richmond 3/21/65. Paroled Lynchburg, Va., 5/23/65. Former resident of Baltimore; destination Baltimore. Took oath Washington, D.C., 8/1/65. Postwar, Civil Engineer, Georgetown, D.C., 1900. d. 7/00. Bur. Oak Hill Cem., Washington.

BRICKHEAD, _____: Pvt., Co., unknown. On postwar roster.

BRIGHTWELL, JOSEPH WILLIAM: Pvt., Co. D. b. circa 1847. Res. of Tex., Baltimore Co., Md. Entered Old Soldiers' Home, Pikesville, Md., 23/1/98, age fifty-one. Carpenter. d. 10/3/04, age fifty-seven. Bur. Loudon Park Cem., Baltimore.

BRISCOE, ENOCH: Pvt., Co. A. Res. St. Mary's Co. On postwar roster Co. A, 1st Md. Inf., also.

BRITTON, JAMES E.: Pvt., Co. A. Captured Martinsburg, W.Va., 10/15/63; sent to Ft. McHenry; transf. to Pt. Lookout 11/1/63; never arrived. NFR.

BROGDEN, J. SELLMAN: Pvt., Co. C. b. Anne Arundel Co., Md., 8/10/32. Res. Davidsonville, Anne Arundel Co. Enl. Co. H, 1st Md. Inf., 6/18/61; discharged 6/18/62. 5'11", light complexion, light eyes, dark hair. Farmer. Paroled Northern Neck, Va., 5/3/65. Member ANS/MLA. d. 5/30/98. Bur. All Hallows Cem., Davidsonville, Md.

BROGDON, HENRY: Pvt., Co. B. Res. Anne Arundel Co. On postwar roster. Possibly Henry Hall Brogdon (1836–1905). Bur. St. Barnabas' Episcopal Ch. Cem., Prince George's Co., Md.

BROOKE, HENRY: (See page 206.)

BROTHERTON, DAVID: Pvt., Co. C. On postwar roster.

BROWN, FRANCIS: 1st Sgt., Co. D. Res. Princess Anne, Somerset Co., Md. Enl. Harrisonburg, Va., 6/62. Captured, date and place unknown. Exchanged prisoner, Camp Lee, Richmond, 3/19/65. NFR. Possibly Francis L. Brown (1842–1904). Bur. Mt. Olivet Cem., Frederick, Md.

BROWN, RICHARD LOUIS, JR.: Sgt., Co. C. b. Orange Co., Va. 2/22/43. Att. VMI, class of 1863. Enl. Co. C (3rd), 1st Md. Inf., 1861–62. Enl. Co. C, 2nd Md. Cav., date unknown; promoted Lt. on Gen. Albert G. Jenkins's staff and Gen. John McCausland's staff; WIA Monocacy, Md., 7/7/64; present Appomattox CH, Va., 4/9/65. Paroled Winchester 5/65. Moved to Md. Farmer, Anne Arundel Co. 1867–69. Businessman, Baltimore 1879–1900. Member ANS/MLA. Res. of Baltimore 1984. d. Baltimore 5/25/09.

BRUBAKER, R.: Pvt., Co. F. Joined from Co. D., 12th Va. Cav., Jefferson Co., W.Va., 10/23/63. NFR. Not on muster rolls Co. D, 12th Va. Cav.

BRYAN, W. H.: Pvt., Co. C. Res. of Carroll Co., Md; ab. sick with "debilitas" in Richmond hosp. 3/7/65; furloughed for thirty days 3/9/65. NFR.

BUCHANAN, THOMAS E.: Pvt., Co. F. Enl. Co. D, 2nd Va. Inf., 4/18/61; WIA (shoulder) Bull Run, Va., 7/21/61. NFR. Enl. Co. F, 12th Va. Cav., 2/20/62. Captured 10/21/62; sent to Old Capitol; exchanged 10/31/62. Captured near Front Royal, Va., 5/13/63; sent to Ft. McHenry; transf. to Ft. Monroe; exchanged 5/17/63. WIA Todd's Tavern 5/7/64. Transf. to 2nd Md. Cav., 8/13/64. NFR.

BUCKLEY, JOHN: Pvt., Co. D. b. circa 1842. Enl. Co. F, 19th Va. Inf., 5/21/61. Age twenty. Laborer. Dark complexion, hazel eyes, sandy hair. Discharged 9/25/62. Served in Co. C, Davis's Bn. Enl. Co. D, 2nd Md. Cav., Winchester, 7/1/64. Captured Moorefield, W.Va., 8/7/64. On rolls to 8/31/64. NFR. Res. of Baltimore 1894.

BUNTING, JOHN H.: Pvt., Co. unknown. b. circa 1843. Res. of Baltimore. Served in Co. I, 1st S.C. Inf., 1861–63; des. to the enemy 12/63. Age twenty, 5'9", fair complexion, blue eyes, light hair. Took oath, sent north, 12/5/63.

BURCHELL, JOHN: Pvt., Co. B. Forwarded to PM, Staunton, Va., 7/24/63, as des.: "a citizen of N.Y. and a deserter from the U.S. Army and having been a frequent prisoner in Castle Thunder, Richmond, is considered a dangerous character." Captured and sent to Ft. McHenry 8/26/63; took oath, released 9/14/63. 5'11", dark complexion, brown hair, brown eyes. Res. of N.Y.

BURKE, FRANCIS WILLIAM "POLK": 2nd Lt., Co. D. b. Va. or Md. 8/14/46. Student, age fifteen, Harpers Ferry, W.Va., PO, Jefferson Co., per 1860 census. Enl. as Pvt., Co. F, 1st Va. Cav., date unknown. Captured Clarke Co. 12/26/62; sent to Camp Chase; exchanged 4/1/63. Captured Berryville, Va., 4/21/63; sent to Ft. McHenry; transf. to Ft. Monroe; exchanged 4/28/63. Transf. to Co. D, 2nd Md. Cav., and elected 2nd Lt; present 12/63; paid 8/8/64 for 11/25/63–7/25/64; paid 1/1/65. Paroled Harrisonburg 5/8/65. Age nineteen, 5'7", light complexion, dark hair, gray eyes. Brother of John R. Burke. Member Pat Cleburne Camp, CV, Waco, Tex. d. Waco, Tex., 12/16/20. Bur. Oakwood Cem., Waco, Tex.

BURKE, JOHN M.: Pvt., Co., A. Res. of Baltimore. Enl. Co. H, 1st Md. Inf., 5/30/61; discharged 5/16/62. On postwar roster. Res. Waverly, Baltimore Co., 1894. Member ANS/MLA.

BURKE, JOHN REDMOND: Capt., Co. D. b. Md. circa 1837. Stonecutter, age twenty-three, Harpers Ferry, W.Va., PO, Jefferson Co., per 1860 census. Enl. Co. K, 2nd Va. Inf., 4/20/61. Transf. to Co. F, 1st Va. Cav., 8/12/61; detailed Gen. J. E. B. Stuart's headquarters as scout 12/11/61–4/62.

Known as the "Potomac Scout." WIA (leg) 8/20/62; present until ab. detached 10/20/62 until captured near Shepherdstown, W.Va., 11/9/62; sent to Ft. McHenry; exchanged 12/4/62. Captured Berryville, Va., 4/4/63; sent to Ft. McHenry; transf. to Ft. Monroe; exchanged 4/19/63. Wrote Secretary of War requesting authority to raise co. of cavalry in the Valley from nonconscripts 5/9/63; AWOL through 12/31/63; ab. sick in Staunton, Va., hosp. 2–3/64. General Stuart wrote on 3/19/64, "He is a man of sterling worth[,] intelligence, intrepid daring, and an inflexibility of resolve that would never swerve from the path of duty no matter how perilous." Paid 4/5/64; two bay mares killed, Leesburg, Va., 7/15/64. Transf. to Co. D, 2nd Md. Cav., and elected Capt. 8/31/64; ab. sick with scabies in Richmond hosp. 2/3–3/26/65. Paroled Staunton, Va., 5/1/65. Age twenty-eight, 5'7½", dark complexion, black hair, hazel eyes. Bur. Elmwood Cem., Shepherdstown, no dates. Brother of Francis W. Burke.

BURKE, NICHOLAS: Capt., Co. A. b. circa 1812. Mexican War Veteran. Res. of Baltimore. Enl. circa 6/1/63; present Harrisonburg, Va., 11/27–12/14/63; present 5/15/64; in Lynchburg, Va., 6/18/64; paid 7/22/64; present 8/31/64; paid 9/16/64; AWOL sixty-four days 10/25/64; dropped 1/3/65; submitted resignation 1/27/65; paid 2/2/65 while in Richmond hosp. Paroled Baltimore Co. 7/26/65. 5'8", light complexion, dark hair, blue eyes. Deputy Warden; Jail Detective; and Rent Collector, Baltimore. d. 1/10/81, age sixty-nine.

BURNS, DANIEL: Pvt., Co. D. Des., arrested Hancock, Md., 7/23/63; sent to Wheeling. Age thirty-four, 6'3¾", dark complexion, gray eyes, auburn hair. Miner. Res. of Cincinnati, Oh. Transf. to Camp Chase; took oath, released 1/0/65.

BURNS, IGNATIUS: Pvt., Co. F. Enl. Big Spring, Va., 7/27/64. NFR.

BURNS, JAMES: Pvt., Co. B. Captured Newtown, Va., 10/8/63; sent to Ft. McHenry; escaped 10/22/63. NFR.

BURNS, JOHN: Pvt., Co. D. Captured Moorefield, W.Va., 8/7/64; sent to Wheeling. Age twenty-two, 6', fair complexion, gray eyes, red hair. Laborer. Res. New Orleans, La. Transf. to Camp Chase; exchanged 3/12/65. NFR.

BURNS, PATRICK: Pvt., Co. D. Enl. Winchester 7/1/64; horse killed Clear Spring, Md., 7/18/64, paid $3,000. Captured Moorefield, W.Va., 8/7/64. NFR until exchanged. Paid Richmond 3/20/65. NFR.

BURNS, PATRICK J.: Pvt., Co. A. b. Ireland. Captured Martinsburg, W.Va., 10/15/63. "Volunteered to get out of Castle Thunder. Was in service 3 months when he was captured." Sent to Ft. McHenry; released 4/23/65.

BURTON, JAMES W.: Sgt., Co. B. Res. Golden Hill, Dorchester Co., Md. Captured 10/13/63; sent to Ft. McHenry; transf. to Pt. Lookout 11/1/63, but entry cancelled. NFR.

BUSHBAUM, HENRY: Cpl., Co. C. On postwar roster.

CAHILL, JOHN: Pvt., Co. D. Des., arrested Gettysburg, Pa., 11/1/63; sent to Ft. Mifflin, Pa.; took oath, released 12/24/63 to join U.S. Marine Corps. 5'6½", fresh complexion, brown hair, hazel eyes. Res. Richmond.

CALLAN, JOHN: Pvt., Co. F. Enl. Big Spring, Va., 7/17/64; KIA Moorefield, W.Va., 8/7/64.

CAMBLE, THOMAS: Pvt., Co. F. Enl. Big Spring, Va., 7/27/64. NFR.

CARDER, JOSEPH F.: Pvt., Co. E. b. 1841. Enl. Co. I, 13th Va. Inf., 5/18/61. Age twenty-two, Laborer. Discharged 5/20/62. Reenl. Co. A, 33rd Va. Inf., 6/24/62. In Comm. Dept. 8/63. Transf. to Co. E, 2nd Md. Cav., 4/1/64. Paroled Lynchburg, Va., 4/15/65.

CAREY, THOMAS W.: Sgt., Co. D. b. circa 1841. Res. of Baltimore. Captured Moorefield, W.Va., 8/7/64; sent to Wheeling. Age twenty-three, 5'7", dark complexion, gray eyes, dark hair. Transf. to Camp Chase; exchanged 3/27/65. Paroled Winchester 4/28/65. Former res. of Baltimore; destination: "Go N. of Pa. Line."

CAREY, TIMOTHY W.: Sgt., Co. C. b. circa 1841. Res. Frederick, Md. Enl. Co. A, 1st Md. Inf., 5/22/61. Reenl. 2/8/62; paid 2/21/62. NFR. Enl. Co. F, 2nd Md. Inf., date unknown; WIA (back) and captured Gettysburg, Pa., 7/3/63; transf. to General Hosp. 7/14/63. NFR. Enl. Co. C, 2nd Md. Cav., date unknown. Paroled Winchester 4/19/65. Age twenty-four, 5'7", dark complexion, dark hair, gray eyes. Res. of Baltimore 1894. Member ANS/MLA. d. 1897.

CARLISLE, GEORGE A.: Pvt., Co. F. b. circa 1845. Enl. Big Spring, Va., 7/27/64. Captured Moorefield, W.Va., 8/7/64; sent to Wheeling. Age nineteen, 5'8", fair complexion, hazel eyes, dark hair. Miller. Res. of Baltimore Co. Transf. to Camp Chase; exchanged 3/27/65. Paroled Richmond 4/10/65. Took oath Richmond 4/13/65. Former res. of Baltimore; destination Baltimore.

CARPENTER, LEE: 3rd Sgt., Co. D. Enl. Richmond 9/10/63; des. 8/15/64; on rolls to 8/31/64. NFR.

CARR, WILLIAM: Pvt., Co. A. b. Ireland circa 1827. Enl. Co. A, 1st Md. Inf., 5/21/61; discharged 8/22/62. Age thirty-five, 5'6½", dark complexion, blue eyes, dark hair. Laborer. Paid 8/27/62; signed by mark. On postwar roster.

CASTLEMAN, CHARLES W.: Pvt., Co. F. Enl. Big Spring, Va., 7/27/64. NFR.

CASTLEMAN, THOMAS: Pvt., Co. F. Enl. Big Spring, Va., 7/27/64. NFR. Possibly Thomas Butler Castleman (10/11/48–5/20/18), Clarke Co., Va.

CAVANAUGH, PATRICK: Pvt., Co. B. Paroled Winchester 4/28/65. Age twenty-one, 5'9", fair complexion, blue eyes. Res. of Shenandoah Co., Va.

CAVE, WILLIAM W.: Pvt., Co. C. Captured, date and place unknown; sent to Ft. Del.; exchanged 8/1/63. Captured Madison CH, Va., 9/24/63; sent to Old Capitol; transf. to Pt. Lookout; in hosp. there 12/1–31/63. NFR.

CHAMBERS, JAMES H.: Sgt., Co. A. Paid Richmond 9/14/63. Captured Martinsburg, W.Va., 10/15/63; sent to Ft. McHenry; transf. to Pt. Lookout; exchanged 3/3/65. NFR.

CHAPMAN, WILLIAM: Pvt., Co. F. Enl. Big Spring, Va., 7/27/64. NFR.

CHERRY, JAMES: Pvt., Co. F. Served in Co. G, 1st Md. Inf., 1861–62. Probably James F. Cherry, Enl. Co. F, 12th Va. Cav., by 7/31/62. Captured and sent to Ft. McHenry 8/29/62; exchanged 10/2/62. Ab. Newtown, Va., 11/62. NFR; present 5/64. NFR.

CLARK, DAVID J.: Pvt., Co. A. Res. Clarksville, Howard Co., Md. On postwar roster.

CLARK, DUNCAN CHINK: Pvt., Co. C. Captured Hampshire Co., W.Va., 3/23/64; sent to Wheeling. Age nineteen, 5'6", fair complexion, gray eyes, light hair. Student. Res. of Baltimore; transf. to Camp Chase; sent to City Pt. for exchange 2/25/65. NFR. Res. of Baltimore 1894. Member ANS/MLA.

CLARK, JAMES LOUIS: Capt., Co. F. b. Savannah, Ga., 12/12/40. Att. Rugby Acad. and U. of Va. Lawyer, Baltimore. Appointed Capt. and QM, 1st Md. Inf., 11/20/61; dropped 2/24/62. Captured Baltimore 7/21/62; exchanged 8/11/62. Applied for Lt. in C.S. Regular Army 9/29/62 and 1/1/62. Appointed Lt. and Ord. Officer, Stuart Horse Arty., 1/24/63. Served on staff of Gen. J. E. B. Stuart. Appointed Capt., Co. F, 12th Va. Cav., 6/17/63; horses killed under him at Todd's Tavern, Va., 5/6/64, and Ashland, Va., 6/1/64. Transf. to Co. F, 2nd Md. Cav., as Capt., 7/27/64; horse killed Frederick, Md., 7/28/64. Captured Moorefield, W.Va., 8/7/64; sent to Wheeling. Age twenty-three, 5'9", light complexion, blue eyes, light hair. Transf. to Camp Chase and Pt. Lookout; exchanged 2/24/65. Paid Richmond 2/25/65; paid 3/6 and 3/24/65; commanded Bn. to end of war. Surrendered Appomattox CH, Va., 4/9/65; destination Baltimore. Harry Gilmor wrote of him in

1866, "He was a perfect tiger in a fight." Moved to Columbine, Routt Co., Colo.; returned to Baltimore. d. 9/4/10. Bur. Loudon Park Cem., Baltimore. (Photograph in Hartzler 1992)

CLARK, JOHN: Sgt., Co. A. Ab. sick with palpitation of the heart in Richmond hosp. 9/22/64; furloughed for forty days 10/4/64. NFR.

CLARK, JOHN: Pvt., Co. C. Served in Lucas's 15th Bn. S.C. Arty. 1861–64. Captured Piedmont, Va., 6/5/64; sent to Camp Morton; took oath, joined U.S. Army 3/14/65.

CLARK, JOHN O.: Pvt., Co. C. Res. Mathews Store, Howard Co., Md. On postwar roster.

CLARK, THOMAS: 3rd Sgt., Co. A. Enl. Richmond 6/12/63. Captured Martinsburg, W.Va., 10/15/63; sent to Ft. McHenry; transf. to Pt. Lookout; exchanged 9/19/64. In Richmond hosp. 9/20–21/64 and 10/3/64; furloughed for forty days 10/5/64 and thirty days 12/13/64; admitted to Richmond hosp. with debility 4/3/65, captured same day; sent to Newport News, Va.; admitted Richmond hosp. 7/7/65. Took oath, released 8/22/65.

CLARK, THOMAS: Pvt., Co. D. Enl. Richmond 6/12/63; present dismounted 8/31/64. NFR.

CLARKE, JOHN D.: Capt., Co. F. Captured Smithfield, W.Va., 8/28/64; sent to Ft. Del.; released 5/22/65. 5'8", light complexion, brown hair, blue eyes. Res. Baltimore; destination Baltimore.

CLASH, CORNELIUS V.: 4th Cpl., Co. D. b. circa 1843. Enl. Co. H, 1st Va. Inf., 5/15/61, age eighteen; discharged 4/62. Enl. Richmond 7/23/63; paid Staunton, Va., 4/6/64; present 8/1/64; issued clothing 10/10/64 and 10/15/64. Paroled New Market, Va., 5/6/65. Member Pickett Camp, CV, Richmond. d. 4/29/96.

CLEARY, DOUGLAS: 1st Lt., Co. E. Res. of Baltimore. On roster.

CLEM, JOHN A.: Pvt., Co. unknown. b. Edith, Shenandoah Co., Va., 7/16/46. Worked at Caroline Furnace until it was destroyed. Enl. 2nd Md. Cav., served to the end of the war. Farmer, Shenandoah Co., 1865–70. Merchant, Woodstock, Va.; moved to Staunton, Va. d. 11/26/14. Bur. Thornrose Cem., Staunton.

CLOUD, MONTJOY: Pvt., Co. C. On postwar roster.

COAKLEY, JOHN: Pvt., Co. E. Enl. Harrisonburg, Va., 5/31/63; ab. sick with "scorbutus" in Richmond hosp. 9/22/64; furloughed for forty days 10/4/64; transf. to Staunton, Va., hosp. NFR.

COBOURN, JAMES M.: 2nd Lt. , Co. A. Captured Cedar Creek, Va., 9/19/64; sent to Ft. Del.; released 5/10/65. 5'10", fair complexion, light hair, gray eyes. Res. Shenandoah Co., Va.

COE, CHARLES HANSON PITTS: Pvt., Co. D.

On postwar roster. Res. of Baltimore.

COLUMBINI, LUIGI: Pvt., Co. unknown. Des. to the enemy, Winchester, 10/15/63; sent to Ft. Mifflin, Pa.; took oath, released 11/5/63. 5'2", fair complexion, light hair, hazel eyes. Res. of Winchester.

COMBS, BENJAMIN: Pvt., Co. unknown. Captured Moorefield, W.Va., 8/7/64; sent to Wheeling. Age fourteen, 5'5½", dark complexion, dark hair, dark eyes. Farmer, Hampshire Co., W.Va., Transf. to Camp Chase; paroled for exchange 2/25/65. NFR.

CONDELL, SAMUEL C.: Pvt., Co. C. b. Baltimore circa 1841. Res. of Baltimore. Enl. Co. F, 1st Md. Inf., 5/22/61; discharged 8/17/62. Age twenty-one, 5'7", fair complexion, blue eyes, brown hair. Laborer. Reenl. Co. C, 2nd Md. Cav., New Market, Va., 7/13/63. Captured Winchester 9/4/63; sent to Ft. McHenry; transf. to Pt. Lookout; paroled for exchange 9/19/64. Admitted Richmond hosp. with debility 9/20/64; exchanged 10/4/64; present Camp Lee, Richmond, 10/31/64; issued clothing 11/2/64 and 12/1/64. Captured Charlottesville 4/5/65; sent to Ft. Monroe; transf. to Pt. Lookout; released 6/10/65. 5'7", light complexion, brown hair, blue eyes.

CONLEY, WILLIAM P.: Pvt., Co. C. Enl. Co. F, 1st Md. Inf., 5/26/61; paid Richmond 8/28/63. Enl. date and place unknown; issued clothing 9/10/64. Paroled Romney, W.Va., 5/10/65. Age thirty-eight, 6', dark complexion, dark hair, gray eyes. Res. "Camel [Campbell?] Co., Va."

COOK, ROBERT: Pvt., Co. unknown. On postwar roster.

COOK, STEVE J.: Sgt., Co. A. Admitted Richmond hosp. 6/6/63 as Pvt. Promoted Sgt. Captured Smithfield, W.Va., 8/28/64; sent to Old Capitol; transf. to Camp Chase and Pt. Lookout; released 6/24/65. 5'6½", fair complexion, grayish hair, blue eyes. Res. Washington, D.C.

COOLEY, AMBROSE: Pvt., Co. F. Served in 1st Md. Inf., on postwar roster. Enl. Big Spring, Va., 7/27/64; issued clothing 9/10/64. Captured 11/17/64; sent to Ft. McHenry; took oath, released 2/9/65. Res. of Harford Co., Md.

COOLEY, WILLIAM L.: Pvt., Co. D. On postwar roster. Res. Harford Co., Md., 1905.

COOPER, JAMES M.: 2nd Lt., Co. A. WIA Winchester 9/19/64. Captured Cedar Creek, Va., 9/20/64; arrived Ft. Del. 9/25/64. NFR.

COOPER, SAMUEL: Pvt., Co. C. Captured Berryville, Va., 2/11/64; sent to Wheeling. Age twenty-one, 5'8", fair complexion, dark eyes, dark hair. Blacksmith. Res. St. Mary's Co., Md. Transf. to Camp Chase and Ft. Del.; exchanged, date unknown. Paid Richmond 4/14/64. NFR.

COOPER, WILLIAM: Pvt., Co. D. Enl. Richmond 8/15/63. Captured Charles Town, W.Va., 9/15/63. On rolls to 10/31/64. NFR. May have been KIA as not on Federal POW rolls. Res. of Annapolis, Anne Arundel Co., Md.

COX, C. M.: Pvt., Co. E. Surrendered Appomattox CH, Va., 4/9/65. Paroled again Winchester 4/16/65. Age twenty-seven, 5'4", fair complexion, dark hair, hazel eyes. Former res. of Cincinnati, Oh.; destination Baltimore.

CRAWFORD, GEORGE WILLIAM: Pvt., Co. D. b. Locust Grove, Va., 1847. Res. of Md. On roster. Enl. Co. F, 43rd Bn. Va. Cav., 12/23/64. Paroled Louisa CH, Va., 4/15/65. d. Trevilian, Va., 1936.

CREEL, BARNETT: Pvt., Co. A. Captured Martinsburg, W.Va., 10/15/63; sent to Ft. McHenry; transf. to Pt. Lookout; exchanged 3/3/65. NFR.

CROSS, GEORGE W.: Pvt., Co. A; issued clothing 10/15/64. Paroled Winchester 4/21/65. Age twenty-six, 5'4", fair complexion, light hair, blue eyes. Res. of Baltimore. Took oath Harpers Ferry, W.Va., 4/23/65; destination Baltimore.

CROUGHAN, MICHAEL: Pvt., Co. F. Enl. Big Spring, Va., 7/27/64. NFR.

CROWLING, MICHAEL: Pvt., Co. C. Captured Smithfield, W.Va., 8/28/64; sent to Old Capitol; transf. to Camp Chase; received 6/2/64. NFR.

DALEY, JOHN: Pvt., Co. D. Enl. Richmond 5/30/63; des. to the enemy Martinsburg, W.Va., 7/3/64; sent to Ft. McHenry; desired to take oath 9/64; in hosp. there with "acute diarrhoea" 1/27–5/2/65. NFR. d. 3/5/84. Bur. Loudon Park Cem., Baltimore.

DANIELS, WILLIAM C.: Pvt., Co. C. Captured Piedmont, Va., 6/5/64. Under guard Staunton, Va., 6/8/64. NFR.

DARNELL, J. L.: Pvt., Co. B; issued clothing 9/10/64; WIA; in Richmond hospitals 9/23–10/1/64. NFR.

DAVIDSON, WILLIAM: Pvt., Co. G. Paroled Harpers Ferry, W.Va., 4/22/65. Took oath Washington, D.C., 5/15/65. Res. of Georgetown, D.C. d. Washington 7/11/24. Bur. Arlington Natl. Cem., Va.

DAVIS, JAMES W.: Pvt., Co. G. Captured Somerset Co., Md., 10/20/64; sent to Ft. McHenry; transf. to Pt. Lookout; released 5/9/65. Res. of Cambridge, Dorchester Co., Md.

DAVIS, MOSCOW: Pvt., Co. C. On postwar roster.

DAVIS, WILLIAM M.: Pvt., Co. C. Captured Moorefield, W.Va., 87/64; sent to Wheeling. Age twenty-five, 6'2", light complexion, blue eyes, sandy hair. Res. of Rappahannock Co., Va. Transf. to Camp Chase and Pt. Lookout; exchanged 3/27/65. Paroled Winchester 4/29/65. Possibly the

William M. Davis (8/27/34–3/26/01) bur. Pleasant Grove Methodist Ch. Cem., Frederick Co., Md.

DECHAINE, AUGUSTUS WESLEY: Pvt., Co. D. Enl. Richmond 10/14/63. Captured Charles Town, W.Va., 10/19/63; sent to Wheeling. Age twenty-seven, 5'6½", florid complexion, blue eyes, auburn hair. Cabinet Maker. Res. Louisville, Ky. Transf. to Camp Chase and Johnson's Island; released 6/13/65, age twenty-five.

DELISLE, WILLIAM: Pvt., Co. A. Enl. Richmond 4/15/63. Captured Martinsburg, W.Va., 10/15/63; sent to Ft. McHenry; transf. to Pt. Lookout; exchanged 3/6/64. In Richmond hosp. 3/6–7/64; present Camp Lee, Richmond, 3/19/64; issued clothing Harrisonburg, Va., 9/20/64; in Liberty, Va., hosp. 10/8/64; issued clothing 10/19/64 and 11/12/64; in Richmond hosp. 12/1–2/64; WIA (left leg), admitted Charlottesville hosp. 12/20/64. Admitted Richmond hosp. 3/25/65; furloughed for thirty days 4/26/65; admitted to Charlottesville hosp. 4/2/65 with chronic ulcers on leg; transf. to Lynchburg, Va., hosp. 4/5/65. NFR.

DENMEAD, AQUILA: Pvt., Co. F. Enl. Big Spring, Va., 7/24/64. NFR.

DENNISON, GEORGE W.: Pvt., Co. C. b. circa 1838. Enl. Co. G, 13th Va. Inf., 5/28/61. Age twenty-three. Plasterer. Discharged as nonresident 5/28/62. Enl. Co. C, 2nd Md. Cav., New Market, Va., 7/23/63. Captured Middletown, Md., 9/20/63; sent to Ft. McHenry; transf. to Pt. Lookout. Age twenty-four, 5'6", light complexion, blue eyes, dark hair. Res. of Baltimore. Exchanged 11/15/64. Issued clothing 12/3/64; present Camp Lee, Richmond, 12/17/64. NFR.

DENT, GEORGE H., JR.: Pvt., Co. B. b. Charles Co., Md. Enl. Co. I, 1st Md. Inf., 7/11/61; discharged 6/15/62. Enl. Co. C, 43rd Va. Bn. Cav. (Mosby), 11/14/63. Age twenty, 6', florid complexion, dark hair, hazel eyes; present through 2/64. NFR. Paroled Northern Neck, Va., 5/1/65, as Pvt., Co. B, 2nd Md. Cav. Res. Pope's Creek, Charles Co., Md., 1909. Bur. Christ Episcopal Ch. Cem., Wayside, Charles Co., no dates.

DERNAY, JAMES: Pvt., Co. unknown. b. N.Y. circa 1843. Reared in Norfolk, Va. Res. of Washington, D.C. City Fireman, Richmond, postwar. Killed in Richmond 9/20/71, age twenty-eight. Obituary only record of service.

DERRIES, JOHN: Pvt., Co. F. Enl. Big Spring, Va., 7/27/64. NFR.

DESNEY, JOHN: Alias JOHN KERREGAN, PAT KERREGAN, and JOHN FOX. Pvt., Co. D. Captured Luray, Va., 12/7/63; sent to Ft. Del.; sent to Washington, D.C., for trial as des. from Stanton's Legion N.Y. Volunteers.

DEVRIES, WILLIAM: Pvt., Co. C. On postwar roster.

DIBRILL, CHARLES L.: Pvt., Co. C; present 12/63. In Lynchburg, Va., hosp. 2/27/64; furloughed 3/1/64; issued clothing 9/30/64. NFR.

DIGGES, EUGENE: Capt., Co. B. b. Charles Co., Md., 10/27/38. Gd. Georgetown U. 1857. Gd. U of N.Y. Law School. Res. Allen's Cut, Port Tobacco, Charles Co. Enl. Co. I, 1st Md. Inf., 6/16/61; appointed 2nd Lt. 7/19/61; present 9–12/61; WIA Harrisonburg, Va., 6/6/62; discharged 8/62. Served in Topographical Engineers; in Richmond, unassigned, 8/63. Elected Capt., Co. B. 2nd Md. Cav. Captured Martinsburg, W.Va., 10/15/63; sent to Ft. McHenry; transf. to Pt. Lookout and Ft. Del.; sent to Hilton Head Island, S.C. (one of the "Immortal 600"); transf. to Ft. Pulaski, Ga., Hilton Head Island, S.C., and Ft. Del.; released 6/1/65. 5'10", fair complexion, blue eyes, brown hair. Res. Charles Co. Took oath 6/5/65. Lawyer and State's Attorney, Charles Co.; moved to San Antonio, Tex. 12/79; State Attorney and State Librarian for Tex. Member J. B. Hood Camp, CV. d. Austin, Tex., 6/29/99. (Photograph in Hartzler 1992)

DINEY, WILLIAM: Pvt., Co. D. Paroled Winchester 5/15/65. Former res. of Baltimore; destination Baltimore.

DISNEY, WILSON E.: Pvt., Co. unknown. b. 10/18/27; issued clothing 9/10/64. NFR. Res. Princeland, Anne Arundel Co., Md. d. 9/26/88. Bur. Disney family cem., Anne Arundel, Md.

DIXON, J. J.: Pvt. Co. B. Des. to the enemy in western Va. 1/64. Age thirty, 5'9", light complexion, blue eyes, light hair. Farmer. Res. Danville, Va. Took oath, sent north, 1/10/64.

DOBBS, THOMAS E.: Pvt., Co. A. Captured flag 10/18/63; issued clothing 9/30/64. Captured Woodstock, Va., 10/7/64; sent to Pt. Lookout; released 4/20/65. Res. Baltimore.

DOBSON, WILLIAM H.: Pvt., Co. G "See 14th La. Inf.," on records.

DONAHUE, MICHAEL: Pvt., Co. C. Des. Ash Hollow, Va., 10/1/63. Arrested Harrisburg, Pa., 10/7/63; sent to Philadelphia same day. NFR.

DONALD, J. W.: Pvt., Co. A. Paroled Winchester 4/27/65.

DONALDSON, JOHN alias JOHN SHAY: Pvt., Co. D. Des. to the enemy Martinsburg, W.Va., 1/64; sent to Ft. Del; transf. to Washington, D.C., 1/17/64, to stand trial as des. from 11th Mass. Inf.

DONLEY, CHARLES A.: Pvt., Co. C. Captured Piedmont, Va., 6/5/64; sent to Camp Morton. Took oath; joined U.S. Service 3/22/65.

DOOLEY, THEODORE W.: Pvt., Co. D. Enl. Mt. Jackson, Va., 11/1/63. Captured Moorefield, W.Va., 8/7/64, horse killed; sent to Wheeling. Age seventeen, 5'3", fair complexion, blue eyes, dark

hair. Res. Jefferson Co., Va. Transf. to Camp Chase and Pt. Lookout; exchanged 3/27/65. Paid Richmond 3/31/65. Paroled Harrisonburg, Va., 5/8/65. Age seventeen, 5'4", light complexion, dark hair, gray eyes.

DORAN, WILLIAM: Pvt., Co. D. Enl. Richmond 9/10/63; present 11/63; ab. on horse detail and time expired; on rolls 12/31/63–8/31/64. NFR.

DORSEY, ALBERT A.: Pvt., Co. F. Enl. Big Spring, Va., 7/27/64; issued clothing 9/30/64. Paroled Harpers Ferry, W.Va., 4/24/65 as Pvt., Co. E, 2nd Md. Cav. Res. Howard Co., Md., 1880.

DORSEY, BERNARD: Pvt., Co. F. On postwar roster.

DORSEY, WILLIAM: 3rd Lt., Co. F. On postwar roster. Res. of Mathews Store, Howard Co., Md.

DOSIER, CHARLES: Pvt., Co. D. Enl. Mt. Jackson, Va., 4/1/64. Captured Winchester 9/19/64. NFR. May have been KIA; not on Federal POW rolls.

DOWNS, JOHN H.: Pvt., Co. E. Captured, date and place unknown; issued clothing as paroled POW 11/19/62. Paroled Winchester, 4/19/65, as Regimental QM. Age thirty-three, 6'1", fair complexion, brown hair, blue eyes.

DUFFEY, JAMES G.: Pvt., Co. C. Enl. in La. unit 9/61. Enl. Co. C, 2nd Md. Cav., date unknown. Captured Winchester 4/26/64; sent to Camp Douglas; took oath, released 4/4/65. 5'11", fair complexion, brown hair, blue eyes. Res. Orleans Parish, La.

DUNAHO, MICHAEL: Pvt., Co. D; issued clothing 8/1/64. NFR.

DUNNEGAN, PHILLIP: Pvt., Co. F. On postwar roster.

DUVAL, FRANCIS Mc.: Pvt., Co. F. Enl. Co. F, 17th Va. Inf., 5/28/61, age twenty-six. Bookkeeper. Discharged for leaving the breastworks, Yorktown, in the face of the enemy, by order of Gen. A. P. Hill, 4/30/62. Enl. Co. F, 2nd Md. Cav., date unknown. Captured Monocacy, Md., 7/10/64, or Middletown, Md., 7/11/64; sent to West Buildings Hosp., Baltimore; transf. to Ft. McHenry and Pt. Lookout; exchanged 11/15/64. Paroled Fairfax Co., Va., 4/27/65. Age twenty-nine, 5'11", dark complexion, dark brown hair, dark eyes. Member ANS/MLA, 1894. Res. of Baltimore.

EDWARDS, ELI H.: Pvt., Co. E. b. Baltimore circa 1830. Enl. Richmond 11/10/63. Age thirty-three, 5'8", light complexion, light hair, blue eyes. Carpenter. Des. to the enemy 8/24/64. Took oath, sent to Philadelphia, Pa.

ELLIS, HENRY: Pvt., Co. E. Captured, date and place unknown. POW, received at Ft. Del. 7/30/63; left at Ft. Del.; on list of POWs transf. to

CHARLES
FAVOUR

*(Daniel D.
Hartzler)*

Pt. Lookout 9/29/63. NFR.

EMMART, GEORGE: Pvt., Co. C. b. Baltimore Co. circa 1840. Enl. Baltimore Light Arty. 3/6/62; discharged 1/1/64. Age twenty-four, 5'6", fair complexion, gray eyes, sandy hair. Clerk. Enl. Co. C, 2nd Md. Cav., date unknown. In Richmond hosp. 6/15/64; issued clothing 9/30/64. Paroled Winchester 5/10/65. Age twenty-five, 5'7", light complexion, light hair, blue eyes. Res. of Baltimore; destination Baltimore.

EMMERICH, GEORGE H.: Pvt., Co. C. On postwar roster. Res. of Baltimore. Member ANS/MLA, 1903.

EMMERICH, JOHN W.: Cpl., Co. C. On postwar roster. Res. of Baltimore.

EMORY, GEORGE: Pvt., Co. A. b. Washington, D.C., circa 1845. Enl. Harrisonburg, Va., 6/64. Captured Beverly, W.Va., 10/29/64; sent to Wheeling. Age nineteen, 5'10", fair complexion, blue eyes, dark hair. Salesman. Res. of Baltimore. Transf. to Camp Chase; received 11/4/64. NFR; exchanged under John H. Emory's name 3/65; present Camp Lee, Richmond, 3/28/65. NFR.

EMORY, JOHN H.: Pvt., Co. B. Enl. New Market, Va., 7/62, by Capt. Davis. Captured Shenandoah Co., Va., 5/12/64; sent to Wheeling. Age twenty-one, 6'2", dark complexion, blue eyes, dark hair. Clerk. Res. of Baltimore. Transf. to Camp Chase; d. there of pneumonia 2/12/65. Bur. Camp Chase Cem., grave #1198.

ENGLEFIELD, GILES: Pvt., Co. E. Captured Piedmont, Va., 6/5/64; arrived Camp Morton 6/21/64. NFR.

EVANS, JOHN: Pvt., Co. D. Captured Martinsburg, W.Va., 10/10/63; sent to Ft. McHenry; took oath, released 10/25/63.

FAVOUR, CHARLES F. or R. (photo): Pvt., Co. F. b. Philadelphia, Pa., 1844. Enl. Co. I, 30th Va. Inf., 7/22/61. Transf. to Md. Line 4/62. NFR. Enl. Co. F, 12th Va. Cav., 7/22/62. Transf. to Co. F, 2nd

Md. Cav., 4/29/64. Captured Frederick Co., Va., 5/3/64; sent to Wheeling. Age twenty, 5'9½", fair complexion, hazel eyes, black hair. Student; res. Harford Co., Md. Transf. to Camp Chase; exchanged 2/27/65. Paroled Winchester 5/17/65; destination Harford Co. PO Employee, Baltimore postwar. Alive 1898.

FEAST, LOUDON: Pvt., Co. E. Res. of Baltimore. Enl. Co. C, 1st Md. Inf., 5/17/61; discharged when co. disbanded 8/6/62. Served in Secret Service under Gen. Winder. Captured and sent to Johnson's Island; exchanged. Enl. Co. E, 2nd Md. Cav., 3/1/64. NFR. Member ANS/MLA. 1894. Res. Washington, D.C. d. 11/16/12. Bur. Arlington Natl. Cem., Va.

FELIS, CARLIS: Pvt., Co. F. Captured Shenandoah Co., Va. 12/10/63; sent to Wheeling. Age twenty-eight, 5'6", florid complexion, brown eyes, dark hair. Soldier. Res. of France; sent to Cumberland, Md., 4/27/64. NFR.

FENTON, HENRY T.: Sgt., Co. B. Paroled Richmond 4/65. Age twenty-three, 5'5", fair complexion, blue eyes, light hair. Clerk.

FENTON, JOHN J.: Pvt., Co. B. Enl. Capt. Preston's Co. A, 1st S.C. Arty.; 2/22/61; requested transf. 5/16/63; transf. 1864; issued clothing 8/1/64; paid for 5/1–8/31/64, Richmond, 9/26/64. NFR. Member ANS/MLA. d. 6/25/12.

FERRELL, BENJAMIN: Pvt., Co. D; ab. sick with pneumonia in Charlottesville hosp. 6/26/64; furloughed for sixty days 6/29/64; paid for 5/1–6/8/64 Richmond 8/28/64. NFR.

FIELD, EUGENE WILLIAM: Ord. Sgt. b. circa 1830. Res. of Baltimore. Enl. Co. C, 2nd Md. Cav., date unknown; promoted Ord. Sgt.; signed requisitions for Ord. 3/30/63 and at Mt. Jackson, Va., 11/19/63; KIA Ishamch Day's house on Bel Air and Harford Roads, Md., near Joshua Price house, 7/16/64, age thirty-four. Bur. Loudon Park Cem., Baltimore.

FIPPS, F.: Pvt., Co. F. On postwar roster.

FISHER, CHARLES D.: Pvt., Co. F. b. Westminster, Md., 1/20/48. Enl. Big Spring, Va., 7/27/64. Captured Moorefield, W.Va., 8/7/64; sent to Wheeling. Age seventeen, 5'10", fair complexion, gray eyes, light hair. Student. Res. of Baltimore Co. Transf. to Camp Chase; took oath, released 3/15/65. Age eighteen, 5'8", light complexion, blue eyes, light hair. Clerk, Baltimore, postwar; later in grain business. Killed in RR accident 11/29/06.

FITZGERALD, JOHN: Pvt., Co. E. Captured Hampshire Co., W.Va., 4/14/64; sent to Wheeling. Age nineteen, 6', fair complexion, gray eyes, brown hair. Machinist. Res. St. Louis, Mo. Transf. to Camp Chase. Took oath, enl. U.S. Navy

7/21/64.

FITZPATRICK, _____: Pvt., Co. A. Res. of Baltimore. KIA near Winchester 6/10/63. Harry Gilmor called him "one of the bravest of the brave."

FITZPATRICK, DANIEL: Pvt. Co. F. On postwar roster.

FLETCHER, MADISON W.: 3rd Cpl., Co. D. Enl. Richmond 10/19/63; present 12/31/63–8/31/64; issued clothing 9/30/64. NFR.

FOMAN, CHARLES: Pvt., Co. F. On postwar roster.

FOMAN, PERRY: Pvt., Co. F. On postwar roster.

FORD, _____: Pvt., Co. unknown. Res. of Baltimore. KIA near Summit Point, W.Va., 9/63.

FORD, EDWIN: Pvt., Co. C. Res. of St. Mary's Co., Md. On postwar record.

FORD, FLEMMING: Pvt., Co. C. b. Henrico Co. circa 1846. Enl. Richmond 12/29/63. Age seventeen, 5'9", light complexion, blue eyes, light hair. Farmer. Ab. sick with rheumatism in Staunton, Va., hosp. 2/1–29/64. Captured Frederick Co., Va., 4/26/64; sent to Wheeling. Age seventeen, 5'8", florid complexion, blue eyes, light hair. Laborer. Res. of Richmond. Transf. to Camp Chase; exchanged 3/12/65. NFR.

FORD, HENRY: Pvt., Co. B. Enl. Zarvona's Md. Zouaves 6/15/61; disbanded 6/15/62. In Richmond hosp. 5/27–28/64. NFR.

FOREBARGER, JAMES H.: Pvt., Co. C. Enl. 1st Md. Arty., date unknown. Captured Hagerstown, Md., 7/12/63; sent to Elmira; transf. to Pt. Lookout; exchanged 10/29/64. On postwar roster.

FOREMAN, CHARLES: Pvt., Co. unknown. Captured near Charles Town, W.Va., 9/63. NFR.

FORNEY, GEORGE W.: 2nd Lt., Co. C. Resigned 11/28/63; approved 12/13/63. May have served in Co. A, 11th Va. Cav.

FOUNTAIN[E], J.: Sgt., Co. A. Enl. Richmond 6/63; paid 10/31/63. Captured, date and place unknown. Paroled POW, Camp Lee, Richmond, 3/28/65. NFR.

FRANKLIN, JOHN: Pvt., Co. A. Captured Martinsburg, W.Va., 10/15/63, horse killed; sent to Ft. McHenry; transf. to Pt. Lookout; exchanged 3/1/65. Admitted Richmond hosp. with "debilitas" 3/2/65; furloughed for thirty days 3/8/65; paid Richmond 3/13/65. NFR.

FREBERGER, JAMES H.: Pvt., Co. C. Enl. Mt. Jackson, Va., 3/63. Captured Frederick, Md. 7/7/64; sent to Ft. McHenry; transf. to Pt. Lookout; exchanged 10/64. Present Camp Lee, Richmond, 10/31/64; issued clothing 11/17/64. Paroled Winchester 4/19/65. Age twenty-nine, 5'7", dark complexion, dark hair. Res. of Baltimore.

FREBERGER, WILLIAM T.: Pvt., Co. C. On post-

war roster. Res. of Baltimore.

GADD, WILLIAM T.: Pvt., Co. unknown. b. Baltimore circa 1836. Enl. Co. B. 21st Va. Inf., 7/9/61. age twenty-five, 5'11½", dark hair, dark eyes; ab. sick Winchester 11–12/61. NFR. On postwar roster.

GAULT, CYRUS, JR.: Pvt., Co. F. Enl. in unknown unit at Frederick, Md., 9/1/62. Enl. Co. G, 12th Va. Cav., 2/25/64. Transf. to Co. F, 2nd Md. Cav., 4/29/64; horse killed near Pine Grove Ch., Spotsylvania Co., Va., 5/15/64, paid $1,100. Joined Martinsburg, W.Va., 7/27/64; horse killed Magnolia, Harford Co., Md., 7/11/64, paid $4,000; WIA (chest and right wrist, injuring flexor tendons), date and place unknown; admitted Richmond hosp. 9/21/64; furloughed to Luray, Va., for twenty days 11/28/64 and sixty days 1/24/65; paid 3/21/65. NFR.

GEEGAN, LOUIS A.: Pvt., Co. C; issued clothing 9/24/63; ab. on detail as Clerk in Richmond hosp. 3/4–5/3/65. Captured Richmond 5/3/65. Took oath Richmond 5/18/65. Former res. of Baltimore; destination Baltimore.

GETLING, FREDERICK: Pvt., Co. D. Enl. Richmond 9/10/63. Captured Smithfield, W.Va., 2/17/64; on rolls to 8/31/64. May have been KIA; not on Federal POW rolls.

GILBERT, WILLIAM C.: Pvt., Co. unknown. Carpenter, age twenty-one, Northern Dist. Augusta Co., per 1860 census. Enl. Co. G, 5th Va. Inf., 3/23/62 and des. May have served previously in Lee's Md. Cav; des. to the enemy Eastville, Va., 5/1/64. 5'9½", fair complexion, gray eyes, light hair. Res. of Staunton, Va. Sent to Ft. Monroe. Took oath, sent to Philadelphia, Pa., 5/18/64.

GILLAND, STEPHEN R.: Pvt., Co. F. Enl. Co. B, 1st Md. Inf., 5/21/61; discharged 5/28/62. Enl. Co. K, 32nd N.C. Inf., 7/62, as substitute; des. Richmond 7/62. NFR. Enl. Co. F, 2nd Md. Cav., Big Spring, Va., 7/27/64. NFR.

GILMOR, ARTHUR: Pvt., Co. F. b. circa 1846. Enl. Big Spring, Va., 7/27/64. Captured Moorefield, W.Va., 8/7/64; sent to Wheeling. Age twenty, 5'8½", dark complexion, dark hair, gray eyes. Clerk. Res. of Baltimore. Transf. to Camp Chase and Pt. Lookout; d. on board the *City of Albany*, near Jamestown, Va., 3/26/65, en route to being exchanged.

GILMOR, C. GRAHAM: Pvt., Co. F. b. Baltimore circa 1842. Enl. Co. B, 21st Va. Inf., 1861. Age nineteen, 5'8½", light hair, blue eyes. Discharged as nonresident 2/17/62. Enl. Co. F, 12th Va. Cav., 3/13/62. Transf. to Co. F, 2nd Md. Cav., 4/29/64; joined 7/27/64. Paroled Mt. Jackson, Va., 4/21/65. Age twenty-four, 5'10", fair complexion, light hair, gray eyes. Took oath Baltimore 5/8/65. Member ANS/MLA. In Old Soldiers' Home, Pikesville, Md., 1894. Receiving pension, Pulaski Co., Ark., 1911.

GILMOR, HARRY WARD: Lt. Col. b. "Glen Ellen," near Carney, Md., 1/24/38. Businessman Baltimore, Wisc., and Nebr. Res. Towson, Md., 1861. Arrested as a spy in Baltimore, 8/61, and held two weeks. Enl. as Pvt., Co. G, 7th Va. Cav., 8/31/61; promoted Sgt. Maj. Organized Co. F, 12th Va. Cav., 3/27/62; elected Capt. 4/10/62; present Jackson's Valley Campaign and Western Va. Raid. Captured Reistertown, Md., 9/12/62; sent to Ft. McHenry; exchanged 2/13/63. Served briefly on Gen. J. E. B. Stuart's staff as ADC; present Kelly's Ford, Va., 3/17/63. Resigned 5/7/63 and raised 2nd Md. Cav.; promoted Maj. 5/27/63; horse killed Newtown, Va., 6/13/63, paid $600; present Gettysburg campaign; signed for forage 8/1/63 and 8/13/63; signed for Ord. 8/17/63; signed for forage Staunton, Va., 8/27/63, and Louisa CH, Va., 9/30/63; WIA (leg) near Charles Town, W.Va., 10/15/63, but remained on duty; signed for clothing Staunton, Va., 11/14/63; paid Mt. Jackson, Va., 1/19/64; present 3/3/64; paid 5/1/64; WIA (back) near Mt. Jackson 5/12/64, but remained on duty; present New Market, Va., 5/15/64 and 5/29–30/64; present Piedmont, Va., 6/5/64; present 6/10–12/64; signed for forage New Market, 6/28/64; present 7/3/64 and on Gen. Jubal Early's raid into Md., 7/8–14/64; present Chambersburg, Pa.; WIA Clear Spring, Md., 7/29/64; present Oldtown, Md., 8/64; Commanding 1st and 2nd Md. Cav.'s, Moorefield, W.Va., 8/6–7/64; WIA (collarbone broken) near Bunker Hill, W.Va., on Martinsburg Pike, four miles from Winchester, 9/3/64, while commanding his bn. and the 18th Va. Cav; ab. wounded through 10/25/64; present 10/30 and 11/30/64. Captured near Moorefield, W.Va., 2/5/65; sent to Ft. Warren guarded by seven men, by order of Gen. Philip Sheridan; released 7/24/65. 6'¾", dark complexion, blue eyes, dark hair. Wrote *Four Years in the Saddle,* 1866. Clerk, Baltimore, 1871; State Weigher, 1873; Police Commissioner of Baltimore 1874–79; Insurance business, Baltimore. d. 3/4/83. Bur. Loudon Park Cem., Baltimore. Brother of Meredith and Richard T. Gilmor.

GILMOR, HOFFMAN: Pvt., Co. F. b. 3/3/44. Enl. Big Spring, Va., 7/27/64; WIA (arm) 8/64. Harry Gilmor, a cousin, removed pieces of bone from his upper arm. Captured near Moorefield, W.Va., 2/5/65; sent to Ft. McHenry as "guerilla not to be exchanged during the war." Released 5/1/65. Age twenty, 5'9", fair complexion, brown hair, hazel eyes. Res. of Baltimore; destination Baltimore.

d.12/21/12. Bur. Loudon Park Cem., Baltimore. (Photograph in Hartzler 1992)

GILMOR, MEREDITH: 2nd Lt., Co. A. b. circa 1844. Enl. 2/63. Captured Martinsburg, W.Va., 7/22/63; sent to Wheeling. Age eighteen, 6'½", florid complexion, gray eyes, auburn hair. Farmer, Baltimore Co. Transf. to Camp Chase and Johnson's Island; released 5/16/65. Res. of Baltimore; destination Baltimore. Served as Pvt., Co. C, 10th U.S. Infantry 2/2/80–2/1/85. Reenl. Ft. Marcy, N.M., in Co. C, 22nd U.S. Infantry 3/1/85; discharged for disability 7/8/85. "Aneurism of the abdominal aorta." In U.S. Old Soldiers' Home, Washington, D.C., 1886. d. Govansville Hotel, Baltimore Co., Md., 9/21/00. Bur. Westminster Cem., Baltimore. Brother of Harry W. and Richard T. Gilmor.

GILMOR, RICHARD TILGHMAN: Capt., Co. C. b. "Glen Ellyn," Baltimore Co., Md., circa 1840. Res. Towson, Baltimore Co. Arrested during Baltimore riots 4/19/61, held for $13,000 bail; released and ordered to go south, but was stopped at Ft. Monroe and confined aboard U.S.S. *Cumberland*; released and ordered to go to Baltimore; went to Richmond instead. Appointed 2nd Lt., Co. H, 1st Md. Inf., 6/18/61; present 9–12/61. NFR. Enl as Pvt., Co. F, 12th Va. Cav., 2/15/62; elected 2nd Lt. 2/25/62; paid 7/22/62. Transf. to Co. C, 2nd Md. Cav., as 1st Lt. by 10/63; present 10/15/63; captured flag near Charles Town, W. Va., 10/18/63; promoted Capt.; paid 6/12/64; signed for clothing, Lynchburg, Va., 6/18/64; WIA Middletown, Md., 7/64; paid 8/8/64; signed for forage for twenty-four horses 8/31/64; absent on leave 11/64. Paroled Campbell CH, Va., 5/27/65. Returned to Baltimore 8/65. WIA twice per postwar roster. Bailiff in Baltimore Criminal Ct. Member ANS/MLA. Entered Old Soldiers' Home, Pikesville, Md., 1892; d. there 8/23/08. Bur. Loudon Park Cem., Baltimore. Brother of Harry W. and Meredith Gilmor. (Photograph in Hartzler 1992)

GILMOR, WILLIAM "WILLIE": Pvt., Co. C. Enl. New Market, Va., 8/62; present 11/63; WIA (arm), Shenandoah Valley 12/63; present 2/11/64. Captured Moorefield, W.Va., 8/7/64; sent to Wheeling. Age twenty, 5'8¾", dark complexion, blue eyes, brown hair. Clerk. Res. of Baltimore. Transf. to Camp Chase and Pt. Lookout; exchanged 3/27/65; present Camp Lee, Richmond, 3/28/65. Paroled Mt. Jackson, Va., 4/21/65. Age twenty-one, 5'10", dark complexion, dark hair, blue eyes. Took oath Winchester 5/31/65. Former res. of Baltimore; destination Baltimore.

GLENN, WILLIAM Y.: Pvt., Co. F. Res. of

Baltimore. On postwar roster. Enl. 2nd Md. Arty., 10/25/61; present through 12/31/61. NFR.

GLOCKER, ALBERT CAMPBELL: Pvt., Co. A. b. Baltimore 5/1/46. Enl. 5/63; present Gettysburg, Pa., Piedmont, Va., and Chambersburg, Pa., Raid. Captured Moorefield, W.Va., 8/7/64; sent to Wheeling. Transf. to Camp Chase and Pt. Lookout; exchanged 3/27/65. Paroled Burkville, Va., 4/25/65. Lawyer, Baltimore, 1870–89. Member ANS/MLA. d. 1889, age forty-five.

GLOVER, THOMAS J.: Pvt., Co. B. Captured Mt. Jackson, Va., 9/15/63; sent to Ft. Del.; released 5/11/65. 5'11", fair complexion, dark hair, blue eyes. Res. of Rockingham Co., Va.

GLYNN or GLENN, PATRICK: Pvt., Co. D. b. Ireland circa 1837. Captured Harrisonburg, Va., 12/20/63; sent to Wheeling. Age twenty-six, 5'7¾", dark complexion, hazel eyes, red hair. Transf. to Camp Chase; took oath, released 3/20/65.

GOING(S), ROZIER: Pvt., Co. E. Enl. Woodstock, Va., 9/1/63. Captured near Winchester 4/26/64, horse killed; sent to Wheeling. Age twenty-one, 5'10", florid complexion, blue eyes, dark hair. Carpenter. Res. Washington, D.C. Transf. to Camp Chase; exchanged 3/1/65. In Richmond hosp. 3/10/65; paid Richmond 3/30/65. Paroled Richmond 4/28/65; destination Washington, D.C.

GOLDSBOROUGH, EUGENE YARBIG: Pvt., Co. C. b. circa 1846. Res. of Carroll Co., Md. Enl. Co. A, 1st Md. Inf., 5/21/61; discharged by 8/11/62. Enl. Co. C, 2nd Md. Cav., date unknown. Captured Newtown, Va., 1/12/64; sent to Wheeling. Age twenty, 5'11', fair complexion, hazel eyes, dark hair. Druggist. Res. of Carroll Co., Md. Transf. to Camp Chase and Ft. Del.; d. there of acute rheumatism 2/21/65; no effects. Bur. Finn's Point, N.J., National Cem.

GORMAN, (alias) ARISTO _____: Pvt., Co. C. KIA Oldtown, Md., 8/64. Res. of La. Joined from a La. regiment. Bur. on the field.

GORMAN, D.: Pvt., Co. A. Enl. Staunton, Va., 2/63; paid 10/31/63. Captured, date and place unknown. Paroled POW Camp Lee, Richmond, 3/28/65. NFR.

GORSUCH, NATHAN: QM Sgt; present 2/11/64. Paroled Lynchburg, Va., 4/15/65, as Pvt., Co. C. Res. Baltimore Co., Md.

GORSUCH, THEODORE: Pvt., Co. B. Ordered transferred to CSN 2/26/63, but never carried out. Captured Williamsport, Md., 7/14/63; sent to Ft. Del; transf. to Ft. Columbus and Pt. Lookout; exchanged 2/21/65. NFR.

GRAHAM, JOHN T.: Co. D; discharged for underage 3/16/64. NFR.

GREEN, ALEXANDER: Pvt., Co. A. Captured

Piedmont, Va., 6/5/64; POW under guard Staunton, Va., 6/8/64. NFR.

GROVE, PHILIP D.: Asst. Surgeon. Appointed Asst. Surgeon 9/17/62; assigned to Danville, Va., hosp.; assigned to 2nd Md. Cav., 5–6/63. Captured Martinsburg, W.Va., 10/15/63; sent to Ft. McHenry; exchanged 11/21/63. Assigned to Staunton, Va., hosp. NFR.

GROVER, JOHN H.: Pvt., Co. B. Captured Piedmont, Va., 6/5/64; sent to Camp Morton; exchanged 3/23/65. Captured in Richmond hosp. 4/3/65. Paroled 4/12/65. Took oath, sent to Washington, D.C., 4/14/65; transportation furnished to New Orleans, La., 4/17/65.

GUINN, PATRICK: Pvt., Co. B. Captured Piedmont, Va., 6/5/64; sent to Camp Morton; exchanged 3/23/65. NFR.

HACK, H. R.: Pvt., Co. A. Paroled Mt. Jackson, Va., 4/21/65. Age twenty-two, 5'6", fair complexion, light hair, blue eyes.

HACKETT, JOHN: Pvt., Co. D. Enl. Richmond 10/13/63; horse killed, Darkesville, Md., 7/2/64. Captured Moorefield, W.Va., 8/7/64; sent to Wheeling. Age twenty-six, 5'10", dark complexion, blue eyes, brown hair. Steamboatman. Res. of Baltimore. Transf. to Camp Chase and Pt. Lookout; exchanged 3/27/65. NFR.

HAGAN, R.: Pvt., Co. F. Enl. Big Spring, Va., 7/27/64. NFR.

HAHN, REUBEN H.: Pvt., Co. F. Enl. Co. A, 1st Md. Inf., 5/21/61; discharged 5/21/62. On postwar roster.

HAHN, REUBEN T.: 4th Sgt., Co. D. Enl. Co. F, 12th Va. Cav., 6/12/62. Transf. to Co. D, 2nd Md. Cav., as 4th Sgt., circa 4/29/64; presence or ab. not stated 7/27/64. NFR. (See entry page 235, Hahn, Reuben T. or H.)

HALL, THEODORE F.: Pvt., Co. C. Paroled Winchester 4/19/65. Age twenty-one, 5'9", fair complexion, fair hair, blue eyes.

HALPIN, THOMAS P.: Pvt., Co. F. Enl. Co. G, 1st Md. Inf., 5/23/61; discharged 6/62. Enl. Co. F, 12th Va. Cav., 7/1/62. Transf. to Co. F, 2nd Md. Cav., 4/29/64. Captured Haw's Shop, Va., 5/28/64; sent to Pt. Lookout. NFR until paroled Winchester 4/19/65. Age twenty-three, 5'11", fair complexion, dark hair, gray eyes.

HALSEY, WILLIAM: Pvt., Co. D. Enl. Richmond 10/13/63. Captured Winchester 10/18/64. On rolls. NFR. May have been KIA; not on Federal POW rolls.

HAMILTON, F. JACOB: Pvt., Co. unknown. Enl. Co. G, 12th Va. Cav., 7/21/62. Transf. to 2nd Md. Cav., 4/29/64. Captured near Harpers Ferry, W.Va., 7/16/64; sent to Old Capitol; transf. to Elmira; took oath, released 9/13/64. 5'7½", fair complexion, light blue eyes, light brown hair. Res. of Baltimore.

HAMILTON, WILLIAM CAMPBELL: Pvt., Co. F. Gd. Georgetown U. 1832. Res. of Charles Co., Md. Enl. Co. G, 12th Va. Cav., 6/9/62. Transf. to Co. F, 2nd Md. Cav., 4/29/64; presence or ab. not stated 7/27/64. NFR.

HAMMOND, C.: Pvt., Co. F. Enl. Big Spring, Va., 7/27/64. NFR.

HAMSBER, WILLIAM: Cpl., Co. A. Captured Berkeley Co., W.Va., 10/10/63; sent to Ft. McHenry; transf. to Pt. Lookout. Admitted to hosp. there with "remittent fever" 5/24/64; d. 7/13/64. Bur. Pt. Lookout Confederate Cem.

HANCOCK, JOHNATHAN H.: Pvt., Co. C. Captured Shenandoah Co., Va., 5/12/64; sent to Wheeling. Age thirty-nine, 5' 11½", fair comlexion, blue eyes, dark hair. Merchant. Res. Luzen, Pa. Transf. to Camp Chase; d. there of pneumonia 2/3/65. Bur. Camp Chase Natl. Cem., Oh.

HANS, HENRY: Sgt., Co. C. Enl. Richmond 6/8/63; ab. sick with "chilbrans" in Richmond hosp. 1/1–2/29/64; issued clothing 12/7/64. NFR.

HANSDAFFER, JOHN: Pvt., Co. E. Captured Moorefield, W.Va., 8/7/64; sent to Wheeling. Age twenty-two, 5'5", fair complexion, gray eyes, light hair. Clerk. Res. of Baltimore. Transf. to Camp Chase; took oath, released 1/25/65.

HARDING, BABE: Pvt., Co. C. On postwar roster. Res. of Howard Co., Md. Possibly Basil Harding (3/26/30–11/27/66). Bur. Central Chapel Methodist Ch. Cem., New London, Frederick Co., Md.

HARDING, CHARLES A.: Pvt., Co. C. M.D. Res. of Va. Appointed Asst. Surgeon, 1st Md. Inf., 10/11/61; declined appointment; present 2/11/64. NFR.

HARDING, JOHN W.: Pvt., Co. A. Enl. Big Spring, Va., 7/27/64. Captured Smithfield, W.Va., 8/28/64; sent to Old Capitol; transf. to Camp Chase. Took oath; enlisted in U.S. Army 4/22/65.

HARDING, NICHOLAS: Pvt., Co. C. Horse killed, Clear Spring, Md., 7/28/64. Captured Moorefield, W.Va., 8/7/64; sent to Wheeling. Age twenty-one, 5' 6½", dark complexion, blue eyes, sandy hair. Farmer. Res. of Carroll Co., Md. Transf. to Camp Chase and Pt. Lookout; exchanged 3/27/65. Paid 4/1/65. Paroled Staunton, Va., 5/11/65. Age twenty-one, 5'8", light complexion, light hair, blue eyes.

HARRINGTON, C. M.: Pvt., Co. A. Enl. Richmond 5/63; paid 10/29/63. Captured Smithfield, W.Va., 8/28/64, horse killed. NFR until paroled POW, Camp Lee, Richmond, 2/27/65; paid 3/2/65. Paroled Winchester 4/17/65. Age twenty-six, 5'9½", fair complexion, brown hair, blue eyes.

HARRISON, C. J.: Pvt., Co. A. Ab. sick with debility in Charlottesville hosp. 12/17/64. NFR.

HARRISON, JOHN SPENCER: 1st Lt., Co. B. b. circa 1838. Res. of Church Hill, Queen Anne's Co., Md. Paid as Sgt. Richmond 7–8/63; paid for 6/29–9/1/63 Richmond 9/15/63; 1st Lt. comanding co. 9/19/63. Captured Piedmont, Va., 6/5/64; sent to Camp Morton; transf. to Johnson's Island; released 5/13/65. Age twenty-seven, 5'5", fair complexion, light hair, blue eyes. d. 5/17/65, in 28th year. Bur. "Meadow Vale" Cem. (Seney Cem.), Queen Anne's Co., Md.

HARSHBERGER, S. D.: Pvt., Co. D. Enl. New Market, Va., 10/29/63; present 12/31/63–8/31/64. Paroled New Market, Va., 4/20/65. Age nineteen, 6', light complexion, light hair, blue eyes.

HASSON, JOHN: Lt., Co. A. b. circa 1841. Enl. Co. F, 12th Va. Cav., 9/15/62. Captured Front Royal, Va., 5/13/63; sent to Ft. McHenry; transf. to Ft. Monroe; exchanged 5/17/63. Captured Shepherdstown, W.Va., 7/15/63; sent to Pt. Lookout; exchanged 12/25/63; AWOL 2/2–3/31/64, however, transf. to Co. A, 2nd Md. Cav. Captured Hampshire Co., W.Va., 3/23/64; sent to Wheeling. Age twenty-two, 5'9", fair complexion, dark hair, dark eyes. Clerk. Res. Cecil Co., Md. Transf. to Camp Chase; transf. to City Point, Va., for exchange 2/25/65. NFR.

HAWKINS, C. M.: Pvt., Co. C. Enl. New Market, Va., 7/10/63. Captured, date and place unknown. Paroled POW Camp Lee, Richmond, 2/27/65. NFR.

HEIMILLER, WILLIAM: Cpl., Co. A. Enl. Co. D, 1st Md. Inf., 5/22/61. In Richmond hosp. 7/7–16/62. NFR. Co. disbanded 8/62. Enl. Co. A, 2nd Md. Cav., Richmond, 6/14/63. Captured Berkeley Co., W.Va., 10/16/63; sent to Ft. McHenry; transf. to Pt. Lookout; in smallpox hosp. there 1/2–18/64; reported dead 7/13/64; exchanged 9/22/64. Admitted Richmond hosp. with "remittent fever" the same day; furloughed for forty days to Sampson Co., N.C., 10/4/64. Paroled Harpers Ferry, W.Va., 5/15/65. Took oath Alexandria, Va., 8/8/65. Age twenty-eight, 5'10½", light complexion, blue eyes, brown hair. Farmer. Res. of Baltimore; destination Baltimore. Res. of Baltimore 1894. Member ANS/MLA.

HELM, WILLIAM: Pvt., Co. G. Captured Piedmont, Va., 6/5/64; sent to Camp Morton; took oath, released 9/17/64. 5'7½", dark complexion, dark hair, hazel eyes.

HENRY, JOHN WINDER: Pvt., Co. A. b. 9/3/45. Captured Martinsburg, W.Va., 10/15/63; sent to Ft. McHenry; transf. to Pt. Lookout; took oath, released 3/31/64. d. 3/12/23. Bur. Springhill Cem., Easton, Md.

HERBERT, CHARLES: Pvt., Co. D. Enl. Richmond 10/13/63. Captured Winchester 11/11/63, on rolls to 8/31/64. NFR. May have been KIA; not on Federal POW rolls.

HERBERT, LAWRENCE M.: Pvt., Co. D. Captured Winchester 11/18/63; sent to Wheeling. Age twenty, 5'10", dark complexion, dark hair, dark eyes. Machinist. Res. Norfolk, Va. Released 5/4/65. 6', dark complexion, dark hair, hazel eyes. Res. Norfolk, Va.

HERRON, GEORGE S.: Pvt., Co. C. Captured Moorefield, W.Va., 8/7/64; sent to Camp Chase; released 4/20/65. Res. of Harford Co., Md.

HIPSLEY, THOMAS: Pvt., Co. unknown. Enl. Co. K, 1st Va. Cav., 4/21/61. Transf. to Co. D, 12th Va. Cav. On postwar roster. Member ANS/MLA. Res. of Baltimore 1894.

HITCHCOCK, ROBERT FIELDING: Pvt., Co. D. Enl. Co. B, 1st Md. Inf., 4/21/61, age fourteen; discharged for underage 9/21/61. Enl. Co. D, 2nd Md. Cav., Richmond, 10/13/63; ab. on horse detail 8/31/64; in Richmond hosp. 11/22–25/64; issued clothing 11/29/64. NFR. Member ANS/ MLA. Entered Old Soldiers' Home, Pikesville, Md., 1/7/08, age sixty. Carpenter. d. 3/28/15, age sixty-seven. Bur. Loudon Park Cem., Baltimore.

HOBBS, JOHN: Pvt., Co. F. Enl. Big Spring, Va., 7/27/64. NFR.

HOBBS, WILLIAM H.: Pvt., Co. A. Served as Drummer, Lucas's Bn. S.C. Heavy Arty., 1861–64. Enl. Co. A, 2nd Md. Cav., date unknown. Captured Piedmont, Va., 6/5/64; sent to Camp Morton; released 5/22/65. 5'7", florid complexion, black hair, gray eyes. Res. of Washington, D.C. Member ANS/MLA. In Old Soldiers' Home, Pikesville, Md., 1894.

HODGE, WILLIAM: Pvt., Co. D. Enl. Richmond 10/13/63. Captured Moorefield, W.Va., 8/7/64; on rolls to 8/31/64. May have been KIA; not on Federal POW rolls.

HOLLYDAY, FLOYD S.: Pvt., Co. unknown. On postwar roster.

HOLMES, JOHN W.: Pvt., Co. A. Captured Martinsburg, W.Va., 10/15/63; sent to Ft. Mc-Henry; transf. to Pt. Lookout; d. there 7/12/64. Mother requested body be removed to Washington, D.C., 7/11/65.

HOLMES, JULIUS CHARLES: 2nd Lt., Co. B. b. Baltimore 2/10/42. Enl. Richmond Fayette Arty. 4/25/61. Carpenter. Transf. to CSN 8/63. Elected 2nd Lt., Co. B, 2nd Md. Cav., date unknown; WIA (saber cut to head) and captured Strasburg, Va., 10/27/63; sent to Wheeling. 5'8", light complexion, blue eyes, dark hair. Res. of Strasburg, Va. Transf. to Camp Chase, Rock Island, and Johnson's Island; released 5/16/65. Res. of Baltimore. Member ANS/MLA. Inspector of Public Buildings, Washington, D.C.; Builder,

Charles Town, W.Va., 1913. d. 5/12/14. Bur. Edge Hill Cem., Charles Town.

HOLTZ, RANDOLPH: Pvt., Co. A. Paroled New Market, Va., 4/21/65. Age twenty-seven, 5'6", florid complexion, brown hair, blue eyes. Res. near Salem, Va.

HOOD, JOHN D.: Pvt., Co. D. Enl. Winchester 7/1/64. Captured Moorefield, W.Va., 8/7/64; on rolls to 8/31/64. May have been KIA; not on Federal POW rolls.

HOOK, ROBERT BRUCE: Pvt., Co. F. Enl. Big Spring, Va., 7/27/64. Captured Great Falls , Va., 10/21/64; sent to Old Capitol; took oath, released 12/25/64. Res. of Reistertown, Baltimore Co., Md.

HOOVEY, JOHN: Pvt., Co. B. Enl. Richmond 8/64; des. to the enemy, Harpers Ferry, W.Va., 9/20/64. Age twenty-two, 5'11", dark hair, gray eyes, light hair. Res. of Mobile, Ala. Sent to Old Capitol; took oath 9/30/64; transportation furnished to Chicago, Ill.

HORN, H. C.: Pvt., Co. F. Paroled Winchester 4/21/65. Age twenty, 5'11", fair complexion, black hair, hazel eyes. Res. of Baltimore Co., Md.

HORN, WILLIAM C.: Pvt., Co. F. Enl. Big Spring, Va., 7/27/64. Paroled Winchester 4/21/65; sent to Old Capitol as witness 6/1/65; took oath, released 7/8/65.

HUDDLESTON, WILLIAM GREEN: 2nd Lt., Co. E. b. Ala. 3/8/43. Served in Capt. Thom's Co., C.S. Marine Corps. Enl. Mobile, Ala., 3/28/61; served at Gosport Naval Yard, Norfolk, 11/29/61; served on C.S.S. *Virginia* 11/61–5/62; on rolls through 10/1/62. NFR. Enl. as Pvt., Co. E, 2nd Md. Cav.; present Gainesville, Va., 1864; promoted 2nd Lt. NFR. Farmer. d. Jacksonville, Tex., 10/10/29. Bur. Jacksonville City Cem.

HUFFMAN, HENRY: Pvt., Co. E. b. Saxony, Germany, circa 1841. Captured Harrisonburg, Va., 12/20/63; sent to Wheeling. Age twenty-four, 5'4½", florid complexion, hazel eyes, dark hair. Transf. to Camp Chase; took oath, joined U.S. Navy 7/20/64.

HUNTINGTON, SANFORD G.: Pvt., Co. C. b. 3/17/39. Bank Teller, Alexandria, Va., per 1860 census. Enl. Alexandria Arty. 7/12/61; present 8/18/63. NFR. Transf. to Co. C, 2nd Md. Cav., date unknown. Captured Front Royal, Va., 12/11/63; sent to Wheeling. Age twenty-three, 5'6", dark complexion, black eyes, black hair. Res. of Fairfax Co., Va. Transf. to Camp Chase and Ft. Del.; released 6/19/65. Dark complexion, blue eyes, brown hair. Res. of Alexandria. d. 7/30/67. Bur. St. Paul's Episcopal Ch. Cem., Alexandria.

HURST, EMANUEL: 2nd Lt., Co. F. Enl. Co. F,

12th Va. Cav., 4/10/62; dropped 1/28/63. NFR. On postwar roster.

HURST, THOMAS F.: Pvt., Co. F. Enl. Woodstock, Va., 9/1/63; horse killed near Winchester 4/21/64. Captured near Winchester 4/26/64; sent to Wheeling. Age twenty-one, 5'8", light complexion, blue eyes, auburn hair. Res. Washington, D.C. Transf. to Camp Chase; exchanged 2/27/65. In Richmond hosp. 3/10/65; paid 3/28/65. Paroled Richmond 4/18/65. Res. of Washington, D.C.

JACKSON, L. M.: Pvt., Co. B. In Farmville, Va., hosp. 3/28–29/65. NFR.

JAMES, WALTER: Pvt., Co. A. Des. to the enemy in Western Va. 1/64. Age twenty-three, 5'4½", light complexion, blue eyes, light hair. Clerk. Res. of Harrisonburg, Va. Took oath, sent north, 1/15/64.

JEFFERSON, MARVIN: Pvt., Co. A. Took oath City Point, Va., 4/12/65; transportation furnished to Philadelphia, Pa.

JEFFERSON, WARREN: Pvt., Co. A. b. Pa. Enl. 1st S. C. Arty. 10/23/61. Transf. to Co. A, 2nd Md. Cav., 1864. Captured Piedmont, Va., 6/5/64; sent to Camp Morton; exchanged 3/23/65. Took oath Alexandria, Va., 4/11/65. 5'11", fair complexion, brown hair, hazel eyes. Res. of Washington, D.C.

JENKINS, DAVID W.: Pvt., Co. D. Captured Winchester 11/4/63; sent to Wheeling. Age twenty-two, 5'9", dark complexion, hazel eyes, dark hair. Res. of Winchester. Transf. to Camp Chase and Rock Island; exchanged 3/27/65. Paroled Winchester 4/18/65. Age twenty-two, 5'8", fair complexion, blue eyes, brown hair. Res. of Winchester.

JENKINS, W. W.: Pvt., Co. C. Enl. New Market, Va., 8/12/63; paid 12/31/63. Captured, date and place unknown; exchanged POW Camp Lee, Richmond, 2/18/65. NFR. Res. of Baltimore.

JESTER, WILLIAM: Pvt., Co. D. On postwar roster. Res. of Church Creek, Dorchester Co., Md.

JOHNSON, ANTHONY: Pvt., Co. B. Captured Piedmont, Va., 6/5/64; sent to Camp Morton. Exchanged 3/23/65. Paroled Danville, Va., 4/13/65. Took oath 5/20/65.

JOHNSON, BENJAMIN F.: Pvt., Co. B. Captured near Winchester 8/4/63; sent to Camp Chase. Age twenty-seven, 5'9½", florid complexion, blue eyes, brown hair. Corker. Res. of St. Tammany Parish, La. Transf. to Ft. Del.; escaped 7/1/64. NFR.

JOHNSON, BENJAMIN F.: Pvt., Co. D. Enl. Winchester 7/1/64; issued clothing 9/30/64. Captured Charles Town, W.Va., 11/25/64; on rolls. NFR. May have been KIA; not on Federal POW rolls.

JONES, THOMAS: Pvt., Co. C. Captured Piedmont, Va., 6/5/64; sent to Wheeling 7/64. NFR.

Res. of Frederick Co., Md.

KAHLER, CHARLES PORTERFIELD: Pvt., Co. E. Captured Moorefield, W.Va., 8/7/64; sent to Wheeling. Age twenty-one, 5'10", dark complexion, brown hair, brown eyes. Civil Engineer. Res. of Baltimore. Transf. to Camp Chase; took oath, released 2/27/65.

KANE, JAMES C. (photo page 248): Pvt., Co. unknown. b. Baltimore circa 1841. On postwar roster. Enl. Co. D, 43rd Bn. Va. Cav. (Mosby), 10/11/64, age twenty-three. Paroled Winchester 4/22/65. Took oath Winchester 6/2/65; destination Baltimore. Employee, Pacific Gas Improvement Co., San Francisco, Calif., 1895. Brother of John C. Kane.

KANE, JOHN C.: Pvt., Co. Unknown. Served in Stuart Horse Arty; on postwar roster. Enl. Co. D, 43rd Va. Bn. Cav.; issued clothing 4th Quarter 1864. NFR. Vice President, Silverton Days Mining and Tunnel Co., Silverton, Colo., 1895. Brother of James C. Kane.

KEARNEY, HENRY WAMPLER: Lt., Co. B. b. "Rocky Marsh" near Shepherdstown, W.Va., 7/31/38. Enl. Co. D, 12th Va. Cav., 3/17/62; present with Gilmor 2/64; present with 12th Va. Cav., 7–8/64. NFR. On postwar roster. Paroled Winchester 4/18/65 as Lt., Co. D, 12th Va. Cav. 6', florid complexion, blue eyes, red hair. d. Alexandria, Va., 12/19/04. Bur. Ivy Hill Cem., Alexandria.

KEIDEL, HERMAN F.: Adj. b. 1832. Clerk, Baltimore 1861. Enl. Co. F, 12th Va. Cav., 5/20/62. Transf. to 2nd Md. Cav. as Adj. 7–8/63. Captured Shanghai, W.Va., 10/15/63; sent to Ft. McHenry; transf. to Pt. Lookout and Ft. Del.; released 6/12/65. 5'11", fair complexion, gray eyes, light hair. Res. of Baltimore. Res. Catonsville, Md. postwar.

KEINNINGHAM, S. E.: Pvt., Co. B. Enl. Richmond 11/23/63; paid 12/31/63; ab. sick with debility in Richmond hosp. 9/5–12/21/64. Paroled Lynchburg, Va., 4/13/65, and Richmond 4/22/65.

KELBAUGH, JEHU "HENDERSON": Cpl., Co. C. b. 1837. Enl. Co. C, Lucas's 15th Bn. S.C. Arty., 4/29/61. Reported transf. to Md. Line 4/2/64. Joined Co. C, 2nd Md. Cav., date unknown. Captured Piedmont, Va., 6/5/64; sent to Camp Morton; released 5/22/65. 5'7½", florid complexion, dark hair, hazel eyes. Res. of Baltimore. Took oath Baltimore 6/5/65. Trunkmaker, Baltimore, postwar. d. 7/25/13. Bur. Loudon Park Cem., Baltimore.

KELLEY, CHARLES W.: Pvt., Co. D. b. Alexandria, Va., 4/12/43. Enl. Alexandria, Va., Artillery 9/8/61. Transf. to Co. D, 2nd Md. Cav., after 8/31/63. Captured Front Royal, Va., 12/11/63; sent to Wheeling. Age twenty, 5'9", light complexion, light eyes, light hair. Transf. to

Camp Chase; took oath, released 4/25/64. Riverman. d. Alexandria, Va., 11/24/01. Bur. First Presbyterian Cem., Alexandria.

KELLY, CHARLES: Pvt., Co. C. Des. to the enemy in Western Va. 12/63. Age twenty-eight, 5'7", dark complexion, brown eyes, dark hair. Sailor. Res. of New Orleans, La. Took oath, sent north, 12/5/63.

KELLY, EDWARD F.: Pvt., Co. F. Enl. Winchester 9/6?; des. to the enemy Winchester 9/20/64. Age twenty-two, 5'10", brown hair, blue eyes. Clerk. Res. of Baltimore; sent to Old Capitol. Took oath; transportation furnished to Baltimore 9/30/64.

KELTON, CARLTON BROWN: Pvt., Co. C. b. Baltimore 1838. Res. Calvert Co., Md. Enl. Co. D, 1st Md. Inf., 1861; discharged 8/17/62; paid 11/29/62. Enl. Co. C, 1st Md. Cav., date unknown. Captured Gettysburg, Pa., 7/3/63; sent to Ft. Del; transf. to Ft. Columbus and Pt. Lookout; exchanged 3/3/65. (Another may have been exchanged in his place; see page 129.) On postwar roster. NFR. Member ANS/MLA, 1894. Prospector and Sheriff, Tombstone, Ariz.; Member Ariz. Legislature. d. Baltimore 5/04.

KEMP, ROBERT: Sgt., Co. F. On postwar roster.

KEMP, WILLIAM H.: 2nd Lt., Co. C. b. Baltimore Co., Md., 1821. Capt. of "Lake Guard," Md. Militia, Mt. Washington, Md., 1861. Enl. Co. F, 12th Va. Cav., 4/9/62. Captured Berryville, Va., 11/29/62; sent to Old Capitol; exchanged 3/29/63. Paid Richmond 3/31/63; promoted 1st Sgt; present 7–8/63; AWOL 9/21/63. Transf. to Co. C, 2nd Md. Cav., date unknown; present 12/63; present 2/11/64; paid as 2nd Lt. 1/12–3/12/64 on 4/30/64; present 7/64; KIA Moorefield, W.Va., 8/7/64.

KENNEDY, WILLIAM: Pvt., Co. F. Enl. Big Spring, Va., 7/27/64. Captured Smithfield, W.Va., 8/28/64; sent to Camp Chase; transf. to Pt. Lookout for exchange 3/26/65. NFR.

KERNAN, JAMES LAWRENCE: Pvt., Co. unknown. b. Baltimore 7/29/38. Att. Loyola Col., Baltimore, and Mt. St. Mary's Col., Emmittsburg, Md. Dry Goods Clerk, B&O RR, Baltimore. Enl. 2nd Md. Cav., date unknown, per postwar account. Transf. to Baltimore Light Arty. Captured 10/64. NFR. Hotel and Theater Owner, Baltimore, 1912.

KIDD, THOMAS J.: 1st Cpl., Co. F. b. circa 1845. Enl. Co. F, 12th Va. Cav., 4/1/62. Captured Leesburg, Va., 10/15/63; sent to Ft. McHenry; transf. to Pt. Lookout; exchanged 4/27/64. Admitted to Richmond hosp. with "debilitas" 5/1/64; furloughed for thirty days 5/6/64; ab. 7–8/64, however, present 7/30/64. Paroled Winchester 4/21/65. Age twenty, 5'11", light complexion, dark hair, hazel eyes. Res. of Baltimore.

KING, R. S.: 2nd Lt., Co. C. Paroled Woodstock, Va., 5/5/65. Age twenty-one, 5'11", fair complexion, dark hair, black eyes.

KIRBY, JAMES: Pvt., Co. E. b. Richmond circa 1844. Enl. Richmond 1/30/64. Age seventeen, 5'6", light complexion, light hair, gray eyes. Carpenter. NFR.

KITZMILLER, C.: Pvt., Co. D. Enl. Richmond 7/1/63; discharged 8/23/63. Apparently reenl; ab. detailed in Armory, Richmond, 12/31/63–8/31/64. NFR.

KLINE, FERDINAND: Bugler. Des. to the enemy in Western Va. 1/64. Age thirty-four, 5'10", dark complexion, hazel eyes, dark hair. Shoemaker. Res. of New Orleans, La. Took oath, sent north from New Creek, W.Va., 1/25/64.

KNIGHT, LOUIS W.: Pvt., Co. D. b. Baltimore 10/21/44. Enl. 8/5/63. Transf. to 2nd Md. Arty. 8/31/64. Captured Tom's Brook, Va., 10/9/64; sent to Pt. Lookout; released 5/3/65. Gd. U. of Md. Medical School 1866. M.D., Baltimore, 1900. Member ANS/MLA, 1900. Res. of Baltimore 1905. Member Isaac Trimble Camp, CV, Baltimore, 1911.

KOBRIDGE, THEODORE: Pvt., Co. B. Captured Middletown, Va., 11/9/63; sent to Wheeling. Age twenty-three, 5'9", dark complexion, hazel eyes, dark hair. Farmer. Res. of Baton Rouge, La. Transf. to Camp Chase; released 11/15/63.

KOFFMAN, GEORGE: Pvt., Co. E. Captured Falls Church, Va., 9/1/64; sent to Old Capitol; transf. to Elmira 10/24/64. NFR.

KREMER, FREDERICK M.: Pvt., Co. D. Enl. Co. G, 13th Va. Inf., 5/28/61. Age twenty-one. Painter. Discharged 5/28/62. Served in Engineer Corps 1862–63. Enl. Luray, Va., 7/14/64; present, dismounted, 8/31/64; issued clothing 9/30/64. Paroled Staunton, Va., 4/10/65. Took oath Winchester 5/27/65. Age twenty-five, 5'5", dark complexion, dark hair, blue eyes. Former res. of Baltimore; destination Virginia. Member ANS/ MLA. Res. of Baltimore 1894. Entered Old Soldiers' Home, Pikesville, Md., 9/6/01, age fifty-one. Painter.

KREPPTS, M. J.: Pvt., Co. E. Enl. Richmond 7/1/63; ab. detailed in Armory, Richmond, 12/31/63–8/31/64. NFR.

KUHN, JOHN A.: Pvt., Co. A. Captured Smithfield, W.Va., 8/28/64; sent to Old Capitol; transf. to Camp Chase; d. there of pneumonia 1/20/65. Bur. Camp Chase National Cem., Oh., grave #819.

LAKIN, CHARLES HENRY: Pvt., Co. F. b. 9/14/34. Enl. Co. F, 12th Va. Cav., 2/21/62. Cap-tured Sharpsburg, Md., 9/17/62; sent to Ft. McHenry; transf. to Ft. Monroe; exchanged 3/13/63. Transf. to Co. F, 2nd Md. Cav., 4/29/64; joined 7/27/64. Paroled New Market, Va., 4/20/65. 5'6", fair complexion, blue eyes, dark hair. d. 6/3/01. Bur. Mt. Olivet Cem., Frederick, Md.

LAMAR, ROBERT: Pvt., Co. F. On postwar roster.

LAMY, JULES: Pvt., Co. G. b. France circa 1838. Enl. Richmond 1/29/64. Age twenty-five, 5'8½", dark complexion, blue eyes, brown hair. Perfumer. NFR.

LANDES, ISAAC: Pvt., Co. C; ab. sick in Petersburg, Va., hosp. 3/5–23/65. In Richmond hosp. 3/27–28/65. Paroled New Market, Va., 4/20/65, and Winchester 5/2/65. Age nineteen, 5'10", light complexion, light hair, blue eyes. Res. of New Market.

LANE, JOHN: Pvt., Co. E. Captured Smithfield, W.Va., 8/26/64; sent to Camp Chase; transf. to Pt. Lookout; released 6/14/65.

LANNERS, JOHN H.: Pvt., Co. A. Captured Moorefield, W.Va., 8/7/64; sent to Wheeling. Age twenty-seven, 5'9", fair complexion, blue eyes, light hair. Shoemaker. Res. of Baltimore. Transf. to Camp Chase and Pt. Lookout; exchanged 3/27/65. Paroled Staunton, Va., 5/1/65. Age twenty-eight, 5'9", fair complexion, light hair, gray eyes. Res. of Baltimore.

LARKER, T.: Pvt., Co. A. In Richmond hosp. 9/22–23/64. NFR.

LAYTON, JOHN H.: Pvt., Co. C. Captured Moorefield, W.Va., 8/7/64; sent to Wheeling. Age twenty-four, 5'10", fair complexion, brown eyes, dark hair. Carpenter. Res. Madison Co., Va. Transf. to Camp Chase and Pt. Lookout; exchanged 3/27/65. NFR.

LEE, GEORGE W.: Sgt., Co. D. Enl. as 2nd Cpl., Richmond, 8/16/63. In Richmond hosp. 12/14–31/63; horse killed Taylorsville, Md., 7/27/64. Captured Moorefield, W.Va., 8/7/64; sent to Wheeling. Age nineteen, 5'9", dark complexion, gray eyes, dark hair. Printer. Res. of Richmond. Transf. to Camp Chase and Pt. Lookout; exchanged 3/27/65; present Camp Lee, Richmond, 3/28/65, as Sgt. NFR.

LEE, JOHN W.: Pvt., Co. E. Captured Smithfield, W.Va., 8/28/64; sent to Pt. Lookout; released 6/14/65. 5'8¾", florid complexion, brown hair, gray eyes. Res. of Baltimore; transportation furnished from Washington, D.C., to Baltimore 6/15/65.

LEGG, JAMES E.: b. 9/25/35. Pvt., Co. unknown. Enl. Co. A, 12th Va. Cav., 8/17/61. Captured near Luray, Va., 7/13/62; sent to Old Capitol; transf. to Ft. Monroe; exchanged 8/5/62. Transf. to 2nd Md. Cav., 5/3/64. Joined 43d Bn. Va. Cav. by 12/64. Paroled Westmoreland CH, Va., 5/5/65. Receiving pension Fairfax Co., Va., 1914. Res. of Alexandria, Va.; d. there 7/9/15. Bur. Ivy Hill Cem., Upperville, Va.

LEHMANN, ROBERT E.: Pvt., Co. F. Enl. Big Spring, Va., 7/27/64; WIA (left elbow joint) and captured Smithfield, W.Va., 8/28/64; sent to West Buildings Hosp., Baltimore. Transf. to Pt. Lookout; exchanged 11/15/64; furloughed for thirty days 11/16/64; issued clothing 11/28–30/64. In Richmond hosp. with "anchylosis left elbow joint" 3/4–5/65. Paroled Lynchburg, Va., 4/13/65. Entered Old Soldiers' Home, Pikesville, Md., 12/7/09, age seventy-six. Carpenter. Member ANS/MLA. Res. of Pikesville. d. 1/20/10. Bur. Howard Co., Md.

LESLIE, J. T.: Pvt., Co. A. Paroled Harpers Ferry, W.Va., 4/23/65.

LEVY, JAMES C.: Sgt., Co. B. Paid for 11/1–12/31/63 on 1/9/64; ab. sick with "Parotitis" in Charlottesville hosp. 1/8–19/64; brown horse killed, Front Royal, Va., 2/11/64, paid 3/11/65. NFR.

LEWIS, EDWARD T.: Pvt., Co. A. Enl. Richmond 6/4/63. Captured Martinsburg, W.Va., 10/15/63; sent to Ft. McHenry; transf. to Pt. Lookout; exchanged 3/18/65. Paroled Staunton, Va., 5/1/65. Age twenty-three, 5'6", florid complexion, brown hair, gray eyes. Res. of Washington, D.C.

LITTLEJOHN, CLIFTON W.: Pvt., Co. D. b. 1847. Enl. Mt. Jackson, Va., 4/1/64; present 8/31/64; issued clothing 9/30/64. Paroled Winchester 4/19/65. Age eighteen, 5'7", fair complexion, dark hair, hazel eyes. Res. of Loudoun Co., Va., Member Clinton Hatcher Camp, CV, Leesburg, Va., 1888. d. 3/9/93. Bur. Union Cem., Leesburg.

LOGSDON, NIMROD: Pvt., Co. F. Enl. Big Spring, Va., 7/27/64. NFR.

LORD, W.: Cpl., Co. G; WIA (right leg), admitted to Charlottesville hosp. 11/23/64; transf. to Lynchburg, Va., hosp. 4/5/65. NFR.

LOVEDAY, CHARLES L.: Pvt., Co. F. Enl. Co. F, 12th Va. Cav., 5/20/62. Captured near Luray, Va., 7/12/62; sent to Old Capitol; exchanged, date unknown. Present 11–12/63. Transf. to Co. F, 2nd Md. Cav., 4/29/64; presence or ab. not stated 7/27/64. NFR. In Old Soldiers' Home, Pikesville, Md., 1894.

LOWERY, ROSS: Pvt., Co. B. Captured Shenandoah Co., Va., 11/15/63; sent to Wheeling. Age seventeen, 5'8", florid complexion, gray eyes, light hair. Bricklayer. Res. of Richmond. Transf. to Camp Chase. Took oath, joined U.S. Navy 7/21/64.

LUCAS, JAMES BUCHANAN: Pvt., Co. B. b. 1848; issued clothing 9/30/64. Paroled Harpers Ferry, W.Va., 4/21/65. Age seventeen, 5'4½", light complexion, blue eyes, light hair. Res. of Washington Co., Md. d. 1908. Bur. Elmwood Cem., Shepherdstown, W.Va.

MACON, PATRICK: Pvt., Co. D. Horse killed

Charles Town, W.Va., 4/26/64; in Richmond hosp. 3/27/65; paid $2,700 for horse 3/29/65. NFR.

MAJORS, G. W.: Pvt., Co. G. Captured, date and place unknown. d. of "chronic diarrhoea," Camp Chase, 3/26/65. Bur. Camp Chase Natl. Cem., Oh., grave #1760.

MANLEY, NELIUS: Pvt., Co. B. Captured Berryville, Va., 10/31/63; sent to Wheeling. Age twenty-one, 5'5", dark complexion, black eyes, black hair. Res. Charles Co., Md. Transf. to Camp Chase and Rock Island; escaped 11/7/64. NFR.

MARLEY, GEORGE: Pvt., Co. G. Captured Martinsburg, W.Va., 11/63; sent to Ft. Del.; sent to Washington, D.C., 1/17/64 for trial as des. from Co. C, 99th N.Y. Inf.,

MARSHALL, GEORGE: Pvt., Co. G. Captured Birds Nest, Va., 10/9/63; sent to Ft. McHenry. Escaped 10/22/63. NFR. Res. Cambridge, Dorchester Co., Md.

MARRIOTT, HENRY: Lt., Co. E. Enl. Co. H, 1st Md. Inf., 6/18/61; discharged 5/21/62. On postwar roster. Body removed from Mineral Co., W.Va., 1874, reburied Loudon Park Cem., Baltimore.

MARTIN, GEORGE: Pvt., Co. F. Enl. Big Spring, Va., 7/27/64. Captured Great Falls, Va., 10/21/64; sent to Old Capitol as "suspected spy." Sent to Col. James A. Hardee for orders. NFR.

MARTIN, HUGH: Pvt., Co. C. Enl. Richmond 10/63. NFR until paroled POW, Camp Lee, Richmond, 3/19/65. NFR. M.D., Baltimore.

MATTHEWS, WILLIAM H., JR.: Pvt., Co. B. Paid for 2/17–6/30/64 on 9/24/64. NFR.

McALEESE, FRANCIS L.: Pvt., Co. D. Res. of St. Mary's Co., Md. Served in Co. A, 1st Md. Inf., per postwar roster. Enl. Co. F, 35th Bn. Va. Cav., date unknown. Captured Frederick Co., Va. 11/15/63; sent to Wheeling. Age eighteen, 5'8", fair complexion, light hair, blue eyes. Student. Transf. to Camp Chase and Ft. Del.; escaped 7/3/64. NFR. Enl. Co. D, 2nd Md. Cav., date unknown. Paroled Winchester 4/18/65. Age twenty, 5'10", fair complexion, brown hair, gray eyes. Destination Baltimore.

McALEESE, JAMES P.: 2nd Lt., Co. F. Served in Co. A, 1st Md. Inf., on postwar roster. Reenl. Co. F, 2nd Md. Cav., date unknown. Captured Moorefield, W.Va., 11/7/64; sent to Wheeling. Age twenty-five, 6', dark complexion, hazel eyes, dark hair. Merchant. Res. of Baltimore. Transf. to Camp Chase; released 6/12/65.

McATEE, J. M.: Pvt., Co. A. In Richmond hosp. 5/10–11/64. NFR.

McCABE, GEORGE WILLIAM E.: Pvt., Co. G. b. circa 1840. Res. of Baltimore. Enl. Pelham's Bty., Stuart Horse Arty., 7/9/62. Transf. to Co. G, 2nd Md. Cav., date unknown; WIA and in Charlottes-

ville hospital 3/24–5/20/64; WIA (saber cut left parietal region) Monocacy, Md., 7/9/64. Captured Frederick, Md., 7/10/64; sent to West Buildings Hosp., Baltimore; transf. to Ft. McHenry and Pt. Lookout; exchanged 7/64. Transf. to Co. K (2nd), 1st Va. Cav., 8/64. Transf. to Co. K, 1st Md. Cav., 8/15/64; WIA (head), captured, Smithfield, W.Va., 8/28/64. Age twenty-four; sent to Ft. McHenry; transf. to Pt. Lookout; exchanged 3/18/65; present Camp Lee, Richmond, 3/19/65. NFR. d. by 1903.

McCARROLL, WILLIAM J.: 1st Lt., Co. D. Whilte in Richmond hospital, paid for 3/1–4/30/64 in Richmond hosp. 2/15/64 and for 5/1–30/64 on 1/17/65; dropped for AWOL 1/3/65. NFR.

McCAUL, _____: Pvt., Co. unknown; present 8/1/64. NFR.

McCLERNAN, JOHN H.: Pvt., Co. B. On postwar roster. Res. of Baltimore.

McCLERNAN, SAMUEL T.: Pvt., Co. C. Served in 2nd Md. Arty. Enl. Co. C, 2nd Md. Cav., date unknown. Captured Moorefield, W.Va., 8/7/64; sent to Wheeling. Age twenty-six, 5'10½", florid complexion, blue eyes, brown hair. Carpenter. Res. of Baltimore. Transf. to Camp Chase and Pt. Lookout; exchanged 3/27/65. Admitted Richmond hosp. with pneumonia same day. Captured in Richmond hosp. 4/3/65. Paroled Richmond 4/17/65. Took oath Richmond 7/1/65. Formerly of Baltimore; destination Richmond.

McCOOL, DENNIS: Pvt., Co. A. Captured Moorefield, W.Va., 8/7/64; sent to Wheeling. Age twenty-two, 5'10", florid complexion, blue eyes, auburn hair. Gunsmith. Res. of New Orleans, La. Transf. to Camp Chase and Pt. Lookout; exchanged 3/27/65. NFR.

McCURDIE, J. W.: Pvt., Co. D. Enl. Richmond 1/7/64; present dismounted 8/31/64. NFR.

McDERMOTT, JOHN: Pvt., Co. B. Des. to the enemy in Western Va. 1/64. Age twenty-six, 5'10", dark complexion, blue eyes, brown hair. Mechanic. Res. of Richmond. Took oath, sent north 1/15/64.

McDONALD, JOHN: Pvt., Co. A. Paroled Winchester 4/20/65. Age twenty-two, 5'7", fair complexion, dark hair, hazel eyes. Took oath Harpers Ferry, W.Va., 4/23/65. Former res. of N.Y.; destination N.Y.

McENTEE, JAMES J.: Pvt., Co. D. Served in Capt. Valentine's Co., 1st S.C. Inf., Enl. Co. C, 2nd Md. Cav., 1864. Captured in Richmond hosp. 4/3/65; sent to Newport News, Va.; released 7/4/65. Member ANS/MLA. Res. Baltimore. d. 6/4/94.

McGEARY, J.: Pvt., Co. B. Captured Halltown, W.Va., 7/15/63; sent to Baltimore. Transf. to City Point,Va., for exchange 8/24/63. NFR.

McGRAW or MAGRAW, STEPHEN C.: 4th Cpl., Co. F. Res. of Baltimore. Enl. Big Spring, Va.,

7/27/64. Captured Moorefield, W.Va., 8/7/64; sent to Wheeling. Age sixteen, 5'9", dark complexion, blue eyes, dark hair. Farmer. Res. of Baltimore Co. Transf. to Camp Chase. Paroled to report to PM, Baltimore 4/7/65; released 4/17/65.

McGUGGIN, BERNARD: Pvt., Co. E. "While under the influence of liquor at Pikesville, Md., was induced to enlist 14 July 1864." Des. to 8th Ill. Cav., Leesburg, Va., 7/15/64; sent to Old Capitol; transf. to Elmira; took oath, released 2/13/65. 5'6", ruddy complexion, blue eyes, dark brown hair. Res. of Baltimore.

McKAIG, WILLIAM WALLACE, JR.: Capt., Co. A. b. Cumberland, Md. 5/5/42. Attended VMI 1859–61. Res. of Cumberland, Md. Served as Drillmaster, Richmond 4–6/61. Claimed to have served in the battle of Bull Run, Va., 7/21/61. Appointed 2nd Lt. Co. I, 1st Va. Inf., 9/14/61; resigned 4/26/62. Served in the 12th Va. Cav. Appointed 1st Lt., Co. A, 2nd Md. Cav., circa 6/1/63. Captured Hampshire Co., W.Va., 3/23/64; sent to Wheeling. 5'11", fair complexion, light hair, gray eyes. Cadet. Res. of Allegany Co., Md. Transf. to Camp Chase; exchanged 2/25/65. Promoted Capt. Paroled Winchester 4/24/65. Age twenty-two, 6', fair complexion, light hair, blue eyes. Iron Manufacturer, Cumberland, Md.; Mayor of Cumberland; Col., Md. Natl. Guard. Shot and killed in Cumberland 10/17/70. Bur. Rose Hill Cem., Hagerstown, Md.

McKEE, CHARLES W.: Pvt., Co. E. Captured Moorefield, W.Va., 8/7/64; sent to Wheeling. Age twenty-two, 5'11", dark complexion, gray eyes, red hair. Carpenter. Res. of Baltimore. Transf. to Camp Chase and Pt. Lookout; exchanged 3/27/65. NFR.

McKENNY, JAMES M.: Pvt., Co. D. Enl. Richmond 10/1/63. Captured Charles Town, W.Va., 10/18/63; on rolls 12/31/63–8/31/64. NFR. May have been KIA; not on Federal POW rolls.

McKIEMER, F. M.: Pvt., Co. A. Paroled Harpers Ferry, W.Va., 4/30/65.

McLAUGHLIN, THOMAS: Pvt., Co. B; issued clothing 9/10/64. Captured Harrisonburg, Va., 9/30/64; sent to Pt. Lookout. Took oath, joined U.S. service, 10/8/64.

McMAHON, ANDREW: Pvt., Co. A. Captured Piedmont, Va., 6/5/64; sent to Camp Morton. Took oath, joined U.S. service, 3/22/65.

McMINN, PETER: Pvt., Co. E. b. Richmond circa 1844. Enl. Richmond 1/30/64. Age sixteen, 5'8", dark complexion, gray eyes, brown hair. Carpenter. NFR.

McMULLEN, LAMBERT G.: 3rd Sgt., Co. F. Enl. Co. D, 1st Md. Inf., 6/12/61; WIA (arm) Bull Run, Va., 7/21/61; discharged, date unknown. Enl. Co. F, 12th Va. Cav., 3/8/62. Captured Bunker Hill, W.Va., 9/5/62; sent to Wheeling. Age twen-

ty, 5'9", light complexion, gray eyes, brown hair. Clerk. Res. of Jefferson Co., Va. Transf. to Camp Chase and Cairo, Ill; exchanged 9/29/62. Captured Shepherdstown, W.Va., 7/13/63; sent to Baltimore; transf. to Pt. Lookout; exchanged 12/25/63. Transf. to Co. F, 2nd Md. Cav., 4/29/64; presence or ab. not stated 7/27/64. NFR.

McWILLIAMS, JOHN: Pvt., Co. C. b. Baltimore 1/10/36. Clerk and Iron Moulder. Enl. Co. G, 13th Va. Inf., 5/28/61; promoted Sgt. Maj.; discharged 5/28/62 as nonresident. (Promoted Lt. in Md. Co. in postwar account.) Captured Winchester 9/19/64; exchanged 2/65. In Secret Service, Wilmington, N.C. Paroled Richmond 4/15/65 as Pvt. Express Agent, Weldon, N.C.; Clerk, Baltimore, 1865; Clerk of Court, Baltimore, 1878–79.

MEALY, PATRICK: Pvt., Co. A. Captured Moorefield, W.Va., 8/7/64; sent to Wheeling. Age twenty-six, 5'11", fair complexion, gray eyes, dark hair. Laborer. Res. of Baltimore. Transf. to Camp Chase and Pt. Lookout; exchanged 3/27/65. NFR.

MEDARY, SAMUEL: Pvt., Co. A. Enl. Richmond 4/12/63; WIA (left forearm about one inch below elbow joint), captured Martinsburg, W.Va., 10/15/63; sent to West Buildings Hosp., Baltimore; bullet removed 11/8/63; transf. to Ft. McHenry and Pt. Lookout; exchanged POW, Camp Lee, Richmond, 3/19/65. Admitted Richmond hosp. with pneumonia 3/30/65. NFR.

MENZZO, JOSEPH: Pvt., Co. D. Enl. Richmond 10/1/63. Captured Charles Town, W.Va., 10/15/63. NFR. May have been KIA; not on Federal POW rolls.

MERRIZI, ROCHO: Pvt., Co. G. Des. to the enemy 10/18/63; sent to Ft. Mifflin, Pa.; took oath, released 10/28/63.

MILLER, FRANK C.: Pvt., Co. B. Captured 12/25/63; sent to Old Capitol; took oath, sent to N.Y. 3/14/64. 5'9½", dark complexion, black hair, dark eyes. Res. of New Orleans, La.

MILLER, HENRY: Pvt., Co. C. On postwar roster.

MILLER, JAMES C.: Pvt., Co. D. b. 1846. Enl. Mt. Jackson, Va., 10/13/63. Captured Moorefield, W.Va., 8/7/64; sent to Wheeling. Age eighteen, 5'7", fair complexion, gray eyes, dark hair. Laborer. Res. of Charles Town, Jefferson Co., W.Va. Transf. to Camp Chase and Pt. Lookout; exchanged 3/27/65. Paroled Winchester 4/18/65. Age eighteen. d. 1928. Bur. Edge Hill Cem., Charles Town.

MILLER, WILLIAM: Pvt., Co. D. Res. of Carroll Co., Md. Enl. Co. E, 1st Md. Inf., 5/22/61; discharged 8/5/62. Enl. Co. D, 2nd Md. Cav., Richmond, 6/12/63; paid 8/31/63; present 12/31/63–8/31/64. NFR.

MINTY, J. M.: Pvt., Co. E. Des. to the enemy Frederick, Md., 7/9/64; sent to Ft. McHenry;

desired to take oath 9/64. NFR.

MITCHELL, JAMES: Pvt., Co. D. On postwar roster.

MITCHELL, JAMES W. : Pvt., Co. F. Enl. Co. F, 12th Va. Cav., 5/10/62. Enl. Co. F, 1st Md. Cav., without authority; ordered back 12/62. Transf. to Co. F, 2nd Md. Cav., 4/29/64; WIA (left side), date and place unknown; issued clothing 7/64; ab. sick with ulcer on left leg 3/6/65; furloughed for sixty days 3/18/65. Paroled Richmond 4/65. Age twenty-four, 5'6", dark complexion, dark hair, dark eyes. Shoemaker. Res. of Baltimore; d. there 1/26/19. Bur. Loudon Park Cem., Baltimore.

MITCHELL, WILLIAM: Pvt., Co. unknown. Des. to the enemy Franklin Co., Pa., 5/16/64; sent to Ft. Del.; transf. to Washington, D.C., for trial as des. from Co. K, 93rd N.Y. Inf.,

MODLIN, W. W.: 2nd Sgt., Co. D. Enl. Richmond 8/3/63; des. 6/15/64, on rolls to 8/31/64. NFR.

MONAGHAN, PATRICK: Pvt., Co. C. Captured Chambersburg, Pa., 8/2/64; sent to Ft. Del.; released 5/3/65. 5'5", light complexion, light hair, blue eyes. Res. of Baltimore.

MONTAGUE, THOMAS: Pvt., Co. B. Captured Piedmont, Va., 6/5/64; sent to Camp Morton. Took oath, enlisted in U.S. service 3/22/65.

MONTROSE, CHARLES: Pvt., Co. B. Res. of Baltimore. Captured Baltimore 7/20/63; sent to Ft. McHenry; took oath, released 10/25/63.

MOOG, JACOB J.: Pvt., Co. F. Captured Moorefield, W.Va., 8/7/64; sent to Wheeling. Age eighteen, 5'7½", light complexion, gray eyes, dark hair. Farmer. Res. of Harford Co., Md. Transf. to Camp Chase and Pt. Lookout; exchanged 3/27/65. NFR.

MOOG, JAMES: Pvt., Co. F. Enl. Big Spring, Va., 7/27/64. NFR.

MOORE, HENRY: Pvt., Co. C. Captured Piedmont, Va., 6/5/64; sent to Camp Morton 6/21/64. NFR.

MOORE, JAMES H.: Pvt., Co. E. Paid for 7/4–8/31/63 on 8/15/64; WIA and admitted Richmond hosp. 9/2/64; furloughed for sixty days; furloughed for twenty-five days 12/28/64. Paroled Winchester 4/16/65. Age twenty-one, 5'9½", light complexion, brown hair, blue eyes. Res. of Wheeling. Took oath same day. Former res. of Baltimore; destination Baltimore.

MOORE, THOMAS: Pvt., Co. B. Att. Georgetown U. Class of 1866. Enl. 1863; present Gettysburg, Pa., 7/3/63. Took oath, joined U.S. service 10/15/64. Res. of Ga.

MOORE, W. D.: Pvt., Co. E; WIA Gettysburg, Pa., 7/2–3/63; DOW in Staunton, Va., hosp. 9/1/64. Bur. Thornrose Cem., Staunton.

MOORE, WILLIAM B.: Pvt., Co. D. Enl. Richmond 9/10/63; AWOL 12/31/63–8/31/64. NFR. Member R. E. Lee Camp No. 1, CV, Richmond. d. 1917.

MOORE, WILLIAM S., JR.: Pvt., Co. D. b. Tazewell Co., Va., 5/15/40. Enl. Co. B, 40th Tenn. Inf., as Sgt. Captured Island No. 10, Tenn.; sent to Camp Douglas; exchanged 1862. Enl. Richmond 8/23/63; ab. sick with "debilitas" in Staunton, Va., hosp. 2/8/64. NFR; present Piedmont, Va., Lynchburg, Va., Monocacy, Md., Moorefield, W.Va., and Winchester in postwar account. Res. Wayne Co., W.Va., 1884.

MORGAN, CHARLES S.: Pvt., Co. B. Captured Falling Waters, Md., 7/14/63; sent to Old Capitol. Took oath, sent north 12/20/63. 5'6¼", light complexion, light hair, gray eyes. Res. of Buffalo, N.Y.

MORRIS, JOHN M.: Pvt., Co. B. Enl. 8/11/63. Captured Frederick, Md., 7/10/64; sent to Old Capitol; transf. to Elmira. Took oath 12/16/64. "Desires to go to Pottsville, Pa., where his mother and other relatives reside." Despite taking oath, he was not released until 5/19/65. 5'6½", light complexion, light hair, blue eyes. Res. of Reading, Pa.

MORRIS, WILLIAM T.: Pvt., Co. E. May have served in Co. E, 1st Md. Inf.; on postwar roster. Possibly the Wm. T. Morris (12/3/44–10/13/11) bur. St. Luke's Methodist Ch. Cem., Talbot Co., Md.

MORRISON, GEORGE W.: Pvt., Co. B. b. 9/11/40. Enl. 9/62. Paroled Harpers Ferry, W.Va., 5/16/65. Age twenty-five, 5'6", light complexion, light hair, gray eyes. Took oath Harpers Ferry, W.Va., 5/24/65. M.D., Chelsia, Indian Terr., 1914. Member Stand Watie Camp, CV.

MOULTON, WILLIAM: Pvt., Co. F. Enl. Big Spring, Va., 7/27/64, on rolls; however, captured Point of Rocks, Md., 7/23/64; sent to Old Capitol; transf. to Elmira. Ordered released 10/28/64.

MULLANEY, PATRICK: Pvt., Co. C. Served in Lucas's 15th Bn., S.C. Heavy Arty., 1861–64. Enl. Co. C, 2nd Md. Cav., date unknown. Captured Moorefield, W.Va., 8/7/64; sent to Wheeling. Age twenty-four, 5'6¾", fair complexion, blue eyes, dark hair. Res. of Ireland. Transf. to Camp Chase. Took oath, joined U.S. Army 4/22/65.

MURDOCK, WILLIAM: Pvt., Co. A. Captured Moorefield, W.Va., 8/7/64; sent to Wheeling. Age twenty, 5'8", dark complexion, brown eyes, brown hair. Cooper. Res. of New Orleans, La. Transf. to Camp Chase and Pt. Lookout; exchanged 3/27/65. NFR.

MURPHY, DANIEL E.: Pvt., Co. G. Enl. 8/63. Captured Newtown, Va., 10/9/63; sent to Ft. McHenry; transf. to Pt. Lookout; took oath, released 4/18/64. Res. of Baltimore.

MURPHY, FRANK: Pvt., Co. C. On postwar roster.

MURPHY, GEORGE: Pvt., Co. C. On postwar roster. Res. of Carroll Co., Md. Possibly George W. Murphy (4/9/36–4/11/15) bur. Hyattstown Methodist Ch. Cem., Frederick Co., Md.

MURPHY, M. (1): Pvt., Co. D. On postwar roster.

MURPHY, M. (2): Pvt., Co. D. Enl. Richmond 10/13/63; ab. sick with "syphilis cousic," in Gordonsville, Va., hosp. 8/31/4. transf. to Charlottesville hosp.; RTD 9/27/64; issued clothing 11/11/64. NFR.

MURRAY, GEORGE: Pvt., Co. F. Enl. Big Spring, Va., 7/27/64. Captured Moorefield, W.Va., 8/7/64; sent to Wheeling. Age sixteen, 5'9", light complexion, blue eyes, light hair. Farmer. Res. of Carroll Co., Md. Transf. to Camp Chase; released by order of President Lincoln 12/1/64.

MURTAY, J.: Pvt., Co. D. Captured Frederick, Md., 7/7/64; sent to Ft. McHenry; released 5/9/65. Res. of Washington, D.C.

MYERS, CHARLES THOMAS: Pvt., Co. C. On postwar roster. Res. of Frederick Co., Md. (See entry page 265.)

NELSON, NATHAN, JR.: Pvt., Co. E. b. circa 1845. On postwar roster. Res. New Market, Md. d. Clarksville, Ill., 2/13/69, age thirty-two. Bur. Methodist Ch. Cem., New London, Md.

NEWKIRK, J. V.: Pvt., Co. F. Enl. Big Spring, Va., 7/27/64; issued clothing 9/10/64. NFR. Res. of Frederick Co., Md.

NORWOOD, LEWIS: Pvt., Co. A. On postwar roster.

NORWOOD, W.: Pvt., Co. D; ab. sick with dysentery in Richmond hosp. 10/1/64; furloughed for sixty days 10/5/64. NFR.

NORWOOD, WILLIAM: Pvt., Co. A. b. 3/31/34. Enl. Richmond 4/15/63. Captured Martinsburg, W.Va., 10/15/63; sent to Pt. Lookout; exchanged 3/18/65; present Camp Lee, Richmond, 3/19/65; paid 3/23/65. Paroled Winchester 4/18/65. Age thirty-one, 5'6", fair complexion, dark hair, gray eyes. Took oath Harpers Ferry, W.Va., 5/5/65. d. 3/30/14. Bur. Providence Meth. Ch., Kempstown, Frederick, Co., Md.

NOSSETT, CYRUS MILTON: Pvt., Co. unknown. b. Shenandoah Co., Va., 6/26/44. Enl. Co. C, 11th Va. Cav., date unknown. Captured Cool Spring, Clarke Co., Va. 8/5/63; sent to Wheeling, W.Va. Age eighteen, 5'6¾", dark complexion, dark hair, gray eyes. Farmer. Shenandoah Co., Va., Transf. to Camp Chase and Ft. Del.; released 5/14/65. d. Winchester 10/7/10, age sixty-seven. Obituary only record. Bur. Sunrise Ch. Cem., Relief, Frederick Co., Va.

OATES, CHARLES T.: Pvt., Co. C. Enl. Co. A, 1st Md. Inf., 5/22/61; discharged 5/24/62. Enl. Co. C, 2nd Md. Cav., date unknown; horse killed Frederick, Md., 7/8/64, paid $3,500. Captured Moorefield, W.Va., 8/7/64; sent to Wheeling. Age twenty-two, 5'6", dark complexion, brown eyes, dark hair. Student. Res. of Frederick, Md. Transf. to Camp Chase and Pt. Lookout; exchanged

3/27/65. Paid 4/1/65. Paroled Winchester 5/10/65. Age twenty-three, 5'8", dark complexion, hazel eyes, auburn hair. d. date unknown. Bur. Catholic Ch. Cem., Frederick Co., Md., no dates.

O'BRIEN, DENNIS: Cpl., Co. B. Enl. Co. B, 1st Md. Inf., 5/21/61; discharged by 8/11/62, when regt. disbanded. Enl. Co. B, 2nd Md. Cav., date unknown; paid Richmond 3/28/63. Captured Berryville, Va., 10/31/63; sent to Wheeling. Age twenty-five, 5'8", light complexion, blue eyes, light hair. Res. of Baltimore. Transf. to Rock Island; took oath, joined U.S. Navy 1/25/64.

O'BRIEN, JOHN: Pvt., Co. B. b. Manchester, England, circa 1841. Enl. Richmond 2/6/64. Age twenty-three, 5'10½", light complexion, gray eyes, dark hair. Horse killed, Summit Point, W.Va., 5/23/64, paid $2,500 3/27/65. NFR.

O'CONNELL, CHARLES: Pvt., Co. D. Enl. Winchester 7/1/64. Captured Charles Town, W.Va., 10/18/64. NFR. May have been KIA; not on Federal POW rolls.

O'CONNELL, DAVID JOSEPH: Pvt., Co. D. Res. of Baltimore. Served in Lucas's 15th Bn., S.C. Heavy Arty., 1861–64. Enl. Co. D, 2nd Md. Cav., date unknown; ab. sick with "inter fever" in Richmond hosp. 5/20/64; furloughed for sixty days 5/29/64. Captured Piedmont, Va., 6/5/64; sent to Camp Morton; exchanged 3/23/65. NFR.

O'CONNELL, EDWARD: Pvt., Co. D. Captured Piedmont, Va., 6/5/64; sent to Camp Morton. d. of "Inflammation of the lungs" there 12/5/64. Bur. Greenlawn Cem., Camp Morton, Ind., grave #1185.

O'NEAL, JAMES: Pvt., Co. D. Res. Havre-de-Grace, Harford Co., Md. Enl. Staunton, Va., 8/1/63. Captured Rockville, Md., 7/7/64; sent to Old Capitol; transf. to Elmira. In post hosp., Elmira, 7/13/65; released 7/26/65. 5'10", dark complexion, dark hair, dark eyes. Res. of Macon, Ga.

ORIN, WALTER: Pvt., Co. B. Captured Piedmont, Va., 6/5/64; sent to Camp Morton; exchanged 3/23/65. Paroled Alexandria, Va., 4/11/65. Took oath same day; transportation furnished to Baltimore.

ORNDERF, JOHN: Pvt., Co. D. Captured Martinsburg, W.Va., 10/15/63; sent to Ft. McHenry; transf. Pt. Lookout; arrived 11/2/63; exchanged, date unknown. Paroled Richmond 5/15/65.

OWENS, NORVAL WILSON: Capt. and QM. b. 1841. Res. of Anne Arundel Co., Md. On postwar roster. d. 1918.

OWENS, WILLIAM H.: Pvt., Co. B. May have served in Co. G, 1st S.C. Inf., 1861–64. Enl. date unknown. Captured Piedmont, Va., 6/5/64; sent to Camp Morton; released 6/12/65. 5'9", dark complexion, dark hair, blue eyes. Res. of Baltimore; destination Baltimore.

OWINGS, NICHOLAS W.: Capt. and QM. b. Md. 3/27/24. Res. of Owings Mill, Baltimore Co. Present 2/11/64; ab. sick with piles in Winchester hosp. 7/28–8/6/64. Paroled Edwards' Ferry, Md., 5/9/65. Took oath 5/23/65. d. Frederick, Md. 1/31/83. Bur. Mt. Olivet Cem., Frederick, Md.

OWINGS, THOMAS: Pvt., Co. unknown. b. 1836. Res. of Anne Arundel Co., Md. On postwar roster. May also have served in Stuart Horse Arty. d. 1925.

PACE, H. B.: Sgt., Co. A. Enl. Richmond 5/16/63. NFR until paroled POW, Camp Lee, Richmond, 3/18/65. NFR.

PAGE, WILLIAM: Pvt., Co. B. Res. of Charles Co., Md. In Richmond hosp. 5/27–28/64. NFR.

PANGLE, WATSON: Pvt., Co. G. Paroled Winchester 4/29/65. Age twenty-six, 5'10", light complexion, dark hair, blue eyes. Res. Cedar Creek, Frederick Co., Va.

PARSONS, JOSEPH F.: Pvt., Co. F. Des., captured, Frederick, Md., 7/7/64; sent to Ft. McHenry; took oath, released 10/14/64.

PATTERSON, E.: Pvt., Co. C; ab. sick with "debilitas" in Richmond hosp. 3/6/65; furloughed for thirty days 3/8/65. NFR.

PEAY, B. C.: Pvt., Co. A. On postwar roster.

PENDLETON, FRANK: Pvt., Co. A; present as Color Bearer 7/4/64. NFR.

PEREGOY, H.: Pvt., Co. F. Enl. Big Spring, Va., 7/27/64. NFR.

PETERS, THOMAS: Pvt., Co. D. Res. of Park Mills, Frederick Co., Md. On postwar roster.

PETTIS, A.: Pvt, Co. F. Enl. Big Spring, Va., 7/27/64. NFR.

PETTIT, ALLEN O.: Pvt., Co. B. b. circa 1840. Res. of Baltimore. Enl. Co. F, 2nd Va. Inf., 5/1/61; ab. sick in hosp. 11–12/61. NFR. Enl. Co. F, 12th Va. Cav., 4/1/62. Transf. to Co. B, 2nd Md. Cav., date unknown; in arrest 3–8/64. Paroled Winchester 5/31/65. Member ANS/MLA, 1894. Res. of Baltimore. d. 10/11/08.

PHELPS, MARTIN: Pvt., Co. A. Des. to the enemy in W.Va. 1/64. Age twenty-five, 5'7", dark complexion, blue eyes, dark hair. Engineer. Res. of Macon, Ga. Took oath, sent north 1/25/64.

PHILLIPS, GEORGE H.: Pvt., Co. E. b. Henrico Co., Va., circa 1844. Enl. Richmond 1/27/64. Age seventeen, 5'5", light complexion, blue eyes, brown hair. Clerk. Paid 9/26/64. NFR.

PHILLIPS, JOHN: Pvt., Co. C. On postwar roster.

PHILLIPS, WILLIAM: Pvt., Co. D. Enl. Richmond 9/10/63. Ordered transf. to Co. E, 4th Va. Inf., by Gen. Jubal Early 7/38/64, but never carried out; horse killed Moorefield, W.Va., 8/7/64, paid $2,500; present 8/31/64; issued clothing 9/10 and 9/15/64; paid 2/20/65. NFR.

PHIPPS, JOHN S.: Color-bearer. Res. of Anne Arundel Co., Md. Enl. Big Spring, Va., 7/24/64. Captured Smithfield, W.Va., 8/28/64; sent to Old Capitol; transf. to Camp Chase and Pt. Lookout; released 6/12/65. 5'8½", light complexion, light brown hair, dark blue eyes. Issued transportation from Washington, D.C., to Annapolis, Md., 6/15/65.

POE, JOHN LEWIS: Pvt., Co. C. b. 1/29/39. Enl. Co. E, 49th Va. Inf., 5/61. Enl. Co. C, 2nd Md. Cav., 8/63. Captured Moorefield, W.Va., 8/7/64; sent to Wheeling. Age twenty-five, 5'5", dark complexion, blue eyes, dark hair. Farmer. Rappahannock Co., Va. Transf. to Camp Chase and Pt. Lookout; exchanged 3/27/65. NFR. Farmer near Amissville, Rappahannock Co., Va. d. 3/26/1936. Bur. Leeds Cem. near Hume, Va.

POWELL, GEORGE: Pvt., Co. C. On postwar roster.

PRICE, JOHN "BUCK": Pvt., Co. C. Captured Jefferson Co., W.Va., 11/5/64; sent to Ft. Warren; released 6/15/65. Res. of Baltimore; destination Baltimore.

PULLEN, HENRY: Pvt., Co. C. On postwar roster.

PURNELL, GEORGE WASHINGTON: 2nd Lt., Co. B. b. Snow Hill, Worcester Co., Md., 4/14/41. Att. Snow Hill Acad., U. of Va. (1858–59), and Princeton Col. (1859–61). Enl. Capt. Thomas Sturgis Davis's Co., Davis's Md. Bn. Cav., Richmond, 6/20/63; promoted 2nd Lt. Co. B, 2nd Md. Bn. Cav., 9/63. Captured Piedmont, Va., 6/5/64; sent to Camp Chase. 5'8", dark complexion, dark hair, hazel eyes. Res. of Snow Hill. Transf. to Johnson's Island; released 6/15/65. Took oath Baltimore 8/12/65. Applied for Presidential Pardon from Snow Hill 8/32/65. Businessman, Worcester Co. Gd. U. of Va. (LLD 1868). Lawyer, Worcester Co., Md. Member ANS/MLA. d. Snow Hill 5/8/99; bur. there, All Hallows Epis. Ch. Cem. (Photograph in Hartzler 1992)

PYNE, AYLMER C.: Pvt., Co. D. Enl. Winchester 7/1/64; present through 8/31/64; horse killed Fisher's Hill, Va., 9/22/64, paid $2,300 3/11/65. Paroled Richmond 4/11/65. Machinist. Res. of Richmond.

QUINN, JOHN SKINNER: Pvt., Co. C. b. 9/6/32. Res. of Baltimore; ab. sick with "diabetis" in Richmond hosp. 11/18/64; furloughed for sixty days 11/24/64; readmitted Richmond hosp. 1/10/65. NFR. d. 9/25/05. Bur. Mt. Olivet Cem., Frederick, Md.

RADY, HENRY: Cpl., Co. E. Captured Martinsburg, W.Va., 10/15/63; sent to Ft. McHenry; transf. to Pt. Lookout; arrived 11/2/63. NFR.

RAILING, GEORGE H.: Pvt., Co. C. b. 2/19/40. Res. of Frederick Co., Md. Captured Hagerstown, Md., 7/12/63; sent to Pt. Lookout; exchanged 4/6/64. Captured Smithfield, W.Va., 8/28/64; sent to Old Capitol; transf. to Camp Chase, Pt. Lookout 3/26/65; released 5/28/65. d. 4/2/30. Bur. Mt. Olivet Cem., Frederick, Md.

RATCLIFFE, GEORGE E.: 1st Lt., Co. E. b. Baltimore circa 1839. Enl. Co. B, 21st Va. Inf., 6/15/61. Age twenty-two, 5'10", light hair, brown eyes. NFR. Appointed 1st Lt., Co. E, 2nd Md. Cav., date unknown. Enl. as Pvt., Co. D, 43rd Bn. Va. Cav. (Mosby), 10/4/64. Paroled Winchester 4/22/65. Age twenty-three, 5'10", light complexion, light hair, brown eyes. Res. Salem, Va. Took oath Harpers Ferry, W.Va., 5/22/65; destination Baltimore.

READ, B. E.: Pvt., Co. E. Served in 39th Va. Inf., Enl. 9/63 in postwar account. Lutheran Minister, Webster Grove, Mo., 1914.

REAGS, P. A.: Pvt., Co. A. Paroled Mt. Jackson, Va., 4/21/65.

REARDON, MICHAEL: Pvt., Co. D. Captured 12/25/63; sent to Old Capitol. Took oath, transportation furnished to Philadelphia 3/19/64. 5'10½", dark complexion, black hair, blue eyes. Res. of Montreal, Canada.

REED, EUGENE: 2nd Lt., Co. unknown. Captured near Martinsburg, W.Va., 10/15/63. NFR.

REED, WILLIAM: Pvt., Co. F. Captured Martinsburg, W.Va., 10/15/63; sent to Ft. McHenry; transf. to Pt. Lookout; reportedly d. 12/13/63, however, exchanged 3/6/64. Present 7/31/64. NFR. May be the same William Reed who served in Davis's Bn., Md. Cav.

REESE, GIDEON DAVIS: Pvt., Co. unknown. On postwar roster.

REILEY, PATRICK: Sgt., Co. C; issued clothing 9/30/64. Paroled Winchester 4/19/65. Age twenty-five, 5'10", fair complexion, light hair, gray eyes.

REILLY, JOHN: Pvt., Co. A. Captured Hampshire Co., W.Va., 4/14/64; sent to Wheeling. Age twenty-six, 6'½", fair complexion, gray eyes, light hair. Carpenter. Res. of Baltimore. Transf. to Camp Chase; released 5/12/65. 6', florid complexion, black hair, blue eyes. Res. of Baltimore.

REYNOLDS, CHARLES W.: Pvt., Co. D. Enl. Richmond 8/17/63. Captured Winchester 11/18/63; sent to Wheeling. Age seventeen, 5'6", fair complexion, gray eyes, fair hair. Student. Res. of Norfolk, Va. Transf. to Camp Chase and Ft. Del.; escaped 7/1/64; ab. on horse detail 8/31/64; ab. sick with "debilitas" in Charlottesville hosp., 10/11–13/64, and Richmond hosp., 11/10–11/64. NFR.

REYNOLDS, WILLIAM L.: Pvt., Co. D. Res. of Baltimore. Enl. Co. B. 43rd Bn. Va. Cav. (Mosby), 12/1/63; present through 12/63. NFR. Enl. Co. D, 2nd Md. Cav., Mt. Jackson, Va., 8/7/64; AWOL 8/31/64; ab. sick with syphilis (primary) in Charlottesville hosp. 10/4–5/64; issued clothing 10/20/64. NFR. Paroled Bowling Green, Va., 5/16/65, as member of Co. B, 43rd

Bn. Va. Cav; sent to Essex Co., Va.

RIBY, F. M.: Pvt., Co. unknown. Served in Co. G, 12th Va. Cav. Transf. to 2nd Md. Cav. NFR.

RICAMORE, GEORGE C.: Pvt., Co. D. b. 4/23/49. Res. of Clarke Co., Va. Enl. Mt. Jackson, Va., 10/18/63. Ordered transf. to Co. B, 12th Va. Cav., 8/18/64; however, present 8/31/64. Paroled Winchester 4/19/65 as member Co. B, 12th Va. Cav. 5'7", dark complexion, blue eyes, brown hair. d. 8/25/22. Bur. Greenhill Cem., Berryville, Va.

RICE, CHARLES: Pvt., Co. D. Enl. Mt. Jackson, Va., 9/10/63; AWOL 8/31/64. Paroled Staunton, Va., 5/1/65. Age sixteen, 5'3", light complexion, brown hair, gray eyes. Res. of Richmond. Took oath Richmond 6/15/65. Laborer, Tredegar Iron Works, Richmond.

RICHARDS, _____: Sgt., Co. unknown. On postwar roster.

RICHARDSON, THOMAS alias THOMAS MOORE: Pvt., Co. G. Captured Luray, Va., 12/7/63; sent to Ft. Del.; sent to Washington, D.C., 1/17/64, for trial as des. from 90th Pa. Inf.

RICHARDSON, WILLIAM H.: 1st Lt., Co. F. b. Henrico Co., Va., circa 1838. Enl. as Pvt., Co. F, 12th Va. Cav., 5/26/62; present 7–8/63 and 3–4/64. Transf. to Co. F, 2nd Md. Cav., 4/29/64; appointed 1st Lt.; horse killed, Clear Spring, Md., 7/29/64. Captured Moorefield, W.Va., 8/7/64; sent to Wheeling. Age twenty-seven, 5'11¾", fair complexion, blue eyes, light hair. Res. of Harford Co., Md. Transf. to Camp Chase; exchanged 3/12/65. Paid 3/22/65. Paroled Staunton, Va., 5/27/65. Res. of Austin, Tex., 1918; d. there 9/16/24. Bur. Oakwood Cem., Austin.

RICHY, GEORGE: Pvt., Co. B. Paroled Winchester 5/18/65. Age twenty-three, 6'3", dark complexion, dark hair, hazel eyes. Res. Bedford Co., Va.

RICKETTS, DANIEL: Pvt., Co. A. Captured Hampshire Co., W.Va., 4/14/64; sent to Wheeling. Age twenty-one, 5'8", fair complexion, brown eyes, light hair. Moulder. Res. of Richmond. Transf. to Camp Chase; released 5/8/65.

RIDDLE, CHARLES C.: Pvt., Co. C. Captured Strasburg, Va., 12/11/63; sent to Wheeling. Age twenty-two, 5'10", dark complexion, hazel eyes, dark hair. Res. of Greene Co., Va. Transf. to Camp Chase and Ft. Del.; released 6/15/65.

RIDER, GEORGE J.: Pvt., Co. C. Enl. New Market, Va., 8/6/63. Captured Middletown, Va., 9/20/63; sent to Ft. McHenry. Age twenty, 5'11", fair complexion, gray eyes, light hair. Farmer, Frederick Co., Md. Transf. to Pt. Lookout; exchanged 2/15/65; present Camp Lee, Richmond, 2/18/65. NFR.

RIELY, FRANK M.: Pvt., Co. F. Res. of Washington, D.C. Enl. Co. F, 12th Va. Cav., 6/1/62. Transf.

to Co. F, 2nd Md. Cav; presence or ab. not stated 7/27/64; KIA Winchester 9/19/64.

RIELY, W.: Pvt., Co. A. Captured Piedmont, Va., 6/5/64. Under guard Staunton, Va., 6/8/64. NFR.

RIFE, JOSEPH H.: Pvt., Co. C. b. 10/23/42. Paroled Winchester 4/28/65. Age nineteen, 5'10", fair complexion, fair hair, hazel eyes. Res. of New Market, Va. Member Neff–Rice Camp, CV, New Market. d. near Broadway, Rockingham Co., Va., 2/16/11. Bur. Emanuel Ch. Cem., Broadway.

ROADES, JOHN: Pvt., Co. G. Des., arrested Franklin Co., Pa., 5/18/64; sent to Ft. Del.; sent to Washington, D.C., for trial 1/17/64 as des. from Co. A, 125th N.Y. Inf.,

ROBESON, GEORGE W.: Pvt., Co. K. b. Washington Co., Md., circa 1843. Captured Beverly, W.Va., 10/29/64; sent to Wheeling. Age twenty-one, 5'10", fair complexion, black eyes, dark hair. Farmer. Res. of Washington Co., Md. Transf. to Camp Chase; received 11/1–4/64. NFR.

ROBERTS, J. S.: Pvt., Co. D. Enl. Mt. Jackson, Va., 1/1/64. Captured Clarke Co., Va., 6/10/64; sent to Wheeling. Age twenty, 5'9", dark complexion, gray eyes, black hair. Baker. Res. of Augusta Co. Transf. to Camp Chase; exchanged 3/12/65. NFR.

ROBEY, WILLIAM: Pvt., Co. G. Paroled Winchester 4/17/65. Age twenty-eight, 5'9", light complexion, brown hair, gray eyes. Res. of Md.

ROBINSON, THOMAS J.: Pvt., Co. A. Captured Martinsburg, W.Va., 10/15/63; sent to Ft. McHenry; transf. to Pt. Lookout; d. 11/7/64 on U.S.S. *Baltic* of "chronic diarrhoea," en route for exchange. Bur. Finn's Point Natl. Cem., N.J.

ROBINSON, WILLIAM H.: Pvt., Co. C. Res. of Baltimore. Captured Hampshire Co., W.Va., 5/13/63; sent to Wheeling. Age twenty-six, 5'1", florid complexion, auburn hair, gray eyes. Shoemaker. Transf. to Camp Chase, Johnson's Island, and Pt. Lookout. NFR.

ROBY, HENRY ALBERT: Sgt., Co. B. Res. of Baltimore. Enl. Richmond 8/8/63. In Staunton, Va., hosp. with camp itch 2/27/64. Transf. to 2nd Md. Arty. 4/21/64. Paroled Lynchburg, Va., 4/13/65. Served in Spanish–American War 1898. Res. of Baltimore 1900.

RODERICK, JOHN: Pvt., Co. D. Enl. Richmond 7/1/63. Captured near Harpers Ferry, W.Va., 7/18/64. On rolls to 8/31/64. NFR. Possibly John Phillip Roderick (3/14/38–12/23/24), bur. Edge Hill Cem., Charles Town, W.Va.

RODLEY, EDWARD SMITH: Pvt., Co. D. b. Baltimore 1841. Captured Piedmont, Va., 6/5/64; sent to Camp Morton; released 5/22/65. 5'4", dark complexion, black hair, black eyes. Res. of Baltimore. Butcher, Baltimore. d. 11/10/82.

RODRICK, JACOB: Pvt., Co. D. b. Harpers Ferry,

W.Va., 12/17/42. Enl. Mt. Jackson, Va., 9/1/63. Captured Winchester 11/16/63; sent to Wheeling. Age twenty-one, 5'11", fair complexion, gray eyes, dark hair. Laborer. Res. of Winchester. Transf. to Camp Chase and Ft. Del.; escaped 7/1/64. Captured Moorefield, W.Va., 8/7/64; sent to Wheeling. Age twenty-one, 5'9½", dark complexion, hazel eyes, brown hair. Transf. to Camp Chase and Pt. Lookout; exchanged 3/27/65. Paroled Winchester 4/18/65. Took oath Harpers Ferry, W.Va., 5/5/65. Res. of Harpers Ferry. In RR Construction 1866–72; RR Conductor, B&O RR 1873–1913. d. Lexington, Va., 6/26/16. Bur. Stonewall Jackson Cem., Lexington.

ROGERS, EDWARD J.: Pvt., Co. A. Volunteered from Capt. Kite's Co. H, 2nd Bn. Va. Militia 2/18/62; paid Richmond 11/13/63 for 5/1–10/31/63. Served in Co. F, 12th Va. Cav; ab. on detail 7–8/64. NFR.

ROGERS, SAMUEL: Pvt., Co. unknown. KIA Clear Spring, Md., 7/29/64. Res. of Green Spring, Md. NFR.

RONEY, JOHN C.: Pvt., Co. A. Served in Co. G, 1st S.C. Inf., 1861–62. Enl. 2nd Md. Arty. 1862; ab. sick 12/62. Enl. Co. A, 2nd Md. Cav., date unknown. In Richmond hosp. 11/14–15/64 and 11/18–19/64. NFR.

ROSS, DAVID M.: Capt., Co. C. b. circa 1835. Res. of Kent Co., Md. Enl. Co. K, 12th Va. Cav., 1862; AWOL 9–10/62. Transf. to Co. C, 2nd Md. Cav., and elected Capt., date unknown; signed for ord. stores 3/30/63 and 10/18/63; present 12/30/63, 2/11/64 and 6/10/64; ab. detailed for 115 days by Gen. Jubal Early to gather grain and cattle for his army. Paroled Staunton, Va., 5/24/65. Age twenty-nine, 6', fair complexion, black hair, blue eyes.

ROUSSELOT, C. A.: 2nd Lt., Co. D. Resigned 2/23/64. Capt. Burke endorsed his application "incompetent to fulfill the duties of an officer". Approved 2/29/64. NFR.

ROWAN, MARTIN: Pvt., Co. B. Des. 9/29/63. Captured Martinsburg, W.Va., 10/16/63; sent to Ft. Mifflin; took oath, employed by U.S. government 1/1/64. 5'6", fresh complexion, dark red hair, hazel eyes. Res. of Richmond.

ROWLAND, H. R.: Pvt., Co. A. On postwar roster.

ROYSTER, WILLIAM A.: Pvt., Co. B. Captured Piedmont, Va., 6/5/64; sent to Camp Morton. Exchanged 3/12/65. Paroled Winchester 4/19/65. Age sixteen, 5'3", fair complexion, light hair, blue eyes.

RYAN, WILLIAM HENRY (photo next page): Pvt., Co. C. b. 1846. Coachmaker. Res. of Baltimore. Enl. Co. A, 1st Md. Inf., date unknown; paid Richmond 2/19/62; discharged when regiment disbanded 8/11/62. Enl. Co. C, 2nd Md. Cav., date unknown. Captured near Hawkinstown, Shenan-

WILLIAM
HENRY RYAN

*(Daniel D.
Hartzler)*

doah Co., Va., 5/12/64; sent to Wheeling. Age eighteen, 5'6", fair complexion, dark eyes. Transf. to Camp Chase; exchanged 2/27/65. Des., arrested Accotink, Va., 3/30/65; sent to Old Capitol. Took oath, sent to Washington, D.C., 4/1/65.

SCHAUB, HENRY or HENIRICK: Pvt., Co. E. b. Germany circa 1841. Enl. Richmond 1/29/64. Age twenty-three, 5'9", dark complexion, blue eyes, light hair. Baker. NFR.

SCHECKELL, MARENUS W.: Pvt., Co. C. Served in Co. E, 1st Va. Inf., but not on muster rolls. Enl. Co. C, 2nd Md. Cav., date unknown. Captured Middletown, Va., 9/22/63; sent to Ft. McHenry; took oath, released 10/30/63 by order of President Lincoln. Age twenty-two, 5'6", fair complexion, gray eyes, black hair. Clerk. Res. of Georgetown, D.C.

SCHNEIDER, GEORGE W.: Sgt., Co. D. Enl. as 1st cpl., Richmond, 9/13/63; promoted Sgt. Captured Moorefield, W.Va., 8/7/64, gray horse killed; sent to Wheeling. Age twenty-three, 6'1", light complexion, blue eyes, light hair. Carpenter. Res. of Baltimore. Transf. to Camp Chase and Pt. Lookout; exchanged 3/27/65. Paid $3,000 for gray horse 3/29/65. Paroled Staunton, Va., 5/1/65. Member ANS/MLA. 1907. Res. of Baltimore.

SCHOPPERT, JOHN HENRY: Pvt., Co. D. b. Martinsburg, W.Va., 1844. Employee, U.S. Arsenal, Harpers Ferry, W.Va., 1861. Enl. C.S.A. Ord. Dept. 9/61. Served under Gen. Imboden. Enl. 1863. Paroled Winchester 6/3/65. Age twenty, 5'7", light complexion, dark hair, dark eyes. Res. of Berkeley Co. Internal Revenue Service employee. d. 5/8/24. Bur. Elmwood Cem., Shepherdstown, W.Va.

SCOTT, CHANNING M.: 1st Sgt., Co. C. b. circa 1843. Enl. 1st Md. Arty. 9/1/62. Enl. Co. C, 2nd Md. Cav., 1/5/63; paid Richmond 9/14/63 and 10/13/63. "Came to Richmond in charge of prisoners from the Valley." Paroled Richmond

5/15/65. Member ANS/MLA. d. Old Soldiers' Home, Pikesville, Md., 6/28/92, age forty-nine. Bur. Loudon Park Cem., Baltimore.

SCULLY, PATRICK: Pvt., Co. F. Enl. Big Spring, Va., 7/27/64; des. to the enemy Hancock, Md., 9/64; took oath, released Baltimore 12/23/64. Former res. of Baltimore; destination Baltimore.

SEDDEN, FRANK: Pvt., Co. C. Captured Hampshire Co., W.Va., 7/30/63; sent to Wheeling. Age nineteen, 5'10", dark complexion, dark hair, dark eyes. Farmer. Res. of King William Co., Va. Transf. to Camp Chase; released 6/6/65. Age twenty-one, 5'11", dark complexion, black hair, black eyes. Res. of Caroline Co., Va.

SEIBERT, JOSEPH: Pvt., Co. C. Captured Luray, Va., 10/2/64; sent to Pt. Lookout; exchanged 2/15/65. NFR.

SERVIS, THOMAS BROWNE: Pvt., Co. unknown. Res. of Baltimore. On postwar roster.

SEVERE, FRANCIS S.: Pvt., Co. A. Served in Co. A, 12th Ala. Inf., 1861–63; paid Richmond 9/26/64 for 11/1/63–2/29/64. NFR. Member ANS/MLA, 1887. Res. of Baltimore. Entered Old Soldiers' Home, Pikesville, Md., 7/00, age sixty-eight. Seaman. NFR.

SEWARD, GEORGE H.: Pvt., Co. C. Captured Hagerstown, Md., 7/30/64; sent to Ft. Del.; released 3/1/65 by order of the War Department.

SEXSMITH, TRUMAN: Pvt., Co. C. Captured Hampshire Co., W.Va., 7/30/63; sent to Wheeling. Age twenty-three, 5'7", light complexion, gray eyes, red hair. Printer. Res. of Wetzel Co., Va. Transf. to Camp Chase; took oath, released 3/25/65.

SHAFFER, GEORGE W.: Sgt., Co. A. Enl. New Market, Va., 5/15/63; issued clothing 9/20/64. Captured Edinburg, Va., 10/9/64; sent to Pt. Lookout; exchanged 2/15/65; present Camp Lee, Richmond, 2/27/65. Paroled Augusta, Ga., 5/6/65. Took oath 5/20/65.

SHAFFER, GEORGE WILLIAM: Pvt., Co. K. Res. of Baltimore. Paroled New Market, Va., 4/20/65. Member ANS/MLA. Res. of Baltimore 1894. d. 3/20/09.

SHARP, J.: Pvt., Co. D. In Richmond hosp. 11/24–25/64. NFR.

SHAW, JOHN: Pvt., Co. G. Captured Luray, Va., 12/7/63; sent to Ft. Del.; arrived 12/17/63. NFR. Possibly John W. Shaw, who d. 6/18/93, age sixty-two, eight months, twenty-five days; bur. Mt. Hope Cem., Woodsboro, Frederick Co., Md.

SHEAN, MICHAEL H.: Pvt., Co. B. Captured Piedmont, Va., 6/5/64; sent to Camp Morton. Took oath, joined U.S. service 3/22/65.

SHEEHAN, JAMES JOHN: Pvt., Co. D. Enl. Richmond 10/13/63. Captured Moorefield, W.Va., horse killed, 8/7/64; sent to Wheeling. Age thirty-one, 5'9", dark complexion, dark hair, dark eyes. Blacksmith. Res. of Richmond. Transf. to Camp Chase and Pt. Lookout; exchanged 3/27/65. Paid 3/28/65. NFR. May have lived in Millington, Kent Co., Md.

SHEARER, GEORGE E.: Capt., Co. D. Captured Winchester 8/8/63; sent to Ft. McHenry; escaped 5/15/64 while under sentence of fifteen years hard labor. NFR.

SHELL, WILLIAM: Pvt., Co. C. Captured 8/9/63; sent to Ft. McHenry; took oath, released 9/25/63.

SHIPLEY, JOSHUA: Pvt., Co. A. Captured Clarke Co., Va., 1/3/64; sent to Wheeling; transf. to Camp Chase and Ft. Del.; released 6/21/65. 5'6", light complexion, light hair, blue eyes. Farmer. Res. of Baltimore.

SHUGART, JOHN ZACHARIAH: Pvt., Co. D. Enl. Shepherdstown, W.Va., 7/1/64; WIA (lost leg) Moorefield, W.Va., 8/7/64; ab. wounded through 8/31/64. NFR. d. Mecklenburg Co., Va., 8/10/03, age fifty-seven. Bur. Chase City, Va.

SIMS, JOHN J.: Pvt., Co. B. b. circa 1840. Res. St. Mary's Co., Md. Enl. Co. D, 1st Md. Inf., 5/22/61; discharged by 8/11/62 when regt. disbanded. On postwar roster. d. Old Soldiers' Home, Pikesville, Md., 4/1/89, age forty-nine. Res. Baltimore. Bur. Loudon Park Cem., Baltimore.

SLEEPER, LOUIS: Pvt., Co. C; ab. sick with catarrh in Richmond hosp. 12/24/64–1/9/65. Paroled Winchester 4/28/65. Age twenty-six, 5'8", fair complexion, brown hair, hazel eyes. Res. of Baltimore.

SMITH, CHARLES: Pvt., Co. G. b. Cumberland Co., Va., circa 1847. Enl. Richmond 1/29/64. Age seventeen, 5'4½", dark complexion, hazel eyes, brown hair. Farmer. NFR.

SMITH, EDWARD: Pvt., Co. E. b. Liverpool, England circa 1840. Enl. Richmond 1/6/64. Age twenty-three, 5'7", florid complexion, dark hair. Laborer. NFR.

SMITH, H.: Pvt., Co. D. Enl. Richmond 9/10/63. Captured Front Royal, Va., 1/11/64; on rolls to 8/31/64. May have been KIA; not on Federal POW rolls.

SMITH, HARRY alias JOHN SNYDER: Pvt., Co. unknown. Captured Martinsburg, W.Va., 11/63; sent to Ft. Del.; sent to Washington, D.C., to stand trial as a des. from 170th N.Y. Inf.

SMITH, JAMES: Pvt., Co. C. Served previously as Gunner, CSN. Des., arrested Martinsburg, W.Va., 2/15/64; sent to Wheeling. Age twenty-three, 5'6", dark complexion, dark hair. Farmer. Res. of Liverpool, England. Transf. to Camp Chase. Took oath, enlisted in U.S. Navy 7/20/64.

SMITH, JEFF: Lt., Co. D. On postwar roster.

SMITH, JOHN: Pvt., Co. E. b. Ireland circa 1847. Enl. Richmond 1/29/64. Age eighteen, 5'6", light complexion, gray eyes, red hair. Laborer. NFR.

SMITH, VIRGIL: Pvt., Co. D. Captured Johnstown, Pa., 7/22/63; sent to Wheeling. Age nineteen, 5'11", dark complexion, gray eyes, dark hair. Farmer. Res. of Tishamingo Co., Miss. Transf. to Camp Chase; d. there of smallpox 4/8/64. Bur. Camp Chase Natl. Cem., Oh., grave #131.

SMITH, WILLIAM: Pvt., Co. B. Des. to the enemy 10/1/63. Arrested Harrisburg, Pa., 10/7/63; sent to Ft. Mifflin, Pa.; took oath to work for U.S. government 1/1/64. 5'7", fresh complexion, dark hair, hazel eyes. Res. of Richmond.

SMITH, WILLIAM: Pvt., Co. D. Paroled Winchester 4/19/65. Age nineteen, 5'8", fair complexion, dark hair, blue eyes.

SNIVELY, GEORGE T.: Pvt., Co. B. On postwar roster.

SNIVELY, GRIFFIN B.: Pvt., Co. F. Enl. Big Spring, Va., 7/27/64; des. Martinsburg, W.Va., date unknown. In Chambersburg, Pa., jail 9/9–10/64; sent to Ft. Mifflin; took oath, released 9/17/64. 5'7½", dark complexion, brown hair, hazel eyes. Res. of Baltimore Co., Md.

SNODGRASS, _____: Pvt., Co. C. On postwar roster.

SNOWDEN, GEORGE T.: Capt., Co. unknown. Captured Moorefield, W.Va., 1/3/65; sent to Wheeling. Age twenty-four, 5'10", florid complexion, gray eyes, light hair. Surveyor. Res. of Howard Co., Md. Escaped 7/18/65.

SOTECKI, ISADORE A.: Pvt., Co. B. Enl. Co. D, 1st Md. Inf., 6/1/61; discharged 7/2/62. Enl. Co. B, 2nd Md. Cav., date unknown. Captured Piedmont, Va., 6/5/64; sent to Camp Morton; released 6/12/65. 5'8", dark complexion, dark hair, dark eyes. Res. of Baltimore; destination Baltimore. Member ANS/MLA. d. 5/10/17. Bur. Loudon Park Cem., Baltimore.

SOUTHERLAND, LEIGH M.: Pvt., Co. A. b. Charleston, Md., 2/18/43. Employee, Patent Office, Washington, D.C. Res. of Charles Co., Md. Enl. Co. H, 1st Va. Inf., 5/20/61. Transf. to 1st Md. Arty. 5/1/64; discharged 10/31/64; on postwar roster. Farmer, Charles Co., Md. 1865–81; Sheriff, 1881–84. Member George Emack Camp, CV, 1906. Bur. Mt. Rest Cem., La Plata, Md., no dates.

SPAULDING, SAMUEL EGGLESTON: Pvt., Co. unknown. b. 1836. Gd. Georgetown U. 1859. M.D. Res. of Leonardtown, St. Mary's Co., Md. Served in McNeil's Rangers. On postwar roster 2nd Md. Cav. Served as 2nd Lt. Co. F, 59th Va. Inf. d. 8/22/99, age sixty-three. Bur. Old St. John's Cem., Hollywood, Md.

SPEDDEN, JOHN R.: Pvt., Co. A. Res. of Baltimore. Served in Co. C, 27th S.C. Inf.; on postwar roster. Member ANS/MLA. Res. of Baltimore. Entered Old Soldiers' Home, Pikesville, Md., 1/2/92, age fifty-three. Painter. Discharged.

SPRIGG, JOHN M: 2nd Sgt., Co. F. Enl. Co. F, 12th Va. Cav., 8/1/62; WIA Upperville, Va., 6/21/63. Transf. to Co. F, 2nd Md. Cav., 4/29/64; presence or ab. not stated 7/27/64. Paroled New Orleans, La., 7/18/65.

SPRINGER, A. G.: Pvt., Co. C. Captured Front Royal, Va., 12/3/63; sent to Ft. Del.; released 5/10/65. 5'9", light complexion, light hair, brown eyes. Res. of St. John, N.B., Canada.

SPIRL, MICHAEL: Pvt., Co. unknown. Captured near Harpers Ferry, W.Va., 7/30/64; sent to Old Capitol. NFR.

STANLEY, ALFRED J.: Cpl., Co. A. Enl. 6/9/63. Captured Martinsburg, W.Va., 10/15/63; sent to Ft. McHenry; transf. to Pt. Lookout; exchanged by 3/64; issued clothing 3/23/64; paid 5/18/64. Captured Clarke Co., Va., 6/10/64; sent to Wheeling. Age twenty-five, 5'5½", dark complexion, dark eyes, black hair. Seaman. Res. of Richmond. Transf. to Camp Chase; exchanged 3/12/65. NFR.

STANSBURY, JOSEPH W.: 1st Sgt., Co. A. Enl. 9/5/62; paid 12/31/63. Captured near Washington, D.C., 7/14/64; sent to Old Capitol; transf. to Elmira; released 5/17/65. 6', light complexion, light hair, blue eyes. Res. of Baltimore. Someone using his name was a paroled POW, Camp Lee, Richmond, 3/19/65.

STAPLES, JOHN M.: Pvt., Co. A. Captured Piedmont, Va., 6/5/64; sent to Camp Morton. d. of "Inflammation of the lungs" 2/4/65. Bur. Greenlawn Cem., Camp Morton, Ind., grave #1357.

STEPHENS, WILLIAM M.: Pvt., Co. D. Enl. Richmond 7/1/63; present 12/31/63–8/31/64; horse killed Frederick, Md., 7/7/64, paid $2,000; horse killed Moorefield, W.Va., 8/7/64, paid $2,500; issued clothing 9/30/64; paid 10/6/6/4; ab. sick with scabies in Richmond hosp. 12/28/64–3/27/65. Paroled Harrisonburg, Va., 5/8/65. Age twenty, 5'8", light complexion, light hair, blue eyes.

STEWARD, GEORGE W.: Pvt., Co. C. Application to ANS/MLA is only record of service. Res. of Baltimore 1890. Entered Old Soldiers' Home, Pikesville, Md., 5/5/96, age fifty-three. Carpenter. Dropped.

STEWART, COLUMBUS J., JR.: 3rd Cpl., Co. F. b. Baltimore circa 1844. Res. of Baltimore. Enl. Co. F, 5th Va. Cav, Dover, Pa., 5/1/63; WIA Louisa CH, Va., 6/11/64. Transf. to Co. F, 2nd Md. Cav., by 7/27/64; horse killed Chambersburg, Pa., raid.

Captured Moorefield, W.Va., 8/7/64; sent to Wheeling. Age twenty, 5'9", dark complexion, black eyes, dark hair. Transf. to Camp Chase and Pt. Lookout; exchanged 3/27/65. Paid $3,500 for horse 4/1/65. Paroled Winchester 4/20/65. Hardware Merchant, Baltimore 1865–1900. Member ANS/MLA. d. 7/6/00.

STINE, JOSEPH A.: 1st Sgt., Co. F. Served in 1st Md. Arty. 1861–62. Enl. Co. F, 12th Va. Cav., 6/1/62. Transf. to Co. F, 2nd Md. Cav., 4/29/64; presence or ab. not stated 7/27/64. Captured Moorefield, W.Va., 8/7/64; sent to Wheeling. Age nineteen, 5'10½", dark complexion, gray eyes, brown hair. Clerk. Res. of Baltimore. Transf. to Camp Chase and Pt. Lookout; exchanged 3/27/65. Paroled and took oath Winchester 5/9/65, age twenty; destination Baltimore. Member ANS/MLA, 1894. Res. of Baltimore.

STOCKSDALE, F. G.: Pvt., Co. C. On postwar roster. Member ANS/MLA, 1894. Res. of Baltimore. d. 5/1/02.

STOCKSDALE, GEORGE W.: Pvt., Co. C. On postwar roster.

STONEBRAKER, EDWARD L.: Pvt., Co. unknown. Res. of Washington Co., Md. On postwar roster. Brother of Joseph R. Stonebraker, 1st Md. Cav.

STOUTSENBERGER, ALBERT C. (See Strasburger, Albert.)

STRASBURGER, ALBERT: Pvt., Co. C. On postwar roster. Possibly Albert C. Stoutsenberger, Co. B, 35th Bn. Va. Cav. Res. of Frederick Co., Md. Captured Berryville, Va., 11/29/62; sent to Old Capitol; exchanged 3/29/63. Captured Gettysburg, Pa., 7/3/63; sent to Ft. McHenry; transf. to Ft. Del. and Pt. Lookout; released 5/10/65. 5'7", fair complexion, dark hair, hazel eyes.

STREET, JOHN F.: Pvt., Co. F. Enl. Co. A, 1st Md. Inf., 5/21/61; discharged 8/17/62. Enl. Co. F, 12th Va. Cav., 5/20/62. Transf. to Co. F, 2nd Md. Cav., 4/29/64. Captured Winchester 9/19/64; sent to Pt. Lookout; exchanged 2/16/65. Present Camp Lee, Richmond, 2/17/65. Paroled Richmond 4/10/65. Took oath Richmond 4/15/65. Former res. of Baltmore; destination Baltimore. Member ANS/MLA. d. 5/5/03, age sixty-four. Bur. Loudon Park Cem., Baltimore.

STURMAN, JOHN F.: Pvt., Co. C. Captured Moorefield, W.Va., 8/7/64; sent to Wheeling. Age twenty-four, 5'5", dark complexion, black eyes, black hair. Student. Res. of Baltimore. Transf. to Camp Chase and Pt. Lookout; exchanged 3/27/65. NFR.

SUDLER, JOHN EMORY: Capt., Co. E. b. Kent Co., Md., 3/4/39. Farmer, age twenty-one, Still Pond, Kent Co., Md., per 1860 census. On postwar roster 1st Md. Cav. Appointed Capt., Co. E,

2nd Md. Cav., date unknown; WIA (ankle) Chancellorsville, Va., 5/3/63; WIA Cedar Creek, Va., 10/13/64; present Appomattox CH, Va. Paroled Mechanicsville, Va., 5/28/65. Member Isaac Trimble Camp, CV, Baltimore. d. circa 1910. Bur. St. James Episcopal Ch. Cem., Anne Arundel Co., Md.

SULLIVAN, JOHN: Pvt., Co. E. b. Dublin, Ireland, circa 1828. Enl. Richmond 2/6/64. Age thirty-five, 5'9½", florid complexion, blue eyes, brown hair. Seaman. NFR.

SULLIVAN, JOSEPH D.: Pvt., Co. B. Res. of Baltimore. Enl. 2nd Md. Arty. 8/5/63. In Staunton, Va., hosp. with "chronic diarrhoea" 2/23/64. Transf. to Co. B, 2nd Md. Cav., 4/21/64. Captured Woodstock, Va., 10/9/64; sent to Pt. Lookout; exchanged 3/28/65. Paroled, took oath, Winchester 4/17/65. Age twenty-six, 5'8", light hair. Res. of Baltimore.

SWANK, L. S.: Pvt., Co. D. Enl. Richmond 10/1/63; lost horse 5/64; present 8/31/64; issued clothing 9/10/64. Paroled Montgomery, Ala., 5/30/65. 5'6", light complexion, dark hair, dark eyes.

TALBOTT, JOSHUA FREDERICK COCKY: Pvt., Co. F. Res. of Lutherville, Baltimore Co., Md. Enl. Big Spring, Va., 7/27/64; present 9/19/64. Paroled Danville, Va., 5/16/65. Took oath Marietta, Ga., 8/26/65. Member U.S. Congress 1912. Member ANS/MLA. Res. Lutherville, Md. (Photograph in Hartzler 1992)

TALIAFERRO, FELIX TAYLOR: Pvt., Co. unknown. b. 11/45. Attended VMI for eight months, class of 1865. Res. of Orange Co. Enl. Co. B, 12th Va. Cav., date unknown. Transf. to 2nd Md. Cav. 9/28/63. Transf. back to Co. B, 12th Va. Cav., 8/64. NFR. Auditor, Central RR of N.J. d. Elizabeth, N.J., 3/5/04.

TAY, J. L.: Pvt., Co. A. In Petersburg, Va., hosp. with acute dysentery 6/3–6/64. NFR.

TAYLOR, MAKLE: Pvt., Co. unknown; present 5/64. NFR.

TEAGLE, JOHN: Pvt., Co. D. Enl. Richmond 9/10/63. Captured Charles Town, W.Va., 9/18/63; on rolls 12/31/63–8/31/64. NFR. May have been KIA; not on Federal POW rolls.

TELLO, P. MANLY: Pvt., Co. unknown. Att. college in Md. before the war. Captured near Berryville, Va., date unknown; sent to Johnson's Island. Escaped to Canada. Alive in Pittsburgh, Pa., 1918. Postwar account only record.

TERRELL, D.: Pvt., Co. D. In Richmond hosp. with pneumonia 8/29–9/13/64. NFR.

TERRETT, BERRY: Pvt., Co. D. Enl. Richmond 9/10/63; ab. sick in Richmond hosp. 1–8/64. Captured Beverly, W.Va., 10/29/64. Res. of Hanover Co., Va.; sent to Clarksburg. Age eighteen, 5'10",

blue eyes, dark hair. Farmer. Transf. to Camp Chase; released 6/12/65. Res. of Henrico Co., Va.

TERRY, J. C.: Pvt., Co. B. In Richmond hosp. with "debilitas" 3/7/65; furloughed for thirty days 3/9/65. NFR.

THOMAS, CHARLES F.: Pvt., Co. A. Captured Moorefield, W.Va., 8/7/64; sent to Wheeling. Age twenty-two, 6', fair complexion, blue eyes, black hair. Clerk. Res. of Baltimore. Trans. Camp Chase; released 6/12/65.

THOMAS, CHARLES P.: Pvt., Co. A; issued clothing 9/10/64. NFR.

THOMAS, EDWARD: Pvt., Co. B. Captured Piedmont, Va., 6/5/64; sent to Camp Morton; released 5/11/65. 5'6", dark complexion, dark hair, blue eyes. Res. of Richmond.

THOMAS, EDWARD alias AMOS HILL: Pvt., Co. G. Captured Sir John's Run, W.Va., date un-known; sent to Ft. Del.; transf. to Washington, D.C., 1/16/64 for trial as a des. from the 12th Mass. Infantry.

THOMAS, JAMES EDWARD: Pvt., Co. B. b. circa 1839. Enl. Co. G, 7th Va. Cav., 4/1/62. Transf. to Co. F, 2nd Md. Cav., 4/21/64. Captured Winchester 7/20/64; sent to Wheeling. Age twenty-five, 5'8", dark complexion, dark hair, blue eyes. Farmer. Res. of Charles Co., Md. Transf. to Camp Chase; took oath, released 4/3/65.

THOMAS, R. H.: 1st Sgt., Co. D. Enl. Richmond 8/15/63; present 12/31/63–8/31/64. Paroled Columbia, Va., 6/1/65.

THOMPSON, GEORGE: Pvt., Co. F. Enl. Big Spring, Va., 7/27/64. NFR.

THOMPSON, R.: Pvt., Co. A. Captured Piedmont, Va., 6/5/64. POW under guard Staunton, Va., 6/8/64. NFR. Possibly Robert Thompson, b. 1843, who served in Co. A, Davis's Bn. Md. Cav.

TILGHMAN, JOHN: Pvt., Co. F. Enl. Big Spring, Va., 7/27/64. NFR.

TODD, MERRYMAN or MELVIN: Sgt., Co. C; present 10/18/63; present 2/11/64. Captured Orleans, Va., 3/18/64; sent to Old Capitol; transf. to Ft. Del.; released 6/10/65. 5'11", dark complexion, light hair, hazel eyes. Res. of Marion, Del. Living Brown's Valley, Tuba Co. [sic], state unknown, 1913. Brother of William H. Todd.

TODD, WILLIAM H.: Pvt., Co. C; present 10/18/63. Captured Shenandoah Co., Va. 5/12/64; sent to Wheeling. Age twenty, 6'2", fair complexion, gray eyes, light hair. Farmer. Baltimore Co. Transf. to Camp Chase; exchanged 2/27/65. Admitted Richmond hosp. with "debilitas" 3/7/65; furloughed for thirty days 3/9/65. Paroled Winchester 4/23/65. Age twenty-one, 6'2", light complexion, brown hair, blue eyes. Destination Baltimore Co. Member ANS/MLA, 1894. Res. of

Warren, Baltimore Co. Superintendent, Old Soldiers' Home, Pikesville, Md., 1913. Brother of Merryman or Melvin Todd.

TONGUE, WILLIAM G. D.: Pvt., Co. A. b. Baltimore Co., Md., 1843. Clerk, Baltimore Co. Enl. Co. G, 13th Va. Inf., 5/28/61; discharged as nonresident 5/28/62. Went to Bainbridge, Ga., 7/62, and worked in father's cotton factory two years. Enl. Stuart Horse Arty. 1864. NFR. On postwar roster Co. A, 2nd Md. Cav. Res. of Bainbridge, Ga., 1895.

TORPEY, JAMES: Pvt., Co. A. b. New Orleans, La., circa 1842. Enl. Co. K, 6th La. Inf., 6/4/61; des. 1/29/62. Enl. Co. A, 2nd Md. Cav., date unknown; des. Captured Hampshire Co., W.Va., 4/14/64; sent to Wheeling. Age twenty-one, 5'9", fair complexion, brown hair, dark eyes. Coopersmith. Res. of New Orleans, La. Transf. to Camp Chase; took oath; enlisted in U.S. Navy 7/20/64.

TRAINOR, E. alias HIRAM ROSS: Pvt., Co. G. Captured Page Valley, Va., 12/5/63; sent to Ft. Del.; sent to Washington, D.C., for trial 1/17/64 as des. from 12th Mass. Inf.

TRAVERS, ALONZO: 2nd Sgt., Co. A. On postwar roster. Enl. Co. F, 43rd Bn. Va. Cav., 12/13/64. Paroled Winchester 4/22/65. Age thirty-three, 5'11", dark complexion, dark hair, black eyes. Res. of Baltimore. Took oath Winchester 5/3/65; destination Richmond. Grocer. d. Alexandria, Va., 5/17/15, age sixty-six.

TRAVERS, J. H.: Pvt., Co. F. Enl. Big Spring, Va., 7/27/64. NFR.

TRAVERS, JOHN M.: Pvt., Co. C. Res. of Baltimore. Enl. Co. D, 1st Md. Inf., 5/22/61. Discharged 12/23/61. Enl. Letcher's Va. Bty. Richmond 2/17/62. Printer. Transf. to Co. C, 2nd Md. Cav., 4/29/64. Captured Piedmont, Va., 6/5/64; sent to Camp Morton; released 4/20/65. 5'5", light complexion, black hair, hazel eyes. Res. of Baltimore. Took oath 5/9/65 "Leaving Middle Military Department." Member ANS/MLA, 1894. Res. of Baltimore. d. 5/29/10.

TRIPPE, CHARLES: Pvt., Co. unknown. Served previously in Lee's Md. Cav. Captured Kearneysville, W.Va., 9/30/63; sent to Ft. McHenry; took oath, released 10/4/63. Res. of Pittsburgh, Pa.

TROUT, WILLIAM: Pvt., Co. C. Captured Berryville, Va., 9/20/63; sent to Ft. McHenry; transf. to Pt. Lookout; exchanged 1/64. Paroled, took oath, Millwood, Va., 4/28/65. Former res. of Baltimore; destination Baltimore.

TRUEHEART, J. G.: Pvt., Co. A. Paroled Winchester 4/19/65. Age sixteen, 6'3", fair complexion, light hair, blue eyes.

TUCK, RICHARD W.: Pvt., Co. C. On postwar roster.

TUCKER, GEORGE W.: Pvt., Co. F. Application to ANS/MLA is only record. Also claimed service in 12th Va. Cav. d. 12/4/06.

TULLY, JOHN: Pvt., Co. D. Enl. Richmond 10/13/63; present 12/31/63–8/31/64; horse killed Smithfield, W.Va., 8/28/64, paid $2,500; issued clothing 9/30/64; paid 2/24/65. NFR.

TURPIN, HENRY W.: Asst. Surgeon. b. 1848. Att. Georgetown U. 1861–64. Res. of Washington, D.C. Enl. 2nd Md. Cav., fall of 1864. Served as Clerk in Medical Dept., Richmond. Captured Bristol, Tenn., 9/4/64. Appointed Acting Asst. Surgeon 12/6/64, while a POW; exchanged 1/8/65. Paroled Bristol 4/30/65. Took oath Nashville, Tenn., 5/2/65. 5'9", gray eyes, light hair. M.D., Washington, D.C. Entered Old Soldiers' Home, Pikesville, Md., 4/3/17.

TURPIN, RICHARD: Pvt., Co. D. Enl. Richmond 9/10/63; AWOL 12/31/63–8/31/64. NFR.

TURPIN, THOMAS L.: Pvt., Co. unknown. Member ANS/MLA, 1894. Res. of Baltimore. Only record of service. Also served as Drummer in Co. D, 59th Va. Inf., 1/1/62–10/31/64; discharged for being underage.

UKHORN, JOSEPH H. K.: Pvt., Co. C. b. Baltimore circa 1840. Enl. Co. G, 13th Va. Inf., 7/6/61; discharged as nonresident 5/28/62. Age twenty-two, 6', light complexion, light eyes, light hair. Machinist. Enl. Co. C, 2nd Md. Cav., New Market, Va., 8/63. Captured White Hall, Va., 8/20/63; sent to Ft. McHenry; transf. to Pt. Lookout; exchanged 11/15/64. Issued clothing Camp Lee, Richmond, 1/22/64. NFR.

UPSHUR, LEVIN: Sgt., Co. E. (Also see entry page 295.) Captured Smithfield, W.Va., 8/28/64; sent to Camp Chase; transf. to Pt. Lookout; released 6/21/65. 5'8½", fair complexion, auburn hair, blue eyes. Res. Worcester Co., Md.; transportation to Baltimore furnished by PM, Washington, D.C., 6/22/65. Member ANS/MLA. Entered Old Soldiers' Home, Pikesville, Md. d. by 1894.

VOGLE, JOHN A.: Pvt., Co. D. Res. of Smithsburg, Washington Co., Md. Enl. Wise (Va.) Arty. Martinsburg, W.Va., 4/19/61; present as Blacksmith 8/31/61. Transf. to Co. D, 2nd Md. Cav., 6/5/62; des. Chambersburg, Pa., 7/12/64, using alias CHARLES NORTHRUP; sent to Ft. Del.; took oath; released 12/8/64.

WADE, W. E.: Pvt., Co. A. On roster. Enl. Co. A, 43rd Bn. Va. Cav., date unknown. Captured Upperville, Va., 9/24/63; sent to Ft. McHenry. 6', dark complexion, dark hair, dark eyes. transf. to Pt. Lookout; d. there of consumption 3/19/64. Bur. Pt. Lookout Confederate Cem., Md.

WALKER, JAMES: Pvt., Co. D. Enl. Co. B, 28th Bn. Va. Inf., 3/7/62. Transf. to Co. D, 2nd Md.

Cav., date unknown. Captured near Bethesda Ch., Va., 5/26/64; exchanged, date unknown. Paroled Lynchburg, Va., 4/15/65.

WALKER, THADDEUS J.: Pvt., Co. D. Enl. Richmond 9/10/63; paid 2/29/64 and 4/6/64; AWOL 8/31/64. Captured, date and place unknown; exchanged; present as paroled POW Camp Lee, Richmond, 10/31/64. Paroled Lynchburg, Va., 4/15/65.

WALSH, ROBERT: Pvt., Co. D. Enl. Richmond 8/1/63; des. 5/30/64. On rolls to 8/31/64. Paroled Winchester 4/24/65. Age twenty-four, 5'6", fair complexion, light hair, blue eyes. Res. of Shenandoah Co., Va.

WARD, WILLIAM B.: Pvt., Co. A. Res. of Friendship, Anne Arundel Co., Md. On postwar roster.

WARD, WILLIAM W.: Pvt., Co. A. b. Georgetown, D.C., circa 1840. Enl. Co. I, 1st Md. Inf., 6/15/61; discharged 6/15/62. Age twenty-two, 5'7", light complexion, brown eyes, light hair. Farmer. Enl. Co. A, 2nd Md. Cav., 3/5/63; ab. sick with fever and "diarrhoea" in Richmond hosp. 7/31/64; furloughed to Harrisonburg, Va., for thirty days 8/20/64. NFR.

WARFIELD, ADOLPH: Pvt., Co. F. Res. of Baltimore. Enl. Big Spring, Va.; 7/27/64; KIA Clear Spring, Md., 7/29/64.

WATSON, SAMUEL H.: Pvt., Co. B. b. Va. circa 1828. Potter, age thirty-two, Northern Dist., Augusta Co., per 1860 census. Enl. Co. M, 5th Va. Inf., 5/61; discharged 6/61. Enl. Co. B, 2nd Md. Cav., date unknown. Captured Eastville, Va., 5/2/64; sent to Ft. Monroe; took oath, released 5/10/64. 5'7¼", dark complexion, black eyes, black hair. Res. of Staunton, Va. Sent to Cincinnati, Oh. Potter, age forty-two, 2nd Dist., Augusta Co., per 1870 census.

WEAVER, HIRAM S.: Pvt., Co. C. Res. of Funkstown, Washington Co., Md. Enl. Co. A, 1st Md. Inf., 6/2/61; discharged 5/21/62. On postwar roster Co. C, 2nd Md. Cav. Captured, date unknown; sent to Ft. McHenry; transf. to Ft. Monroe 12/29/62; exchanged. (Also see entry page 299.)

WELCH, JOHN L.: Pvt., Co. A. b. St. Mary's Co., Md. Enl. Co. C, 1st Md. Inf., 5/24/61; discharged 6/14/62. Age twenty-six, 5'8¾", dark complexion, hazel eyes, dark hair. Merchant. Enl. Co. A, 2nd Bn. Md. Cav., date unknown. Captured Piedmont, Va., 6/5/64; sent to Camp Morton; released 5/23/65. 5'8¼", dark complexion, dark hair, hazel eyes. Res. of Baltimore.

WELLS, JOHN B.: 1st Lt., Co. A. b. circa 1841. Enl. Co. G, 13th Va. Inf., 7/6/61; discharged as nonresident 5/28/62. Arrested as spy Berlin, Md., 1/20/63; sent to Ft. Del.; exchanged, date unknown. Enl. Co. A, 2nd Md. Cav., date unknown;

ab. sick with syphilis in Richmond hosp. 2/1– 8/31/64; horse killed Gordonsville, Va., 9/10/64, paid $3,000; ab. sick with "diarrhoea" in Harrisonburg, Va., hosp. 9/19–11/30/64; horse killed near Liberty Mills, Va., 12/20/64; paid $3,000. Paroled Staunton, Va., 5/1/65. Age twenty-four, 5'9", dark complexion, brown hair, hazel eyes. Took oath Winchester 6/19/65. Former res. of Baltimore; destination Baltimore. Member ANS/MLA, 1894. Res. of Baltimore. d. 3/11/12.

WELSH, EDWARD: Pvt., Co. A. Enl. Richmond 4/63. Captured, date and place unknown. Paroled POW Camp Lee, Richmond, 2/19/65. NFR.

WELSH, ENOCH O.: Pvt., Co. A. Res. of Bristol, Anne Arundel Co., Md. On Postwar roster.

WELSH, MARTIN L.: Pvt., Co. E. Enl. Co. E, 1st Md. Inf., 5/23/61; discharged 8/17/62. Captured Martinsburg, W.Va., 10/10/63; sent to Ft. McHenry; took oath, released 10/28/63. Issued clothing 8/1/64. NFR.

WEST, JACK: Pvt., Co. unknown; present 5/64. NFR.

WHITAKER, B.: Pvt., Co. unknown. Res. of Baltimore. KIA 9/25/64. Bur. Masonic Cem., Jefferson Co., W.Va.

WHITE, STEPHEN: Pvt., Co. C. On postwar roster.

WHITLEY, WILLIAM F.: Cpl., Co. B. b. Yorkshire, England, circa 1826. Res. of Federalsburg, Dorchester Co., Md. Enl. Co. H. 17th Va. Inf., 4/27/61; discharged for overage 7/24/62. Enl. Co. B, 2nd Bn. Md. Cav., date unknown. Admitted Richmond hosp. 11/28/64; furloughed for thirty days 11/29/64. NFR. Wood Carver, Baltimore postwar. Entered Old Soldiers' Home, Pikesville, Md., 10/23/93, age sixty-seven; expelled for stealing 11/5/93. Entered Old Soldiers' Home, Richmond 10/8/95; dismissed 10/17/95. d. 12/95.

WILLIAMS, EDWARD, JR. "NED": Sgt. Maj. Gd. Georgetown U. 1852. Res. of Georgetown, D.C. Enl. Co. A, 1st Md. Inf., 5/21/61; appointed 1st Lt., Co. C, 19th Bn. Va. Arty., 4/13/62; present 10/31/62; co. disbanded. Served in 12th Va. Cav., but does not appear on muster rolls. Appointed Sgt. Maj., 2nd Md. Cav., date unknown. Captured flag at Charles Town, W.Va., 10/18/63. Captured Shenandoah Co., Va., 5/18/64; sent to Wheeling. Age twenty-eight, 5'8", florid complexion, blue eyes, light hair. Transf. to Camp Chase; exchanged 2/25/65. Ab. sick with "debilitas" in Richmond hosp. 3/7/65; furloughed for thirty days 3/9/65. Paroled Winchester 4/21/65. Age twenty-nine, 5'9", fair complexion, light hair, blue eyes. Member Alexander Young Camp, CV, Frederick, Md., circa 1900.

WILLIAMS, GEORGE W.: Pvt., Co. B. Res. of Baltimore. Served in Lucas's Bn. S.C. Heavy

Arty., 1861–64. Enl. Co. B, 2nd Md. Cav., date unknown. Captured Mt. Crawford, Va., 10/3/64; sent to Pt. Lookout; took oath; joined U.S. Army 10/14/64.

WILLIAMS, JAMES: Pvt., Co. E. Paroled Winchester 4/29/65. Age eighteen, 5'11", fair complexion, dark hair, blue eyes. Res. of Flint Hill, Rappahannock Co., Va.

WILLIAMS, JAMES B.: Pvt., Co. D. Captured Martinsburg, W.Va., 10/15/63; sent to Ft. McHenry; transf. to Pt. Lookout 11/1/63. NFR.

WILLIAMS, PATRICK H.: Pvt., Co. C Enl. Co. E. 1st Md. Inf., 5/23/61; discharged by 8/11/62 when regt. disbanded. Enl. Co. C, 2nd Md. Cav., date unknown. Captured Berlin, Md., 1/25/63; sent to Ft. McHenry as a spy; transf. to Ft. Del.; exchanged 5/4/63. NFR.

WILLIS, _____: Pvt., Co. unknown; present 9/64. NFR.

WILSON, GEORGE L.: Pvt., Co. F. Served in Co. K, 9th La. Inf., Captured near Winchester 4/26/64; sent to Wheeling. Age thirty-four, 5'10", dark complexion, hazel eyes, auburn hair. Overseer. Res. of Carroll Parish, La. Transf. to Camp Chase; d. there of erysipelas 12/18/64. Bur. Camp Chase Cem., Oh., grave #628.

WILSON, GEORGE WASHINGTON: Pvt., Co. unknown. May have served in Lucas's Bn. S.C. Heavy Arty. Captured Eastville, Va., 4/1/64; sent to Ft. Monroe. 5'10 7/8", dark complexion, brown eyes, dark hair. Res. of Cincinnati, Oh. Took oath, sent to Cincinnati 5/18/64.

WILTSHIRE, JAMES B.: Pvt., Co. B. Captured Winchester 10/15/63; sent to Ft. McHenry; transf. to Pt. Lookout 11/1/63. NFR.

WINDER, WILLIAM SIDNEY: Pvt., Co. F. Res. of Annapolis, Anne Arundel Co., Md. Enl. Big Spring, Va., 7/27/64. NFR. Served as Capt. and AAG on Gen. J. H. Winder's staff. Entered Old Soldiers' Home, Pikesville, Md., 10/4/04, from Baltimore. Age seventy-two. Clerk. d. 2/14/13. Bur. St. Thomas P. E. Ch. Cem., Baltimore.

WINGROVE, THOMAS: Pvt., Co. E. b. Richmond, circa 1847. Enl. Richmond 1/28/64. Age sixteen, 5'6¼", light complexion, blue eyes, light hair. Laborer. NFR.

WINFREE, WILLIAM H.: Pvt., Co. E. Res. of Oak Forest, Cumberland Co., Va., per 1860 census. Ab. sick with debility and rheumatism "producing & enlargement of large joint of upper extremity & disease of the heart" in Farmville, Va., hosp. 3/1/64. Age forty-five. Furloughed to Oak Forest, Cumberland Co., Md., for sixty days 7/5/64; extended thirty days 9/6/64, 10/7/64, and 11/8/64; issued clothing 11/23/64. NFR.

WOLFE, NICHOLAS S.: 5th Sgt., Co. D. Enl. Co.

E, 1st Md. Inf., by 1862. In Lynchburg, Va., hosp. 8/11/62; discharged. Enl. Co. D, 2nd Md. Cav., Richmond, 9/1/63; paid 12/31/63; ab. sick with fever in Staunton, Va., hosp. 3/2–17/64; WIA and admitted Charlottesville hosp. 6/6/64; transf. to Lynchburg, Va., hosp. same day; d. there 7/20/64. Bur. Old Town Cem., Lynchburg.

WOOD, CHARLES S.: Pvt., Co. F. On postwar roster.

WOOLFOLK, A. M.: Asst. Surgeon. Res. of Bayou Grosse Tete, Talbot Co., Md. M.D. in Washington, DC. Appointed 6/63. Captured Prince George's Co., Md., 7/12/64; sent to Old Capitol; transf. to Ft. Del.; exchanged 8/12/64. NFR.

WRIGHT, GEORGE S.: Pvt., Co. B. Captured Mt. Jackson, Va., 3/5/65; sent to Pt. Lookout 3/9/65; transf. to Ft. Del.; released 6/22/65. 5'9", sallow complexion, dark hair, brown eyes. Res. Warren Co., Va.

YOUNG, EDWARD D.: Pvt., Co. B. b. Washington Co., Md., circa 1840. Res. of Washington Co., Md. Enl. Richmond 9/29/63. Age twenty-three, 5'6", dark complexion, hazel eyes, dark hair. Printer. NFR.

YOUNG, GEORGE LEWIS: Pvt., Co. C. b. Md. 1842. Enl. Alexandria, Va. Arty. 4/17/61. Transf. to Co. C, 2nd Md. Cav., 9/12/63. Paroled Winchester 4/27/65. Age twenty-four, 5'6", dark complexion, dark hair, brown eyes. Res. of Fairfax Co. Member R. E. Lee Camp, CV, Alexandria, Va. d. Alexandria 12/13/13. Bur. Sydenstricker Methodist Ch. Cem., Fairfax Co., Va.

YOUNG, JOHN: Pvt., Co. B. b. New Orleans, La., circa 1841. Enl. Co. E, 7th La. Inf., 6/7/61, age twenty. Machinist. Captured Fredericksburg, Va., 5/3/63; sent to Ft. Del.; exchanged 5/23/63. Captured Gettysburg, Pa., 7/3/63; exchanged, date unknown. Enl. Co. B, 2nd Md. Cav., date unknown. Captured Front Royal, Va., 8/3/64; sent to Wheeling. Age twenty-three, 5'8", dark complexion, gray eyes, dark hair. Steamboatman. Res. of New Orleans, La. Transf. to Camp Chase and Ft. Del.; released 5/11/65.

ZIMMERMAN, WILLIAM A.: Pvt., Co. F. Res. of Baltimore. Enl. 8/21/63. Captured Smithfield, W.Va., 8/28/64; sent to Camp Chase; transf. to Pt. Lookout for exchange 3/26/65. NFR.

ZIMMERMAN, WILLIAM E.: Pvt., Co. D. Enl. Breathed's Bty. Horse Arty., Richmond 12/1/62. Transf. to Co. D, 2nd Md. Cav., 4/64. NFR. Res. of Baltimore 1905.

Bibliography

In citing works in the footnotes, the following abbreviations have been used: MHS, Maryland Historical Society; MSA, Maryland State Archives; OR, U.S. War Department Official Records of the War of the Rebellion; WFCHS, Winchester–Frederick County Historical Society; WLU, Washington and Lee University.

Manuscripts

Augusta County Historical Society, Staunton, Virginia
   Cemetery Listings.
Dana Bible Collection, Mohawk, Tennessee
   Papers on Gen. J. C. Vaughn's Brigade and the battle of Piedmont.
Garth Bowling, La Plata, Maryland
   Records of Confederate soldiers buried in Charles County, Maryland.
John M. Brice Collection, Pasadena, Maryland
   Roster of Confederate Soldiers from Anne Arundel County, Maryland.
Stephen R. Brockmiller Collection, Baltimore
   "Elgar L. Tschiffely Book, Co. A, First Maryland Cavalry." Diary July 1863–April 9, 1865.
   William I. Rasin Letter, March 20, 1912.
   James R. Wheeler Letters.
Erick F. Davis Collection, Baltimore
   Material on Thomas Sturgis Davis.
Duke University, Durham, North Carolina
   Bradley T. Johnson Papers.
   Thomas T. Munford Papers.
Frederick Historical Society, Frederick, Maryland
   Jacob Engelbrecht Diary, 1863.
George Washington University, Washington, D.C.
   Constitution and Roll of Members of the Confederate Veterans Association of the District of Columbia, 1894.
   Constitution and By-Laws and Roll of Members of the Confederate Veterans Association of the District of Columbia, 1910.
   Constitution and By-Laws and Roll of Members of the Confederate Veterans Association of the District of Columbia, 1922.
Harvey Griff Collection, Walton, Massachusetts
   John S. B. Burroughs Letter, 1863.
Hagerstown, Maryland, Civil War Round Table
   Civil War Dead, Elmwood Cemetery, Shepherdstown, West Virginia.

Harrisonburg–Rockingham County Historical Society, Dayton, Virginia
  Records of Neff-Rice Camp, United Confederate Veterans, New Market, Virginia.
Daniel D. Hartzler Collection, New Windsor, Maryland
  "A Souvenir of the Unveiling of the Confederate Monument June 3, 1933, at Mt. Olivet
    Cemetery, Frederick, Maryland."
  John C. Carroll Letters.
  Davis's Battalion, Maryland Cavalry, Company A, Postwar Roster.
  First Maryland Cavalry, Company D, Postwar Roster.
  Frank L. Hering Letter, July 24, 1864.
  United Confederate Veterans, George M. Emack Camp, Hyattsville, Maryland Records.
Hollywood Cemetery, Richmond, Virginia
  R. E. Lee Camp of Confederate Veteran Soldiers' Home Burial Ledgers.
Howard County Historical Society, Ellicott City, Maryland
  Brice, Carroll A. "Confederate Service."
  Anna Dorsey Cooke Collection. A listing of Dorseys who served in the Confederate Army
    and Navy.
  Howard County, Maryland, Cemetery Records. 7 vols.
  Reunion Records of Company A, First Maryland Cavalry, held July 18, 1899, at "Oakdale,"
    the home of Edwin Warfield.
  "Scrapbook of Company A, First Maryland Cavalry." United Daughters of the Confederacy,
    Chapter #1856, compilers, 1947.
Charles T. Jacobs Collection, Washington Grove, Maryland
  Cemetery Records of Confederate Soldiers Buried in Montgomery Co., Maryland.
  "Colonel Ridgely Brown." United Daughters of the Confederacy, Ridgely Brown Chapter,
    1945.
  Confederate Burials in Arlington National Cemetery, Virginia.
  Reunion Program, Company A, First Maryland Cavalry. 1899.
Library of Congress, Washington, D.C.
  Keidel, Herman F. War Record, 1861–65.
  Kenton Harper Papers.
Maryland Historical Society, Baltimore, Maryland
  R. G. Harper Carroll Letters.
  Confederate Army and Navy Society, Maryland Line Association. Records.
  Confederate Maryland Line Soldiers' Home Record Books.
  Confederate Veterans, Ridgely Brown Camp Roster.
  Christian Conradt. "War Experiences."
  Jubal A. Early Military Correspondence.
  First Maryland Cavalry, Company B Roster.
  First Maryland Cavalry, Company E Muster Roll.
  Maj. Charles Howard Papers.
  Kenley Papers.
  R. Stuart Latrobe Papers.
  Lunsford Lomax Military Correspondence.
  Maryland United Daughters of the Confederacy. Applications.
  Maryland United Daughters of the Confederacy. Records of Maryland Confederate Soldiers.
  Mason E. McKnew Letter, November 28, 1864.
  Ridgely Family Civil War Scrapbook.
  C. W. Shriver Papers.
  United Confederate Veterans, Franklin Buchanan Camp, Baltimore. Records.
  United Confederate Veterans, Isaac R. Trimble Camp, Baltimore. Records 1900.
  Wilson, William Bowley. "Reminiscences."

Maryland State Archives, Annapolis
  Charles Kettlewell Letters, 1862–65.
Museum of the Confederacy, Eleanor Breckinridge Library, Richmond, Virginia
  Confederate Dead in Northern Cemeteries.
  Confederate Memorial Society, Confederate Roll of Honor. 345 vols.
  Gordonsville Hospital Records, June 1, 1863–May 5, 1864.
  James R. Herbert Diary, June–July 1863.
  Bradley T. Johnson Papers.
  Maj. Gen. Fitzhugh Lee Report.
  Henry Carter Lee Diary, 1864–65.
  Otho Scott Lee Diary, 1862–63.
  Lucas Brothers. "The Murray Confederate Association, Composed of the Surviving
    Members of Co. H, First Maryland Infantry, C.S.A. and Co. A, Second Maryland
    Infantry, C.S.A., Commanded by Captain Wm. H. Murray." Unpublished, April 1885.
  Capt. Wilson Cary Nicholas Records.
  Oakwood Cemetery Records.
  John Ridgely Letters.
National Archives, Washington, D.C.
  Compiled Service Records of Confederate Soldiers Who Served in Organizations from the
    State of Maryland, Microfilm No. M 321, Rolls 1–22.
  Jedediah Hotchkiss Papers.
  Dr. Richard P. Johnson, Chief Surgeon, Valley District of Virginia, C.S.A., First Maryland
    Cavalry. Casualty Report. "Battle of Greenland Gap, Grant County, West Virginia."
  Thomas T. Munford Papers.
Frederick D. Shroyer Collection, La Vale, Maryland
  First Maryland Cavalry, Company C, Muster Roll, January 1–February 29, 1864.
  First Maryland Cavalry Materials.
  Lefevre, Hamilton. "Record of My Service to the Confederacy in the War of the Rebellion."
Staunton City Records, Staunton, Virginia
  Thornrose Cemetery Record of Burials 1861–65.
Daniel C. Toomey Collection, Ferndale, Maryland
  Biographical Sketches of the Members of Maryland Line Confederate Home, January 1900.
Robert J. Trout, Myerstown, Pennsylvania
  Stuart's Horse Artillery Records.
United States Army, Military History Institute, Carlisle Barracks, Pennsylvania
  S. Z. Ammen. "Maryland Troops in the Confederacy."
University of Virginia, Alderman Library, Charlottesville, Virginia
  Gordonsville Receiving Hospital Prescription Book May 1864–March 1865.
  Hanover Junction Hospital Records 1863–64.
  University of Virginia, Confederate Cemetery List.
Virginia Military Institute, Lexington, Virginia
  Alumni and Faculty Records.
  William H. Shriver Collection. "First Person Story."
Virginia State Library, Richmond, Virginia
  First Maryland Infantry Discharges.
Washington and Lee University, Leyburn Library, Lexington, Virginia
  Otho Scott Lee Collection. "Reminiscences of Four Years Service in the Confederate Army,"
    1861–62.
Winchester–Frederick County Historical Society, Winchester, Virginia
  Kate Sperry Diary, 1861–66.

Periodicals

Anne Arundel County History Notes. Anne Arundel County Historical Society.
Chronicles of St. Mary's. St. Mary's County Historical Society, 1991–97.
Confederate Veteran. 40 vols. 1893–1932.
Maryland Historical Magazine. Various vols. 1963–99.
Southern Historical Society Papers. 52 vols. 1876–1930.

Newspapers

Baltimore Sun
Richmond Daily Dispatch
Richmond Daily Examiner
Richmond Dispatch
Richmond Enquirer
Richmond Sentinel
Richmond Times-Dispatch
St. Mary's Beacon
St. Mary's Enterprise
St. Mary's Gazette
St. Mary's Journal

Published Works

Alleghany County, Maryland, Rural Cemeteries. Genealogical Society of Alleghany County. Parsons, W.Va.: McClain Printing Co., 1990.
Angus, Felix, ed. *The Book of Maryland: Men and Institutions.* Baltimore: Maryland Biographical Association, 1923.
Armstrong, Richard L. *Seventh Virginia Cavalry.* Lynchburg, Va.: H. E. Howard, Inc., 1992.
Anderson, George M. "The Civil War Courtship of Richard Mortimer Williams and Rose Anderson of Rockville." *Maryland Historical Magazine,* Vol. 80 (1985).
Arps, Walter E. Jr. *Maryland Mortalities 1876–1915: From the Baltimore Sun Almanac.* Decorah, Iowa: The Annundsen Publishing Co., 1983.
Atkinson, George W., and Alvardo F. Gibbons. *Prominent Men of West Virginia.* Wheeling, W.Va.: W. L. Collin, 1890.
Baltimore County Historical Society. *Baltimore Cemeteries.* 4 vols. Silver Spring, Md.: Family Line Publications, 1985–86.
Baltimore: Its History and Its People. 3 vols. New York: Lewis Historical Publishing Co., 1912.
Barringer, Paul B. *University of Virginia: Its History, Influences, Equipment and Characteristics with Biographical Sketches and Portraits of Founders, Benefactors, Officers and Alumni.* New York: Lewis Publishing Co., 1904.
Battles and Leaders of the Civil War. Vols. 1-6. New York and London: Thomas Yoseloff, Inc., 1887, reprint 1956.
Bearss, Ed, and Chris M. Calkins. *Battle of Five Forks.* Lynchburg, Va.: H. E. Howard, Inc., 1985.
Beck, Brandon R., and Charles S. Grunder. *The Second Battle of Winchester June 12–15 1863.* Lynchburg, Va.: H. E. Howard, Inc., 1989.

Beitzel, Edwin W. *Point Lookout Prison Camp for Confederates.* Abell, Md.: privately published, 1972.

Beneath These Stones: Cemeteries of Caroline County, Maryland. 3 vols. Easton, Md.: Upper Shore Genealogical Society of Maryland, 1985.

The Biographical Cyclopedia of Representative Men of Maryland and the District of Columbia. Baltimore: National Biographical Publishing Co., 1879.

Bolling, Alexander R. *The Bolling Family.* Baltimore: Gateway Press, 1990.

Booth, George W., comp. *Illustrated Souvenir: Maryland Line Confederate Soldiers' Home, Pikesville, Maryland.* 1894.

_____. *Personal Reminiscences of a Maryland Soldier in the War Between the States.* Baltimore: Press of Fleet, McGinney & Co., 1898.

Bowie, Effie G. *Across the Years in Prince George's County, Maryland.* Baltimore: Genealogical Publishing Co., 1975.

Brown, Dakota B. *Data on Some Virginia Families.* Berryville, Va.: Virginia Book Company, 1979.

Buckler, Edward St. C. Jr., comp. *Hough Family.* Annapolis, Md.: undated.

Burtz, Shirley V., and George E. Burtz, comps. *Prince George's County, Maryland, Marriages and Deaths in Nineteenth Century Newspapers.* 2 vols. Bowie, Md.: Heritage Books, Inc., 1995.

Bushong, Dean M., and Millard K. Bushong. *Fightin' Tom Rosser, C.S.A.* Shippensburg, Pa.: Beidel Printing House, Inc., 1983.

Calkins, Chris M. *The Battles of Appomattox Station and Appomattox Court House.* Lynchburg, Va.: H. E. Howard, Inc., 1987.

Carroll County, Maryland, Cemeteries. 2 vols. Westminster, Md.: Carroll County Genealogical Society, 1989–90.

Carroll, David H., and Thomas G. Boggs. *Men of Mark in Maryland.* 4 vols. Baltimore: B. F. Johnson, Inc., 1907–11.

Cooke, John E. *Outlines from the Outposts.* Chicago: R. R. Donnelly & Sons, Inc., 1961.

Cottom, Robert I. Jr., and Mary Ellen Heyward. *Maryland in the Civil War: A House Divided.* Baltimore: The Johns Hopkins University Press, 1994.

Crute, Joseph H. Jr. *Confederate Staff Officers, 1861–1865.* Powhatan, Va.: Derwent Books, 1982.

Cryser, Leona. *Deaths and Burials in St. Mary's County, Maryland.* Bowie, Md.: Heritage Books, Inc., 1995.

Davis, Stephen, and Robert Pollard III. 1990. "Allen C. Redwood and Sophie Bledsoe Herrick in 'The Discovery of a Secret, Significant Relationship.' " *Maryland Historical Magazine,* Vol. 85 (1990).

Devine, John E. *Thirty-fifth Battalion Virginia Cavalry.* Lynchburg, Va.: H. E. Howard, Inc., 1985.

Diaries, Letters, and Recollections of The War Between the States. Vol. 3. Winchester, Va.: Winchester–Frederick County Historical Society, 1955.

Driver, Robert J. Jr. *First and Second Rockbridge Artillery.* Lynchburg, Va.: H. E. Howard, Inc., 1987.

_____. *First Virginia Cavalry.* Lynchburg, Va.: H. E. Howard, Inc., 1991.

_____. *Tenth Virginia Cavalry.* Lynchburg, Va.: H. E. Howard, Inc., 1992.

_____. *Second Virginia Cavalry.* Lynchburg, Va.: H. E. Howard, Inc., 1995.

Dryden, Ruth T. *Cemetery Records of Somerset County, Maryland.* San Diego, Calif.: R. T. Dryden, 1988a.

_____. *Cemetery Records of Worcester County, Maryland.* San Diego, Calif.: R. T. Dryden, 1988b.

Earle, Swepson. *The Chesapeake Bay Country.* Baltimore: Thomsen-Ellis Co., Publishers,

1923.

Eastern Shore of Maryland: Portrait and Biographical Record. New York: Chapman
Publishing Co., 1898.

Eminent and Representative Men of Virginia and the District of Columbia. Madison, Wis.:
Brant & Fuller, 1893.

Emory, Frederic. *Queen Anne's County, Maryland.* Baltimore: J. H. Furst Co., 1950.

Evans, Clement A., ed. *Confederate Military History.* 12 vols. Atlanta: Confederate Publishing
Co., 1898.

*Fifth Regiment, Infantry, Maryland National Guard, U.S. Volunteers. Board of Officers of the
Regiment.* Baltimore: Press A. Hoen & Co., 1899.

Fresco, Margaret K. *Marriages and Deaths: St. Mary's County, Maryland, 1634–1900.* Ridge,
Md.: privately published, 1982.

_____. *Doctors of St. Mary's County, Maryland.* Privately published, 1992.

Frye, Dennis E. *Twelfth Virginia Cavalry.* Lynchburg, Va.: H. E. Howard, Inc., 1988.

Garnett, Theodore S. *Riding with Stuart: Reminiscences of an Aide-de-Camp.* Shippensburg,
Pa.: White Mane Publishing Co., Inc., 1994.

Gill, John. *Reminiscences of 4 Years as a Private Soldier in the Confederate Army 1861–1865.*
Baltimore: Sun Printing Office, 1904.

Gilmor, Harry. *Four Years in the Saddle.* New York: Harper & Brothers Publishers, 1866.

Goldsborough, William W. *The Maryland Line in the Confederate Army 1861–1865.* Baltimore:
Press of Guggenheimer, Weil & Co., 1900.

Grimsley, David A. *Battles in Culpeper County, Virginia, 1861–1865.* Culpeper: Raleigh T.
Green, comp. and publisher, Exponent Printing Office, 1900.

Gunney, John T. *Cemetery Inscriptions of Anne Arundel County, Maryland.* 2 vols. Pasadena,
Md.: Anne Arundel County Genealogical Society, 1982–87.

Hanson, George A. *Old Kent: The Eastern Shore of Maryland.* Baltimore: John S. Des Forges,
1876.

Hartzler, Daniel D. *Marylanders in the Confederacy.* Silver Spring, Md.: Family Line
Publications, 1986.

_____. *Medical Doctors of Maryland in the Confederate States Army.* Gaithersburg, Md.: Olde
Soldier Books, Inc., 1988.

_____. *A Band of Brothers.* Privately published, 1992.

The History of the College of William and Mary: From its Foundation, 1693, to 1870.
Baltimore: John Murphy & Co., 1870.

Hoar, Jay S. *The South's Last Boys in Gray.* Bowling Green, Ohio: Bowling Green State
University Press, 1981.

Holdcraft, Jacob M. *Names in Stone: 75,000 Cemetery Inscriptions from Frederick County,
Maryland.* Baltimore: Genealogical Publishing Co., 1985.

Hollywood Memorial Association. *Register of Confederate Dead Interred in Hollywood
Cemetery.* Richmond: Clement & Jones, Printers, 1869.

Howard County, Maryland, Records. Howard County Historical Society, 1979–88.

Howard, McHenry. *Recollections of a Maryland Confederate Soldier and Staff Officer.*
Baltimore: Williams & Wilkins Co., 1914.

Hull, Susan R. *Boy Soldiers of the Confederacy.* New York and Washington: The Neale
Publishing Co., 1905.

Jones, Elias. *New Revised History of Dorchester County, Maryland.* Cambridge, Md.:
Tidewater Publishers, 1966.

Keen, Hugh C., and Horace Mewborn. *Forty-third Battalion Virginia Cavalry: Mosby's
Command.* Lynchburg, Va.: H. E. Howard, Inc., 1993.

Kerr, John B. *Genealogical Notes of the Chamberlaine Family of Maryland.* Baltimore County,
Md.: undated.

Kirby, Walter J. *Roll Call: The Civil War in Kent County, Maryland.* Silver Spring, Md.: Family Line Publications, 1985.

Klapthor, Margaret B., and Paul D. Brown. *The History of Charles County, Maryland.* La Plata, Md.: Charles County Tercentenary, Inc., 1958.

Klein, Frederick J. *Just South of Gettysburg: Carroll County, Maryland, in the Civil War.* Westminster, Md.: The Newman Press, 1963.

Klein, Margaret C. *Tombstone Inscriptions of Orange County, Virginia.* Baltimore: Genealogical Publishing Co., Inc., 1979.

Knause, William H. *The Story of Camp Chase.* Nashville, Tenn.: Publishing House of the Methodist Church, South, 1906.

Krick, Robert K. *Lee's Colonels: A Biographical Register of the Field Officers of the Army of Northern Virginia.* Dayton, Ohio: Press of the Morningside Bookshop, 1979.

Kummer, Frederick A. *The Free State of Maryland.* 4 vols. Baltimore: The Historical Record Association, 1941.

Kutz, Lucy F., and Benny Ritter. *A Roster of Confederate Soldiers Buried in Stonewall Cemetery, Winchester, Virginia.* Winchester: Farmers & Merchants Bank, 1962.

Lowdermilk, Will H. *History of Cumberland, Maryland.* Washington, D.C.: James Anglim, 1878.

Markham, Jerald H., comp. *List of Confederate Veterans Buried in Hollywood Cemetery from Camp Lee Soldiers' Home, 1894–1946.* Unpublished, undated.

_____, comp. *Lynchburg, Va.'s War Dead: Diuguid's Records, May 1861–April 1865.* Unpublished, undated.

Markham, Virginia G. *Descendants of Godfrey Gatch of Baltimore County, Maryland.* Baldwin City, Kans.: 1972.

Marshall, Nellie M., comp. *Tombstone Records of Dorchester County, Maryland 1678–1964.* Dorchester County Historical Society, 1965.

Mazzeo, Michael J. "The Simmons and Welch Families of Charles County, Maryland." Unpublished, undated.

McClellan, Henry B. *The Life and Campaigns of Major-General J. E. B. Stuart.* Boston: Houghton, Mifflin & Co., 1885.

McDonald, Archie P., ed. *Make Me a Map of the Valley: The Civil War Journal of Stonewall Jackson's Topographer.* Dallas: Southern Methodist University Press, 1973.

McGill, John, comp. *The MacGill-McGill Family of Maryland.* Washington, D.C.: privately published, 1948.

McKim, R. M. *A Soldier's Recollections.* New York: Longman, Green & Co., 1910.

McLeod, Martha N., ed. *Brother Warriors: The Reminiscences of Union and Confederate Veterans.* Washington, D.C.: The Darling Printing Co., 1940.

Men of Mark of Maryland: Biographies of Leading Men in the State. 4 vols. Washington, D.C.: Johnson Wynne Co., 1907.

Mettam, Henry Clay. "Civil War Memories of the First Maryland Cavalry, C.S.A." *Maryland Historical Magazine,* Vol. 58 (1963).

Mickle, William E. *Well Known Confederate Veterans.* New Orleans, La.: 1907.

Miller, Samuel H. *Confederate Hill, Loudon Park Cemetery.* Baltimore: 1962.

Miller, Thomas C., and Hu Maxwell. *West Virginia and Its People.* 3 vols. New York: Lewis Historical Publishing Co., 1913.

Moore, Robert H. *First and Second Stuart Horse Artillery.* Appomattox, Va.: H. E. Howard, Inc., 1998.

Mosby, John S. *Stuart's Cavalry in the Gettysburg Campaign.* New York: Moffett, Yard & Co., 1908.

Nash, J. Ogden. *The Immortal 600.* Roanoke, Va.: Stone Printing & Manufacturing Co., 1911.

National Society of Daughters of the Revolution, Bee Line Chapter. *Tombstone Inscriptions in*

Jefferson County, West Virginia. Missouri, W.Va.: Walsworth Publishing Co., 1981.

Neff, Ray A. *Valley of the Shadow*. Terre Haute, Ind.: Rana Publications, 1989.

Newman, Harry W. *Charles County Gentry*. Washington, D.C.: undated.

_____. *Anne Arundel Gentry*. Annapolis: privately published, 1970.

_____. *Maryland and the Confederacy*. Annapolis: privately published, 1976.

Nichols, James L. *General Fitzhugh Lee: A Biography*. Lynchburg, Va.: H. E. Howard, Inc., 1989.

O'Brien, Jerry, Mildred O'Brien, and Merle L. Gibson, comps. "Calvert County Maryland Old Graveyards." Calvert County, Sunderland, Genealogical Newsletter, Maryland, 1986.

Opie, John N. *A Rebel Cavalryman with Lee, Stuart and Jackson*. Chicago: W. B. Conrey Co., 1899.

O'Sullivan, Richard. *Fifty-fifth Virginia Infantry*. Lynchburg, Va.: H. E. Howard, Inc., 1989.

Ownings and Allied Families 1685–1985. 3rd ed. Baltimore: Gateway Press, Inc., 1985.

Paca, Edmund C., ed. "Tim's Black Book: The Civil War Diary of Edward Tilghman Paca Jr., C.S.A." *Maryland Historical Magazine,* Vol. 89 (1994).

Pippenger, Wesley E. *John Alexander: A Northern Neck Proprietor, His Family, Friends and Kin*. Baltimore: Gateway Press, Inc., 1990.

Pompey, Sherman L. "Muster List of the American Rifles of Maryland, Baltimore Artillery, Deas Maryland Artillery, Maryland Guerilla Zouaves and Captain Walter's Company Zarvona Zouaves." Unpublished, 1915.

Porter, John C., ed. *Washington (D.C.) Past and Present: A History*. 5 vols. New York: Lewis Publishing Co., 1930.

Portrait and Bibliographical Record of Harford and Cecil Counties, Maryland. New York and Chicago: Chapman Publishing Co., 1897.

Queen Anne's County, Maryland: Its Early History and Development. Baltimore: Maryland Historical Society, 1950.

Rich, Edward R. *Comrades Four*. New York and Washington: Neale Publishing Co., 1907.

Ridgely, Helen W. *Historic Graves of Maryland and the District of Columbia*. New York: The Grafton Press, 1905.

Rudy, James S. *Blue and Gray: Georgetown University and the Civil War*. Washington, D.C.: The Georgetown University Alumni Association, 1961.

Ruffner, Kevin C. *Border State Warriors: Maryland's Junior Officer Corps in the Union and Confederate Armies*. Ann Arbor, Mich.: University of Michigan Press, 1992.

_____. "More Trouble than a Brigade: Harry Gilmor's 2nd Maryland Cavalry in the Shenandoah Valley." *Maryland Historical Magazine,* Vol. 89 (1994).

Sargent, Jean A., ed. *Stones and Bones: Cemetery Records of Prince George's County, Maryland*. Bowie, Md.: Genealogical Society, Inc., 1984.

Scharf, J. Thomas. *History of Western Maryland*. 2 vols. Baltimore: Regional Publishing Co., 1968.

Shiples, Linwood P. Sr. *The Shipleys of Maryland*. Baltimore: King Brothers, Inc., 1971.

Sketches of Maryland Eastern Shoremen. Silver Spring, Md.: Family Line Publications, 1985.

Smythe, Samuel G., comp. *A Genealogy of the Duke-Shepherd-Van Metre Family*. Lancaster, Pa.: Press of the New Era Printing, 1909.

Soderberg, Susan C. *A Guide to Civil War Sites in Maryland: Blue and Gray in a Border State*. Shippensburg, Pa.: White Mane Books, 1998.

Sons of Confederate Veterans Album. Houston, Tex.: Heritage Publishers Services, 1986.

Stackpole, Edward J. *Sheridan in the Shenandoah*. New York: Bonanza Books, 1961.

Stonebraker, Joseph R. *A Rebel of '61*. New York and Albany: Wyncoop, Hallenbeck, Crawford Co., Printers, 1899.

Talbert, Bart R. *Maryland: The South's First Casualty*. Berryville, Va.: Rockbridge Publishing Co., 1995.

Thomas, Armstrong. *The Thomas Brothers of Mattapany.* Washington, D.C.: 1963.

Tidwell, William A. *Come Retribution: The Confederate Secret Service and the Assassination of Abraham Lincoln.* Jackson, Miss.: University of Mississippi Press, 1988.

Tilghman, Oswald. *History of Talbot County, Maryland.* 2 vols. Baltimore: Williams & Winkins Co., 1915.

Tombstone Records of Harford County, Maryland. 2 vols. Bel Air, Md.: Daughters of the American Revolution, Gov. William Paca Chapter, 1961–64.

Tombstone Inscriptions of Talbot County, Maryland. 4 vols. Easton, Md.: Upper Shore Genealogical Society of Maryland, 1989–93.

Truitt, Reginald V., and Millard G. Les Callette. *Worcester County: Maryland's Arcadia.* Snow Hill, Md.: Worcester County Historical Society, 1977.

United Confederate Veterans, Jefferson County Camp. *Military Operations in Jefferson County, Virginia and West Virginia 1861–1865.* Charlestown, W.Va.: Farmers Advocate Print, 1911.

U.S. War Department. *The War of the Rebellion: A Compilation of the Official Records of the Union and Confederate Armies.* 128 vols. Washington, D.C.: U.S. Government Printing Office, 1880–1901.

Virginia Military Institute. *Virginia Military Institute Register of Former Cadets.* Lexington: 1957.

Wallace, Lee A. Jr. *First Virginia Infantry.* Lynchburg, Va.: H. E. Howard, Inc., 1985.

_____. *A Guide to Virginia Military Organizations, 1861–1865.* Lynchburg, Va.: H. E. Howard, Inc., 1986.

_____. *Seventeenth Virginia Infantry.* Lynchburg, Va.: H. E. Howard, Inc., 1990.

Warfield, J. D. *The Founders of Anne Arundel and Howard Counties, Maryland.* Baltimore: Regional Publishing Co., 1967.

Warner, Nancy M. *Carroll County, Maryland: A History 1837–1976.* 1971.

Wearmouth, Robert J. *Abstracts from the "Port Tobacco Times" and "Charles County Advertiser" 1861–1884.* 4 vols. Bowie, Md.: Heritage Books, Inc., 1996.

Williams, Thomas J. C., et al. *A History of Washington County, Maryland.* 2 vols. Hagerstown: Mail Publishing Co., Printers, 1906.

_____. *History of Frederick County, Maryland.* 2 vols. Hagerstown: L. R. Titsworth & Co., 1910.

Winchester–Frederick County Historical Society. *Diaries, Letters, and Recollections of the War between the States.* Winchester, Va.: 1955.

Yeary, Mamie. *Reminiscences of the Boys in Gray.* Printers of Morningside, 1986.

Acknowledgments

The history of the Maryland Confederate cavalry units could not have been written without the assistance of many interested individuals.

Daniel D. Hartzler of New Windsor, Maryland, shared his vast collection of information on Marylanders and permitted the use of many of the photographs in this book. I am also indebted to him for his hospitality during my visits to his home.

George Sherwood of Frederick, Maryland, provided a roster of Maryland artillerists, some of whom later served in one of the Maryland cavalry battalions. Robert J. Trout of Myerstown, Pennsylvania, provided the same information on Marylanders who had served in the Stuart Horse Artillery.

Robert E. Lyons of Baltimore researched obituaries and cemetery records in the Baltimore area. Mike and Donna Williams of Baltimore tracked down elusive photographs and records in the collections of the Maryland Historical Society.

Jack Kelbaugh of Annapolis provided information on his Civil War ancestor and material from his collection and writings; he graciously lent me rare books from his library.

Charles T. Jacobs of Washington Grove, Maryland, provided cemetery records and other material on the Confederate soldiers from Montgomery County. Charles E. Chambers of Houston, Texas, gathered pension and cemetery records on Marylanders who had moved to the Lone Star state. Garth Bowling of La Plata, Maryland, provided information on the Bowlings and cemetery data from Charles County. Margaret K. Fresco of Ridge, Maryland, provided data on St. Mary's County Confederates.

Erick Davis of Baltimore provided information on his ancestor Thomas Sturgis Davis and his battalion. Frederick D. Shroyer of La Vale, Maryland, shared his collection of First Maryland Cavalry material and photographs of the Maryland Line Camp at Hanover Junction. Raymond Watkins of Falls Church, Virginia, provided cemetery listings from his vast collection.

Roger Keller of Hagerstown, Maryland, researched the cemeteries of Washington County. Stephen R. Brockmiller of Baltimore lent me his collection of material on the First Maryland Cavalry. Robert K. Krick of the Fredericksburg–Spotsylvania National Battlefield Park located the burial site of a Maryland cavalryman buried in Fredericksburg and provided data on the surgeons of the units.

Al Gough Jr. of Leonardtown, Maryland, provided information on his ancestors and other men from St. Mary's County. Philip M. Reitzel of the Howard County Historical Society took time from his busy schedule to allow me a full day of research on the holdings of the society and provided follow-up information on members of the Howard County Light Dragoons.

Hugh C. Keen III of Tulsa, Oklahoma, shared information on Marylanders who had later served with John S. Mosby. Ben Ritter of Winchester, Virginia, provided cemetery listings and photographs of Marylanders who had settled in that area. Jeff Weaver of Arlington, Virginia, researched the Keidel papers in the Library of Congress for me.

Richard B. Kleese of Strasburg provided information on the officers and men who served in Davis's Battalion and later in the Twenty-third Virginia Cavalry.

My thanks to the many others who provided family-related material for my research!

My special thanks to Jim and Marian Krupka of Catonsville, Maryland, for their hospitality during my research visits to the Baltimore area.

The librarians and staff of the Virginia Military Institute, Washington and Lee University, Museum of the Confederacy, the Waynesboro (Virginia) library, and others deserve special mention. Special thanks to Betsy Brittigan of the Washington and Lee library for her efforts to obtain rare and out-of-print books for my research.

Index

Notes: Entries in the muster rolls are not indexed.

Page number in *italics* indicates photograph.